W9-BEX-807

Botanica's Pocket
ORCHIDS

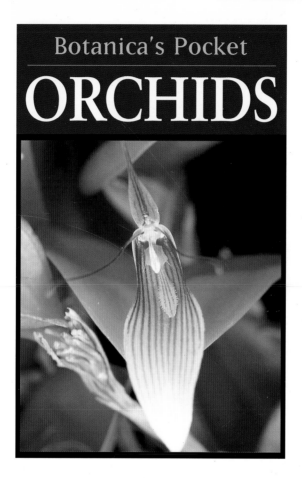

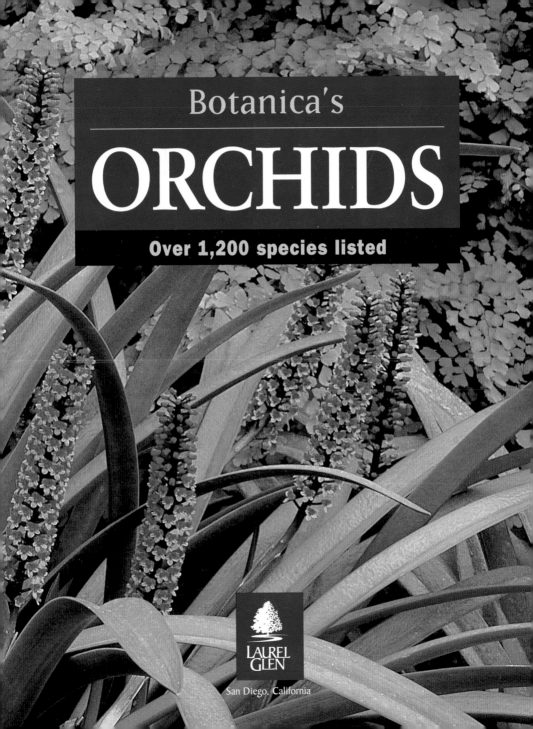

Botanica's

ORCHIDS

Over 1,200 species listed

LAUREL GLEN

San Diego, California

Laurel Glen Publishing
An imprint of the Advantage Publishers Group
5880 Oberlin Drive, San Diego, CA 92121–4794
www.laurelglenbooks.com

Copyright © 2002 Random House Australia
Copyright under International, Pan American, and Universal
Copyright Conventions. All rights reserved. No part of this
book may be reproduced, or transmitted in any form or by
any means, electronic or mechanical, including photocopying,
recording, or by any information storage-and-retrieval system,
without written permission from the publisher. Brief passages
(not to exceed 1,000 words) may be quoted for reviews.

All notations of errors or omissions should be addressed to
Laurel Glen Publishing, editorial department, at the above
address. All other correspondence (author inquiries,
permissions and rights) concerning the content of this book
should be addressed to Random House Australia, 20 Alfred
Street, Milsons Point, NSW 2061, email
random@randomhouse.com.au

Library of Congress Cataloging-in-Publication Data

Botanica's orchids: over 1,200 species listed
    p. cm
    ISBN 1-57145-721-6
    1. Orchids. 2. Orchid culture. I. Laurel Glen
    Publishing

SB409.B74 2002
635.9'344~~dc21

                                        2002030198

2 3 4 5 6 08 07 06 05 04

Creative Consultants:	Bill Lavarack
	Wayne Harris
Consultants:	Gary Yong Gee
	Howard Wood
	Wolfgang Rysy
Managing Editor:	Joanne Holliman
Assembly:	Peta Nugent, Vicky Short
Production Manager:	Linda Watchorn
Publishing Assistant:	Anabel Pandiella
	Monika Paratore
Publisher:	James Mills-Hicks
Printed by:	Sing Cheong Printing Co.
	Ltd, Hong Kong
Film separation:	Pica Digital Pte Ltd,
	Singapore

Contents

Introduction

For many people the word "orchid" conjures up images of exotic, expensive, delicate, and rare flowers, but the truth is far from this romantic image. The Orchidaceae family probably comprises the most species of all the families of flowering plants. Estimates of the total number of orchid species vary widely, however, figures such as 20,000 or 30,000 are often mentioned. This represents about ten per cent of the world's flowering plants.

Orchids are also among the most adaptable plants. They are not restricted to tropical jungles, as the uninitiated sometimes imagine. Orchids can be found growing naturally on every continent, except Antarctica.

Where Orchids Grow

Orchids occur in environments as diverse as Arctic tundras, dry savannas, and tropical jungles. Only the driest deserts, the coldest mountain tops, or permanent snowfields have proved unsuited to orchids. They are most abundant in the tropical jungles of Central and South America and in Southeast Asia, and the islands of the Malay Archipelago.

New Guinea may well be the richest orchid area on the planet. The number of species there is not known with any certainty as new species are discovered on a frequent basis, but estimates are usually around the 3000–3500 mark. Other areas, such as Borneo, Colombia, Venezuela, or Brazil, may have a similar density.

The factors that combine to promote a bountiful supply of orchids are the topography and geography of these places. All these regions have high reliable rainfall and, being close to

A colony of *Habenaria propinquior* on Cape York peninsula in northeast Australia.

Ansellia africana, a tropical African species from dry, open woodlands.

the equator, there is little difference between the summer and winter temperatures. All of them have rugged terrains, which gives rise to a diversity of lowland and highland climates.

When looking for orchids in forest country, light is often the key. A lowland rain forest may have few species over much of its area, but the numbers increase dramatically when the forest canopy is broken by a large stream or a rock face. In these situations light is much more available and air movement is good—two conditions that most orchids appreciate.

In many tropical regions orchids will colonize disturbed areas, such roadside embankments or landslide remains. On a forest tree different types of epiphytes occupy different parts of the tree— larger epiphytes will be found on the major branches, but smaller, delicate species grow in the outer canopy, and these are known as "twig epiphytes."

Some species grow almost exclusively in clumps of peat formed by epiphytic ferns. Emergent trees that protrude well above the canopy are usually rich in orchids, as are isolated trees left in paddocks after clearing.

The lush, tropical rain forest is not the only orchid habitat. Although they are not as numerous or diverse else-where, epiphytic orchids are common in savannas, such as those in Africa and northern Australia, and dry forests. Some of the finest orchid specimens inhabit these areas; for example, the Cooktown orchid, *Dendrobium bigibbum*, from Australia, and *Ansellia africana* from Africa.

Temperate meadows, grasslands, heathlands, and open forests support numerous terrestrial orchids. Both North America and Europe have an abundance of interesting species. Orchids in these situations have underground storage organs, such as tubers. They take advantage of wet seasons to grow and flower, then drop their leaves and survive the dry or cold

Grammatophyllum speciosum, perhaps the largest orchid species, in the Botanic Gardens in Lae, Papua New Guinea.

parts of the year by retreating to these underground parts. These orchids are sometimes most prolific where the soil is moist, such as at the foot of boulders or along stream banks, but many are simply scattered at random across the country side. Often plants in grassy habitats flower more profusely after there has been a wild fire.

The Big and the Small

What is the largest orchid in the world? Often the answer given is *Grammatophyllum speciosum* from Southeast Asia and New Guinea. It has a huge mass of pseudobulbs up to 10 ft (3 m) long and a large plant of this species could easily tip the scales at about a ton. The tallest orchid may be *Dendrobium steatoglossum* from New Caledonia or *Selenipedium chica* from South America, both of which may reach 16$\frac{1}{2}$ ft (5 m) tall.

Equally, the title of the "smallest" requires definition. The Australian *Bulbophyllum globuliforme*, with pseudobulbs less than $\frac{1}{8}$ in (3 mm)

across and virtually no leaf, may qualify, but one of these plants comprises many small pseudobulbs connected by a rhizome. Other species, such as some belonging to *Corybas*, consist of just a small tuber, a small leaf about $\frac{1}{3}$ in (1 cm) across, and a single flower. One of these species is probably small enough as a whole to take the prize.

Orchid flowers are similarly variable in size. The smallest may belong to the genus *Oberonia*, where flowers less than $\frac{1}{25}$ in (1 mm) across are common. The largest could possibly be *Sobralia xantholeuca*, which has flowers with a diameter of 10 in (25 cm). But there are flowers, such as *Paphiopedilum sanderianum*, which deserve special mention—they have pendulous, twisted petals up to 40 in (1 m) long.

The History of Orchids

The first definite references to orchids are in early Chinese writings from about 800 BC. Later, in about 500 BC, the writings of Confucius extol the virtues of the perfume of *lan* (the Chinese name for orchids). Orchids that are identifiable from these early recordings include various species of *Cymbidium*, as well as *Dendrobium moniliforme* and *Bletilla striata*. Chinese art from about AD 1200 also features orchids.

In Europe the earliest known interest in orchids dates back to the ancient Greeks, but the interest was a little more earthy than that of the Oriental cultures. The paired tubers of the local terrestrial species were thought to resemble testicles, for which the Latin word is *orchis—from* this word came the names orchid and Orchidaceae.

Orchids were introduced into cultivation in Europe in the middle of the eighteenth century. By the early 1800s, they were becoming popular among the well-to-do who could afford a glasshouse. Unfortunately, most of these early importations had a short life as a large number died on the long journey from the Americas or Asia.

An orchid nursery and importing business was established by Conrad Loddiges in 1812. This flourished for 40 years and other importers followed, included H. Low, J. Veitch and Sons, and Frederick Sanders. These firms employed collectors in America, Asia, and Africa, and new species, including some that were extremely spectacular, flooded into Europe in the latter half of the nineteenth century.

Many tales have been told of the adventures of the orchid collectors from this period. Romantic characters, such

Bletilla striata, one of the first species to be mentioned in early Chinese writings.

Dendrobium speciosum, a species that survives wild fires by growing on rock faces.

as Wilhelm Micholitz, battled hostile natives, wild animals, and tropical diseases, as well as rival collectors, to be the first to ship any spectacular new find to their employers in England. In 1890, a plant of *Dendrobium striaenopsis* attached to a skull was auctioned in London, causing a sensation. Huge numbers of orchids were taken from the wild—one collector proudly told how he obtained his *Odontoglossum* plants:

After two months work we had secured about ten thousand plants, cutting down to obtain these some four thousand trees, moving our camp as the plants became exhausted in the vicinity.

Clearly these practices could not continue indefinitely, and World War I finally put a stop to them. After the war things had changed. Most of the spectacular species had been discovered and were in cultivation, but more than that, fashions had changed.

What began to emerge were techniques for growing orchids from seed and producing hybrids. Large free-flowering hybrids became available and these grew more readily in cultivation than the species. At the same time the focus of orchid growing had shifted from a few wealthy noblemen in England to the west coast of the USA where it was taken up by a much wider cross section of the population, and soon spread to all the developed nations. Orchid societies sprang up in dozens of countries around the world.

The Orchid Plant

It is difficult to generalize about the structure of the orchid plant. They have adapted to grow in an extremely diverse array of habitats in all sorts of climates, and the structure of each species has diversified to suit the prevailing conditions. Many orchids grow on trees and these are known as epiphytes. When they grow on rocks they are called lithophytes, and in the ground, terrestrials.

Epiphytes and lithophytes face particular problems, the main one being that the substrate in which they grow does not retain moisture. Storage organs, such as swollen stems (pseudobulbs) or succulent leaves, have evolved to solve this problem. The pseudobulbs may be almost globular or elongated, but there is an endless array of variations in the sizes and shapes recorded.

A colony of *Dendrochilum*, an epiphyte, on a tree branch.

Roots have also adapted to help with water economy. Many epiphytes have thicker roots than seems necessary, but these are able to anchor the plant to the substrate and rapidly absorb large quantities of water when it rains. Other epiphytes take advantage of clumps of ferns that produce large amounts of moisture-holding peat, or they grow in thick mats of moss or in leaf litter in the forks of trees.

Terrestrial orchids contend with different problems, depending on the habitat in which they grow. Those from open habitats, such as the veld in Africa or coastal heathlands in Australia, often have to cope with a dry season with little available moisture. In North America they may have to survive harsh winters, including being covered with snow. These orchids have met the challenge by developing underground storage organs, such as tubers, corms, or swollen roots.

The range of adaptations in orchids seems endless and in this lies a large part of their charm to gardeners. Many have large, colorful flowers, but there

A colony of *Pterostylis taurus*, a terrestrial orchid, in a pocket of soil on a rock ledge.

A massive clump of *Bulbophyllum baileyi*, a lithophyte, growing over a rock.

are even more that are less beautiful, but are weird, strange, unusual, interesting, or even bizarre in form.

The Orchid Flower

Orchids belong to the group of flowering plants known as monocotyledons. These have one seedling leaf and their floral parts come in threes—three sepals, three petals, three stamens, and an ovary made up of three carpels. Orchids, however, have modified this basic structure. The stamens are reduced in number to one in most cases, but there are two in the slipper orchids as well as a few other species. The stamen is fused to the female parts, known as the stigma, to form a "column." In addition, one of the petals is often larger and more brightly colored than the others. This petal is known as the "lip" or "labellum," and it is usually the most attractive part of the orchid flower. The lip is usually positioned on the flower to provide a landing platform for a pollinator.

Orchids have developed numerous strategies in the struggle for survival, but two stand out and are responsible for the form of orchid flowers as we know them. These are pollination by animals, mainly insects but occasionally birds, and by the dispersal of seeds through wind. To achieve these strategies the flowers must be colorful and relatively large to attract the pollinator and the seeds must be tiny enough to float on the wind.

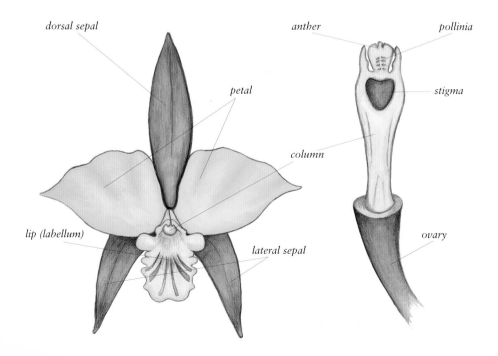

dorsal sepal

anther

pollinia

petal

stigma

column

lip (labellum)

lateral sepal

ovary

Zygosepalum lindeniae, an orchid with a large, showy flower.

A large, colorful orchid flower has one purpose—to attract a pollinator. It does this by one of several methods, including imitating a specific female insect to attract the male of the species. The male effects pollination when it attempts to mate with the orchid flower. An orchid may also imitate the flower of a non-orchid species which grows in the same area, and in doing so fools the pollinator of the non-orchid species by attracting the insect to its own flower. However, the simplest method of attracting a pollinator is having flowers that reward an insect with nectar.

The adaptations for the wind dispersal of seeds are less obvious, but equally important to the survival of the orchids. In most non-orchid plants the seeds store nutrients to help the seedlings survive the first few days after germination, before it has developed leaves to tap into the sun's energy. However, to be able to float on the breeze orchid seeds must be small and light, which means there is no room for them to carry stored nutrients, so the orchid seed has little chance of survival when it finally comes to rest. To overcome this, orchids produce large numbers of seeds—some orchid seed capsules release over half a million seeds. A few of these seeds may land in a suitable niche, where the conditions are moist and sheltered, so the seedling can get going.

As an additional method of survival, orchid seedlings have a symbiotic association with a fungus known as mycorrhiza. The fungus provides the growing seedling with food, but to survive the seed must land in a place where the fungus is present. So of the half a million seeds released by a capsule, perhaps one or two, but very often none, will survive.

Quite by accident, the pollination methods of orchids have attracted a new form of pollination. The large, attractive flowers make the plants desirable to people. Orchid growers made use of the knowledge of seed germination to grow seeds in a sterile flask where no diseases can reach them and where simple foods, such as sugars, are provided. By doing this, a large proportion of the seeds survive. The technique allowed the development of the spectacular hybrids that are so familiar in florist shops. There are now around 100,000 artificially made hybrids available, and about 1000 new ones are added each year.

Orchid Conservation

As with many other plants and animals, orchids face an uncertain future in their natural habitats. About six per cent (almost 2000) of the world's orchid species are considered directly threatened. In addition, many more have had their populations significantly reduced by land clearing. A few really well-known species are threatened, including *Paphiopedilum rothschildianum*, *Odontoglossum crispum* and *Vanda coerulea*.

The total forest cover of the world has reduced by one half in the past 100 years. Estimates are that the remaining forest is disappearing at a rate of about one per cent per year. The clearing has been very patchy, so that while large areas remain in the Congo and Amazon, in other areas, such as the Philippines and Vietnam, only about 20 per cent of the original forest remains. The rain forests in the eastern part of Madagascar are an even worse example. They are the home of many interesting and unique orchids, but recent estimates suggest that only eight per cent of these forests remain.

Two forms of action are required to conserve orchids—the preservation of land and the prevention of collecting from the wild. The land must be preserved in orchid-rich habitats and also managed and policed to prevent illegal removal of orchids. The land preserved should be representative and each nation should aim at reserving a minimum of ten per cent of its natural habitat. The reserves should be large enough to allow ecosystems to function.

The removal of orchids (and, of course, other plants and animals) from their habitats must be controlled. This is the responsibility of each nation, but wealthy nations should assist developing nations to achieve this.

One method of providing assistance is through international treaties. The most important of the international treaties is the Convention on International Trade in Endangered Species (CITES), which seeks to control trade of threatened species between nations. The theory is that while the less-developed nations, where most orchids grow, may not have the resources to control illegal collecting and export, the wealthy nations that import the plants do have resources and, with their cooperation, the illegal trade can be stopped.

Many threatened species are grown and propagated in cultivation. Surely these could be re-introduced to areas

Vanda coerulea, adored for its blue flower, but becoming rare in the wild.

Paphiopedilum rothschildianum, a rare species from a threatened habitat.

where they are now gone? However, the plants in cultivation represent only a small fraction of the original gene pool and many have been bred for several generations to enhance their appearance. The modified flowers may not be recognizable to the pollinators, or may have lost their survivability in other ways.

What can individual orchid lovers do? The following are a few simple rules to follow:

- Support the creation of new national parks and other reserves.
- Join an orchid society and learn about orchids.
- Become familiar with, and obey, the relevant laws concerning collecting orchids from the wild.
- Do not purchase any plants you suspect may have been collected from the wild.
- Learn as much as you can about the orchids from your area, including how to identify them.
- Report any interesting new finds in your area to the appropriate scientific institution.
- Propagate new plants from rare species in your collection and make them available to other growers.
- If you hear of land clearing where orchids grow, see if you can organize your society to salvage plants, but be sure to obtain the relevant permits.
- Never tell people you do not know well the localities of any rare species you find.

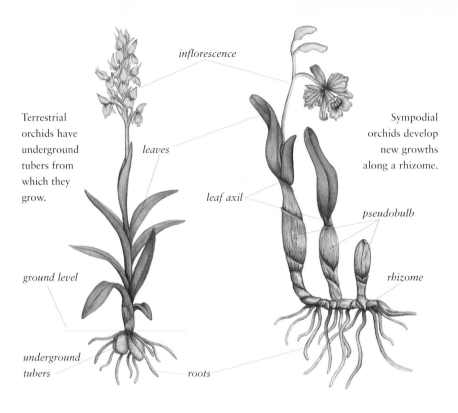

inflorescence

Terrestrial
orchids have
underground
tubers from
which they
grow.

leaves

Sympodial
orchids develop
new growths
along a rhizome.

leaf axil

pseudobulb

ground level

rhizome

underground
tubers

roots

How to Grow Orchids

Orchids are sometimes regarded as delicate plants, difficult to grow, and requiring a tropical climate. Nothing could be further from the truth. They are hardy, adaptable survivors that, with a little care, will reward the grower with bright, showy flowers. While many of the popular orchids come from tropical areas, some are from high altitudes and will grow well in cool climates. So the climate of the plant's origin will to some extent dictate the species of orchids you are able to grow.

In general, though, orchids are forgiving and will perform well if a few simple rules are followed. These rules are discussed below, but because orchids come from a diverse range of climates, specific information about a particular species' needs is provided in the descriptions of the genera and species. For more information consult your local orchid nursery or, even better, join an orchid society. You will find many of these on the Internet, which can also be an excellent source of information.

ORCHID HOUSES

The outlay for a glasshouse may be considerable, but it should be remembered that a large number of plants

Monopodial orchid grow steadily every year from the main stem.

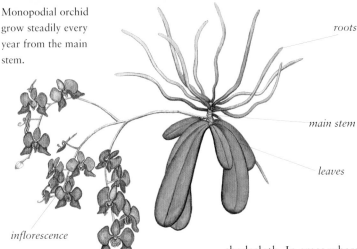

roots

main stem

leaves

inflorescence

may be accommodated within one. The type of orchid house you'll need and the degree of complexity in providing a suitable environment is dependent on the conditions of your area. For example, in the tropics and subtropics, a small collection can be maintained outdoors, with some shading provided. In the cooler areas, the glasshouse may need fans for air movement, heaters for winter warmth, and even cooling systems during summer. It is a common practice in North America to grow orchids in the basement of a house by providing them with light, humidity, warmth, and air circulation. The best advice for your location can be gained from your local orchid society or nursery.

If you are becoming a serious grower and wish to have a large collection, some insect control measures will be required. This is done most easily by constructing an orchid house using a shadecloth. In areas where heavy rain is more or less constant, a translucent roof may be needed to protect plants.

POTS, BASKETS, AND SLABS
Depending on the type of orchid you are growing, it may be planted in a pot or basket, or on a mount such as a slab, or on a tree. Whatever type of container or mount is used, it must provide excellent drainage and must be a suitable size for the plant.

Modern plant pots are now made of polypropylene, which has many advantages over other plastic and ceramic pots, the latter having been very popular for decades. Today's pots are lightweight, flexible, and seldom crack or break when dropped or stored for long periods. They are available in a wide range of sizes and shapes, including square-slatted baskets for genera such as *Vanda*, or net pots suitable for *Barkeria*, where aeration is beneficial. Many orchids can be potted in shallow or "squat" pots. These require less

Orchids growing on teak posts in Lae
Botanic Gardens, Papua New Guinea

potting mix. One popular type of
pot, especially for orchids that have
pendulous racemes or a flower spike
growing down through the compost
such as in *Stanhopea*, is the wood-
slatted or wire basket. These can be
lined with materials such as coconut
fiber or old pieces of shade cloth, to
retain the mix.

Many orchid plants do not do well
in containers and perform much better
on slabs or mounts. There are a number
of different mounts available, from
broken pieces of ceramic pots and
sheets of polystyrene foam, to various
wood and tree-fern pieces. One of the
most popular mounts is natural cork

bark, but old, weathered hardwood
pieces from a paling fence also make
an excellent mount. Pieces of hardwood
branches with bark attached may also
be used. For those plants that appreciate
more moisture at the roots, pieces of
tree fern are popular.

When deciding to mount a plant,
consider the ultimate size to which
it will grow and select the mount size
accordingly. This prevents having to
remount too frequently—if you do
need to remount, simply attach the
old mount to the new one. The plant
should be firmly attached so that there
is no movement which would damage
new root growths. Nylon fishing line
is a favorite, but wire staples, adhesives
such as "liquid nails," and hot gun glues

can all be used. New root growth can sometimes be encouraged by placing a layer of sphagnum moss between the plant and the mount. In the early stages it is sometimes beneficial to lay the slab and plant horizontally so that more moisture is retained around the plant. When new root growth appears, the plant can be hung vertically.

Most of these points with regard to slab culture can be applied to growing orchids outdoors as epiphytes in suitable climates. However, if you are attaching a plant directly to a tree in the garden, the tree or shrub should have bark that does not peel off on an annual basis, and it should not contain a lot of toxic substances, such as resin. It is also better for most species to be mounted on the side of the trunk that does not receive direct sunlight, although some plants will take full sun. Try attaching the plant to the underside of the tree branches or in a position where two branches meet.

There are many thousands of trees or shrubs that would make suitable host plants—palms make excellent mounts, as do frangipanis and citrus trees. In climates that have a distinct cool season, select a tree that is deciduous. At all times, partial shade is preferable and it is better to avoid trees with a dense canopy.

POTTING MIXES

Given the wide range of environments and the materials available, there are almost endless recipes for the "ideal" potting mix. There are several criteria to bear in mind. The medium

- should have sufficient water-holding capacity, enough to keep the plant from drying out between waterings.
- must have adequate aeration between the particles of the mix. It is best to keep all the particles at about the same size to prevent packing and subsequent loss of porosity.
- should be free from diseases and weed seeds, and the pots should be thoroughly cleaned beforehand.
- should have good stability so it will last until the plant has outgrown the container. Once the medium starts to break down the incidence of fungal and bacterial diseases will increase, becoming detrimental to the healthy growth and survival of the plant.
- should contain essential elements for plant nutrition. Organic matter, such as peat, has this ability, but additives, such as coarse sand, do not.
- should have a pH value that suits the type of plant being grown. Most epiphytes grow happily in a slightly acidic mix. Some *Paphiopedilum* species favor a slightly alkaline mix. Control the pH by adding dolomite lime or powdered limestone to make it more alkaline, or a weak acid solution to make it more acidic.

There are two basic mixes. One is for epiphytes or lithophytes and the other is for the terrestrial orchids.

Epiphyte mixes

There are three basic types of epiphyte mixes—bark, sphagnum moss, and peat and perlite. By far the most common is granulated bark, which can be purchased in a variety of grades and is usually made from radiata pine, redwood or Douglas fir. The small size (less than 1/3 in / 1 cm) is used for seedlings and the largest (up to 1 1/4 in / 3 cm) for mature plants. Avoid using fibrous or flaky bark and any that contains resin. Numerous pieces can be added to this basic mix, including broken brick, charcoal, polystyrene, graded gravel, scoria, and firm fiber.

Sphagnum moss is also popular. It is used alone or combined with any number of mixes. It is capable of holding a great deal of water, which it releases gradually on drying. It should not be allowed to dry out altogether as it can be difficult to resaturate. Sphagnum moss is excellent for small seedlings, plants from cool altitudes, and plants that are ailing. It appears to contain antifungal chemicals, which help to prevent root rot. Its main disadvantage is that it breaks down quickly if fertilizer is used and if the water used is not similar to rain water in quality.

Peat and perlite is becoming very popular. Perlite is a substance derived from heating a mineral to about 1650°F (900°C) and it is widely used in agriculture. It is inert, it does not absorb nutrients or salts, and it holds a small amount of moisture. Use the coarsest grade available with a good-quality, fibrous peat. This mix is usually acidic, and powdered dolomite —at a rate of about 1 1/2 oz per 1 3/4 pints (5 g per L) of mix—will lift the pH closer to neutral (around 5 or 6). The proportions of the mix depend on the frequency of watering, but a ratio of 75 per cent perlite and 25 per cent peat is typical. Pots dry out more slowly when using this mix so less watering may be required.

Terrestrial mixes
There are two types of terrestrial orchids, evergreen and deciduous, and they require different cultural treatments depending on their origin. However, there are certain generalities that apply to both.

- The mix should be well-drained and contain some composted plant material such as peat, bark compost, or fern fiber.
- A basic mix consists of one part leaf mulch or wood shavings, one part friable loam, and two parts coarse sand with a small portion of a slow-

Various potting mixes: sphagnum moss and perlite (top left); coarse perlite (top right); medium-grade bark (bottom left); fine-grade bark (bottom right).

A group of sympodial orchids (catteleyas)
potted in a bark mixture.

release nitrogenous fertilizer, such
as "hoof and horn" or "blood and
bone."

- The proportion of sand may vary
depending on the condition and
moisture requirements of the plants.
- Organic mulch may be added to
simulate forest-floor conditions
for rain forest species.
- The pH of the mix should be adjusted
according to the directions that apply
to epiphyte mixes. For example, if
acidic add powdered dolomite to
bring it close to neutral.
- Top the mix with fine washed gravel
or chopped pine needles to prevent
water being splashed on the plants.
This will reduce the risk of fungal or
bacterial infections being spread.

Both evergreen and deciduous terrestrial
orchids should be repotted in new
compost every two years. The peat
and perlite mix described for epiphytic
species may also be used successfully
for terrestrial orchids.

One of the most frequently asked
questions by novice orchid growers is,
in fact, when to repot an orchid. The
answer is quite simple: when the plant
becomes too big for its pot, or when
the mix becomes stale at the roots. It
does not hurt to take the plant out of
the pot, say, every two years, to check
the condition of the roots. If the roots
are not showing any vigor or are
obviously rotting, then immediate
remedial action is required. Normally,
repotting should be done when the
roots are beginning active growth,
usually in spring and early summer.

A commercial nursery with an open-weave shadecloth, allowing good air movement.

FERTILIZING

Most orchid mixtures do not provide the plant with nutrients and, even when they are included, they may be depleted within three months. Generally, orchids require less fertilizer than most other plants, and the best regime for orchids is "little and often." Ideally, small doses of fertilizer could be applied at every watering. An application of fertilizer for three waterings out of four at about half the strength recommended on the packet will ensure good growth.

For growers in warm areas, where growth barely ceases at any time, fertilizer may be applied year-round. When a plant is in active growth from spring to early autumn, the sunlight levels are at their highest and the plants should be fertilized regularly with a high-nitrogen fertilizer to encourage rapid growth. A more balanced fertilizer should be applied during autumn until growth ceases in winter. This aids new growth and promotes flower production. Fertilizing can be withheld in winter until new growth appears in spring.

Orchids do not require any specific fertilizer, but a liquid one is preferable and more reliable. Most commercially available fertilizers include all of the major elements of nitrogen (N), phosphorous (P), and potassium (K), as well as trace elements. The proportions of the major elements are indicated on the packaging as a ratio—a high-nitrogen fertilizer will appear as a N:P:K ratio of 25:10:10 or similar, and a more balanced fertilizer will have a ratio of 10:10:10. Of the minor elements, calcium and magnesium are the most important as they are essential for cell growth and photosynthesis. Dolomite lime, which contains both calcium and magnesium, may be added to bark-based mixtures every six months or so, to provide these elements.

AIR MOVEMENT, LIGHT AND TEMPERATURE

These three factors must be maintained at their optimal levels to ensure good growth and flowering. Each species of orchid has different requirements but, generally, gentle air movement is essential for the health of the plant—if stale conditions persist, bacterial and fungal diseases will proliferate. In closed situations, electric fans can be effective. Plant houses constructed with open-weave material, such as shadecloth, should not need any extra assistance.

Light and temperature are closely correlated and the amounts needed by a species depends on the plant's origins. Most orchids are very tolerant and will grow well in a range of conditions. Consult your local nursery or orchid society to find out more information.

WATERING AND HUMIDITY

Most epiphytes come from regions that experience high rainfall and humidity for at least part of the year. These plants require watering several times a week during the growing season. If plants are mounted, daily misting during this time is also essential. For species from regions with distinct seasonal changes, where there is little or no moisture for several months of the year, a watering rest period is required for a few weeks each year, particularly during the cold months. However, if the pseudobulbs show signs of excessive shrivelling, give the plant a good watering. Recommence regular watering when new growth begins.

Terrestrial orchids that are deciduous should receive no water during the time the leaves have died back, but the mix may be kept just damp to prevent the tubers from shrivelling. Most rain forest or evergreen terrestrials can be watered year-round, with perhaps a rest of only a couple of weeks during winter. Recommence watering during spring and increase the frequency during summer.

PESTS AND DISEASES

Orchid plants are attacked by a range of insect pests, and by fungal, bacterial, and viral infections, similar to those that other garden plants suffer from. Many of these can be controlled by good cultural practices and orchid houses that exclude insects.

The most common insect pests are spider mites, aphids, mealy bugs, and scale insects. Most of these can be controlled by a systemic insecticide—one that enters the system of the plant—made specifically for the particular infestation. If you use chemicals such as these, adhere to the manufacturer's specifications and take adequate precautions against the harmful effects of these toxic chemicals for yourself and others, including pets, who may come into contact with treated plants.

Many insect pests can be controlled without the use of strong chemicals. Aphids can be controlled by maintaining a high humidity in the plant house, especially in times of high temperature. In addition, they can be hosed off the young shoots and inflorescences. Mealy bugs and scale insects are the most difficult to control. They are often transported to the plant by ants which will actively "farm" the insects for their sugary secretions. Scale can be controlled with white oil and minor infestations of mealy bugs can be removed by dabbing them with a cotton bud dipped in alcohol. Controlling the ant population is a more proactive way of maintaining the health of your plants.

Where plants are grown in open gardens, they may be attacked by a range of other leaf-eating insects, such as grasshoppers. These can be controlled by commercial spray compounds. Slugs and snails can decimate new growth overnight. Cleanliness around the plants will eliminate their hiding places and reduce their numbers. Searching by torchlight in the evening will expose them so they can then be caught and

disposed of. Commercially available baits are effective but these can be hazardous for pets.

Several viral diseases are known to infect orchids. The leaves will show these infections in a number of ways, including abnormal streaking or areas of dead tissue. Each virus has its own symptoms and some will present with similar symptoms. If you suspect a viral infection, the plant should be tested, but bear in mind there is no cure for a virus-infected plant and it should be burned to prevent the infection spreading. Viruses are transmitted mostly by insects, such as aphids and thrips, so control of leaf-sucking insects is important. Sterilization of pruning tools by either flaming or standing in a bleach solution will guard against the human element of transmission.

Bacterial and fungal infections are more likely to occur when there is insufficient air movement. They usually enter the plant through damaged tissue, so every cut or chewed surface should be dusted routinely with a suitable powder. Some plants, particularly *Phalaenopsis* species, are susceptible to crown rot disease, which occurs when water is allowed to remain in the leaf axils overnight. The remedy is simple— do not allow water to remain on the plants overnight. Remember, fungal and bacterial infections spread rapidly and require immediate attention to prevent further damage.

Dendrobium bigibbum (Cooktown orchid) in a tropical garden. Garden orchids are often subject to insect attack.

PROPAGATION

Once infected with "orchidmania" a grower is usually keen to add to their collection. Orchids can be propagated by vegetative means or by a process which involves the raising of seedlings.

Vegetative propagation—epiphytes
Sympodial orchids have rhizomes, which produce roots that attach the plant to the substrate, and pseudobulbs with leaves and flowers. The rhizome can be cut cleanly with a sharp, sterile knife and the pieces separated, leaving a minimum of about three stems or pseudobulbs on each.

In some plants the rhizome rarely branches and the pseudobulbs may be very close together. If the rhizome is cut behind three or four pseudobulbs it will produce a similar result—a lead and a "back cut." This will stimulate dormant buds to produce new growths on the back cut. The forward-growing section can be potted in a similar medium to that used for the back cut.

For some orchids, like *Cymbidium* species, old, leafless pseudobulbs can be used for propagation. When dividing, simply remove the leafless pseudobulb and place in a mix similar to that used for the parent plant. New growths will emerge from the dormant eyes of the pseudobulb. These can be potted once it has produced healthy roots.

Monopodial orchids can be treated similarly, except a "top cut" is taken. In genera such as *Vanda* and *Aerides*, the plant continues an upward growth with roots forming along the stem.

An orchid before division (top) and after the plant has been divided (bottom).

A "top cut" is taken at a position where the separated top will have three or four roots. This is then potted in a similar mix. The parent plant will produce new growth from nodes along the axis. Some monopodial orchids may produce new shoots from the leaf axils naturally and these can be separated from the original plant when they have developed sufficient roots.

Propagation by offshoots
Some orchids, particularly *Dendrobium* species, produce offshoots which are called "aerials," "anoks," or "keikis." These arise from buds in the leaf axils, usually towards the top of the plant. Remove them with a sharp knife when they have a well-developed head and

good roots. Keikis can be encouraged to produce roots by tying a small pod of sphagnum moss immediately below the junction of the keiki and the plant's main stem. Older leafless, canes or pseudobulbs can be detached and laid on a bed of sphagnum moss, where they will invariably produce offshoots.

Terrestrials
Many colony-forming terrestrials multiply by producing "daughter" tubers, usually at the end of a long underground stem. Collect these when repotting the parent plant. For species that only renew the existing tuber each

Seedlings in a flask.

Seedlings in community pots.

year, some success has been achieved by what is termed "daughter tuber removal." When the plant reaches maturity it is carefully taken from the pot and the newest tuber is removed and replanted. The original tuber usually has enough time and energy to produce a second tuber.

Propagation from seed
By far the great majority of new plants are produced from seed. Seed raising requires specialist equipment and knowledge and is not recommended for the beginner. Orchid growers can purchase a flask of seedlings, or buy advanced seedlings that have been established in a pot after deflasking.

Seed capsules are sown onto a sterile agar medium that contains the essential nutrients and hormones needed for germination and growth, and placed in a flask. The flasks should not be opened, except under sterile conditions or when the seedlings are ready to be deflasked. The plants are ready for deflasking when they have good root and shoot development. The best time to deflask is during spring or autumn.

To deflask, the glass may need to be smashed. Gently wash off the agar mix in lukewarm water. Pot the seedlings together in a community pot with either seedling bark, peat and perlite, or sphagnum moss. Cover the plants with a plastic bag or bottle for a few weeks, then harden them through gradual exposure to your orchid house conditions. When they are growing strongly, pot them into individual small seedling pots.

Top 20 orchids for special purposes

FRAGRANT ORCHIDS

Aerides odorata

Angraecum eburneum

Bifrenaria harrisoniae

Brassavola nodosa

Cattleya intermedia

Dendrobium formosum

Dendrochilum cobbianum

Lycaste aromatica

Maxillaria tenuifolia

Miltonia spectabilis

Neofinetia falcata

Oncidium ornithorhyncum

Paphiopedilum concolor

Phalaenopsis pulchra

Prosthechea fragrans

Sophronites purpurata

Stanhopea oculata

Trichopilia marginata

Vanda lamellata

Zygopetalum maculatum

SMALL ORCHIDS FOR CONFINED SPACES

Aerangis fastuosa

Ascocentrum ampullaceum

Bulbophyllum miram

Comparettia falcata

Dendrobium cuthbertsonii

Dryadella zebrina

Ionopsis utricularioides

Leptotes bicolor

Masdevallia uniflora

Maxillaria sophronitis

Mediocalcar decoratum

Mystacidium aliciae

Neolehmannia porpax

Ornithocephalus iridifolius

Pleurothallis mirabilis

Promenaea xanthina

Restrepia antennifera

Sarcochilus ceciliae

Schoenorchis fragrans

Sophronitis coccinea

Trichoglottis atropurpurea

ORCHIDS FOR COOL CLIMATES

Ada aurantiaca

Anguloa uniflora

Arethusa bulbosa

Bletilla striata

Cautlanzinia pendula

Cochlioda noetzliana

Coelogyne cristata

Cymbidium eburneum

Cypripedium calceolus

Dendrobium kingianum

Disa uniflora

Laelia autumnalis

Lycaste deppei

Masdevallia tovarensis

Miltoniopsis roezlii

Oncidium ornithorhyncum

Paphiopedilum insigne

Pterostylis nutans

Rossioglossum grande

Zygopetalum maculatum

ORCHIDS FOR INTERMEDIATE/ HOT CLIMATES

Aerides lawrenciae

Ansellia africana

Brassia caudata

Broughtonia sanguinea

Bulbophyllum medusae

Cattleya intermedia

Coelogyne mayeriana

Dendrobium bigibbum

Ludisia discolor

Myrmecophilia tibicinis

Oncidium sphacelatum

Paphiopedilum glaucophyllum

Phaius tankervilleae

Phalaenopsis schilleriana

Renanthera monachica

Rhyncholaelia digbyana

Sophronitis purpurata

Spathoglottis plicata

Trichoglottis atropurpurea

Vanda luzonica

Lycaste aromatica

Using the Species Guide

Genus heading: Arranged alphabetically by genus. A genus contains species with a number of common characteristics.

Genus description: Usually contains general information about the species within the genus, such as range, cultivation details, and hybrid details.

Author: The person who first described the genus or species. The names are usually abbreviated. Where a species has been changed from one genus to another, the name of the original author appears in brackets and the name of the botanist who changed its status follows.

syn: An abbreviation for synonym(s), botanical names no longer accepted but still lingering in use.

Species description: Usually includes details of habitat, distribution, size of plant and flower, flowering season, and other details not apparent from the photograph.

ACAMPE

The ten species in this genus are monopodial epiphytes. They range from east Africa to the Malay Peninsula, occurring north to China and on the islands of the Indian Ocean. They grow at low altitudes, occasionally a little higher. They are medium to large in size with thick leaves that form two ranks. The erect inflorescences are usually branched with densely packed flowers. The lip is saccate or may have a short spur.

CULTIVATION
The large, fleshy roots of these species require room to grow and good aeration. For this reason it is best to grow them in a basket or pot with coarse, well-drained mixture. Most of the species prefer warm conditions and do well in bright light with good air movement. Water these plants throughout the year.

Acampe ochracea
syn. *A. dentata*

This robust species occurs from Sri Lanka and India to Myanmar and Thailand, growing at low to moderate altitudes. It is up to 40 in (1 m) tall, with fleshy leaves about 6–8 in (15–20 cm) long and 1 in (2.5 cm) wide. The branched inflorescences are 10–12 in (25–30 cm) long, and ½ in (12 mm) across. Each branch bears two or six flowers during autumn.
ZONES 11–12. H.

Acampe pachyglossa

Acampe pachyglossa

The debate about whether this species and *Acampe praemorsa* are the same plant is yet to be resolved. *A. pachyglossa* is very similar to *A. rigida*, and is recorded in east Africa from Kenya to the KwaZulu-Natal province of South Africa, and on the island of Madagascar. It grows between sea level and 3000 ft (900 m). It is a robust species with stems up to 1 ft (30 cm) tall and thick leaves up to 1 ft (30 cm) long and ¾ in (18 mm) wide. Each inflorescence is densely packed with 15 to 25 flowers that are about ¾ in (18 mm) across. Flowering is from late winter to early summer. ZONES 11–12. I-H.

Phalaenopsis amboinensis

Phalaenopsis amabilis
syn. *P. grandiflora*, *P. gloriosa*

The moth orchid is from the south of the Philippines, Sumatra, Java, Borneo, New Guinea, and northeast Australia. There are two subspecies and one or more varieties recognized, and the subspecies *rosenstromii* from New Guinea and Australia has slightly smaller flowers. *P. amabilis* is an epiphyte or lithophyte that grows year-round in warm, moist conditions in shaded or semi-shaded, humid locations at low to moderate altitudes. It has the largest flowers in the genus, up to 3½ in (8 cm) across. Numerous, long-lasting flowers are borne on an arching, branched inflorescence up to 40 in (1 m) long. Flowering may occur at any time of the year but there is an emphasis on spring and summer. This plant may be kept warm and moist year-round and be provided with good drainage. A greenhouse is essential in all but subtropical and tropical climates. ZONES 10–12. I-H.

Phalaenopsis amboinensis

This species occurs on the Moluccas and Sulawesi, where it grows in shady, humid forests with year-round rainfall at low altitudes. The thick-textured, long-lasting flowers are about 1½ in (4 cm) across and have orange-to-brick-red markings in a pattern on a white or yellow background. There are two to four fleshy leaves up to 10 in (25 cm) long and 4 in (10 cm) across. ZONES 11–12. H.

Phalaenopsis bellina
syn. *P. violacea var. bellina*

Recognized as a separate species as recently as 1995, this plant is restricted to the Malay Peninsula and Borneo. It grows at low altitudes in shady, humid habitats, such as beside streams. It is pendulous with rounded leaves up to 10 in (25 cm) long and 4½ in (12 cm) across. The flowers open progressively with one, two or three open at any one time. They are about 2 in (5 cm) across and are the most fragrant of the genus. They have a strong, fruity perfume. ZONES 11–12. H.

Phalaenopsis bellina

Species head: The botanical name of the species. The species are ordered within a genus alphabetically by this name.

Common name: A number of plants are known by an accepted common name. These appear in quotation marks.

var.: An abbreviation for variety, a botanical classification below the species rank. Sometimes "ssp." may appear. This stands for subspecies.

Cultivation conditions: Guidelines based on the average minimum night temperatures the species will tolerate in cultivation. Some will grow outside the range if care is taken, for example, if the plant is kept away from cold winds.
C = Cool = 45–50°F (7–10°C)
I = Intermediate = 50–65°F (10–18°C)
H = Hot = 65–70°F (18–21°C)

Caption: The orchid's botanical name.

Hardiness zones: Zones based on the maps on pages 33 to 35. These are sometimes modified by the effects of altitude to produce cooler zones than those shown on the map.

HARDINESS ZONE MAPS

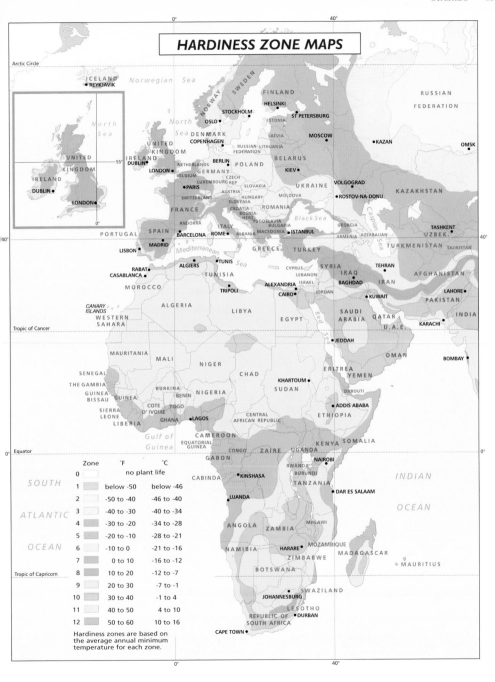

Zone	°F	°C
0	no plant life	
1	below -50	below -46
2	-50 to -40	-46 to -40
3	-40 to -30	-40 to -34
4	-30 to -20	-34 to -28
5	-20 to -10	-28 to -21
6	-10 to 0	-21 to -16
7	0 to 10	-16 to -12
8	10 to 20	-12 to -7
9	20 to 30	-7 to -1
10	30 to 40	-1 to 4
11	40 to 50	4 to 10
12	50 to 60	10 to 16

Hardiness zones are based on the average annual minimum temperature for each zone.

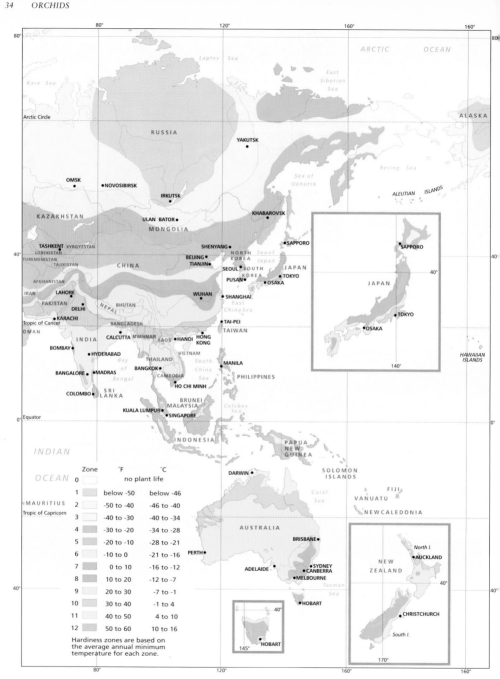

Zone   °F   °C

0   no plant life

1   below -50   below -46

2   -50 to -40 -46 to -40

3   -40 to -30 -40 to -34

4   -30 to -20 -34 to -28

5   -20 to -10 -28 to -21

6   -10 to 0   -21 to -16

7   0 to 10   -16 to -12

8   10 to 20   -12 to -7

9   20 to 30   -7 to -1

10   30 to 40   -1 to 4

11   40 to 50   4 to 10

12   50 to 60   10 to 16

Hardiness zones are based on
the average annual minimum
temperature for each zone.

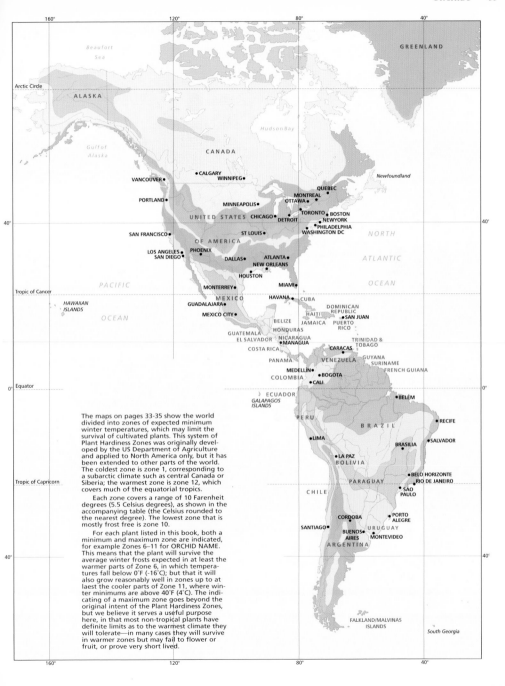

The maps on pages 33-35 show the world divided into zones of expected minimum winter temperatures, which may limit the survival of cultivated plants. This system of Plant Hardiness Zones was originally developed by the US Department of Agriculture and applied to North America only, but it has been extended to other parts of the world. The coldest zone is zone 1, corresponding to a subarctic climate such as central Canada or Siberia; the warmest zone is zone 12, which covers much of the equatorial tropics.

Each zone covers a range of 10 Farenheit degrees (5.5 Celsius degrees), as shown in the accompanying table (the Celsius rounded to the nearest degree). The lowest zone that is mostly frost free is zone 10.

For each plant listed in this book, both a minimum and maximum zone are indicated, for example Zones 6–11 for ORCHID NAME. This means that the plant will survive the average winter frosts expected in at least the warmer parts of Zone 6, in which temperatures fall below 0˚F (-16˚C); but that it will also grow reasonably well in zones up to at laest the cooler parts of Zone 11, where winter minimums are above 40˚F (4˚C). The indicating of a maximum zone goes beyond the original intent of the Plant Hardiness Zones, but we believe it serves a useful purpose here, in that most non-tropical plants have definite limits as to the warmest climate they will tolerate—in many cases they will survive in warmer zones but may fail to flower or fruit, or prove very short lived.

ACACALLIS LINDL.

A

This genus contains two species, both of which are native to the South American countries of Brazil, Colombia, Venezuela, Guyana, and Peru. Both of the—species bear blue flowers that are produced on a creeping rhizome.

Acacallis cyanea LINDL.

This is a small epiphyte with pseudobulbs about 2 in (5 cm) high. It produces a solitary leaf, about 8 in (20 cm) long, and flowers about 2½ in (6 cm) across. It grows best on a slab of cork or tree fern, and prefers intermediate to hot conditions with high humidity. This species may be difficult to cultivate. **ZONES 10–12. I–H.**

Acacallis cyanea

ACAMPE LINDL.

The ten species in this genus are monopodial epiphytes. They range from east Africa to the Malay Peninsula, occurring north to China and on the islands of the Indian Ocean. They grow at low altitudes, occasionally a little higher. They are medium to large in size with thick leaves that form two ranks. The erect inflorescences are usually branched with densely packed flowers. The lip is saccate or may have a short spur.

CULTIVATION

The large, fleshy roots of these species require room to grow and good aeration. For this reason it is best to grow them in a basket or pot with coarse, well-drained mixture. Most of the species prefer warm conditions and do well in bright light with good air movement. Water these plants throughout the year.

Acampe ochracea

(LINDL.) HOCHR.

syn. *A. dentata* LINDL.

This robust species occurs from Sri Lanka and India to Myanmar and Thailand, growing at low to moderate altitudes. It is up to 40 in (1 m) tall, with fleshy leaves about 6–8 in (15–20 cm) long and 1 in (2.5 cm) wide. The branched inflorescences are 10–12 in (25–30 cm) long, and ½ in (12 mm) across. Each branch bears two to six flowers during autumn. **ZONES 11–12. H.**

Acampe ochracea

Acampe pachyglossa

Acampe pachyglossa RCHB.F.

The debate about whether this species and *Acampe praemorsa* are the same plant is yet to be resolved. *A. pachyglossa* is very similar to *A. rigida*, and it is recorded in east Africa from Kenya to the KwaZulu Natal province of South Africa, and on the island of Madagascar. It grows between sea level and 3000 ft (900 m). It is a robust species with stems up to 1 ft (30 cm) tall and thick leaves up to 1 ft (30 cm) long and ¾ in (18 mm) wide. Each inflorescence is densely packed with 15 to 25 flowers that are about ¾ in (18 mm) across. Flowering is from late winter to early summer. **ZONES 11–12. I-H.**

A

Acanthephippium sylhetense

Acanthephippium sylhetense LINDL.

Widely distributed from India to south China and Taiwan, this species grows at altitudes up to 2700 ft (800 m). The stems have a swollen base and are up to 4¾ in (12 cm) long and 1¼–1¾ in (3–4 cm) across at the widest. The two to three leaves are up to 16 in (40 cm) long and 4 in (10 cm) wide. The inflorescence is erect, up to 8 in (20 cm) long, with a few flowers, each about 1¾ in (4 cm) long. Flowering occurs during spring.
ZONES 10–12. I.

Acanthephippium splendidum J. J. SM.
syn. *A. papuanum* SCHLTR., *A. vitiense* L. O. WILLIAMS

This species occurs from the Indonesian island of Sulawesi to Papua New Guinea, then across to the Pacific Islands, as far east as Tonga. It grows on the rain forest floor from sea level to an altitude of about 4300 ft (1300 m). The plant is about 32 in (80 cm) tall. The pseudobulbs are cigar-shaped, about 4¾ in (12 cm) tall. There are two or three rather broad leaves, each about 12–15 in (30–40 cm) long. The inflorescence arises from the base of the new growth and bears three to five fleshy flowers, each about 1¾ in (4 cm) long.
ZONES 11–12. H.

Acanthephippium splendidum

ACANTHEPHIPPIUM BLUME

There are approximately 15 species in this genus. They range over a wide area, from India through China and the Malay Archipelago to the Pacific Islands as far east as Fiji. All the species are terrestrial, growing at low to moderate altitudes on shady rain forest floors. The stems or pseudobulbs tend to be a cylindrical or bottle-shaped with two or three large broad leaves at the apex. The flowers are relatively large and urn-shaped, with the sepals connate, forming a tube.

CULTIVATION

Being terrestrial, these plants should be grown in a well-drained, sandy mixture with leaf mould or other organic content. They should be kept in a humid atmosphere, in complete shade or highly filtered light. Water and fertilize heavily throughout the year, especially when the plants are in active growth.

A

ACIANTHUS R. BR.

The species of this genus occur in eastern Australia, including Tasmania, and in New Zealand. They are terrestrials that grow in areas where there is adequate shade and moisture, and a seasonal climate change—they lie dormant during the height of summer but grow actively between late summer and early spring. Several of the species produce large matlike colonies, and new plants are obtained by the daughter tubers. These plants are easy to cultivate in a standard terrestrial mix. When dormant during summer, the tubers must be watered less after the leaves have died.

Acianthus caudatus R. BR.

This species can be found in moist, open forests in eastern Australia, from the Tropic of Capricorn to Tasmania and west to South Australia. It is a distinctive species with long sepals up to 1¼ in (3 cm) long. It grows naturally in colonies, but it may be difficult to maintain in cultivation. Flowering occurs from early winter to spring. **ZONES 8–9. C–I.**

Acianthus fornicatus

Acianthus caudatus

Acianthus fornicatus R. BR.

This species ranges along the eastern seaboard of mainland Australia, from Queensland to New South Wales. It forms colonies in moist, open forest habitats. The single leaf is about 1¾ in (4 cm) across. It is heart-shaped and a dark-green color above the leaf and purplish below. Up to 14 small flowers, about ⅓ in (1 cm) long, are carried on a stem up to 8 in (20 cm) high. This species is easy to grow and flowers occur from autumn to early spring. **ZONES 8–10. C–I.**

A

ACINETA LINDL.

There are about 20 species in this genus, ranging from Mexico through Venezuela and Ecuador to Peru. They are robust, epiphytic plants with pseudobulbs that are large, egg-shaped to cylindrical, and heavily furrowed. These are topped by two or three large leaves up to 2 ft (60 cm) long. The inflorescences are similar to those of *Stanhopea*, that is, pendulous in shape, so they grow best in slatted baskets or on slabs of tree-fern fiber.

Acineta superba
(H. B. K.) RCHB.F.

This species has pseudobulbs up to 5¹/₂ in (13 cm) long, with leaves up to about 2 ft (60 cm) long. Its inflorescence has five or more flowers, each about 3 in (7.5 cm) across. *A. superba* flowers have a spicy fragrance and appear during spring.
ZONES 10–11. I–H.

Acineta superba

ACRIOPSIS REINW. EX BLUME

This epiphytic genus comprises some six species, distributed from north India through Southeast Asia, the Indonesian and Philippine islands, Papua New Guinea, northeast Australia to the Solomon Islands. The plants are mostly lowland species that grow in brightly lit situations. The pseudobulbs are densely clustered and egg-shaped with a few leaves at the apex. The branched inflorescence arises from the base of the pseudobulb and has numerous small flowers.

CULTIVATION

Most of these species come from hot, humid climates. Bright light, even full sunlight, is acceptable in some cases. Slab culture seems best—if potted, the plants should be given a coarse medium. Watering throughout the year is recommended.

Acriopsis liliifolia (KOEN.) ORMEROD
syn. several names, including *A. javanica* REINW. EX BLUME,
A. papuana KRAENZL., *A. philippensis* AMES

Acriopsis liliifolia

The roots are a feature of this species. They grow upwards in large numbers, serving as a trap for falling leaves and debris. This provides the plant with nutrients. It is a widespread species with virtually the same distribution as the genus. It grows at low altitudes up to about 5300 ft (1600 m), usually in exposed conditions. The pseudobulbs are ovoid in shape, up to 2³/₄ in (7 cm) long and 1¹/₄ in (3 cm) wide, with two to four leaves. The branched inflorescence carries anywhere up to 200 flowers, each less than ¹/₃ in (1 cm) across. **ZONES 11–12. H.**

A

Ada allenii

Ada aurantiaca

ADA LINDL.

This small genus of about 16 species is distributed from Costa Rica and Panama to Venezuela and Peru. They are mostly epiphytes (some are occasionally lithophytes) that occur at high altitudes. These plants have pseudobulbs with well-developed leaflike leaf sheaths. For successful cultivation, they require cool to intermediate conditions.

Ada aurantiaca LINDL.

This species grows at high elevations in the Andes in Colombia, Ecuador, and Venezuela. The pseudobulbs are compressed and elliptic in shape, about 3¼ in (8 cm) long, with one or two leaves up to 12 in (30 cm) long. The inflorescences grow up to 14 in (35 cm) long and carry one to many flowers, each about 1 in (2.5 cm) long. Clusters of flowers appear from winter to early spring. This species requires cool cultivation conditions. It may be mounted or grown in a pot. Water amply during growth periods. **ZONES 9–10. C–I.**

Ada allenii (L. O. WILLIAMS & SCHWEINF.) N. H. WILLIAMS
syn. *Brassia allenii* L. O. WILLIAMS & C. SCHWEINF.

This is a distinctive species from Panama. It occurs in cloud forests up to 3300 ft (1000 m) on the Atlantic slopes of the mountains. The plants, up to 14 in (35 cm) tall, do not have pseudobulbs. The eight to 14 leaves form the shape of a broad fan. The erect to arching inflorescence is usually shorter than the leaves and it bears five to eight flowers. These fragrant flowers grow about 2½ in (6 cm) long. **ZONE 11. I.**

Ada glumacea (LINDL.) N. H. WILLIAMS
syn. *Brassia glumacea* LINDL., *Oncidium glumaceum* (LINDL.) RCHB.F.

This epiphytic species occurs in Colombia and Venezuela. The pseudobulbs are about 2 in (5 cm) tall and are topped by a single leaf up to 20 in (50 cm) long. The inflorescence is as long as, or longer than, the leaves. It bears a few flowers, each about 2 in (5 cm) across. This species flowers from winter to spring. **ZONES 9–10. C–I.**

Ada glumacea

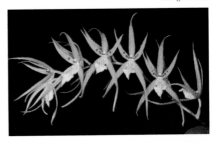

A

AERANGIS RCHB.F.

This genus comprises about 60 monopodial species that are equally spread between eastern Africa and Madagascar, with one species extending to Sri Lanka. They grow along the banks of streams at a range of altitudes, from sea level to 6500 ft (1950 m). The majority prefer dense shade and a humid environment. Mostly they have short stems and long or short inflorescences. Their predominantly white, star-shaped flowers have a long spur and are often fragrant during the evening.

CULTIVATION

Several of these species are popular cultivation plants because they are delightful miniatures with relatively large flowers. They prefer temperatures ranging from intermediate to warm, and most of them should be grown in shade and kept in humid conditions year-round. They should be watered freely when the leaves or flower buds are developing, but kept relatively dry for about two months each year. A slab is the best foundation as many of these plants have pendulous inflorescences.

Aerangis biloba

Aerangis biloba
(LINDL.) SCHLTR.

This small, slender species comes from tropical west Africa, where it grows in rain forests in full sun or partial shade. The leaves crowd the apex of a short stem and are about 3¼–7 in (8–18 cm) long. The inflorescence is longer than the leaves, is pendulous, and has up to 15 fragrant, waxy flowers, each 1–2 in (2.5–5 cm) across. Flowering is during spring.
ZONES 11–12. H.

A

Aerangis confusa

Aerangis confusa J. STEWART

This species occurs in central and southwestern Kenya and northern Tanzania. It grows low in shady situations on the trunks of trees, in moderate to high altitudes. It has a short stem up to 4 in (10 cm) long, with up to 12 leaves about 9⅔ in (24 cm) long. The leaves are 2 in (5 cm) wide near the apex, tapering towards the end. The pendulous inflorescences have up to 12 flowers, each about 1¼–1¾ in (3–4 cm) across, with a spur up to 2.5 in (6 cm) long. Flowering is reported during spring and autumn. **ZONES 9–11. C–I.**

Aerangis fastuosa

Aerangis fastuosa (RCHB.F.) SCHLTR.
syn. *Angraecum fastuosum* RCHB.F.

This miniature species occurs on Madagascar in humid, evergreen forests at an altitude of 3300–5000 ft (1000–1500 m). The leaves are up to 3¼ in (8 cm) long and ¾ in (18 mm) wide. The inflorescence comprises one to three flowers, each about 2 in (5 cm) across, with a spur to about 3¼ in (8 cm) long. Flowering occurs during spring, and the flowers last about three weeks. **ZONES 9–10. C–I.**

Aerangis fuscata (RCHB.F.) SCHLTR.

This species is incorrectly identified in many collections as *A. umbonata*. It is found on Madagascar and is an epiphyte that grows on twigs and smaller branches in a range of habitats from sea level to a 4500-ft (1350-m) altitude. The short stems have leathery leaves about 4 in (10 cm) long. The inflorescences are pendulous, up to about 8 in (20 cm) long, with many fragrant flowers up to 1–1½ in (2.5–3.5 cm) across. Flowering occurs during summer. **ZONES 11–12. H.**

Aerangis fuscata

A

Aerangis hyaloides (RCHB.F.) SCHLTR.

syn. *A. pumilio* SCHLTR.

This miniature is no more than 3¼ in (8 cm) tall. Restricted to shady conditions of moss forests on the island of Madagascar, this species grows from sea level to an altitude of about 3300 ft (1000 m). The leaves are about 2–2¾ in (5–7 cm) long and up to ¾ in (18 mm) wide. The inflorescences are up to 2¾ in (7 cm) long and bear 12 to 25 flowers, each about ⅓ in (1 cm) across, with a short spur. Flowering is during winter in cultivation.
ZONES 11–12. H.

Aerangis hyaloides

Aerangis kirkii

Aerangis kirkii (RCHB.F.) SCHLTR.

This small epiphyte occurs at low altitudes in tropical east Africa, from Kenya to Mozambique. It grows in shady conditions along streams and in coastal vegetation. It has a short stem with two to seven leaves, each up to 6 in (15 cm) long and 1¼ in (3 cm) wide near the apex. The inflorescences bear two to six flowers, each about 1¾ in (4 cm) across. These have a spur up to 2¾ in (7 cm) long. Flowering occurs during spring.
ZONES 11–12. H.

A

Aerangis kotschyana (RCHB.F.) SCHLTR.

This small epiphyte is widespread across tropical Africa, from Guinea through Kenya to Mozambique. It grows in savannas and forests from sea level to 5000 ft (1500 m), often in light shade. The short stem bears anything up to 20 leaves, each $2^1/_2$–8 in (6–20 cm) long and $^4/_5$–$3^1/_4$ in (2–8 cm) wide. The inflorescences are pendulous with ten to 20 flowers up to 2 in (5 cm) across. The spur is 5–10 in (13–25 cm) long, and is prominently twisted like a corkscrew. **ZONES 10–12. H.**

Aerangis kotschyana

Aerangis mystacidii (RCHB.F.) SCHLTR.

syn. *Angraecum saundersiae* H. BOLUS

This species occurs in South Africa, Swaziland, Zimbabwe, Mozambique, Malawi, and Zambia. It grows at low altitudes in shady conditions along streams and in gorges. The short stems have four to eight leathery leaves , each up to $3^1/_4$ in (8 cm) long and $1^1/_4$ in (3 cm) wide near their apexes. The inflorescences are pendulous and bear four to 15 flowers about $^4/_5$ in (2 cm) across with a spur to about $2^3/_4$ in (7 cm) long. **ZONES 10–12. H.**

Aerangis mystacidii

A

AERANTHES LINDL.

This monopodial genus of about 40 species occurs on Madagascar and adjacent islands. They grow from sea level to about 5000 ft (1500 m), mostly under the shade of humid rain forests. Most *Aeranthes* are small to medium in size, and their leaves, growing from a short stem, form a fan shape. The inflorescences are long and wiry and some of the flowers are quite large. In most species the flowers open in succession. They have a spur that is usually short and club-shaped.

CULTIVATION

As most of these species have pendulous inflorescences, it is best to grow them on a slab or in a hanging pot or basket. If a pot is used, the medium should be very open and free draining. They require humid conditions and intermediate to warm temperatures and should be grown under shade or filtered light. Water freely while the plants are actively growing, but keep slightly drier for a short period each year.

Aeranthes grandiflora LINDL.
syn. *A. brachycentrum* REGEL

The large flowers are a feature of this species, which is restricted to Madagascar where it grows in rain forests stretching from the coast to the central plateau, up to an altitude of 4000 ft (1200 m). The plants have a short stem with leaves up to 1 ft (30 cm) long and 1¼ in (3 cm) wide. The inflorescence may grow over 40 in (1 m) and the flowers open successively over a period of three months or more. The flowers are up to 4 in (10 cm) across and up to 5½ in (13 cm) long. Flowering occurs from winter to autumn. **ZONES 10–12. I–H.**

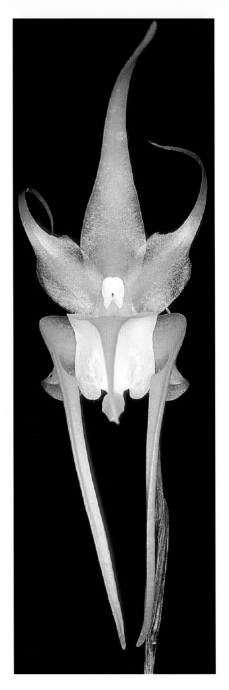

Aeranthes grandiflora

Aeranthes ramosa ROLFE
syn. *A. vespertilio* COGN.

This species is restricted to the moss forests of Madagascar at about 4500 ft (1350 m) above sea level. Here there is constant humidity and reliable rainfall. The short stem has about four or five leaves about 1 ft (30 cm) long and 1¼ in (3 cm) wide. The inflorescences are branched and pendulous, up to 5 ft (1.5 m) long, with numerous flowers, each up to 2 in (5 cm) across. Flowering occurs in February (summer) on Madagascar. **ZONES 10–11. C–I.**

Aeranthes ramosa

A

AERIDES LOUR.

This genus includes about 20 species of monopodial orchids occurring from India to Papua New Guinea, as far north as China and the Philippines. They are epiphytes that in situations where there is bright light and most of them grow at low to moderate altitudes. Their branched climbing stems may grow from 1 ft (30 cm) to more than 5 ft (1.5 m), and have straplike leathery or succulent leaves that act as storage organs in the absence of pseudobulbs. The numerous fragrant flowers develop mostly on pendulous inflorescences, and are often white, pink, and purple. There is usually a forward-projecting spur.

CULTIVATION

Large slabs, baskets, or hanging pots are best to cater for the pendulous inflorescence growth habit and the rampant root growth. The roots may be allowed to roam outside the container. The plants require bright light and constant humidity, with temperature requirements depending on the altitude range from which they come. Generally they should be watered throughout the year and fertilized when in active growth. Care should be taken when repotting to avoid damage to the roots.

HYBRIDS

Aerides crassifolia

Aerides have been used quite extensively to make intergeneric hybrids with a number of genera, including *Vanda*, *Phalaenopsis*, *Ascocentrum* and *Rhynchostylis*.

Aerides crassifolia PARISH EX BURB.
syn. *A. expansum* RCHB.F.

This species is recorded from low to moderate altitudes in Myanmar, Thailand and Indochina. It is a robust species with leaves 7 in (18 cm) long and 2 in (5 cm) wide. The arching or pendulous inflorescences grow up to 2 ft (60 cm) long. They bear many fragrant flowers, each about 1¾ in (4 cm) across. Flowering occurs during summer. In cultivation this plant benefits from a slightly drier period during winter. **ZONES 11–12. H.**

A

Aerides crispa LINDL.

syn. *A. brookei* BATEMAN, *A. lindleyanum* WIGHT

This species from India and Sri Lanka grows at moderate altitudes and has stems up to 5 ft (1.5 m) long. The well-spaced leaves are up to 8 in (20 cm) long and 2 in (5 cm) wide. The sweetly fragrant flowers are 1¼ in (3 cm) wide and are borne on semi-erect inflorescences as long as 3 ft (90 cm). The inflorescences are occasionally branched with numerous flowers. Flowering occurs during summer.
ZONES 10–11. I.

Aerides falcata

Aerides crispa

Aerides falcata LINDL.

syn. *A. larpentae* HORT.,
A. mendelii HORT. EX B. S. WILLIAMS

This species occurs naturally in the Himalayan foothills from Assam in India to Nepal and Indochina. It grows at low to moderate altitudes. The stems of this medium- to large-sized species may reach lengths of up to 6 ft (1.8 m). The leaves are from 6–14½ in (15–36 cm) long and 1¾ in (4 cm) wide, and are arranged in two ranks. The arching to pendulous inflorescences are up to 20 in (50 cm) long, with numerous fragrant flowers, each about 1¾ in (4 cm) across. Flowering occurs during summer.
ZONES 10–12. I–H.

A

Aerides flabellata

Aerides houlletiana

Aerides flabellata ROLFE EX DOWNIE
syn. *Vanda flabellata* (ROLFE EX DOWNIE) CHRISTENSON

Considered by some authorities to belong to the genus *Vanda*, this
species occurs in Indochina and the Yunnan province in China. It grows
at moderate altitudes. The stem extends up to 1 ft (30 cm) long with
leaves 6–12 in (15–30 cm) long but less than ⁴/₅ in (2 cm) across. The
lateral inflorescence has three to seven flowers, each about ³/₄ in (18 mm)
across. It flowers during spring. **ZONES 9–11. I–H.**

Aerides houlletiana RCHB.F.
syn. *A. ellisii* J. ANDERSON, *A. falcata* **var.** *houlletiana* (RCHB.F.) VEITCH

Considered by some authorities to be a form of *A. falcata*, this species
occurs in Thailand and Indochina at low to moderate altitudes, often in
shaded situations. It differs from *A. falcata* through flower color and the
narrower leaves. The numerous flowers are about ³/₄ in (18 mm) across
and are borne on a pendulous inflorescence about 10 in (25 cm) long.
Flowering occurs mostly during spring and early summer. In cultivation
it should be grown under partial shade. **ZONES 11–12. I–H.**

Aerides krabiensis

Aerides krabiensis
SEIDENF.

This species was separated from *A. multiflora* in 1971. It occurs in Thailand and down the Malay Peninsula on exposed limestone cliffs under full sun at low altitudes. It forms small clumps of stems, up to 8 in (20 cm) long, with thick leaves, about 4¾ in (12 cm) long and ⅓ in (1 cm) wide, that have a V-shaped cross section. The inflorescence is arching with 12 to 15 flowers up to ⅘ in (2 cm) wide. When cultivated in conditions that are less extreme than in the natural habitat, these plants tend to have larger flowers. **ZONES 11–12. H.**

Aerides lawrenciae

Aerides lawrenciae RCHB.F.

Growing in brightly lit situations at low altitudes on the island of Mindanao in the Philippines, *A. lawrenciae* is a robust species up to 5 ft (1.5 m) tall. It sometimes becomes pendulous. The leaves are up to 1 ft (30 cm) long and 2 in (5 cm) wide. The pendulous inflorescence has up to 30 strongly fragrant flowers, each about 1¾ in (4 cm) across. Flowering occurs during autumn. **ZONES 11–12. H.**

A

Aerides multiflora ROXB.

syn. several names, including *A. affine* LINDL.,
A. roseum LODD. EX PAXTON

This species is widespread in low-altitude areas from Nepal, Bhutan, and northeast India to Indochina. The stems, which are usually less than 10 in (25 cm) long, form large clumps in its natural habitat. The leaves are up to 1 ft (30 cm) long and $^4/_5$ in (2 cm) wide. The densely flowered inflorescences are up to 1 ft (30 cm) long, and are either arching or pendulous. The waxy, fragrant flowers are about $^4/_5$ in (2 cm) across. Flowers appear during summer. **ZONES 11–12. H.**

Aerides odorata LOUR.

syn. many names, including
A. latifolia (THUNB. EX SW.) SW.,
A. cornutum ROXB.

This widespread species occurs in many areas from the northwestern regions of the Himalayas to Indochina and the Asian islands of Borneo, Java, Sulawesi, and the Philippines. It grows in brightly lit situations, mostly at low altitudes, but it has been reported as growing as high as 6700 ft (2000 m) in the Philippines. It is a robust species that reaches as tall as 5 ft (1.5 m) and forms dense clumps. The inflorescence is semi-pendulous with up to 40 fragrant flowers, each about 1 in (2.5 cm) across. **ZONES 10–12. I–H.**

Aerides odorata

Aerides quinquevulnera LINDL.

syn. several names, including A. album SANDER, A. marginatum RCHB.F.

This species grows in the Philippines and Papua New Guinea. It can be found in brightly lit situations up to a 6700-ft (2000-m) altitude. The stems may reach 40 in (1 m) and the leathery leaves grow up to 1 ft (30 cm) long and 1¾ in (4 cm) wide. The inflorescences are pendulous with up to 30 fragrant flowers, each about 1 in (2.5 cm) across. Flowering occurs during autumn and lasts for about two weeks. **ZONES 10–12. I–H.**

Aerides quinquevulnera

Aerides rosea LODD. EX LINDL. & PAXTON

syn. A. fieldingii B. S. WILLIAMS, A. williamsii WARNER

Previously known as A. fieldingii, this species is widespread throughout the Himalayan region at moderate altitudes. It forms clumps of stems up to 1 ft (30 cm) long. The leaves are also up to 1 ft (30 cm) long and 1¼ in (3 cm) wide. The inflorescence is pendulous, occasionally branched, with many densely packed flowers, each about 1 in (2.5 cm) across. It flowers during summer. **ZONES 10–12. I.**

Aerides rosea

A

AMBLOSTOMA SCHEIDW.

This is a very small genus of epiphytic or lithophytic orchids that are indigenous to the Andes of South America. They are best cultivated in pots with a suitable well-drained mix or mounted on tree-fern slabs.

Amblostoma cernua

Amblostoma cernua
SCHEIDW.
syn. *A. tridactylum* SCHEIDW.

This species occurs in Mexico, Bolivia, Brazil, and Peru. The pseudobulbs form clusters and have a narrow spindle shape. They are up to 8 in (20 cm) tall. Several thin-textured and erect leaves are borne near the top of the pseudobulb and reach about 10 in (25 cm) long. The inflorescence is about 6 in (15 cm) tall with many small flowers, each about ¼ in (6 mm) wide. This plant requires intermediate growing conditions with year-round moisture. It grows best in a pot or mounted on a tree-fern slab. Flowering is during summer. **ZONES 9–10. I.**

AMESIELLA SCHLTR. EX GARAY

This genus is endemic to the Philippines and comprises two epiphytic species of monopodial orchids. These grow anywhere from about 1000–7200 ft (300–2160 m) above sea level.

Amesiella monticola J. E. COOTES & D. P. BANKS

This species is tolerant of cool conditions and occurs at an altitude of 6000–7300 ft (1800–2200 m) in central Luzon, one of the northern Philippine islands. It is found on the fringes of rain forests. It is small, only 1–2 in (2.5–5 cm) tall, with leaves up to 4 in (10 cm) long. The inflorescence bears up to three flowers about 2½ in (6 cm) across and it has a nectary up to 4½ in (11 cm) long.
ZONES 10–11. I.

Amesiella philipinnensis AMES

This species, endemic to the Philippines, grows at an altitude of 1300–4700 ft (400–1400 m). It has a similar growth habit to *A. monticola*, but it is generally smaller and less robust. The spur is shorter too. Flowers appear during spring. **ZONES 11–12. I–H.**

Amesiella monticola

Amesiella philipinnensis

ANACAMPTIS RICH.

This genus consists of one small terrestrial species that is widespread over Europe. It has a pyramid-shaped inflorescence with pink flowers.

CULTIVATION

Because of its special habitat requirements, this species is very difficult to grow in cultivation. Collection of this species from the wild is prohibited over much of its range.

Anacamptis pyramidalis

Anacamptis pyramidalis

(L.) RICH.

A

This attractive species grows mostly in the warm, dry grassland and shrubland from sea level to 6300 ft (1900 m) around the Mediterranean Sea— from north Africa and Spain to Turkey and Israel with outlying occurrences in England, Germany, and the Swedish islands of Oeland and Gotland. It occurs as far east as Iran and the Caucasus range. It is 8–18 in (20–45 cm) tall, including the inflorescence of many small flowers about ⅔ in (15 mm) wide. The flowers are pink to dark red—the more northern the distribution, the darker its color. It has four to ten leaves arranged in a rosette at the base of its stem. Its inflorescence has a pyramidal form at first, but becomes cylindrical. Flowering is from April to July.
ZONES 8–10. I.

ANCISTROCHILUS ROLFE

This genus comprises two species that grow in west Africa, Uganda, and Tanzania. Vegetatively, they resemble *Pleione*. In cultivation these species require intermediate conditions with plenty of water—enough to prevent the pseudobulbs from shrivelling—while actively growing and when the leaves fall. The inflorescence emerges from the base of the mature pseudobulbs at about the time the leaves fall.

Ancistrochilus rothschildianus O'BRIEN

This species occurs in tropical Africa from Guinea and Sierra Leone to Uganda. The pseudobulbs are conical in shape, and up to about 2 in (5 cm) in diameter. Two thin-textured leaves emerge from the top of the pseudobulbs which may be up to 8 in (20 cm) long. The inflorescence has two to five flowers and is up to 9 in (22 cm) tall. The flowers are up to 3⅔ in (9 cm) wide. This species is best grown in a shallow pan with a well-drained, moisture-retentive mix. Flowering may occur at any time. **ZONES 11–12. I–H.**

Ancistrochilus rothschildianus

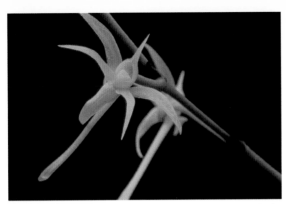

Angraecum calceolus

ANGRAECUM BORY

This monopodial genus comprises some 200 species, with over half occurring in Madagascar; the remainder in tropical Africa, the islands of the western Indian Ocean, and Sri Lanka. They vary in size from miniature to large, and almost all of them have white, cream, or light, green flowers. The size of the flowers ranges from as small as $\frac{1}{2}$ in (12 mm) to as wide as 9 in (22 cm) across. The genus is characterized by a prominent spurred lip.

CULTIVATION

Different conditions apply as the climatic zone and the habitat details vary from species to species within the genus. In general, slab or pot culture is suitable for most species. Larger plants may be grown in a garden bed in suitable climates, but drainage must be good. Most species benefit from a resting period in the cooler months when watering should be reduced.

Angraecum calceolus
THOUARS

This species occurs on the islands of Madagascar, Reunion, Mauritius, and the Seychelles, from sea level to about 6700 ft (2000 m). It grows in shady conditions in humid forests, usually on the bases of trees and shrubs. The short stem has up to ten leaves $6\frac{1}{2}$–8 in (16–20 cm) long and $\frac{2}{3}$ in (15 mm) wide. The inflorescence is branched and about 1 ft (30 cm) long. It bears four to six flowers, each about $\frac{4}{5}$ in (2 cm) across, and a spur $\frac{1}{3}$–$\frac{1}{2}$ in (10–12 mm) long. It flowers from late spring to the end of summer in the wild.
ZONES 10–12. I–H.

Angraecum chevalieri
SUMMERH.

This small epiphyte occurs in west Africa, including Nigeria, Ghana, Côte d'Ivoire, Guinea, and Uganda. It grows on the larger branches of rain forest trees where it receives bright light. It is only about $4\frac{3}{4}$ in (12 cm) long. The leaves are $1\frac{3}{4}$–$2\frac{3}{4}$ in (4–7 cm) long and $\frac{1}{3}$ in (1 cm) wide. The inflorescence is very short and the flowers are about $1\frac{1}{4}$ in (3 cm) long with a spur up to $\frac{4}{5}$ in (2 cm) long. Flowering is from June to July in its natural habitat.
ZONES 11–12. H.

Angraecum chevalieri

Angraecum compactum

Angraecum compactum SCHLTR.

As the name implies this is a small plant. It is quite widespread on Madagascar, occurring in humid forest conditions up to 6700 ft (2000 m) above sea level. Its branching stems may reach 1 ft (30 cm) long, and it has six to 14 leaves about $2^3/_4$ in (7 cm) long and $^1/_3$ in (1 cm) wide. The inflorescence is short with one to three flowers (most often two), each flower about $1^1/_4$ in (3 cm) across. The spur has a U-shaped bend and is about 4 in (10 cm) long. The flowers release a spicy fragrance during the evenings. Flowering is during summer in cultivation.
ZONES 10–12. I–H.

Angraecum didieri (BAILL. EX FINET) SCHLTR.

This species grows in the humid forests of Madagascar, from the lowlands to the plateau at about 5000 ft (1500 m). It mostly occurs above 2000 ft (600 m). Its stem is usually short, but may grow to 8 in (20 cm) long. The five to seven leaves are up to $2^3/_4$ in (7 cm) long. The flowers are borne singly and are about $2–2^1/_2$ in (5–6 cm) across with a spur up to about $5^2/_3$ in (14 cm) long. Flowering in the wild is from October to January (spring to summer). **ZONES 9–12. I–H.**

Angraecum didieri

Angraecum eburneum BORY

syn. *A. virens* LINDL.

This large, robust species occurs on the east coast of Madagascar, the Mascarene and Comoros islands, and in Kenya and Tanzania, although the African mainland plants are considered a separate variety, or even species, by some authorities. It grows at low altitudes on rocks or on trees. The stems are branched, form clumps, and are 5 ft (1.5 m) or more tall. The leaves are rigid, up to 1 ft (30 cm) long and $1^1/_4$ in (3 cm) wide. The inflorescences are more or less erect with 15 to 30 large flowers about $1^3/_4$–$2^1/_2$ in (4–6 cm) across. The lip is held uppermost and the spur is $2^3/_4$ in (7 cm) long. Flowering in cultivation is during early winter. **ZONES 11–12. H.**

Angraecum eburneum

A

Angraecum eichlerianum

KRAENZL.

This robust, epiphytic species occurs at low altitudes in the rain forests of tropical west Africa. It forms clumps and has stems reaching 2 ft (60 cm) or more in length. The stems are covered on their lower part by old leaf bases. The leaves are 2³/₄–4 in (7–10 cm) long and ⁴/₅–1³/₄ in (2–4 cm) wide. The flowers are borne singly and are about 3¹/₄ in (8 cm) across. The spur is 1¹/₄–1³/₄ in (3–4 cm) long. Flowers occur during summer in cultivation.
ZONES 11–12. H.

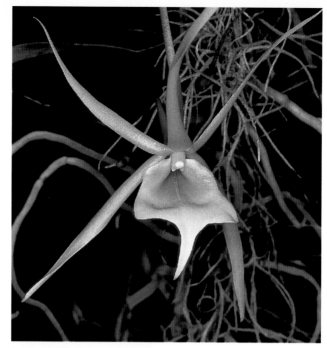

Angraecum eichlerianum

Angraecum leonis (RCHB.F.) ANDRE

syn. *A. humboltii* ROLFE EX ROLFE, *Aeranthes leonis* RCHB.F.

This medium-sized epiphyte occurs in Madagascar and the Comoros Islands. It grows from sea level to 3000 ft (900 m). The stems are short with four or five leaves 2–10 in (5–25 cm) long and about ⁴/₅ in (2 cm) across. The inflorescences bear one to seven star-shaped flowers, each about 1³/₄–3²/₃ in (4–9 cm) across. The spur is up to 3²/₃ in (9 cm) long.
ZONES 11–12. I–H.

Angraecum leonis

A

Angraecum magdalenae

Angraecum scottianum

Angraecum magdalenae SCHLTR. & H. PERRIER

The natural habitat of this medium-sized species is leaf litter pockets on exposed boulders at an altitude of 2700–6700 ft (800–2000 m) on Madagascar. These areas have a cool, dry season that lasts for five months. The plants have a short branched stem that may grow to 14 in (35 cm) on old plants. The leaves, 10–12 in (25–30 cm) long and 1¾–2 in (4–5 cm) wide, are arranged in a fan shape. The inflorescences arise from below the leaves and have one to five flowers, each about 2¾–4 in (7–10 cm) across. The S-shaped spur is about 4 in (10 cm) long. Flowering is during summer. **ZONES 9–10. C–I.**

Angraecum sesquipedale

Angraecum scottianum RCHB.F.
syn. *A. reichenbachianum* KRAENZL.

This small species is restricted to the Comoros Islands, north of Madagascar. It is an epiphyte, growing on the trunks and lower branches of trees, often in exposed positions in full sunlight at altitudes of about 1700 ft (500 m). The slender stems are up to 8 in (20 cm) long with six to 15 terete leaves, 2½–4 in (6–10 cm) long and about ¼ in (6 mm) in diameter. The flowers are about 2½ in (6 cm) across. They are borne singly or on a short inflorescence of a few flowers, and open successively. Flowering is during June and July in the wild. **ZONES 11–12. I–H.**

Angraecum sesquipedale THOUARS
"COMET ORCHID"

The large flowers and the extremely long spur of this popular species are its main features. It grows at low altitudes on the east coast of Madagascar on trees or rocks where there is good air movement and light shade. The stems are usually unbranched and may grow to over 40 in (1 m) with leaves up to 15 in (40 cm) long and 2¾ in (7 cm) wide along its length. The inflorescences have about four flowers, each 6¾–9 in (17–22 cm) across and with a spur to about 14 in (35 cm) long. Flowering is from June to November (winter to spring) in the wild. When repotting the roots should be disturbed as little as possible. **ZONES 11–12. H.**

A

ANGULOA RUIZ & PAVON

This genus of about nine species occurs in Venezuela, Colombia, Ecuador, and Peru. They grow at moderate to high altitudes, mostly on the forest floor in leaf litter under light shade. They are related to the genus *Lycaste*. The leaves are deciduous and the single-flowered inflorescences are produced from the base of the leafless pseudobulbs. The long-lasting flowers are showy and have a waxy texture.

CULTIVATION

These species are suited to cultivation in cool to intermediate conditions. They do well in a well-drained mixture that retains some moisture—some growers add sphagnum moss or rich garden soil. Bright filtered light is best. The plants should be watered heavily while the growths are forming, but watering should be greatly reduced after the leaves have fallen.

Anguloa clowesii LINDL.

This species occurs in Venezuela and Colombia at moderate to high altitudes, growing terrestrially in leaf mould on the forest floor. The pseudobulbs are clustered, conical, and up to 5$^{1}/_{2}$ in (13 cm) tall. They have several plicate leaves about 18–32 in (45–80 cm) long. The inflorescence are up to 12 in (30 cm) long with a single, showy, waxy, long-lasting flower up to 3$^{1}/_{4}$ in (8 cm) long. Flowering is from spring to early summer. **ZONES 9–10. C–I.**

Anguloa virginalis
LINDEN EX SCHLTR.
syn. *A. turneri* B. S. WILLIAMS

This species comes from Colombia and the northern part of South America. It grows at moderate to high altitudes, and has been much confused with *A. uniflora* and *A. eburnea*, both of which have predominantly white flowers. The flower color of *A. virginalis* is white marked with closely set pink or brown spots. The pseudobulbs are clustered, conical, and about 6 in (15 cm) long, with one or two leaves up to 18 in (45 cm) long and 6$^{1}/_{4}$ in (16 cm) wide. The inflorescences have a single, large, showy, waxy, sweetly scented, long-lasting flower about 4 in (10 cm) across. Flowers appear during spring. **ZONES 9–11. C–I.**

Anguloa virginalis

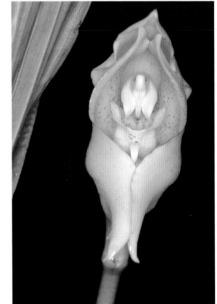

Anguloa clowesii

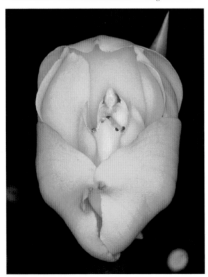

ANIA LINDL.

This genus is related to, and often united with, *Tainia*. There are about eight species, all terrestrials, with conical pseudobulbs, each having one leaf. The inflorescence arises from the base of the old pseudobulb. They occur in rain forests from Thailand, down to the Malay Peninsula, and on the Asian islands of Sumatra, Java, and Borneo.

A

Ania penangiana (HOOK.F.)
SUMMERH.

syn. *Tainia hookeriana* KING & PANTL.

This is a very widespread species from Southeast Asia, ranging from northeast India through China, Thailand, and Vietnam to the Malay Peninsula. It grows on the forest floor in tropical semi-evergreen forests at altitudes between 2000 and 2800 ft (600 and 830 m). The pseudobulbs are up to 2 in (5 cm) high with leaves up to 20 in (50 cm) long. The inflorescence, which arises from the pseudobulb bases, is up to 40 in (1 m) high and carries five to 15 flowers. Flowers are about 1¾ in (4 cm) wide. Flowers appear mostly during winter.
ZONES 10–11. I–H.

Ania penangiana

A

Anoectochilus formosanus

Anoectochilus yatesae

Anoectochilus yatesae
F. M. BAILEY

This small species grows on the rain forest floor at low to moderate altitudes in the northeast corner of Australia, often near streams or in leaf litter pockets on rocks. A short creeping stem has two to six oval leaves, up to about 2½ in (6 cm) long and 1¾ in (4 cm) wide, with attractive silver veining on dark green-maroon color. The inflorescence is up to 6 in (15 cm) tall with a few white flowers. Flowering is during the dry season. **ZONES 10–11. I.**

Ansellia africana

ANOECTOCHILUS BLUME
"JEWEL ORCHIDS"

These small terrestrial species are grown for their attractively veined leaves, hence their often used common name. They consist of a creeping rhizome that lies on or just under the leaf litter. From it, a short stem grows vertically with a few dark red leaves that have a light veining and a velvet sheen. The relatively large flowers are few, but the midlobe of the lip is usually strongly fringed. Most of these species grow at low to moderate altitudes, in deep shade on rain forest floors.

CULTIVATION
The plants must be given a humid environment with semi to heavy shade away from excessive air movement. The substrate should remain moist after watering. In cultivation, slugs and snails may be a problem.

Anoectochilus formosanus HAYATA

This small species grows in Taiwan at moderate altitudes on shady forest floors. The plant, including its erect inflorescence, is about 6 in (15 cm) tall. The leaves are about 1¼–1¾ in (3–4 cm) long and ⅘–1¼ in (2–3 cm) across. They are a dark reddish-green color with an attractive veining on the velvety surface. **ZONES 9–10. I–H.**

ANSELLIA LINDL.

Now regarded as one variable species, this genus was previously thought to include several species. It is widespread in tropical Africa, growing in a range of habitats.

CULTIVATION
While *Ansellia* plants often grow in seasonally very dry climates, in cultivation evenly moist conditions seem best. Bright light is required for flowering. The root system may be quite massive, so large pots or baskets with freely draining medium are recommended.

Ansellia africana LINDL.
syn. several names, including *A. gigantea* RCHB.F.

This robust species occurs in tropical Africa, as far south as the KwaZulu Natal province of South Africa. It grows in open woodlands at altitudes from sea level to 7300 ft (2200 m) in areas that have a seasonal climate. It has cylindrical pseudobulbs 20–48 in (50–120 cm) long with leaves on the upper part. The flowers are 1¼–2 in (3–5 cm) across, sweetly scented, yellow with a variable amount of dark spotting, and borne on a branched or unbranched inflorescence of ten to 100 flowers. **ZONES 10–12. I–H.**

A

APLECTRUM NUTTALL

This genus has two species, one in eastern USA, the other in Japan. This distribution is explained through the movement of glaciers over 20,000 years ago, which may have wiped out related plants in the area between these two countries. Unlike most North American terrestrial orchids, *Aplectrum* is a member of a large division of the orchid family that includes most of the tropical tree-dwelling species grown by orchidists. This genus, however, is not suited to cultivation. The plants have an underground storage stem or corm, formed anew each year. From this the roots, leaves, and flower stems arise. The single leaf appears during winter. Inflorescences with multiple flowers appear during spring.

Aplectrum hyemale (MUHLENBERG
EX WILLDENOW) NUTTALL
"PUTTY ROOT"

This native of northeastern USA grows in deciduous forests that are rapidly vanishing. Its common name arose because early colonists valued the mucilaginous flesh of the corms, using it for glue, medicine, and even food. As the winter leaf vanishes, the flower stalk rises to 20 in (50 cm), carrying up to ten flowers, each 1 in (2.5 cm) wide. Albino forms of this species are also known. The plant is dormant through summer to early autumn and flowers during spring. **ZONES 5–7. C.**

Aplectrum hyemale

APOSTASIA BLUME

This genus, along with the related *Neuweidia*, is considered by some botanists not to belong in the Orchidaceae family because it has two fertile stamens and a very poorly developed column. *Apostasia* are all terrestrial herbs that grow in shady, humid places in tropical Asia and Australia. They have several narrow leaves and white to yellow flowers with petals that do not have well-developed lips. Although rarely cultivated, a rich, well-drained mixture and humid, shady conditions would most likely be needed for successful growth.

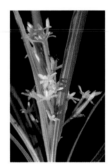

Apostasia wallichii

Apostasia wallichii R.BR.
syn. *A. stylidioides* (F. MUELL.) RCHB.F., *A. papuana* SCHLTR., *A. alba* ROLFE

This small terrestrial species has a wide distribution from Sri Lanka to Papua New Guinea and northeast Australia. It grows at low altitudes on the forest floor in shaded conditions. The stems are up to 40 in (1 m) tall, but more commonly about 8–12 in (20–30 cm) tall. It has numerous narrow, grasslike leaves just as long. The erect or pendulous inflorescence is about $3^{1}/_{4}$ in (8 cm) long with five to 25 flowers, each about $^{1}/_{3}$ in (1 cm) across. Flowering occurs usually during the wet season. **ZONES 11–12. H.**

A

ARACHNIS BLUME

The seven species in this genus are scrambling epiphytic monopodial orchids. They occur naturally in Southeast Asia and the Malay Archipelago. They feature long stems and sprays of large, striped, long-lasting flowers. The genus is related to *Vanda* and *Renanthera*.

CULTIVATION

These species require mostly full sun and hot, humid conditions with good air movement. The large size and scrambling nature of the plants make them unsuited to pot culture in a glasshouse. They grow best out in the open in a tropical garden.

HYBRIDS

These species have been crossed with *Vanda* and *Renanthera* species to produce flowers well suited to the cut-flower trade.

Arachnis flosaeris (L.) RCHB.F.
syn. *A. moschifera* BLUME

This is a large, scrambling monopodial species from the Malay Peninsula, the Asian islands of Sumatra, Java and Borneo, and the Philippines. It grows at low altitudes, often in full sunlight, scrambling over trees or rocks. The stems are up to 33 ft (10 m) long with numerous leathery leaves about 4–8 in (10–20 cm) long and 1–2 in (2.5–5 cm) across. The horizontal or pendulous inflorescences are up to 5 ft (1.5 m) long, and they carry several flowers that open progressively. Each flower is about $3-3^2/_3$ in (7.5–9 cm) wide and $4^1/_2$ in (11 cm) long.
ZONES 11–12. H.

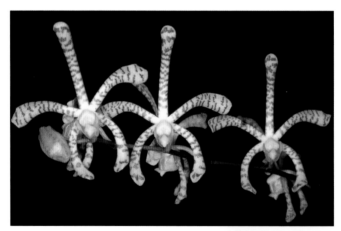

Arachnis flosaeris

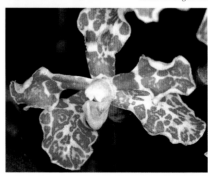

Arachnis longicaulis

Arachnis longicaulis (SCHLTR.) L. O. WILLIAMS
syn. *Vandopsis longicaulis* SCHLTR.

This species occurs in Papua New Guinea and, probably, in Irian Jaya. It grows on trees and rocks in the Central Range at an altitude of 500–4300 ft (150–1300 m). This robust, branching species may reach up to 80 in (2 m) long. It is usually pendulous with widely spreading leaves about 8 in (20 cm) long. The inflorescences are about as long as the leaves and bear up to ten flowers, each about $2^1/_2$ in (6 cm) across. The flowers are long lasting.
ZONES 11–12. H.

ARETHUSA L.

This genus contains only one North American species. As is the case with the genera *Aplectrum* and *Pogonia*, its closest relative is native to Japan. *Arethusa* is named after a nymph from classical mythology. It grows in cool woodlands, and like several other American terrestrial orchids, it arises from a perennial corm. It produces a single flower in early spring and one leaf after flowering.

Arethusa bulbosa

Arethusa bulbosa L.

This inhabitant of sphagnum peat bogs is now in danger of extinction over much of its range—the northeast region of the USA and the Maritime Provinces of Canada. The flower is up to 15 in (40 cm) high and over 1¹/₄ in (3 cm) wide. Like three other purple, spring-blooming species, *Calopogon*, *Calypso*, and *Pogonia*, it attracts bees with a yellow "beard" on its lip. This resembles pollen. The attractive flower looks like the head of a small animal because of the way its upright dorsal sepal and two petals contrasts with the reflexed lip. **ZONES 4–7. C.**

A

ARPOPHYLLUM LA LLAVE & LEX.

This genus comprises about five species, all of which occur in Mexico with some extending further south to Colombia. The plants have a slender short stem topped by a single, thick and tough leaf. All the species produce a compact, many-flowered, erect spike, and are either epiphytes, lithophytes, or, sometimes, terrestrials.

CULTIVATION

All the species grow at intermediate elevations and require potting in a well-drained mixture kept moist throughout the year. They also require bright light in order to flower well.

Arpophyllum alpinum

Arpophyllum alpinum
LINDL.

This species occurs in Mexico, Guatemala, and Honduras. The pseudobulbs arise at short intervals along a creeping rhizome and may grow up to 15 in (40 cm) tall. The single leaf is rigid and fleshy and may be up to 24 in (60 cm) long. The inflorescence is produced on a long stalk and the cylindrical raceme, up to 6 in (15 cm) long, is dense with many flowers. The flowers are less than ¾ in (18 mm) across. Flowering is during spring.
ZONES 10–11. I–H.

Arpophyllum giganteum
HARTWEG EX LINDL.

This species has a more widespread distribution than *A. alpinum*—it occurs in Costa Rica, Colombia and Jamaica. It is also much larger and more robust. The plants may be up to 28 in (70 cm) tall, and flowers are up to ¾ in (18 mm) across. Flowering is during spring.
ZONES 10–11. I–H.

Arpophyllum giganteum

Arundina graminifolia

ARUNDINA BLUME

This is a small genus of about eight species extending from southern China and the Himalayas, Sri Lanka, Malaysia, and Indonesia to the Pacific Islands as far as Tahiti. It is not present in the Philippines. All are terrestrial herbs and may be cultivated outdoors in gardens in warm regions.

Arundina graminifolia (D. DON) HOCHR.

This species is a large, erect, terrestrial plant that is about 60–100 in (1.5–2.5 m) tall. Its stems are to about ¾ in (18 mm) in diameter. The leaves are grasslike, about 12 in (30 cm) long. The inflorescence is terminal, up to 12 in (30 cm) long. Flowers are about 3⅔ in (9 cm) wide. Flowering occurs throughout the year and the species may be cultivated in garden beds with well-drained soil. This species has become naturalized in the Hawaiian islands. **ZONE 12. H.**

A

ASCOCENTRUM SCHLTR.

This genus comprises about ten species that occur in the Himalayan area, Southeast Asia, the Philippines, and the islands of Borneo and Java. They are monopodial species, mostly small or miniature, and they grow mainly at low to moderate altitudes (except for *A. pumilum* which grows in cloud forest at high altitudes). They have many small, showy flowers featuring bright orange, red, or yellow colors.

CULTIVATION

With the exception of *A. pumilum*, these species grow well in intermediate to hot climates in brightly lit conditions. Generally they require year-round watering and humid conditions, although a resting period of a few weeks in winter, when the plants are kept a little drier, is beneficial to flowering. They are amenable to pots, baskets, or slabs. If potted, a well-drained medium is required.

HYBRIDS

While only a handful of hybrids have been created within this genus, they have been used extensively in crosses with *Vanda* (*Ascocenda*), producing bright colors on small, easy-to-handle plants. They have also been crossed with other genera, for example, *Aerides* × *Ascocentrum* × *Vanda* (*Christiera*), or *Ascocentrum* × *Rhynchostylis* × *Vanda* (*Vascostylis*).

Ascocentrum ampullaceum (ROXB.) SCHLTR.

This colorful miniature grows at low to moderate altitudes from northeast India and Nepal through the Yunnan province of China to Indochina. The plant has a short stem with several more or less spotted leaves, about 5–6 in (13–15 cm) long and $\frac{1}{3}$ in (1 cm) wide. The erect inflorescence carries up to about 45 densely packed flowers, each about $\frac{4}{5}$ in (2 cm) across. Flower color ranges from pink to orange. A drier, cool resting period is required to encourage good flowering.
ZONES 10–12. I–H.

Ascocentrum ampullaceum

A

Ascocentrum curvifolium (LINDL.) SCHLTR.

This species occurs in the Himalayas from India and Nepal to Indochina. It grows at low to moderate altitudes, and has a longer stem than most species in this genus. The leaves are strap-shaped, about 4–12 in (10–30 cm) long and ⅔ in (15 mm) wide. The inflorescence is erect and bears numerous flowers, each up to ⅘–1¼ in (2–3 cm) across. Flowering occurs during spring. A cooler, slightly drier resting period in winter is required for good flowering. **ZONES 10–12. I–H.**

Ascocentrum garayi CHRISTENSON

In cultivation this species is often incorrectly labelled *A. miniatum*. True *A. garayi* occurs in Indochina at low to moderate altitudes. It is a small plant, growing to about 6 in (15 cm) tall, with leathery leaves 4½ in (11 cm) long and ⅔ in (15 mm) wide. The upright inflorescence has numerous orange flowers about ½ in (12 mm) across. Flowering occurs during spring. **ZONES 10–12. H.**

Ascocentrum curvifolium (left)

Ascocentrum garayi

A

Ascoglossum calopterum

ASCOGLOSSUM SCHLTR.

This is a genus of two species—one occurring in Ambon, Indonesia, the other in Papua New Guinea. It is related to *Vanda* and has a similar growth habit. The cultivation conditions are also similar to other vandaceous species and these plants may be grown either mounted on hardwood or cork slabs, or in a hanging basket with a coarse, free-draining mix.

Ascoglossum calopterum (RCHB.F.) SCHLTR.

This species is endemic to Papua New Guinea. It grows in a variety of habitats, from mangrove swamps to rain forests, from sea level to about 2000 ft (600 m). The erect stems are up to about 20 in (50 cm) tall, and have six to 12 lax leaves on the upper part of the stem to about 10 in (25 cm) long. The inflorescence has two to seven branches with each branch carrying up to 15 flowers. The flowers are about 1 in (2.5 cm) high. Flowering occurs throughout the year and lasts for several weeks. **ZONE 12. H.**

Aspasia principissa RCHB.F.

This species ranges from Nicaragua to Colombia and is found in wet forests at moderate altitudes. The ellipsoidal and laterally compressed pseudobulbs are 6 in (15 cm) long and have stalks. The paired leaves are leathery and grow to about 12 in (30 cm) long. The erect inflorescences, about 9¼ in (23 cm) tall, have a few flowers. These are about 3 in (7.5 cm) long and are lightly fragrant. Flowering occurs during late spring and summer. **ZONES 11–12. I–H.**

Aspasia principissa

ASPASIA LIND.

This genus of about eight epiphytic or lithophytic species grows from Guatemala to Brazil. They are all medium-sized plants with showy, long-lasting flowers.

CULTIVATION

These species are easy to grow. They may be either mounted or grown in pots with a well-drained mix. They require warm conditions and abundant moisture during active growth periods.

Aspasia lunata LINDL.

This Brazilian species has compressed pseudobulbs spaced 2–3 in (5–7.5 cm) apart on a rhizome, and about 2 in (5 cm) tall. The leaves are about 8 in (20 cm) long, and the flowers about 1½ in (3.5 cm) long. The inflorescence appears during spring and bears one or two flowers. **ZONE 11–12. I–H.**

Aspasia lunata

B

BAPTISTONIA BARB. RODR.

This genus contains only one species, endemic
to Brazil. It grows at altitudes of 165–2600 ft
(50–780 m) in the subtropical, coastal
mountain rain forests near Rio de Janeiro and
Sao Paulo. When cultivated it should be kept in
intermediate conditions. It also needs to be
watered well during the growing season. This
plant may be grown in hanging baskets, pots,
or mounted on tree-fern slabs.

Baptistonia echinata BAR. RODR.

The pseudobulbs of *B. echinata* are tightly
clustered and about 4 in (10 cm) long and
½ in (12 mm) in diameter. Two leaves, each
about 7 in (18 cm) long, are present at the
apex of the pseudobulbs. Many flowers are
produced on a pendulous, often branched,
inflorescence. The flowers are up to about
1 in (2.5 cm) wide. Flowers appear during
spring. **ZONES 10–11. I.**

Baptistonia echinata

Barbosella dusenii

BARBOSELLA SCHLTR.

This is a genus of about 20 species. They are
widespread from Central America to southern
Brazil. These plants are small, and they either
creep or form tufts. Most grow in high
altitudes and require cool to intermediate
conditions with constant, year-round
moisture. They may be grown either mounted
on tree-fern slabs, especially the creeping
types, or in small pots containing sphagnum.

Barbosella dusenii (A. SAMP.) SCHLTR.

This species from the coastal
mountains of southeast Brazil has
flowers about ⅘ in (2 cm) high. The
plant may be accommodated in a
small pot or mounted on a tree-fern
slab. It should not be allowed to dry
out and it must be kept in a cool,
humid environment. **ZONES 8–10. C.**

BARKERIA KNOWLES & WESTCOTT

The 15 species of this genus were once considered part of *Epidendrum*. They were separated from that group because there are some differences in the shapes of their columns, rostellums, and pseudobulbs. Most of the *Barkeria* species grow from Mexico to Guatemala but at least one of the species extends into Panama. The majority of them grow at moderate altitudes, often in bright light, as epiphytes or lithophytes. Their pseudobulbs are narrow and cylindrical, almost reedlike, and their flowers grow on the leafless stems, usually during winter.

CULTIVATION

As most of these species are deciduous, they require drier conditions during winter. A slab of cork or a similar material is best for mounting, but care should be taken to ensure the roots are not wet for any extended periods. Bright light, even full sun, is recommended.

Barkeria dorotheae

Barkeria lindleyana

Barkeria dorotheae
HALBINGER

This is a rare and restricted orchid in its native habitat— the low-altitude regions of the Jalisco state in western Mexico. It is epiphytic, and grows at the bottom of large cacti or small trees, or on rocks. Its pseudobulbs are spindle-shaped and leafless when in flower. The flowers are large and showy, appearing early to mid summer. Lateral branches may develop on the inflorescences, and these may continue the flowering period into late summer. **ZONES 11–12. H.**

Barkeria lindleyana
BATEMAN EX LINDL.
syn. *Epidendrum lindleyanum*
(BATEMAN EX LINDL.) RCHB.F.

This epiphytic species occurs from Mexico to Costa Rica at low to high altitudes. The pseudobulbs grow in clusters. They are cylindrical to spindle shaped, and are up to about 2 in (5 cm) long. The leaves may range from 1¾–6 in (4–15 cm) long and ⅔–1¾ in (1.5–4 cm) broad. The erect to arching inflorescences may be up to 2 ft (60 cm) long. They comprise anywhere from a few to many flowers, each one 2–2¾ in (5–7 cm) wide. **ZONES 10–12. I–H.**

B

Barkeria skinneri

Barkeria skinneri (BATEMAN EX LINDL.) PAXT.
syn. *Epidendrum skinneri* BATEMAN EX LINDL.

This species occurs in both Guatemala and the
state of Chiapas in Mexico. It grows on oak
trees at low to moderate altitudes. Its
pseudobulbs are narrow and cylindrical, and
they may be up to 6 in (15 cm) long. From
these, several leaves arise, each growing up to
6 in (15 cm) long and $^4/_5$ in (2 cm) wide. The
inflorescence may be either branched or
unbranched, up to 12 in (30 cm) long, with
few to many flowers, each about $1^3/_4$ in (4 cm)
wide. Flowering occurs during autumn and
winter. It grows best on a slab under bright
light. **ZONES 10–12. I.**

Barkeria spectabilis BATEMAN EX LINDL.
syn. *Epidendrum skinneri* (BATEMAN EX LINDL.) RCHB.F.

This is the showiest species of the genus. It
grows on oak trees in the state of Chiapas in
Mexico, Guatemala, and El Salvador, at
elevations of 5000–8300 ft (1500–2500 m). Its
pseudobulbs are narrow and cylindrical, about
6 in (15 cm) long. The leaves are $1^3/_4$–$5^2/_3$ in
(4–14 cm) long and $^2/_3$–$1^3/_4$ in (1.5–4 cm) wide.
Its inflorescence may have few or many
flowers, and these vary in size as well as color,
although white and lilac are predominant.
ZONES 9–10. C–I.

Barkeria spectabilis

Barkeria whartoniana

Barkeria whartoniana
(SCHWEINFURTH)
SOTO ARENAS
syn. *Epidendrum
whartonianum*
SCHWEINFURTH

This species comes
from the Isthmus
of Tehuantepec in
southern Mexico.
It grows at low
altitudes in exposed
conditions on rocks
in deciduous forests.
It is a rare species,
therefore, to conserve
it in its habitat, it
should not be
purchased if it has
been collected from
the wild.
ZONES 11–12. H.

B

BIFRENARIA LINDL.

These species of this genus have previously been placed in the genera *Lycaste* and *Maxillaria*. *Bifrenaria* now comprises about 24 species which occur in Brazil and other South American nations. Most are epiphytes, growing in rain forests at low to moderate altitudes. The pseudobulbs grow in clusters, and are ovoid in shape with four angles. They have one or two long, broad leaves. Their inflorescences arise from the pseudobulb base and produce one to three, usually large, waxy flowers.

CULTIVATION

These species do well in pots or hanging baskets with a standard epiphytic mix. In general, intermediate conditions are recommended. These plants grow best in bright light and should be watered heavily when the pseudobulbs are developing. When the pseudobulbs are mature and conditions cooler, allow a drier resting period.

Bifrenaria inodora LINDL.
syn. *B. fragrans* R. BR.

This epiphytic species is similar to *B. harrisoniae*, except the flowers are apple-green in color. It grows at low to moderate altitudes in Brazil. The pseudobulbs are 2½ in (6 cm) tall, each producing a single leaf. The single flowers are about 3 in (7.5 cm) across. They are waxy and long-lasting and may be fragrant. Flowering occurs during late winter and summer.
ZONES 10–12. I–H.

Bifrenaria harrisoniae (HOOK.F.) RCHB.F.
syn. *Maxillaria harrisoniae* (HOOK.F.) LINDL.,
Lycaste harrisoniae (HOOK.F.) B. S. WILLIAMS

This species occurs naturally in the lowlands of Brazil but it has become a popular cultivated species. It is usually an epiphyte, but it also grows over rocks under full sunlight in exposed situations. Its pseudobulbs have four angles, are ovoid in shape, and up to about 3 in (7.5 cm) tall. A single, leathery leaf, up to 1 ft (30 cm) long and 4 in (10 cm) wide, is present on each pseudobulb. Two single, waxy, fragrant, long-lasting flowers, about 3 in (7.5 cm) wide, arise from the pseudobulb bases. Flowers appear during spring and early summer. This species does well in a hanging pot in intermediate conditions in filtered light, requiring less water during winter. **ZONES 10–11. I–H.**

Bifrenaria inodora
Bifrenaria harrisoniae

B

Bifrenaria tetragona (LINDL.) SCHLTR.

syn. *Lycaste tetragona* LINDL., *Maxillaria tetragona* LINDL.

This species comes from the mountainous areas
in southern Brazil. It grows at low to moderate
altitudes. Its clustered pseudobulbs have four
angles, are ovoid in shape, and are about 4 in
(10 cm) tall. A single leaf, about $9^2/_3$–18 in
(24–45 cm) long and $3^1/_4$ in (8 cm) wide, is
present on each pseudobulb. The inflorescences
arise from the base of each pseudobulb and
bear one to three flowers. Each waxy, long-
lasting flower is about 2 in (5 cm) across but,
unfortunately, they have a rather unpleasant
smell. Flowers occur during summer.
ZONES 10–11. I–H.

Bifrenaria tetragona

Bifrenaria tyrianthina (LODD.) RCHB.F.

syn. *Lycaste tyrianthina* LODD., *L. d'allemagnei* HORT., *Maxillaria tyrianthina* HORT.

This species comes from the mountainous regions of southern Brazil,
where there is a significant dry season. Its pseudobulbs are clustered,
have four angles, and are ovoid in shape. They are $2^1/_2$–$5^1/_2$ in (6–13 cm)
tall and have a single, leathery leaf that is up to about 11 in (28 cm)
long and $3^1/_4$ in (8 cm) wide. Its inflorescences are up to 4 in (10 cm)
long and have two or three fleshy, long-lasting flowers, each about
2–$2^3/_4$ in (5–7 cm) wide. In cultivation this species grows well in a
range of temperatures. **ZONES 9–11. I–H.**

Bifrenaria tyrianthina

B

BLETIA RUIZ AND PAVON.

This genus of about 40 terrestrial or lithophytic species is limited to the American tropics. The pleated leaves arise from an underground corm. *Bletia* is distantly related to *Arethusa*.

Bletia purpurea (LAM.) DE CANDOLLE

Bletia purpurea

This attractive, purple-flowered species occurs in southern Florida, throughout the Caribbean and Central America, and the northern part of South America. In Jamaica it flourishes in the stony soil beside roads. Up to five leaves, as large as 3 ft (90 cm) long, grow annually from a corm, which is 2 in (5 cm) across. The inflorescences reach 40 in (1 m), and carry several flowers, about 2 in (5cm) wide. The lip displays several yellow crests. This species is readily cultivated in a standard terrestrial mix. It should be allowed a watering rest period when the leaves die back. **ZONES 11–12. I–H.**

BLETILLA RCHB.F.

There are about nine species, all terrestrial, in this genus. They occur in eastern Asia, including China, Japan, and some nearby islands. Most grow at moderate to high altitudes, in brightly lit situations. They have a cormlike pseudobulb with deciduous, pleated leaves and an erect inflorescence of a few flowers.

CULTIVATION

These plants should be potted in a rich, well-drained terrestrial mixture and grown in bright light or full sun. They tolerate cold temperatures, but should be protected from severe frost. Watering should be greatly reduced when the leaves are absent during winter.

Bletilla striata

Bletilla striata (THUNB.) RCHB.F.
syn. many names, including *Bletia striata* (THUNB.) DRUCE.

This terrestrial species from the eastern Himalayas, China, and Japan grows in full sun or light shade at moderate to high altitudes. The plant is up to 20 in (50 cm) tall and has broad, pleated leaves arising from an ovoid and compressed pseudobulb. Its erect inflorescence may have up to eight flowers, each about 2 in (5 cm) wide. They are usually pink or, occasionally, white. Flowering occurs during spring. *B. striata* is easy to grow in temperate areas, where it is best potted with well-drained soil and placed in the open.
ZONES 8–10. C–I.

BOLLEA RCHB.F.

This genus comprises about 11 species that occur mostly in the Andes of South America. They are epiphytes that live in wet cloud forests at altitudes between 3300 and 6000 ft (1000 and 1800 m). None of the species have pseudobulbs so they should not be allowed to dry out for any length of time in cultivation. They are best grown in a pot with a well-drained, water-retentive mix in cool to intermediate conditions.

Bollea coelestis

RCHB.F.

"BLUE ORCHID"

This orchid has a spectacular, highly fragrant flower. It is found on the slopes of the Andes in Colombia. The plants are tufted with six to ten leaves for each growth. The leaves are up to 1 ft (30 cm) long. Its inflorescence is much shorter than the leaves, and bears a single flower, up to 4 in (10 cm) across, during the summer. **ZONES 8–10. C.**

Bollea coelestis

Bonatea speciosa

BONATEA WILLD.

There are about 20 species in this terrestrial genus, which is related to *Habenaria* but is different in some of the flower details. The distribution of the species extends from Yemen and Ethiopia through eastern Africa to the Cape of Good Hope.

CULTIVATION

Several species of this genus are cultivated. They may be grown in a pot with a standard terrestrial mixture that drains well. They should be kept dry throughout winter, after flowering, and watered regularly when growth begins again in spring.

Bonatea speciosa WILLD.

This robust terrestrial species occurs in the sandy soils from sea level to 4000 ft (1200 m) above in southern and eastern South Africa. The plant, including its inflorescence, is up to 40 in (1 m) tall. It has broad, dark-green leaves, about ½–⅘ in (12–20 mm) long. These develop along the stem. The inflorescence has numerous densely packed flowers, each about 2 in (5 cm) across with a spur ⅘–2 in (2–5 cm) long. A feature of the flowers is the lower petal lobes. These may reach 1½ in (3.5 cm) in length. Flowering time is variable in the wild, depending on the location. **ZONES 9–11. I–H.**

BRACHYCORYTHIS LINDL.

This genus comprises some 35 species that occur mostly in the higher
altitudes of tropical Africa, with a few growing in Asia. The species are
terrestrial with tuberous roots. The base of the flower lip is boat-shaped
while the upper part is flattened and often has two equal-sized lobes.

CULTIVATION

The species of this genus are not widely cultivated. If they are, they
should be kept fairly dry when they die down to an underground tuber
after flowering, up until new shoot grow some months later.

Brachycorythis buchananii (SCHLTR.) ROLFE
syn. *B. parviflora* ROLFE, *Platanthera buchananii* SCHLTR.

This species occurs in grasslands and swamps across central Africa and
south to Zimbabwe, at an altitude of about 6700 ft (2000 m). It is
8–20 in (20–50 cm) tall and has numerous leaves up to 2 in (5 cm) long
and $4/5$ in (2 cm) wide. Its inflorescence is up to $5\frac{2}{3}$ in (14 cm) long with
many densely packed flowers, each flower about $1/4$ in (6 mm) long.
Flowering occurs during summer. **ZONES 9–10. C–I.**

Brachycorythis buchananii

Brachycorythis pleistophylla
RCHB.F.

syn. *B. leopoldii* KRAENZL., *B. pulchra*
SCHLTR.

This species occurs across tropical
Africa, as far south as northeast
South Africa, and on Madagascar.
It grows in grasslands and
woodlands at altitudes of
3300–9000 ft (1000–2700 m).
The plants are up to 3 ft (90 cm)
tall with numerous leaves along
the stem, the largest being about
$2\frac{1}{2}$ in (6 cm) long and $2/3$ in
(15 mm) wide. Its inflorescence
has many flowers, each about
$3/4$ in (18 mm) long, which are
loosely packed. Flowering occurs
during late spring and early
summer. **ZONES 9–10. C–I.**

Brachycorythis pleistophylla

BRASSAVOLA R. BR.

This genus of about 15 showy epiphytic species ranges from Mexico and the Caribbean south to Argentina. Most are plants of low to moderate altitudes. The pseudobulbs are slender and usually short, with a single (occasionally two) long, slender or terete leaves. The flowers are large and spidery, mostly in shades of white, cream, and green. They are long-lasting and fragrant at night. This combination of features attracts the nocturnal hawk moth that pollinates the species. One to several flowers are borne at the the junction of the slender stem and the single leaf. They last for several weeks. These species are related to *Rhyncholaelia* and *Cattleya*.

CULTIVATION

Plants of this genus are popular with collectors. Most are pendulous to some extent, and a hanging pot, basket, or slab suit them best. These plants may grow into large clumps so they require room to expand. Intermediate conditions with high humidity, good air movement, and bright light are the best growing conditions. They should be watered heavily throughout the growing season, but less so after flowering—the stems and leaves, however, should not be allowed to shrivel.

HYBRIDS

These species are easy to hybridize with members of the *Cattleya* alliance. Numerous horticultural hybrids, often involving several different genera, are on record.

Brassavola cucullata

Brassavola flagellaris

Brassavola cucullata (L.) R. BR.
syn. *Epidendrum cucullatum* L., *Brassavola cuspidata* HOOK.F.

This epiphytic species from Central America, the West Indies, and northern South America grows into large clumps. It occurs in rain forests from sea level to 6000 ft (1800 m). The slender stems may be up to 8 in (20 cm) long with a single terete leaf, about 8–12 in (20–30 cm) long, which may be arching or pendulous. The flowers appear singly or, occasionally, in pairs or triplets and are long-lasting. They are up to 7 in (18 cm) wide and are fragrant at night. They appear mostly during winter. **ZONES 10–12. I–H.**

Brassavola flagellaris BARB. RODRIGUES
"WHIP-LEAF ORCHID"

This species grows on trees and rocks at low to moderate altitudes in a restricted area of eastern Brazil. Its 20-in (50-cm) long, narrow, terete leaves resemble a whip, and this image gives rise to the species' scientific and common names. Its slender stems are erect, about 8 in (20 cm) tall. Its inflorescences are about 6 in (15 cm) long and each has five to 15 flowers, each flower about $2^{3}/_{4}$ in (7 cm) wide. These flowers are fragrant and long-lasting, and appear from spring to early summer. **ZONES 10–12. I–H.**

B

Brassavola martiana LINDL.

syn. several names, including *B. amazonica* POEPPIG & ENDLICHER, *B. multiflora* SCHLTR.

This species is recorded from the hot, steamy low-altitude regions of the Amazon Basin and the northern part of South America. Its slender stems are 4–10 in (10–25 cm) long, erect or slightly bent over, with a single pendulous, terete leaf, 10–20 in (25–50 cm) long. It has four to six, occasionally more, flowers per inflorescence. These flowers are fragrant at night, long-lasting, and about $3^1/_4$ in (8 cm) wide. Flowering occurs during summer. **ZONES 11–12. H.**

Brassavola nodosa (L.) LINDL.

syn. several names, including *Epidendrum nodosum* L., *Brassavola gillettei* JONES

This species was one of the earliest of the New World (American) orchids to be recorded, dating back to 1691. It is a popular orchid to cultivate. Its distribution is Central America, West Indies, Colombia and Venezuela, growing at low altitudes, often in rather dry conditions. The slender stems are up to 6 in (15 cm) long, with a single, narrow, fleshy leaf. The leaf is up to 12 in (30 cm) long with a groove on the upper surface. The inflorescence produces one to several flowers, each $3^1/_4$ in (8 cm) across, which are long-lasting and fragrant at night. Flowering occurs throughout the year. **ZONES 11–12. I–H.**

Brassavola perrinii LINDL.

syn. *B. rhomboglossa* PABST

This species grows in Bolivia, Brazil, Paraguay and, possibly, Argentina in a range of habitats at low to moderate altitudes. There has been much confusion between this species and *B. tuberculata*. *B. perrinii*, however, does not have dark purple-red spots on its sepals and is a smaller plant with smaller leaves and more flowers than *B. tuberculata*. Its slender stems are about $3/_4$–6 in (2–15 cm) long with a single, narrow leaf up to $9^1/_2$ in (24 cm) long. Each inflorescence has one to two flowers, about $2^1/_2$–$3^1/_4$ in (6–8 cm) wide. It flowers during summer. **ZONES 10–12. I–H.**

Brassavola martiana

Brassavola nodosa

Brassavola perrinii

B

Brassavola subulifolia

Brassavola subulifolia LINDL.

This charming epiphyte, restricted to Jamaica, was known for a long time as *B. cordata* because of its heart-shaped lip. Its flowers are relatively small but are produced in large numbers and make a splendid show when in bloom—up to eight flowers are borne on an inflorescence, each flower over 4 in (10 cm) in diameter. Its slender stem is up to 8 in (20 cm) long with a leaf measuring about 1 ft (30 cm) long but less than 1/3 in (1 cm) across. The leaf has a prominent groove on the upper surface. **ZONES 10–12. I–H.**

BRASSIA R. BR.

This is a genus of about 30 species occurring throughout tropical America. Most of them are epiphytes living in wet rain forest conditions from sea level to 5000 ft (1500 m).

CULTIVATION

This genus is easy to grow in baskets or pots. Use a mix that drains well and keep at intermediate temperatures. Water freely during the growing season but less often during dormancy.

Brassia arcuigera RCHB.F.

syn. *B. longissima* (RCHB.F.) NASH

This large plant has a stout, creeping rhizome and it occurs in Ecuador, Costa Rica, Panama, and Peru. Its pseudobulbs are a compressed ovoid shape, and are up to 7 in (18 cm) long. There is a single leaf about 20 in (50 cm) long. An inflorescence arises from the base of the pseudobulbs and bears up to 15 flowers. These are usually large with long sepals growing up to $9^2/_3$ in (24 cm) long. This plant should be grown under light shade. Flowers appear during spring. **ZONES 10–12. I–H.**

Brassia caudata (L.) LINDL.

This species, named for its long flower "tails," grows on trees or rocks. It is widely distributed in Florida, the Caribbean islands, and Central and South America. Its pseudobulbs, up to 6 in (15 cm) long, have two or three leaves, each up to 1 ft (30 cm) long. The gracefully arching inflorescence is up to 18 in (45 cm). It carries up to 12 flowers, each up to 8 in (20 cm) long. The flowers are fragrant and last for several weeks. Flowering occurs during autumn to early winter. **ZONES 11–12. I–H.**

Brassia arcuigera

Brassia caudata

B

Brassia lanceana

Brassia lanceana LINDL.

This species is found from Panama to Brazil
and Peru. It grows at low to moderate
altitudes. Its pseudobulbs are shaped like
compressed oblongs, and are about 5½ in
(13 cm) tall. The plant has two straplike leaves
up to 1 ft (30 cm) long. The inflorescence is
up to 2 ft (60 cm) tall and bears seven to
12 fragrant flowers, each about 5½ in (13 cm)
across. Flowering occurs during autumn.
ZONES 10–12. I–H.

Brassia peruviana POEPP. & END.

This large species appears to be endemic to
Peru. It has smaller pseudobulbs than other
species in the genus, measuring up to 2 in
(5 cm) long. The pseudobulbs are shaped like
globes. Its leaves are large, up to 2 ft (60 cm)
long. The raceme carries up to nine flowers,
which are medium in size for the genus. This
plant will tolerate slightly drier conditions than
the rest of the species in this genus. Flowering
occurs from late spring to summer.
ZONES 10–11. I–H.

Brassia peruviana

BROUGHTONIA R. BR.

There are about five species in this West Indian genus. Most are plants of humid, lowland environments with a distinct dry season. The pseudobulbs usually grow in clusters, are shaped like a flattened ovoid, and have two leathery leaves. The inflorescences are produced from the apex of the pseudobulbs and these contain a few brightly colored, rounded flowers.

CULTIVATION

The species in this genus grow best mounted on slabs of cork or similar material, but may be grown in pots with a well-drained medium. They require heavy watering during the growing season, but this should be decreased considerably when the pseudobulbs are mature. Intermediate to hot conditions with bright light and good air movement are recommended.

HYBRIDS

This genus is related to the *Cattleya* alliance and quite a number of hybrids have been created with that group.

Broughtonia domingensis

Broughtonia sanguinea (SW.) R. BR.

syn. *Epidendrum sanguinea* SW., *Broughtonia coccinea* LINDL.

This species, native to Jamaica, grows epiphytically at low altitudes. Its clustered pseudobulbs are ovoid to cylindrical and are 1–2 in (2.5–5 cm) tall. The two leaves are 3¼–8 in (8–20 cm) long and ⅘–2 in (2–5 cm) broad. Its inflorescence is up to 18 in (45 cm) long, is rarely branched, and bears five to 15 flowers. The brilliant red or, occasionally, yellow flowers are grouped near the end of the inflorescence and are about 1 in (2.5 cm) wide. Flowers appear from autumn to spring.
ZONES 11–12. I–H.

Broughtonia domingensis (LINDL.) ROLFE.

syn. *Laeliopis domingensis* (LINDL.) LINDL., *Broughtonia lilacina* NORTHROP.

This species from the lowland areas of Jamaica is considered by some authorities to also be a synonym of *B. negrilensis*. Its ovoid pseudobulbs reach 2½ in (6 cm), with one to three leaves, each about 7 in (18 cm) long and 1¼ in (3 cm) wide. The inflorescence may be as long as 40 in (1 m) and has up to 15 lilac flowers, about 2 in (5 cm) wide. The gullet of its ruffled lip is white. Flowering is from autumn to winter.
ZONES 11–12. I–H.

Broughtonia sanguinea

B

BULBOPHYLLUM THOUARS

With nearly 3000 species, this is one of the largest genera in the orchid family. It has a widespread distribution, mostly in the tropics, but also extends into temperate zones. It is found in the Americas, Africa and Madagascar, Southeast Asia (where it has its greatest diversity), Papua New Guinea, eastern Australia, and the western Pacific Islands.

Botanists are attempting to subdivide the genus into more manageable units. There are already more than 70 sections, some of which have been raised to generic level by some authorities. Pending a universally accepted taxonomic review of the genus, any alternative generic names are indicated in the synonymy under those species.

CULTIVATION

Being a genus with a large range of species from many different habitats, it is impossible to provide anything but generalized information about cultivation. Most species are epiphytes but a few are lithophytes. Generally, species with pseudobulbs growing quite close together are shallow rooted, so the pots may be shallow. The mixture should be free draining and able to retain adequate moisture. Species with widely spaced pseudobulbs may be grown in shallow hanging baskets or mounted on slabs which must be kept moist for most of the year, particularly during the growing season. All these plants appreciate high humidity, moderate warmth, and some shade—good light, however, is needed for flowering.

Bulbophyllum affine LINDL.

This species occurs from northern India and Nepal to China and Taiwan. It grows at altitudes up to 6700 ft (2000 m) but is more common at lower elevations. The pseudobulbs are cylindrical in shape and are spaced about 2–2³/₄ in (5–7 cm) apart. The rhizome and the base of the pseudobulbs are clothed with long, stiff bristles. The leaves are up to 7 in (18 cm) long. One flower arises from the base of the pseudobulbs on a pedicel about 2³/₄ in (7 cm) tall. The flower is about 1 in (2.5 cm) across. This species is best grown in a hanging basket or mounted on a slab. **ZONES 8–11. I–H.**

Bulbophyllum affine

Bulbophyllum ambrosia (HANCE)
SCHLTR.

This attractive species originates from Vietnam and China. Its pseudobulbs are cylindrical, orange-yellow in color, about 1½ in (3.5 cm) tall, and spaced 2–2¾ in (5–7 cm) apart on the rhizome. There is a single leaf about 5½ in (13 cm) long. A solitary flower, 1 in (2.5 cm) in diameter, is borne on a scape about 3 in (7.5 cm) tall. Because this species tends to ramble, it is best grown in a hanging basket or on a mount. Place under shade in warm to intermediate and humid conditions. **ZONES 10–11. I–H.**

Bulbophyllum ambrosia

Bulbophyllum auratum (LINDL.)
RCHB.F.

syn. *Cirrhopetalum auratum* LINDL.,
Bulbophyllum campanulatum ROLFE

Bulbophyllum auratum

This species is native to Thailand, the Malay Peninsula, the islands of Sumatra and Borneo, and the Philippines. Its pseudobulbs are about 1 in (2.5 cm) tall and about ½ in (12 mm) apart on a creeping rhizome. The single leaf is about 5½ in (13 cm) long. Its flowers are arranged in a whorl and each is about 1¾ in (4 cm) long. The inflorescence is about 6 in (15 cm) tall. It is easy to grow either on a mount or in a pot or basket. It thrives in warm to intermediate conditions with high humidity. Flowers occur during summer and autumn. **ZONES 11–12. I–H.**

B

Bulbophyllum barbigerum   *Bulbophyllum biflorum*

Bulbophyllum baileyi

Bulbophyllum baileyi F. MUELL.

This species occurs in Queensland in northeast Australia and in Papua New Guinea. It grows as an epiphyte or lithophyte in a range of habitats—from lowland rain forest, where it is commonly seen in massive clumps, to about 3300 ft (1000 m), where it is less frequent. Its rhizomes are covered with coarse bracts and its pseudobulbs are about 1¾ in (4 cm) tall and ovoid in shape. An upward-facing, single flower arises from a 4-in (10-cm) stalk and is about 1¾ in (4 cm) across. This species is best grown on a mount and requires warm, humid conditions—it is cold sensitive. It flowers from late winter into spring.
ZONES 10–12. I–H.

Bulbophyllum barbigerum LINDL.

This species is a native of tropical Africa, occurring around the Gulf of Guinea and extending from Sierra Leone to Gabon. It is found in rain forests growing from sea level to as high as 7700 ft (2300 m). Its pseudobulbs are spaced about 1 in (2.5 cm) apart on a rhizome, have a flattened ovoid shape, and are 1¾ in (4 cm) long. Its inflorescence carries many flowers and may be up to 8 in (20 cm) long. Its leathery leaves are about 3 in (7.5 cm) long. This species requires warm, humid conditions to grow well. It may be mounted on a slab or maintained in a shallow pan or pot.
ZONES 10–12. H.

Bulbophyllum biflorum TEIJSM. & BINN.

This is a widespread species that extends from Thailand, Malaysia, and Indonesia to the Philippines. It grows as an epiphyte at altitudes up to 2700 ft (800 m). The pseudobulbs on the form from the Philippines grow close together; on the other forms they are up to 2½ in (6 cm) apart on a rhizome. They all have four distinct angles, and may be up to 1¾ in (4 cm) tall. There is a single leaf about 5½ in (13 cm) long, and the flowers occur in pairs on a semi-pendulous inflorescence. Each flower is about 4 in (10 cm) long. Cultivated, this species is easily grown in a shallow pot or hanging basket in warm to intermediate conditions and bright light. Flowering is during autumn.
ZONES 11–12. I–H.

Bulbophyllum brienianum (ROLFE) J. J. SM.

This species grows in Malaysia, the islands of
Borneo and Sumatra, and the Philippines. Its
pseudobulbs are about ¾ in (18 mm) tall and
egg-shaped. The solitary leaf is about 2½ in
(6 cm) long. The inflorescence is about 8 in
(20 cm) long and carries five to ten flowers in
an umbel. These are fragrant and about 1¾ in
(4 cm) long. This species may be cultivated in
pots or hanging baskets in intermediate to hot
conditions. Flowering is during winter.
ZONES 11–12. I–H.

Bulbophyllum brienianum

B

Bulbophyllum burfordiense

Bulbophyllum carunculatum

Bulbophyllum burfordiense GARAY, HAUER & SIEGERIST **syn.** *B. grandiflorum* OF SOME AUTHORS NON BLUME

This very distinctive species occurs from Sumatra through Papua New Guinea to the Solomon Islands. It grows at moderate elevations, from about 330–2700 ft (100–800 m). Its ovoid to conical pseudobulbs are about 2 in (5 cm) apart, and about 1¾–2¾ in (4–7 cm) high. The single leaf is up to 6 in (15 cm) long and the single, 4-in (10-cm) long flower arises on a scape up to 8 in (20 cm). This species requires warmth and adequate moisture to grow and flower. Flowering occurs during spring. **ZONES 11–12. H.**

Bulbophyllum carunculatum GARAY, HAMER & SIEGERIST

This species is found on the Indonesian island of Sulawesi and in the Philippines. It is robust, growing up to 18 in (45 cm) tall. Its pseudobulbs are up to 2½ in (6 cm) tall and they have a single leaf about 16 in (40 cm) long and 2¾ in (7 cm) wide. The flowers are carried on an upright inflorescence about 18 in (45 cm) tall. Up to 12 flowers appear in succession, each about 3⅔ in (9 cm) long. **ZONES 10–12. I–H.**

B

Bulbophyllum cupreum   *Bulbophyllum dayanum*

Bulbophyllum cupreum LINDL.

This species originates from Myanmar and
Thailand. Its pseudobulbs are often spaced 4 in
(10 cm) or more apart on a slender rhizome.
They are ellipsoidal in shape and about 3 in
(7.5 cm) tall. The solitary leaf is thick and
leathery, and about 8 in (20 cm) long. The
short inflorescence is either pendulous or
horizontal. It is about 2½ in (6 cm) long and
densely packed with small flowers about ½ in
(12 mm) long. This species is best cultivated
in a wire hanging basket or on a slab where
its rambling habit can be accommodated. It
requires warm to intermediate conditions
with ample watering. Flowering is during
spring. **ZONES 11–12. I–H.**

Bulbophyllum dayanum RCHB.F.

This unusual species is distributed from north
India to Myanmar, Thailand, Cambodia, and
Vietnam. It grows at altitudes of about
1700–4300 ft (500–1300 m). Its egg-shaped
pseudobulbs are about 1¾ in (4 cm) tall and
may be clustered or closely spaced along a
rhizome. Its leaves are fleshy and up to 4 in
(10 cm) long. They are usually a reddish or
purplish color underneath. The inflorescence
has a very short stalk and it carries two to four
flowers, each about 1¾ in (4 cm) in diameter.
The flowers appear during spring and summer,
and they have the unfortunate character of
being somewhat foul smelling. Cultivation of
this species requires warmth, shade, moisture,
and humidity year-round. **ZONES 11–12. I–H.**

B

Bulbophyllum dearei REICH.F.

This attractive species is distributed from west
Malaysia through the island of Borneo to the
Philippines. It grows at elevations up to 3300 ft
(1000 m). Its pseudobulbs grow close together
and are about 2 in (5 cm) tall. The single leaf
is rigid and leathery, and is up to 6 in (15 cm)
long. The single flowers are borne on an
inflorescence that is generally shorter than the
leaves. The flowers are about 4¾ in (12 cm)
across, are heavily textured and long-lasting.
Flowering occurs during spring and early
summer. This species responds well to
cultivation in a shallow pot or hanging basket.
ZONES 11–12. I–H.

Bulbophyllum dearei

Bulbophyllum digoelense

Bulbophyllum digoelense J. J. SM.

This species, endemic to the lowlands of Papua
New Guinea, flowers progressively over a
period of months. Up to 12 flowers may
appear on an inflorescence during this time.
The inflorescence is long, up to 20 in (50 cm),
and the flowers open widely, to about 3 in
(7.5 cm) across. The pseudobulbs are 1¾ in
(4 cm) apart and are about 1¾ in (4 cm) tall.
The single leaf is up to 10 in (25 cm) long. This
species is amenable to cultivation in a hanging
basket or shallow pot. Flowering occurs from
spring to autumn. **ZONE 12. H.**

Bulbophyllum falcatum (LINDL.) RCHB.F.
syn. *Megaclinium falcatum* LINDL.

This species occurs in tropical Africa, from Sierra Leone through Guinea
and Zaire to Uganda. It is an epiphyte found from sea level to about
4000 ft (1200 m). The pseudobulbs are angular, about 2 in (5 cm) apart
on a rhizome and about 2½ in (6 cm) tall. The two leaves at the apex
are up to 6 in (15 cm) long. The inflorescence is a flattened rachis, about
5½ in (13 cm) long, which bears flowers placed alternately on either

Bulbophyllum falcatum

side. The flowers are
about ½ in (12 mm)
long and have an
unpleas-antly foul
odor. It is an easy
species to grow in a
pot or basket.
Flowering is during
the spring
and summer.
ZONES 11–12. I–H.

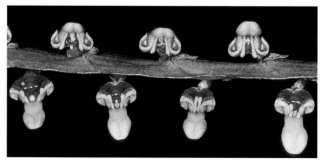

Bulbophyllum fascinator

Bulbophyllum fletcherianum

Bulbophyllum fascinator ROLFE

This species occurs from northeast India through Indochina and the islands of Sumatra and Borneo to the Philippines. Its pseudobulbs are about $^4/_5$ in (2 cm) high and they bear a solitary leaf about 3 in (7.5 cm) long. The scape is about 4 in (10 cm) high and carries one or two flowers with lateral sepals up to 7 in (18 cm) long. **ZONES 10–12. I–H.**

Bulbophyllum fletcherianum HORT.

This is probably the largest species in the genus. It is endemic to Papua New Guinea and grows anywhere from 800–2660 ft (240–800 m) above sea level. It forms large, spreading colonies on rock faces, and also grows on the low branches of trees near streams. Its large creeping rhizome produces pseudobulbs about $2^1/_2$–$3^2/_3$ in (6–9 cm) apart. These are erect, up to 4 in (10 cm) tall and $3^1/_4$ in (8 cm) wide at the base. The single, terminal leaf may be up to 5 ft (1.5 m) long and 7 in (18 cm) wide. The inflorescence is stout and carries a crowded raceme of 20 to 40 flowers. This species is difficult to maintain in cultivation but some success has been achieved by mounting plants on long tree-fern poles that are kept moist. The plants are very slow growing. Flowering is from late winter to spring. **ZONE 12. H.**

Bulbophyllum fraudulentum GARAY, HAMER & SIEGERIST
syn. *B. arfakianum* OF SOME AUTHORS NON KRAENZLIN

This attractive epiphyte is endemic to Papua New Guinea where it grows at elevations of 165–1300 ft (50–400 m). Its creeping rhizome branches regularly and produces four-sided pseudobulbs spaced about 1 in (2.5 cm) apart. These are often purple and about $^4/_5$ in (2 cm) high. They have a solitary leaf up to about 2 in (5 cm) long. The solitary flower, also about 2 in (5 cm) long, is held horizontally. It is borne on an erect stem up to about 6 in (15 cm) tall. Flowering time is sporadic throughout the year. **ZONE 12. I–H.**

Bulbophyllum fraudulentum

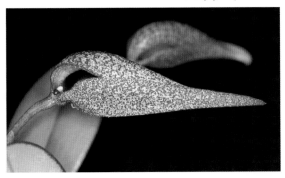

B

Bulbophyllum fritilariiflorum J. J. SM.

This species, endemic to
Papua New Guinea, has a
similar growing habit to
B. fraudulentum. The
inflorescences are about
5¹/₂ in (13 cm) tall, and the
flower may be up to 3 in
(7.5 cm) long. **ZONE 12. I–H.**

Bulbophyllum frostii
SUMMERH.

syn. *Cirrhopetalum frostii*

(SUMMERHOYES) GARAY, HAMER & SIEGERIST

This species from Vietnam,
Thailand, and the Malay
Peninsula, is small with
pseudobulbs spaced about
¹/₂ in (12 mm) apart on a
creeping rhizome. They are
about ⁴/₅ in (2 cm) high. The
single leaf is about 1³/₄ in
(4 cm) long. Clusters of small
flowers up to ⁴/₅ in (2 cm)
long arise from the rhizome on
a short stalk. This plant may be
cultivated on a slab or grown in
a pot. Flowering is during
winter. **ZONES 11–12. I–H.**

Bulbophyllum globuliforme NICHOLLS

This species is endemic to parts
of Australia—southeast
Queensland and northeast New
South Wales. It grows in rain
forests, mostly above 1700 ft
(500 m), and is one of the
smallest orchids. Its tiny
globular pseudobulbs are less
than ¹/₁₅ in (1 mm) in diameter.
The leaf is about the same
length, and is often shed early.
The inflorescence, up to ²/₃ in
(15 mm) tall, has a single
flower about 1¹/₄ in (3 cm)
across. Cultivate on a hardwood mount and water
frequently. Flowers appear
during spring. **ZONE 9. C–I.**

Bulbophyllum fritilariiflorum

Bulbophyllum globuliforme

Bulbophyllum frostii

Bulbophyllum gracillimum (ROLFE) ROLFE

syn. *B. leratii* (SCHLTR.) J. J. SM., *Cirrhopetalum gracillimum* ROLFE

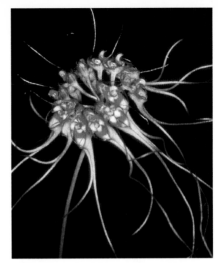

This species is very widespread, from Thailand to Indonesia, Papua New Guinea, Australia, the Solomon Islands, New Caledonia, and Fiji. It is an epiphyte that grows in lowland rain forests from sea level to about 500 ft (150 m). It grows in deep shade, often low down on a tree trunk. Its creeping rhizome has small pseudobulbs spaced ½ in (12 mm) apart and about ½ in (12 mm) high. These have four angles when mature. One or two slender inflorescences are produced. They are about 14 in (35 cm) long and carry up to 12 flowers in an umbel. The flowers are very slender, about 1¾ in (4 cm) long, and appear from spring through summer. This species is easily grown in a shallow pot or basket and should be given good shade and high humidity in a warm environment. **ZONE 12. H.**

Bulbophyllum gracillimum

Bulbophyllum graveolens F. M. BAILEY

This is a robust and striking species from the southern part of Papua New Guinea. It grows in rain forests from 330–2000 ft (100–600 m) in altitude. It has a creeping rhizome with large, fleshy green pseudobulbs spaced about 1¾ in (4 cm) apart. These may be up to 4 in (10 cm) high and they support a large, leathery leaf about 24 in (60 cm) long. The inflorescence is up to 8 in (20 cm) long. It is erect or slightly arching and ends in a horizontal fan of up to ten flowers, each of which is about 2 in (5 cm) long. The flowers are long-lasting. Flowering is during summer. A large pot will be required for mature plants. **ZONE 12. I–H.**

Bulbophyllum graveolens

B

B

Bulbophyllum guttulatum (HOOK.F.)
BALAKRISHNAN

syn. *B. umbellatum* LINDL., *B. leopardinum* (WALL.) LINDL.

This species ranges from Nepal in the Himalayas through Vietnam to Taiwan. The plants are reasonably compact with leaves to about 2 in (5 cm) long. The inflorescence is about the same size as the leaves and carries up to eight flowers in an umbel. These are about ½ in (12 mm) high. **ZONE 10. I.**

Bulbophyllum lasiochilum PAR. & RCHB.F.

syn. *B. breviscarpum* ROLFE, *Cirrhopetalum lasiochilum* (PAR. & RCHB.F.) HOOK.F.

This is an easy-to-grow orchid occurring in Myanmar, Thailand, and Malaysia. The pseudobulbs are ovoid in shape and about ⅘ in (2 cm) tall. They are spaced 1¼ in (3 cm) apart on a creeping rhizome. The solitary leaf is about 2 in (5 cm) long. The solitary flower is borne on a stalk about 1¾ in (4 cm) long. It is easily cultivated on slabs or in pots in warm to intermediate conditions with ample water during the growing season.
ZONES 11–12. I–H.

Bulbophyllum guttulatum

Bulbophyllum lasiochilum

B

Bulbophyllum lepidum

Bulbophyllum levyae

Bulbophyllum lobbii

Bulbophyllum lepidum (BLUME) J. J. SM.

syn. many names, including *Ephippium lepidum*
BLUME, *Cirrhopetalum lepidum* SCHLTR.

This species is widespread from Indochina to
the Moluccas in Indonesia. Its pseudobulbs are
closely spaced on the rhizome, are globular in
shape, and are about ⁴/₅ in (2 cm) tall. The
single leaf is about 5¹/₂ in (13 cm) long. The
inflorescence is up to 6 in (15 cm) high and
carries eight to ten flowers up to about 1 in
(2.5 cm) long. Flowering is during autumn.
ZONE 12. H.

Bulbophyllum levyae GARAY, HAMER & SIEGERIST

This is a large plant that is up to 16 in (40 cm)
tall. It is a native of Papua New Guinea, where
it grows in rain forests at an altitude of about
2700 ft (800 m). Its pseudobulbs are closely
spaced and its leaves are about 10 in (25 cm)
long. The inflorescence is about 16 in (40 cm)
tall and carries three or four flowers, about
1¹/₂ in (3.5 cm) wide. **ZONE 12. I–H.**

Bulbophyllum lobbii LINDL.

This well-known species occurs in Thailand, the
Malay Peninsula, and the islands of Sumatra,
Java, and Borneo. It grows as an epiphyte at
elevations between 3300 and 6000 ft (1000
and 1800 m). Its pseudobulbs are spaced up to
3¹/₄ in (8 cm) apart and are about 2 in (5 cm)
tall with sheaths that split into persistent
yellowish fibres. The leathery
leaves are up to 10 in (25 cm)
long. It has large, fragrant
and distinctive flowers that
are up to 3 in (7.5 cm) in
diameter. They arise from a
scape up to 4 in (10 cm) long.
It is easily cultivated in a
shallow pot or basket in
warm to intermediate
conditions. Flowering is
during late spring or summer.
ZONES 11–12. I–H.

B

Bulbophyllum longiscapum

Bulbophyllum longiscapum ROLFE

This species is very similar to *B. digoelense* and is found at low elevations from the Solomon Islands through to Tonga, Samoa, and Fiji. It has a progressive flowering lasting several months. **ZONE 12. H.**

Bulbophyllum longiflorum

Bulbophyllum longiflorum THOUARS
syn. *B. unbellatum* J. J. SM, *B. clavigerum* (FITZGERALD) DOCKRILL.

This is a very widespread species, ranging from Uganda and Madagascar to the Malay Peninsula, the Philippines, Papua New Guinea, Australia, New Caledonia, Fiji, Tahiti, and Guam. The species inhabits rain forests from sea level to about 5300 ft (1600 m). The plant is a creeping epiphyte with pseudobulbs to about 1¾ in (4 cm) long and spaced 2 in (5 cm) apart on the rhizome. The single leaf is up to 6 in (15 cm) long. Its inflorescence is up to 8 in (20 cm) long and bears six to eight flowers that form a semi-circle at the end of the peduncle. The flowers are about 1¾ in (4 cm) long. Flowering occurs from late summer to autumn. Culture is as for the genus. Warm conditions should be maintained. **ZONES 11–12. H.**

Bulbophyllum longissimum (RIDL.) RIDL.
syn. *Cirrhopetalum longissimum* RIDL.

This epiphyte from Thailand grows at low elevations. It is a spectacular species with four to ten flowers that may be up to 8 in (20 cm) long. The closely spaced pseudobulbs are conical in shape and are up to 1 in (2.5 cm) long. The single leaf is up to 6 in (15 cm) long. **ZONE 12. H.**

Bulbophyllum longissimum

B

Bulbophyllum medusae

Bulbophyllum masdevalliaceum

Bulbophyllum melanoglossum

Bulbophyllum masdevalliaceum KRAENZL.

syn. *B. blumei* (LINDL.) J. J. SM.

This is a most attractive species with a wide distribution, from west Malaysia, Sumatra, and Borneo to the Philippines, Papua New Guinea, Australia, and the Solomon Islands. It is most common in coastal forests but may occur as high as 2700 ft (800 m). The rhizome is creeping and frequently branches. The pseudobulbs are about 2 in (5 cm) apart and up to 1¾ in (4 cm) high. The solitary leaf is up to 4 in (10 cm) long. The inflorescence has a single flower on an erect peduncle about 4½ in (11 cm) long. The flower is about 2½ in (6 cm) long. Flowering is from winter to spring.
ZONE 12. H.

Bulbophyllum medusae (LINDL.) RCHB.F.

This species is epiphytic and lithophytic. It grows in limestone rocks in Thailand, western Malaysia, the islands of Sumatra and Borneo, Singapore, and the Philippines. Its pseudobulbs are spaced about 1¾ in (4 cm) apart and are up to 1¾ in (4 cm) high. The single leaf is up to 8 in (20 cm) long. The inflorescence is erect or arching and may be up to 8 in (20 cm) tall with a moplike head of many flowers, each about 6 in (15 cm) long. This species flowers during autumn and winter.
ZONES 11–12. I–H.

Bulbophyllum melanoglossum HAYATA

This species is endemic to Taiwan, growing at an altitude of about 5000 ft (1500 m). The pseudobulbs are spaced about 2 in (5 cm) apart on a rhizome. They are about 1 in (2.5 cm) tall. The single leaf is about 2½ in (6 cm) long. The inflorescence is up to 4 in (10 cm) high and carries up to 15 flowers arranged in an umbel. The flowers are about ⅔ in (15 mm) long. Flowering is from late spring to early summer. **ZONE 10. I.**

B

Bulbophyllum mirum J. J. SM.

syn. *Cirrhopetalum mirum* (J. J. SM.) SCHLTR., *Rhytionanthos mirum* (J. J. SM.)
GARAY, HAMER & SIEGERIST

This species is from Indonesia and western Malaysia. It grows at
altitudes between 4000 and 5000 ft (1200 and 1500 m). This
compact plant has pseudobulbs about ⁴/₅ in (2 cm) tall that grow
about ⁴/₅ in (2 cm) apart. The leaves are about 3 in (7.5 cm)
long. The inflorescence is very short and carries two flowers
about 3 in (7.5 cm) long. Flowering is during winter.
ZONES 11–12. I–H.

Bulbophyllum mirum

Bulbophyllum nematopodum F. MUELL.

This species is endemic to
northeast Queensland in
Australia, where it grows in
rain forests at elevations
above 2700 ft (800 m). It
forms small, dense clumps and
has pseudobulbs that may be
ovoid or flask shaped, about
⁴/₅ in (2 cm) high. The leaves
are about 5¹/₂ in (13 cm) long.
The flowering stem is about
3 in (7.5 cm) tall and carries
a single nodding flower, about
¹/₃ in (1 cm) across. Flowering
is during spring.
ZONES 10–11. I.

Bulbophyllum nutans

(LINDL.) RCHB.F.

syn. *Bulbophyllum othonis* (KUNTZE)
J. J. SM. *Cirrhopetalum nutans* LINDL.

This small plant is from the
Philippines. Its pseudobulbs
are about ¹/₃ in (1 cm) tall.
They grow about ⁴/₅ in
(2 cm) apart on a rhizome.
The inflorescence is long, up
to 8 in (20 cm), with many
flowers, each about ⁴/₅ in
(2 cm) long. Flowers appear
during autumn.
ZONE 12. I–H.

Bulbophyllum nematopodum

Bulbophyllum nutans

Bulbophyllum nymphopolitanum KRAENZL.

This species is endemic to the Philippines where it grows at elevations up to 3300 ft (1000 m). It is mostly an epiphyte. Its pseudobulbs are ovoid in shape and are up to 1¼ in (3 cm) high. The solitary, leathery leaf is up to 6 in (15 cm) long. The inflorescence bears up to four flowers, each up to 3⅔ in (9 cm) high. Flowering is during winter. **ZONE 12. H.**

Bulbophyllum odoratissimum (J. E. SMITH) LINDL.

This species is distributed from India and Nepal to Laos and Vietnam. The pseudobulbs are about 1 in (2.5 cm) tall and are widely separated on the rhizome. The single leaf is about 3 in (7.5 cm) long. The capitate inflorescence about 3 in (7.5 cm) long, carries many flowers. This species is pleasantly fragrant when it flowers during the autumn and winter. **ZONES 10–11. I.**

Bulbophyllum nymphopolitanum

Bulbophyllum orientale SEIDENF.

This species, a native of Thailand, is similar in most respects to *B. cupreum*. The pseudobulbs of *B. orientale* are about 1¼ in (3 cm) apart on the rhizome and about 1¾ in (4 cm) tall. The single leaf is about 6 in (15 cm) long. The inflorescence is densely flowered. Flowering occurs during spring. **ZONES 11–12. I–H.**

Bulbophyllum odoratissimum

Bulbophyllum orientale

B

Bulbophyllum picturatum

Bulbophyllum propinquum

Bulbophyllum picturatum (LODDIGES EX LINDL.) RCHB.F.

syn. *Cirrhopetalum picturatum* LODDIGES EX LINDL.

This species occurs from India to Vietnam at altitudes of about 3300 ft (1000 m). The clustered pseudobulbs are ovoid in shape and are up to 2 in (5 cm) tall. The rigid, solitary leaf is up to 7 in (18 cm) long. The inflorescence is up to 10 in (25 cm) tall and carries eight to ten flowers in an umbel at the apex. The flowers are about 2½ in (6 cm) long and are slightly fragrant but short-lived. Flowers appear during spring.
ZONES 11–12. I–H.

Bulbophyllum piestoglossum VERM.

This species is endemic to the Philippines. It grows as an epiphyte at elevations of 2000–4300 ft (600–1300 m). The pseudobulbs are spaced about 2 in (5 cm) apart on the rhizome and are about 1¾ in (4 cm) tall.

The single leaf is about 5²/₃ in (14 cm) long. The single flower is about 2 in (5 cm) across and is borne on a scape up to 3 in (7.5 cm) high. Flowers appear during summer.
ZONES 11–12. I–H.

Bulbophyllum propinquum
KRAENZL.

This species, a native of Thailand, has a similar growth habit to *B. cupreum*. Its pseudobulbs are about 1¾ in (4 cm) high, and are spaced about 1¾ in (4 cm) apart on the rhizome. The single leaf is about 5½ in (13 cm) long. Its inflorescence is similar in size and shape to *B. cupreum* and is densely flowered. Flowering is during winter.
ZONES 11–12. I–H.

Bulbophyllum piestoglossum

Bulbophyllum repens

Bulbophyllum retusiusculum

Bulbophyllum rothschildianum

Bulbophyllum rufinum

B

Bulbophyllum repens GRIFF.

This species occurs in Thailand, Myanmar, and India at moderate altitudes. Its pseudobulbs are small and close together. The single leaf is about ½ in (12 mm) long, and the inflorescence is densely flowered and is about 1¾ in (4 cm) high. **ZONES 10–11. I–H.**

Bulbophyllum retusiusculum RCHB.F.

This is a widespread and variable species, ranging east from Nepal to China, Indochina, and Taiwan. Its pseudobulbs are ovoid, about 1¼ in (3 cm) high, and spaced about the same distance apart on the rhizome. The single leaf is up to 4 in (10 cm) long. Six to 12 flowers on a radiating umbel are borne on a scape up to about 4 in (10 cm) long. **ZONES 10–12. I–H.**

Bulbophyllum rothschildianum
(O'BRIEN) J. J. SM.

This species from India and Thailand has pseudobulbs spaced about 1¼ in (3 cm) apart on a rhizome. The pseudobulbs are around 1¾ in (4 cm) high and they support a solitary leaf up to 6 in (15 cm) long. The inflorescence carries two to six flowers, each up to 6 in (15 cm) long. Because of its rambling nature, this species is best grown in a large pot or basket. Flowering occurs between spring and autumn. **ZONES 10–11. I–H.**

Bulbophyllum rufinum RCHB.F.

This species from Thailand resembles *B. cupreum* in its growth habit. The inflorescence, however, is longer and more sparsely flowered. **ZONES 11–12. I–H.**

Bulbophyllum schinzianum KRAENZL.

This robust species from equatorial Africa—Liberia through to Nigeria and Zaire—grows in rain forests from sea level up to about 2700 ft (800 m). The pseudobulbs have four prominent angles and are about 2 in (5 cm) tall. They are spaced about 1³/₄ in (4 cm) apart on the rhizome. The large and leathery leaf reaches up to 10 in (25 cm) long and 2 in (5 cm) wide. The tall inflorescence, up to 40 in (1 m), bears 11 to 100 flowers, which open progressively. These are about 1¼ in (3 cm) long and they appear during autumn. This species requires large pots to accommodate its spreading growth. **ZONES 11–12. I–H.**

Bulbophyllum schinzianum

B

Bulbophyllum sichyobulbon PAR. & RCHB.F.

A rambling, easy-to-grow plant from Myanmar and Thailand, this species is found at elevations up to 4000 ft (1200 m). Its pseudobulbs are conical, and they are up to 2 in (5 cm) high with a spread about 2 in (5 cm) apart. The leaves are thick and leathery, up to 6 in (15 cm) long. The inflorescence has a scape up to about $^1/_2$ in (12 mm) long. It carries many small, closely packed flowers, each up to about $^1/_4$ in (6 mm) wide. This species may be grown in hanging baskets, shallow pots, or mounted. It requires warm conditions with high humidity.
ZONES 9–11. I–H.

Bulbophyllum sichyobulbon

Bulbophyllum vaginatum (LINDL.) RCHB.F.

This species with a distribution from Thailand, Malaysia, and the islands of Sumatra, Java, and Borneo, is similar to *B. medusae*. Its pseudobulbs are up to 2 in (5 cm) apart and about $^4/_5$ in (2 cm) long. They are ovoid in shape. The thick, stiff leaf is up to 5$^1/_2$ in (13 cm) long. The flowering scape is about 4 in (10 cm) high and carries up to 15 flowers. Flowering is gregarious but occurs mostly during spring and early summer. **ZONES 11–12. I–H.**

Bulbophyllum vaginatum

Bulbophyllum weinthallii

Bulbophyllum wendlandianum

Bulbophyllum weinthallii R. ROGERS

This species is endemic to southeast Queensland and northeast New South Wales in Australia. It requires the Hoop Pine (*Araucaria cunninghamii*) tree that grows on the ranges and tablelands as its host. Its crowded pseudobulbs are conical to ovoid in shape, and up to about 1$^3/_4$ in (4 cm) high with a leaf to about 1$^1/_4$ in (3 cm) long. The flower stems are very short with a single flower up to about 1$^3/_4$ in (4 cm) across. This species may be difficult to grow as it needs cool, moist conditions for successful cultivation. A tree-fern slab gives the best results. Flowering is during autumn.
ZONE 9. C.

Bulbophyllum wendlandianum (KRAENZL.)

DAMMER
syn. *Cirrhopetalum collettii* HEMSLEY EX HOOK.F.

This species, found in Myanmar and Thailand, is similar to, but smaller than, *B. rothschildianum*. The pseudobulbs are about 1$^1/_4$ in (3 cm) high and are spaced about 1 in (2.5 cm) apart on the rhizome. Its single leaf is about 3$^2/_3$ in (9 cm) long. The inflorescence is about 6 in (15 cm) tall and carries two to four flowers about 4 in (10 cm) long. Flowering is during autumn.
ZONES 10–11. I–H.

Cadetia taylori

C

Cadetia wariana

CADETIA GAUDICH.

This epiphytic or lithophytic genus of about
65 species centers around Papua New Guinea,
with some species occurring in nearby regions
such as Australia, the Solomon Islands, the
Moluccas, and the Asian island of Borneo.
These plants grow in rain forests, usually at
low to moderate altitudes. They are miniatures
with a slender pseudobulb and a single leaf.
The flowers are mostly white or pink and are
borne from a group of bracts at the stem's
apex. The genus is related to *Dendrobium*.

Cadetia taylori (F. MUELL.) SCHLTR.

syn. *Bulbophyllum taylori* F. MUELL., *Dendrobium uniflos*
F. M. BAILEY

This species grows epiphytically or on rocks in
rain forests at low to moderate altitudes in
northeast Queensland, Australia, and Papua
New Guinea. Its narrow and cylindrical
pseudobulbs are 1–4 in (2.5–10 cm) tall with
a single, rigid leaf about ⅘–2 in (2–5 cm) long
and ⅓ in (1 cm) wide. The flower is borne
from a long stalk and is about ⅓ in (1 cm)
across. Flowering occurs throughout the year
with an emphasis on summer and autumn.
ZONES 10–12. I–H.

Cadetia wariana SCHLTR.

This miniature, mat-forming species is recorded
in northern Cape York Peninsula in Australia,
the islands of Torres Strait, and southern Papua
New Guinea. It grows on trees or rocks under
semi-shade and in humid rain forests at low to
moderate altitudes. The pseudobulbs are about
⅓ in (1 cm) tall with a single, glossy leaf about
the same length. The flowers are less than ¼ in
(6 mm) wide. These may appear at any time of
the year but are more profuse during autumn.
This species is easy to grow into a large plant
on a slab of cork or in a small pot. It should
be watered year-round, kept under filtered
sunlight, and exposed to good air movement.
ZONES 11–12. H.

CALADENIA R. BR.

This genus has about 160 species but some botanists have sub-divided them into three different genera. This is controversial and the old, familiar names are used here. (Some species below may be accepted as belonging to other genera in the future.) *Caladenia* occurs in southern and eastern Australia, with one species reaching the eastern tropics. Outlying species occur in New Zealand, Indonesia, and New Caledonia. They are all terrestrial plants with underground tubers that give rise to a single, hairy leaf and an inflorescence of one to several colorful flowers.

CULTIVATION

Caladenias are generally difficult to grow. They require a terrestrial mix which contains leaf litter from *Eucalyptus* forests and coarse sand. The plants need to be kept moist while the leaf is in evidence, usually during winter and spring, but watering should be reduced when the leaf dies back. Tubers may be removed and stored over the resting season for repotting when new growth is beginning.

Caladenia colorata

Caladenia carnea R. BR.
"PINK FINGERS"

This species occurs over a wide range in the southeastern states of Australia. It grows in open forests at low to moderate altitudes with a distinct dry season. The single leaf is about 4 in (10 cm) long and sparsely hairy. The inflorescence arises from an underground tuber to heights of up to 1 ft (30 cm). It produces one or two flowers, each about 1¼–2 in (3–5 cm) across. Flower color ranges from almost white to pink, but there is always a red barring on the upper part of the lip. Flowers appear at any time from winter to late spring, depending on the climate.
ZONES 8–11. C–I.

Caladenia colorata D. L. JONES

This species is restricted to the Australian state of South Australia, growing around the Murray River region and the Mount Lofty Ranges. It grows in woodlands where there is good winter rainfall. The leaf is lanceolate, so it is narrow and tapering towards the end. It is hairy and up to 4 in (10 cm) long. The inflorescence is 1¼–2 in (3–5 cm) tall and bears a single flower about 2 in (5 cm) across. Flowering occurs during spring. This species is now regarded as endangered due to land clearing.
ZONES 9–10. C–I.

Caladenia carnea

C

Caladenia filamentosa
R. BR.

"DADDY LONG LEGS"

This species occurs in Australia, from southeast Queensland to Tasmania and across to South Australia. It grows in the open forests between the coast and the Great Dividing Range. It has a single, narrow, hairy leaf up to 8 in (20 cm) long. The inflorescence is up to 18 in (45 cm) tall with one to four flowers. These flowers, up to 2³/₄ in (7 cm) long, feature extremely long, slender, drooping petals and sepals. Flowering occurs from late winter to early summer. **ZONES 8–10. C–I.**

Caladenia flava R. BR.
"COWSLIP ORCHID"

This species is restricted to the southwest corner of Western Australia. It grows in dense colonies, sometimes consisting of thousands of plants, in a variety of habitats ranging from coastal woodlands to granite outcrops inland. The leaf is hairy, growing up to 4³/₄ in (12 cm) long and ¹/₂ in (12 mm) wide. The inflorescence is 4–10 in (10–25 cm) tall and bears one to four flowers, each up to 2 in (5 cm) across. The flowers are yellow with variable reddish-brown markings. Flowers appear from winter to summer, with the best flowering occurring if fire has swept through its habitat during the previous summer. **ZONES 9–11. I.**

Caladenia filamentosa

Caladenia flava

C

Caladenia latifolia R. BR.
"PINK FAIRIES"

This species occurs across southern
Australia, including Tasmania. It
grows in sandy coastal heathlands
and open forests, often forming
large, densely packed colonies.
The hairy leaf, up to 8 in (20 cm)
long and 1 in (2.5 cm) wide, often
lies along the ground. The 16-in
(40-cm) tall inflorescence has one
to four flowers. Each flower is up
to 1½ in (3.5 cm) across. and they
appear from late winter to spring.
ZONES 8–9. C–I.

Caladenia latifolia

Caladenia tentaculata

Caladenia tentaculata SCHLTR.

Until recently this species was regarded as part
of *C. dilatata*. It occurs across southern
Australia from Victoria to Western Australia.
It grows on heathlands and in open forests,
in areas with cool, wet winters and hot, dry
summers. Its single, hairy leaf is about 8 in
(20 cm) long and ⅘ in (2 cm) broad. The
inflorescence is up to 20 in (50 cm) tall and
bears one or two flowers. Each flower grows
up to 4 in (10 cm) across and has narrow floral
parts. Flowering occurs from spring to early
summer. **ZONES 9–10. C–I.**

C

Calanthe argenteostriata

Calanthe argenteostriata
C. Z. TANG & S. J. CHENG

This species is restricted to southeast China. It grows at moderate altitudes in crevices or on wooded slopes in rocky limestone regions. The pseudobulbs are more or less conical, about ⅔ in (15 mm) across. The leaves are ovate, about 7–10 in (18–25 cm) long and 2–4 in (5–10 cm) across. Their upper surfaces are dark green with a few silver-grey longitudinal stripes. The inflorescence is erect, up to 2 ft (60 cm) long, with ten or more flowers, each about 1¼ in (3 cm) long. Flowers appear during spring. **ZONES 9–11. I.**

CALANTHE R. BR.

This widespread genus of about 150 terrestrial species occurs from Africa to Tahiti, and from Japan to Australia, as well as most areas in between. Many of the plants prefer shaded areas, although some grow in strong light. All have a pseudobulb that sits above ground and long, broad, pleated leaves that are deciduous in some species and evergreen in others. The flowers are attractive, and are borne on long spikes arising from the base of the pseudobulb.

CULTIVATION

Evergreen species should be kept evenly moist throughout the year, be grown in a moisture-retentive but well-drained mix, and placed under semi-shade. Deciduous species, such as *C. vestita*, should be rested from watering when the leaves drop. When resting it is best to keep them cool but placed under brighter than usual light.

Calanthe cardiglossa

Calanthe cardiglossa SCHLTR.
syn. *C. hosseusiana* KRAENZL., *C. fuerstenbergiana* KRAENZL. EX SCHLTR.

This deciduous species grows in Laos, Vietnam, Cambodia, and Thailand, in areas of low to moderate altitudes. Its pseudobulbs are ovoid but often constricted around the middle. They are up to 2½ in (6 cm) tall. The leaves are pleated and they are up to 10 in (25 cm) long and 2 in (5 cm) across. The inflorescence is erect, up to 12 in (30 cm) long, with ten to 20 flowers, each about 1 in (2.5 cm) across. The petals and sepals are white or pink. Flowers appear during autumn. **ZONES 10–12. I–H.**

C

Calanthe gibbsiae

Calanthe gibbsiae ROLFE

This species is restricted to the Asian island of Borneo. It grows in the lowland hill forests on limestone ridges, at low to moderate altitudes. **ZONES 10–11. I–H.**

Calanthe rubens RIDL.

syn. *C. vestita* LINDL. **var.** *fournieri* ROLFE; *Calanthe elmeri* AMES

This attractive species from Thailand, the Malay Peninsula, and the Philippines grows at low to moderate altitudes. It is related to *C. vestita* and has pseudobulbs with four angles. They are up to 6 in (15 cm) tall and have a prominent constriction near the top. The leaves are deciduous, growing up to 12 in (30 cm) long and 2 in (5 cm) wide. The long inflorescence is erect, about 1 ft (30 cm) long, and bears about 12 flowers, each measuring 1¼ in (3 cm) wide. The flowers vary in color from white to pink. Flowering occurs during autumn. **ZONES 10–11. I–H.**

Calanthe sylvatica

Calanthe sylvatica (THOUARS) LINDL.

syn. several names, including *C. violacea* ROLFE, *C. masuca* (D. DON.) LINDL.

This variable species is extremely wide ranging, occurring in tropical and southern Africa, on Madagascar and other islands of the Indian Ocean, in India, most of Southeast Asia including southern China, and on the Indonesian islands of Sumatra and Java. It grows at low to high altitudes on the floor of humid rain forests. Its conical pseudobulbs are about ⅘ in (2 cm) across, and are spaced closely together. The leaves are broadly ovate in shape, and up to about 16 in (40 cm) long and 6¾ in (17 cm wide). The inflorescence is erect, up to about 30 in (75 cm), and bears numerous flowers, each about 1¾ in (4.5 cm) across. The flower colors range from white to pale pink or mauve. Flowering occurs during spring. **ZONES 9–12. I–H.**

Calanthe rubens

C

Calanthe triplicata (WILLEM.) AMES
syn. many names, including *C. veratrifolia*
(WILLD.) R. BR.

This extremely widespread and variable species
occurs from Madagascar and India to
Southeast Asia, the Malaysian Archipelago,
Australia, and the Pacific Islands. It usually
grows in humid, shaded habitats at sea level to
a 6700-ft (2000-m) altitude. Its ovoid-shaped
pseudobulbs are spaced closely together and
are about 1¼ in (3 cm) wide. The broad leaves
are dark green, and up to 20 in (50 cm) long
and 6 in (15 cm) across. The inflorescence is
erect, up to 40 in (1 m) tall, and has numerous
flowers that crowd towards the end of it. The
flowers are about 1¼ in (3 cm) long and occur
from spring to autumn. In Australia, the
flowers appear during December, hence it is
known there as the "Christmas orchid".
ZONES 9–12. I–H.

Calanthe triplicata

Calanthe vestita

Calanthe vestita LINDL.
syn. *C. pilosa* (DE VRIESE), *C. regnieri* RCHB.F.

This widely cultivated, deciduous species from Myanmar and Thailand
has many forms and varieties. The form pictured here is often referred to
as the variety *rubro-oculata*. Other forms have pink or white flowers, or
flowers with white petals and sepals and a colorful lip. The pseudobulbs
are up to 8 in (20 cm) tall, and are constricted around the middle. The
leaves are broad, and are about 18–24 in (45–60 cm) long. They appear
after the flowers. Fifteen flowers, usually less than 2¾ in (7 cm) long,
are borne on an erect or nodding inflorescence, about 24–32 in (60–80
cm) long. The long-living flowers appear during winter.
ZONES 10–12. I–H.

CALEANA R. BR.

This genus consists of one to three species, depending on which classification is followed. They are restricted to the sandy soils near the coast and the mountains of southeast and southern Australia. They are all terrestrial, with one leaf arising from an underground tuber. An inflorescence produces a few flowers in which the lip is held uppermost.

CULTIVATION

These species have proved difficult to maintain and are not recommended for cultivation.

Caleana major

Caleana major R. BR.

"FLYING DUCK ORCHID"

This species is found in eastern and southern Australia, ranging from Queensland to Tasmania and South Australia. When the flower is observed from the side it resembles a duck in flight—the lip at the top looks like the head—hence the species' common name. It grows in the sand and sandstone soils of heathlands and open forests between the coast and the mountains. The leaf is up to $4^3/_4$ in (12 cm) long, often lying on the ground. It is predominantly green with some red beneath. The inflorescence is up to 20 in (50 cm) tall and bears one to five flowers, each of which is about 1 in (2.5 cm) long. Flowers appear from spring to summer.
ZONES 9–11. I.

CALOCHILUS R. BR.
"BEARDED ORCHIDS"

The lips of most of the 12 species in this genus have long hairs, giving rise to their common name. The genus is most common in Australia, both in the temperate south and the tropical north, with one species in Papua New Guinea, one in New Zealand, and one in New Caledonia. They are all terrestrial and have a single, fleshy leaf arising from an underground tuber. The inflorescence is tall and bears several flowers, usually with only one or two open at a time.

CULTIVATION

Calochilus species have proved difficult to maintain and are not recommended for cultivation.

Calochilus caeruleus W. O. WILLIAMS

The home of this species are the lowland coastal tea-tree forests of northern Australia and southern Papua New Guinea, where it is hot and humid. In these habitats there is a reliable wet season in summer and autumn and dry season in winter and spring. Its narrow leaf is up to 16 in (40 cm) long, is fleshy with three corners in cross section. The slender inflorescence may be up to 32 in (80 cm) tall, and bears four to 12 flowers, each opening progressively so that only one or two are open at the same time. The flowers are about ⅘ in (2 cm) long. Flowering occurs from summer to autumn during the wet season. **ZONE 12. H.**

Calochilus robertsonii BENTH.

This species occurs in the southeast and southwest regions of Australia and in New Zealand. It grows in open forests, from the sandy coastal regions to the mountains. The leaf is narrow, fleshy, three-cornered in cross section, and is up to 16 in (40 cm) long. Its inflorescence is up to 18 in (45 cm) tall, bearing one to nine 1¼-in (3-cm) wide flowers. These appear during winter and spring. **ZONES 9–10. C–I.**

Calochilus caeruleus

Calochilus robertsonii

CALOPOGON R. BR.

This genus comprises four similar North American terrestrial species—three occur only in the southeast while the fourth, *C. tuberosus*, is widespread in eastern North America. All have a tall, multi-flowered inflorescence and several slim leaves arising from a small, buried corm. *Calopogon* is well known for its unique deceptive pollination mechanism. The lip is uppermost on the purple flowers, and it displays yellow "hairs" which attract young, naive bees. Mistaking these hairs for pollen, a bee lands on the hinged lip, which droops, dropping the bee precisely onto the flattened column below. In the process, the pollen adheres to the bee's back, enabling distribution.

Calopogon tuberosus

Calopogon tuberosus (L.) BRITTON, STERNS, & POGGENBERG.

syn. *C. pulchellus* (SALISBURY) R. BR., *Limodorum tuberosum* L.

"GRASS PINK"

This tall, conspicuous species is the only widespread member of the genus, ranging from maritime Canada through east and midwest USA to Cuba and the Bahamas. The pink-flowered trio of *Arethusa*, *Pogonia*, and *Calopogon* bloom during spring in northern bogs. This species is the most spectacular, most common, and most versatile of the group, and also grows on road shoulders and in wet fields. The plant may be as tall as 4 ft (1.2 m) and may carry up to 25 flowers, each more than 1¼ in (3 cm) in diameter. Flowers appear from spring in the north to summer in the south. **ZONES 6–12. C–I–H.**

CALYPSO SALISB.

This genus has only one species. It grows in temperate parts of the northern hemisphere and may be grown in a mixture of leaf mould and coarse sand, or in sphagnum moss. It should be watered during growth periods, but allowed to dry out during spring and early summer. It requires cool conditions.

Calypso bulbosa (L.) OAKES

syn. many names, including *C. borealis* SW., *C. japonica* MAXIM., *C. occidentalis* HELLER.

This plant forms dense colonies in the damp areas and marshes of coniferous forests. It is up to about 8 in (20 cm) tall. A single leaf may be 1¼–2½ in (3–6 cm) long and 1–2 in (2–5 cm) across. It is ovoid in shape, and has undulated margins. The leaf develops in late summer and persists through winter, lying close to the ground. There is an underground corm about ⅓–⅘ in (1–2 cm) across. Its single, nodding flower is about 1¼–1⅔ in (3–4 cm) long. Flowers appear in early spring and are frost tolerant. **ZONES 5–8. C.**

Calypso bulbosa

CATASETUM L. C. RICH. EX KUNTH

There are about 70 species in this genus, and they are distributed from the West Indies and Central America to Argentina and Peru. The plants have substantial spindle-shaped pseudobulbs with several deciduous leaves. The inflorescences arise from the base of the pseudobulbs. There are separate male and female flowers, usually borne on separate inflorescences. The female flowers are mostly green in color, not varying much between different species, while the male flowers vary in shape and color. The top of the column is sensitive to touch and this causes pollen to be ejected explosively.

CULTIVATION

During active growth the plants should be heavily watered. They prefer high humidity but care should be taken with young shoots as they are susceptible to rot. After the leaves have fallen, a cooler, drier resting period is required. Often full sunlight triggers female flower growth while more shade produces male flowers. Any well-drained orchid mix will usually be successful. Wooden baskets are used by many growers for this genus.

Catasetum barbatum (LINDL.) LINDL.

syn. many names, including *C. brachibulbon* SCHLTR., *C. comosum* COGN., *C. crinitum* LINDL.

This species occurs in the northern part of South America, in Colombia, Venezuela, Guyana, and Brazil. It grows at low altitudes, usually as an epiphyte but occasionally as a terrestrial. The pseudobulbs are spindle-shaped, growing up to 4³/₄ in (12 cm) long. They have about six leaves, each 9³/₄ in (24 cm) long and 2½ in (6 cm) wide. The pseudobulbs also have around 12 fragrant male flowers about 1¾ in (4 cm) wide. Female flowers are slightly smaller, about 1½ in (3.5 cm) across. Flowers appear at almost any time of the year. **ZONES 11–12. I–H.**

Catasetum barbatum

Catasetum expansum

Catasetum expansum
RCHB.F.

syn. *C. cliftonii* HORT., *C. platyglossum* SCHLTR.

This species is restricted to Ecuador, where it grows in dry forests at low altitude. Its pseudobulbs are spindle-shaped, reaching up to 8 in (20 cm) tall. They have several leaves, up to 18 in (45 cm) long. The male inflorescence is up to 12 in (30 cm) long and bears about six flowers, each 3¼ in (8 cm) wide. The female inflorescence has fewer flowers that are smaller than the male flowers. Flowering occurs mostly during spring and summer.
ZONES 11–12. H.

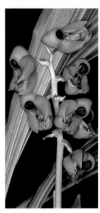

C

Catasetum fimbriatum

Catasetum fimbriatum

(MORREN) LINDL. & PAXTON

syn. several names, including
C. *cogniauxii* LINDEN, C. *wredeanum*
SCHLTR.

The home of this species is Brazil
(excluding the Amazon Basin) and
nearby countries. It grows as an
epiphyte at low altitudes. Its
pseudobulbs are ovoid, clustered,
and are up to 4¾ in (12 cm) long
and 2 in (5 cm) wide. They have
eight leaves, each up to 18 in
(45 cm) long and 3¼ in (8 cm)
wide. The male inflorescence is up
to 18 in (45 cm) long and bears
about 20 fragrant flowers, each
up to 2¾ in (7 cm) across. The
female flowers are slightly smaller,
about 2½ in (6 cm) across.
Flowers appear from summer to
autumn. **ZONES 11–12. I–H.**

Catasetum laminatum LINDL.

This species from Mexico grows
at moderate altitudes in deciduous
forests, where there is a dry winter
and spring and a wet summer and
autumn. Its pseudobulbs are up to
8 in (20 cm) long with about ten
leaves each. The leaves are up to
14 in (35 cm) long and 3¼ in (8
cm) wide. The male inflorescence
bears about seven flowers, each
about 3¼ in (8 cm) across. About
four flowers, each with a lip
positioned uppermost on the
flower, are borne on the female
inflorescence. Flowers appear
during summer from the developing pseudobulb. **ZONES 10–11. I.**

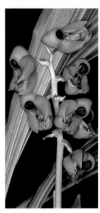

Catasetum planiceps

Catasetum planiceps LINDL.

syn. C. *recurvatum* LINK, KLOTZSCH & ED. OTTO, C. *hymenophorum* COGN.

This species grows on rocks or in the ground. It occurs in
coastal areas and the foothills of the mountains from north
Brazil to Venezuela and Peru. Its pseudobulbs are spindle-
shaped, and up to 6 in (15 cm) long. They have about eight
leaves up to 14 in (35 cm) long. The male inflorescence is
about 10 in (25 cm) long and bears around four flowers,
each 1½ in (3.5 cm) wide. Flowering occurs from spring to
summer. Although a terrestrial species, it should be provided
the same conditions as other species in this genus when
cultivating. **ZONES 11–12. H.**

Catasetum laminatum

C

Catasetum saccatum LINDL.

syn. several names, including *C. colossus* SCHLTR.,
C. secundum KLOTZSCH

The hot, steamy lowlands of the Amazon River
in Brazil create the ideal habitat for this
species. It is often reported growing on dead
trees under full sunlight. The pseudobulbs are
spindle-shaped, up to about 10 in (25 cm) long.
They have eight leaves, about 16 in (40 cm)
long and 3¼ in (8 cm) wide. The male
inflorescence is up to 2 ft (60 cm) long. It is
pendulous, and bears up to 20 flowers. These
are about 3¼ in (8 cm) across. The female
inflorescence is erect and has fewer flowers.
Flowering occurs throughout the year with an
emphasis on summer and autumn. **ZONE 12. H.**

Catasetum tenebrosum KRAENZL.

This species' habitat is the trees or rocks under
full sunlight at moderate altitudes in Peru and
western Brazil. Its pseudobulbs are spindle-
shaped, growing up to 5⅔ in (14 cm) long with
six to eight leaves up to 12 in (30 cm) long.
The male inflorescence is usually shorter than
the leaves, bearing four to 12 flowers. The
flowers are about 2 in (5 cm) across. Flowers
appear in late spring. In cultivation this species
requires only a brief rest. **ZONES 10–11. I–H.**

Catasetum saccatum

Catasetum tenebrosum

CATTLEYA LINDL.

This genus is one of the most popular for the orchid hobbyist as well as the general gardener. They produce flamboyant, spectacular hybrids that are generally tolerant of most conditions. The genus comprises about 70 species and many varieties and forms. Many thousands of hybrids are registered by enthusiasts. The species are widespread in the American tropics, with two main centers of diversity—coastal Brazil, the largest area, and the Andes. There is also significant *Cattleya* occurrences in Mexico and other Central American countries.

CULTIVATION

Cattleya species are among the easiest of all orchids to grow, with most being very tolerant of poor conditions and neglect. They will grow in almost any compost provided it drains well and the medium does not become stale around the roots. The most common medium used is pine bark. Some of these species are suitable for slab culture, but most grow in gardens mounted on a suitable host tree. They need light shade and water during the growing season, and all the species do well in warm or intermediate conditions in bright light with some shading during the hottest parts of the year. They require copious amounts of water from the time the roots show signs of new growth and throughout the growing season. When new growth has reached maturity, watering should be reduced. Fertilizer may be applied during the growing season—these species need heavy feeding. Repot when the mix becomes stale or when the plant outgrows the pot or mount.

HYBRIDS

More hybrids have been registered for this genus than for any other orchid group. They are created by breeding between the species in the genus and by combining *Cattleya* species with other closely related genera. The following list indicates some of these complex hybrids. (*See* pages at end of *Cattleya* entries for hybrid pictures.)

Cattleya × *Brassavola* = *Brassocattleya (Bc.)*

Cattleya × *Brassavola* × *Laelia* = *Brassolaeliacattleya (Blc.)*

Cattleya × *Brassavola* × *Laelia* × *Sophronites* = *Potinara (Pot.)*

Cattleya × *Broughtonia* = *Cattleytonia (Ctna.)*

Cattleya × *Broughtonia* × *Laelia*
      × *Sophronites* = *Hawkinsara (Hksna.)*

Cattleya × *Epidendrum* = *Epicattleya (Epc.)*

Cattleya × *Laelia* = *Laeliocattleya (Lc.)*

Cattleya × *Laelia* × *Sophronites* = *Sophrolaeliocattleya (Slc.)*

Cattleya × *Sophronites* = *Sophrocattleya (Sc.)*

Note: The abbreviation in parentheses is the accepted contracted form for the hybrid.

Cattleya aclandiae LINDL.

This species is endemic to Brazil. It grows on small trees in arid conditions near the ocean. This climate is hot and bright but benefits from regular mists rolling in from the ocean. The plants are dwarf in habit, up to 8 in (20 cm) high. Two or three fleshy leaves are up to 3 in (7.5 cm) long. Its inflorescence has one or two flowers, each up to 4 in (10 cm) across. Flowers appear from autumn to winter. This species does well mounted on cork or tree-fern slabs but may be potted. It requires good light, warmth, and humidity, with ample water during the growing season and less when at rest. **ZONE 12. I–H.**

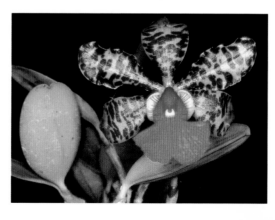

Cattleya aclandiae

C

Cattleya amethystoglossa LINDEN & RCHB.F. EX WARNER

This species is endemic to Brazil, where it grows on coastal rocks and trees in full sun. The plant is tall, producing stems up to 40 in (1 m) high. When fully grown it may produce up to 30 flowers. These emerge during spring and have a diameter of about 4 in (10 cm). Because of its size C. *amethystoglossa* is best potted in a free-draining mix. It likes good light, warmth, and humidity, with ample water during the growing season; less when at rest. **ZONE 12. I–H.**

Cattleya amethystoglossa

Cattleya aurantiaca (BATEMAN) DON.

This species ranges from Mexico to Nicaragua. It grows on rocks and trees in exposed situations where it is both extremely hot and cold. The stems, up to 16 in (38 cm) tall, have two leaves and up to 12 flowers. These flowers are the smallest of the genus, about 1¼ in (3 cm) wide and come in a number of color variants. The flowers appear from summer to autumn. **ZONES 11–12. I–H.**

Cattleya aurantiaca

Cattleya bicolor LINDL.

Endemic to Brazil, this species grows in large clumps on trees and rocks. It reaches a height of about 30½ in (76 cm) and has two leaves about 6 in (15 cm) long. Three to ten fragrant flowers are borne at its apex and are up to 4 in (10 cm) across. This species blooms during autumn. **ZONE 12. I–H.**

Cattleya bicolor

C

Cattleya bowringiana

Cattleya bowringiana VEITCH

This easy-to-grow species comes from Honduras and Guatemala. There it grows on trees and rocks near fast-moving streams. The plant is about 24 in (60 cm) tall and has two or more thick leaves, each up to 8 in (20 cm) long. Its pseudobulbs are swollen in shape near the base. Five to 20 flowers are produced, and each one is up to 3¼ in (8 cm) wide. Flowers appear in autumn and early winter. **ZONE 11. I–H.**

Cattleya dormaniana RCHB.F.

This species from Brazil grows 2000 and 3300 ft (600 and 1000 m). It is smaller and less robust than C. *bowringiana*. Its pseudobulbs, about 12 in (30 cm) long, are narrow at the base and bear two ellipsoidal leaves, each about 5⅔ in (14 cm) long. One or two flowers are produced on a spike about 4 in (10 cm) long. The flowers are about 3¼ in (8 cm) across and appear during autumn. This species may be grown mounted on tree-fern slabs. **ZONE 11. C–I.**

Cattleya dormaniana

C

Cattleya forbesii LINDL.

This is a very adaptable and easy-to-grow species. It occurs in Brazil—in the swampy coastal areas or forested riverbanks from sea level to about 670 ft (200 m). It grows mostly as an epiphyte and occasionally a lithophyte. Its stems are thin, up to 16 in (40 cm) high, with two leaves. The inflorescence has two to five flowers, each about 4 in (10 cm) across. It flowers during spring and summer. **ZONE 12. I–H.**

Cattleya forbesii

Cattleya intermedia

Cattleya granulosa LINDL.

This species, endemic to Brazil, occurs mostly in hot, humid lowlands, often near the ocean. The slender pseudobulbs are up to 2 ft (60 cm) tall with two leaves, each about 7 in (18 cm) long. It bears one to nine flowers on an 8-in (20-cm) spike during autumn or early winter. The flowers are about 4 in (10 cm) wide. **ZONE 12. I–H.**

Cattleya intermedia GRAHAM EX HOOKER

This species from Brazil, Paraguay, and Uruguay grows close to the ocean, mainly as an epiphyte. It occurs from sea level to about 1000 ft (300 m) above. Its pseudobulbs are cylindrical and are up to 20 in (50 cm) tall with two or three leaves at the apex. This species produces up to nine fragrant flowers during spring and early summer. These are up to $5^{1}/_{2}$ in (13 cm) across. **ZONE 12. I–H.**

Cattleya granulosa

Cattleya labiata LINDL.

This robust plant from the Brazilian mountains has stout, clublike pseudobulbs. They are as long as 1 ft (30 cm), and up to 1¼ in (3 cm) wide. Their shape is compressed laterally and is strongly furrowed. From the apex a single, stiff leaf, also up to about 1 ft (30 cm) long, is produced. Two to five fragrant flowers appear during autumn or winter and these are up to 7 in (18 cm) across. **ZONE 11. I–H.**

Cattleya loddigesii LINDL.

This species is found in Brazil and Paraguay. It grows in a variety of habitats—on rocks and on trees, in both sunny and shady situations. The slender pseudobulbs reach about 16 in (40 cm) tall and have two elliptic leaves at the apex. Two to nine flowers are produced and these are about 4 in (10 cm) in diameter. Flowering time is from summer to autumn. **ZONE 12. I–H.**

Cattleya lueddemanniana RCHB.F.

This outstanding species is a native of Venezuela. Its cylindrical pseudobulb carries a single, narrow, stiff leaf. It has three or four large flowers, to about 8 in (20 cm) across. **ZONE 12. I–H.**

Cattleya labiata

Cattleya loddigesii

Cattleya lueddemanniana

C

Cattleya luteola

Cattleya maxima

Cattleya luteola LINDL.

This is one of the smallest-growing *Cattleya* species. It is found in the Amazon Basin in Brazil, Peru, and Ecuador. It has a creeping rhizome that produces pseudobulbs that are cylindrical to ovoid in shape, up to about 3 in (7.5 cm) tall, and have a single leaf at their apexes. The inflorescence carries two to six flowers that are shorter than the leaf, about 2 in (5 cm) across. Flowering occurs throughout the year. This species does well mounted on cork, tree-fern, or hardwood slabs.
ZONES 11–12. I–H.

Cattleya maxima LINDL.

This species occurs in the dry coastal forests of Ecuador and northern Peru. It is both an epiphyte and lithophyte. Its pseudobulbs are cylindrical but sometimes the upper half is club-shaped. They are up to $10^{3}/_{4}$ in (27 cm) long. A single leaf about 10 in (25 cm) long is borne at the apex. The erect inflorescence may bear between five and 15 flowers, each about 5 in (12.5 cm) across. Flowering time is during autumn and winter. **ZONE 10. I–H.**

C

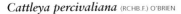
Cattleya percivaliana

Cattleya schilleriana

Cattleya skinneri

Cattleya percivaliana (RCHB.F.) O'BRIEN

This species from Venezuela is found growing mostly as a lithophyte in full sun on rocks near rivers at altitudes of about 4300–6300 ft (1300–1900 m). It has club-shaped pseudobulbs up to 6 in (15 cm) long that have a single leaf. Two to four flowers, about 5 in (12.5 cm) are produced during winter. **ZONES 11–12. I–H.**

Cattleya schilleriana RCHB.F.

This small epiphyte is endemic to Brazil, where it grows on mossy rocks and trees from sea level to about 2700 ft (800 m). Its pseudobulbs are club shaped and up to about 6 in (15 cm) tall. They bear two leaves. Both the pseudobulbs and the leaves may have red-purple spots. Up to five fragrant, long-lasting flowers appear in late spring and summer, and these are up to 4 in (10 cm) across. This species grows best mounted on tree-fern slabs or in hanging baskets with a free-draining medium. Keep in a humid, intermediate environment. **ZONE 12. I–H.**

Cattleya skinneri BATEMAN

This is a common orchid in Costa Rica—it is that country's national flower. It is also found in Mexico and northern South America. Its club-shaped pseudobulbs are about 1 ft (30 cm) tall. From their apexes grow two leaves, each measuring up to 6 in (15 cm) long. Two to 12 flowers appear during spring, and these may be up to 3 in (7.5 cm) across. **ZONES 11–12. I–H.**

C

Cattleya trianaei J. LINDEN & RCHB.F.

This species is endemic to the mountains of Colombia. It is an epiphyte with club-shaped pseudobulbs up to 1 ft (30 cm) tall. One leaf, up to 1 ft (30 cm) long, is borne at the apex. The plant usually has three to four flowers up to $9\frac{1}{2}$ in (23 cm) across. Flowering occurs during winter.
ZONE 11. I–H.

Cattleya trianaei

Cattleya velutina RCHB.F.

This species occurs in Brazil, Peru, Venezuela, and Guyana, often in exposed situations at an elevation of about 1000–2700 ft (300–800 m). Its pseudobulbs are grooved, reedlike, and reach 16 in (40 cm) in height. Two or three leaves arise from the apex of the pseudobulbs. There are also one to four flowers, up to about $3\frac{2}{3}$ in (9 cm) across. These have a spicy, sweet fragrance. In cultivation, this species may be difficult to maintain as it needs bright light, high humidity, and excellent drainage. It may be either potted or mounted on a slab. Flowering occurs from autumn to winter.
ZONES 11–12. I–H.

Cattleya velutina

Cattleya walkeriana GARDN.

A number of *Cattleya* species are endemic to Brazil, including this one. It grows naturally on rocks or small trees near streams at elevations up to 6700 ft (2000 m). It is often exposed to full

Cattleya walkeriana

sunlight and high temperatures. Its club-shaped pseudobulbs are up to $4\frac{1}{2}$ in (11 cm) high. These are well spaced on a stout, creeping rhizome, and each one bears a single leaf up to $4\frac{3}{4}$ in (12 cm) long. An inflorescence, up to 8 in (20 cm) long, bears one to three flowers. These long-lasting flowers are up to 4 in (10 cm) across and appear during autumn or spring. This species is very adaptable and may be mounted, or grown in pots or hanging baskets.
ZONES 11–12. I–H.

Hksna. Alice Iwanaga 'Ruby Lips'

Bc. Binosa 'Lyn'

Ctna. Cherry Vanilla

Pot. Dals Emperor 'Jori'

Sc. Dals Good One

C

Slc. Dream Cloud

Slc. Jillian Lee 'Kitty'

Lulu 'Pink Blush'

Blc. Love Sound 'Dogashima'

Epc. Morning Star

Blc. Princess Beautiful

Lc. Scarlet Imp 'Paradise'

C

CATTLEYOPSIS LEMAIRE

This genus of three species is closely related to both *Cattleya* and *Laelia*. They occur in the West Indies, mostly growing in hot, humid environments. Cultivation for this genus is as for *Cattleya* and *Laelia*.

Cattleyopsis lindenii (LINDL.) COGNIAUX
syn. *Laelia lindenii* LINDL., *C. delicatula* COGNIAUX

This epiphytic or lithophytic species occurs in both Cuba and the Bahamas. Its pseudobulbs have an oval–cylindrical shape, and they are up to 3¼ in (8 cm) long. There are usually one to three rigid, fleshy leaves, each up to 4½ in (11 cm) long and 1½ in (3.5 cm) across. The inflorescence is up to 2 ft (60 cm) tall and bears 12 flowers, each up to 1½ in (3.5 cm) long. Flowering may occur at any time during the year, but is more profuse from late spring to early autumn (May to September in its native habitat). **ZONES 11–12. H.**

Cattleyopsis lindenii

CAULARTHRON R.AF.

This small genus comprises only two or three species from South America and the islands of the West Indies. They are epiphytes that grow in seasonally dry forests close to sea level. Cultivation is similar to that of *Cattleya,* with a dry resting period after flowering.

Caularthron bicornutum
(HOOK) R. E. SCHULTES

This species occurs in Brazil, Colombia, Venezuela, and the West Indies. Its pseudobulbs are long and cylindrical, and up to 1 ft (30 cm) long. The erect inflorescence may carry only a few or up to 20 showy flowers, each about 2½ in (6 cm) across. Flowering occurs most often during the spring.
ZONES 11–12. I–H.

Caularthron bicornutum

CENTROSTIGMA SCHLTR.

These robust, terrestrial species occur at high
altitudes in tropical Africa. The genus consists
of three species and is related to *Habenaria*.
The major difference between the two genera
is the stigma—the stigma of *Habenaria* species
does not have two elongated arms. The lips of
Centrostigma flowers also have longer spurs.
The plant has rounded tubers that grow below
the ground and an erect, leafy stem.

CULTIVATION

Cultivate as for *Habenaria* in a standard
terrestrial mixture.

Centrostigma clavatum SUMMERH.

This species is recorded in the upland areas of
Malawi, southern Tanzania, and Zambia. It
grows in perennially wet grasslands above an
altitude of about 3300 ft (1000 m). Its stems
are up to 20 in (50 cm) tall. It is similar to
C. occultans, but the lateral lobes of its lip are
swept upwards and the spur is shorter, about
3¼ in (8 cm) long. Flowering occurs from mid
to late summer. **ZONES. 9–11 C–I.**

Centrostigma clavatum

Centrostigma occultans

Centrostigma occultans
SCHLTR.

syn. *Habenaria occultans* RCHB.F.,
C. schlechteri (KRAENZL.) SCHLTR.

This robust terrestrial species
occurs in upland areas above
3000 ft (900 m) in northeast
South Africa, Angola, south
Tanzania, Zambia, Malawi,
and Zimbabwe. It grows in
wet, boggy grassland. Its
stems reach up to about 2 ft
(60 cm) tall with about eight
leaves, each around 5½ in
(13 cm) long and ⅘ in (2 cm)
wide. The inflorescence bears
three to six flowers. These are
about 1¼ in (3 cm) long, have
fimbriate lateral lip-lobes, are
held horizontally, and have a
spur about 6 in (15 cm) long.
Flowering occurs during
summer. **ZONES 9–11. C–I.**

C

Cephalanthera kotschyana

Cephalanthera kotschyana RENZ
& TAUBENHEIM
"KOTSCHY'S HELLEBORINE"

This rare species is endemic to the eastern part of Turkey. It thrives in moist environments, and grows in various types of mountain woodlands at moderate altitudes. It is around 1–2 ft (30–60 cm) tall, including its flowers. It has three to six egg-shaped leaves about 3–4 in (7.5–10 cm) long and $^4/_5$–1$^3/_4$ in (2–4 cm) wide on its upper part. Its inflorescence is 3$^1/_4$–8 in (8–20 cm) long and is densely packed with flowers. The flowers are pure white in color and are about 1$^3/_4$ in (4 cm) wide. This species flowers from late spring to winter, depending on the altitude. **ZONES 7–9. C–I.**

CEPHALANTHERA RICH.

This genus is closely related to *Epipactis*, and both genera are known by the common name "helleborine". There are about 15 species in *Cephalanthera*. All of them except one occur in the European/North African/Asiatic region. These plants grow mostly in calcareous soils, maintaining a symbiotic relationship with a mycorrhizal fungus. Every year during spring, new shoots grow from an underground rhizome. The inflorescences bear just a few, relatively large flowers. These are connected to a stem by twisted ovaries, whereas *Epipactis* has flower stalks. Pollination occurs through bees brushing against the pollinia, but this is not a very sophisticated method as the two pollinia do not have sticky rostellums.

CULTIVATION

Because of their lifelong dependence on mycorrhiza, it is difficult to grow these species in cultivation. They may grow for a year or so, but rarely do they survive a long time. Limestone will need to be added to their compost medium.

Cephalanthera kurdica BORNM.
"KURDIC HELLEBORINE"

This species, ranging from southeast Turkey to Iraq and Iran, grows in light oak or pine woodlands at an elevation of 2700–7000 ft (800–2100 m). Its total height of 8–28 in (20–70 cm) includes the inflorescence. It has several elliptic leaves up to 2 in (5 cm) long that grow on the lower part of the plant. Most of the plant's upper part displays pink flowers, each about 2 in (5 cm) in diameter, with short spurs. Flowers appear from the end of spring to early summer, depending on the altitude. **ZONES 7–9. C–I.**

Cephalanthera kurdica

C

Cephalanthera longifolia

Cephalanthera longifolia
(L.) FRITSCH
"SWORD-LEAVED HELLEBORINE"

This species has a wide distribution, from north Africa through north Spain and France to England, middle Europe and the Mediterranean regions. It also spreads east to the Caucasus Mountains, Iran, the Himalayas, and China. It grows in the calcareous soils of deciduous forests, preferring those with beech and oak trees, from sea level to 6700 ft (2000 m). Its inflorescences arise amid long, lanceolate leaves, and are 8–24 in (20–60 cm) tall. They bear ten to 15 pure white flowers, each 1¼ in (3 cm) across. Flowers appear between late spring and winter. **ZONES 7–10. C–I.**

Cephalanthera rubra (L.) RICH.
"RED HELLEBORINE"

The wide distribution of this species includes north Africa, the eastern parts of Spain and France, southern England, across middle Europe to Estonia, and from the Mediterranean Sea region to Turkey, Russia, and the Caucasus Mountains. It is found in open beech, mixed, and coniferous forests and wood meadows in calcareous soil. It grows from sea level to about 6000 ft (1800 m) in the Alps, or to 8300 ft (2500 m) in Morocco. Its stem is 1–2 ft (30–60 cm) tall and has three to six lanceolate leaves, each about 2–4 in (5–10 cm) long and ½–1¼ in (1–3 cm) wide at the lower end. The inflorescence comprises five to 15 bright-pink to lilac-red flowers, each about 1¾ in (4 cm) across. Flowers appear in late spring in the south and mid summer in the north. **ZONES 4–10. C–I.**

Cephalanthera rubra

CERATOSTYLIS BLUME

This genus, related to *Eria*, comprises about 100 small epiphytic plants and ranges from India to Papua New Guinea. Most of the species have small flowers, and a few are popular with orchid growers. They are easy to grow in a hanging pot or basket that can accommodate the often pendulous growth. In cultivation, hot, humid, and moderately shady conditions, perhaps with a short resting period, are recommended.

Ceratostylis incognita J. T. ATWOOD
& J. BECKNER

This epiphytic species is restricted to the island of Luzon in the Philippines. It grows at 2500–5000 ft (750–1500 m) in brightly lit situations. The plant is up to 1 ft (30 cm) long, is pendulous, or nearly so, and has branching stems. The leaves are narrow, terete and are up to 10 in (25 cm) long. The flowers are solitary, borne along the stems and about ⅔ in (15 mm) across. **ZONES 10–11. I–H.**

Ceratostylis incognita

Ceratostylis retisquama

Ceratostylis retisquama RCHB.F.
syn. *C. rubra* AMES

This species is restricted to the Philippines, where it grows on the islands of Luzon and Mindanao at low altitudes. The stems are semi-pendulous, branched, and up to 16 in (40 cm) long. It has fleshy leaves up to 4¾ in (12 cm) long and ⅓ in (1 cm) wide. The flowers are borne singly near the base of the stems. They are about 1¾ in (4 cm) across and have a very small lip. Flowering occurs several times throughout the year. **ZONES 11–12. I–H.**

CHILOGLOTTIS R. BR.

This genus of about 30 terrestrial species is restricted to New Zealand and Australia. They grow in open forests and heathlands. They have two leaves arising from an underground tuber. They also have a solitary flower with a lip that is the most obvious feature of the flower—ornamented with callii that resemble an insect. The flower stalks grow longer after pollination to assist in scattering the seed.

CULTIVATION

These species are relatively easy to grow in a potting mixture comprising sandy loam and leaf litter.

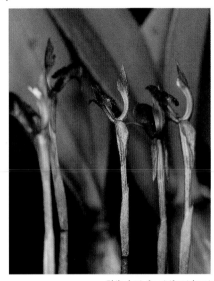

Chiloglottis formicifera (above)

Chiloglottis formicifera

FITZGERALD

"ANT ORCHID"

This species is recorded in southeast Queensland and northeast New South Wales in Australia. It grows at low altitudes in wet, open forests under shade in the leaf litter on the forest floor. It forms large, free-flowering colonies. Its light-green leaves grow to $2\frac{1}{2}$ in (6 cm) long and $\frac{4}{5}$ in (2 cm) wide. The single flower, about $\frac{4}{5}$ in (2 cm) across, is borne on a stem about 4 in (10 cm) tall. The callii on the lip resembles an ant, hence its common name. Flowering is during spring. **ZONES 9–10. C–I.**

Chiloglottis valida

D. L. JONES

"BIRD ORCHID"

Often known by its common name, this species was once considered part of *C. gunnii*. It occurs in southeast Australia from New South Wales to South Australia and Tasmania. It is also found in New Zealand. It grows in tall, shady open forests and other moist habitats from the coast to the mountains, sometimes in moss or leaf litter. Several plants may form a colony in suitable habitats, with numerous colonies growing near each other. It has two dark-green leaves up to 4 in (10 cm) long and $1\frac{1}{4}$ in (3 cm) across. The single flower is only a few centimetres above the leaves and about $1\frac{3}{4}$ in (4 cm) wide. Flower color ranges from green to dark purple-brown, and the flowers appear from spring to summer. **ZONES 8–10. C–I.**

Chiloglottis valida

CHILOSCHISTA LINDL.

The plants in this genus consist of a root system, a very short stem, and usually no leaves—the roots contain chlorophyll and have taken over the function of the leaves. The well-developed root system radiates out like the spokes of a wheel over the trunks of host trees. The inflorescence is more or less erect with several white or yellow flowers.

CULTIVATION

These plants are amenable to cultivation on a slab of cork or similar material. They require semi-shade and frequent watering, but they should be allowed to dry out between waterings.

Chiloschista parishii SEIDENF.

Previously regarded as *C. lunifera*, *C parishii* was separated from that species because it has quite different flower markings—dark-colored spots. It is found in northeast India, Bhutan, Myanmar, Thailand and, possibly, southern China, growing at low to moderate altitudes. It often has a pair of small leaves that wither before flowers appear. The inflorescence is unbranched with 20 or more flowers, each about ⅓ in (1 cm) across. Flowering occurs during spring.
ZONES 11–12. I–H.

Chiloschista parishii

Chiloschista ramifera
SEIDENF.

This species is distinguished from the other species described here by the longer, branched inflorescence and the two leaves that are about 2¾ in (7 cm) long, which are present during flowering. The inflorescence is up to 10 in (25 cm) long. It is pendulous and has many branches with numerous flowers. The flowers are not spotted like other species in the genus, and they are ⅓ in (1 cm) across. Flowers appear during spring. **ZONES 10–12. I–H.**

Chiloschista trudelii
SEIDENF.

This species is restricted to Thailand, growing at low to moderate altitudes. Its inflorescence is shorter than the other *Chiloschista* species described here, and it is erect, in contrast to the pendulous *C. ramifera*. The erect, fleshy inflorescence is 3¼–4 in (8–10 cm) tall, has branches and comprises a few flowers, each about ⅓ in (1 cm) across. **ZONES 10–12. I–H.**

Chiloschista ramifera

Chiloschista trudelii

C

C

CHONDRORHYNCHA LINDL.

This genus of about 30 species ranges from southern Mexico to the Andes of South America. They are largely inhabitants of highland rain forests so they require relatively cool conditions when cultivated. The genus is characterized by a lack of pseudobulbs, leaves arranged in a fan shape, and single-flowered inflorescence arising from the axil of a leaf sheath.

CULTIVATION

These species should never be allowed to dry out and they should be grown in intermediate conditions with high humidity. They are generally intolerant of disturbances so repotting should be done only when absolutely necessary. Live sphagnum moss is an ideal medium.

Chondrorhyncha viridisepala SENGHAS

This species from Colombia has flowers about 2 in (5 cm) long. Flowering occurs throughout the year.
ZONES 11–12. C–I.

Chondrorhyncha viridisepala

CHYSIS LINDL.

This genus comprises about six epiphytic species growing from Mexico to Peru. Its pseudobulbs are club-shaped, pendulous, elongated, and consist of several internodes. The many thin-textured leaves concentrate more towards the apex of the pseudobulbs. The inflorescence arises from nodes on the new growth and carries several showy flowers.

CULTIVATION

These plants are particularly suited to cultivation in hanging baskets using a mix that drains freely. During growth periods they require high humidity and ample water. The plants are deciduous when growth is complete, and at this time they should be kept cool and watered less frequently.

Chysis bractescens

Chysis laevis

Chysis bractescens LINDL.

This species ranges from Mexico to Nicaragua, from sea level to an altitude of about 2800 ft (850 m). Its pseudobulbs are up to 1 ft (30 cm) long with several leaves up to 16 in (40 cm) long and 2½ in (6 cm) wide. Inflorescences arise from the lower nodes of old pseudobulbs and each carries four to eight flowers, about 3 in (7.5 cm) wide. These fragrant and long-lasting flowers appear during early summer. **ZONES 11–12. I–H.**

Chysis laevis LINDL.

This species is similar vegetatively to C. *bractescens*, with a similar distribution. The main difference between the two is the color of the flowers. This species also has fragrant and long-lasting flowers, and they appear from spring to early summer. **ZONES 11–12. I–H.**

Chysis tricostata SCHLTR.

This species characteristically has three ridges on its labellum. It is found in Costa Rica and Nicaragua. Flowers appear from spring to early summer. **ZONES 11–12. I–H.**

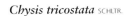

Chysis tricostata

C

Cirrhaea saccata

CIRRHAEA LINDL.

This genus comprises about six epiphytic species occurring in central and southern Brazil. They are plants of cooler mountain regions. Characteristically, the pseudobulbs are ovoid and strongly ribbed with a single, deeply veined leaf at the apex. An elongated, pendulous inflorescence arises from the base of the pseudobulbs and it bears many flowers.

CULTIVATION

If potted, these species should be suspended so that the pendulous inflorescence may hang freely. They require conditions similar to those for *Cattleya*.

Cirrhaea saccata LINDL.

This species occurs in southeast Brazil. Its pseudobulbs are up to about 3 in (7.5 cm) tall. They have a leaf about 1 ft (30 cm) in length and a spike that bears up to 20 flowers, each about 2 in (5 cm) across. Flowering occurs during summer. **ZONES 11–12. I–H.**

CLEISOSTOMA BLUME

This genus of monopodial epiphytic orchids comprises about 90 species. They range from India to Australia and the Pacific Islands, growing mainly in lowland areas. Most of the species are small with an elongated stem that is either erect or hanging. The flowers are small, but many are colorful. They grow on branched or unbranched inflorescences.

CULTIVATION

These plants are usually grown on a slab or in a pot, according to the form of the plant. They grow best in humid conditions with regular watering. The plants should be allowed to dry out between watering.

Cleisostoma arietinum (RCHB.F.) GARAY
syn. *Sarcanthus aeietinus* RCHB.F., *Sarcanthus recurvus* ROLFE

This small epiphyte occurs from northeast India to Indochina. The stems are up to 3½ in (9 cm) long. The 2¾-in (7-cm) terete leaves grow at right angles to the stem, as do the inflorescences, which are longer than the leaves. They bear numerous flowers, about ¼ in (6 mm) long. **ZONES 11–12. I–H.**

Cleisostoma arietinum

CLOWESIA LINDL.

This genus was originally described by John Lindley in 1843, but most botanists treated it as part of *Catasetum* until 1975, when its status was recognized by Calaway Dodson. It is distinguished from *Catasetum* through its flowers—it does not have separate male and female flowers. *Clowesia* comprises about six species distributed from Mexico to Ecuador. The leaves are deciduous and the inflorescences are pendulous.

CULTIVATION

Most of these species grow best in a well-drained pot in intermediate conditions. Watering should be frequent while in growth, but a drier resting period is required when the plants have stopped growing.

Clowesia rosea

Clowesia warscewiczii (RCHB.F.) DODSON
syn. *Catasetum scurra* RCHB.F., *Catasetum warscewiczii* LINDL. & PAXT.

This species from Costa Rica, Panama, Colombia, and Venezuela grows at low to moderate altitudes. Its wrinkled pseudobulbs are ovoid-shaped, and are to about 3½ in (9 cm) in length. They have four to six leaves up to 16 in (40 cm) long and 2¾ in (7 cm) wide. The inflorescences are pendulous, and about 1 ft (30 cm) long. They bear few to many fragrant, long-lasting flowers, each about 1½ in (3.5 cm) across. Flowering occurs from summer to autumn. **ZONES 11–12. I–H.**

Clowesia rosea LINDL.
syn. *Catasetum roseum* (LINDL.) RCHB.F.

This species from Mexico (and possibly other locations in central and northern South America) grows at altitudes of 1600–4300 ft (500–1300 m) in oak forests and subtropical deciduous forests. Its pseudobulbs are up to 4 in (10 cm) long and 1 in (2.5 cm) wide at the base. They have five or more leaves about 6–16 in (15–40 cm) long and 1¼–2½ in (3–6 cm) wide. The inflorescence is pendulous with six or seven flowers, each about ⅘ in (2 cm) long. Flowers appear in spring. **ZONES 10–11. I–H.**

Clowesia warscewiczii

C

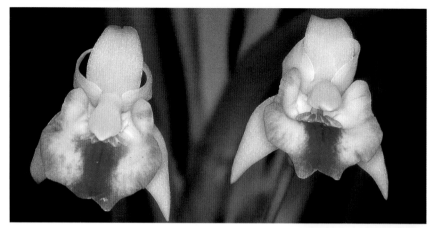

Cochleanthes candida

COCHLEANTHES RAF.

This genus comprises about 15 species ranging from Costa Rica to Peru. They are epiphytes that grow in forests at elevations between 1600 and 5000 ft (500 and 1500 m). These medium-sized plants do not have pseudobulbs, and their leaves are arranged like a fan. A single flower may appear on the inflorescence at any time during the year.

CULTIVATION

Intermediate conditions with high humidity is the best growing environment for this species. The plants should not be allowed to dry out. Live sphagnum moss is the ideal medium.

Cochleanthes amazonica

Cochleanthes amazonica (RCHB.F. & WARSC.) R. E. SCHULTES & GARAY

This species occurs in Colombia, Ecuador, Peru, and Brazil. The plants form fanlike clumps and their leaves are up to 8 in (20 cm) long. A single flower is borne on a short spike and may be as long as 3 in (7.5 cm). Flowering is from late autumn to winter. **ZONES 11–12. I.**

Cochleanthes candida
(LINDL.) SCHULTES & GARAY

This Brazilian species grows as an epiphyte or among leaf litter on the forest floor. The plant is similar vegetatively to *C. amazonica*, except the flower is smaller, about 2 in (5 cm) tall. Flowering is from late autumn to winter. **ZONES 11–12. I.**

Cochlioda noezliana

COCHLIODA LINDL.

This genus of about five species comprises small- to medium-sized epiphytes or lithophytes from the Andes in Ecuador, Peru, and Bolivia. They occur at elevations between 6700 and 11,600 ft (2000 and 3500 m) and require cool conditions for successful cultivation. These species have been hybridized with *Odontoglossum*, *Oncidium*, and *Miltonia* to form the hybrid genera *Odontioda*, *Oncidioda*, and *Miltonioda* respectively. They may be grown in pots with a well-drained medium or live sphagnum moss. Adequate shading must be provided during summer.

Cochlioda noezliana
(MAST.) ROLFE

This species ranges from central Peru to northern Bolivia. The ovoid, flattened pseudobulbs are up to 3 in (7.5 cm) tall. They have a single leaf about 10 in (25 cm) long. The arching inflorescence is up to 18 in (45 cm) long and bears many flowers, which are up to 2 in (5 cm) in diameter. Flowers appear from summer to autumn. **ZONES 9–10. C.**

COELIA LINDL.

This genus of about five species is distributed from Mexico and the West Indies to Guatemala, Honduras, El Salvador, and Panama. They are mostly epiphytic species but also occur as terrestrials or even lithophytes.

CULTIVATION

They grow best in pots with a well-drained mix. These orchids don't take well to having their roots disturbed, so repotting should only be done when absolutely necessary. They should be kept in an environment of high humidity, and moist, intermediate conditions.

Coelia bella (LEMAIRE) RCHB.F.
syn. *Bothriochilus bellus* LEMAIRE

This terrestrial species comes from Mexico, Honduras and Guatemala. It lives in rain forests up to a 5000-ft (1500-m) elevation. The plant is up to 32 in (80 cm) tall and has ovoid- to globose-shaped pseudobulbs that are about 2 in (5 cm) long. Several membranous leaves, about 20 in (50 cm) long, emerge as a cluster from the top of the pseudobulb. The inflorescence arises from the base of the pseudobulb and it is shorter than the leaves, up to 6 in (15 cm) long. It bears two to several fragrant flowers, about 2 in (5 cm) wide. Flowers appear during summer.
ZONES 11–12. I–H.

Coelia macrostachya

Coelia macrostachya LINDL.

This species occurs in Mexico, Guatemala, Honduras, Panama, and Costa Rica. The pseudobulb is more or less egg-shaped, and extends into a slender stalk up to about 4 in (10 cm) long. There are usually has three leaves, each up to about 3 ft (90 cm) long and about 1 in (2.5 cm) wide. The inflorescence is densely flowered and may be up to 2 ft (60 cm) tall. Its fragrant flowers are small, about 1/4 in (6 mm) long. The flowers appear during summer.
ZONES 11–12. I–H.

Coelia bella

COELOGYNE LINDL.

This genus is thought to consist of up to 150 species scattered from India to the Pacific Islands and as far north as southern China and the Philippines. They occupy habitats from sea level to over 8300 ft (2500 m), usually growing under semi-shade where there are moist conditions throughout most of the year. Virtually all of them are epiphytes, although some grow on rocks or even in soil in grasslands and in shrubby areas. They have short, fat pseudobulbs, sometimes very smooth and cylindrical. These may be closely or widely spaced on a creeping rhizome. Each pseudobulb bears one or two leathery leaves. The flower stems emerge from the bases of the pseudobulbs or from the apex of a developing new growth. They are usually arching or pendulous, although they sometimes bear just a single flower. The flowers come in many shapes and sizes, mostly in shades of green, cream, brown, dull purple, and sometimes pure white. They often have orange markings on the lip. Most of the flowers are fragrant.

Coelogyne asperata

CULTIVATION

Coelogyne species are generally very attractive orchids that grow easily in a range of different climates. Many will grow into large, bulky plants, producing numerous sprays of sweetly scented blooms. Some do well in cool conditions and will grow happily outdoors in a sheltered spot protected from frost. Many have long, straggling growths and these would suit being planted in a hanging basket rather than a pot. They like a fairly coarse, soil-free compost and plenty of water while actively growing during summer. Reduce watering during winter to encourage good flower growth. To propagate, divide the plants after flowering.

Coelogyne asperata LINDL.
syn. *C. pustulosa* RIDL., *C. lowii* PAXTON

This large, robust species ranges from the Malay Peninsula through the Malay Archipelago to the Solomon Islands. It grows from sea level to a 6700-ft (2000-m) altitude in rain forests as an epiphyte or, occasionally, a terrestrial on rocks or in grassland. The egg-shaped pseudobulbs are usually spaced closely together, and are up to about 10 in (25 cm) long and $3\frac{2}{3}$ in (9 cm) across, but usually smaller. They bear two large leaves. The inflorescence is borne on a developing new shoot before the leaves are formed. They carry six to 35 flowers, each about $1\frac{3}{4}$–$2\frac{3}{4}$ in (4–7 cm) across, and are slightly fragrant. Flowering occurs once or twice a year at varying times in different areas.
ZONES 9–12. I–H.

C

Coelogyne barbata

Coelogyne barbata GRIFF.

This epiphytic or lithophytic species occurs
in the foothills of the Himalayas in northern
India, Nepal, and Bhutan at an altitude of
about 3300–6000 ft (1000–1800 m). Its
pseudobulbs grow in clusters, are ovoid- to
pear-shaped, and are up to 4 in (10 cm) tall.
Two leaves, about 10–16 in (25–40 cm) tall
and 2–4 in (5–10 cm) across, arise from the
pseudobulb. The erect inflorescences arise from
between the leaves and bear about ten flowers,
each about 2¾ in (7 cm) across. They have a
musk scent and are long-lasting. Flowers
appear from winter to spring.
ZONES 9–10. I.

Coelogyne brachyptera RCHB.F.

syn. *C. parishii* HOOK.F.

Originating from Myanmar and Indochina,
this species is found at low to moderate
altitudes. The long, narrow, almost cylindrical
pseudobulbs are about 4–6 in (10–15 cm) long
and less than ⅓ in (1 cm) wide. The flowers
are fragrant and are about 2 in (5 cm) across.
They are borne on a pendulous or erect
inflorescence of about five flowers.
ZONES 10–12. I–H.

Coelogyne brachyptera

Coelogyne carinata

Coelogyne carinata ROLFE

This attractive small, epiphytic species grows in
low-altitude rain forests in Papua New Guinea.
The pseudobulbs are about 1¼ in (3 cm) tall
with one or two leaves about 6–8 in (15–20
cm) long. The inflorescence arises from new
growth and bears up to eight flowers, one or
two opening at a time. Each flower is about
1 in (2.5 cm) across. Flowering in cultivation
occurs during summer. **ZONES 11–12. H.**

C

Coelogyne celebensis J. J. SM.
syn. *C. platyphylla* SCHLTR.

This robust species is restricted to the island of
Sulawesi in Indonesia, where it grows in rain
forests at low to moderate altitudes. The ribbed
pseudobulbs are spaced about 2 in (5 cm) apart
and are 2½–5⅔ in (6–14 cm) long. They have
one or two leaves, about 1–2 ft (30–60 cm)
long and 3¼–5⅔ in (8–14 cm) across. The
inflorescence develops from new growth and
has three to seven flowers about 2¾ in (7 cm)
across. These open successively and appear
from autumn to winter in the wild.
ZONES 11–12.

Coelogyne celebensis

Coelogyne chloroptera

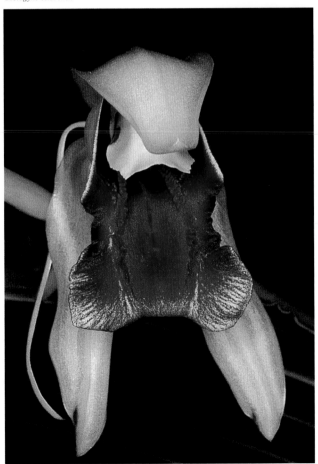

Coelogyne chloroptera RCHB.F.

This species grows
on trees and rocks
in rain forests at
an altitude of about
4000 ft (1200 m) on
the Philippine islands
of Luzon and Negros.
Its pseudobulbs are
pear-shaped, and
about 2½ in (6 cm)
tall. They bear two
leaves up to 8 in
(20 cm) long and
2 in (5 cm) wide.
The inflorescences
arise from new
growth. They are
erect and comprise
up to 12 flowers,
each about 1¾ in
(4 cm) across. The
flowers are fragrant
and waxy and appear
during spring.
ZONES 9–11. I–H.

C

Coelogyne cristata LINDL.

The habitat of this species is Nepal and the mountains of
northern India. It grows at moderate to high altitudes. Its
pseudobulbs are spaced closely together and are up to $3^1/_4$ in
(8 cm) long and $1^3/_4$ in (4 cm) across. They bear two leaves.
The inflorescence is arching to pendulous and comprises up
to ten strongly fragrant flowers, each about 3 in (8 cm) across.
Several color variations of this species are recorded. In
cultivation the plant requires intermediate to cool conditions.
Flowering is from late winter to spring. **ZONES 9–10. I.**

Coelogyne dayana RCHB.F.

Recorded on the Malay
Peninsula and the islands of
Sumatra and Borneo (and
possibly Thailand), this
species grows epiphytically
in river valleys at low to
moderate altitudes. Its
pseudobulbs are conical,
up to 8 in (20 cm) long. The
inflorescences are pendulous,
20–40 in (50–100 cm) long,
and bear numerous flowers,
each $2^1/_2$ in (6 cm) across. The
flowers release a musk scent
and are long-lasting. The main
flowering season occurs
during spring.
ZONES 10–12. I–H.

Coelogyne fimbriata LINDL.
syn. many names, including
C. ovalis LINDL., *C. fuliginosa* LINDL.,
C. laotica GAGNEP.

This widespread species
occurs in the Himalayas, from
India and Nepal to southern
China, the Malay Peninsula,
Malaysia, and the islands of
Sumatra and Borneo. It grows
at low to high altitudes, but is
most abundant around the
5000-ft (1500-m) level. The
egg-shaped pseudobulbs are
usually spaced wide apart on
the rhizome and are about
$4/_5$–$3^2/_3$ in (2–9 cm) long and
$4/_5$ in (2 cm) across. Two
leaves are borne on the
pseudobulbs. The
inflorescence bears two to five
flowers, but often only one
opens at a time. The flowers
are about $1^1/_4$–$1^3/_4$ in (3–4 cm)
wide and they have a
prominent fringed margin on
the lip. Flowering may occur
at any time of the year,
depending on the altitude.
ZONES 8–12. I–H

Coelogyne cristata

Coelogyne dayana

Coelogyne fimbriata

C

Coelogyne fragrans

Coelogyne flaccida LINDL.

This epiphyte grows in the Himalayas from India and Nepal to southern China. It is found in mountain forests at moderate altitudes with a distinct dry season. Its pseudobulbs are spaced closely together, have a conical shape, and are up to 4¾ in (12 cm) long and 1 in (2.5 cm) wide. Two leaves arise from the pseudobulbs. The pendulous inflorescence bears eight to ten fragrant flowers, each up to 1¾ in (4 cm) across. Flowers appear during spring. **ZONES 9–11. I.**

Coelogyne flaccida

Coelogyne fragrans SCHLTR.

This is a common epiphytic, occasionally terrestrial, species that grows in Papua New Guinean rain forests up to an altitude of 6700 ft (2000 m). Its pseudobulbs are spaced closely together, and are about 2½–4 in (6–10 cm) long. They have one or two leaves at the apex. The inflorescence appears when the leaves on new growth are developing. It consists of up to six fragrant flowers which open successively or, in the highlands, at the same time. They are about 3¼ in (8 cm) across. The flowers appear at any time throughout the year and they last for up to two weeks. **ZONES 9–12. I–H.**

Coelogyne lawrenceana ROLFE

syn. *C. fleuryi* GAGNEP.

Endemic to Vietnam, where it grows at moderate altitudes, this species has ovoid-shaped pseudobulbs about 4 in (10 cm) tall. They are clustered and have two leaves. The inflorescence is arching and bears about three fragrant, waxy flowers, each 4 in (10 cm) across. Flowering occurs during spring.
ZONES 10–11. I.

Coelogyne lawrenceana

Coelogyne mayeriana
RCHB.F.

Green flowers are usually thought of as uninteresting, but this species and its relative, *C. pandurata*, prove this view wrong. *C. mayeriana* occurs on the Malay Peninsula and on the Indonesian island of Sumatra. It may also grow on Borneo. It is either an epiphyte or terrestrial and is found at low altitudes, often near mangroves. Its pseudobulbs are well spaced apart on the rhizome. They are about 1¼–3⅔ in (3–9 cm) long and 1¼–2 in (3–5 cm) wide and have two leaves. The flowers are about 2½ in (6 cm) across and have a strikingly marked lip. They appear at almost any time of the year. **ZONES 11–12. H.**

Coelogyne mayeriana

Coelogyne merrillii AMES

This species is restricted to the Philippines, where it grows on Luzon and Negros islands at altitudes between 1000 and 7700 ft (300 and 2300 m). It grows mostly on rocks. The pseudobulbs are ovoid in shape and up to 2 in (5 cm) tall with two leaves, up to 10 in (25 cm) long and 2¾ in (7 cm) across. The erect inflorescence arises from new growth and bears several flowers up to 2 in (5 cm) across. **ZONES 9–11. I–H.**

Coelogyne merrillii

Coelogyne mooreana ROLFE

syn. *C. psectrantha* GAGNEP.

Endemic to Vietnam, this species grows at moderate to high altitudes. Its pseudobulbs are widely spaced apart and are shaped like narrow eggs. They are about 3¼ in (8 cm) tall and 1 in (2.5 cm) wide. The upright inflorescence develops from a new growth and bears up to eight fragrant flowers, each about 3¼ in (8 cm) across. Flowering occurs from spring to early summer. **ZONES 9–10. C–I.**

Coelogyne mossieae ROLFE

This species is apparently restricted to northern India, where it grows at low to moderate altitudes. Its ovate pseudobulbs are about 2 in (5 cm) long. They crowd closely together and each has two leaves about 7 in (18 cm) long. The inflorescence arises from new shoots and bears up to ten fragrant flowers, each about 1¾ in (4 cm) across. Flowering occurs from spring to early summer. **ZONES 9–10. I.**

Coelogyne nitida

(WALL.) LINDL.

syn. *C. ochracea* LINDL.

This species grows at high altitudes in north India, Nepal, Bhutan, Myanmar, Laos, and the Yunnan province in China. Its pseudobulbs are up to 4 in (10 cm) long and 1 in (2.5 cm) wide. They are about 1 in (2 cm) apart and have two leaves. The erect inflorescence is formed from a developing new growth and bears six to eight flowers, each 1¾ in (4 cm) across. The highly fragrant flowers appear in late winter and spring. **ZONES 8–10.**

Coelogyne mooreana

Coelogyne mossieae

Coelogyne nitida

C

Coelogyne pandurata

Coelogyne prolifera

Coelogyne pandurata LINDL.

This green-flowered species comes from the Malay Peninsula, and the Asian islands of Sumatra and Borneo. It grows epiphytically or as a terrestrial at low to moderate altitudes. Its pseudobulbs are spaced well apart and tend to be flattened in shape. They are up to $7^2/_3$ in (19 cm) long and about $2^3/_4$ in (7 cm) across. They have two leaves. The inflorescence develops from new growth and bears up to 15 flowers. The fragrant flowers are about $4–5^1/_2$ in (10–13 cm) wide and occur throughout the year. The wide gaps between this species' pseudobulbs makes it difficult to contain it in a pot, so slab cultivation is best.
ZONES 10–12. I–H.

Coelogyne prolifera LINDL.

This epiphytic species ranges from north India and Nepal through the Yunnan province in China to Indochina. It grows in fairly open forests at moderate to high altitudes. The narrow, ovoid-shaped pseudobulbs are well spaced along the rhizome. They are about $4/_5–1^3/_4$ in (2–4 cm) long with two leaves. The inflorescence is about as long as the leaves and has six flowers, each about $1/_3–1$ in (1–2.5 cm) across. Flowers appear during winter.
ZONES 9–10. C–I.

Coelogyne speciosa (BLUME) LINDL.

The islands of the Malay Archipelago provide the habitat for this variable species. It is an epiphyte, occasionally a terrestrial, that grows in rain forests at altitudes of 2300–6700 ft (700–2000 m). Its pseudobulbs are spaced close together and up to $2^3/_4$ in (7 cm) long. The one to two leaves are up to 16 in (40 cm) long and $3^1/_4$ in (8 cm) wide. The inflorescence arises from a new shoot and bears three to eight, occasionally more, flowers. These vary in length from $2^1/_2–3^2/_3$ in (6–9 cm) across. Flowering occurs throughout the year.
ZONES 9–11. I.

Coelogyne speciosa

C

Coelogyne stricta (D. DON) SCHLTR.

syn. *C. elata* LINDL.

This species occurs in India, Nepal, Bhutan, and Myanmar at moderate to high altitudes. The pseudobulb is almost cylindrical in shape and about 3¼–6 in (8–15 cm) long and ⁴/₅–2 in (2–5 cm) wide. It has two leaves and an erect inflorescence with 12 to 15 flowers, each about 1¼ in (3 cm) across. Flowers appear during spring. **ZONES 9–10. C–I.**

Coelogyne stricta

Coelogyne tomentosa LINDL.

syn. *C. massangeana* RCHB.F., **according to some authorities**

This species occurs at low to moderate altitudes in Thailand, on the Malay Peninsula, and on the Indonesian island of Java. It has ovoid pseudobulbs about 2½ in (6 cm) long and 1¼ in (3 cm) wide. Its musk-scented flowers, about 4 in (10 cm) across, are borne on a pendulous inflorescence about 18 in (45 cm) long. **ZONES 10–12. I–H.**

Coelogyne tomentosa

C

Coelogyne trinervis LINDL.

syn. *C. cinnamomea* TEIJSM. & BINN., *C. angustifolia* RIDL., *C. pachybulbon* RIDL.

This widespread species is recorded from Indochina to the Indonesian islands. It grows at low to moderate altitudes on trees or rocks. Its pseudobulbs are spaced closely together and are ovoid shaped. They are 2–3¼ in (5–8 cm) long and have one or two leaves. The upright inflorescence has four to eight flowers, each about 1¾ in (4 cm) across. Their scent has been variously described as both "disagreeable" and "light and pleasant." **ZONES 9–12. I–H**

Coelogyne trinervis

Coelogyne viscosa RCHB.F.

syn. *C. graminifolia* PAR. & RCHB.F.

The range of this species extends from Assam in India, through southern China and Indochina to the Malay Peninsula. It grows on rocks or trees at moderate altitudes. Its ovoid-shaped pseudobulbs are spaced only about ⅘ in (2 cm) apart on the rhizome. They are up to 2½ in (6 cm) tall and have two long, narrow leaves, about 12–16 in (30–40 cm) long. The inflorescence arises from a developing shoot and bears two to four fragrant flowers, each about 1¾ in (4 cm) across. Flowering occurs during summer. **ZONES 9–10. I.**

Coelogyne viscosa

COMPARETTIA POEPP. & END.

Most of the ten species in this genus are spectacular, colorful, and small. They are found mostly in the Andes of Colombia and Ecuador with one species, *C. falcata*, extending to the West Indies and Mexico. All of them are epiphytes with small, terete pseudobulbs and a single, leathery leaf. The inflorescence may be single or branched, and arises from the base of the pseudobulbs. They bear a few, proportionately large, showy flowers.

CULTIVATION

These species do best when mounted on a hardwood or tree-fern slab. They prefer intermediate conditions and frequent watering.

Comparettia speciosa

Comparettia falcata

Comparettia falcata POEPP. & ENDL.

This species is the most widespread of the genus. Its pseudobulbs are very small and clustered with a single, leathery leaf up to about 4 in (10 cm) long. The inflorescence is slender and erect, and bears three to eight flowers at the apex. The flowers, about $\frac{4}{5}$ in (2 cm) long, appear from autumn to winter. **ZONES 10–12. I.**

Comparettia macroplectron RCHB.F. & TRIANA

This species from Colombia is similar vegetatively to *C. falcata*, but it has larger flowers, up to about 2 in (5 cm) long. The blooms are also a different color. Flowering occurs from summer to autumn. **ZONE 11. I.**

Comparettia speciosa RCHB.F.

This species occurs in Ecuador and northeast Peru. It is similar to the other species in the genus, but it is readily distinguished by its bright-orange flowers, which are up to 2 in (5 cm) in diameter. It flowers during autumn. **ZONES 10–12. I.**

Comparettia macroplectron

CONDYLAGO LUER

This monotypic genus allied to *Pleurothallis* occurs at high altitudes in Colombia. The plants are tufted and lack pseudobulbs. The leaves are up to about 4 in (10 cm) long. The inflorescence is up to 10 in (25 cm) long, hangs loosely and is flexuous. It carries many flowers which open successively and are about ⅔ in (15 mm) long.

CULTIVATION

These plants should be kept in cool conditions. They may be maintained in small pots with live sphagnum moss being a good medium. They should not be allowed to dry out.

Condylago rodrigoi LUER

This species is only 3 in (7.5 cm) tall. Its inflorescence is a similar length. Flowering time is autumn. **ZONE 12. C–I.**

Condylago rodrigoi

CORALLORHIZA (HALLER) CHATELAINE

"CORAL ROOT"

This genus of ten terrestrial species, mostly from North America, is known as saprophytic because the plants have no leaves and make little chlorophyll. Instead of roots, they have tangled underground rhizomes which are invaded by strands of mycorrhiza. This fungus digests decaying material in the soil, which nourishes the plants with carbohydrates. Because they do not rely on energy from the sun, *Corallorhiza* species usually flourish in dark woods. The perennial underground stems produce inflorescences unpredictably and the species is virtually impossible to cultivate.

Corallorhiza maculata   *Corallorhiza trifida*

Corallorhiza maculata (RAFINESQUE) RAFINESQUE

"SPOTTED CORAL ROOT"

This is the most common and widespread member of the genus. It inhabits northeast USA and spreads west across Canada and south to the mountains, with a separate population in upland areas of south Mexico and Guatemala. Its stem, usually about 12 in (30 cm) tall, may reach 32 in (80 cm). It carries up to 40 white flowers with purple markings. These may not open fully but they tend to reach a diameter of about ⅔ in (15 mm). The plant is usually self-pollinating and all the flowers bear fruit. The flowers unexpectedly pop up during late spring and summer. **ZONES 4–10. C–I.**

Corallorhiza trifida CHATELAINE

var. *verna* (NUTTALL) FERNALD.

"EARLY CORAL ROOT"

This species has an unusual distribution—it is circumpolar (around the North Pole), dipping into the USA in the northeast and at the Rocky Mountains. The spring-flowering southern variety occurs in the mid-Atlantic region. Its stem is less than 1 ft (30 cm) tall, and bears up to 20 flowers, each less than ⅓ in (1 cm) in diameter. Its greenish color indicates the presence of some chlorophyll—its stems are a clear yellow-green color and the flowers are unmarked; the other species in the genus have brown or purple markings. The plant shown here grew in marshy ground in the Pocono Mountains in Pennsylvania. **ZONES 3–7. C–I.**

CORYANTHES HOOK.

"BUCKET ORCHIDS"

This genus of 30 quite extraordinary orchids occurs in lowland tropical America. The common name arose because of the shape of the lips. They are mostly epiphytes, and have large, ribbed pseudobulbs with two or three thin leaves. The flowers are borne in sharply pendulous racemes and their intricate structure is unique among orchids. Grow these orchids in a well-drained mix in a basket so that the pendulous inflorescence may emerge freely. They may be difficult to maintain in cultivation and they require hot, humid conditions.

Coryanthes macrantha
(HOOK.) HOOK.

This species has a disjointed distribution—Trinidad in the West Indies and northeast Peru. Its pseudobulbs are ovoid to spindle-shaped, growing up to $5^1/_2$ in (13 cm) tall. The inflorescence, about 8 in (20 cm) long, often bears only two flowers. These are about $5^1/_2$ in (13 cm) long and have a sweet fragrance. The flowers appear from winter to spring.
ZONE 12. H.

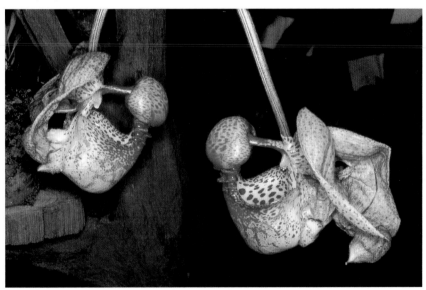

Coryanthes macrantha

CORYBAS SALISB.

This genus ranges from the mountains of northeast India through Southeast Asia to Papua New Guinea, the Pacific Islands, Australia, and New Zealand. In the tropics the species usually grow in mountainous areas at moderate to high altitudes. In Australia and New Zealand they often grow at sea level. Almost all the plants grow in leaf litter or in moss in shady, moist habitats. The plants are terrestrial, and consist of a small, round tuber, a single leaf that is usually heart-shaped, and a single flower situated on, or very close to, the leaf. The flower consists of a large dorsal sepal and a large lip. The other parts are comparatively small in size.

CULTIVATION

Many of these species are relatively easy to grow, particularly those that form colonies. A standard terrestrial mix with sandy loam and leaf mould (in Australia *Eucalyptus* leaf mould is preferable) is best. The plants should be kept dry while in active growth. The timing of this varies, depending on when the rains fall in the natural habitat. When well grown, the plants multiply rapidly by forming new tubers.

Corybas cerasinus

Corybas cerasinus
D. L. JONES & B. GRAY

This species was once known as *C. neocaledonicus*, but it was separated from that species in 2001. It is found in the mountainous areas in north Queensland, Australia, known as the Wet Tropics. It grows in the leaf litter of moist, open forests and it forms large colonies of numerous plants, only a few of which are in flower at one time. The single, heart-shaped leaf, about ⅓–1 in (1–2.5 cm) long and ⅓ in (1 cm) across, is held close to the solitary flower. The floral parts are hidden by a dorsal sepal about ⅓ in (1 cm) long. Flowering occurs during autumn and winter. **ZONES 10–12. I–H.**

Corybas fimbriatus (R. BR.) RCHB.F.

This species is widespread in eastern Australia, from north Queensland to Tasmania. It grows in a range of habitats from coastal scrubs to mossy rocks in the mountains. It usually grows in leaf litter under shade, and often forms large colonies. The leaf is light green in color, heart-shaped, and is up to 1¾ in (4 cm) across, but usually smaller. The single flower, up to 1¼ in (3 cm) long, is dominated by its dorsal sepal and lip. Flowers appear during autumn and winter. **ZONES 9–10. C–I.**

Corybas fimbriatus

CRYPTOSTYLIS R. BR.

This genus of about 20 terrestrial species comes from the Malay Archipelago to Australia and the Pacific Islands. They often grow in wet or boggy conditions. The leaves are usually ovate and arise from thick, fleshy roots. The flowers are borne on an erect inflorescence of several flowers. The lip is uppermost and the other perianth segments are very small. The Australian species attract male *Ichneumon* wasps for pollination by a process known as "pseudocopulation"—the plant mimics the female insect to attract the male.

CULTIVATION

Most species grow readily in a terrestrial mixture with coarse sand and leaf mould from the forests where the plants originally grew. The mix should be kept evenly moist. Repot only when absolutely necessary as these plants react badly to root disturbance.

Cryptostylis erecta R. BR.

This species occurs along the east coast of Australia, from about the Tropic of Capricorn to Victoria. It grows in sandy or peaty soil in open forests or on coastal heathlands. The leaves are distinctive, up to 7 in (18 cm) long and 1¼ in (3 cm) across. The leaves are dark green above and purple below. The 18-in (45-cm) inflorescence bears two to 12 flowers, each of which is about 1¼ in (3 cm) long. Flowers appear during spring and summer.
ZONES 9–11. I.

Cryptostylis subulata (LABILL.) RCHB.F.

This species is widespread in Australia, from north Queensland along the east coast to Tasmania and west to South Australia. It usually grows in swamp and stream margins, but may also grow in moist situations in open forests. In the southern part of the Great Dividing Range it grows at a lower altitude than in the tropical regions. The leaves are usually held erect and are up to 6 in (15 cm) long and 1¼ in (3 cm) across. Its inflorescence is up to 32 in (80 cm) tall and bears three to 20 flowers, each about 1 in (2.5 cm) long.
ZONES 9–11. I–H.

C

Cryptostylis erecta (above)
Cryptostylis subulata (right)

CUITLANZINIA LA LLAVE & LEX.

This monotypic genus from the mountains near the Pacific coast in western Mexico grows as an epiphyte in oak and oak–pine forests at altitudes between 4700 and 7300 ft (1400 and 2200 m). Its large pseudobulbs have two leathery leaves, up to 10 in (25 cm) long. The racemes are up to 8 in (20 cm) long and carry up to 15, often crowded, flowers. The highly fragrant flowers are about 2 in (5 cm) across.

CULTIVATION

Because of the pendulous nature of the inflorescence, these plants are best suited to hanging baskets. The plants should be grown in cool to intermediate conditions in a free-draining mix. They benefit from cool night temperatures.

Cuitlanzinia pendula
LA LLAVE & LEX

This is the only species in the genus. The flowers appear in spring and early winter.
ZONE 10. C–I.

Cuitlanzinia pendula

CYCNOCHES LINDL.

"SWAN ORCHIDS"

The common name of this genus arose because the slender column and down-turned apex resemble a swan. The genus comprises about 23 epiphytic species from the American tropics. They grow in hot, humid lowland conditions. The inflorescences bear separate male and female flowers. In some species the male and female flowers appear similar, while in others they look very different.

C

Cycnoches loddigesii

Cycnoches loddigesii

LINDL.

syn. *C. cucullata* LINDL.

This species from Brazil and the north of South America lives in hot, steamy lowland habitats. Its pseudobulbs are more or less cylindrical, and up to 10 in (25 cm) long. They have five to seven pleated leaves, up to about 16 in (40 cm) long and 2¾ in (7 cm) across. The arching inflorescence bears nine or more flowers with the male and female flowers appearing superficially similar. The male flowers are the larger ones, about 4¾ in (12 cm) across. Flowering occurs during summer. **ZONE 12. H.**

Cycnoches ventricosum

Cycnoches ventricosum BATEM.

This large, epiphytic species comes from low to moderate altitudes in Mexico and Panama. Its pseudobulbs are cylindrical to spindle-shaped, growing up to 12 in (30 cm) long and 1¼ in (3 cm) wide. The five to six leaves are up to 14 in (35 cm) long. There are both male and female flowers on one inflorescence. Flowers of both sexes are fragrant, waxy, and long-lasting. While superficially similar, the male flowers are up to 4 in (10 cm) wide, and the females slightly smaller with a stouter column. Flowering occurs from summer to early autumn. **ZONES 11–12. I–H.**

C

Cymbidiella pardalina

CYMBIDIELLA ROLFE

There are three species in this genus, and they are restricted to Madagascar. They grow at low to moderate altitudes in constantly humid conditions. As the name implies, the plants resemble and are related to *Cymbidium*. They are distinguished from that genus by their epiphytic habit and the shape of the flowers.

CULTIVATION

The best growing medium for these plants is a pot with a well-drained mix. They prefer warm, humid conditions with bright light. No watering rest period is necessary. When repotting, avoid damaging the roots.

Cymbidiella pardalina (RCHB.F.) GARAY

syn. *C. rhodochila* (ROLFE) ROLFE, *Grammangis pardalina* RCHB.F., *Cymbidium rhodochilum* ROLFE

This species grows in humid, low- to moderate-altitude rain forests on Madagascar. It usually grows in the peat of the fern *Platycerium madagascariensis*. Its pseudobulbs are ovoid, and are 3–6 in (7.5–15 cm) long and 1–1½ in (2.5–3.5 cm) wide. They have five to ten straplike leaves, up to 40 in (1 m) long and ⅘ in (2 cm) wide. The inflorescence arises from the bases of the pseudobulbs and has 20 or more showy flowers, each about 2¾ in (7 cm) across. Flowering in cultivation occurs during spring and summer. **ZONES 11–12. I–H.**

CYMBIDIUM sw.

This is one of the most important genera in cultivation—its history extends back to the times of Confucius in ancient China. Thousands of hybrids have been developed from this genus of more than 40 species. Its natural habitat ranges from India to Japan in the northern hemisphere and Australia in the southern hemisphere. They grow as epiphytes or on rocks, generally in areas of moderate to high rainfall, although *C. canaliculatum* extends into semi-arid regions in Australia. They occur from sea level to about 10,000 ft (3000 m), with the majority growing at a medium altitude where the climate is relatively cool. They are mostly large and showy plants.

CULTIVATION

Cymbidium hybrids grow and flower well in cool climates, needing protection only during the coldest months of the winter in northern Europe and America. For many people living in such areas, the word orchid is synonymous with *Cymbidium*. As long as an area is frost free, these hybrids may be grown in a garden setting. They grow best under strong light but partly shaded conditions. For most species and hybrids, a well-drained mixture that retains some moisture without becoming soggy, is preferred. Potting mixtures vary, but they often contain bark, peanut husks, charcoal, and perlite. The mixture should be able to retain its structure for about three years before repotting is necessary. Water heavily during summer but reduce watering during winter. Never allow the plant to dry out completely. Regular feeding with a diluted fertilizer during the growing season is recommended.

HYBRIDS

There have been thousands of hybrids made from this genus over a period of more than 100 years. These originated from fewer than 20 parent species; the vast majority from seven or eight species, including *C. lowianum*, *C. eburneum*, *C. hookerianum*, *C. insigne*, *C. sanderae*, and *C. floribundum*. Hybridists have been looking to create more floriferous plants with larger and more colorful flowers, compact upright spikes, on more compact plants. There has also been a significant trend, however, to create a large range of smaller, compact hybrids that take up less space. Most of the hybrids are large with numerous flowers borne on long, arching spikes that often need staking. The flowers vary in size from 2–6 in (5–15 cm) wide, come in a variety of colors, and appear mostly during winter and spring. The flowers last for several weeks.

Cymbidium aloifolium

Cymbidium aloifolium (L.) SW.

This widespread species occurs from India and Sri Lanka through south China, Myanmar, Thailand, and Hong Kong to west Malaysia and Java. It is a medium-sized plant with thick, rigid leaves measuring up to 40 in (1 m) long. The inflorescence is pendulous and bears up to 45 flowers, each about 1¾ in (4 cm) across. The sepals and petals are pale yellow to cream in color with a central maroon stripe. The lip of the flower is cream or white with the side and midlobe veins being maroon. Flowering occurs from late spring to early summer. This species is easy to grow in warm climates. **ZONES 9–10. I–H.**

C

Cymbidium atropurpureum

Cymbidium bicolor LINDL.

This species is very similar in appearance to *C. aloifolium* but it has a more extensive range—from Indonesia to the Philippines. It also occurs in southern India, Sri Lanka and Nepal. Both species grow in the forks and branches of large trees from sea level to about 5000 ft (1500 m). It can be distinguished from *C. aloifolium* by the mottled rather than stripped maroon color of the labellum's side and midlobes. The flowers of *C. bicolor* appear from late winter to early summer. This is an easy-to-grow species, preferring intermediate conditions. It may be grown on a suitable tree where it will get good light in a moist situation. **ZONES 11–12. I–H.**

Cymbidium bicolor

Cymbidium atropurpureum (LINDL.) ROLFE

This large epiphytic species is distributed from Thailand, Malaysia, and Indonesia to the Philippines. It grows mostly in the forks of trees, sometimes on rocks, in lowland forests, often near the sea. In Sabah on the island of Borneo and on Sumatra, however, it may occur as high as 7300 ft (2200 m). The most distinctive color variation of this variable species is found in the Philippines and in lowland Sabah, where they have wine-red sepals and petals. Plants from western Malaysia and Thailand have greenish sepals. The inflorescence is pendulous and up to 28 in (70 cm) long. The plants flower intermittently, although the main period is during late spring. This species is hardy in tropical and subtropical regions, where it may be grown in the garden attached to a suitable host tree. **ZONES 11–12. I–H.**

Cymbidium canaliculatum R. BR.

This species is endemic to Australia, ranging
from northern Western Australia to Cape York
Peninsula in Queensland and south to central
New South Wales. It has the capacity to
withstand drought and is more commonly
found in the drier habitats of its range. It is less
common near the coast in those areas. It can be
found almost always in rotting hollow logs or
in the forks of suitable hosts, frequently a
Eucalyptus species. The leaves are distinctive,
being very thick and leathery. They are erect
and form a strong V–shape in cross section.
The racemes are pendulous, up to 20 in
(50 cm) long, and the flower color is variable.
The most common form has greenish sepals
and petals with brown spotting, but the most
sought-after forms have deep purple sepals and
petals. Flowers appear from late spring to early
summer. These plants will tolerate full sun and
may be grown outdoors in warm climates. It is
advisable to withhold watering during the
colder months of winter. **ZONES 10–12. I–H.**

Cymbidium dayanum

Cymbidium canaliculatum

Cymbidium dayanum RCHB.F.

syn. *C. simonsianum* KING & PANTLING

This species is a particularly attractive and
rewarding plant to grow. It is medium-sized
with smallish pseudobulbs and graceful arching
foliage. It ranges from northern India through
southeast China, Taiwan, and Japan to the
Philippines. It also occurs in Thailand and
Cambodia and probably in Laos, Vietnam,
west Malaysia, Sabah in Borneo, and Sumatra.
It generally prefers a cooler climate, growing at
elevations of more than 6700 ft (2000 m),
where it is found most often in rotting stumps
and logs. In cultivation it does well in part
shade in a normal *Cymbidium* mix. Flowers
appear at any time but the peak period is
usually late summer through to spring.
ZONES 9–11. C–I.

C

Cymbidium devonianum PAYLAN

This small-growing species occurs at moderate
altitudes from India to Nepal and northern
Thailand. Its short, stout, crowded stems give
rise to leathery leaves about 16 in (40 cm) long
and 1¾ in (4 cm) broad. It has pendulous
inflorescences up to 16 in (40 cm) long that
produce numerous closely spaced flowers, each
about 1¼ in (3 cm) across. The color of the
flowers varies from green to light brown, with
a red to maroon lip. Flowers appear in late
spring. **ZONES 9–10. C–I.**

C. eburneum LINDL.

C. eburneum is one of the most attractive
orchids in this genus and has been used
extensively in hybridization. In fact, it was one
of the parents (the other is C. lowianum) of the
first artificial Cymbidium hybrid. This

Cymbidium devonianum

epiphytic species is distributed from northern India and Nepal to
China and northern Myanmar. It occurs in damp forests at
altitudes of 1000–5700 ft (300–1700 m). It has a short
inflorescence which usually carries a single, large, and sweetly
lilac-scented flower about 3¼–4¾ in (8–12 cm) in diameter.
Flowering occurs in mid winter. **ZONES 9–10. C.**

Cymbidium eburneum

Cymbidium elegans

Cymbidium elegans LINDL.
syn. C. longifolium D.DON

This species' distribution is from northeastern India and Nepal
through northern Myanmar to southwest China. It grows on rocks
overhanging streams at elevations of 5000–8300 ft (1500–2500 m).
It is distinctive because its inflorescence is sharply pendulous and
the densely crowded racemes have pendulous, narrow, funnel-
shaped flowers. The flowers are about 1¼ in (3 cm) in diameter
and are lightly scented. **ZONES 9–10. C.**

Cymbidium ensifolium

Cymbidium erythrostylum ROLFE

Little is known of the inaccessible habitat of this species. Endemic to Vietnam, it is found at an elevation of about 5000 ft (1500 m). It is an epiphyte, lithophyte, and a terrestrial. Its arching leaves are up to about 20 in (50 cm) long. The inflorescence is slender, erect to arching, and carries up to ten flowers, each with a diameter about 2½ in (6 cm). They have a narrow, triangular appearance with the petals tending to lie close to the lateral lobes of the labellum and column, therefore not opening widely. This is one of the most attractive species in the genus and the flowers are long-lasting. The flowering period is autumn through to winter. **ZONE 11. C.**

Cymbidium ensifolium (L.) SW.

C

This species has a wide distribution from southern India and Sri Lanka through China, Thailand, Vietnam, Cambodia, Malaysia, and Indonesia to the Philippines and Papua New Guinea. It is a terrestrial species occurring in lightly shaded forests. It comes in a wide variation of color and form and has been cultivated in Japan and China for more than 2000 years. It is much prized for its strongly scented flowers and for the variegated leaves of some cultivars. *C. ensifolium* is a medium-sized plant with small pseudobulbs. Its erect inflorescence bears three to nine flowers towards the upper half. The flowers are about 1¼–2 in (3–5 cm) in diameter. Flowering is sporadic in warmer climates; the main period is from late winter to spring. **ZONES 10–12. C–I.**

Cymbidium erythrostylum

C

Cymbidium floribundum LINDL.
syn. *C. pumilum* ROLFE

This species grows naturally as a lithophyte in rocky gorges, or as an epiphyte. It occurs at an altitude of 5000–9300 ft (1500–2800m) in the mountains of southern China and on the island of Taiwan. It is tolerant of dry conditions and forms large clumps in open situations. Many variations are known in cultivation, and of particular value are the forms with variegated leaves. It has also been important in the breeding of miniature hybrids. Its small pseudobulbs have leaves up to 20 in (50 cm) long and ⅔ in (15 mm) broad. The erect to arching inflorescence, about 8 in (20 cm) long, bears up to 30 or 40 closely spaced flowers. The flowers have a diameter about 1¼–1¾ in (3–4 cm). This species is easily grown but is reluctant to flower in warmer climates. Flowering occurs from spring to early summer. **ZONES 9–10. C.**

Cymbidium floribundum

Cymbidium iridioides D. DON

This species grows at altitudes between 4000 and 7300 ft (1200 and 2200 m) from northern India and Nepal to southwest China and Myanmar. It is a large epiphyte that grows on mossy trees and in tree hollows with abundant humus and leaf litter. The leaves may be up to nearly 40 in (1 m) long. The sub-erect to arching inflorescence bears seven to 20 flowers, each up to 4 in (10 cm) across. This species is best grown in intermediate conditions with reduced watering during the winter months. **ZONES 9–10. C–I**

Cymbidium hookerianum RCHB.F.
syn. *C. grandiflorum* GRIFFITH

This species extends from Nepal and northeast India to southwest China. It grows as an epiphyte or lithophyte in dense forests at altitudes of 5000–8700 ft (1500–2600 m). It has a long, arching inflorescence, up to 28 in (70 cm), that bears six to 15 strongly scented flowers. These are apple-green in color with red spots, and may be up to 5⅔ in (14 cm) across. This plant requires cool conditions in order to flower from late winter to early spring. **ZONES 9–10. C.**

Cymbidium hookerianum

Cymbidium iridioides

C

Cymbidium kanran

Cymbidium lowianum

Cymbidium kanran MAKINO

This terrestrial species grows under shade in the open forests of southern China, Taiwan, the Ryukyu Islands, southern Japan, and southern Korea. It can be found at altitudes between 2700 and 6000 ft (800 and 1800 m). The erect inflorescence is about 20 in (50 cm) tall, and bears ten or more flowers. These are borne on the upper half of the stem, and rise above the leaves. The color of the flowers is variable but the most common is olive green with some red-brown in the central vein of the sepals and petals. They are strongly scented and are about 2–3 in (5–7.5 cm) across. *C. kanran* is closely allied to *C. sinense* but can be easily distinguished by its very long, narrow, finely tapering sepals. Flowers appear during winter. **ZONES 7–9. C–I.**

Cymbidium lowianum (RCHB.F.) RCHB.F.

This large species is one of the commonly used parents of many *Cymbidium* hybrids. Its natural habitat is high in the mountains in Myanmar and southern China. Its leaves are set in two rows and are up to 28 in (70 cm) long and ⅘ in (2 cm) wide. They arise from crowded pseudobulbs, which are compressed in shape and are about 5½ in (13 cm) long. The flower spikes are up to 5 ft (1.5 m) tall and bear numerous large blooms, each about 3¼–4 in (8–10 cm) wide. They are light green to brown in color with a prominent red blotch at the tip of the lip. Flowering occurs during spring. **ZONES 9–10. C–I.**

Cymbidium madidum

Cymbidium madidum LINDL.

This robust species with large pseudobulbs is restricted to Australia, occurring in moist forests from Cape York Peninsula to northern New South Wales. It grows most often in rotting stumps and branches, forks of trees, and in clumps of elkhorn ferns. The erect to arching leaves may be up to 32 in (80 cm) long. The pendulous inflorescence is up to 4 ft (1.2 m) long. It may bear up to 50 or 60 flowers, each nearly 1 in (2.5 cm) wide. The flowers have a slight, sweet scent. The sepals and petals are colored apple-green to yellow. Flowers appear from late winter to spring. This species will tolerate some direct sun and will also grow and flower under heavy shade. It performs well outside, mounted in the fork of a large tree in a suitable climate. **ZONES 9–11. I–H.**

Cymbidium sanderae (ROLFE) CRIBB
& DU PUY
syn. *C. parishii* RCHB.F., **var.** *sanderae* ROLFE

This species, endemic to Vietnam, occurs at
elevations of about 5000 ft (1500 m). It
grows on trees. Its leaves are about 20 in
(50 cm) long and 1 in (2.5 cm) broad. The
pseudobulbs are ovoid. The robust
inflorescence is 12–20 in (30–50 cm) long
and is sub-erect to arching. The three to
15 lightly scented flowers are about 3¼ in
(8 cm) in diameter. Flowers appear from
late winter to spring. **ZONE 10. C.**

Cymbidium sanderae

Cymbidium sinense

Cymbidium suave

Cymbidium sinense (JACKSON IN ANDR.) WILLD.

This robust species has been in cultivation in
China and Japan for several centuries. It is
highly prized for its diverse flower color and
variegated leaves. Its distribution is from
Bangladesh through China, northern Myanmar,
northern Thailand, Taiwan, and the Ryukyu
Islands, at elevations between 1000 and 7700
ft (300 and 2300 m). It is a terrestrial species
favoring the shade or semi-shade of dense
mixed or evergreen forests. It has erect
inflorescences up to 32 in (80 cm) tall. These
bear up to 20 flowers that grow in the upper
part of the scape that rises well above the
foliage. The strongly scented flowers are about
2 in (5 cm) in diameter. There is a wide
variation of form within the species, particularly
in flower color, which may range from deep
purple-brown to green. Flowers appear from
autumn to spring. **ZONES 9–10. C–I.**

Cymbidium suave R. BR.

This medium-sized species from Australia
grows from sea level to about 4000 ft (1200 m)
on the eastern slopes of the Great Dividing
Range from northern Queensland to southern
New South Wales. Its most common habitat is
Eucalyptus woodland. It grows in rotting
branches and logs and in the forks of large
trees, where it forms an extensive root system.
When the species grows on *Melaleuca* (paper
bark) trees, its root system penetrates between
the bark layers. Its pseudobulbs are slender.
The racemes are pendulous and up to about
1 ft (30 cm) long. They have up to 40 closely
spaced flowers, each ¾–1 in (18–25 mm)
across. The flowers have a sweet scent. This
species likes bright light and its flowers appear
from late winter in northern Queensland,
through to summer in southerly regions.
ZONES 8–11. C–I–H.

Cymbidium tigrinum PARISH EX HOOK.F

This species occurs on bare rocks and in crevices within open forests at altitudes of 5000–9000 ft (1500–2700 m). It has a distinct distribution, occurring in Myanmar and northeast India. The plant is a small lithophyte that is up to 6 in (15 cm) tall. Its spherical to broad-ovoid pseudobulbs are strongly compressed bilaterally. They are about $1\frac{1}{4}$ in (3 cm) in diameter. The leaves are up to 8 in (20 cm) long and $1\frac{1}{2}$ in (3.5 cm) broad. The inflorescence, up to 10 in (25 cm) long, bears two to five large flowers, about $1\frac{3}{4}$–2 in (4–5 cm) wide. The petals of these form a partial hood over the column. The honey-scented flowers appear during spring and early winter. **ZONES 9–10. C.**

Cymbidium tigrinum

Cymbidium tracyanum

Cymbidium tracyanum
L. CASTLE

This species occurs in eastern and northern Myanmar, northern Thailand, and China at altitudes of 4000–6300 ft (1200–1900 m). It grows on damp rocks and in trees in shaded forests, often near water. The leaves are up to 40 in (1 m) long. Its sub-erect to arching inflorescence is up to 52 in (1.3 m) long. It bears ten to 20 flowers about 6 in (15 cm) wide. They have a strong, sweet scent and appear from spring through to winter. **ZONES 9–10. C.**

C

Cym. Bingo

Cym. Dag × Wyanga

Cym. Del Playa 'Yvonne'

Cym. Dr Len 'Geyserland'

Cym. Cronulla

Cym. Jubilation 'Geronimo'

C

Cym. Kiata × Ruby Eyes

Cym. Nancy Maxwell Shirley

Cym. Summer Clouds

Cym. Ming Pagoda

Cym. Towering Giant

Cym. Royal Fair 'Krista'

CYNORKIS THOUARS

This genus of terrestrial orchids is related to *Habenaria*. It comprises some 125 species, most of which grow on Madagascar and its adjacent islands. About 17 are found on the African continent. The majority of the species grow in moist habitats under semi-shade, from sea level to moderate altitudes. They have tuberous roots, usually one or two leaves, and an upright inflorescence with several small flowers. The flowers have a three- to five-lobed lip with a prominent spur.

CULTIVATION

These plants are relatively easy to grow in a shallow pot with a well-drained but moisture-retentive mixture.

Cynorkis fastigiata THOUARS

This is one of a few orchids that could be called a weed. It is a nuisance in many orchid collections because it spreads rapidly by seed. It originally came from Madagascar, the Comoro Islands, the Seychelles, and Mauritius. It grows on the margins of or near rivers in forests from sea level to 4700 ft (1400 m). It has a single, straplike leaf. The inflorescence bears a few

flowers, each about 1/3–4/5 in (1–2 cm) long. They vary in color from pink to white or pale yellow. Flowering occurs throughout the year. **ZONES 9–12. C–I–H.**

Cynorkis ridleyi T. DURAND & SCHINZ.

This species is recorded on Madagascar and the Comoro Islands. It grows in rain forests at an altitude of 2700–6700 ft (800–2000 m). **ZONES 9–11. C–I.**

Cynorkis fastigiata

Cynorkis ridleyi

Cynorkis uncata (ROLFE) KRAENZL.

This species from Kenya and Tanzania occurs in upland rain forests. It can be found growing in humus between rocks at an altitude of 3000–5500 ft (900–1650 m). The plant reaches anywhere from 4 to 14 in (10 to 35 cm) tall. It has two spreading leaves, each about 1 3/4–6 1/2 in (4–16 cm) long and 1/3–2 in (1–5 cm) wide. The inflorescence is rather open and bears three to 17 flowers, each about 1/3 in (1 cm) wide. The flower spur is less than 1/3 in (1 cm) long. Flowering occurs during late autumn and early winter. **ZONES 9–10. I.**

Cynorkis uncata

CYPRIPEDIUM L.

"SLIPPER ORCHIDS" OR "LADY'S SLIPPER ORCHIDS"

The 45 species that make up this genus occur on three continents—Europe, Asia, and America. The main concentration is in the Himalayas, and there are about 15 species in North America and three species in Europe. Many tropical orchids once classified as a *Cypripedium* now belong to other genera, such as *Paphiopedilum*, *Phragmedium* and *Selenipedium*, although all are still referred to as "slipper orchids".

Both the scientific and common names of this genus derive from the way the lip of the flower forms a hollow pouch shaped like the toe of a slipper, albeit a very bulbous one. It is the lip's upper opening that attracts bees and causes pollination. The area around the opening is very slippery so the insect falls easily into it. Only bees of the right size are able to get through the basal openings, where the stigma and pollinia are situated. As a bee passes through, pollination is effected.

CULTIVATION

Cypripedium species, like all orchids, are protected in the wild in most countries. As the true species are difficult to obtain and maintain, it is probably best to grow the specially created hybrids. Only artificially propagated plants may be used in cultivation. Most of the hybrids are crosses involving *C. calceolus*, *C. candidum*, *C. cordigerum*, *C. henryi*, *C. parviflorum*, and *C. reginae*. They are easy to grow and suitable for outdoor cultivation. They need good light, but should be shaded by walls or trees during the hottest part of the day. The soil should comprise calcareous, clayed humus with limestone grit (pH-value about 6–7), and be well-aerated and not compressed. They need good drainage with little ground moisture, in humid conditions.

Cypripedium acaule

Cypripedium acaule AITON

syn. *C. hirsutum* MILL., *C. humile* SALISB.

This species' distribution is limited to the northeastern parts of Canada and the USA. It grows in a range of habitats, from dry pine forests to wet sphagnum bogs, but always in strongly acidic soil under moderate shade. It forms large colonies and has a short underground rhizome. From this a very short, erect stem grows, followed by two plicate, elliptic, bright-green leaves, about 4–10 in (10–25 cm) long and 2–6 in (5–15 cm) wide. The inflorescence is about 8–18 in (20–45 cm) long. It usually has a single flower about 2½ in (6 cm) wide. The flowering period occurs between spring and summer. In cultivation *C. acaule* is difficult to grow and must have acidic soil and a pine humus that does not decompose rapidly. **ZONES 4–7. C.**

C

Cypripedium bardolphianum
W. W. SM. & FARRER

syn. *C. nutans Schltr.*

This species grows in moss along mountain streams and under trees in gorges at high altitudes in western China—in areas with a cold winter. It is not known in cultivation. The elliptic leaves are 2–2½ in (5–6 cm) long and about 1 in (2.5 cm) wide. The 3-in (7.5-cm) long inflorescence arises between the leaves and has a single flower about 1¼ in (3 cm) across. It has been said that the lip fits the description of the grotesque, warty nose of Bardolph in Shakespeare's *Henry V*. The flowers appear during June and July. **ZONES 6–8. C..**

Cypripedium bardolphianum

Cypripedium calceolus L.
syn. many names, including *C. boreale* SALISB., *C. ferrugineum* GRAY, *C. microsaccus* KRAENZL.

This is the most attractive and best-known orchid of Europe. It is general widely distributed in north Spain, in one area of the British Isles, and through northern and middle Europe, as north as Siberia. It also ranges to north China and Japan's Honshu Island. It is found from sea level to 8300 ft (2500 m) in partly shaded forests with lime-rich soil. Because of its attractiveness, it was heavily collected and is now very rare and endangered in the wild. It reaches up to 1–2 ft (30–60 cm) tall and has two to four ovate leaves on the basal part of the stem. It has one or, rarely, two flowers up to about 6 in (15 cm) across. It flowers for only two weeks between late autumn and early winter. *C. calceolus* has been cultivated for centuries but it is not easy to grow. The soil it grows in must consist of perfectly crumbled calcareous clay containing small pieces, up to sand-grain size, of limestone. **ZONES 3–9. C.**

Cypripedium calceolus

C

Cypripedium cordigerum

Cypripedium flavum

Cypripedium cordigerum D. DON

This lady's slipper ranges along the Himalayas from northern Pakistan to Nepal, Bhutan, and Tibet at altitudes of 7000–13,300 ft (2100–4000 m). It grows in shady and wet forests or open glades or can be found under shrubs. It has a stem height of up to 2 ft (60 cm). Its two to five elliptic leaves are well-spaced along the stem. The inflorescence bears one or, rarely, two flowers. The flower size is variable, between 1¾ and 2½ in (4 and 6 cm). Flowers appear in summer. This species is hardy, but it is very difficult to establish in a garden. It is easier to cultivate its hybrids. **ZONES 5–7. C.**

Cypripedium flavum P. F. HUNT & SUMMERH.
syn. *C. luteum* FRANCH.

This species grows in open woodlands or under scrub at high altitudes. It is limited to the southwest provinces of China and grows as a single plant or in clusters. Its stout

rhizomes produce leafy stems anywhere between 8 and 24 in (20 and 60 cm) tall. Its six to ten ovate leaves are well-spaced along the stem. The leaves are about 4–6¾ in (10–17 cm) long and 2–4 in (5–10 cm) wide and the largest are borne on the upper part of the plant. The flowers are about 1¾ in (4 cm) wide and are pale to dark in color, sometimes flushed with red. The lip is sometimes more or less spotted red. The broad, ovate staminode may be all yellow, or may be yellow marked with a red-brown color, or may be red-brown all over. *C. flavum* is not easy to grow and needs a lot of care. The soil must be calcareous and rich in humus, but must not hold too much moisture. **ZONES 5–7. C.**

Cypripedium formosanum HAYATA
syn. *C. japonicum var. formosanum* (HAYATA) S. S. YING
"FORMOSA LADY'S SLIPPER"

Cypripedium formosanum

This beautiful lady's slipper, limited to high altitudes on Taiwan, grows in damp places in open areas and in forests. It has stems 4–10 in (10–25 cm) tall. At the apex are two nearly round leaves with 11 to 13 radiating veins spreading out like a fan. They are 4–5½ in (10–13 cm) long. The single flower is 2½–2¾ in (6–7 cm) across. It is borne on a peduncle about 4 in (10 cm) long. This species flowers in spring. It is considered to be easy to grow, but it needs calcareous soil with a relatively heavy substrate. Frequent watering and heavy fertilizing is necessary during the growing season. **ZONES 5–7. C.**

C

Cypripedium macranthos SW.
syn. *C. calceolus* **var.** *rubrum* GEORGI
"LARGE FLOWERED LADY'S SLIPPER"

This species has a wide distribution, from Russia through
Siberia to Korea, northeast China, and Japan. It grows between
sea level and 8000 ft (2400 m) under light shade in the damp
surroundings of forests and in meadows or under shrubs. Its
leafy stem is 6–16 in (15–40 cm) tall and bears three to five
ovate leaves, each 4–5⅔ in (10–14 cm) long and 1¾–2½ in
(4–6 cm) wide. The inflorescence usually has a single flower
about 2½–2¾ in (6–7 cm) across. Flowers appear in summer.
C. macranthos needs a compost mix of coarse sand, gravel-like
pumice and well-crumbled loam with a little rotten wood. Very
good drainage is important. **ZONES 3–7. C.**

Cypripedium plectrochilum

Cypripedium macranthos

Cypripedium plectrochilum FRANCH.
"RAM'S HEAD LADY'S SLIPPER"

This species occurs in the
coniferous or mixed forests
at high altitudes in southwest
China. It grows under semi-
shade in stony ground, usually
containing limestone. Its
slender, erect stem is up to
7 in (18 cm) long and bears
three lanceolate leaves. From
the top a single-flowered
inflorescence is produced. The
flower is about 1 in (2.5 cm)
across and is dominated by
the whitish lip with a conical
elongation at the apex. It
flowers during summer. An
alpine house is recommended
for this species to have a
chance of growing it in
cultivation. **ZONES 5–7. C.**

C

Cypripedium reginae

Cypripedium reginae WALT.

syn. *C. album* AITON, *C. spectabile* SALISB.

"QUEEN LADY'S SLIPPER"

Reginae means "queen", and this slipper orchid is one of the showiest. As a result of this, it has been depleted in the wild. It occurs in northeast America, growing in wet, neutral to calcareous soils in meadows, bogs, and swamps. It forms colonies of stems about 14–32 in (35–80 cm) tall. The three to seven leaves are strongly ribbed and have an elliptic-lanceolate form. The inflorescence normally bears a single flower, about 3¼ in (8 cm) across. It is white with a typically more or less rose-purple colored shoe. Flowers appear in summer. *C. reginae* is relatively easy to cultivate. It requires regular feeding and moist, but not overly wet, conditions. **ZONES 3–9. C.**

Cypripedium tibeticum

Cypripedium tibeticum KING EX ROLFE

syn. *C. corrugatum* FRANCH., *C. compactum* SCHLTR.

"TIBET LADY'S SLIPPER"

The distribution of this species extends from Bhutan to Tibet and southwestern China. It grows in open montane meadows or light coniferous or mixed forests at high altitudes. *C. tibeticum* is related to *C. macranthos*, but it is far more difficult to cultivate. It has about six leaves—the lowermost reduced to sheaths, the uppermost ovate and measuring up to 6 in (15 cm) long to 3 in (7.5 cm) wide. The stem is up to 1 ft (30 cm) long. There are one or, occasionally, two flowers about 3 in (7.5 cm) wide. The flowers are overtopped by a leafy bract. Flowering time is during summer. This species is intolerant of being too wet during winter. **ZONES 5–7. C.**

CYRTOPODIUM R. BR.

There are about 30 species in this genus of epiphytes or terrestrials. They occur from Florida in the USA through the West Indies and Central America to Argentina. They are related to *Eulophia* and have long, cigar-shaped pseudobulbs with several long, thin-textured leaves. The inflorescences are branched and erect, and arise from the base of the pseudobulbs. The flowers are moderately large and often rather drab in color.

CULTIVATION

A mixture suitable for terrestrial species such as *Cymbidium* may be used. The plants should be given a dry, cool resting period when not in active growth. Some species may grow into large plants so they will need a lot of room in an orchid house.

Cyrtopodium gigas

Cyrtopodium gigas (VELL.) HOEHNE

This species comes from Brazil and Argentina where it grows at low to moderate altitudes in the mountains. The pseudobulbs are spindle-shaped, sometimes measuring over 40 in (1 m), but usually shorter. It has several deciduous, long, narrow leaves. The inflorescence is branched, growing up to 40 in (1 m) long. It bears numerous fragrant flowers, each about 1¼ in (3 cm) across. Flowering occurs during autumn and winter. **ZONES 10–12. I–H.**

Cyrtopodium polyphyllum (VELL.) PABST EX F. BARRIOS

syn. *C. paranaense* SCHLTR.

This species grows as a terrestrial in sandy soil and sometimes on rocks at low altitudes in South America from Colombia to Brazil. It is also naturalized in Florida in the USA, where it grows in a few scattered areas in pine forests. In Florida it has been confused with the *C. andersonii*, which is endemic to the West Indies. *C. polyphyllum* forms a large plant with pseudobulbs about 8–24 in (20–60 cm) tall. They are spindle-shaped and have several deciduous long, narrow leaves. The branched inflorescence is 2–3 ft (60–90 cm) long, with numerous fragrant, long-lasting flowers, each about 1–1¾ in (2.5–4 cm) across. Flowering occurs from late spring to early summer. **ZONES 10-12. I-H.**

Cyrtopodium polyphyllum

Cyrtopodium punctatum

Cyrtopodium punctatum (L.) LINDL.

syn. several names, including *C. speciosissimum* HORT. EX DU BUYSSON, *C. tigrinum* LINDEN

This species is usually epiphytic and occurs in Florida in the USA, the West Indies, Central America, Brazil and Paraguay. It may grow into a large plant and has cigar-shaped pseudobulbs up to 16 in (40 cm) long, and long, narrow, leaves up to 28 in (70 cm). The erect and branched inflorescence is up to 5 ft (1.5 m) long and bears numerous flowers, each about 1½ in (3.5 cm) across. Flowering occurs from spring to early summer. **ZONES 10–12. I–H.**

CYRTORCHIS SCHLTR.

There are about 15 species in this monopodial genus which is related to *Angraecum*. They occur in Africa, mostly in open situations with bright light. They have a short- to medium-sized stem with leaves forming two ranks. The roots are often vigorous and thick. The flowers vary from small to large and are star-shaped with a spur. The segments are usually reflexed. The flowers tend to start white but turn yellow or orange.

CULTIVATION

Slab culture is best as it provides good drainage, and the roots are also difficult to contain in a pot. Bright, filtered sunlight encourages growth and flowering. A rather drier resting period is beneficial for most species.

Cyrtorchis arcuata

Cyrtorchis chailluana

Cyrtorchis praetermissa

Cyrtorchis arcuata (LINDL.) SCHLTR.

syn. *Listrostachys whitei* ROLFE, *Angraecum arcuatum* LINDL.

This widespread, variable species occurs over much of central and southern Africa, extending from the west to the east coast and south to the Cape Province in South Africa. It grows on trees or rocks at sea level to 10,000 ft (3000 m) in a variety of habitats, but usually in bright light. The stems are upright, growing up to 1 ft (30 cm) long. The leaves are up to 6 in (15 cm) long, arranged in two ranks. The horizontal or arching inflorescences bear up to 14 fragrant flowers, each about 1¾–2 in (4–5 cm) across. As the segments age they curl back and turn orange. The curved spur is 1¼–3¼ in (3–8 cm) long. Flowering occurs from spring to autumn in the wild. **ZONES 10–12. I–H.**

Cyrtorchis chailluana (HOOK.F.) SCHLTR.

syn. *Listrostachys chailluana* (HOOK.F.) RCHB.F., *Angraecum chailluaum* HOOK.F.

This medium- to large-sized epiphyte comes from the rain forests of west Africa, inland to Uganda. It grows at low to moderate altitudes. Its leaves are up to 10 in (25 cm) long and 1¼ in (3 cm) wide. The inflorescences are up to 10 in (25 cm) long and bear many fragrant flowers, each about 3 in (7.5 cm) across. The spur is up to 6 in (15 cm) long. **ZONES 11–12. H.**

Cyrtorchis praetermissa SUMMERH.

This small- to medium-sized species is widespread over eastern central Africa, spreading as far south as northern South Africa. It grows in woodlands, usually in fairly open situations at an altitude of 3300–7700 ft (1000–2300 m). The stems are up to 8 in (20 cm) long with narrow, stiff, leathery leaves forming two ranks. The inflorescence bears three to 14 flowers, each about ½ in (12 mm) across. The spur is about 1 in (2.5 cm) long. Flowering occurs from spring to autumn. **ZONES 9–11. I.**

D

DACTYLORHIZA NECK. EX NEVSKI
"MARSH ORCHIDS," "SPOTTED ORCHIDS"

The genus *Dactylorhiza* occurs in Europe, western and northern Asia, and North America. It has 33 variable species, which are all terrestrials with two tubers that are divided like fingers. This gives rise to their scientific name. They grow in bogs, grasslands, and pastures. Many of the species have spotted leaves and most of them have pink flowers with darker pink spots. These plants often tend to hybridize naturally, and this may cause problems when trying to identify them.

CULTIVATION

Members of this genus are frost-hardy. They prefer part-shade and require specialist potting mixtures, usually with peat moss, leaf mold, decomposed bark, sand, and loam. The plants should be kept wet during warm weather and somewhat drier during winter. They can be propagated by division in early spring.

Dactylorhiza aristata (FISCHER) SOÓ

This species has a unique distribution—from Korea and Japan, through Russia's Kuril Islands, Kamchatka Peninsula, and Komandorskije Islands to Alaska's Aleutian Islands and mainland. It is the only common orchid along this route that flowers during early July (summer)—its brilliant purple flowers lighten up the still bleak, foggy landscapes. This plant's height is up to 16 in (40 cm). Like its relatives in Europe, it sometimes has spotted leaves. There are two to five leaves, and as many as 30 flowers, each with a diameter to about 1 in (2.5 cm). The flowers are recognizable by the sharp ends of the sepals. **ZONES 3–6. C.**

Dactylorhiza aristata

Dactylorhiza elata

Dactylorhiza elata (POIRET) SOÓ
"ROBUST MARSH ORCHID"

This moisture-loving plant grows in wet grasslands, bogs, and sometimes along roadside ditches from northwest Africa through Spain to northwest France and the Mediterranean island of Corsica. It is a robust species, as its common name suggests. It is about 40 in (1 m) tall and has around eight to 14 unspotted, broadly lanceolate leaves along the stem. The inflorescence is dense with pink to purple-red flowers, each about ⅔ in (15 mm) across. The flowers appear from spring to early summer. **ZONES 8–10. I.**

D

Dactylorhiza foliosa

Dactylorhiza foliosa (VERM.) SOÓ
"MADEIRA ORCHID"

As its common name suggests, this species is endemic to the Portuguese island of Madeira. It grows in marshy grasslands at low to moderate altitudes. It can form large colonies when it grows in a favorable wet, oceanic climate. The plant has a robust stem about 16–24 in (40–60 cm) long. This usually carries 12 unspotted, lanceolate leaves topped by a densely flowered inflorescence. The flowers are about ⅘ in (2 cm) across, and they range in color from pink to purple-red with darker purple spots near the lip base. *D. foliosa* flowers during late spring and early summer and is cultivated in some botanical gardens in Great Britain. **ZONES 7–9. C–I.**

Dactylorhiza incarnata

Dactylorhiza fuchsii

Dactylorhiza fuchsii (DRUCE) SOÓ
"COMMON SPOTTED ORCHID"

The distribution of this common orchid covers much of Europe, including Iceland, but it is absent from southern Spain, southern Italy, and Greece. It grows in the dry to moist calcareous soil of grasslands and light, deciduous or coniferous forests, including borders of forests and beside roads in forests. This plant may be easily confused with *D. maculata*, but it can be distinguished by the long, extended midlobe of the lip. Its stem is 8–24 in (20–60 cm) tall and bears seven to 12 leaves that are heavily spotted and held nearly erect. The inflorescence is 4–8 in (10–20 cm) long and is dense with flowers about ⅔ in (15 mm) across. Flowering occurs during summer. **ZONES 6–8. C–I.**

Dactylorhiza incarnata (L.) SOÓ
"EARLY MARSH ORCHID"

This species is widespread over much of Europe, but not in the southern areas of the Mediterranean. It grows in damp to wet grasslands and in bogs with slightly alkaline soil, but it has become endangered due to land drainage. The stem is up to 2 ft (60 cm) long and bears five to seven unspotted, lanceolate leaves with an apex that forms a hood. The flowers are relatively small for the genus, about ½ in (12 mm) across, and they are dense on the inflorescence—sometimes there are up to 50. The lips have slightly folded-back edges. The flowers appear from late spring to mid summer. **ZONES 6–8. C.**

Dactylorhiza maculata (L.) SOÓ
"HEATH SPOTTED ORCHID"

This species, the leaves of which are always spotted, is one of the most widespread orchids in Europe. It is found in the wet, acidic soils of heathlands and moorland bogs. It is a variable species with several local varieties. It is similar in plant and flower shape to *D. fuchsii*, but is distinguishable by its three, similar-sized lip lobes. A subspecies, *ericetorum*, is the form found in western Great Britain, Ireland and possibly Spain—it is smaller, has fewer flowers, a lighter background color, and dark-purple lines on the lip.
ZONES 5–9. C–I.

Dactylorhiza maculata ssp. *ericetorum*

Dactylorhiza majalis (RCHB.F.) HUNT
& SUMMERH.
"BROAD-LEAVED MARSH ORCHID"

The distribution of this species is middle Europe and the northern parts of southern Europe. It grows in marshy grasslands from sea level to 8300 ft (2500 m) in the Alps. It has robust stems, 8–24 in (20–60 cm) tall, and four to eight broadly lanceolate leaves with purple-brown spots. The inflorescence carries many flowers, each about 2/3 in (15 mm) across. The color of these ranges from light to dark purplish-red with darker spots and lines on a three-lobed lip. The flowers appear from late spring to mid summer. A few local varieties of this species are considered by some botanists to be separate species. The subspecies *purpurella* from the coastal regions of northwest Europe is smaller with bright reddish-purple flowers and a one-lobed lip. **ZONES 6–9. C–I.**

Dactylorhiza majalis ssp. *purpurella*

Dactylorhiza sambucina

Dactylorhiza sambucina (L.) SOÓ
"ELDER-FLOWER ORCHID"

This species grows in the acidic soils of mountainous grasslands and light forests at moderate to high altitudes. Its distribution is the southern end of middle Europe to northern Spain, Italy, Greece and southern Scandinavia. The hollow stem is 4–12 in (10–30 cm) long and carries about four to six lanceolate, unspotted leaves on its lower half. The inflorescence is dense with either yellow or purple-red flowers with a faint scent similar to elder flowers, hence the common name. Often both color forms grow together and there are also plants with mixed colors. Flowering is from spring to early summer. **ZONES 6–8. C–I.**

DENDROBIUM sw.

This is one of the largest of the orchid genera, with about 1200 species occurring from India through Japan, Australia, and New Zealand to Tahiti. New Guinea, with at least 500 species, is particularly rich in *Dendrobium* species, as are India, southern China, and Thailand. The plants grow from the hot, steamy tropical lowlands to altitudes of 10,000 ft (3000 m), and in the semi-arid conditions of northern Australia. They are epiphytes that grow on rocks and in swampy ground. It is likely this genus will be divided into several genera in the near future and many of the familiar *Dendrobium* names may be replaced.

CULTIVATION

Because of the wide range of habitats and growing conditions, it is difficult to be specific about cultivation. Generally, this genus is divided into hot-, intermediate-, and cool-growing species. For hot species the temperature should not drop below 60°F (15°C). Intermediate species are tolerant of temperatures down to 36°F (2°C). Cool species will tolerate lower minimum temperatures, but they do not grow well in hot climates. A very well-drained mixture of bark and charcoal, often with a little added sphagnum moss, is preferred, although slab culture is also commonly used. Most of the species should be given a watering rest period during winter if good flowering is desired. Most of these species may be repotted when new shoots appear, and they may also be divided for propagation at this time.

Dendrobium adae

HYBRIDS

These species have been extensively hybridized with several other types of hybrids to create plants suitable for various climatic conditions or other purposes, such as hobby growing and the cut-flower industry. Some of the hybrids include "soft cane" or "nobile" types, such as the Yamamoto hybrids which prefer hot to intermediate conditions. Phalaenanthe hybrids are mostly hot-growers and they are used widely for cut flowers. Ceratobium hybrids are also hot-growers and they have interesting twisted floral segments. Recently, a series of hybrids has been produced using native Australian species. These require intermediate conditions.

Dendrobium adae
F. M. BAILEY
syn: *D. palmerstoniae* SCHLTR.

This species occurs in the eastern tropics of Australia at moderate altitudes. It grows as a lithophyte or epiphyte and forms small clumps of thin, wiry pseudobulbs up to about 2 ft (60 cm) high. The one to six flowers are about 1 in (2.5 cm) in diameter, and last for two weeks. They have an attractive fragrance, similar to orange blossoms. The color ranges from white, green, and pale yellow to apricot. The flowers appear from late winter to spring. This species is most suited to cool or intermediate conditions with high humidity and semi shade.
ZONES 9–10. C–I.

D

Dendrobium affine

Dendrobium aemulum R. BR.

"BOX ORCHID," "IRON BARK ORCHID"

This epiphytic orchid is from moist areas in eastern Australia. It grows at low to moderate altitudes. Several forms have been recognized, depending on which host tree the plant occupies. Its dark-colored pseudobulbs form small clumps up to 1 ft (30 cm) tall, but often much shorter. The racemes are up to 4 in (10 cm) long and bear up to 12 crystalline white flowers, each up to 1 in (2.5 cm) across. The flowers last for a few days and turn pink as they age. Flowering is from mid winter to spring. This species is best suited to slab culture. **ZONES 9–11. C–I.**

Dendrobium aemulum

Dendrobium affine (DECNE.) STEUD.
syn: *D. dicuphum* F. MUELL.

This species occurs on the Indonesian islands of Tanimbar, Timor (including East Timor), and southern Irian Jaya, and in the Northern Territory in Australia. It grows at low altitudes in areas with a distinct seasonal climate. Its stout pseudobulbs are up to 40 in (1 m) long, but usually shorter. The long, arching racemes bear up to 20 flowers, which vary in width from ⅘–2 in (2–5 cm). The flowers appear during autumn and winter and last for about four to six weeks. This species requires year-round hot conditions with a watering rest period during winter and spring. It may be grown on a slab or in a small pot with a well-drained mixture. **ZONES 10–12. H.**

Dendrobium agrostophyllum F. MUELL.
syn: *D. muellerianum* SCHLTR.

This small- to medium-sized epiphyte or lithophyte is from northeast Australia, where it grows at moderate altitudes in moist, open forests and rain forests. It has a creeping habit with well-spaced, slightly swollen stems up to 20 in (50 cm) long, but usually shorter. Short racemes bear two to ten flowers about ⅘ in (2 cm) across. Flowers appear during spring and they last for about one to two weeks. This species requires a semi-shaded position and a moist atmosphere. If it grows well, it can outgrow its pot rapidly, so it may be better suited to slab culture. **ZONES 9–11. C–I.**

Dendrobium agrostophyllum

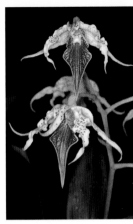

D

Dendrobium albosanguineum

Dendrobium alexandrae

Dendrobium albosanguineum LINDL.

This medium-sized species from Thailand and
Myanmar grows high in the upper branches of
tall trees. It occurs at low to moderate altitudes
in areas with a dry winter. It is regarded as
"under threat" due to habitat clearing and
over-collection. Its pseudobulbs are up to 10 in
(25 cm) long. The inflorescences are short with
two or three flowers up to 3¼ in (8 cm) across.
The flowering season is late spring and the
blooms last for two or three weeks. A watering
rest period during winter and spring is required
for good flowering, but the plant should not
dry out completely. ZONES 10–12. I–H.

Dendrobium alexandrae SCHLTR.

Named by Rudolf Schlechter after his wife,
Alexandra, this attractive species is known in
only one or two areas in Papua New Guinea.
It occurs at low to moderate altitudes in cool,
shady conditions on moss-covered branches. Its
pseudobulbs are narrowly club-shaped, about
20–28 in (50–70 cm) tall and ⅓ in (1 cm)
wide. There are three to four elliptic leaves,
which are light bluish-green underneath. The
inflorescences bear three to seven flowers, each
2–3¼ in (5–8 cm) across. The main flowering
season is autumn and spring and the blooms
last for several weeks. In cultivation this species
requires intermediate to hot conditions with
good air movement, year-round watering, and
high humidity. ZONES 10–12. I–H.

Dendrobium amethystoglossum

Dendrobium amethystoglossum RCHB.F.

This attractive epiphyte or lithophyte comes
from Luzon in the Philippines. It is found on
mossy limestone cliffs at moderate to high
altitudes, where there is year-round humidity
and a dry period during winter. The pendulous
racemes, about 4–6 in (10–15 cm) long, bear
up to 15 fragrant flowers, each about 1¾ in
(4 cm) long, on the top of the stems. The
flowers appear during winter and the blooms
last for about three to four weeks. This plant
should be given a watering rest period through
winter into early spring, but should not be
totally dry for long periods. ZONES 9–12. C–I.

Dendrobium anosmum LINDL.

syn: *D. superbum* RCHB.F.

This is one of the most widespread species in the genus, ranging from India to New Guinea. It grows primarily in lowland areas but may extend above 3300 ft (1000 m) in some places. Its deciduous stems are long, slender, and pendulous, and up to 10 ft (3 m) long. Most often, though, they grow only 20–40 in (50–100 cm) in cultivation. The inflorescences are lateral, lying along the length of the leafless stems, and bear one or two flowers, each 2–4 in (5–10 cm) across. Flowering occurs mostly during the dry season, although it can occur at any time in New Guinea. The flowers last for about two or three weeks. The long, pendulous stems make this species unsuited to a pot, so tie it to a slab or grow it in a hanging basket.
ZONES 10–12. I–H.

Dendrobium anosmum

Dendrobium antennatum

Dendrobium antennatum LINDL.

syn: *D. d'albertisii* RCHB.F.
"ANTELOPE ORCHID"

Four-angled stems are a feature of this medium-sized epiphyte from low-altitude, humid jungles in New Guinea, the Solomon Islands, and northern Australia. The pseudobulbs grow about 1 ft (30 cm) long and have a swollen base and narrow apex from which fleshy leaves are borne. The inflorescences arise from the top of leaf axils and measure up to 1 ft (30 cm) long. They bear several long-lasting flowers about $^4/_5$–2 in (2–5 cm) across. This is a hot-growing species that must have glasshouse conditions to survive outside the tropics. Flowering occurs throughout the year. **ZONES 10–12. H.**

Dendrobium aphyllum

Dendrobium aphyllum (ROXB.) FISCHER

syn: *D. pierardii* ROXB. EX HOOK.

This was one of the earliest *Dendrobium* species to be grown and flowered in England—records of it flowering in the Liverpool Botanic Gardens date back to 1821. It is a deciduous, medium-sized epiphyte or, occasionally, a lithophyte that ranges from India to southern China. It grows in seasonal forests at low to moderate altitudes. The stems are pendulous, and slender, about 28 in (70 cm) long. The fragrant flowers are about 1¼–2 in (3–5 cm) across and last for about three weeks. The flowering season is during spring. The plant produces numerous aerial growths that can be used for propagation. The pendulous habitat makes this species unsuited to pot culture, so a slab or hanging basket is best. The plant must be kept dry during winter and early spring with occasional light watering only.
ZONES 9–12. I–H.

Dendrobium atroviolaceum
ROLFE

This species was first described by R. A. Rolfe in April 1890 from a plant imported from "eastern New Guinea" by Messrs J. Veitch and Sons. Large quantities of the plant were collected and shipped to Europe in the latter part of the nineteenth century. This caused concern for its survival, but recent expeditions suggest there are still numerous specimens in the natural habitat. This species is found on the D'Entrecasteaux Islands and the Louisiade Archipelago off the eastern tip of New Guinea. It grows on rain forest trees at low to moderate altitudes. The pseudobulbs are spindle-shaped and about 4–12 in (10–30 cm) long. A few large, nodding flowers measure 1¾–2½ in (4–6 cm) wide. Flowering can occur at any time but there is an emphasis from autumn to spring. The long-lasting flowers remain in good condition for three months or more. *D. atroviolaceum* is a popular species in many orchid collections and has been used extensively for hybridization. It is easy to grow in hot to intermediate conditions. **ZONES 10–12. I–H.**

Dendrobium atroviolaceum

Dendrobium bellatulum ROLFE

The flowers of this miniature epiphyte are large in relation to the size of the plant. The species is widespread in the mountainous areas of Southeast Asia. It grows at moderate to high altitudes, in deciduous forests where there is bright light and a pronounced seasonal climate. Its clustered, squat pseudobulbs are covered with black hairs and are up to about 2–3¼ in (5–8 cm) long. The inflorescences consist of one to three flowers, each one about 1¾–2 in (4–5 cm) across. These long-lasting and faintly fragrant blooms have a brightly colored labellum that tends to increase in intensity as the flower ages. The flowers are at their most abundant during spring. This species is sometimes regarded as difficult to cultivate. A slab is best as the roots must not become soggy, even when the plant is watered regularly during summer. Allow a watering rest period during winter. **ZONES 9–11. C–I.**

Dendrobium bellatulum

D

Dendrobium bifalce LINDL.
syn: *D. chloropterum* RCHB.F. & S. MOORE

This medium- to large-sized epiphyte or, occasionally, lithophyte grows in large clumps in the lowland areas of New Guinea and its adjacent islands, northern Australia, and the Solomon Islands. It often occurs in situations where there is intense heat and light, even in the baking sun on rocks. Its spindle-shaped pseudobulbs are 2 ft (60 cm) long. The erect inflorescences are up to 8 in (20 cm) long, and bear six to ten flowers, each about $^4\!/_5$ in (2 cm) across. They are waxy and last for a few weeks. The flowers appear throughout the year, but plants grown in cooler climates rarely flower. **ZONES 10–12. H.**

Dendrobium bifalce

Dendrobium bigibbum LINDL.
syn: several names, including *D. phalaenopsis* FITZG., *D. sumneri* F. MUELL.
"COOKTOWN ORCHID"

This epiphyte occurs in lowland areas that have a pronounced seasonal climate in northeastern Australia and southern New Guinea. The slender, purple pseudobulbs are 6–40 in (15 cm– 1 m) long. The leaves are borne from the apex of a stem and are $3^1\!/_4$–$4^3\!/_4$ in (8–12 cm) long and $1^3\!/_4$ in (4 cm) wide. The inflorescences are up to 16 in (40 cm) long and bear numerous, long-lasting purple flowers, each about 2 in (5 cm) in diameter. Flowering is during autumn. This species grows best in a small pot with a well-drained mixture. A watering rest period during winter is essential. **ZONES 10–12. H.**

Dendrobium bigibbum

Dendrobium bracteosum

Dendrobium bracteosum RCHB.F.

syn: *D. chrysolabium* ROLFE, *D. novaehiberniae* KRAENZL.

This is a small- to medium-sized epiphyte from the hot, steamy lowlands on the north coast of New Guinea. It forms dense clumps in exposed areas with bright light in mangroves or other coastal forests. Its slender pseudobulbs are about 14 in (35 cm) long. The flowers are variable in color—one common form has pink petals and sepals with an orange labellum. White, yellow, orange, and red are not uncommon. The flowers last for up to six months and the plants are rarely out of flower. This species requires bright light and regular watering, but it will tolerate dry spells. It grows best in a hanging pot or on a slab.
ZONES 10–12. H.

Dendrobium bullenianum

Dendrobium canaliculatum

Dendrobium bullenianum RCHB.F.

syn: *D. topaziacum* AMES

This is a medium-sized epiphyte from the Philippine islands of Leyte, Luzon, and Bucas Grande. It grows in the hot, steamy lowlands. The 2-ft (60-cm) long pseudobulbs are initially erect but become pendulous as they lengthen. The short inflorescences contain numerous, densely packed flowers, each about $\frac{4}{5}$ in (2 cm) long, on leafless stems. They range in color from yellow to orange with red or purple stripes. The flowering season is during spring and the blooms last for about two weeks. This species grows best in a hanging pot with a well-drained mix or on a slab to accommodate its pendulous habit.
ZONES 10–12. H.

Dendrobium canaliculatum R. BR.

syn: *D. tattonianum* BATEMAN
"TEA TREE ORCHID," "ONION ORCHID"

This miniature species is from northern Australia, the islands of Torres Strait, and southern New Guinea. It grows in melaleuca woodlands and open forests at low altitudes where the climate has a very pronounced dry season during winter and spring. The pseudobulbs have an ovoid shape and are about $1\frac{1}{4}$–$4\frac{3}{4}$ in (3–12 cm) long. Four to five fleshy leaves are at the apex of the pseudobulbs. A long, slender raceme bears anywhere between 30 and 40 flowers, each one about $\frac{4}{5}$–$1\frac{1}{4}$ in (2–3 cm) across. The flower color varies—some authorities consider the lighter form from the southern part of the range as a separate species, *D. tattonianum,* and the darker form from the north as *D. canaliculatum.* Flowers appear during early spring and last for several weeks. This species may be grown in a small pot with a good, well-drained medium or on a slab. It is intolerant of soggy conditions around the roots.
ZONES 10–12. H.

D

Dendrobium capituliflorum

Dendrobium capituliflorum ROLFE

This small epiphyte occurs from New Guinea to Vanuatu, mostly in the lowlands, but it has been recorded at moderate altitudes. It is found in a range of habitats, including coastal rain forests, mangroves, savanna forests, and on rock faces. The stout pseudobulbs are up to about 16 in (40 cm) long, but are more commonly 4–8 in (10–20 cm). Dense, crowded heads of blooms, about ⅘–1¼ in (2–4 cm) across, contain small, tubular flowers, each one about ⅔ in (15 mm) long. The flowers are borne on inflorescences that last for one or two months. There is usually more than one flowering period during the year. This species is easy to grow if given hot to intermediate conditions and year-round watering. **ZONES 10–12. H.**

Dendrobium chryseum ROLFE
syn: *D. aurantiacum* RCHB.F., *D. clavatum* LINDL., *D. flaviflorum* HAYATA

This species is widespread throughout the Himalayas from India to the Yunnan province in China. It grows on trees and rocks at altitudes of 3300–6700 ft (1000–2000 m). Its slender pseudobulbs are up to 30 in (75 cm) long and bear several leaves on the upper part of the stem. After the leaves have dropped the following year, the inflorescences emerge on the old stems. Each one produces four to 15 fragrant flowers, and each flower is about 2–3¼ in (5–8 cm) across. The flowers appear from spring to early summer, but they do not last long. **ZONES 9–10. I.**

Dendrobium chryseum

Dendrobium chrysotoxum

Dendrobium chrysotoxum LINDL.

syn: *D. suavissimum* RCHB.F.

"GOLDEN ARCH ORCHID"

This clump-forming epiphyte occurs at
moderate altitudes in the Himalayas, from
India to southern China. Its stout pseudobulbs
are about 8 in (20 cm) long and have two to
four leaves at the apexes. The arching
inflorescence is about 6–8 in (15–20 cm) long
and comprises 12 to 20 flowers, each about
1¾ in (4 cm) in diameter. Flowering occurs
during spring. This species should be grown in
full sunlight and requires only a short watering
rest period during winter. **ZONES 10–12. I–H.**

Dendrobium crumenatum SW.

syn: *D. schmidtianum* KRAENZL.

"PIGEON ORCHID." "DOVE ORCHID"

D

This orchid was described by
Olaf Swartz in 1799, making it
one of the first *Dendrobium*
species to be recorded. It is
generally found throughout
Southeast Asia, from Myanmar
to the Philippines and Timor.
The pseudobulbs, about 40 in
(1 m) long, have a swollen
base that tapers abruptly into
a long, slender stem. They
often bear numerous aerial
growths that form a tangle,
causing the stems to become
pendulous. The fragrant
flowers, each about 2 in (5 cm)
across, last for one day only,
but the plant compensates for
this—it produces large
numbers of flowers several
times a year in response to a
sudden drop in temperature,
usually when a tropical
rainstorm occurs. This species
is amenable to cultivation, and
does well in a basket, pot, or
on a slab. However, it grows
best on a tree if the climate is
suitable. **ZONES 10–12. H.**

Dendrobium crumenatum

D

Dendrobium crystallinum RCHB.F.

The name of this delicate, deciduous species comes from its unique anther cap, covered with crystalline papillae. It is a medium-sized, pendulous epiphyte that ranges from Myanmar to China. It grows at moderate altitudes in mountain forests with a distinct dry season. Its slender stems are up to 2 ft (60 cm) long. The inflorescences are lateral and short with one to three flowers borne on the leafless stems. The fragrant flowers, about 2 in (5 cm) in diameter, appear during spring. This species will grow in hot climates, but is better suited to intermediate conditions with virtually no watering during winter. **ZONES 10–12. I–H.**

Dendrobium crystallinum

Dendrobium cuthbertsonii

Dendrobium cuthbertsonii F. MUELL.
syn: *D. sophronites* SCHLTR.

The large, colorful flowers on this miniature plant are a feature of this species, which occurs in many highland regions in New Guinea. It grows as an epiphyte or a terrestrial. It is mostly seen on trees and moss-covered shrubs, but has been recorded on roadside banks, mossy rock ledges, and short alpine grasslands. Its pseudobulbs are $\frac{1}{3}$–$3\frac{1}{4}$ in (1–8 cm) long. The flowers, up to $1\frac{1}{2}$ in (3.5 cm) across and 2 in (5 cm) long, are extremely long-lasting, sometimes for up to ten months. The variable flower color includes yellow, orange, and purple combinations, although red is most common. This species requires cool to intermediate temperatures—it is intolerant of hot conditions. It should be grown in a pot with a well-drained mix that retains some moisture. **ZONES 9–11. C–I.**

Dendrobium dearei

Dendrobium dearei RCHB.F.

This medium-sized epiphyte is restricted to the Philippine islands of Luzon (the southern end only), Mindoro, Samar, Dinagat, and Mindanao. It grows in hot, humid tropical forests at low altitudes. Its pseudobulbs are up to 3 ft (90 cm) long. The arching inflorescences, borne from the apex of the pseudobulbs, bear up to ten flowers, each about 2 in (5 cm) in diameter. These last for several weeks and occur during late spring and early summer. Hot, humid conditions are required to grow this species successfully, and it should be watered regularly throughout the year. **ZONES 10–12. H.**

D

Dendrobium densiflorum

Dendrobium discolor

Dendrobium densiflorum LINDL.

Occurring at moderate altitudes in India, Nepal, and Myanmar, this species grows as an epiphyte in mountain forests. Its pseudobulbs are about 1 ft (30 cm) long with a ⁴⁄₅-in (2-cm) diameter, with three to five leaves at the apexes. The pendulous inflorescence, about 8 in (20 cm) long, produces numerous flowers, each about 1³⁄₄ in (4 cm) across. Flowering occurs during spring. This species requires a well-drained mixture, part-shade, intermediate conditions, and plenty of water during summer with a watering rest period during winter. **ZONES 8–11. I–H.**

Dendrobium discolor LINDL.

syn: *D. undulatum* R. BR.
"GOLDEN ORCHID," "RIGO TWIST," "MORESBY GOLD," "BENSBACH YELLOW"

This variable species is from the east coast of Australia, the islands in Torres Strait, and southern New Guinea. It grows at low altitudes. In northern Australia it is quite common near the coast—on rocks under full sun, often in places where it receives salty seaspray, or on trees in vine forests. Its robust pseudobulbs may grow to more than 16½ ft (5 m) long with a diameter of 3¼ in (8 cm). This makes *D. discolor* one of the largest orchid species. Many flowers are borne on the long inflorescences which arise from a few nodes near the apex of the pseudobulbs. The flowers are up to 2 in (5 cm) in diameter and their color ranges from dark chocolate-brown to light yellow. The flowers appear from late winter to early spring and last for up to two months. This large plant may take up a great deal of room in an orchid house. It requires hot conditions, but it will grow in intermediate conditions if kept dry at night and protected from cool winds. **ZONES 10–12. H.**

Dendrobium falcorostrum FITZG.
"BEECH ORCHID"

This medium-sized epiphyte grows almost exclusively on the Antarctic beech, *Nothofagus moorei*, that grows in rain forests at moderate altitudes in eastern Australia. The pseudobulbs are up to 20 in (50 cm) long. The flower spike bears four to 20 flowers, each one up to 1½ in (3.5 cm) wide. The sepals and petals are a snowy, glistening white color and the labellum is white with orange and purple markings. The flowers have a distinct, spicy perfume, which is most evident during warmer times of the day. The flowers appear in late spring and last for about two weeks. **ZONES 9–10. C–I.**

Dendrobium falcorostrum

D

Dendrobium farmeri

Dendrobium farmeri PAXTON
syn: *D. densiflorum* LINDL., **var.** *farmeri*
REGAL

This robust species is an old favorite—it is present in many collections. It occurs naturally from the foothills of the Himalayas in India to the Malay Peninsula. It has four-angled pseudobulbs up to 1 ft (30 cm) long. The pendulous inflorescence, borne from the upper part of a pseudobulb, is 6–8 in (15–20 cm) long. It produces numerous, densely packed flowers, each about 1¼–1¾ in (3–4 cm) across. These vary in color from white to almost pink, but have a yellow lip. The flowers appear during spring and last for about a week only. This plant is easy to grow and flowers if placed in a well-lit position, but not under full sun, and kept dry during the cooler months of the year.
ZONES 10–12. I–H.

Dendrobium fimbriatum HOOK.F.
syn: *D. paxtonii* PAXTON

This large, robust epiphyte is widespread from India to southern China and the Malay Peninsula. It grows in deciduous mountain forests at low to moderate altitudes. The slender pseudobulbs, up to 80 in (2 m) long, are erect at first, but become pendulous as they lengthen. The inflorescences consist of seven to 12 flowers, each 2–3¼ in (5–8 cm) across. Most of the cultivated forms of this species have a dark-maroon area at the base of the flowers' lips. These plants are known as "var. *occulatum*". Other forms have pure yellow flowers. The flowers last for seven to 12 days and appear during late winter or early spring. A watering rest period during the cool months is required for good growth and flowering.
ZONES 9–12. I–H.

Dendrobium fimbriatum

Dendrobium forbesii

Dendrobium formosum

D

Dendrobium forbesii RIDL.

syn: *D. ashworthiae* O'BRIEN

This large, robust epiphyte occurs at moderate altitudes in the mountain rain forests of New Guinea. The pseudobulbs, up to 1 ft (30 cm) long, have a pronounced club shape. The inflorescences bear eight to 15 fragrant flowers, each with a diameter of about 2–2¾ in (5–7 cm). The backs of the sepals are almost smooth, but the ovary is covered with dense hairs. The flowers last for several weeks and may occur at almost any time. In cultivation, keep this species evenly moist throughout the year. **ZONES 9–11. I.**

Dendrobium gouldii

Dendrobium formosum ROXB. EX LINDL.

syn: *D. infundibulum* RCHB.F. NON LINDL.

This medium-sized epiphyte grows at low to moderate altitudes in the Himalayan foothills, from India to Indochina. The climate in these places is moderately seasonal, and the plants often grow in places where they receive strong sunlight. The robust pseudobulbs grow to 18 in (45 cm) long. Short inflorescences bear up to five large and showy flowers, each up to 4¾ in (12 cm) across. These appear during winter and spring and last for several weeks. In cultivation, this plant may be watered slightly less during winter, but it should not be allowed to dry out completely at any time of the year. Some large-flowered forms are known as variety "*giganteum.*" **ZONES 9–11. I–H.**

Dendrobium gouldii RCHB.F.

syn: *D. imthurnii* ROLFE, *D. woodfordianum* (MAID.) SCHLTR. "BOUGAINVILLE WHITE," "GUADALCANAL GOLD"

This large, robust species occurs from New Ireland, an island in the Bismarck Archipelago, to Guadalcanal in the Solomons. It grows abundantly on rocks or trees in coastal and semi-coastal situations, such as coconut plantations. In the Solomons it may grow on limestone cliffs overhanging the sea, and on many of the islands it is a feature on calophyllum trees lining the beaches. Its pseudobulbs are up to 80 in (2 m) tall. The flowers, up to 2 in (5 cm) across, last for about six weeks and vary in color with white, blue, brown, and gold dominating. Often, the form on each island is unique. **ZONES 10–12. H.**

D

Dendrobium helix P. J. CRIBB
"POMIO BROWN," "MUSHROOM PINK,"
"TALASEA LIME YELLOW"

This large epiphyte occurs in
the coastal lowlands of the
eastern and southern coasts
of New Britain, an island in
the Bismarck Archipelago of
Papua New Guinea. It grows
on the calophyllum and other
large trees near the coast and
in lowland rain forests where
there is extremely high rainfall
throughout the year. Its robust
pseudobulbs grow to more
than 80 in (2 m) tall. The
inflorescences produce up to
20 flowers, 2–4 in (5–10 cm)
across, and have corkscrew-
shaped petals and sepals. The
flowers last for about three
months and the flowering
season varies among the many
different forms—most often in
cultivation it is during late
winter and spring. This
species requires room to grow.
When mature, it does best in a
large pot with a well-drained
mix or on a tree in tropical
regions. **ZONES 10–12. H.**

Dendrobium helix

Dendrobium heterocarpum LINDL.
syn: *D. aureum* LINDL.

This deciduous epiphyte is widely distributed
from Sri Lanka to the Indonesian island of
Sulawesi. It grows at moderate to high
altitudes, mostly in areas with a distinct dry
season. The erect or pendulous pseudobulbs
grow up to 2 ft (60 cm) long, but are usually
shorter. The fragrant flowers are borne in
groups of two or three and are 2½ in (6 cm)
across. They open widely and last for several
weeks during spring. This plant does well in
intermediate conditions with a watering rest
period during winter and early spring. Use a
hanging pot, basket, or slab to best accommodate the pendulous stems. **ZONES 9–11. C–I.**

Dendrobium heterocarpum

D

Dendrobium johannis RCHB.F.

This is a small- to medium-sized epiphyte from the northeast of Australia, the islands in Torres Strait, and southern New Guinea. It occurs in lowland areas with a pronounced dry season, in moist, open forests, on the margins of rain forests, and in forests along streams. Its pseudobulbs are up to 1 ft (30 cm) long. The inflorescences, about 8 in (20 cm) long, bear anywhere between two and 20 flowers, each about 1¼–2 in (3–5 cm) in diameter. These flowers appear mostly during autumn and last for about three weeks. This is a hot-growing species and it does best in a small pot with a well-drained mix or on a slab.
ZONES 10–12. H.

Dendrobium johannis

Dendrobium johnsoniae F. MUELL.
syn: *D. macfarlanei* RCHB.F.

The large flowers on this small plant make it one of the most outstanding orchids from New Guinea. It grows as an epiphyte at low to moderate altitudes in mountain forests, often on casuarina trees lining watercourses but also in other places, such as on araucaria trees, where the light level is high. Its slender, club-shaped pseudobulbs are up to 1 ft (30 cm) long.

Dendrobium johnsoniae

The inflorescences bear up to 12 flowers, each 2½–4¾ in (6–12 cm) across. The flowers last for about two months and may appear at any time of the year. In cultivation the roots of this plant are susceptible to rot if the surrounding medium becomes soggy. **ZONES 10–12. I–H.**

D

Dendrobium jonesii RENDLE

Dendrobium jonesii

syn: *D. ruppianum* A. D. HAWKES, *D. fusiforme* (F. M. BAILEY) F. M. BAILEY

This showy species occurs in northeast Australia, where it grows on rocks and trees at low to moderate altitudes. It is distinctive and can be recognized by the brown, spindle-shaped pseudo-bulbs, which are up to 20 in (50 cm) tall. One of its form has stout pseudobulbs and flowers up to 2 in (5 cm) across; while others have flowers about ⅘ in (2 cm) across. All the flowers are fragrant and appear during spring. They last for about seven to ten days. This plant may be grown mounted on slabs or in pots with a well-drained medium. **ZONES 10–11. I.**

Dendrobium keithii RIDL.

This medium- to large-sized epiphyte from Thailand is found at low altitudes in areas with distinct seasonal climates. The pendulous stems grow up to 16 in (40 cm) long. They are

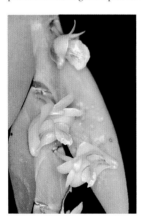

covered along their length with succulent, flattened, and sharp-pointed leaves up to 2 in (5 cm) long. Abundant flowers are borne along the center line of the stems. These are about ⅘ in (2 cm) wide and appear from late winter to spring. The pendulous habit makes the plant suitable to slab culture or a hanging pot with a well-drained mix. It produces aerial growths often, and these may be used for propagation. **ZONES 10–12. H.**

Dendrobium keithii

Dendrobium kingianum
BIDWILL EX LINDL.

This species has been widely used for hybridization. It is one of the best-known species from Australia. It grows at low to moderate altitudes on rocks in exposed situations. The pseudobulbs range in length from 1 in to more than 1 ft (2.5 to 30 cm). The inflorescences are up to 8 in (20 cm) long and carry up to 15 flowers. The color of the flowers ranges from white through various shades of pink to deep mauve. They appear from late winter to spring and last for up to two weeks. Considerable line breeding of the various forms has resulted in many sought-after clones. Because of its adaptability, the species may be grown in a wide range of situations. It makes an excellent rockery plant under semi-shade, and does well in shallow terracotta pots with a coarse mix. **ZONES 8–10. I.**

Dendrobium kingianum

Dendrobium laevifolium

Dendrobium laevifolium STAPF
syn: *D. occulatum* AMES

This miniature epiphyte ranges from New Guinea to Vanuatu. It grows from low to moderate altitudes in damp moss forests. The pseudobulbs are often 1–3¼ in (2.5–8 cm) long, but may occasionally grow up to 5⅔ in (14 cm) long. The inflorescences consist of one or two, sometimes up to four, flowers that last for more than a month. The flowers are large for the size of the plant—⁴/₅–1¾ in (2–4 cm) long. They are somewhat variable in color, with shades of cream, pink, and purple. While this species can be grown in hot conditions, cool to intermediate temperatures are best. It will do well on a slab, but a pot with a well-drained mixture is more ideal. It should be kept moist year-round. **ZONES 9–11. C–I–H.**

Dendrobium lamellatum (BLUME) LINDL.
syn: *D. platycaulon* ROLFE

This is a widespread species ranging from Myanmar through the Asian islands of Java and Borneo to the Philippines. It occurs in rain forests at low to moderate altitudes, usually in semi-shaded, moist environments. Its pseudobulbs are distinctive—flat with two ranks of leaves along most of the stem. The inflorescences arise near the apex of the pseudobulbs and have short racemes of up to six flowers, each about ⅔ in (15 mm) in diameter. They last for about a week and turn from white to yellow as they age. There are often two or more bursts of flowering during autumn and spring. This species does well in cultivation if provided hot or intermediate conditions with year-round moisture and filtered sunlight. **ZONES 10–12 . H.**

Dendrobium lamellatum

D

Dendrobium lasianthera

Dendrobium lasianthera J. J. SM.
syn: *D. ostrinoglossum* RUPP
"SEPIK RIVER BLUE"

This spectacular species is a large, robust epiphyte. It occurs on the north coast of New Guinea at low altitudes in forest along rivers and in swamps, where the climate is hot and extremely humid with year-round rainfall. Its pseudobulbs are up to 10 ft (3 m) long. The inflorescences, 8–20 in (20–50 cm) long, bear up to 30 flowers that come in various color combinations of red, purple, pink, maroon, and white. The flowers are 2–2¾ in (5–7 cm) across and appear at any time of the year. They last for six to 12 weeks. This plant requires plenty of room in an orchid house. It has not proved an easy species to cultivate outside New Guinea but it grows best in a pot with extremely well-drained medium.
ZONE 12. H.

Dendrobium lawesii F. MUELL.

The brightly colored flowers of this epiphyte stand out in the moderate-altitude rain forests of New Guinea. The pseudobulbs are long, narrow, pendulous, and deciduous, and the leaves are about 1 in (2.5 cm) long and ⅓ in (1 cm) wide. The flowers, about 1¾ in (4 cm) long, are bell-shaped and come in a variety of colors, including red, orange, yellow, and mauve. They are borne in clusters of five to eight on leafless stems, are long-lasting, and may appear at any time, but mostly during spring. This species may be grown in cool or intermediate conditions, in shady positions, on a slab or in a pot with a mix that retains moisture without becoming soggy. **ZONES 9–11. I.**

Dendrobium lawesii

Dendrobium lindleyi STEUD.
syn: *D. aggregatum* ROXB.

This epiphyte from moderate to high altitudes ranges from northeast India to southern China. It grows in areas with distinct seasonal climates, often under strong sunlight. The pseudobulbs are up to 4 in (10 cm) long. The pendulous inflorescences bear up to 15 fragrant flowers, each about 1¼ in (3 cm) across. Flowering occurs during spring and the thin-textured blooms last for about a week. This plant is amenable to both hot and intermediate conditions so long as it is given a watering rest period during winter with regular watering during summer and autumn. The plant's habit makes it best suited to a slab; it will grow quickly into a large clump.
ZONES 9–12. I–H.

Dendrobium lindleyi

Dendrobium lineale ROLFE

syn: *D. veratrifolium* LINDL.
"MOROBE SHOWER," "KUI BLUE"

This species occurs at low altitudes along the northeast coast of New Guinea. Its pseudobulbs grow up to about 80 in (2 m) long. The arching inflorescences, up to 30 in (75 cm) long, bear numerous flowers that are variable in color, with white or pale yellow and blue veining predominant. The flowers last for two to three months and each one is up to 2 in (5 cm) across. They appear throughout the year in its habitat, but are more common during late winter and spring in cultivation. Hot conditions with strong light, even direct sunlight, and good air movement are required. This species may be grown in a pot of coarse, well-drained mixture, or on a tree in tropical climates. **ZONES 10–12. H.**

Dendrobium lineale

Dendrobium loddigesii ROLFE

syn: *D. seidelianum* RCHB.F.

This small, deciduous species occurs in Laos and southern China, on Hainan Island, and in Hong Kong. It grows at low to moderate altitudes in areas with a distinct dry season. The slender stems, up to 6 in (15 cm) long, branch freely by means of aerial growths complete with roots. These form dense, tangled clumps or mats on trees or rocks. These clumps may be covered with fragrant flowers, about 1¾–2 in (4–5 cm) across, during spring and summer. Each solitary bloom lasts for about three weeks. The scrambling habit of this species makes it suited to slab culture. The plant must be given a watering rest period during late autumn and winter if it is to flower well. **ZONES 9–11. I–H.**

Dendrobium loddigesii

Dendrobium macrophyllum A. RICH.

syn: *D. veitchianum* LINDL., *D. psyche* KRAENZL., *D. musciferum* SCHLTR.

Dendrobium macrophyllum

This widespread species was first described in 1834, placing it among the earliest orchids from New Guinea to be recorded. It extends from the western end of Java through the Philippines and New Guinea to the Pacific island of Samoa. It is usually found in the canopy of forests in hot, steamy lowlands. It forms huge clumps, making it one of the largest epiphytes to grow in these forests. Its pseudobulbs are up to 2 ft (60 cm) long and its racemes bear up to 25 flowers, each 1¼–2 in (3–5 cm) across. The backs of the sepals, ovary, and pedicel are covered with dense hairs. The flowers last for about two months and are produced throughout the year. **ZONES 10–12. H.**

D

Dendrobium moniliforme (L.) SW.

syn: *D. japonicum* (BLUME) LINDL.,
D. monile (THUNB.) KRAENZL.

This is the species on which the genus is based (the type species). It was first described as *Epidendrum moniliforme* in 1753. It is a small epiphyte or lithophyte that occurs on the Japanese islands of Honshu, Shikoku, and Kyushu, many small islands south of Japan including the Ryukyu Islands, as well as Korea, China, and Taiwan. It is found in forests at moderate to high altitudes where the climate is temperate and moist for most of the year, with a drier period during winter when temperatures regularly reach freezing point. Its strongly fragrant flowers are about 2 in (5 cm) across. They appear during spring and last for about two or three weeks. In cultivation, this plant should be watered regularly but allowed a watering rest period during winter. But do not allow the plant to become completely dry for extended periods. **ZONES 8–11. C–I.**

Dendrobium moniliforme

Dendrobium monophyllum

Dendrobium monophyllum F. MUELL.

This creeping epiphyte or lithophyte occurs in eastern Australia. It grows in rain forests and open forests at low to moderate altitudes, where the climate has wet and dry seasons. The plant usually grows in strong sunlight. The short, thick pseudobulbs are almost conical and are about 2½–3¼ in (6–8 cm) long. They are well spaced apart and produce a single leaf or, occasionally, two leaves. The inflorescences are terminal, long, and slender, and bear up to 20 fragrant flowers, each about ¼ in (6 mm) across. The flowering season is spasmodic but there is an emphasis on late winter and spring. The creeping habit of this species makes it suited to slab culture. **ZONES 9–11. I.**

Dendrobium moschatum (BUCH.-HAM.) SW.

syn: *D. calceolaria* CAREY EX HOOK.F., *D. cupreum* HERBERT

This large, robust epiphyte is found in countries near the Himalayas, including India, Myanmar, Thailand, Laos, and Vietnam. It grows at low to high altitudes in deciduous forests with a seasonal climate. Its pseudobulbs are slender and grow up to 80 in (2 m) long. They are erect at first, but become pendulous

Dendrobium moschatum

as they lengthen. The inflorescences are also pendulous and they bear seven to 15 flowers, each 2–3¼ in (5–8 cm) in diameter. The flowers last for a few days only and appear during late spring. The large size of the plant can be a disadvantage when cultivating as it needs plenty of room. A watering rest period is required from late autumn to spring. **ZONES 9–12. C–I.**

Dendrobium nobile LINDL.
syn: *D. coerulescens* WALL,
D. formosanum (RCHB.F.) MASAMUNE

This is one of the most
popular cultivated orchids.
It occurs naturally in the
Himalayas from India to
southern China as an epiphyte
in deciduous forests, mostly at
moderate altitudes. It is a
widespread species with many
forms and varieties. The
pseudobulbs, up to 2 ft
(60 cm) long, are initially
erect but become pendulous.
Short inflorescences bear two
to four flowers from their
nodes. The flowers, about
$2\frac{1}{2}$–$3\frac{1}{4}$ in (6–8 cm) across,
are waxy, fragrant, last for
three to six weeks, and are
variable in color. The variety
"*virginale*" has a white flower
with a yellow-green patch on
its lip. It is best grown in a
hanging pot or basket with
a mixture that retains some
moisture, but drains freely.
It should be kept dry during
winter and spring until new
growth emerges.
ZONES 10–12. C–I.

Dendrobium nobile

Dendrobium parishii RCHB.F.

This compact, deciduous epiphyte occurs from northeast India
to southern China. It grows in forests at moderate altitudes
where the climate is distinctly seasonal. Its pseudobulbs are
short and thick, often curved or misshapen, and grow about
1 ft (30 cm) long. When the leaves drop the stem is covered
with white leaf bases. The flowers, about $1\frac{3}{4}$–$2\frac{1}{2}$ in (4–6 cm)
across, vary in color, are fragrant, and last for about three or
four weeks. The flowering season is during spring. This species
requires hot to intermediate conditions and may be grown in
a pot or on a slab. **ZONES 10–12. I–H.**

Dendrobium parishii

D

Dendrobium pentapterum

Dendrobium polysema

Dendrobium pseudoglomeratum

T. M. REEVE & J. J. WOOD

This semi-pendulous epiphyte occurs in swamp forests and mountain rain forests from low to moderate altitudes in New Guinea. Its slender stems are up to 28 in (70 cm) long. The inflorescences arise from the stems and consist of six to 15 densely packed flowers, each about 1¼ in (3 cm) long. These brightly colored flowers appear throughout the year in the wild, but in cultivation they appear most commonly during spring. The fragrant flowers last for about two to five weeks. This species is found in a variety of conditions, and this means it is a relatively easy species to cultivate in a range of climates. **ZONES 9–12. I–H.**

Dendrobium pentapterum SCHLTR.

This species occurs in the Madang and Morobe provinces of Papua New Guinea. It is an erect epiphyte, 4–6 in (10–15 cm) tall, that is found in the branches of small trees in lower mountain and secondary forests. A well-grown plant will rapidly form a large clump that will be covered in flowers for most of the year. These long-lasting flowers are greenish-white to cream colored. The plant grows well on a slab or in a pot with a well-drained mix. **ZONES 9–10. I.**

Dendrobium polysema SCHLTR.

syn: *D. pulchrum* SCHLTR., *D. macrophyllum* **var.** *stenopterum* RCHB.F.

This medium- to large-sized epiphyte occurs in eastern New Guinea at moderate altitudes and in the Solomon Islands and Vanuatu from sea level to moderate altitudes. It grows in rain forests with high rainfall throughout the year. Its pseudobulbs, up to 20 in (50 cm) long, are club-shaped. The inflorescences bear up to 12 flowers, each 1¾–2½ in (4–6 cm) across. These long-lasting flowers appear at all times of the year. This plant should be watered regularly, but kept a little drier during winter. It should not, however, be allowed to dry out completely for long periods. **ZONES 9–11. I–H.**

Dendrobium pseudoglomeratum

Dendrobium rhodostictum

Dendrobium rhodostictum F. MUELL.
& KRAENZL.

syn: *D. madonnae* ROLFE

This small- to medium-sized epiphyte or terrestrial from New Guinea and the Solomon Islands grows at moderate altitudes in mountain rain forests or on steep, mossy limestone slopes that drain well. The shape of the pseudobulbs is variable, but usually club-shaped. They are up to 10 in (25 cm) long. The inflorescences form at or near the apex and consist of two to six large flowers, 2½–3⅔ in (6–9 cm) across. These fragrant flowers last for about six weeks and appear during winter and spring. In cultivation this plant should not be allowed to dry out completely. **ZONES 9–11. C–I.**

Dendrobium secundum

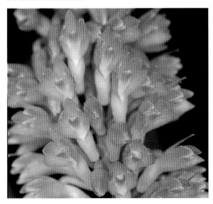

Dendrobium sanderae ROLFE

This species is restricted to the island of Luzon in the Philippines, where it grows as an epiphyte at moderate to high altitudes. There are at least four different varieties of this plant recorded—the form with the largest flower is known as variety "*major.*" The pseudobulbs are 1–3 ft (30–90 cm) long. The inflorescence, which arises from near the apex of the stem, bears up to ten flowers, each about 2½–4 in (6–10 cm) in diameter. The var. *major* flowers during spring and the var. *parviflorum* during autumn. This species should be grown in intermediate temperatures with constant high humidity. A reduced watering period is recommended during winter. **ZONES 9–11. I–H.**

Dendrobium sanderae

Dendrobium secundum (BLUME) LINDL.
syn: *D. bursigerum* LINDL., *D. heterostigma* RCHB.F.

This epiphytic species is often abundant and occurs over an extensive range from Myanmar to the Indonesian islands, as far west as Sulawesi and as far north as the Philippines. It grows at low or, occasionally, moderate altitudes, usually in forests with a distinct dry season. The stout pseudobulbs are semi-erect or pendulous and grow up to 40 in (1 m) long, but are more commonly 8–12 in (20–30 cm). The inflorescences measure up to 4 in (10 cm) long and are densely crowded with flowers, each about ⅘ in (2 cm) long. The flowers usually grow on one side of the inflorescence, which gives rise to the plant's botanical name ("secund" means on one side). Flowers appear during spring and they last for about one to two weeks. White-flowered forms of this species have been recorded. **ZONES 10–12. I–H.**

D

Dendrobium signatum RCHB.F.

syn: *D. hilderbrandii* ROLFE

This attractive species is common in many collections. Its natural habitat ranges from Myanmar to Vietnam and Laos. It usually grows at low to moderate elevations in areas with a seasonal climate. Its pseudobulbs are about 20 in (50 cm) long, and they become pendulous as they lengthen. The flowers, which last for about three weeks, are borne during spring on the leafless pseudobulbs. They are about 1¾–2½ in (4–6 cm) across. This plant does well in a pot or basket with a standard *Dendrobium* species bark mix.
ZONES 9–11. I–H.

Dendrobium signatum

Dendrobium smillieae F. MUELL.

syn: *D. ophioglossum* RCHB.F., *D. hollrungii* KRAENZL.
"BOTTLEBRUSH ORCHID"

This attractive, large epiphyte occurs in moist lowland forests or, occasionally, on rocks in open forests in New Guinea and northeast Australia. It can form large clumps and may grow stems over 40 in (1 m) long. The short inflorescences bear numerous flowers that are extremely densely packed. Each flower is tubular in shape and is about ⅘ in (2 cm) long. This species has two color forms—one with a prominent pink color on the base of the floral segments; the other with white and green coloration. The flowering season is mostly during spring and early summer and the blooms last for about two to six weeks.
ZONES 10–12. H.

Dendrobium smillieae

Dendrobium speciosum

Dendrobium speciosum SM.

"KING ORCHID"

This large, robust epiphyte or lithophyte occurs in Australia from sea level to a moderate altitude. Its pseudobulbs are up to 2 ft (60 cm) long. The inflorescence, up to 2 ft (60 cm) long, bears numerous fragrant flowers, 1–2 cm (2.5–5 cm) in diameter. These flowers are colored white to cream or yellow and they last for about two to three weeks. Flowering is during late winter and spring. This orchid makes an excellent rockery plant in the right conditions. Several varieties of this species have been recorded and some are regarded as separate species by different authorities.
ZONES 9–11. I–H.

D

Dendrobium spectabile

Dendrobium stratiotes RCHB.F.

This spectacular epiphyte occurs in Irian Jaya and on the Molucca and Sunda islands in Indonesia. It is a reasonably large epiphyte that grows at low altitudes. Its pseudobulbs are up to 40 in (1 m) long and have a swollen base and slender apex. The inflorescences, up to 16 in (40 cm) long but usually shorter, bear three to ten large flowers up to 4 in (10 cm) in length, but more often about 2 in (5 cm). The flowers last for up to six weeks. While the main flowering season is during spring, these flowers may occur at any time of the year. This plant is best grown in a large, shallow pot with a well-drained mixture. It requires year-round hot, moist conditions. **ZONES 10–12. H.**

Dendrobium × superbiens RCHB.F.

syn: *D. goldiei* RCHB.F., *D. brandtiae* KRAENZL., *D. vinicolor* ST CLOUD

This natural hybrid between *D. bigibbum* and *D. discolor* occurs mainly on the islands of the Torres Strait and northern Cape York Peninsula in Australia. It grows in vine forests or on rock faces, often near the ocean, in areas of extreme seasonal changes. Its pseudobulbs are up to 40 in (1 m) long. The inflorescences bear up to 20 flowers, each about 2 in (5 cm) in diameter. Flowering may occur at any time of the year, and the blooms last for about two months. In cultivation this species requires bright light, good air movement, and hot, humid conditions. It should be kept dry during winter and spring, with copious amounts of watering during summer and autumn. **ZONES 10–12. H.**

Dendrobium spectabile

(BLUME) MIQ.

syn: *D. tigrinum* ROLFE EX HEMSLEY

The large, spectacular flowers of this species are most unusual; they have distinctive twists in all their parts. The plant is a large, robust epiphyte that occurs in the hot, steamy lowlands of the Pacific Islands, from New Guinea to as far south as Vanuatu. It grows most commonly in tree canopies. Its pseudobulbs are cylindrical. They measure up to 32 in (80 cm) long and ⅘–1¼ in (2–3 cm) in width and up to six leathery leaves emerge at their apexes. This plant bears up to 20 flowers, each 1¾–3¼ in (4–8 cm) across. The flowering season is during winter and the blooms last for several weeks. This species flowers best when it has been established in a pot for several years. **ZONES 10–12. H.**

Dendrobium stratiotes

Dendrobium × superbiens

D

Dendrobium tangerinum

Dendrobium tangerinum P. J. CRIBB

This handsome epiphyte is found on the north coast of Papua New Guinea at low to, occasionally, moderate altitudes. Its pseudobulbs are up to 30 in (75 cm) long. The racemes are up to 1 ft (30 cm) long and they bear up to 15 flowers, each about 1¾–2 in (4–5 cm) long. The flowers last for up to two months and occur all year in the natural habitat, but usually restricted to winter and spring in other climates. When cultivated, this plant requires hot conditions, bright light, even full sun, and regular watering throughout most of the year. Slightly less watering during winter is of some benefit. This species has suffered in the wild over recent years because of habitat clearing and over-collection. **ZONES 9–12. I–H.**

Dendrobium taurinum

Dendrobium taurinum LINDL.

This large, robust, attractive epiphyte is restricted to the Philippines; on Luzon, Palawan and Dinagat islands. It grows on mangroves or on the trees nearby in open forests—in places where there is a hot, wet, and humid climate year-round. Its pseudobulbs may be as long as 10 ft (3 m), but are usually only 40 in (1 m) long. The inflorescences, borne from the upper axils, are up to 2 ft (60 cm) long. They comprise up to 30 well-spaced flowers, each one large and waxy and about 2–2½ in (5–6) cm across. The flowering season is during autumn and winter and the blooms last for about six weeks. This species needs plenty of space when cultivating, so it may be a problem in a small glasshouse. It grows best in a pot with a well-drained mixture. **ZONES 10–12. H.**

Dendrobium tetragonum A. CUNN.

"SPIDER ORCHID"

This small, variable epiphyte occurs in eastern
Australia from sea level to moderate altitudes.
It grows in rain forests and forests along
stream banks, usually in shaded positions. Its
pseudobulbs, up to 16 in (40 cm) long, are
very slender at the base and have a prominent
four-angled, swollen part, about $\frac{2}{3}$ in (15 mm)
wide, at the apex. The inflorescence comprises
two to five flowers, which are $1\frac{1}{4}$–$6\frac{3}{4}$ in
(3–17 cm) long. The larger ones belong to var.
giganteum (*D. capitisyork*). The flowers vary
in color from green to cream, or yellow with
red markings. They last for about two weeks
and appear during winter and spring. This
species is relatively easy to grow if mounted
on a slab and grown in semi-shade. Some
authorities classify it as four separate species.
ZONES 9–12. I–H.

Dendrobium tetragonum

Dendrobium thyrsiflorum

Dendrobium thyrsiflorum RCHB.F.

syn: *D. densiflorum,* **var.** *albolutea* HOOK.F.

Occurring from India to southern China, this medium-sized
epiphyte grows from moderate to high altitudes in deciduous
forests with distinct seasonal changes. Its club-shaped
pseudobulbs are rounded, and grow up to 2 ft (60 cm) long.
The flowers are about 2 in (5 cm) across and are borne on
densely crowded, pendulous inflorescences. The flowering
season is during spring and the blooms last for about a week.
D. thyrsiflorum is relatively easy to grow if given a watering
rest period during winter and early spring. **ZONES 9–11. I–H.**

Dendrobium toressae (F.M. BAILEY) DOCKR.

syn: *Bulbophyllum toressae* F. M. BAILEY, *Dockrillia toressae* (F. M. BAILEY) BRIEGER

"GRAIN OF WHEAT ORCHID"

In many ways, this is one of the smallest members of the genus.
It is a tiny species from the northeast of Australia. It is found
at low to moderate altitudes in rain forests and nearby open
forests. It grows as an epiphyte or a lithophyte in semi-shade
and usually in humid conditions. This species forms dense mats
comprising short rhizomes with small, succulent leaves less than
$\frac{1}{3}$ in (1 cm) long—about the size and shape of a grain of wheat,
hence the common name. The single flowers are about $\frac{1}{4}$ in
(6 mm) in diameter. They may appear at any time of the year
and last for a few days. A slab is the best growing method for
this species. **ZONES 10–12. I–H.**

Dendrobium toressae

D

Dendrobium unicum SEIDENF.

The unusual shape of the flowers is a feature of this medium-sized species that occurs in northern Thailand, Laos, and Vietnam. It grows at altitudes of 2700–5000 ft (800–1500 m) on low shrubs and on rocks in areas with seasonal rainfall and strong light. Its erect or pendulous pseudobulbs are up to 10 in (25 cm) long. They turn a dark color with age. From the apex grow three narrow, deciduous leaves, about 2½ in (6 cm) long. The inflorescences are borne from the upper nodes and consist of two to four bright-orange, sometimes twisted, flowers about 1¾–2 in (4–5 cm) across. They have a tangerine-like fragrance and appear during winter and spring. **ZONES 10–11. I–H.**

Dendrobium unicum

Dendrobium venustum TEIJSM. & BINN.
syn: *D. ciliatum* PARISH EX HOOK.F., *D. rupicola* RCHB.F.

This miniature deciduous epiphyte occurs from Myanmar to Vietnam. It grows at low altitudes in areas with a distinct dry season. It is closely related to *D. delacourii*, but differs because of its longer, narrower pseudobulbs, 4–20 in (10–50 cm) long. These are more or less cylindrical and they become pendulous with age. The erect or arching inflorescences arise from nodes at the apexes of the pseudobulbs. These are up to 1 ft (30 cm) long and bear numerous flowers, each about 1 in (2.5 cm) across. Flowering is during summer. A watering rest period during winter, in which the plants are allowed to dry out for lengthy periods, is required in cultivation. **ZONES 9–12. H.**

Dendrobium venustum

Dendrobium victoriae-reginae LOHER.
syn: *D. coelestre* LOHER.
"BLUE ORCHID"

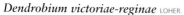

This epiphyte occurs in the Philippines on the Camiguin, Luzon, Mindanao, Mindoro, and Negros islands. It grows at high altitudes in cool, mossy forests, where there is year-round rainfall. Its 4-ft (1.2-m) long pseudobulbs are slender, branched, tangled, and pendulous. The inflorescences, borne on the leafless stems, have two to five or, occasionally, up to 12 waxy flowers, each 1¼–1¾ in (3–4 cm) across. They are an unusual shade of violet-blue, which leads to this species' common name. Flowering occurs throughout the year. The plant requires cool to intermediate temperatures with year-round high humidity in cultivation. **ZONES 9–11. C–I.**

Dendrobium victoriae-reginae

Dendrobium Avrils Gold

D

Dendrobium Gerald McCraith

Dendrobium forbesii × *D. convolutum*

Dendrobium Yukidaruma "Queen"

Dendrobium Jonathons Glory "David"

Dendrobium Lynette Banks "Golden Nugget"

Dendrobium Silver Bells

Dendrobium Champagne Stripes × Classic Gem

D

Dendrobium Queen Cobra × *D. helix*

Dendrobium Blue Sparkle

Dendrobium Mousmee

Dendrobium Hambuhren Gold × Beautiful Egg

D

DENDROCHILUM BLUME

This genus is distributed from Malaysia to the
Philippines, with its greatest diversity in the
Philippines and Borneo. The species grow from
sea level to about 10,000 ft (3000 m), and they
range from coastal mangroves through to
scrubby sub-alpine forest. Most of them are
epiphytes with a few growing as terrestrials
or lithophytes. They are either pendulous or
creeping with elongated rhizomes, or dense to
loosely tufted with closely spaced pseudobulbs
and a solitary leaf. The inflorescence is
terminal and may gracefully arch with a few
to many long-lasting flowers that open at the
same time.

CULTIVATION

This genus is easy to grow in a bark mix with
sphagnum moss or any other free-draining
medium. The plants require plenty of water
during the growing season.

Dendrochilum cobbianum RCHB.F.

This species is endemic to the Philippines where
it grows as a lithophyte in exposed situations at
altitudes of 4700–8300 ft (1400–2500 m). It is
a tufted plant with pseudobulbs up to 3¼ in
(8 cm) long and leaves up to about 1 ft (30 cm)
long. The inflorescence is 18 in (45 cm) long,
and is at first erect, but becomes pendulous
when it reaches about 1 ft (30 cm) in length. It
bears many flowers, each about ½ in (12 mm)
across, with wide-spreading segments. These
fragrant flowers appear from late autumn to
winter. ZONES 9–10. C–I.

Dendrochilum cobbianum

D

Dendrochilum cootesii

Dendrochilum convallariaeforme

Dendrochilum filiforme

Dendrochilum convallariaeforme SCHAUER

syn: *D. bicallosum* AMES

This species, endemic to the Philippines, grows as an epiphyte in mossy forests at altitudes of 1000–6300 ft (300–1900 m). It is a tufted plant with pseudobulbs to about 1¾ in (4 cm) long. Its leaf may be up to 1 ft (30 cm) long. The inflorescence is 1 ft (30 cm) long and becomes pendulous. It bears many flowers up to about ¼ in (6 mm) wide. The flowers appear during late autumn and winter. ZONE 11. I.

Dendrochilum cootesii H. E. PEDERSEN

This species, endemic to the Philippines, grows in moss-covered trees and occurs at altitudes of 4000–6700 ft (1200–2000 m). The plant is tufted with pseudobulbs up to about 2 in (5 cm) long. The single leaf is about 4 in (10 cm) long. The inflores-cence is about 5½ in (13 cm) long, and is gracefully arched to pendulous. The flowers, about ¼ in (6 mm) across, appear from late autumn to winter. ZONE 11. I.

Dendrochilum filiforme LINDL.

This epiphyte grows in the forests of the Philippines at altitudes of about 2000–7500 ft (600–2250 m). The plants are tufted with ovoid-shaped pseudobulbs to about 1¼ in (3 cm) tall. The pendulous inflorescence, up to about 1 ft (30 cm) long, has many flowers, about ¼ in (6 mm) across. Flowering occurs from late summer to winter. ZONE 11. I.

Dendrochilum glumaceum

D

Dendrochilum glumaceum LINDL.

This species occurs in Borneo and the Philippines, where it grows as an epiphyte up to a 7700-ft (2300-m) altitude. The plants are tufted with pseudobulbs up to 1¼ in (3 cm) high. The single leaf grows up to 1 ft (30 cm) long. The gracefully arching inflorescence is up to about 16 in (40 cm) long, and the sweetly scented flowers are about ⅘ in (2 cm) across. Flowering is gregarious throughout the year.
ZONES 11–12. I–H.

Dendrochilum javieri MAGRATH, BULMER & SHAFER

Endemic to the Philippines, this species grows on moss-covered trees at altitudes of 6000–8000 ft (1800–2400 m). Its pseudobulbs are spaced closely together on the rhizome and are up to 1¾ in (4 cm) long. They are narrowly cylindrical to terete in shape. The solitary leaf is narrow and leathery, and about 7 in (18 cm) long. The arching inflorescence appears with the new growth and is about 8 in (20 cm) long. It comprises many crowded flowers, about ½ in (12 mm) across. Flowering is during winter.
ZONE 11. I.

Dendrochilum javieri

Dendrochilum longifolium
RCHB.F

syn: *D. clemsiae* AMES, *D. bartonii* (RIDL.) SCHLTR.

This is the most widespread species of the genus. It ranges from west Malaysia and Singapore to Indonesia, New Guinea, and the Philippines. It grows most often as an epiphyte but may occur as a lithophyte at elevations up to 7300 ft (2200 m). The plant is tufted and is quite robust. Its pseudobulbs are ovoid and grow up to 3⅔ in (9 cm) high. The single leaf is about 1 ft (30 cm) long. The inflorescence gracefully arches and is more than 1 ft (30 cm) long. It carries up to 40 flowers, each about ⅓ in (1 cm) across. Flowering occurs during winter. **ZONES 11–12. I–H.**

Dendrochilum longifolium

Dendrochilum macranthum (SCHLTR.) H. E. PEDERSEN
syn: *D. grandiflorum* SCHLTR., *D. magnum* RCHB.F., *D. latifolium*
var. *macranthum* (SCHLTR.) H. E. PEDERSEN

This epiphyte is endemic to the Philippines, where it grows at altitudes above 4000 ft (1200 m). The plant is tufted and has pseudobulbs which are ovoid. They are up to 3 in (7.5 cm) tall. The single leaf is up to 2 ft (60 cm) long and 3 in (7.5 cm) wide. The inflorescence starts out erect but becomes pendulous as it lengthens. It is up to about 2 ft (60 cm) long and bears many flowers, each about ½ in (12 mm) wide. Flowering occurs during spring and summer. **ZONES 11–12. I–H.**

Dendrochilum pangasinanense AMES

Endemic to the Philippines, little is known about this species natural habitat or altitudinal range. Its pseudobulbs, about 2 in (5 cm) long, are clustered on a short rhizome. The leaf is lanceolate and about 5½ in (13 cm) long. The inflorescence is initially erect, then becomes pendulous. It is about 7 in (18 cm) long and bears many flowers, each about ⅓ in (1 cm) across. Flowering is during summer. **ZONES 11–12. I–H.**

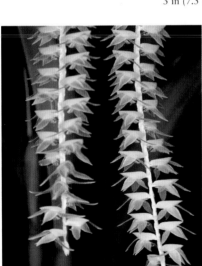

Dendrochilum macranthum

Dendrochilum pangasinanense

Dendrochilum saccolabium KRAENZL.

This species is endemic to the Philippines, where it grows as an epiphyte in forests at altitudes of 670–1160 ft (200–350 m). Its pseudobulbs are clustered on a short rhizome and are up to ⅘ in (2 cm) long. The semi-arching inflorescence is up to 1 ft (30 cm) long and carries up to 40 flowers, each with a diameter of about ¼ in (6 mm). Flowering occurs during winter and early spring. **ZONE 12. I–H.**

D

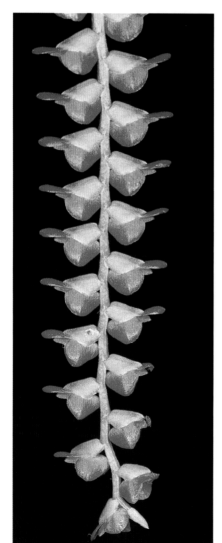

Dendrochilum saccolabium

Dendrochilum tenellum

Dendrochilum tenellum (NEES & MEYER) AMES

This very common species is endemic to the Philippines and grows as an epiphyte in mossy forests at elevations of about 1000–8300 ft (300–2500 m). This is the only species in the genus that has perfectly terete leaves. The plant is tufted with pseudobulbs that are terete, clustered, and up to 3⅔ in (9 cm) long. The rigid leaf is up to 20 in (50 cm) long, and the densely flowered inflorescence grows up to 3⅔ in (9 cm) long. The flowers are very small, about ⅛ in (3 mm) across, and appear from autumn through to summer.
ZONES 11–12. I–H.

Dendrochilum uncatum RCHB.F.

syn: *D. formosanum* (SCHLTR.) SCHLTR.

This tufted plant from the Philippines and Taiwan occurs in mossy forests at altitudes of 3000–8300 ft (900–2500 m). It has ovoid pseudobulbs up to about 1 in (2.5 cm) high. The leaves are up to about 4 in (10 cm) long. The inflorescence is longer than the leaves, arches, and carries many faintly fragrant flowers about ⅓ in (1 cm) wide. Flowering is during autumn and spring. **ZONE 11. I.**

Dendrochilum uncatum

D

Dendrochilum wenzelii AMES

Endemic to the Philippines, this species grows as an epiphyte in forests at altitudes of 1700–6000 ft (500–1800 m). The tufted plant has ovoid- to terete-shaped pseudobulbs up to 1½ in (3.5 cm) high. They grow closely together and have narrow, leathery leaves about 1 ft (30 cm) long. The inflorescence, up to 1 ft (30 cm) long, is semi-arching and bears many flowers about ⅓ in (1 cm) in diameter. Flowering occurs from winter to early spring. **ZONES 10–11. I–H.**

Dendrochilum wenzelii

Dendrochilum yuccaefolium

Dendrochilum yuccaefolium L. O. WILLIAMS

This small species is endemic to the Philippines, where it grows as an epiphyte above 1700 ft (500 m). Very little is known of its ecology or habitat requirements. Its pseudobulbs are about 1¾ in (4 cm) high and the leaves are up to 8 in (20 cm) long. The arching inflorescence is about 6 in (15 cm) long and carries up to 30 flowers, each with a diameter of about ⅔ in (15 mm). Flowering occurs from autumn to early spring. **ZONE 11. I.**

DENDROPHYLAX RCHB.F.

This is a genus of eight epiphytic species restricted to the Caribbean. It is an American offshoot of the Eurasian *Vanda* group. *Dendrophylax* are leafless, nearly stemless orchids, with greenish, flattened roots that take on the photosynthetic role of leaves. Having no water storage capabilities, these species are limited to humid, shady, and swampy habitats. Most of them have large flowers with a long spur.

CULTIVATION

These plants should be grown on a slab or a tree so that sunlight reaches the roots. They should be watered regularly and kept in bright light.

Dendrophylax lindenii (LINDL.) BENTHAM
EX ROLFE.

syn: *Angraecum lindenii* LINDL., *Polyradicion lindenii* (LINDL.) GARAY, *Polyrhiza lindenii* (LINDL.) COGN.
"GHOST ORCHID"

This striking species occurs in Cuba and southern Florida in the USA—it is the only member of the *Vanda* group in the USA. It is at home growing on custard-apple trees in the shadows of the Big Cypress Swamp in Florida. Its size, color, and nocturnal fragrance mark it as a species that is pollinated by night-flying hawkmoths. The flower spike reaches 10 in (25 cm) in length and bears up to ten large, long-lasting white flowers. The lip carries two long, curving spurs about $4^3/_4$ in (12 cm) long, which makes the flower look somewhat like a frog. The flowers have a diameter of about 2 in (5 cm), and each one is borne singly, appearing in succession throughout summer.
ZONES 9–11. I.

Dendrophylax lindenii

DIENIA LINDL.

This genus probably comprises only one species. It is most commonly known by its synonym, *Malaxis latifolia*. It is widespread from India to Malaysia, Indonesia, New Guinea, and Australia, as far north as Japan. It is an inhabitant of rain forests and grows mostly as a deciduous terrestrial along stream banks and near swampy areas.

CULTIVATION

This one species grows readily in a terrestrial mix. After the leaves drop, the plant should receive less water and be allowed a resting period during the cooler months. Watering should be resumed when new growth appears.

Dienia ophrydis
(KOEN.) ORMEROD & SEIDENF.

The three to six thin-textured leaves are up to 1 ft (30 cm) long. These are scattered along the fleshy pseudobulb, which is up to $4/_5$ in (2 cm) high. The inflorescence is up to 1 ft (30 cm) tall and carries many small, densely packed flowers that open sequentially. The flowers are about $1/_4$ in (6 mm) across and appear during summer.
ZONES 11–12. I–H.

Dienia ophrydis

DIMORPHORCHIS (LINDL.) ROLFE

There are two or three species in this unusual genus from lowland hill forests in Borneo. The plants are monopodial and resemble *Vanda* plants in form. The inflorescences are long and pendulous and bear flowers that are well-spaced along their length. There are two different types of flowers on each inflorescence and it is unclear to botanists why this is the case.

CULTIVATION

This genus should be grown in bright light, although full sunlight should be avoided for most of the species. Year-round moisture and good air circulation are recommended. If grown in a pot, a very coarse medium is required. In the tropics they may be grown in the garden successfully, but they will require glasshouse conditions in temperate climates.

Dimorphorchis lowii (LINDL.) ROLFE

syn: several names, including *Vanda lowii* LINDL., *Vandopsis lowii* (LINDL) SCHLTR.

This large species grows overhanging streams in lower hill forests in Borneo, from sea level to a 4300-ft (1300-m) altitude. The stems may reach 40 in (1 m) or more in length and have leathery, straplike leaves up to 28 in (70 cm) long. The pendulous inflorescences, up to 10 ft (3 m) long, bear many well-spaced flowers that come in two types. The lower two or three flowers are about 2½ in (6 cm) across and 2 in (5 cm) high and have a strong fragrance; the remaining flowers are 2¾ in (7 cm) across and 2½ in (6 cm) high, and are not fragrant. Flowering occurs mostly from autumn to early winter. **ZONES 11–12. H.**

Dimorphorchis lowii

DIPLOCAULOBIUM (RCHB.F.) KRAENZL.

This genus comprises more than 100 species
distributed from Malaysia through Indonesia,
New Guinea, and Australia to the western
Pacific Islands. The center of diversity is New
Guinea, with about 90 per cent of the species
endemic to that island. The genus is characterized by closely spaced pseudobulbs with
only one internode and a solitary terminal leaf.
There is a wide range of variation in the
vegetative form, structure, and habit within the
genus. The flowers last for about a day only,
but occasionally longer.

Diplocaulobium arachnoideum

CULTIVATION

Depending on the growth habit, these species
may be grown either mounted or in a pot.
Most of them will require abundant water
during the growing season, with a watering rest
period during the cooler months. Depending
on the altitude of their origin, they may grow
in a range of temperatures but will always
require a humid environment.

Diplocaulobium arachnoideum (SCHLTR.) CARR

This species is endemic to New Guinea,
occurring in wet, humid forests at altitudes of
2700–5000 ft (800–1500 m). Its pseudobulbs,
about 8 in (20 cm) long, are flask-shaped and
narrowly graduated towards the apex. The leaf
is up to 4¾ in (12 cm) long. The flowers open
widely to about 4 in (10 cm). They are
produced singly at various times throughout
spring, summer, and autumn. This plant grows
well either on a mount or in a pot and needs
abundant water and humidity during the
growing season. ZONE 10. I.

Diplocaulobium glabrum

Diplocualobium kirchianum

Diplocaulobium glabrum (J. J. SM.) KRAENZL.

This widely distributed species on the southern coast of New Guinea also
extends into northern Queensland in Australia. It ranges from about sea
level to 1700 ft (500 m). It grows mostly as an epiphyte, occasionally as
a lithophyte. It has a creeping habit and cylindrical to ovoid pseudobulbs
up to 1¾ in (4 cm) high. The solitary leaf is about 1¾ in (4 cm) long.
The solitary flowers are borne on a pedicel up to about 2½ in (6 cm)
high. They open widely, to about 1¼ in (3 cm). The flowers appear at
any time between spring and late autumn. This plant is best cultivated
on a slab of hardwood. ZONE 11. I–H.

D

Diplocaulobium regale

Diplocualobium kirchianum (A. D. HAWKES & HELLER) P. F. HUNT & SUMMERH.

syn: *Dendrobium bulbophylloides* J. J. SM.

This small, creeping member of the genus is common in the mangroves and swamp forests of the southern coast of Papua New Guinea. The plant forms long, crowded strands of pseudobulbs up to ²/₃ in (15 mm) high. Each of these bears a stiff, leathery leaf up to 1¾ in (4 cm) long. One or two flowers on short pedicels are produced from the apex of the pseudobulbs. The flowers are about ⁴/₅ in (2 cm) wide. Flowering may occur at any time but peaks during late spring and summer. This species grows best on a suitable mount such as cork or hardwood. It should be given hot conditions and high humidity. **ZONE 12. I–H.**

Diplocaulobium regale (SCHLTR.) A. D. HAWKES

This is perhaps the most striking species in the genus. It grows at altitudes of 5000–8300 ft (1500–2500 m) in the New Guinean highlands. The plant is up to 28 in (70 cm) tall and has gradually tapering pseudobulbs. The leaves are up to 8 in (20 cm) long. The flower color ranges from white through to dark rose-red. They measure about 3¼ in (8 cm) wide. Flowering may occur at any time. Maintain this species in intermediate conditions with abundant moisture and high humidity. **ZONES 10–11. I.**

DIPODIUM R. BR.

These plants occur from Thailand to Vanuatu, mostly at low to moderate altitudes. They are terrestrial or, in some cases, start out as a terrestrial then climb a tree and eventually become an epiphyte once the basal part of the stem dies. Several species are saprophytes and these lack leaves. All of them have slender stems with overlapping leaves, usually in two ranks. The erect inflorescences have several spotted flowers.

CULTIVATION

The saprophytic species are virtually impossible to grow, however, the other species are amenable to cultivation. The climbing species require a long slab of bark or something similar to which it can attach. Non-saprophytic species may be grown in a standard terrestrial mix, but they sometimes prove difficult to maintain via this method. All of the species should be given moist, humid conditions and filtered light.

Dipodium ensifolium
F. MUELL.

This terrestrial species from northeast Australia grows in stony or sandy soil in open forests from sea level to about 5000 ft (1500 m). The plant reaches about 40 in (1 m) long. It is upright initially, but it becomes sprawling. The leaves form two ranks and are borne along the upper part of the stem. The inflorescence is erect, up to about 6–20 in (15–50 cm) long, and bears two to 20 flowers, each about ⅘–1¾ in (2–4 cm) across. The flowers appear during late spring and early summer.
ZONES 10–12. I–H.

Dipodium ensifolium

Dipodium pictum (LINDL.) RCHB.F.
syn: *D. pandanum* F. M. BAIL.

This species ranges from the Malay Peninsula to the Solomon Islands, including northeast Australia, growing from sea level to 5000 ft (1500 m). It starts life as a terrestrial, then creeps along the forest floor until it finds a tree or vertical rock surface upon which it can climb. Eventually the lower part of the climbing stem dies, leaving the plant to grow as an epiphyte or lithophyte. Its 67-ft (20-m) stems are brittle, and propagation in nature occurs through the parts that break away and then take root. The stems produce overlapping leaves along their lengths. The inflorescences arise from near the apex of the stems and bear up to 20 or 30 flowers, each about 2 in (5 cm) across. **ZONES 10–12. H.**

Dipodium pictum

Dipodium variegatum

Dipodium variegatum M. A. CLEM. & D. L. JONES
"SLENDER HYACINTH ORCHID"

This saprophytic species from southeast Australia grows at low to moderate altitudes in open eucalyptus forests. The plant lacks leaves and chlorophyll and it survives winter as an underground rhizome. Its inflorescences appear mostly during late spring or early summer and grow to about 32 in (80 cm) tall. They bear up to 50 flowers, each about 1 in (2.5 cm) across. In contrast to similar species, the flower stalks and ovaries have spots similar to those on the flowers. The flowers may appear at any time. **ZONES 8–10. I.**

DISA BERGIUS

This large, terrestrial genus is from central and southern Africa. It comprises about 125 species that grow in grasslands, often in wet areas at low to high altitudes. The stems are erect, and the leaves arise from tuberous roots or, in some species, on a sterile shoot separate to the flowering shoot. The erect inflorescence bears a few to many flowers. The flowers vary in size from a few millimetres up to 2 in (5 cm) wide, such as those on *D. uniflora*. The dorsal sepal has a spur and is often the most visible part of the flower. It forms a hood over the column.

CULTIVATION

D. uniflora and a few related species are well known in many collections and several hybrids are now established. These plants require intermediate to cool conditions. They should be potted in a well-drained mix that includes sand and peat or sphagnum moss, and not allowed to dry out. Care needs to be taken to avoid salt build-up in the potting mix—the water should have a pH of 4.5 to 6 with few dissolved salts. Filtered sunlight and good air movement are required.

Disa erubescens RENDLE var. *carsonii* N. E. BR.

syn: *D. carsonii* N. E. BR.

This attractive species is widespread in tropical Africa, from Nigeria to Kenya and from Sudan to Zimbabwe. It grows in moderate- to high-altitude grasslands where drainage is poor. The plant has a sterile shoot about 1 ft (30 cm) long. This produces two or three leaves. The flowering stems are up to 3 ft (90 cm) tall, but usually shorter, and they bear three to eight flowers, each 1¼–2½ in (3–6 cm) across. The flowers appear during December and January. **ZONES 9–10. C–I.**

Disa erubescens var. *carsonii*
Disa fragrans

Disa fragrans SCHLTR.

This robust species is recorded from the mountain ranges that run through eastern South Africa, Zimbabwe, Tanzania, and Kenya. It grows under full sun in grasslands at altitudes of 6700–11,000 ft (2000–3300 m). The plant reaches a height of 20 in (50 cm), of which about 4 in (10 cm) is the inflorescence. This bears numerous flowers, each ⅓–⅔ in (10–15 mm) across. The fragrant flowers occur during summer. **ZONES 8–9. C.**

Disa ochrostachya RCHB.F.

syn: *D. satyriopsis* KRAENZL.

This is a widespread species that ranges from west to east Africa, and from Sudan in the north to Zimbabwe in the south. It grows in wet grasslands or open grassy forests at high altitudes. The plant is 14–40 in (35 cm–1 m) tall. It has two to three reddish-colored leaves, each about 6–8 in (15–20 cm) long and 1¾ in (4 cm) wide. These are borne on a separate shoot. The inflorescence bears up to 200 densely packed flowers, each about ⅓ in (1 cm) across. **ZONES 8–9. C.**

Disa ochrostachya

Disa ornithantha SCHLTR.

This species grows in wet grasslands at an altitude of about 5000 ft (1500 m) in Zimbabwe, Malawi, Zambia, and Tanzania. Its flowering stems are 8–20 in (20–50 cm) tall. The sterile stems are up to 2½ in (6 cm) tall and produce one to three leaves about 6–7 in (15–18 cm) long and ⅓ in (1 cm) wide. The inflorescence is up to 4 in (10 cm) long and bears one to six flowers, each about 1¼ in (3 cm) across. Flowering occurs during late summer. **ZONES 9–10. C–I.**

Disa perplexa LINDER

This species is widespread, but rare, in eastern Africa, from Kenya to Zimbabwe. It grows in wet grasslands at high altitudes. The plant reaches 1–3 ft (30–90 cm) tall and bears leaves with sheaths along the stem. The inflorescence has many flowers, each about ⅓ in (1 cm) across. Flowering occurs during winter. **ZONES 8–9. C.**

Disa ornithantha

Disa perplexa

Disa ukingensis SCHLTR.

This species was considered to be a synonym of *D. englerana* for many years. It is found at high altitudes on the plateau grasslands of southwest Tanzania and northern Malawi. The plant is about 14 in (35 cm) tall. Its inflorescence bears a few flowers, about 1¼ in (3 cm) across. Flowering occurs during late summer and early autumn. **ZONES 8–9. C.**

Disa ukingensis

D

Disa uniflora

Disa walleri

Disa zombica

Disa uniflora BERGIUS
syn: *D. grandiflora* L.F.

This is one of the finest of the horticultural
orchids. It occurs in the Cape provinces of
South Africa and grows along stream banks
and in other wet areas at altitudes of about
330–4000 ft (100–1200 m), where the
conditions vary from full sun to shade. The
plant is up to 40 in (1 m) tall and along the
length of stems are lanceolate leaves about
3¼–8 in (8–20 cm) long. There is usually one
flower, occasionally more, up to 4 in (10 cm)
across. Most of the flowers are a scarlet color,
but pink, orange, and yellow forms also exist.
The long-lasting and fragrant flowers occur
from December to March. **ZONES 9–11. C–I.**

Disa walleri RCHB.F.

This robust species is recorded in central Africa
in Zaire, Tanzania, Malawi, Zambia, and
Zimbabwe. It grows in highland grasslands, or
the margins of swamps and wet areas in
woodlands. It is up to 3 ft (90 cm) tall and
produces leaves along the stem. The
inflorescence has many densely packed flowers
about 1¼ in (3 cm) across. Flowering occurs
during February. **ZONES 9–10. C–I.**

Disa zombica N. E. BR.
syn: *D. nyassana* SCHLTR.

The habitat for this species is wet grasslands at
altitudes of 3300–6700 ft (1000–2000 m) in
Tanzania, Malawi, Mozambique, and
Zimbabwe. The plant grows up to about 20 in
(50 cm) tall and has sterile stems, to about
4½ in (11 cm), with one to three leaves about
4¾–10 in (12–25 cm) long and ⅘ in (2 cm)
wide. The dense inflorescence has 12 to 30
flowers, each about 1¼ in (3 cm) across.
Flowering is during early autumn.
ZONES 9–10. C–I.

DISPERIS SW.

The majority of the 110 species in this genus of terrestrial orchids occur in Africa and Madagascar, with a few in India, Southeast Asia, the Philippines, and New Guinea. The habitats range from forests to grasslands and marshes, often at moderate altitudes. An underground tuber gives rise to rather small leaves that clasp the stem. The inflorescence bears one to many flowers.

CULTIVATION

Many of these species do well in cultivation if grown in shallow pots with a terrestrial mixture.

Disperis fanniniae HARV.

This species occurs in the eastern part of South Africa. It grows in shady conditions on the floor of forests at altitudes of 4000–6700 ft (1200–2000 m). The plant is about 6–18 in (15–45 cm) tall and bears three stem-clasping leaves, about ⅘–3¼ in (2–8 cm) long and ⅓–1¼ in (1–3 cm) across. The inflorescence produces one to eight large flowers. These are predominantly white flushed with pink or green. They are about 1¼ in (3 cm) long and appear from summer to autumn.
ZONES 9–10. C–I.

D

Disperis fanniniae

DIURIS SMITH

This attractive group of more than 50 species occurs mostly in southeast and southwest Australia, with a few species extending into the tropics of Queensland and one in Timor. They grow most often in open forests and grasslands where winter rain dominates the weather pattern. All of the species are deciduous and die back during the dry summer to a fleshy tuber. This then sprouts after the autumn rains. The tubers are replaced annually and some species produce "daughter" tubers. Most of them flower freely.

Diuris orientis

CULTIVATION

This group is easy to cultivate in a standard terrestrial mix. Many will readily produce additional tubers. For those plants that are slow to multiply, the technique of tuber removal may be used to increase numbers.

Diuris orientis D. L. JONES

This species is restricted to southeast Australia—New South Wales, Victoria, Tasmania, and South Australia. It grows at altitudes between sea level and 660 ft (200 m) in open forests and heathlands. Its one to three leaves are semi-erect to lax, grasslike in appearance, and up to 1 ft (30 cm) long. The flowering stem is up to 16 in (40 cm) tall and carries one to six flowers up to 2 in (5 cm) across. Flowering occurs during spring. **ZONES 8–10. C.**

Diuris parvipetala (DOCKR.) D. L. JONES & M. CLEM

Endemic to Queensland in Australia, this species grows in open forests, often in gravelly soils. The plant has two or three leaves, each to about 6 in (15 cm) long. The flower stem is about 1 ft (30 cm) tall and carries one to five flowers about $^4/_5$ in (2 cm) across. Flowering occurs during spring. **ZONE 10. I.**

Diuris parvipetala

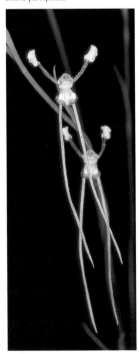

Diuris punctata

Diuris sulphurea

Diuris punctata SMITH

This attractive species is widespread in
Australia, from southeast Queensland through
New South Wales and Victoria to South
Australia. It forms colonies in open forests and
moist grasslands. It is tall with two grasslike
leaves up to 10 in (25 cm) long. The flowering
spike is about 24 in (60 cm) long and carries
two to ten flowers, each about 2½ in (6 cm)
across. The flowers may be fragrant and
appear from spring to early summer. This
species is easy to grow and flowers readily.
ZONES 8–10. C–I.

Diuris sulphurea R. RR.

This species has a wide distribution in
Australia, from southeast Queensland through
New South Wales and Victoria to Tasmania
and South Australia. It occurs from the coastal
regions to the drier western slopes of the
ranges. It produces one to three grasslike leaves
that are lax and up to 20 in (50 cm) long. The
flowering stem is up to 2 ft (60 cm) tall and
bears two to seven flowers, each about 1¼ in
(3 cm) across. Flowering is from late winter
through spring. **ZONES 8–10. C–I.**

DOCKRILLIA BRIEGER

syn: *Dendrobium* **section** *Rhizobium* LINDL.

This genus includes about 30 species—18 are found in eastern Australia, ten in New Guinea, and there are also species in New Caledonia and Vanuatu. They are epiphytes or lithophytes, and grow typically in rain forests and open forests at low to moderate altitudes, often in situations with bright light. Most of them have long, pendulous, terete leaves and thin, wiry stems. The inflorescences consist of many flowers with the three-lobed lip presented uppermost. They also usually have slender, sometimes curled flower segments.

CULTIVATION

These species are popular in cultivation, particularly in Australia. They grow best on slabs because of their rambling habit and pendulous leaves. They prefer bright filtered light and high humidity.

Dockrillia cucumerina (MACLEAY EX LINDL.) BRIEGER

syn: *Dendrobium cucumerinum* MACLEAY EX LINDL. "CUCUMBER ORCHID," "GHERKIN ORCHID"

This species ranges in Australia from southeast Queensland to central eastern New South Wales. It often grows on river oaks (*Casuarina cunninghamii*) from sea level to about 2700 ft (800 m). These plants may form large, dense clumps or strands. The unusual shape of the thick, fleshy leaves, up to 1¾ in (4 cm) long, gives rise to the plant's common names. The racemes are ⅘–1¾ in (2–4 cm) long and bear two to ten flowers, about ⅔ in (15 mm) across, that do not open widely. The flower color is cream to greenish-white with purple striping, and they appear from late spring through summer. **ZONES 9–10. I.**

Dockrillia cucumerina

Dockrillia dolichophylla (D. L. JONES & M. A. CLEM.) M. A. CLEM. & D. L. JONES

syn: *Dendrobium dolichophyllum* D. L. JONES & M. A. CLEM., *D. teretifolium* R. BR. **var.** *aureum* F. M. BAILEY, *D. tereti-folium* R. BR. **var.** *album* C. T. WHITE

This large epiphyte forms long, slender clumps up to 10 ft (3 m) or more. It grows on rocks and trees in moist, shady forests, mostly at moderate altitudes from central Queensland to northern New South Wales in Australia. Its leaves are slender, terete, and up to 40 in (1 m) long. The inflorescences are up to 3¼ in (8 cm) long and bear one to five fragrant flowers up to 2 in (5 cm) in diameter. The flowers are colored yellow with prominent dark purple stripes near the center. They appear during spring. **ZONES 10–11. I.**

Dockrillia dolichophylla

Dockrillia linguiformis

Dockrillia linguiformis (SW.) BRIEGER
syn: *Dendrobium linguiforme* SW.
"TONGUE ORCHID"

This species forms large matlike colonies on
either rocks or trees. It grows from sea level to
an altitude of over 3300 ft (1000 m) in areas
near the central eastern coast of Australia. The
leaf arises from very short stems and is oblong,
fleshy, dark green, usually furrowed, and up
to 1¾ in (4 cm) long and ⅔ in (15 mm) wide.
The racemes are 2–6 in (5–15 cm) long and
bear six to 20 flowers, each up to ⅘ in (2 cm)
across. Flowering is during winter and spring.
ZONES 10–11. I.

Dockrillia racemosa (NICHOLLS) RAUSCHERT
syn: *Dendrobium racemosum* (NICHOLLS) CLEMESHA &
DOCKRILL, *D. beckleri* F. MUELL. **var.** *racemosum* NICHOLLS

This species is confined to the Atherton
Tableland and adjacent regions in northeast
Queensland in Australia. It occurs in rain
forests mostly, preferring exposed situations
at low to moderate altitudes. It forms slender,
erect to semi-erect clumps up to 40 in (1 m)
long. The leaves are 8 in (20 cm) long and ⅔ in
(15 mm) thick. They are fleshy and terete. The
erect inflorescences are to 3¼ in (8 cm) long
and carry eight to 15 flowers, each up to 1 in
(2.5 cm) in diameter. Flowers appear mostly
during spring, but this timing is erratic as the
plant may flower at other times.
ZONES 11–12. I–H.

Dockrillia rigida (R. BR.) RAUSCHERT
syn: *Dendrobium rigidum* R. BR.

This species extends from eastern Cape York
Peninsula in Australia through the islands of
the Torres Strait to New Guinea. It is a very
common lowland species that grows in a
variety of habitats, from mangroves to open
forests. It may form large clumps up to 1 ft
(30 cm) across, but is often smaller. Its wiry,
thin, and branching stems are initially erect but
become pendulous. The leaves, up to 2½ in
(6 cm) long and ⅔ in (15 mm) wide, are fleshy
and have a reddish tinge when they grow in
exposed situations. The inflorescences, up to
about 2 in (5 cm) long, bear two to seven
flowers, each up to ⅔ in (15 mm) in diameter.
The variable flower color is mostly cream to
yellow with red markings. Flowering is
sporadic throughout the year and the blooms
last for two or three weeks. **ZONE 12. H.**

D

Dockrillia rigida

Dockrillia racemosa

D

Dockrillia striolata (RCHB.F.) RAUSCHERT
syn: *Dendrobium striolatum* RCHB.F., *D. milligani* F. MUELL.

This lithophyte from temperate southeast
Australia occurs from the coast to the ranges to
at least 3300 ft (1000 m). It grows on exposed
rocks and may form huge mats. The upright or
pendulous leaves are slender, terete, fleshy, and
somewhat curved and shallowly grooved. They
grow to 4¾ in (12 cm) long. There are usually
numerous inflorescences bearing one or two
flowers, each about 1 in (2.5 cm) in diameter.
ZONES 9–10. C–I.

Dockrillia striolata

Dockrillia teretifolia

Dockrillia teretifolia (R. BR.) BRIEGER
syn: *Dendrobium teretifolium* R. BR.
"PENCIL ORCHID"

This species is restricted to the east coast of
Australia, where it is common in lowlands
where the light is bright and intense. The plant
is an epiphyte or lithophyte. It forms large,
pendulous clumps up to 10 ft (3 m) long and
looks spectacular when in full bloom. The
leaves, up to 2 ft (60 cm) long, are terete and
not grooved. It has one inflorescence per stem,
but there are numerous
inflorescences all over the
whole plant. Each one
carries four to 15 spidery-
looking flowers that open
widely, up to 1½ in
(3.5 cm) across. These
are strongly fragrant and
appear from winter to
spring. **ZONES 10–12. I–H.**

Dockrillia wassellii (S. T. BLAKE) BRIEGER
syn: *Dendrobium wassellii* S. T. BLAKE

This species is endemic to Cape York Peninsula
in northeast Australia. It occurs in lowland
monsoonal rain forests on emergent hoop pines
(*Araucaria cunninghamii*) and, occasionally,
on boulders. The plant forms slender strands
or spreading clumps and has upright leaves
that are 3⅔ in (9 cm) long and ⅓ in (1 cm) in
diameter. The leaves also have five longitudinal
furrows. The erect inflorescence, up to 8 in
(20 cm) long, emerges from near the
base of the leaves. It bears up to
60 densely crowded flowers, each
about 1 in (2.5 cm) across. Flowering
occurs throughout the year but is
most concentrated during late spring
and early summer. While the natural
distribution is in a hot tropical area,
this species will grow in intermediate
conditions. **ZONE 12. I–H.**

Dockrillia wassellii

DRACULA LUER

This genus is closely allied to *Masdevallia*. It comprises about 90 species that are found in the moist forests from Mexico to Peru—their greatest diversity is in Colombia and Ecuador. They have thin leaves with a distinct mid-rib on short stems. The large and colorful flowers are produced on long stems low on the leaf stem. These are often sharply pendulous.

CULTIVATION

These plants require moist, shady conditions in a cool greenhouse. Most grow well in a well-drained mix in hanging baskets, which allows the inflorescence to emerge from the bottom of the basket.

Dracula bella

Dracula bella (RCHB.F.) LUER

This species is restricted to the Western Cordillera of Colombia at altitudes between 6000 and 8300 ft (1800 and 2500 m). It is a large, densely tufted epiphyte with stout stems to about 1¼ in (3 cm) long. The erect leaf is up to 10 in (25 cm) long. The inflorescence has a single flower borne on a descending peduncle to about 7 in (18 cm) long. The tails of the sepals are about 5½ in (13 cm) long. The flowering season is between autumn and spring. **ZONE 10. C–I.**

Dracula bendictii (RCHB.F.) LUER

This medium-sized epiphyte from the Western Cordillera of Colombia occurs at altitudes of 6000–8000 ft (1800–2400 m). The plant is tufted with stems up to about 1¼ in (3 cm) long. The erect leaf is about 7 in (18 cm) long. The inflorescence is congested with flowers, which appear successively on a raceme that is horizontal to pendulous. The tails of the sepal are up to 1¼ in (3 cm) long. Flowers appear between spring and autumn. **ZONE 10. C–I.**

Dracula bendictii

Dracula cordobae LUER

This medium to large epiphyte from Ecuador occurs in wet forests at low altitudes of 1700–2000 ft (500–600 m). The plant is densely tufted with slender stems about 1¼ in (3 cm) high. The erect leaf grows to about 10 in (25 cm) long. The inflorescence is congested with flowers that open successively. They are borne on a raceme up to about 8 in (20 cm) long. The tails of the sepals are 1¾–2¾ in (4–7 cm) long. The flowers appear during autumn and winter. **ZONE 11. I.**

Dracula ligiae LUER & ESCOBAR

This is a large, densely tufted plant from Colombia. It is believed that all the plants in cultivation are divisions of the original plant that was collected from the habitat. Its stems are up to 2 in (5 cm) tall with a leaf up to 10 in (25 cm) long. The inflorescence is loose and has a few flowers that are borne on a raceme up to 8 in (20 cm) or more in length. The tails of the sepals are shorter than those of other species in the genus, up to 1¼ in (3 cm) long. Flowering occurs during spring. **ZONE 10. C–I.**

Dracula sodiroi (SCHLTR.) LUER

This medium- to large-sized epiphyte or terrestrial species is the only *Dracula* to produce more than one flower at a time. It is endemic to Ecuador at altitudes of 6000–8000 ft (1800–2400 m). The stout and erect stems are about 2 in (5 cm) high and bear a leaf about 10 in (25 cm) long. The erect inflorescence is about 8 in (20 cm) tall and bears two or three pendulous flowers about ⅔ in (15 mm) long. These have tails about ⅘ in (2 cm) long. Flowering may occur at any time of the year. **ZONE 10. C–I.**

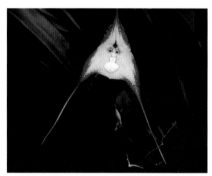

Dracula cordobae

Dracula ligiae

Dracula sodiroi

DRYADELLA LUER

This is a genus of about 40 comparatively small species distributed from Guatemala to southern Brazil. They superficially resemble *Masdevallia*. They are tufted plants with narrow, fleshy leaves. The flowers are produced either singly or successively on short racemes.

CULTIVATION

As these species are essentially plants of habitats that receive abundant moisture, in cultivation they require cool to intermediate conditions with year-round watering. They do well in small pots with a well-drained mix.

Dryadella edwallii

Dryadella simula

Dryadella edwallii (COGN.) LUER

This species occurs high in the mountains of eastern Brazil at about 4300 ft (1300 m). It grows as an epiphyte, and it is small, tufted, and up to 1½ in (3.5 cm) long and ⅛ in (3 mm) wide. The flowers are produced singly and are about 1¼ in (3 cm) across. They appear from late spring to autumn.
ZONES 10–11. C–I.

Dryadella simula (RCHB.F.)

This species is from Ecuador, Colombia, Panama, Costa Rica, Nicaragua, Honduras and Guatemala. It is a small, tufted plant with leaves about 3 in (7.5 cm) long. The flowers, about ½ in (12 mm) across, are produced singly and are often concealed by the leaves. The flowering season is from late spring to summer.
ZONES 10–11. C–I.

Dryadella zebrina (PORSCH.) LUER

The temperate region of southeast Brazil is where this species is found. The pointed leaves are stiff and about 2 in (5 cm) long. Very short spikes are produced and each of them bears a single flower about ⅔ in (15 mm) across. Many flowers are produced at one time and they appear during winter.
ZONE 10. C–I.

Dryadella zebrina

E

Elythranthera brunonis

ELYTHRANTHERA (LINDL.) A. S. GEORGE

This is a genus of two species. Both of them are endemic to southwest Australia and are remarkable for the glossy look of the inner surface of their floral segments. They are deciduous, terrestrial orchids with a solitary basal leaf that is glandular, hairy, and similar to those in *Caladenia*. They grow in open forests and woodlands from the coast to more inland areas. The plants die back during the hot summer and reappear after autumn rain.

CULTIVATION

The genus may be difficult to grow. A well-drained, sandy terrestrial mix is required.

Elythranthera brunonis
(ENDL.) A. S. GEORGE
"PURPLE ENAMEL ORCHID"

The leaf of this species grows to about 32 in (80 cm) long. The thin and wiry flower stem is about 1 ft (30 cm) tall and carries one to three flowers about 1¼ in (3 cm) across. Flowering is during spring and early summer.
ZONES 9–10. C–I

Elythranthera emarginata (LINDL.)
A. S. GEORGE

This species is similar to *E. brunonis* but it is shorter and has pinkish flowers. The leaf is up to 4 in (10 cm) long and the flower stem is about 8 in (20 cm) long. The stem bears one to four glossy flowers about 1¾ in (4 cm) broad. This species is more common in coastal and near-coastal scrubs where there is sandy soil. Flowering is during spring and early summer.
ZONE 9. C–I.

Elythranthera emarginata

EMBREEA DODSON

There is only one species in this genus and it is found in Colombia and Ecuador. These epiphytes grow in very wet cloud forests at altitudes of about 2700–3300 ft (800–1000 m). The genus is characterized by a four-angled pseudobulb with a single leaf and a pendulous, single-flowered inflorescence that is similar in appearance to that of *Stanhopea*.

CULTIVATION

These plants need intermediate conditions with abundant water year-round. They grow best in hanging baskets that allow the pendulous inflorescence to emerge through the bottom of the basket.

Embreea rodigasiana

Embreea rodigasiana (CLAES EX COGN.) DODSON

The pseudobulbs of this species are about 3 in (7.5 cm) tall, and are densely clustered with a single leaf up to about 18 in (45 cm) long and 6 in (15 cm) broad. The flower is about 5¹/₂ in (13 cm) across. Flowering is from summer to autumn. **ZONES 10–11. I.**

E

Encyclia adenocaula

Encyclia adenocaula

(LA LLAVE & LEX.) SCHLTR.

syn: *E. nemoralis* (LINDL.) SCHLTR., *Epidendrum adenocaulum* LA LLAVE & LEX.

This well-known species occurs naturally in Mexico's oak and pine forests at altitudes of 3300–6700 ft (1000–2000 m), where there is a distinct dry season. Its pseudobulbs are clustered, ovoid in shape, and up to 3¼ in (8 cm) long. They produce two or three long, narrow leaves at the apex. The branched inflorescence, up to 40 in (1 m) long, bears many fragrant, long-lasting flowers, each about 4 in (10 cm) across. Flowering is during summer.
ZONES 10–11. I–H.

ENCYCLIA HOOK.

This genus of about 250 epiphytic or lithophytic species is most abundant in Central America and the West Indian islands. It also extends to Florida in the USA and some of the species occur in tropical South America. Most species occur in seasonally dry forests below the 3300-ft (1000-m) altitude. The pseudobulbs produce a few fleshy leaves near the apex. The inflorescences arise from the stem apex and are simple or branched. Many of these plants have showy, but rather small flowers with a lip adnate to the column at the base. These species were regarded as part of *Epidendrum* until the latter part of the twentieth century, and there is considerable confusion around the identification of many of them.

CULTIVATION

Intermediate conditions are best for this genus. Most of its species should be allowed a watering rest period after the new growths have matured—water heavily when in growth. These plants are suited to pots or shallow pans containing a standard, well-drained epiphytic mix. Slabs are equally successful. Bright light similar to that required by *Cattleya* species is best.

Encyclia alata

Encyclia alata (BATEMAN) SCHLTR.

syn: several names, including *Epidendrum alatum* BATEMAN

This species occurs from Mexico to Costa Rica. It grows in semi-deciduous forests below a 3300-ft (1000-m) altitude. Its pseudobulbs are clustered, up to 4¾ in (12 cm) long, and produce two to three straplike leaves up to 20 in (50 cm) long. The branched inflorescence, up to 80 in (2 m) long, bears numerous flowers that have a spicy fragrance. Each flower measures up to 2½ in (6 cm) across, and these appear from spring to autumn. **ZONES 11–12. I–H.**

Encyclia ambigua

Encyclia bractescens

Encyclia ambigua (LINDL.) SCHLTR.
syn: *Epidendrum ambiguum* LINDL., *E. trachychilum* LINDL.

This species occurs in southern Mexico, Belize, Guatemala, and Honduras. It grows at altitudes of 3300–5000 ft (1000–1500 m) in dry oak forests. The pseudobulbs are clustered, ovoid in shape, and up to 3¼ in (8 cm) long. They produce two or three straplike leaves about 1 ft (30 cm) long. The inflorescence is 32 in (80 cm) long and is branched with a few to many fragrant flowers, each about 1¾ in (4 cm) across. Flowering occurs during summer. **ZONES 10–12. I–H.**

Encyclia atrorubens (ROLFE) SCHLTR.
syn: *E. diota* **var.** *atrorubens* (ROLFE) DRESSLER & POLLARD

This species grows in oak forests in Mexico at altitudes of about 4000 ft (1200 m). The pseudobulbs are clustered, conical to almost spherical in shape, with a diameter of about 2 in (5 cm). They produce one or two narrow leaves up to 1 ft (30 cm) long. The branched inflorescence, up to about 40 in (1 m) long, bears many flowers, each 1¼–1¾ in (3–4 cm) across. Flowering is during summer. **ZONES 10–11. I.**

Encyclia atrorubens

Encyclia bractescens
(LINDL.) HOEHNE
syn: *Epidendrum bractescens* LINDL., *E. linearifolium* HOOKER

This species from Mexico, Guatemala, and Honduras grows in rather dry oak forests below an altitude of 4000 ft (1200 m). Its small pseudobulbs are ovoid in shape, about 1¼ in (3 cm) tall, and produce two or three narrow straplike leaves up to 8 in (20 cm) long. The 10-in (25-cm) long inflorescence is either unbranched or has a few branches. It bears two to 15 fragrant, long-living flowers, each about 1 in (2.5 cm) across. Flowering is during spring. **ZONE 11. I.**

E

Encyclia cordigera

Encyclia dickinsoniana

Encyclia cordigera (H. B. K.) DRESSLER
syn: numerous names, including *Epidendrum atropurpureum* WILLD. **and** *E. macrochilum* HOOKER

This most attractive species is present in many collections under the outdated label of *Epidendrum atropurpureum*. It ranges from Mexico to Colombia and Venezuela, and occurs in dry, scrubby forests from sea level to about 3000 ft (900 m). Its pseudobulbs are clustered, conical in shape, and about 4 in (10 cm) tall. There are two straplike leaves up to 16 in (40 cm) long. The inflorescence is either simple or has a few branches. It produces three to 15 flowers, each about 2¾ in (7 cm) long. These are fragrant only when grown in sunlight. The flowers appear from spring to early summer. **ZONES 11–12. I–H.**

Encyclia dichroma (LINDL.) SCHLTR.
syn: *Epidendrum dichromum* LINDL.

This species occurs in Brazil and Suriname, and grows on trees or on rocks in savanna areas, where it is in exposed situations at low to moderate altitudes. The cylindrical to conical pseudobulbs are up to 6 in (15 cm) tall. They have two or three leathery straplike leaves up to about 1 ft (30 cm) long. The inflorescences are long and branched, and bear a few to many fragrant, long-living flowers, each about 2 in (5 cm) across. Flowering is from autumn to early winter. **ZONE 11. I–H.**

Encyclia dickinsoniana (WITHNER) WITHNER
syn: *Epidendrum dickinsonianum* WITHNER

It would appear that most plants in collections labelled *Encyclia guatemalensis* are actually this species. *E. dickinsoniana* occurs from Mexico to Nicaragua in dry oak forests or tropical semi-deciduous forests at low to moderate altitudes. Its clustered pseudobulbs are ovoid to conical in shape, up to 2 in (5 cm) long, and produce two or three straplike leaves up to 1 ft (30 cm) long. The branched or unbranched inflorescence is up to 2 ft (60 cm) long. It bears a few to many flowers, each about 1 in (2.5 cm) across. Flowering occurs from spring to summer. **ZONE 11. I–H.**

Encyclia dichroma

E

Encyclia hanburyi

Encyclia megalantha

Encyclia hanburyi (LINDL.) SCHLTR.

syn: *Epidendrum hanburyi* LINDL.

This species is found in Mexico and, possibly, Guatemala. It grows on trees or, occasionally, on rocks in dry oak forests at altitudes of 4000–6000 ft (1200–1800 m). Its clustered pseudobulbs are conical to ovoid in shape, up to 3¼ in (8 cm) long, and bear one or two leaves up to 8 in (20 cm) long. The inflorescence is either simple or branched. It grows up to 40 in (1 m) long and produces up to 35 flowers, each about 1¾ in (4 cm) across. Flowering is from spring to early summer. **ZONES 10–11. I.**

Encyclia megalantha (BARB. RODR.) PORTO & BRADE

This epiphytic species from Brazil has conical pseudobulbs up to 4 in (10 cm) tall with two straplike leaves about 20 in (50 cm) long. The branched inflorescence produces many flowers, each about 2 in (5 cm) across. It is related to *E. hanburyi* but it has larger flowers with a white lip that is heavily veined with red. **ZONE 11. I–H.**

Encyclia mooreana (ROLFE) SCHLTR.

syn: *Epidendrum mooreana* ROLFE, *E oncidioides* **var.** *mooreana* (ROLFE) AMES, HUBBARD & SCHWEINF.

This is an epiphytic species from Nicaragua, El Salvador, Costa Rica, and Panama. It has attractive, colorful, and fragrant flowers that are about 1¼ in (3 cm) across. These are produced from a large, branched inflorescence. **ZONE 11. I–H.**

Encyclia mooreana

E

Encyclia nematocaulon (A. RICH.) ACUNA
syn: *Epidendrum nematocaulon* A. RICH.,
E. xipheres RCHB.F.

Better known by its synonym *E. xipheres*, this
species is found in the Bahamas, Cuba,
Guatemala, Honduras, El Salvador, and
Mexico. It grows in lowlands in dry scrub
and tropical deciduous forests. The clustered
pseudobulbs are conical and are about 1¼ in
(3 cm) tall. Each produces one narrow leaf
up to 10 in (25 cm) long. The inflorescence
is simple or branched and bears four to 14
flowers, each about 1¼ in (3 cm) across.
Flowering is during spring. **ZONE 12. H.**

Encyclia nematocaulon

Encyclia oncidioides (LINDL.) SCHLTR.
syn: *Epidendrum oncidioides* LINDL., *Encyclia
vellozoana* PABST

There is some confusion between this species
and other similar species that are found in
the northern part of South America. This one
grows at low to moderate altitudes. Its conical
to ovoid pseudobulbs are up to 2½ in (6 cm)
tall, and they produce two to three straplike leaves up to
20 in (50 cm) long. The inflorescence grows up to 60 in
(1.5 m) long and bears numerous flowers, each about
1¼–1¾ in (3–4 cm) across. The flowers appear from
late spring to early summer. **ZONES 10–12. I–H.**

Encyclia oncidioides

Encyclia patens

Encyclia patens HOOKER
syn: several names, including *Epidendrum odoratissimum* LINDL.

This species occurs in Brazil at low to moderate altitudes.
Its elongated pseudobulbs are up to 1 ft (30 cm) long. The
leaves are long, narrow, and leathery. The inflorescence is
sparsely branched, grows a little taller than the leaves, and
bears up to 15 flowers, each about 1 in (2.5 cm) across.
These very fragrant flowers appear from late winter to
summer. **ZONES 10–12. I–H.**

E

Encyclia spatella

Encyclia polybulbon (SW.) SCHLTR

syn: *Epidendrum polybulbon* SW., *Dinema polybulbon* (SW.) LINDL.

This species occurs in Mexico, Cuba, Jamaica, Guatemala, and Honduras. It grows as an epiphyte or, occasionally, on rocks in oak or mixed forests at altitudes of 2000–6700 ft (600–2000 m). It has a creeping rhizome with pseudobulbs spaced up to 1¼ in (3 cm) apart. These are ovoid in shape and about ½ in (12 mm) high. There are two or three apical leaves up to 2 in (5 cm) long. The inflorescence consists of a solitary flower about 1¼ in (3 cm) across. These occur throughout the year. This species is easy to cultivate on a slab of tree fern or cork. **ZONES 10–11. C–I.**

Encyclia spatella (RCHB.F.) SCHLTR.

syn: *Epidendrum spatella* RCHB.F.

This species is restricted to Mexico, where it grows in oak forests, rain forests, or on lava rocks at altitudes of 2500–5000 ft (750–1500 m). Its pseudobulbs are conical and up to 2¾ in (7 cm) long, and usually produce a single straplike leaf up to 1 ft (30 cm) long. The inflorescence is branched and up to 4 ft (1.2 m) long. It bears numerous flowers, each about 1¾ in (4 cm) across. Flowering occurs during summer. **ZONES 10–11. I.**

Encyclia tampensis (LINDL.) SMALL

syn: *Epidendrum tampense* LINDL., *E. porphyrospilum* RCHB.F.
"FLORIDA BUTTERFLY ORCHID"

This species occurs in Florida in the USA as its common name suggests, where it is the most abundant epiphyte, and in the Bahamas. It grows in a variety of lowland habitats, from humid, shady swamps to dead trees under full sunlight. Its pseudobulbs are ovoid and up to 2¾ in (7 cm) tall, and produce one to three narrow leaves up to 16 in (40 cm) long. The simple or branched inflorescence is up to 32 in (80 cm) long, and has many fragrant, long-living flowers, each one about 1½ in (3.5 cm) across. Flowering occurs mostly during early summer but flowers may appear at any time of the year. **ZONES 8–10. I.**

Encyclia polybulbon

Encyclia tampensis

E

EPIDENDRUM L.

The species in this genus may be epiphytic, terrestrial, or lithophytic. There are at least 1000 species and they are found throughout the Americas, from Florida to Argentina. They grow in a range of habitats at a variety of altitudes. The majority do not form pseudobulbs—these have elongated, reedlike stems—but species with pseudobulbs are also present. The inflorescences are produced mostly from the apex, and they may be lateral, branched, or unbranched. The lip of the flower is adnate to the column for most of its length. This genus is still subject to frequent name changes and it is often hard to know which name to use for certain species.

Epidendrum amphistomum

CULTIVATION

The varied conditions under which these species grow in nature make generalizations about cultivation difficult, but intermediate conditions are best for most of them. Use a well-drained mix, perhaps with some leaf litter. The species with reedlike stems may be grown in garden beds in a suitable climate. Watering should be heavy during active growth and somewhat reduced during winter when growth slows. These species have been hybridized with *Cattleya*, *Laelia*, and other related genera to form many complex hybrids.

Epidendrum catillus

Epidendrum amphistomum A. RICHARD

This large epiphyte from Florida in the USA and the Caribbean was previously known under the two names *E. anceps* and *E. secundum*. There remains some debate over the correct name for the Florida population. This species grows at low altitudes in humid environments. It forms dense clumps of slender, leafy stems that are over 40 in (1 m) tall. The leaves, up to 6 in (15 cm) long, are in two ranks. The inflorescence consists of many flowers, each about $1/3$–$4/5$ in (1–2 cm) across, which vary in color from yellow-green to purple. Flowering is throughout the year with an emphasis on late summer. Each inflorescence produces flowers over several years. **ZONES 10–12. I–H.**

Epidendrum catillus
RCHB.F. & WARSZ.

syn: *E. vinosum* SCHLTR.

This epiphyte occurs at altitudes of 2500–5300 ft (750–1600 m). It grows in savanna woodlands and mountain forests in Peru, Ecuador, and Colombia. It is a variable species that may be anywhere from $7^{2}/_{3}$ in to over 40 in (19 cm to over 1 m) tall. The stems have leaves on the apical part and the lower parts of the stems are covered with leaf sheath bases. The leaves are in two rows about $2^{3}/_{4}$ in (7 cm) long and $1^{1}/_{4}$ in (3 cm) wide. The inflorescence is simple or branched with few to many flowers, each about $1^{1}/_{4}$ in (3 cm) across. **ZONES 10–11. I.**

Epidendrum ciliare

Epidendrum ciliare L.

This species ranges from southern Mexico to the northern part of South America. It grows on trees or on rocks, often in full sun, at low to moderate altitudes. The pseudobulbs are cylindrical or cigar-shaped, up to 8 in (20 cm) long, and have one to three leathery, oblong leaves up to 10 in (25 cm) long. The inflorescence arises from the apex of each pseudobulb and has a few to many fragrant, star-shaped flowers, each one up to 4 in (10 cm) across. Flowering is from autumn to spring, and flowers often appear more than once a year. In a collection this species should be grown with *Cattleya* species. **ZONES 10–12. I–H.**

Epidendrum conopseum R. BR.
"GREENFLY ORCHID"

The common name for this species indicates the flower's shape —like an insect. This is the most northerly epiphytic orchid of the USA, extending from northern Florida to North Carolina. It

Epidendrum conopseum

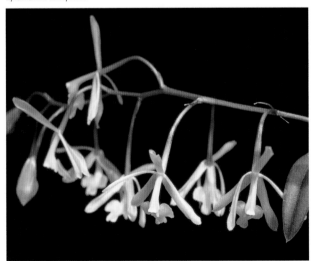

is also found in eastern Mexico. This species is inconspicuous and lives on the large limbs of deciduous trees along with resurrection ferns (*Polypodium*). Its leafy stems are up to 1 ft (30 cm) tall. The inflorescence bears up to 18 flowers, each about 1 in (2.5 cm) in diameter. **ZONES 8–9. I.**

E

E

Epidendrum coriifolium

Epidendrum coriifolium
LINDL.

This species is restricted to Guatemala, although similar species that occur south to Peru are sometimes regarded as part of this species. It grows on trees or rocks at low to moderate altitudes. Its stout stems form dense clumps up to 20 in (50 cm) tall. The leathery leaves are grouped near the apex of the stems and are up to 10 in (25 cm) long and 2 in (5 cm) wide. The inflorescences are up to 10 in (25 cm) tall with numerous flowers, each about 1¼ in (3 cm) across. These are usually presented on one side of the inflorescence on large floral bracts about as long as the flowers. Flowering is from autumn to winter.
ZONES 10–12. I–H.

Epidendrum coronatum
RUIZ & PAVON

syn: *E. amazonicum* SCHLTR., *E. moyobambae* KRAENZL.

Epidendrum coronatum

This widespread species grows in lowlands from Mexico to Peru. Its long, slender stems are up to 3 ft (90 cm) long and have leaves along most of their lengths. These leaves are elliptical, about 6 in (15 cm) long and 1¾ in (4 cm) across. The inflorescence, up to 16 in (40 cm) long, is pendulous and bears many flowers, each 1¼–1¾ in (3–4 cm) across. **ZONES 11–12. H.**

E

Epidendrum densiflorum

Epidendrum denticulatum

Epidendrum densiflorum
HOOKER

This species is closely related to E. *paniculatum* and is considered part of that species by some authorities. It occurs in Central America and grows on trees. Its stems, up to 32 in (80 cm) tall, are canelike and have leaves all along their lengths. The leaves are up to 6 in (15 cm) long and 2 in (5 cm) wide. The terminal inflorescence is branched with numerous flowers, each about ⅔ in (15 mm) across. Flowers appear during spring or autumn. **ZONES 10–12. I–H.**

Epidendrum denticulatum BARB. RODR.

This variable species is found in the mountains of eastern Brazil. It grows as a terrestrial in dry scrubs under full sun at altitudes above 3300 ft (1000 m). The reedlike stems may be up to 40 in (1 m) in length and have ten to 16 leaves. The thick and leathery leaves are up to 3⅔ in (9 cm) long. An apical inflorescence may bear as many as 100 flowers and these may come in several color forms—pink, orange, white, yellow, and cream. The flowers appear from winter through to the following autumn. **ZONES 10–11. I.**

Epidendrum diffusum SW.

This species ranges from Mexico and the West Indies to the northern part of South America. It grows as an epiphyte or lithophyte in open forests at low to moderate altitudes. Its slender stems are up to 1 ft (30 cm) tall and have leaves on the upper half. These leaves are often purple-red in color and are up to 3 in (7.5 cm) long. The erect or arching inflorescence is sometimes branched and has many flowers, each about ⅓ in (1 cm) across. Flowering is from summer to autumn. **ZONES 11–12. I–H.**

Epidendrum diffusum

E

Epidendrum ilense

Epidendrum ilense DODSON

This strange-looking species grows in lowlands in Ecuador, where the conditions are hot and humid. Its inflorescences hang from the tall, slender stems and bear bunches of a few, rather large flowers. These are produced successively over several years. This species is considered endangered in its natural habitat as the areas have been heavily cleared; however, it is firmly established in cultivation. **ZONE 12. H.**

Epidendrum longipetalum
A. RICH. & GALEOTTI

The long, hanging petals give rise to the name of this unusual species from Mexico. It grows in wind-swept cloud forests at moderate to high altitudes. The elong-ated inflorescence bears flowers in succession, so the flowering period lasts for several months. **ZONES 9–11. C–I.**

Epidendrum longipetalum

Epidendrum marmoratum

Epidendrum nocturnum

Epidendrum marmoratum JACQ.

This attractive species is endemic to Mexico, where it grows at moderate altitudes in the southern sierras. The species is unusual for the genus as it has pseudobulbs. Several flowers are produced on an arching or pendulous inflorescence. The flowers are about 1¼ in (3 cm) across. **ZONES 10–11. I.**

Epidendrum nutans

Epidendrum nocturnum JACQ.

The flowers of this species have a strong, pungent fragrance which is produced at night. It occurs from Florida in the USA through the West Indies and Central and South America to Bolivia. It grows in a range of habitats from lowlands to moderate altitudes and from humid forests to dry savannas. The erect, leafy stems are 40 in (1 m) or more tall. The flowers are borne one or two at a time at the end of a short inflorescence. The size of the flowers is variable—they may be 2–4 in (5–10 cm) across, but sometimes they do not open widely. Flowering is throughout the year but takes place most often during summer and autumn. **ZONES 10–12. I–H.**

Epidendrum nutans RUIZ. & PAVON

This species is endemic to Jamaica, where it grows as an epiphyte or lithophyte. It has reedlike stems, about 8 in (20 cm) long. The leaves are about 7⅔ in (19 cm) long and 2 in (5 cm) wide. The fragrant flowers are borne on a pendulous inflorescence and are about 1¾ in (4 cm) wide. Flowering is from autumn through to spring. Because this species may become quite large, it is best planted in a pot with a free-draining mix. **ZONE 12. I–H.**

E

Epidendrum parkinsonianum HOOKER

This is a common epiphytic species ranging from Mexico to Panama. It grows in shady, mixed forests at low to moderate altitudes. Its pendulous stems form hanging clumps up to 80 in (2 m) or more long. The leaves are narrow, almost terete, and fleshy, and are up to 20 in (50 cm) long. The large, fragrant flowers are 6 in (15 cm) or more across. They usually appear one or two at a time on a short inflorescence and are long-living. The flowers appear mostly during summer and autumn.
ZONES 10–11. I.

Epidendrum parkinsonianum

Epidendrum pseudepidendrum RCHB.F.
syn: *Pseudepidendrum spectabile* RCHB.F.

This species occurs in Costa Rica and western Panama, where it grows on trees at low altitudes. Its tall, slender stems are clustered and may be up to about 40 in (1 m) tall. The stems have narrow leaves, up to 8 in (20 cm) long, on their upper halves. One to a few inflorescences bear one to three flowers, up to 2¾ in (7 cm) long. These flowers are glossy and waxy and this, along with the unusual color combinations, creates a spectacular-looking plant. Flowering is during summer and autumn. These plants are now rare in their natural habitat due to over-collection, but because they may be raised from seeds they are freely available in cultivation. **ZONES 11–12. I–H.**

Epidendrum pseudepidendrum

Epidendrum revolutum BAR. RODR.

This is a typical reedlike-stem *Epidendrum*. It is endemic to Brazil, near Rio de Janeiro, where it grows in the lowlands. The stems are up to 2 ft (60 cm) tall with leaves up to about 4¾ in (12 cm) long and 1 in (2.5 cm) wide. The inflorescence is produced from the top of the stems. It is pendulous and carries ten to 13 well-spaced flowers. These are about 1¾ in (4 cm) across and sweetly fragrant. Flowering is during winter. Because of the tall growth habit of this species, it is best to plant it in a tall pot with a coarse, well-drained mix. It prefers hot temperatures and watering should be maintained year-round. **ZONES 11–12. I–H.**

Epidendrum revolutum

Epidendrum rigidum JACQ.

This widespread species ranges from Florida through Central and South America to Brazil and Peru. It grows as an epiphyte in rain forests at low to moderate altitudes. The creeping, branching stems form large straggling mats, and are about 8 in (20 cm) long. The leaves are 3¼ in (8 cm) long and ⅓–⅘ in (1–2 cm) wide on the upper parts. The erect inflorescences bear few to many flowers, each about ⅓ in (1 cm) across. These are almost hidden by large floral bracts. Flowers appear throughout the year, but occur most often during winter and spring. This species is best grown on a slab. **ZONES 10–12. I–H.**

E

Epidendrum rigidum

Epidendrum schomburgkii

Epidendrum schomburgkii LINDL.

This species has been reported from Brazil and Guyana and other localities in South America. It has reedlike stems up to about 30 in (75 cm) long with fleshy leaves along their lengths in two ranks. The leaves are about 4 in (10 cm) in length. The long inflorescence bears flowers at its end, forming a dense head. The flowers are about 1¾ in (4 cm) across. **ZONES 10–11. I.**

Epidendrum secundum JACQ.

syn. many names, including the well-known
E. anceps JACQ.

This large epiphyte ranges from Central America to the northern region of South America. It forms dense clumps of slender, leafy stems to over 40 in (1 m) tall. The leaves, up to 6 in (15 cm) long, are in two ranks. The inflorescence consists of many flowers, each about ⅓–⅘ in (1–2 cm) across. These vary in color from yellow-green to purple. Flowering is throughout the year with an emphasis on late summer. Each inflorescence produces flowers over several years. **ZONES 11–12. I–H.**

Epidendrum secundum

Epidendrum stamfordianum

Epidendrum stamfordianum BATEMAN

This species occurs from Mexico to Panama, Colombia, and Venezuela. It grows at low altitudes in open forests and coffee plantations, in areas with a distinct dry season. The plants have pseudobulbs to about 10 in (25 cm) tall with two to four leathery, ovate leaves up to 5⅔ in (14 cm) long. The inflorescence arises from the basal rhizome and is often branched. It bears many fragrant, long-lasting flowers, each about 1¾ in (4 cm) long. Pink forms are known as well as the normal white and yellow form. Flowering is from winter to spring. **ZONES 11–12. I–H.**

E

Epigeneium amplum

Epigeneium amplum

(LINDL.) SUMMERH.

syn: *Dendrobium amplum* LINDL.,
Sarcopodium amplum (LINDL.) LINDL.,
Katherinea ampla (LINDL.) A. D. HAWKES

Sometimes considered
synonymous with *Epigeneium
coelogyne*, this species occurs
from India to Thailand. It is
found at an altitude of about
5000 ft (1500 m). The
pseudobulbs are 1¼–2 in
(3–5 cm) long, and they are
borne 4–6 in (10–15 cm)
apart on the rhizome. There
are two leaves about 4–6 in
(10–15 cm) long. The single
flower is about 2¾ in (7 cm)
across. Flowering is during
winter. **ZONES 9–10. I.**

EPIGENEIUM GAGNEP.

This genus has often been included in *Dendrobium* or described
as the genus *Sarcopodium*. It comprises about 35 species
distributed from India, China, Taiwan, and Thailand to Borneo,
Indonesia, and the Philippines. The species are mostly epiphytes
that occur in mountain rain forests. They prefer to grow high in
trees where there is bright light. The pseudobulbs are usually
short and often angular on elongated rhizomes with one or two
(occasionally three) leathery leaves. The inflorescences consist
of one or more large, showy, long-lasting flowers that appear
between the leaves. The lip of the flowers is prominently three-
lobed, and there is a short mentum.

E

CULTIVATION

The widely spaced pseudobulbs and rambling habit of many of
these species make it difficult to confine them in a conventional
pot. Baskets or shallow pans with an open epiphyte mix are
best. They should be kept moist all year in a humid, hot
environment. Care should be taken to avoid stale compost
through poor drainage.

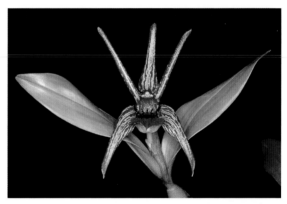

Epigeneium coelogyne

Epigeneium coelogyne (RCHB.F.) SUMMERH.

syn: *Dendrobium coelogyne* RCHB.F., *Sarcopodium coelogyne* (RCHB.F.) ROLFE,
Katherinea coelogyne (RCHB.F.) A. D. HAWKES

This species from Myanmar and Thailand is a rambling epiphyte
that occurs at an altitude of about 4700 ft (1400 m). The
elongated rhizome is clothed in scales and its pseudobulbs,
which are four-angled, are borne at considerable distances from
each other. They are about 2⅔ in (6.5 cm) tall and are topped
by two glossy, leathery leaves up to about 4 in (10 cm) long.
The single-flowered inflorescence arises between these two
leaves. The large flowers are about 4 in (10 cm) in diameter.
These heavily textured and fragrant flowers are produced in late
autumn and early winter and last for a short time. **ZONES 9–10. I.**

E

Epigeneium nakaharaei

Epigeneium nakaharaei (SCHLTR.) SUMMERH.
syn: *Dendrobium nakaharaei* SCHLTR.

This miniature species is found in the central mountain range of Taiwan, at altitudes of about 2700–8000 ft (800–2400 m). It is epiphytic and grows in moist, semi-shade conditions on large trees. The many-angled pseudobulbs are borne on a creeping rhizome and are spaced closely together. They are about 1 in (2.5 cm) tall and have a single terminal leaf, about 1½ in (3.5 cm) long and ⅓ in (1 cm) broad. The solitary flower at the apex of the pseudobulbs is about 1 in (2.5 cm) across. Flowering is during autumn and lasts for a short time. **ZONES 9–11. I–H.**

Epigeneium treacherianum

Epigeneium triflorum

Epigeneium treacherianum (RCHB.F. EX HOOK.F.) SUMMERH.
syn: *Dendrobium treacherianum* RCHB.F. EX HOOK.F., *Sarcopodium treacherianum* (RCHB.F. EX HOOK.F.) ROLFE, *Katherinea treacheriana* (RCHB.F. EX HOOK.F.) A. D. HAWKES

This colorful species is found in Asia, on the island of Borneo and in the Philippines. It grows at low altitudes in the crowns of large trees where moisture and humidity are in abundance. It is epiphytic and has a stout, creeping rhizome with crowded pseudobulbs, about 1¼–3¼ in (3–8 cm) long, that have four to six prominent angles. The two stiff, leathery leaves are up to 4 in (10 cm) long and 1¼ in (3 cm) broad. The inflorescence is 4–6 in (10–15 cm) long and carries up to seven flowers, each 1¼–1¾ in (3–4 cm) in diameter. The flowers are produced during summer and have a fragrance similar to that of desiccated coconut. **ZONE 12. H.**

Epigeneium triflorum (BLUME) SUMMERH.
syn: *Desmotrichum triflorum* BLUME, *Dendrobium triflorum* (BLUME) LINDL., *D. elongatum* LINDL. **var.** *orientale* J. J. SM.

This species and its varieties are restricted to the island of Java in Indonesia. The variety *orientale* (shown here) is common in the mountains in the east and center of the island at altitudes of 3300–6000 ft (1000–1800 m). It forms large clumps on branches where there is strong light. The pseudobulbs, about 1¾ in (4 cm) long and ⅔ in (15 mm) wide, are spaced about 2½–3¼ in (6–8 cm) apart. The leaves are about 8–12 in (20–30 cm) long and ⅘ in (2 cm) wide. The pendulous inflorescence bears six to 17 flowers, each about ⅘–1¼ in (2–3 cm) across. **ZONES 9–11. I.**

EPIPACTIS ZINN
"HELLEBORINES"

This genus of about 35 species extends south from Europe to Ethiopia, and across the northern parts of the Asian continent and Japan to North America. The plants are terrestrial, usually grow in wet habitats, and have fleshy rhizomes and leafy stems, often to 40 in (1 m) tall. The terminal inflorescence bears a few to several colorful flowers, which may be up to 2 in (5 cm) across.

CULTIVATION

These species may be grown in a bed or rock garden containing leaf mold and peat, and either in the sun or under shade. The soil must be alkaline and wet, especially during the growing season. The plants are frost-hardy, and should be kept moist throughout the year. To propagate, divide the plants during spring.

Epipactis albensis NOVAKOVA & RYDLO
"RIVER ELBE HELLEBORINE"

This rare, slender species was described as a separate species in 1967. It is restricted to eastern Germany and the west of the Czech Republic. It grows in acidic, moist soil in very shady, deciduous forests in the river valleys of the Elbe, Moldau, March, and other small streams at low altitudes. The stem is 4–12 in (10–30 cm) tall with three to five lanceolate leaves, 1¼–2½ in (3–6 cm) long and ⅓–⅘ in (1–2 cm) wide at the basal part. The inflorescence has three to 15 self-pollinating flowers with a diameter of nearly ½ in (12 mm). These hang down like small bells and appear from mid summer to autumn.
ZONES 6–7. C–I.

Epipactis albensis

Epipactis gigantea

Epipactis gigantea DOUGLAS EX HOOK
"GIANT HELLEBORINE"

This species gets its botanical name because the plant and its flowers are relatively large compared with other species in the genus. Its distribution is the subalpine regions of northwest America, from southern Canada to Mexico. It grows in open, wet places such as on sandbars of streams or gravelly shores. The stem, up to 40 in (1 m) tall, carries five to ten ovate to lanceolate, plicate leaves on its lower part and five to 15 colorful flowers on the upper part. The flowers have a diameter of 1¾–2 in (4–5 cm) and appear from March to August. "Serpentine night" is an especially attractive cultivar of this species.
ZONES 6–10. C–I.

E

Epipactis helleborine (L.) CRANTZ
"BROAD-LEAVED HELLEBORINE"

This is the most common and widespread orchid in Europe —its distribution includes all of Europe and northwest Africa, and it has been introduced to northeast America. It grows in light, deciduous as well as coniferous forests, shrublands, or wood meadows from sea level to more than 8300 ft (2500 m). The stem is 8–28 in (20–70 cm) long. It has five to nine large, egg-shaped leaves about 2½–4¾ in (6–12 cm) wide. Its many-flowered inflorescence is conspicuously bent below the flowers. The flowers are about ⅔–⅘ in (1.5–2 cm) across, and vary in color from greenish to reddish. The flowering period is during summer.
ZONES 5–10. C–I.

Epipactis helleborine

Epipactis mairei SCHLTR.
"MAIRE'S HELLEBORINE"

The distribution of this robust species is restricted to the central and southwest regions of China. It is found at altitudes of 4000–10,700 ft (1200–3200 m) growing in open areas on grassy, stony slopes or, sometimes, wet meadows. The stems, up to 12–28 in (30–70 cm) long, have brown hairs on their apical half. There are five to eight broad and conspicuously ribbed leaves on the lower part of the stem. The loose-flowered inflorescence carries up to 40 flowers, each with a diameter of about 1¼ in (3 cm). The flowering period is during summer.
ZONES 7–8. C.

Epipactis mairei

Epipactis microphylla

Epipactis microphylla (EHRH.) SW.
"SMALL-LEAVED HELLEBORINE"

This is one of the most slender plants in the genus. It is found in southern Europe—from eastern Spain to Greece and Turkey—and some of the mountainous regions in the middle of Europe, namely from France to Hungary. Although it is widespread it is not common. It grows in shaded woods, mostly on limestone, from sea level to 5700 ft (1700 m). It has gray-green, small leaves about ⅘–1¾ in (2–4 cm) long and ¼–⅘ in (6 mm–2 cm) wide. The stem, 6–14 in (15–35 cm) tall, is hairy and its height includes the length of the inflorescence, which bears five to 20 flowers. The greenish to purplish flowers are ⅓ in (1 cm) across. Flowering is during summer. **ZONES 7–10. C–I.**

E

Epipactis palustris

Epipactis purpurata

Epipactis palustris (L.) CRANTZ
"MARSH HELLEBORINE"

The distribution of this species is over much of
Europe, except in the most southern and
northern regions, and as far east as Iran. It
grows in alkaline soils in wet conditions, such
as marshes, from sea level to 6700 ft (2000 m).
This plant sometimes forms large colonies. Its
stems are 6–10 in (15–25 cm) tall and arise
from a branched, underground rhizome. About
five to 20 attractive flowers, each about ⅔ in
(15 mm) across, are carried loosely on the
inflorescence. The flowers are usually
pollinated by bees, but other insects, such as
ants, have also been recorded as participants
in the process. Flowering is during summer.
ZONES 5–9. C–I.

Epipactis purpurata SM.
"VIOLET HELLEBORINE"

This is one of the largest flowering species in
Europe. Its distribution is restricted to the west
and middle of the continent, particularly in
southern England, northern France, and
southern Germany. It grows on limestone in
shady, deciduous or coniferous forests, and
forms colonies of up to 20 plants, each one
10–30 in (25–75 cm) tall. Its stems have a violet
tinge and are covered with gray hairs. The six
to ten grayish-green, purple-tinged, small leaves
are arranged in a spiral-like pattern along the
stem. The flowers are almost ⅘ in (2 cm) across
and are pollinated by wasps. This species comes
into bloom during late summer or even early
autumn. **ZONES 6–9. C–I.**

ERIA LINDL.

This genus includes some 370 species. It is predominantly from tropical lowlands, ranging from India to the Pacific Islands. It is a diverse group in terms of plant form—it includes small, tufted plants, creeping plants, and large, robust species with swollen pseudobulbs. Most of the species have several leaves; a few have a single leaf. In addition, some plants have a slender, elongated leafy stem 40 in (1 m) or more in length. The flowers may be borne singly or in long or short racemes, and are either terminal or lateral. The distinguishing features of the genus are the eight pollinia and the lip, which is often, but not always, three-lobed, and is mounted on a column foot that usually forms a mentum but never a spur.

CULTIVATION

Many of these plants are extremely attractive when in flower and are easy to grow. It is surprising, therefore, that they are not more common in cultivation. The majority are lowland plants requiring hot temperatures and high humidity, although a few are from higher altitudes. Most thrive best in bright light with year-round watering. They do equally well in pots, hanging baskets, or on slabs. If grown in pots, the medium should be well-drained, but a small amount of moisture-retaining ingredient, such as moss, may be added.

Eria amica RCHB.F.
syn: *E. hypomelana* HAYATA

This species occurs from northeast India and Nepal to the Yunnan province in China and Indochina. It grows on trees at an altitude of 3000–7300 ft (900–2200 m). Its pseudobulbs are more or less cylindrical or ovoid, are spaced closely together, and grow to about 4 in (10 cm) long. They have one to three leaves about 4–6 in (10–15 cm) long. The erect inflorescences arise from the middle or upper part of the stem and have about six to ten loosely packed flowers, each about $\frac{2}{3}$ in (15 mm) across. Flowering is reported during spring. **ZONES 9–11. C–I.**

Eria amica

Eria aporoides LINDL.
syn: *Dendrobium aporoides* (LINDL.) MERR.

This species is restricted to the Philippines, where it grows at low to moderate altitudes as an epiphyte or lithophyte. The stems reach about 10 in (25 cm) long. These are covered with overlapping fleshy leaves, about 1 in (2.5 cm) long, in two ranks. The flowers are about $\frac{1}{3}$ in (1 cm) across and are borne singly on a short inflorescence with four large, orange bracts at its base. The flowers last for about three days and appear throughout the year. **ZONES 11–12. I–H.**

Eria aporoides

E

Eria biflora

Eria biflora GRIFF.

syn: *E. choneana* KRAENZL.

This species occurs at moderate altitudes between India and Borneo, including Indochina, Sumatra, and Java. The pseudobulbs are swollen at the apex, about 6 in (15 cm) long, and have up to five leaves. The inflorescences are extremely short with two or three flowers that do not open widely. These are less than ⅓ in (1 cm) across. Flowering is during autumn. **ZONES 10–11. I–H.**

Eria bractescens

Eria bractescens LINDL.

This species is widely distributed at low altitudes from India and Nepal to Indonesia, New Guinea, the Philippines, and China. Its egg-shaped or cylindrical pseudobulbs, up to 4 in (10 cm) long and 1¼ in (3 cm) wide, have two leaves up to about 8 in (20 cm) long. The inflorescences arise from the apical part of the pseudobulbs and comprise five to 15 flowers, each almost ⅘ in (2 cm) across. The flowers last for about a week. Flowering is during summer. **ZONES 11–12. H.**

Eria fitzalanii F. MUELL.

syn: *E. solomonensis* ROLFE

This species occurs in New Guinea, the Solomon Islands, and northeast Australia. It grows in low-altitude rain forests or open forests under partly shaded or brightly lit conditions. The pseudobulbs are ovoid or elongated, 2–6 in (5–15 cm) long, and covered with brown bracts. There are two to four straplike leaves. The inflorescences are up to 4 in (10 cm) long and bear up to 50 flowers, each less than ⅓ in (1 cm) across. Flowering is during spring and lasts for a few days. **ZONES 11–12. H.**

Eria fitzalanii

E

Eria hyacinthoides

Eria hyacinthoides (BLUME) LINDL.
syn: *E. ebulbe* (BLUME) LINDL.

This epiphyte or lithophyte is an abundant
species on the Malay Peninsula and the islands
of Sumatra, Java, and Borneo. It grows at low
to moderate altitudes. Its conical pseudobulbs
are 2½–4 in (6–10 cm) tall with three leaves
about 10–16 in (25–40 cm) long. The upright
inflorescences bear 30 to 40 flowers, each
about ⅔ in (15 mm) across. Flowering is
during spring. **ZONES 10–12. I–H.**

Eria javanica (SW.) BLUME
syn: several names, including *E. fragrans* RCHB.F.,
E. stellata LINDL.

This widespread species is known from India
to the Malay Peninsula, Indonesia, New
Guinea, and the Philippines. It grows from sea
level to 4000 ft (1200 m). The pseudobulbs, up
to 4¾ in (12 cm) long and ⅘ in (2 cm) wide,
have one or two leaves with a length of about
8–12 in (20–30 cm). The erect inflorescences
are up to 2 ft (60 cm) long and bear numerous
star-shaped and fragrant flowers, each 1–2 in
(2.5–5 cm) across. Flowering is mostly during
spring. **ZONES 10–12. I–H.**

Eria javanica

Eria kenejiana SCHLTR.

This is a little-known species from the upper
Ramu area in Papua New Guinea, where it
grows at low altitudes, often along streams.
The unbranched, brittle, cylindrical stems are
mostly around 2 ft (60 cm) long, but some are
up to 40 in (1 m). The flowers, about ⅔ in
(15 mm) long, are borne laterally from the leaf
axils. There is a prominent group of about five
reflexed bracts, each about ⅓ in (1 cm) long, at
the base of the pedicel. After fertilization, the
ovary rapidly grows from about ⅔ in (15 mm)
to about 2½ in (6 cm) long. The flowers last
for about a week and appear throughout the
year. **ZONES 11–12. H.**

Eria kenejiana

Eria kingii

Eria ornata

Eria kingii F. MUELL.

syn: *E. inornata* T. E. HUNT, *E. hollandiae* J. J. SM.

This robust species occurs from Ambon in Indonesia through New Guinea and northeast Australia to the Solomon Islands. It grows at low altitudes and forms large clumps in rain forest trees or on rocks. The ovoid pseudobulbs are up to 10 in (25 cm) long with three leaves at the apex. The inflorescences arise from the terminal part of each pseudobulb and are about 4¾–12 in (12–30 cm) long. They bear numerous flowers, each about ⅓ in (1 cm) long. Flowering is during spring and lasts for about a week. **ZONES 11–12. H.**

Eria multiflora (BLUME) LINDL.

This epiphytic species occurs in Indonesia in Sumatra, Java, and Bali. It grows at altitudes of 4700–7000 ft (1400–2100 m). The pseudobulbs, spaced about ⅓ in (1 cm) apart, are 8–12 in (20–30 cm) long with five to seven leaves about 8 in (20 cm) long. There are several cylindrical inflorescences per pseudobulb, and these arise from the upper part of the stem. They are horizontal to pendulous, and bear numerous, small pink to white flowers which are packed tightly together. **ZONES 9–11. C–I.**

Eria ornata (BLUME) LINDL.

The large, orange-red bracts are a feature of this rare species from the Malay Peninsula, Thailand, Sumatra, Java, Borneo, and Sulawesi. It grows in brightly lit situations from sea level to 4000 ft (1200 m). Its pseudobulbs, up to 4½ in (11 cm) long and 2 in (5 cm) wide, have three to five fleshy leaves about 1 ft (30 cm) long and 2½ in (6 cm) wide. The erect inflorescences are up to 18 in (45 cm) long. They bear numerous flowers, each about ⅓–⅘ in (1–2 cm) long, the sepals of which have hairy backs. The floral bracts, about 1¼ in (3 cm) long, are more obvious than the flowers. **ZONES 10–12. H.**

Eria xanthocheila RIDL.

syn: *E. wichersii* SCHLTR.

This species occurs in Myanmar, Thailand, on the Malay Peninsula, and on the islands of Sumatra, Java, and Borneo. It grows beside streams at low to moderate altitudes. Its pseudobulbs, spaced about 1 in (2.5 cm) apart on the rhizome, are up to 1 ft (30 cm) long and about ⅓ in (1 cm) wide. They have two or three leaves. The inflorescences, about 4 in (10 cm) long, are held horizontally and bear up to 18 flowers, each about ⅔ in (15 mm) across. Flowering is during summer. **ZONES 11–12. H.**

Eria multiflora

Eria xanthocheila

E

Eriochilus cucullatus

ERIOCHILUS R. BR.

This genus of about six species is endemic to Australia's temperate regions. They inhabit open forests and heathlands, and are deciduous terrestrials with a single ovate leaf. The tubers are dormant during spring and summer and appear after autumn rains.

CULTIVATION

These species require similar cultivation to that of *Caladenia*. A terrestrial mixture with leaf litter from eucalyptus forests and coarse sand is best. The plants should be kept moist while the leaf is in evidence, usually throughout winter and spring, with watering reduced during late spring and summer when the leaf dies back. The tubers may be removed and stored over the resting season and repotted when new growth is about to begin.

Eriochilus cucullatus (LABILL.) RCHB.F.

This widespread species ranges from southeast Queensland through New South Wales and Victoria to Tasmania and South Australia. It grows in a number of habitats, including subalpine regions, open forests, heathlands, and coastal scrubs. The leaf, up to 1¾ in (4 cm) long, may not be completely developed at flowering time. The thin, wiry flower stem, up to 10 in (25 cm) tall, may carry up to five flowers, each up to ⅘ in (2 cm) in diameter. Flowering is from summer to late autumn. **ZONES 8–10. C–I.**

EUANTHE SCHLTR.

This genus consists of a single species that is closely related to *Vanda* and is still considered to be part of that genus by some botanists. The major difference between the two lies in the lip, which is divided into two, rather than three as for *Vanda*.

CULTIVATION

This plant should be grown in conditions similar to those for *Vanda*. It has been used extensively to make fine hybrids with species from that genus.

Euanthe sanderiana (RCHB.F.) SCHLTR.

syn: *Vanda sanderiana* RCHB.F.

The large, colorful flowers of this species make it one of the finest horticultural orchid in the world. It grows in the lowlands, often in exposed positions near the sea, on the island of Mindanao in the Philippines. This monopodial plants is up to 40 in (1 m) tall with straplike leaves up to 16 in (40 cm) long. The erect inflorescence bears up to ten flowers, each up to 4 in (10 cm) across. Flowering is during autumn. **ZONE 12. H.**

Euanthe sanderiana

Euchile citrina

EUCHILE (DRESSLER & POLLARD) WITHNER

The two species that are known for this genus are restricted to Mexico. They are found in dry, oak forests. Both of the species have a characteristic glaucous or bluish appearance.

CULTIVATION

These plants grow best on mounts in cool to intermediate conditions with abundant water during the growing season. They benefit from drier conditions during the winter months.

Euchile citrina (LA LLAVE & LEXARGA) WITHNER

This species from the western area of Mexico grows in dry, open and cool forests at an altitude of 4300–7300 ft (1300–2200 m). Both the plant and its flowers are pendulous. Its pseudobulbs are about 2 in (5 cm) long and have two pendulous leaves up to 8 in (20 cm) long. The usually solitary flowers are borne on a stalk about 4 in (10 cm) long. The flowers grow to about 3 in (7.5 cm) long, and do not open fully, but have a sweet perfume. Flowering time is from autumn to spring. This species is best cultivated on a mount. **ZONE 10. C–I.**

Euchile mariae (AMES) WITHNER

Endemic to northeast Mexico, this species is from altitudes of about 3300–4000 ft (1000–1200 m). Its erect inflorescence is up to 8 in (20 cm) long and produces four or five flowers, each up to 3 in (7.5 cm) in diameter. Flowering is from late spring to summer. These plants may be grown mounted or in a pot with careful attention to watering during the winter months. **ZONE 10. C.**

Euchile mariae

Eulophia andamanensis

Eulophia andamanensis RCHB.F.

syn: *E. keithii* RIDL.

This species occurs on India's Andaman Islands and in Indochina. It grows in rain forests at low altitudes. Its pseudobulbs are about 4 in (10 cm) long and have about five deciduous leaves, each about 1 ft (30 cm) long and ⅓ in (1 cm) wide. The inflorescences arise from the base of the leafless pseudobulbs and are about 12–16 in (30–40 cm) long. They bear ten to 15 flowers, each about ⅔ in (15 mm) across. Flowering is during spring. **ZONES 11–12. H.**

Eulophia angolensis

(LINDL.) RCHB.F.

This species is widespread throughout tropical Africa, from the west to the east coast and south to South Africa. It grows in swamps and seasonally wet grasslands from sea level to 8300 ft (2500 m). The plants are up to 80 in (2 m) tall with a fleshy rhizome and two to four plicate leaves up to 4 ft (1.2 m) long. The inflorescence has many flowers that open progressively over a long period. Each flower grows to about 1¼ in (3 cm) long. Flowering is reported from October to December in Zambia and March to July in Kenya. **ZONES 10–12. I–H.**

EULOPHIA LINDL.

There are over 250 species in this genus distributed throughout the tropics in America, Asia, and Africa, with the majority in Africa. Almost all of them are terrestrial; some with swollen underground rhizomes and some with above-ground pseudobulbs. The leaves are long, narrow or broad, and pleated, and they are sometimes deciduous. The upright inflorescences are tall with numerous flowers. Some species have large, attractive, showy flowers.

CULTIVATION

A well-drained mixture suitable for terrestrial species is required. The plants with pseudobulbs are relatively easy to grow, but those with underground rhizomes are prone to rot if watered at the wrong time. A watering rest period is required during the cooler months, with copious watering when the plants are actively growing. Bright filtered sunlight and good air movement are also necessary, while the temperature requirements vary according to the altitude at which the plants grow in the wild.

Eulophia angolensis

Eulophia bicallosa

Eulophia fridericii

Eulophia petersii

Eulophia bicallosa (D. DON) P. HUNT & SUMMERH.
syn: *E. bicarinata* (LINDL.) HOOK.F.

This is a very widespread, but rather
uncommon species that occurs from the
foothills of the Himalayas through Southeast
Asia and the Malay Archipelago to Australia.
It grows in hot, steamy lowlands. It has a
triangular underground rhizome with a single
grasslike leaf about 16 in (40 cm) long. The
inflorescence is up to 2 ft (60 cm) tall and
bears anywhere from a few to 20 flowers, each
1¼ in (3 cm) across. Flowering is from late
winter to late spring. **ZONES 11–12. H.**

Eulophia fridericii (RCHB.F.) A. V. HALL

This species occurs across tropical Africa in
woodlands at moderate altitudes. The plants
have an underground rhizome and are up to
2 ft (60 cm) tall with leaves up to about 4¾ in
(12 cm) long and 2 in (5 cm) across. The
inflorescence is dense with many flowers, each
about ⅘ in (2 cm) long. Flowering is during
November and December in the wild.
ZONES 10–11. I.

Eulophia petersii RCHB.F.
syn: *E. caffra* RCHB.F., *E. circinnata* ROLFE

This species is widespread in eastern tropical
Africa, growing as far south as the KwaZulu
Natal province in South Africa. It is often
found among granite boulders at moderate
altitudes. It is robust, up to 80 in (2 m) tall,
and has above-ground pseudobulbs about
2½–6 in (6–15 cm) long. The leaves are up to
16 in (40 cm) long and 1¾ in (4 cm) across.
The branched inflorescence is up to 30 in
(75 cm) tall with as many as 50 flowers, each
about 1¼ in (3 cm) long. Flowering is from
late spring to mid autumn. **ZONES 10–11. I.**

Eulophia spectabilis (DENNST.) SURESH.

syn: several names, including *E. squalida* LINDL., *E. nuda* LINDL.

This widespread species occurs from India and Sri Lanka
through China, most of Southeast Asia, and the Malay
Archipelago to the Pacific Islands, as far east as Fiji and Tonga.
It is a species of lowland habitats, usually grasslands, but has
been recorded up to a 5000-ft (1500-m) altitude. Its underground rhizomes are spherical, about 1¼ in (3 cm) across, with
three or four rather broad leaves up to about 20 in (50 cm)
long. The inflorescence, about 40 in (1 m) tall, bears ten to
25 flowers, each about ⅘–1¼ in (2–3 cm) long. The color of the
flowers is variable over the species' range, with combinations of
white, purple, and brown in some areas and red or yellow in
others. Flowering in cultivation is during spring.
ZONES 10–12. I–H.

Eulophia spectabilis

Eulophia walleri

Eulophia walleri (RCHB.F.) KRAENZL.

This species is widespread in
Zaire, Tanzania, Zambia,
Malawi, Zimbabwe, and
Botswana. It grows at
moderate altitudes in
seasonally wet grasslands
and woodlands. The above-
ground pseudobulbs are
squat with grasslike leaves.
The inflorescences are up to
16 in (40 cm) tall and bear
numerous showy flowers
about 2 in (5 cm) long.
Flowering is during summer.
ZONES 9–11. I.

EULOPHIELLA ROLFE

This is a genus of about four species, all of them endemic to Madagascar. The plants are large with creeping rhizomes and long leaves. The inflorescence arises from the base of the plants and carries a number of large, colorful flowers.

CULTIVATION

These species require hot, moist conditions at all times and should not be allowed to become dry at the roots. Because of their rampant growth, large containers may be required. As these plants do not like to be disturbed, repot only when absolutely necessary.

Eulophiella roempleriana

Eulophiella roempleriana (RCHB.F.) SCHLTR.

This large, robust species is found from sea level to 3300 ft (1000 m) on Madagascar. It is restricted to the crowns of pandanus palms. Its creeping rhizome is up to 2½ in (6 cm) in diameter, and the pseudobulbs, up to 10 in (25 cm) long, grow some distance from each other. The four to eight leaves may be up to 4 ft (1.2 m) long and 4 in (10 cm) wide. The inflorescence may be branched and reaches up to 6 ft (1.8 m) in height. It carries up to 30 flowers that open successively over a long period. These are waxy, fragrant and up to 4 in (10 cm) across. Flowering is mostly during spring. **ZONE 11. I–H.**

EURYCHONE SCHLTR.

The two species in this genus are known from
tropical Africa, where they occur in rain forests
at low to moderate altitudes. While these
plants are quite small, the flowers are relatively
large. Cultivation is as for *Angraecum*, to
which these monopodial orchids are related.

E

Eurychone rothschildiana

Eurychone rothschildiana (O'BRIEN) SCHLTR.

This miniature epiphyte occurs in Sierra Leone, Côte d'Ivoire, and
Uganda at low to moderate altitudes in rain forests where there is high
humidity year-round. Its broad, oval leaves are thin and leathery, not
unlike those of *Phalaenopsis* in size and shape. The flowers, about
$2\frac{1}{2}$ in (6 cm) across, are borne on a short inflorescence of up to seven
faintly scented blooms. In cultivation, use a slab or hanging basket so
the flowers may be seen, as they tend to be hidden under the leaves.
ZONES 11–12. I–H.

FLICKINGERIA A. D. HAWKES

syn: *Ephemeranthera* P. HUNT & SUMMERH., *Desmotrichum* BLUME (SCHLECHTER **regarded**
Desmotrichum **as a section of** *Dendrobium*)

This genus of about 65 to 70 species is widely distributed from mainland
Asia and Indonesia to the Philippines, New Guinea, Australia, and the
Pacific Islands. These are creeping epiphytes with a rhizome from which
branching, erect, or pendulous stems arise. These stems have several
internodes with sheathing scale leaves—the last internode is swollen to
form a pseudobulb. There is a solitary leaf at the apex of the pseudobulb
and the inflorescence is terminal to subterminal and consists of one or,
occasionally, two flowers, which last for less than a day. Cultivation of
these species is as for *Dendrobium*.

F

Flickingeria angustifolia (BLUME)
A. D. HAWKES

syn: *Desmotrichum angustifolium* BLUME, *Flickingeria
anamensis* (A. D. HAWKES) A. D. HAWKES, *Flickingeria poilanei*
(GAGNEP.) A. D. HAWKES, *Dendrobium kelsallii* RIDL.

This species occurs on the Malay Peninsula and
Vietnam to Sumatra, Java, and Bali. It grows
epiphytically at low to moderate altitudes. The
branched stems are slender and wiry at the
base, with the apical part swollen into a
pseudobulb about $\frac{2}{3}$ in (15 mm) long and
$\frac{1}{8}$ in (3 mm) thick. The single leaf is $1\frac{3}{4}$–2 in
(4–5 cm) long. The flowers, about $\frac{1}{3}$ in (1 cm)
wide, are borne singly from the apexes of the
pseudobulbs. Their color is variable, ranging
from white to pink or brown.
ZONES 11–12. I–H.

Flickingeria angustifolia

Flickingeria comata

Flickingeria comata (BLUME) A. D. HAWKES
syn: *Dendrobium comatum* (BLUME) LINDL., *Desmotrichum
comatum* BLUME, *Dendrobium thysanochilum* SCHLTR.

This large, branched, erect to pendulous
epiphyte is from lowland rain forests on the
Malay Peninsula, the rest of Malaysia,
Indonesia, New Guinea, Australia, New
Caledonia, Fiji, and Samoa. It is epiphytic or
lithophytic, and usually grows in shaded areas
with high humidity and year-round rainfall.
The slender, erect stems branch several times,
each branch ending in a pseudobulb up to
4 in (10 cm) long and $\frac{2}{3}$ in (15 mm) wide. The
flowers, about $\frac{4}{5}$–$1\frac{1}{4}$ in (2–3 cm) across, have
an elaborately fringed midlobe of the lip. They
are borne terminally from a group of bracts,
one or more at a time. Flowering may occur
at any time of the year and the blooms last for
less than a day. **ZONE 12. H.**

GHI

GALEANDRA LINDL.

This genus comprises about 25 species ranging from Mexico through to Bolivia, with the highest diversity found in the Amazon Basin. Characteristically, these plants have elongated cylindrical pseudobulbs with thin leaves at the nodes. They are epiphytes that grow from about sea level to 1700 ft (500 m). A few are terrestrials or lithophytes in steep, rocky terrains at higher elevations.

CULTIVATION

These species enjoy conditions similar to those given to *Cattleya* species. They grow best in a pot with a well-drained mix and intermediate to hot temperatures.

Galeandra baueri

Galeandra batemanii

Galeandra claesii

Galeandra batemanii ROLFE

This species grows in seasonally dry forests from Mexico to Costa Rica. Its pseudobulbs are up to about 10 in (25 cm) long. The leaves, which are deciduous in the dry season, are about 9 in (22 cm) long. The inflorescence is about 1 ft (30 cm) tall with a simple or branched raceme of a few flowers. The fragrant long-living flowers are up to 3 in (7.5 cm) long. Flowering occurs during summer and autumn. **ZONES 9–12. I–H.**

Galeandra baueri LINDL.

This species is similar to *G. batemanii* and it is sometimes considered synonymous with that species. The difference between the two is the shape of the flower's lip, sepals, petals, and color. *G. baueri* ranges from Mexico to Panama and Suriname. It grows at elevations up to 2700 ft (800 m). Flowering is during summer and autumn. **ZONES 9–12. I–H.**

Galeandra claesii CGN.

The habit of this species from Brazil is similar to the *G. batemanii* and *G. Baueri*, but it is more robust. Its pendulous inflorescence is about 9 in (22 cm) long and bears a few flowers, which are about 2½ in (6 cm) wide. The flowers appear during summer. **ZONES 11–12. H.**

G

GALEARIS RAFINESQUE

This genus of two or three terrestrial species is found in North America and Japan. It is closely related to *Orchis*. The species lack tubers but have numerous fleshy roots. They have a pair of broad leaves and an erect inflorescence with prominent floral bracts and several flowers.

Galearis spectabilis

Galearis spectabilis (L.) RAFINESQUE
syn: Orchis spectabilis L.
"SHOWY ORCHIS," "TWO-LEAVED ORCHIS," "PURPLE-HOODED ORCHIS"

The helmet-shaped hood formed by the sepals and petals of this species gives rise to the generic name (the Latin word *galea* means "helmet"). *G. spectabilis* is a temperate, terrestrial species native to the northeast of North America, extending across the Mississippi River to Arkansas. It is a splendid, early-spring-blooming wildflower from deciduous woodlands. It is up to 14 in (35 cm) tall with two leaves 8 in (20 cm) long and 4 in (10 cm) wide at the base of the stem. A raceme bears up to 15 loosely packed flowers with diameters of about 1 in (2.5 cm). **ZONES 5–7. C.**

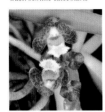

Gastrochilus bellinus

Gastrochilus calceolaris

G

Gastrochilus japonicus

GASTROCHILUS D. DON

This genus of about 15 species ranges from India to eastern Asia, as far as Malaysia and Indonesia. They are almost entirely epiphytic, small monopodial plants with a few leathery leaves and inflorescences of a few flowers.

CULTIVATION

These species may be grown mounted or potted in small baskets with a coarse, well-drained mix. High humidity and frequent watering is required during the growing period.

Gastrochilus bellinus (RCHB.F.) O. KUNTZE

This species occurs in Myanmar and Thailand. The stem is very short and stout with six to eight leathery leaves up to about 8 in (20 cm) long and 1¾ in (4 cm) wide. The erect, very short inflorescence carries four to seven fragrant, densely packed flowers. These are waxy and about 1¾ in (4 cm) wide. Flowering is during late winter and spring.
ZONES 10–11. I.

Gastrochilus obliquus

Gastrochilus calceolaris (J. E. SMITH) D. DON.

This species occurs in the tropical Himalayas, northeast India, Bangladesh, Myanmar, Malaysia, and on the Indonesian island of Java. Its stem is very short and the plant is up to 6 in (15 cm) high. The curved leaves are up to 8 in (20 cm) long. The inflorescence is very short and bears a few fragrant flowers up to about ⅘ in (2 cm) across. Flowering is in autumn.
ZONES 9–12. I–H.

Gastrochilus japonicus SCHLTR.

syn: *G. somai* HAYATA

This species is an epiphyte found in the central mountain range of Taiwan at elevations between 1700 and 5000 ft (500 and 1500 m). Its leaves are thick and leathery and the short inflorescence carries many flowers about ⅘ in (2 cm) broad. Flowering is during autumn. ZONE 10. I.

Gastrochilus obliquus (LINDL.) O. KUNTZE

This species ranges from northeast India to Vietnam. Its growth habit and dimensions are similar to that of *G. calceolaris*. The flowers appear during autumn.
ZONES 9–11. I–H.

Geodorum densiflorum

GEODORUM JACKSON

This genus of about ten species extends from India and Southeast Asia to New Guinea and New Caledonia, with one species present in Australia. These deciduous, terrestrial plants are found in shady forests and rain forests. The crowded, fleshy pseudobulbs grow at the soil surface. The leaves are carried on a short stem. When in flower the inflorescence is nodding, but it straightens during seed maturation.

CULTIVATION

These plants are easy to cultivate in hot climates. They may be grown in pots but do better in gardens with plenty of leaf litter.

Geodorum densiflorum (LAM.) SCHLTR.

syn: **several names, including** *G. pictum* R. BR., *G. neocaledonicum* KRAENZL.

This widespread species is from India, the Malay Archipelago, Australia, and the south-west Pacific Islands. It grows in grassy forests and disturbed sites at low to moderate altitudes. The underground pseudobulbs are spherical, about $1^{1}/_{4}$ in (3 cm) across. There are three to five thin-textured, pleated leaves up to 14 in (35 cm) long. The inflorescence has a characteristic "umbrella handle" shape, with eight to 20 tubular flowers about $^{4}/_{5}$ in (2 cm) across. **ZONES 9–11. I–H.**

GLOSSODIA R. BR.
"WAX LIPS"

This genus consists of two terrestrial species restricted to eastern Australian coastal areas, from the tropics to Tasmania. It grows in heathlands and eucalyptus forests at low to moderate altitudes up to 2700 ft (800 m). The common name is due to the appearance of the lip. These species are related to *Caladenia* and have an underground tuber with a single, hairy leaf and a hairy inflorescence of one or, occasionally, two blue flowers. The plants are dormant during the hot, dry summer months.

CULTIVATION

Grow these plants in similar conditions to those for *Caladenia*. The terrestrial mixture needs to include leaf litter from eucalyptus forests and coarse sand. The plants should be kept moist while the leaf is in evidence and watering reduced when the leaf dies back. Tubers may be removed and stored over the resting season and repotted when new growth is about to begin.

Glossodia major R. BR.

This species occurs in Australia, between the coast and the mountains from central Queensland to South Australia. It often grows in large colonies. The leaf is about 4 in (10 cm) long and $^{4}/_{5}$ in (2 cm) across, and is hairy on both surfaces. The inflorescence is up to 1 ft (30 cm) tall, and bears one or two flowers, each up to 2 in (5 cm) across. The flowers are glossy, purple to mauve or, occasionally, white in color, and appear during late winter and spring. **ZONES 9–10. C–I.**

Glossodia major

G

G

Gomesa crispa (LINDL.) KLOTZSCH. & RCHB.F.
syn: *Rodriguezia crispa* LINDL., *Odontoglossum crispulum* RCHB.F.

This species grows at moderate altitudes in the moist forests of southeast Brazil. The pseudobulbs are tightly clustered, up to about 4 in (10 cm) tall, and carry two soft-textured leaves up to about 8 in (20 cm) long. The inflorescence arches gracefully and is about 8 in (20 cm) long with many flowers. These flowers are fragrant and about ¾ in (18 mm) long. They appear during spring and early summer.
ZONES 9–11. C–I.

Gomesa recurva (LINDL.) R. BR.
syn: *Rodriguezia recurva* (R. BR.) LINDL., *Odontoglossum recurva* (R. BR.) RCHB.F.

This species grows in the cool, moist mountains of southeast Brazil. It is similar in many respects to *G. crispa*, but the racemes are more dense and the sepals and petals do not have wavy (crisped) margins. The fragrant flowers, about ⁴⁄₅ in (2 cm) long, appear in winter. **ZONES 9–11. C–I.**

Gomesa crispa

Gomesa recurva

GOMESA R. BR.

This is a genus of about ten small species from Brazil. They are epiphytic or lithophytic orchids with pseudobulbs and arching or pendulous inflorescences. These are dense with many green to white flowers that last for a long time.

CULTIVATION

These plants may be either mounted or grown in pots using a well-drained mix.

GONGORA RUIZ & PAVON

This genus has a wide distribution, from Mexico and Central America to Peru and Bolivia. Its habitat ranges from the lowlands up to at least 6300 ft (1900 m) in the Andes. Most species grow as epiphytes but some also occur as lithophytes. The plants are characterized by long inflorescences with many strongly perfumed flowers. The pseudobulbs are ovoid, have prominent ribs, and carry two or three thin-textured leaves at the apex.

CULTIVATION

These species may be grown in baskets or pots that allow the inflorescences to hang down.

Gongora galeata (LINDL.) RCHB.F.

This species is endemic to Mexico. Its ribbed pseudobulbs are up to 2¾ in (7 cm) long with leaves up to 1 ft (30 cm) long. The pendulous inflorescence emerges from the base of a pseudobulb and grows up to 10 in (25 cm) long. It carries ten to 20 strongly perfumed flowers about 1¾ in (4 cm) wide. Flowering is during summer. **ZONES 10–11. I–H.**

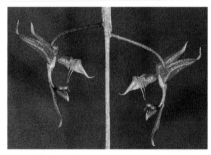

Gongora histrionica

Gongora leucochila

Gongora galeata

Gongora histrionica RCHB.F.

This species from Costa Rica, Panama, and Colombia is found at altitudes of 330–2500 ft (100–750 m). It has deeply ridged pseudobulbs, about 2¾ in (7 cm) tall, that carry two leaves up to about 16 in (40 cm) long and 4¾ in (12 cm) broad. The inflorescence, up to 16 in (40 cm) long, carries up to 25 flowers, each about 2 in (5 cm) broad. Flowering is from spring to the end of summer. **ZONES 11–12. I–H.**

Gongora leucochila LEMAIRE

This species occurs from Mexico to Costa Rica and, possibly, Panama. It grows at altitudes of 670–4000 ft (200–1200 m). The deeply ridged and angular pseudobulbs are conical and about 2¾ in (7 cm) high. The leaves are up to 16 in (40 cm) long and 4¾ in (12 cm) wide. The pendulous inflorescence is about 8 in (20 cm) long and carries up to 15 flowers about 2 in (5 cm) broad. Flowering is during spring and summer. **ZONES 11–12. I–H.**

G

G

Gongora pleiochroma

Gongora pleiochroma
RCHB.F.

This South American species is distributed from Colombia to Peru and, possibly, Brazil and Guyana. It is found on the eastern slopes of the Andes at a low altitude of 2000–3300 ft (600–1000 m). Its pseudobulbs are deep-furrowed, angular, ridged, and conical to elongated with a star-shaped cross section. They are up to 3¼ in (8 cm) tall. The two leaves are about 1 ft (30 cm) long. The 16-in (40-cm) long inflorescence carries 15 to 25 flowers. The color of the flowers varies from dark red to yellow, and speckled red on a yellow background. Flowering is during spring and summer. **ZONES 11–12. H.**

Gongora rufescens JENNY

This species is known only from Colombia. It has deep ridges on its conical to elongated pseudobulbs, which are about 2¾ in (7 cm) high. Two leaves form at the apexes, and these are about 1 ft (30 cm) long. The inflorescence is about 20 in (50 cm) long and carries 15 to 20 flowers about 2 in (5 cm) wide. Flowering is during spring. **ZONES 10–11. I.**

Gongora rufescens

Gongora scaphephorus
RCHB.F. & WARSE.

This epiphytic species extends from Colombia through to Peru. It grows in humid rain forests at altitudes of about 2000–3300 ft (600–1000 m). Its conical to spherical pseudobulbs are slightly ridged and up to 3¼ in (8 cm) high. Two leaves, up to 14 in (35 cm) long and 4 in (10 cm) wide, emerge from the apexes of the pseudobulbs. The inflorescence is up to 32 in (80 cm) long and carries up to 80 flowers, each about 2 in (5 cm) across. Flowering is during spring and summer.
ZONES 10–11. I.

Gongora truncata LINDL.

This species is widely distributed in Mexico, Belize, and Honduras. Its conical to spherical pseudobulbs are about 2½ in (6 cm) high and 1¼ in (3 cm) in diameter. They are slightly ridged. Two or three leaves emerge from the apexes of the pseudobulbs and these are up to about 10 in (25 cm) long and 3 in (7.5 cm) wide. The 1-ft (30-cm) long inflorescence carries ten to 12 flowers, each about 2 in (5 cm) wide. The flowers appear during spring and summer.
ZONES 11–12. I–H.

G

Gongora scaphephorus

Gongora truncata

G

GOODYERA R. BR.

This genus of small terrestrial species is from the northern Temperate Zone and the tropical forests of Southeast Asia, New Guinea, Australia, and the Pacific Islands. Most of the species grow in shady conditions on forest floors at low altitudes. The plants consist of a creeping rhizome that bends upwards to form the leafy shoots. The flowers are borne on an erect inflorescence that arises from the apexes of the shoots.

CULTIVATION

Some species have attractive leaves and are grown for this reason alone. A shallow pan with a large surface area is best as these species creep along the surface rather than grow deep —they may outgrow a normal pot. A well-drained mix of loam and leaf mold with leaf litter on the surface is required. These plants should be grown in shaded, humid conditions and kept evenly moist. Propagate by dividing the rhizome.

Goodyera hispida

Goodyera hispida LINDL.

The attractive pattern of its leaves are a feature of this species, found from northern India to Indochina. It grows in shady conditions on forest floors at low to moderate altitudes. It has several leaves up to 2¾ in (7 cm) long and 1 in (2.5 cm) across. These are dark green with attractive silver veins and a crystalline appearance. The inflorescence is about 4 in (10 cm) long and bears numerous flowers, each about ⅛ in (3 mm) across. Flowering is during summer. **ZONES 10–11. I.**

GRAMMANGIS RCHB.F.

There are only two species in this genus. Both of them are robust epiphytes found in Madagascar. The plants have large pseudobulbs and long inflorescences with many fleshy, medium-sized flowers. The three-lobed lip does not have a spur.

CULTIVATION

These plants require bright light, intermediate to hot conditions, and heavy watering with a watering rest period after flowering. The roots should be disturbed as little as possible when repotting.

Grammangis ellisii (LINDL.) RCHB.F.

syn: *Grammatophyllum ellisii* LINDL., *Grammangis fallax* SCHLTR.

This species grows in coastal rain forests, often overhanging rivers, in Madagascar. Its pseudobulbs are 4–8 in (10–20 cm) long and about 1¾–2½ in (4–6 cm) in diameter. There

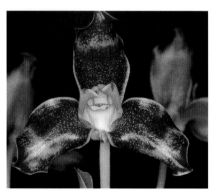

Grammangis ellisii

are three to five leaves 6½–16 in (16–40 cm) long and ⅓–1¾ in (1–4 cm) wide. The inflorescences arise from the bases of the pseudobulbs and are up to 2 ft (60 cm) long. They bear nearly 40 flowers, each about 2–2½ in (5–6 cm) across. **ZONES 11–12. H.**

GRAMMATOPHYLLUM BLUME

This genus of about 12 large epiphytes occurs from Southeast Asia to New Guinea and the Pacific Islands. It grows mostly in hot, humid coastal environments. It is related to *Cymbidium* and has short to elongated pseudobulbs and long spikes of large, showy flowers. Many of the species have thick roots that grow upwards, catching leaf litter and other detritus.

CULTIVATION

These plants may be grown readily in a large pot with an epiphytic mixture and placed in bright but filtered light in hot conditions. Some of the species may grow large and these will require plenty of room in an orchid house.

Grammatophyllum scriptum BLUME

This large, clump-forming epiphyte occurs from the Philippines, the Moluccas, and New Guinea to the Solomons and Pacific Islands, as far east as Fiji. It grows at low altitudes in hot, steamy conditions in coastal forests and coconut plantations. Its pseudobulbs are ovoid, laterally compressed, and up to about 10 in (25 cm) tall. They have five to eight broad leaves up to 2 ft (60 cm) long. The inflorescence arises from the bases of the pseudobulbs and is up to 80 in (2 m) tall. It bears 20 to 90 flowers, each about 2¾ in (7 cm) across. The color of the flowers varies and the lowest ones on the plant are sterile and often malformed. Flowering is mostly during summer. **ZONE 12. H.**

Grammatophyllum scriptum

Grammatophyllum stapeliiflorum (TEIJSM. & BINNEND.) J. J. SM.

syn: *Cymbidium stapeliiflorum* TEIJSM. & BINNEND., *Grammangis stapeliiflora* SCHLTR.

This species occurs on the Malay Peninsula, Borneo, Sumatra, Java, Sulawesi, and in the Philippines. It grows epiphytically at low altitudes in rain forests. The ovoid, laterally compressed pseudobulbs are crowded and grow up to about 6 in (15 cm) long and 2½ in (6 cm) wide. They have two or three leathery leaves up to 1 ft (30 cm) long and about 2½ in (6 cm) across. The pendulous inflorescence carries up to ten flowers, each about 2 in (5 cm) across. **ZONE 12. H.**

G

Grammatophyllum stapeliiflorum

GRAPHORKIS THOU.

This genus has only a few species and these are centered around Madagascar, with one species occurring in tropical Africa. They are epiphytes with numerous conical to ovoid pseudobulbs. Four to six leaves are produced from the base of the apex of each pseudobulb. The branched inflorescence arises from the base before the leaves are formed. The inflorescence bears numerous flowers.

CULTIVATION

These species require hot conditions with abundant moisture and humidity during the growing season, and good shade cover. They may be grown in small pots with a well-drained medium.

Graphorkis conclor var. *alphabetica*

Graphorkis conclor
var. *alphabetica* F. N. RASM.

This small species from Madagascar has pseudobulbs about 1 in (2.5 cm) tall. The leaves grow to about 5¹/₂ in (13 cm). The inflorescence, about 6 in (15 cm) long, carries five to eight flowers, each about ⁴/₅ in (2 cm) broad. Flowering is from spring to autumn. **ZONES 11–12. I–H.**

Grastidium insigne

GRASTIDIUM BLUME

syn: *Dendrobium* **section** *Grastidium* (BLUME) J. J. SM.

This group of about 200 species is regarded by many botanists as part of *Dendrobium*. They occur from Myanmar to Fiji, but New Guinea is clearly the center of distribution, with more than 150 species. The stems are long and slender with leaves along their length. The flowers are produced in pairs and grow laterally along the stem. They last for only a day or two. The lip is three-lobed and there is a prominent mentum.

CULTIVATION

Growing requirements are similar to those required by *Dendrobium* species.

Grastidium insigne (BLUME) M. A. CLEM. & D. L. JONES

syn: *Dendrobium insigne* (BLUME) RCHB.F. EX MIQ., *Dichopus insignis* BLUME

This long, straggling epiphyte is from lowland habitats in New Guinea and its adjacent islands —as far east as the Solomon Islands and west as Ambon in Indonesia. It grows in the hot, steamy environments of mangroves and adjacent forests or coconut plantations. Its slender, brittle stems, up to 28 in (70 cm) long, are at first erect then become pendulous. The ovate leaves are about 2½ or 2¾ in (6 or 7 cm) long. The inflorescences bear one or two flowers on short peduncles. The flowers are 1–2 in (2.5–5 cm) across and last for a day. Flowering is spasmodic throughout the year, but the peak is during summer. **ZONE 12. H.**

G

Grastidium tozerense (LAVARACK) M. A. CLEM. & D. L. JONES

syn: *Dendrobium tozerensis* LAVARACK

This small- to medium-sized species forms large clumps and grows as a lithophyte or, less commonly, as an epiphyte in the ranges of Cape York Peninsula in northeast Australia. It occurs at low altitudes under full or filtered sunlight in areas where there is a distinct dry season during winter and spring. The slender, brittle stems are 8–24 in (20–60 cm) long. The narrow leaves, up to 3¼ in (8 cm) long, are borne in two ranks on the upper half of the stem. The flowers are about 1¼ in (3 cm) across and last for less than a day. It is common for three anthers to be present on this species. The flowering season is spasmodic throughout the year. **ZONE 12. H.**

Grastidium luteocilium

Grastidium luteocilium (RUPP) RAUSCHERT

syn: *Dendrobium luteocilium* RUPP

When large, this plant looks spectacular in flower with numerous blooms produced in pairs along the length of the stems. It is a large, robust epiphyte that occurs in the humid tropical lowlands of northeast Queensland in Australia, and on the islands of Torres Strait and New Guinea. Its slender stems reach almost 80 in (2 m) in length, although about 40 in (1 m) or less is the more common length. The broad leaves are 1¾–5½ in (4–13 cm) long. The fragrant flowers, about ⅘ in (2 cm) across, last for only a day, but there are several bursts of flowering throughout the year. Flowering may be triggered by bursts of rain that suddenly reduce the temperature. **ZONE 12. H.**

Grastidium tozerense

GROBYA LINDL.

This genus is endemic to Brazil and it is related to *Cyrtopodium*. It comprises three species that grow in humid rain forests as small epiphytes with pseudobulbs.

CULTIVATION

These plants may be grown mounted and should be given abundant waterings and high humidity during the growing period. Alternatively, they may be potted with a well-drained mix.

Grobya amherstiae LINDL.

This small species grows at altitudes of 2000–3000 ft (600–900 m) in eastern Brazil. It has densely tufted, ovoid to spherical pseudobulbs about 1¾ in (4 cm) high. About five or six leaves are present near the top of the pseudobulbs. These are up to 16 in (40 cm) long. The erect or arching inflorescence is about 6 in (15 cm) long. The flowers are about 1¼ in (3 cm) long. Flowering is during spring and summer. **ZONES 11–12. I–H.**

Grobya amherstiae

G

HABENARIA WILLD.

This large genus has about 500 species. Its distribution is virtually worldwide, occurring in temperate and tropical grasslands in Africa, Asia, and the Americas. The greatest numbers of the species are in areas with seasonal rainfall. They are all terrestrial plants with underground tubers and a few leaves at the base or along the stem. The inflorescence bears a few to many flowers. White and green are the predominant flower colors, but a few species are more brightly colored.

CULTIVATION

A mixture of peat, soil, sand, and leaf mold is usually successful when growing these species. The plants require a watering rest period when not actively growing, usually after flowering, and copious watering when the new leaves appear.

Habenaria praecox

Habenaria edgari

Habenaria edgari SUMMERH.

This species occurs in Tanzania, Zaire, and Zambia. It grows in grasslands at moderate to high altitudes. The plant is up to 26 in (65 cm) tall. There are usually two large leaves at the base, which are more or less orbicular in shape. These are about 1¼ in (3 cm) across and are held closely to the ground. The inflorescence is about 8 in (20 cm) long and bears two to four flowers, each about 2 in (5 cm) across. Flowering is during December in its habitat. **ZONES 9–10. C–I.**

Habenaria praecox LAVARACK & DOCKRILL

This species grows in the sandy coastal soils of melaleuca (paperbark) woodlands in northeast Queensland, Australia. Rainfall in this habitat is seasonal, but hot and humid conditions prevail throughout the year. The plant grows up to about 20 in (50 cm) tall when in flower. There are two to four erect leaves, about 2–4 in (5–10 cm) long, at the base of the stem, and these appear shortly before the flowers. The inflorescence bearing three to 35 flowers, each about ⅓ in (1 cm) across. Flowering is early during the wet season, which is about December in the wild. **ZONE 12. H.**

Habenaria praestans

Habenaria praestans RENDLE

This robust species occurs in eastern tropical Africa at moderate to high altitudes. It grows in grasslands under full sun, and is about 40 in (1 m) tall. The largest of the six to 12 leaves is 3¼–12 in (8–30 cm) long; the lowest-growing two or three leaves are reduced to bracts. The inflorescence is 4–8 in (10–20 cm) long and is densely packed with up to 30 flowers, each about 1¾ in (4 cm) long. The spur is about 1 in (2.5 cm) long. Flowering is during February in its habitat. **ZONES 9–10. C–I.**

Habenaria propinquior RCHB.F.

This species occurs in coastal sandy melaleuca (paperbark) woodlands along the northeast coast of Australia, the islands of the Torres Strait and, possibly, southern New Guinea. The habitat in these areas experiences seasonal rainfall, with the bulk of the rain falling from December to April. The plant is about 6–16 in (15–40 cm) tall and usually has two basal leaves that stand erect, about 1¼–2¾ in (3–7 cm) long. The inflorescence has ten to 25 flowers, each about ⅓ in (1 cm) across. Flowering is during the middle of the wet season in the wild. **ZONE 12. H.**

Habenaria propinquior

H

Habenaria rhodocheila HANCE
syn: *H. pusilla* RCHB.F., *H. militaris* RCHB.F.

This species is from Indochina and southern China. It grows in low to moderate altitudes, often in leaf

litter on rocks. The plant is about 8–12 in (20–30 cm) tall with about six leaves around 4¾ in (12 cm) long and ⅘ in (2 cm) wide near the base of the stem. The inflorescence is about 1¾–4¾ in (4–12 cm) long with five to 15 flowers, each around 2 in (5 cm) long. The spur is also about 2 in (5 cm) long. The color of the flowers varies from orange or yellow to red. Flowering is during autumn. **ZONES 10–12. I–H.**

Habenaria rumphii (BROGN.) LINDL.
syn: *H. stauroglossa* KRAENZL., *H. holtzei* F. MUELL.

This widespread species occurs from Southeast Asia to New Guinea and Australia. It grows in grassy, open forest habitats in the lowlands. The plant is about 16 in (40 cm) tall with three to five narrow leaves 2¾–5⅔ in (7–14 cm) long. These are well spaced along the stem.

The inflorescence is densely packed with flowers, each about ⅓–⅔ in (10–15 mm) long. Flowering is during the wet season in the wild. **ZONE 12. H.**

Habenaria tentaculigera RCHB.F.

This tropical African species grows in the wet environments of woodlands and grasslands at moderate to high altitudes. The plant is 8–24 in (20–60 cm) tall. Five to 11 leaves clasp the stem. These are 1¼–3¼ in (3–8 cm) long and about ⅘ in (2 cm) wide, but the lowest two are reduced to bracts. The inflorescence is 2–8 in (5–20 cm) long and bears three to 12 flowers, each about 1¾ in (4 cm) long. Flowering is from December to February in the habitat. **ZONES 8–10. C–I.**

Habenaria triplonema SCHLTR.

This species occurs in northern Australia and New Guinea at low to moderate altitudes. It usually grows in grassy, open hillside forests. The plant is 1–2 ft (30–60 cm) tall with three spreading to erect basal leaves, about 2½–4¾ in (6–12 cm) long and ⅓–1 in (1–2.5 cm) wide. The inflorescence bears eight to 20 flowers, each about 1¾ in (4 cm) long. Most of this length is the spur, which is ⅘–1¼ in (2–3 cm) long. Flowering is from summer to early autumn—the wet season in most of its habitat. **ZONES 11–12. H.**

Habenaria rumphii

Habenaria tentaculigera

Habenaria triplonema

Hexisea bidentata

Hexisea imbricata (LINDL.) RCHB.F.

This species from Venezuela is similar to *H. bidentata*, but differs by having pseudobulbs that are not prominently grooved. Some authorities believe the two species are synonymous. The flowers are a similar size to *H. bidentata*. **ZONE 12. I–H.**

H

HEXISEA LINDL.

This genus comprises about six species from Central America, the Amazon Basin, and Colombia. They are epiphytes that grow in moist forests at altitudes of 670–1700 ft (200–500 m). The genus is characterized by having flattened, swollen pseudobulbs. The inflorescences arise from the stem apexes.

CULTIVATION

These plants are easily cultivated on slabs or in pots with a well-drained mix. They prefer intermediate conditions.

Hexisea bidentata LINDL.

This species is widespread on the eastern side of the Andes, from Mexico to Brazil. Its grooved pseudobulbs are clustered and grow to about 18 in (45 cm) tall. Two leaves, about 4½ in (11 cm) long, are produced at the apex of each swollen stem section. The terminal inflorescences are about 1¾ in (4 cm) long. They bear two to six flowers, each about 1 in (2.5 cm) across, but these may not open widely. Flowering is mostly during summer, but may occur at any time. **ZONES 11–12. I–H.**

Hexisea imbricata

HIMANTOGLOSSUM K. KOCH

"LIZARD ORCHIDS"

There are five or six very attractive species in this genus. The characteristic feature is the shape of the lip's central lobe, which is extremely long, narrow, and more or less divided at the tip. The botanical name refers to this straplike lip, and the common name is also a reference to the lip's shape, which looks like a lizard's tongue. This genus is widespread, but fairly uncommon, from western Europe to western Asia and in a small strip in northwest Africa. Flies and bees attracted by the plants' strange scent (some smell like goats) have been observed to act as pollinators.

CULTIVATION

In general, all the species are rare in nature and are rarely grown. In areas with an accumulation of *H. hircinum* plants, such as in France, seed spread in garden lawns sometimes grows into adult plants.

Himantoglossum adriaticum

H

Himantoglossum adriaticum H. BAUMANN

"ADRIATIC LIZARD ORCHID"

This species grows in the northern Adriatic regions as far north as southern Austria and Hungary. It is found in the calcareous soil of dry grasslands and open, scrub-covered hills from sea level to 4300 ft (1300 m). For a long time it was misinterpreted as a loose-flowered form of *H. hircinum*, but there are some differences. The midlobe of the lip is about ⅓ in (1 cm) shorter than that of *H. hircinum*, it is not twisted, the tip is deeply split, and the base has a short furrow. All these aspects resulted in its classification as a separate species in 1978. Both species reach a height of 12–32 in (30–80 cm). *H. adriaticum* carries up to 40 flowers, the length of which is about 1¾–2 in (4–5 cm), during May and June. **ZONES 6–8. C.**

Himantoglossum calcaratum

(BECK) SCHLTR.

"SPURRED LIZARD ORCHID"

This species, restricted to southern Yugoslavia, grows on limestone in grasslands and in light oak woodlands at low to moderate altitudes. In general it has the same habit as *H. hircinum*, but the flowers are the largest of the genus, about 3¼–4¾ in (8–12 cm) long. The midlobe of the lip is deeply split at the tip. The thick spur is about ⅓ in (1 cm) long. Flowering is late in summer. **ZONES 6–8. C.**

Himantoglossum hircinum (L.) SPRENG.

"GOAT'S LIZARD ORCHID"

This plant has the widest distribution of the genus. It occurs from southern Italy to northwestern Africa, Spain, and France, as well as some areas in southern England and southern Germany. It grows between sea level and, in Morocco, up to 6000 ft (1800 m). It is found in dry grasslands, near scrubs, woodland borders and, commonly, on disused vine terraces. It is up to 32 in (80 cm) tall. Most of its seven to 12 leaves form a rosette that withers during the flowering period. The inflorescence appears in spring and carries 40 to 120 flowers. In contrast to other species, the midlobe of its lip is not split. The flowers appear from late spring to summer, and have a rather unpleasant goatlike smell, especially during the evening. **ZONES 6–10. C–I.**

Himantoglossum calcaratum

Himantoglossum hircinum

HOLCOGLOSSUM SCHLTR.

Members of this genus of about eight species were considered, until recently, to belong to *Vanda*. The difference between the two are the details of the flower and the leaves, which in *Holcoglossum* are terete or almost terete. These species occur in Southeast Asia, mostly at moderate to high altitudes.

CULTIVATION

Holcoglossum grow well in conditions similar to those for *Vanda*, although a slab may be more suitable due to the often pendulous nature of the plants.

Holcoglossum amesianum

Holcoglossum kimballianum

Holcoglossum amesianum (RCHB.F.) CHRISTENSON

syn: *Vanda amesiana* RCHB.F.

This small epiphyte is found in the Yunnan province in China, Myanmar, Laos, Thailand, Cambodia, and Vietnam. It grows in full sun in forests or on rocks at altitudes of 4000–6700 ft (1200–2000 m). The short stem has four to seven semi-terete leaves, each 4–12 in (10–30 cm) long and up to $\frac{1}{3}$ in (1 cm) wide. The erect inflorescence is occasionally branched and bears many fragrant flowers. Only a few open at any one time, and each flower measures about $1\frac{1}{4}$ in (3 cm) across. The color varies and they appear mostly during summer, but may occur at any time.
ZONES 9–11. C–I.

Holcoglossum kimballianum (RCHB.F.) GARAY

syn: *Vanda kimballiana* RCHB.F.

This medium-sized epiphyte occurs in the Yunnan province in China, Myanmar, and Thailand. It is found at altitudes of 3300–5300 ft (1000–1600 m). The stem is pendulous and usually has four or five terete leaves, each 1–2 ft (30–60 cm) long. The erect inflorescences are up to 1 ft (30 cm) tall and bear around 20 flowers. These are fragrant, long-living, 1–1$\frac{3}{4}$ in (2.5–4 cm) across, and open at the same time. Flowering is during March in its habitat.
ZONES 10–11. C–I.

H

HOMALOPETALUM ROLFE

This is a genus of about four very small species of orchids that occur in the West Indies, Cuba, Guatemala, and Costa Rica. The pseudobulbs are arranged regularly along the rhizome in alternating rows.

CULTIVATION

These plants are best mounted on a slab or loosely potted in a well-drained mix. They should not be allowed to dry out.

Homalopetalum pumilio (RCHB.F.) SCHLTR.

This small species is found in Mexico, Costa Rica, and Guatemala. It grows as a lithophyte or epiphyte in woodlands up to about 6700 ft (2000 m). The height of the plant, including the pseudobulbs and leaves, is about 1½ in (3.5 cm). It has a single flower on a slender apical stalk about 2 in (5 cm) long. Flowering is during autumn. **ZONES 11–12. I–H.**

Homalopetalum pumilio

Huntleya wallisii

HUNTLEYA BATEM. EX LINDL.

This genus of about ten species is found from Costa Rica to Bolivia. They are epiphytes found in wet cloud forests at elevations of 1700–4000 ft (500–1200 m). Characteristically, the genus lacks pseudobulbs and the plants have a fanlike appearance. The inflorescence, which arises from the axils of the leaf sheaths, carries a solitary flower.

CULTIVATION

These species may be grown on slabs, so long as adequate humidity and moisture can be maintained, or grown in baskets. They should not be allowed to dry out.

Huntleya wallisii (RCHB.F.) ROLFE.

The leaves of this species are up to 1 ft (30 cm) long. The flower may be 8 in (20 cm) in diameter. The flowers appear during summer or autumn. **ZONES 9–10. I.**

IONOPSIS H. B. K.

This is a genus of five species occurring in lowland tropical America. They are epiphytes that grow from sea level to about 2700 ft (800 m). They have a single leaf on a pseudobulb with one internode. The leaf is flat or terete and the inflorescence emerges from the axil of the leaf.

CULTIVATION

These plants grow best on slabs with adequate moisture year-round and intermediate conditions.

Ionopsis utricularioides (SW.) LINDL.

This is a widespread species from Florida in the USA and the West Indies to Mexico, Venezuela, and Brazil. The stiff, leathery leaves are up to 6½ in (16 cm) long. The small pseudobulbs are about ⅔ in (15 mm) long. The inflorescence may be up to 2 ft (60 cm) long and carries many flowers up to about ⅘ in (2 cm) long. Flowers appear year-round, peaking during summer and autumn. Cultivation is best achieved on slabs with good light conditions. ZONES 10–12. I–H.

Ionopsis utricularioides

ISABELIA BARB. RODR.

This genus contains five species found growing as epiphytes in the humid forests of Brazil. They form mats and have closely spaced pseudobulbs, each surrounded by a fibrous network. The single apical leaf is very narrow. The short inflorescence has a single flower that emerges from the apexes of the pseudobulbs.

CULTIVATION

These species may be grown on slabs or in shallow pots or pans under intermediate conditions.

Isabelia virginalis BARB. RODR.

The ovoid pseudobulbs of this species grow up to about ½ in (12 mm) long. The branching rhizome forms a dense mat on the slab or substrate. The leaves are solitary, awl-shaped, and grow up to about 3 in (7.5 cm) long. The flowers, about ¼ in (6 mm) long, do not open fully or last long. Flowering is during winter. ZONES 11–12. I–H.

Isabelia virginalis

ISOCHILUS

R. BR.

This genus of about seven species occurs in tropical America, from Cuba and Mexico to Argentina. These epiphytes grow in moist lowland forests at about 330–1300 ft (100–400 m). The genus is characterized by its slender, canelike stems with narrow leaves arranged in pairs at the nodes. The inflorescence is terminal and lacks a stalk.

CULTIVATION

They are best cultivated under intermediate conditions in pots with a well-drained mix.

Isochilus linearis (JACQ.) R. BR.

syn: *Epidendrum lineare* JACQ.

This species is widespread in tropical America, found mostly in lowland areas. Several plants form dense clumps of slender stems up to 34 in (85 cm) in length. The stems are at first erect but soon become arching or pendulous, and they are dense with narrow leaves about 2½ in (6 cm) long. The inflorescence may have one to several flowers about ½ in (12 mm) long. These vary in color from nearly white to deep rose-purple. Flowering may occur at any time throughout the year, often more than once annually. **ZONES 11–12. I–H.**

Isochilus linearis

Isochilus major

CHAM. & SCHLTR.

This species occurs from Mexico to Panama and on Jamaica. It grows in moist forests and cloud forests at altitudes from sea level up to 6700 ft (2000 m). It is closely similar to *I. linearis* in habit, but has larger lanceolate leaves and a larger raceme of flowers. Flowers may appear at any time of the year, and often more than once annually. **ZONES 11–12. I–H.**

Isochilus major

ISOTRIA RAFINESQUE
"WHORLED PEGONIAS"

This genus comprises two terrestrial species limited to eastern USA. Both usually have five leaves that appear in a single whorl, hence its common name. This arrangement, unique among orchids, closely resembles the foliage of a common wildflower, the Indian cucumber-root (*Medeola virginiana*). (To distinguish them, mature specimens of the cucumber-root carry two tiers of leaves in contrast to the orchids which have one.) The roots of *Isotria* are fuzzy and extremely long. The flower has long sepals and arises from the center of the whorl.

Isotria medeoloides

Isotria medeoloides (PURSH)
RAFINESQUE

This is considered the rarest endemic species in the northeast and mid-Atlantic regions of the USA. It survives in scattered colonies of very small groups in deciduous woodlands, sometimes under large ferns. It is usually difficult to find, but intensive searches in recent years have discovered new stations. Habitat destruction, however, remains a threat to its survival. It occurs with *Medeola*, which it is thought to mimic, hence its botanical name. The leaves of *Isotria medeoloides* open, peel away and reveal one or, sometimes, two flower buds.
ZONES 6–8. C.

Isotria verticillata
(MUHLENBERG EX WILLDENOW)
RAFINESQUE

This lovely species grows in a variety of habitats in the eastern part of the USA, but it is not common. It is sometimes the shy companion of the more common and more spectacular colony-forming *Cypripedium acaule*. Both species bloom at the same time—during spring. The blunt leaves of *Isotria verticillata* distinguish the plant from its rare sister, *I. medeoloides*. They are frequently neighbors in woodland habitats.
I. verticillata grows to 1 ft (30 cm). It has five to six leaves arranged in a whorl, each one about 3⅔ in (9 cm) long. The flower diameter is up to 3⅔ in (9 cm).
ZONES 4–8. C–I.

Isotria verticillata

JKL

JUMELLA SCHLTR.

The 60 monopodial species of this genus are restricted to Madagascar and nearby islands, except for *J. filicornoides*. They grow at a range of altitudes from sea level up to about 6700 ft (2000 m). They have short or relatively long stems and the leaves are arranged along their length or in a fan shape. The flowers have narrow segments and a lanceolate lip that does not envelop the column as it does in the related genus *Angraecum*. The inflorescences bear a single flower.

CULTIVATION

These plants may be grown on a slab or in a pot with a well-drained medium. Many of the species benefit from a slight watering rest period after flowering, but all of them should be watered copiously when in growth.

Jumella arachnantha

Jumella arachnantha (RCHB.F.) SCHLTR.

This medium- to large-sized epiphyte is restricted to the Comoro Islands northwest of Madagascar. It grows at altitudes from 4000 to 6000 ft (1200 to 1800 m). The stems reach about 8 in (20 cm) but are usually shorter. The leaves are about 16–24 in (40–60 cm) long and 1¾–2½ in (4–6 cm) wide, and are arranged in a fan shape. The slender inflorescences are up to 8 in (20 cm) long and bear a single flower about 2 in (5 cm) across. The spur is about 2¾ in (7 cm) long. The flowers are produced profusely during spring. **ZONES 9–10. I.**

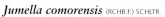

Jumella comorensis (RCHB.F.) SCHLTR.

syn: *Angraecum comorensis* (RCHB.F.) FINET., *Aeranthes comorensis* RCHB.F.

In cultivation, a large plant of this attractive species is rarely without flowers. It is an epiphyte from moist forests at low altitudes on the Comoro Islands, northwest of Madagascar. The stems are branched and up to 10 in (25 cm) long. These become pendulous. The leaves, 2¾ in (7 cm) long and ½ in (12 mm) wide, form two ranks along the stem. The flowers, about 1¾ in (4 cm) across, are borne singly along the stem. The spur is about 4½ in (11 cm) long. **ZONES 11–12. H.**

Jumella comorensis

Jumella filicornoides (DE WILDERMAN) SCHLTR.

This species occurs on the coast of east Africa, from the KwaZulu Natal province in South Africa north to Kenya. It grows at low altitudes in the south and up to 6000 ft (1800 m) in tropical areas. It is usually found high up on large trees in riverine forests or, occasionally, on rocks. Its slender stems, up to 16 in (40 cm) long, form dense clumps. The stiff and shiny leaves, about 4¾ in (12 cm) long, are borne on the apical half of the stems. There are one to three upright inflorescences, each with a single flower about 1–1¼ in (2.5–3 cm) across. The flowers have a mild fragrance, similar to the smell of cloves, during the night, plus a spur about 1¼ in (3 cm) long. Flowering is during February in the habitat. **ZONES 10–11. I–H.**

J

Jumella filicornoides

KEFERSTEINIA RCHB.F.

This genus extends from Mexico to Bolivia, with its maximum diversity and abundance in the Andes in Colombia and Ecuador. The species occur mostly as epiphytes or, rarely, as terrestrials in wet forests at altitudes of about 1000–8300 ft (300–2500 m). These plants are characterized by a lack of pseudobulbs, and leaves and leaf sheaths that form a fanlike shape. The inflorescences arise from the axils of the leaf sheaths.

CULTIVATION

Because these species lack pseudobulbs, they require constant watering year-round and should not be allowed to dry out. They enjoy intermediate, humid conditions. They may be grown in a pot with a well-drained but water-retentive medium, such as sphagnum moss.

Kefersteinia graminea (LINDL.) RCHB.F.

This medium-sized species from Venezuela, Colombia, and Ecuador is up to about 1 ft (30 cm) high. It has spreading leaves and several inflorescences that arise from the leaf axils. The inflorescences bear one to three flowers on short stems. The flowers, about 2 in (5 cm) in diameter, appear during spring and summer. **ZONES 10–11. I.**

Kefersteinia graminea

KOELLENSTEINIA RCHB.F.

This genus of about 16 species occurs from Panama to Brazil and Bolivia. They have small, inconspicuous pseudobulbs surrounded by the bases of narrow leaves. The inflorescence is produced laterally, often with the new growth. These plants grow as terrestrials in wet cloud forests at altitudes of 3300–6700 ft (1000–2000 m).

CULTIVATION

These species like intermediate conditions with constant moisture year-round; they should not be allowed to dry out. They may be grown in pots with a well-drained medium.

Koellensteinia graminea (LINDL.) RCHB.F.

This epiphyte occurs in northern South America, from Colombia to Brazil. The plant is small with short stems. It has one to three narrow, grasslike leaves up to 8 in (20 cm) long. The erect or arching inflorescence has racemes or panicles and bears few flowers. It may be up to 10 in (25 cm) long with the flowers up to $\frac{4}{5}$ in (2 cm) broad. Flowering is during spring. **ZONES 11–12. I–H.**

Koellensteinia graminea

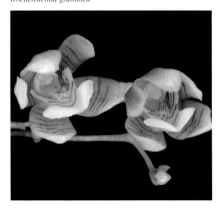

Laelia albida

LAELIA LINDL.

This genus previously comprised more than 60 species, but it has recently been revised and now contains only a few Central American species. Most of the other species have been transferred to *Sophronitis*.

CULTIVATION

The growth habit of *Laelia* species resembles that of *Cattleya* species, to which they are closely related, and they may be grown under similar conditions. Most grow in a pot with a well-drained mix, but some may be mounted. They do not require high humidity while actively growing, but when dormant reduce watering and provide cooler temperatures.

Laelia albida BATEMAN EX. LINDL.

This species from Mexico grows in oak or oak–pine forests or tropical, deciduous forests that occur inland or up to altitudes of 6700 ft (2000 m) on the Pacific Ocean side of the country. Its pseudobulbs are narrow and wrinkled with two leaves up to about 4 in (10 cm) long. The narrow inflorescence, up to 20 in (50 cm) long, carries up to ten flowers about 1¾ in (4 cm) across. Flowering is during winter. This species may be mounted or potted. **ZONES 9–10. C–I.**

Laelia anceps LINDL.

This species, endemic to Mexico and Honduras, occupies a variety of habitats, from coffee plantations and pastures to oak and oak–pine forests at altitudes up to 5000 ft (1500 m). There are many varieties of this species with a wide range of pseudobulb size and inflorescence length. The pseudobulbs may reach a height of about 4 in (10 cm). The leaves, up to 10 in (25 cm) long and 2½ in (6 cm) wide, come either singly or in pairs. The inflorescence may reach up to nearly 40 in (1 m) in length and carries two to five flowers up to 4 in (10 cm) across. Flowering is during autumn and early winter. This is an easy-to-grow species that adapts well to a variety of conditions. Cultivate in a large pot with a well-drained mix. **ZONES 9–11. C–I.**

Laelia anceps

Laelia autumnalis

Laelia autumnalis LINDL.

This species is endemic to Mexico and grows in open oak forests at altitudes of about 5000–8300 ft (1500–2500 m). It occurs mostly as an epiphyte but is also found as a lithophyte. The ovoid pseudobulbs are up to 4 in (10 cm) long. These carry two leaves up to about 6 in (15 cm) long. The flowering stem arises from the apexes of the pseudobulbs and may be more than 40 in (1 m) long. They may carry up to 15 flowers, each about 5$^1/_2$ in (13 cm) wide. Flowering is from autumn to winter. **ZONES 9–11. C–I.**

Laelia rubescens

Laelia rubescens LINDL.

This species from dry woodland areas ranges from Mexico to Guatemala, El Salvador, Honduras, Nicaragua, Costa Rica, and Panama. It is often found in exposed, full-sun situations between sea level and 5700 ft (1700 m). Its pseudobulbs, up to 3 in (7.5 cm) tall, are distinctive—they are strongly compressed and often wrinkled. They have a single, tough leaf up to about 8 in (20 cm) long. The flower stem, up to 1 ft (30 cm) long, arises from the apex of the pseudobulbs. The eight to 12 flowers, each up to 3 in (7.5 cm) across, are colored from white to pink or lavender. Flowering is during autumn. This species is best cultivated on a mount with reduced watering during the dormant period. **ZONES 10–11. I–H.**

LANIUM LINDL.

This small genus of about four species comes from northern
South America. It is part of the *Laelia* group and the species
occur as either epiphytes or lithophytes. They have a moderately
long, creeping rhizome.

CULTIVATION

Due to their creeping rhizome, these species are best mounted
on a slab or potted in shallow pans or pots with a free-draining
mixture. Abundant moisture and humidity is required year-
round in intermediate to hot conditions.

L

Lanium avicula LINDL.

Lanium avicula

This species is from Brazil and the Amazonian region of Peru.
It is a small, creeping plant with pseudobulbs to about ¾ in
(18 mm) tall. These carry two rigid, leathery leaves up to about
1¼ in (3 cm) long. The erect inflorescence arises from the apex
of the pseudobulbs and is up to 6 in (15 cm) tall. It carries
several to many flowers about ½ in (12 mm) wide. The long-
lasting flowers open widely and appear mostly during autumn.
ZONE 12. I–H.

LEPTOTES LINDL.

This genus comprises about three very attractive, small species from Brazil, Paraguay, and Argentina. They are epiphytes with small pseudobulbs and fleshy, terete leaves. The inflorescence arises from the base of the pseudobulbs and carries flowers that are proportionally large for the plants' sizes.

CULTIVATION

These species may be either mounted or grown in shallow pans with a free-draining mix in intermediate to hot conditions. While in active growth they should be given adequate moisture and humidity.

Leptotes unicolor

Leptotes bicolor LINDL.
syn: *Tetramicra bicolor* (LINDL.) BENTH.

This species from southern Brazil and Paraguay grows in subtropical rain forests at altitudes of 1700–3000 ft (500–900 m). Its pseudobulbs are stemlike, clustered, and up to 1 in (2.5 cm) tall. The fleshy, terete leaves may be up to $5^{1}/_{2}$ in (13 cm) long. The short inflorescence carries up to six fragrant flowers, each about 2 in (5 cm) across. The flowers appear during winter and spring. **ZONES 10–11. I.**

Leptotes tenuis RCHB.F.

This species from Brazil's cool mountains is small and has a pendulous habit. Its short, one-leaf stem is about 2 in (5 cm) long. The flowers are about $2/_3$ in (15 mm) wide and they appear during winter and spring. **ZONES 9–10. C–I.**

Leptotes unicolor BARB. RODR.

This species from the cool mountains of Brazil has similar features to *L. tenuis*. The inflorescence becomes pendulous, is about 2 in (5 cm) high, and bears two or three flowers, each about $2/_3$ in (15 mm) across. Flowering is during winter and spring. **ZONES 9–10. C–I.**

Leptotes bicolor

Leptotes tenuis

LIPARIS L. C. RICH.

There are some 250 species in this genus, which occur on all continents except Antarctica. These plants are closely related to *Malaxis*. They grow in temperate climates as terrestrials and in humid, tropical climates as epiphytes or terrestrials. The pseudobulb may be below or above ground and have one or more leaves, and an inflorescence of small flowers colored red, orange, yellow, and green.

CULTIVATION

Terrestrial species may be grown in a mix of loam, leaf mold, and sand. Epiphytic species need a well-drained mix of bark or similar material. These plants need mostly humid, shady conditions and reduced watering when not actively growing.

Liparis caespitosa (THOUARS) LINDL.

syn: a large list, including *Malaxis caespitosa* THOUARS, *Liparis angustifolia* (BLUME) LINDL.

The distribution of this small species extends from Africa to the Pacific Islands, as far north as southern China. It grows in rain forests at altitudes of 1300–5700 ft (400–1700 m). The ovoid, wrinkled pseudobulbs are about $\frac{1}{3}$–$\frac{4}{5}$ in (1–2 cm) long. The single leaf is about 8 in (20 cm) long and $\frac{1}{e}$ in (1 cm) wide. The erect inflorescence is usually as long as the leaf and bears numerous flowers, each about $\frac{1}{8}$ in (3 mm) across. Flowering is from winter to spring. **ZONES 10–12. I–H.**

Liparis condylobulbon

Liparis condylobulbon RCHB.F.

syn: *Liparis confusa* J. J. SM.

This widespread species occurs from Thailand to Fiji, as far north as the Philippines and Taiwan, and most of the places in between. It grows on trees or rocks in rain forests from sea level to a 5000-ft (1500-m) altitude. Its pseudobulbs are flask-shaped and grow about 8 in (20 cm) long. These have one or two leaves, each about 6–8 in (15–20 cm) long and $\frac{1}{3}$–$\frac{4}{5}$ in (1–2 cm) wide. The inflorescence arises from the apex of the pseudobulbs. It is 4–8 in (10–20 cm) long and bears numerous flowers, each about $\frac{1}{4}$ in (6 mm) across. The timing of flowering is variable across the range, but it is usually during the wet season. **ZONES 11–12. I–H.**

Liparis formosana RCHB.F.

syn: *L. nervosa*, **var.** *formosana* (RCHB.F.) HIROE

This species is found in Taiwan and Japan at altitudes of 1000–1700 ft (300–500 m). It grows as a terrestrial in shady forests. It is about 6 in (15 cm) tall with conical to cylindrical pseudobulbs. The inflorescence has 15 or more flowers. Flowering is during February to May in its natural habitat. **ZONE 11. I.**

Liparis caespitosa

Liparis formosana

Liparis habenarina

Liparis latifolia

Liparis habenarina (F. MUELL.) BENTH.

This terrestrial species occurs in Australia, from the New South Wales–Queensland border to the Northern Territory, and on the islands of Torres Strait. It grows in open forests under light shade at low to moderate altitudes. The conical pseudobulbs lie underground and are about ⅘–1¼ in (2–3 cm) tall. There are usually two or three leaves, which are 4–10 in (10–25 cm) long and ⅘–1¾ in (2–4 cm) across. The erect inflorescence is 6–8 in (15–20 cm) tall and bears eight to 20 flowers, each about ⅓ in (1 cm) across. Flowering is during the wet season. **ZONES 11–12. I–H.**

Liparis latifolia (BLUME) LINDL.
syn: *Malaxis latifolia* BLUME, *Liparis robusta* HOOK.F.

This epiphytic species has a wide distribution over southern China, Southeast Asia, Timor, and New Guinea. It grows in rain forests at altitudes of 830–5700 ft (250–1700 m). The pseudobulbs have a somewhat flattened,

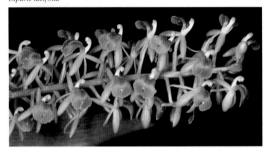

conical shape. They are about 3⅔ in (9 cm) long and usually have one leaf 6–12 in (15–30 cm) long. The erect inflorescence is about as long as the leaf and bears numerous flowers, each about ⅓ in (1 cm) across. The color of the flowers varies from red-brown to green and they appear during summer. **ZONES 11–12. I–H.**

Liparis liliifolia (L.) L. C. RICHARD.

This is one of the most common wild orchids in eastern USA. Like the genus *Spiranthes*, it is likely to colonize disturbed areas such as road shoulders. The plant is up to 10 in (25 cm) tall. The pseudobulbs are ⅘ in (2 cm) long and ⅓ in (1 cm) across. The two leaves are up to 7 in (18 cm) long. A raceme bears up to 27, loosely placed flowers, each with a diameter about ⅘ in (2 cm). These have an attractive form despite their dull color and large lips. Flowering is during spring. **ZONES 4–6. C.**

Liparis liliifolia

Liparis loeselii

Liparis loeselii (L.) L. C. RICHARD.
"LOESEL'S TWAYBLADE," "FEN ORCHID"

This species occurs in both the northeast of North America and western Europe. It dislikes acidic substrate, so it is commonly found in alkaline bogs. The place where it most often grows, however, is on cobbled lake shores. The plant illustrated here was found at the southern edge of its North American range—on a bed of limestone tailings from a disused iron furnace in the New Jersey pine barrens. The species is up to 10 in (25 cm) tall. Its pseudobulbs are about 4 in (10 cm) long and 2 in (5 cm) across. There are up to 12 flowers, each about $\frac{1}{3}$ in (1 cm) across. **ZONES 4–6. C.**

Liparis parviflora (BLUME) LINDL.
syn: *Malaxis parviflora* BLUME, *Liparis flaccida* RCHB.F., *L. tembelingensis* CARR

This species comes from the Malay Peninsula, Sumatra, Java, Borneo, and the Philippines. It grows from sea level to a 6700-ft (2000-m) altitude. The ovoid pseudobulbs are each up to 4 in (10 cm) tall and $1\frac{1}{2}$ in (3.5 cm) across, with two leaves up to 1 ft (30 cm) long and $1\frac{1}{4}$–2 in (3–5 cm) across. The erect inflorescence becomes pendulous and is 8–20 in (20–50 cm) long. It bears numerous flowers, each about $\frac{1}{4}$ in (6 mm) long. Flowering is during summer. **ZONES 11–12. H.**

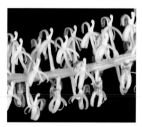

Liparis parviflora

Liparis perpusilla

Liparis perpusilla HOOK.F.

This miniature species occurs in Sikkim in north India at altitudes of 6700–8700 ft (2000–2600 m). Its pseudobulbs are about $\frac{1}{3}$–$\frac{2}{3}$ in (10–15 mm) long, with four to five leaves about $\frac{4}{5}$ in (2 cm) long. The erect inflorescence is $2\frac{1}{2}$–$3\frac{1}{4}$ in (6–8 cm) tall and bears a few flowers, each about $\frac{1}{8}$ in (3 mm) across. Flowering is from summer to autumn. **ZONES 10–11. I.**

Liparis swensonii
F. M. BAILEY
syn: *Liparis reflexa* (R. BR.) LINDL.,
var. *parviflora* NICHOLLS

This species occurs on either side of the New South Wales–Queensland border in Australia. It grows mostly on rocks in exposed situations at moderate altitudes. The ovoid pseudobulbs are $\frac{4}{5}$–$1\frac{1}{4}$ in (2–3 cm) across. There are one or two leaves about $2\frac{1}{2}$–10 in (6–25 cm) long and $\frac{4}{5}$ in (2 cm) across. The erect inflorescence is about 8 in (20 cm) long and bears ten to 30 flowers, each about $\frac{1}{3}$ in (1 cm) across. Flowering is from autumn to winter. **ZONES 10–11. I.**

Liparis swensonii

LISTERA R. BR.

This genus from the northern Temperate Zone comprises about 25 diminutive and delicate terrestrial species. When walking in northern woods near bogs or mossy rocks they make a pleasant, accidental discovery. The flowers are well worth an inspection with a magnifying glass—they have a complicated trigger mechanism that "explodes" the pollinia onto the backs of tiny insects, and the lip is long and often forked.

Listera cordata (L.) R. BR.
"HEART-LEAVED TWAYBLADE"

This small species is one of the most widespread orchids in the world, yet it is seldom seen. Its distribution is in northern Europe, Asia, and America. The plant illustrated here was growing in wet, mossy woods on an island off southwest Nova Scotia. The species' height is up to 10 in (25 cm). Its two leaves are heart-shaped and about ¼ in (6 mm) in diameter at the mid-stem section. There are up to 25 green to reddish-purple flowers. These appear during summer and persist after pollination has occurred.
ZONES 3–6. C.

Listera cordata

LOCKHARTIA HOOKER

This genus of about 30 species ranges from Mexico to the southern part of South America, and also to Trinidad and Tobago. They grow mostly as epiphytes, and are characterized by slender stems surrounded by flattened sheaths and leaves that are loosely spaced together and arranged alternately on either side of the stems to give a braided appearance. The inflorescences are borne near the top of the stem and emerge as racemes or panicles that have few flowers.

CULTIVATION

These species may be grown on slabs or in small pots or baskets. They should receive water year-round and be kept in hot to intermediate conditions.

Lockhartia lunifera

Lockhartia lunifera (LINDL.) RCHB.F.

This species from Brazil has erect to pendulous stems about 8 in (20 cm) tall. The plant is dense with leaves about ⅖ in (2 cm) long and triangular in shape when looked at in profile. The short inflorescence carries one to three flowers about ⅖ in (2 cm) long. Flowering is during summer and autumn. **ZONES 10–11. I–H.**

Lockhartia acuta

Lockhartia acuta (LINDL.) RCHB.F.

This species from Panama, Colombia, Venezuela, and Trinidad and Tobago has arching or pendulous stems up to almost 2 ft (60 cm) in length. The leaves are about ⅖ in (2 cm) long. The inflorescences are produced from the upper leaf axils, have numerous branches, and bear many flowers less than ½ in (12 mm) across. Flowering is mostly during summer. **ZONES 11–12. I–H.**

Lockhartia oestedii

Lockhartia oestedii RCHB.F.

This species occurs from Mexico to Guatemala, Honduras, Costa Rica, and Panama. In all respects it is more robust than *L. lunifera*. Its stems are up to 18 in (45 cm) long. The leaves are about 1 in (2.5 cm) long. The short inflorescence emerges from the upper leaf axils and has one to three flowers up to about 1 in (2.5 cm) long. These appear at any time during the year. **ZONES 11–12. I–H.**

Ludisia discolor

Ludisia discolor (KER-GAWL.) A. RICH.

syn: *Haemaria discolor* (KER-GAWL.) LINDL., *Goodyera discolor* KER-GAWL.

This attractive species ranges from India to Southeast Asia. It grows at low to moderate altitudes. The elliptic leaves are 1¾–2¾ in (4–7 cm) long and 1¼ in (3 cm) wide. They are produced along a fleshy, brittle stem that creeps along the ground and bends up to form leafy shoots. The inflorescences are borne from the apexes of the shoots. Each one is about 1¼–3¼ in (3–8 cm) long and has two to ten flowers about ⅘ in (2 cm) long. Flowering is during spring. **ZONES 11–12. I–H.**

Leaves of *Ludisia discolor*

LUDISIA A. RICH.

"JEWEL ORCHIDS"

There is only one species in this genus, and it has many variations in form. It is popular for its beautiful leaves, which have a dark, reddish-green background, often with attractive red to golden veins on the upper surface. The leaf surface also has an attractive sheen when light hits it.

CULTIVATION

A shallow pan with a large surface area is best for this species, as it has shallow roots and creeps along the surface. It will soon outgrow a normal pot. A well-drained mix of loam and leaf mold with leaf litter on the surface is required. It should be grown in shaded, humid conditions and kept evenly moist. Plants may be propagated by simply breaking the rhizome.

LYCASTE LINDL.

This genus of 45 species occurs from Mexico to Peru at altitudes from sea level to about 8300 ft (2500 m). They are epiphytic or lithophytic and are related to *Maxillaria*. Their pseudobulbs are crowded and usually ovate, with two or three leaves and short spines at the apexes. The leaves are pleated and for most of the species they are deciduous during flowering. The inflorescences arise from the bases of the pseudobulbs and bear a single, large, waxy flower that lasts for about four weeks. As many as 15 flowers per pseudobulb may be produced at one time, making this species most spectacular.

Lycaste aromatica

Lycaste candida

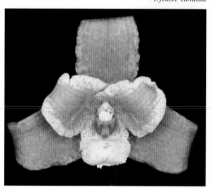

CULTIVATION

A variety of mixes are suitable for the epiphytic orchids, so long as they are well-drained. The plants should be watered freely when in active growth, but be allowed a watering rest period when the growths mature. Watering is resumed when new roots appear. Light requirements for these species range from shade to almost full sun but, as a general rule, shady conditions are best.

HYBRIDS

Many interesting hybrids have been created between the species in this genus and also with the species in *Anguloa*. As well as the desire to produce large flowers with good color, *Lycaste* breeders are aiming for hybrids that flower often, are scentedm, and are small plants. Some examples of popular hybrids using these plants are shown at the end of the species selection.

Lycaste aromatica (GRAHAM EX HOOKER) LINDL.
syn: *Maxillaria aromatica* HOOKER

This species occurs in Mexico, Guatemala, and Nicaragua. It grows on rain forest trees or on limestone cliffs at altitudes of 3000–5000 ft (900–1500 m). Its pseudobulbs are 2¾–4 in (7–10 cm) long, ovate and somewhat flattened. The deciduous leaves are up to 22 in (55 cm) long and 4 in (10 cm) across. There are up to 15 cinnamon-scented flowers, each about 2½ in (6 cm) across. Flowering is mostly during spring. **ZONES 9–11. C–I.**

Lycaste candida LINDL.

This species occurs in Nicaragua, Costa Rica, and Panama. It grows as an epiphyte in wet mountainous forests at an altitude of about 2700 ft (800 m). Its pseudobulbs are ovoid and compressed, and up to 2½ in (6 cm) long. The deciduous, pleated leaves are up to about 8 in (20 cm) long. There are usually several inflorescences per pseudobulb, and each one has a single flower about 2 in (5 cm) across. Flowering is mostly during winter. **ZONES 10–12. I–H.**

Lycaste ciliata

L

Lycaste cochleata

Lycaste ciliata (RUIZ & PAV.) LINDL.

syn: *Maxillaria ciliata* RUIZ & PAVON

This species from Colombia, Ecuador, Peru, and Bolivia occurs at altitudes of 3300–8000 ft (1000–2400 m). It is found as a lithophyte on the walls of gorges or on old tree stumps where the roots grow in the decaying wood. Its ovoid pseudobulbs are about 3¼ in (8 cm) tall and have two deciduous leaves up to 10 in (25 cm) long. The waxy, fragrant flowers are about 4 in (10 cm) across and appear during spring. **ZONES 9–10. C–I.**

Lycaste cochleata LINDL. EX PAXT.

Mangrove swamps and other lowland areas are the habitat for this species from Mexico and Guatemala. Its pseudobulbs are about 3⅔ in (9 cm) tall. The waxy, fragrant flowers are about 2 in (5 cm) across. Flowering occurs during spring. **ZONES 11–12. I–H.**

Lycaste cruenta LINDL.

syn: *Maxillaria cruenta* LINDL., *Lycaste balsamea* A. RICH. EX LINDL.

This large epiphyte or lithophyte occurs in Mexico, Guatemala, and El Salvador at moderate to high altitudes. Its pseudobulbs have a strong spine, and are ovoid, compressed, and up to 4 in (10 cm) long. The deciduous leaves are up to 18 in (45 cm) long and 6 in (15 cm) across. There are several waxy, cinnamon-scented flowers per pseudobulb, each about 2½ in (6 cm) across. Flowering is during spring. **ZONES 10–11. I.**

Lycaste cruenta

Lycaste deppei

(LODD.) LINDL.

syn: *Maxillaria deppei*
LODD.

This distinctive
species occurs in
Mexico, Guatemala,
and Nicaragua at
about a 4000-ft
(1200-m) altitude.
The pseudobulbs,
about 2½–4 in
(6–10 cm) long and
2 in (5 cm) across,
lack spines and are
ovoid and
compressed. The
leaves, 8–20 in
(20–50 cm) long and
3¼–4 in (8–10 cm)

Lycaste deppei

wide, are sometimes deciduous. There are up
to nine fragrant flowers per pseudobulb, each
3⅔ in (9 cm) across. The flowers appear
throughout the year, but most often during
spring and autumn. The plant flowers best
after a long winter watering rest period.
ZONES 10–11. I.

Lycaste dowiana ENDRES & RCHB.F.

This attractive, small species occurs from
Guatemala to Panama and, possibly, in some
areas of South America. The leaves are not
deciduous when in flower. The flowers are
2 in (5 cm) across and are borne in succession
—up to five per pseudobulb open at any one
time—throughout summer and autumn. A
watering rest period during winter is not
necessary for this species. **ZONES 10–11. I.**

Lycaste dowiana

Lycaste lasioglossa

Lycaste lasioglossa RCHB.F.

This large-flowered species is recorded from
Guatemala and Mexico, although it is believed
to be extinct in the latter country. It is reported
to be a terrestrial species. Its pseudobulbs, up
to 4 in (10 cm) long, lack spines and are ovoid
and compressed. The leaves are not deciduous
and grow up to 22 in (55 cm) long and 4¾ in
(12 cm) across. Each pseudobulb has up to
12 flowers, about 3⅔ in (9 cm) across.
Flowering is during spring. **ZONE 10. I.**

L

Lycaste macrophylla

Lycaste xytriophora

Lycaste macrophylla (POEPP. & ENDL.) LINDL.

This species occurs extensively in Central and South America from low altitudes up to 8000 ft (2400 m). It is extremely variable with some seven subspecies, all differing in flower color. The leaves are not deciduous. The pseudobulbs are ovoid, and up to 4 in (10 cm) long and 1¼–2½ in (3–6 cm) wide. Each one bears up to ten flowers about 3¼–4¾ in (8–12 cm) across. Flowering is from March to July in its natural habitat. In cultivation, this species tolerates a range of temperatures but should have slightly reduced watering during winter.
ZONES 10–12. I–H.

Lycaste tricolor KLOTZSCH

This small species occurs in Costa Rica and Panama in cloud forests at altitudes of 2000–3300 ft (600–1000 m), where the moisture levels are high. Its pseudobulbs, up to 2¾ in (7 cm) tall, lack spines and are heavily ribbed. There are three to four leaves that may not be deciduous when the flowers are present. Each pseudobulb produces several waxy, fragrant flowers at one time. These are about 2 in (5 cm) across and appear during spring. **ZONES 10–11. I.**

Lycaste xytriophora LINDEN & RCHB.F.

This species comes from Ecuador. It grows on rocks in the Andes at altitudes of 2000–6000 ft (600–1800 m). Its ovoid and compressed pseudobulbs are up to 4 in (10 cm) long and 2 in (5 cm) across. They have long spines with one to three leaves around 12–20 in (30–50 cm) long. There are several waxy and fragrant flowers per pseudobulb, and each flower is about 3 in (7.5 cm) wide. Flowering is from spring to summer. **ZONES 10–11. I.**

Lycaste tricolor

Lycaste Alwine Miller "Claret"

Lycaste Kodama "Sunrise" × *L. cruenta*

Lycaste Macama "Atlantis"

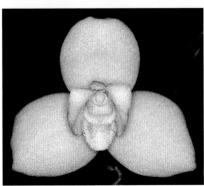

Lycaste Shoalhaven "Beryl"

L

MACODES BLUME

This genus of about ten terrestrial species is one of the "jewel orchids," so-called due to their attractive leaves. They occur from the Malay Peninsula to New Guinea and the Pacific Islands. They grow at low to moderate altitudes on rain forest floors, where light levels are low and humidity is high. They have a creeping stem and short, vertical stems with large, attractively veined leaves. The inflorescences arise from the stem apexes and have several asymmetrical flowers with the lip positioned uppermost.

CULTIVATION

A large, shallow pan is best for these species to accommodate the creeping habit and shallow root system. The potting mix should contain a rich loam, sand and leaf litter and be free draining. Grow in shady, humid conditions and keep evenly moist, without over-watering, throughout the year. Slugs and snails may be a major pest on these plants.

Macodes dendrophila SCHLTR.

This small, attractive species occurs on the island of New Guinea and Bougainville. It grows in the forks and holes of trees, where some leaf litter has lodged, or as a terrestrial in moist cloud forests. It has been reported at

Macodes dendrophila

altitudes of 2000–4000 ft (600–1200 m). The erect stems are about 1 ft (30 cm) long and have three to five attractively veined leaves up to 4 in (10 cm) long and 2 in (5 cm) wide. The small flowers are densely packed on an erect inflorescence about 7 in (18 cm) tall. Flowering in its habitat is mostly from September to January (spring to summer). **ZONES 10–11. I–H.**

Macodes sanderiana (KRAENZL.) ROLFE

syn: *Anoectochilus sanderiana* KRAENZL.

This is perhaps the most attractive of the jewel orchids. It grows in leaf litter on rocks in the lowlands of Papua New Guinea, the Solomon Islands, and Vanuatu. It has an erect stem about 2 in (5 cm) tall. There are about four broad leaves up to 3¼ in (8 cm) long and 2 in (5 cm) wide. These have a dark olive–green to maroon background with silver, green, or pink veins. When caught by light the leaves display a glistening sheen. The terminal inflorescence is up to 5⅔ in (14 cm) long with many small flowers. Flowering is during autumn. **ZONES 11–12. H.**

Macodes sanderiana

Macradenia multiflora

MACRADENIA R. BR.

This is a genus of about 15 relatively small orchids ranging from Guatemala to Brazil. They have cylindrical pseudobulbs with a single leaf at the apexes. The pendulous inflorescences are produced from the bases of the pseudobulbs.

CULTIVATION

These plants may be grown mounted or potted in a well-drained mix. They should be watered throughout the year and grown in intermediate temperatures with moderate humidity.

Macradenia multiflora (KRAENZL.) COGN.

This species is endemic to Brazil. It has clustered pseudobulbs about 2 in (5 cm) long. The solitary leaf is about 8 in (20 cm) long. The pendulous inflorescence, which carries many flowers, is up to 1 ft (30 cm) long. The flowers are about 1¼ in (3 cm) wide. Flowering is during summer.
ZONES 11–12. I–H.

MACROCLINIUM RCHB.F.

Macroclinium was previously a subsection of *Notylia*, but it is now recognized as a separate genus. The species are distributed from Mexico through Central America to Colombia. The plants are small and have a fan-shaped habit.

CULTIVATION

These species are best cultivated on slabs. They require year-round moisture and humidity, with a little less watering during the cooler months. They suit warm or intermediate climates best.

Macroclinium xiphophorus (RCHB.F.) DODSON

This species is a native of Ecuador and Peru. It is a miniature with a fan of flat, rigid leaves that have a base color of green to dark red, mottled with gray–green. The plant is about 1¼ in (3 cm) tall. Its small pseudobulbs are barely perceptible. The inflorescence is about 1¼–2 in (3–5 cm) long with several flowers about 1 in (2.5 cm) long at the end. New branches come from old flower stems in the following year. Flowering is during spring and summer. **ZONES 10–11. I.**

M

Macroclinium xiphophorus

MASDEVALLIA RUIZ & PAVON

This genus comprises about 350 species that occur over most of Central and South America. Many of them grow at high altitudes in the Andes. The stems are short with a single, fleshy leaf. The inflorescences have one to several flowers, and are either erect or pendulous. The most obvious parts of the flower are the sepals —they have connate bases that form a tube. In many species the tips of the sepals are drawn out into long tails. The petals and lip are small. Most of the species have showy and interesting flowers. This genus is related to other genera, such as *Pleurothallis* and *Dracula*.

CULTIVATION

Some of the high-altitude species have proved very difficult to cultivate, but others are quite amenable, including all those described below. They require cool to intermediate and humid conditions with good ventilation and air movement. They will grow in pots, except for the group that has inflorescences hanging straight down. These will require a basket so the flowers can be seen. A well-drained epiphytic mixture with some sphagnum moss added is usually recommended. All the species should be watered evenly throughout the year and kept under shade. Propagation is by the division of large clumps when new growth commences.

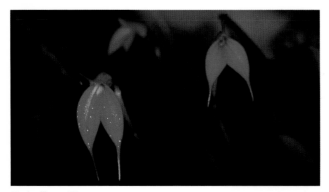

Masdevallia amabilis

Masdevallia amanda

Masdevallia amabilis RCHB.F.

This species grows at an altitude of about 8300 ft (2500 m) in northern Peru. It is reported to grow on rocks under full sun. The leathery, oblong leaves are up to 7 in (18 cm) long. The flowers are borne singly on an erect stem up to 1 ft (30 cm) tall. The flowers are about 1 in (2.5 cm) across, and the color varies from purple to white. Flowering is during winter. **ZONES 9–10. C–I.**

Masdevallia amanda RCHB.F. & WARSZ.

The "amanda" part of the name of this miniature plant might lead one to think it is a hybrid, but it is a species from Colombia. Its narrow leaves are up to 3¼ in (8 cm) tall. The inflorescences are taller than the leaves and bear one to four flowers, each about ⅔ in (15 mm) across. The rhizomes grow upwards, and for that reason a slab might be a better growing method than a pot. **ZONES 9–10. C–I.**

Masdevallia angulata RCHB.F.

This species from Ecuador and Colombia grows at moderate altitudes. It forms large clumps. The flowers are sometimes prolific, making an attractive display, and also tend to be semi-pendulous. Flowering is from late winter to spring with individual flowers lasting for about six weeks. The plant may remain in flower for about three months.
ZONES 9–10. C–I.

Masdevallia attenuata RCHB.F.

This species occurs at moderate to high altitudes in Costa Rica and Panama. Several plants form dense clumps, and they have glossy, green, leathery leaves about 2¾ in (7 cm) long. The inflorescences are usually shorter than the leaves and bear a single, long-lasting flower about 1 in (2.5 cm) long. Flowering is from winter to spring.
ZONES 9–10. C–I.

Masdevallia angulata

Masdevallia attenuata

M

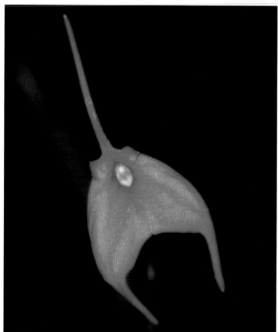

Masdevallia barlaeana
RCHB.F.

This miniature, tufted species has medium-sized but brilliantly colored flowers. It grows on rocks in moss and leaf litter at high altitudes in the Andes of Peru. The leaves are about 4¾ in (12 cm) long. The erect inflorescence is up to 8 in (20 cm) tall and bears a single flower. The floral tube is about ⅔ in (15 mm) long, with the tails of the sepals about 1½ in (3.5 cm) long. Flowering is during spring.
ZONES 9–10. C.

Masdevallia barlaeana

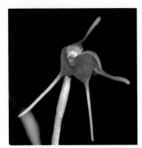

Masdevallia bicolor

Masdevallia caesia

M

Masdevallia caloptera

Masdevallia bicolor RCHB.F.

This species is recorded from Peru and Venezuela, growing epiphytically at high altitudes. It is a miniature plant about 4 in (10 cm) tall. The leaves are about 3¼ in (8 cm) long. The inflorescence bears one to two or three medium-sized (but large in relation to the plant) flowers. The tube made by the sepals is up to ⅓ in (1 cm) long and the tails are up to 1¼ in (3 cm) long. **ZONES 8–10. C.**

Masdevallia caesia ROEZL

This pendulous species is from southwest Colombia. The leaves are blue–green in color, and are long, narrow and pendulous. The flowers are large with long-tailed sepals. **ZONES 9–10. C.**

Masdevallia caloptera RCHB.F.

syn: *M. biflora* REGEL

This miniature species comes from northern Peru. It grows in moist forests at an altitude of about 6700 ft (2000 m). The leaves are erect, up to 3¼ in (8 cm) tall. The inflorescence is also erect and measures about 4¾ in (12 cm) long. There are three to several rather small flowers. The floral sepals form a tube about ⅓ in (1 cm) long, and the tails of the sepals are about ½ in (12 mm) long. **ZONES 9–10. C.**

Masdevallia caudata LINDL.

syn: *Maxillaria shuttleworthii* RCHB.F.

This medium-sized epiphyte comes from Venezuela, Colombia, Ecuador, and Peru. It grows in cloud forests with high moisture levels at altitudes of 6700–8300 ft (2000–2500 m). The leathery leaves are 4¾ in (12 cm) long and 1¼ in (3 cm) across. The inflorescences are shorter than the leaves and each one bears a single flower up to 7 in (18 cm) long. This measurement includes the long sepal tails, which are up to 2¾ in (7 cm) in length. Flowering is during winter. **ZONES 8–10. C.**

Masdevallia caudata

Masdevallia civilis

Masdevallia colossus

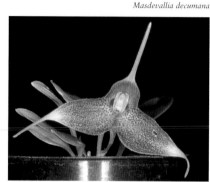

Masdevallia decumana

Masdevallia civilis RCHB.F. & WARSZ.
syn: several names, including *M. aequuiloba* REGEL, *M. fragrans* WOOLWARD

This small epiphyte occurs in Venezuela, Colombia, Ecuador, and Peru, where it is found at an altitude of about 8300 ft (2500 m). It grows as a terrestrial or in leaf mold on rocks. The leaves are up to 5⅔ in (14 cm) long and have rounded ends. The single flower is borne on a stem up to 2½ in (6 cm) tall. Its sepals are about 1 in (2.5 cm) long with short tails. Flowering is during spring. **ZONES 8–9. C.**

Masdevallia colossus LUER

This medium- to large-sized species forms dense, matted tufts. It comes from northern Peru and Ecuador. The stems are stout, about 2 in (5 cm) tall, and they each have a single, erect, and thick leaf about 7 in (18 cm) long. The inflorescence has a single flower on an erect peduncle up to about 4 in (10 cm) long. These long and fleshy flowers have a disagreeable odor. Each flower has a span of about 6 in (15 cm), over half of which is the length of the sepals, including the tails, which is about 3⅔ in (9 cm). Flowering is during autumn and winter. **ZONES 9–11. C–I.**

Masdevallia decumana KÖNIGER

This species from northern Peru and southern Ecuador features large flowers on a small plant. It grows at altitudes of 4700–8700 ft (1400–2600 m). Its broad leaves on short stalks have semi-circular apexes. The inflorescence is longer than the leaves and bears a single flower. The dorsal sepal forms a small hood and the lateral sepals are broad and widely spread with long tails. Often there are several bursts of flowering over the two or three months of winter. **ZONES 9–10. C–I.**

M

Masdevallia floribunda

Masdevallia herradurae

Masdevallia hirtzii

Masdevallia floribunda LINDL.

syn: *M. galeottiana* A. RICH. & GALEOTTI, **M.** *myriostigma* E. MORR.

This is one of the species in the genus that prefers warm-growing conditions. It is found at altitudes of 3000–4300 ft (900–1300 m) in Mexico, Guatemala, Honduras, and Costa Rica. Its leathery leaves are about 3²/₃ in (9 cm) long. The erect to semi-pendulous inflorescence bears a single flower about 1 in (2.5 cm) long. Flowering is during summer. **ZONES 10–11. I–H.**

Masdevallia herradurae LEHMANN & KRAENZL.

This miniature species is found in the mountains of Colombia. It flowers freely, and the small flowers are borne on stems that are shorter than the leaves. The sepals have long tails. **ZONES 9–10. C–I.**

Masdevallia hirtzii LUER & ANDREETA

This medium-sized epiphyte from the mountains of Ecuador is found at an elevation of about 5000 ft (1500 m). The plant forms small clumps with the leaf-bearing stems up to about ⁴/₅ in (2 cm) high. The erect, leathery leaf is up to 4 in (10 cm) long. The solitary flower is borne on an erect stem about 2¹/₂ in (6 cm) high. The tube of the flower is about 1 in (2.5 cm) long and the tails are about ⁴/₅ in (2 cm) long. In the wild, flowering may occur at any time. **ZONE 10. C–I.**

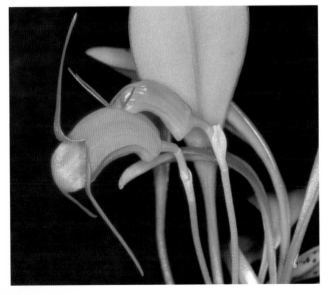

Masdevallia instar LUER & ANDREETA

This species occurs in both Ecuador and Peru at altitudes of 7000–9300 ft (2100–2800 m). It is a medium-sized plant that is epiphytic in habit, and it forms dense, matted tufts. The stems are about 2 in (5 cm) in length and the single leaf is up to 4 in (10 cm) long. A slender, erect peduncle, up to about 4 in (10 cm) long, bears a solitary flower, the dorsal sepal of which is about ¾ in (18 mm) long. Flowering is during spring. **ZONES 8–10. C–I.**

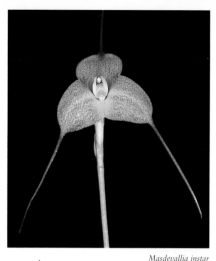

Masdevallia lepida RCHB.F.

This species grows in the cool, moist cloud forests of western Venezuela and eastern Colombia. It is found above 8300 ft (2500 m). The stems are ⅘–3¼ in (2–8 cm) long, the leaf is 2½–6 in (6–15 cm) long, and the inflorescence is 2¾–7½ in (7–19 cm) long. The inflorescence bears a flower about 1 in (2.5 cm) across and 4 in (10 cm) long from the tip of the dorsal sepal to the tip of the lateral sepals. The variable flower color ranges from light yellow–brown to yellowish–white, dotted or spotted with red–brown. This species may be difficult to cultivate as it prefers cold conditions. The flowers are often smaller in cultivation. **ZONES 9–10. C.**

Masdevallia instar

Masdevallia lepida

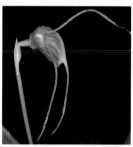

Masdevallia mendozae LUER

This species is found in Ecuadorian cloud forests at an altitude of about 7300 ft (2200 m). It is a small epiphyte that forms small clumps. The stems are about ⅘ in (2 cm) high. The erect, leathery leaf is about 2 in (5 cm) long. The inflorescence is about 1¼ in (3 cm) high and bears a single flower. The floral tube is about 1 in (2.5 cm) long, and the tails about ¹⁄₁₀ in (2 mm) long. Flowering is during winter and spring. **ZONE 10. C–I.**

Masdevallia mendozae

Masdevallia nidifica RCHB.F.

This miniature, epiphytic species occurs in
Costa Rica, Colombia, Ecuador, and Peru at
altitudes of about 1700–6700 ft (500–2000 m).
The leaves are up to 2 in (5 cm) long. The
inflorescence is about as long as the leaves and
bears a single, small flower. The tube formed
by the sepals is about $\frac{1}{3}$ in (1 cm) long and the
sepal tails are up to $1\frac{1}{4}$ in (3 cm) long.
ZONES 10–11. I.

Masdevallia nidifica

Masdevallia pachyura RCHB.F.

This species occurs at high altitudes on the
western slopes of the Andes in Ecuador. The
inflorescence is taller than the leaves and has
four to seven fleshy flowers with short tails.
ZONES 9–10. C–I.

Masdevallia peristeria RCHB.F.

This medium-sized epiphyte or terrestrial
occurs in Colombia at an altitude of about
6700 ft (2000 m). It grows low down on tree
trunks. Its leathery leaves are about $4\frac{3}{4}$ in
(12 cm) long. The short inflorescence has a
single flower, up to $4\frac{3}{4}$ in (12 cm) across, that
opens widely. The flower lasts for about seven
weeks and appears during spring.
ZONES 9–10. C.

Masdevallia pachyura

Masdevallia picea LUER

This species, noted for its foul-smelling odor, is
endemic to Peru, where it occurs at altitudes of
about 7000–9300 ft (2100–2800 m). It is a
robust plant with a dense, mat-forming habit.
The stout stem is up to about
$3\frac{1}{4}$ in (8 cm) high with a single,
thick, tough leaf up to 6 in
(15 cm) long and about 1 in
(2.5 cm) wide. A peduncle, up
to 1 in (2.5 cm) long, bears a
large flower. The sepals are thick
and fleshy, with the dorsal sepal
up to 1 in (2.5 cm) long.
Flowering occurs during spring.
ZONES 8–10. C–I.

Masdevallia peristeria

Masdevallia picea

Masdevallia prodigiosa

Masdevallia schroederiana

Masdevallia tovarensis

Masdevallia triangularis

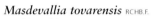

Masdevallia prodigiosa
KÖNIGER

This recently discovered species from northern Peru has relatively large flowers in comparison to the size of the plant. It grows in cloud forests at an altitude of about 6700 ft (2000 m). The leaves are about 2¾ in (7 cm) long. The flowers, borne singly on short inflorescences, are about 2½ in (6 cm) long. These last for about three weeks and there are several bursts of flowering throughout the year. Flowering is prolific in cultivation. **ZONES 9–10. C.**

Masdevallia schroederiana HORT.

This species was first introduced into cultivation in England from Peru prior to 1890, but not much is known about its habitat. Its leaves are up to 6 in (15 cm) long. The flowers are large for the plant size. The sepal tube is about ⅔ in (15 mm) long and the sepal tails reach 3¼ in (8 cm) in length. Flowering occurs during early spring and it lasts for four or five weeks. Experience suggests this species is particularly susceptible to hot weather. **ZONES UNCERTAIN. C.**

Masdevallia tovarensis RCHB.F.
syn: *M. candida* KLOTZSCH & KARST.

This epiphytic species is found in Venezuela at an altitude of about 6000 ft (1800 m). Its glossy, green leaves are up to 5½ in (13 cm) long. The inflorescence holds the one to five flowers above the height of leaves. The flowers open widely and are about 1 in (2.5 cm) across and 2¾ in (7 cm) long. Flowering is during winter. In order for this plant to flower again in the following year, the flowering stems should not be removed. **ZONES 9–10. C.**

Masdevallia triangularis LINDL.

This medium-sized species is an epiphyte that grows in cloud forests at altitudes of 4700–7700 ft (1400–2300 m) in Colombia and Venezuela. The leaves are up to 6 in (15 cm) long. The flowers are borne singly above the leaves. The free part of the sepals is about ⅘ in (2 cm) long and the tails are up to 1¾ in (4 cm) long. Flowering occurs during summer, and there is more than one flowering from each growth. **ZONES 9–10. C.**

M

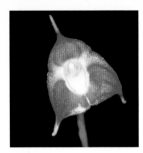

Masdevallia uniflora

Masdevallia urosalpinx

Masdevallia uniflora RUIZ & PAVON

This was the first species of the genus to be discovered and described; its recording dates back to 1794. It is a small plant found at an altitude of about 10,000 ft (3000 m) in the Andes of Peru. The leaves are up to 6 in (15 cm) tall. The inflorescence is a little taller than the leaves and bears a single flower about 1¼ in (3 cm) long. The flower color varies from pink to white. **ZONES 9–10. C.**

Masdevallia urosalpinx LUER

This species, endemic to Peru, is a medium-sized epiphyte. It has a dense, mat-forming habit. The erect and leathery stem, about 1 in (2.5 cm) long, carries a single leaf about 4 in (10 cm) long. The solitary inflorescence bears a flower on a slender peduncle that is up to 2 in (5 cm) long. The dorsal sepal is about 1¼ in (3 cm) long. Flowering is during spring. **ZONES 8–10. C–I.**

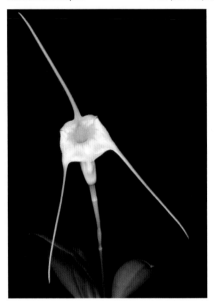

Masdevallia velifera

Masdevallia wagneriana

Masdevallia velifera RCHB.F.

This species comes from moderate to high altitudes in Colombia. Its leaves are clustered, narrow, and up to 8 in (20 cm) long. The inflorescence is shorter than the leaves and has a single flower about 2½ in (6 cm) long with an unpleasant odor. Flowering is during winter. **ZONES 9–10. C.**

Masdevallia wagneriana LINDL.

This miniature species from the mountains of Venezuela grows at an altitude of about 6000 ft (1800 m). The leathery leaves are elliptic, and about 2 in (5 cm) in length. The sub-erect inflorescence has a single flower about 2½ in (6 cm) long, which is large for the size of the plant. The sepal tail is up to 1¾ in (4 cm) long. Flowering is during spring. **ZONES 9–10. C–I.**

Masdevallia Ann Jessop × Drac. vampira

Masdevallia Peach Fuzz

Masdevallia Sunny Angel

Masdevallia Vietchiana

M

MAXILLARIA RUIZ & PAVON

This is one of the larger genera in the orchid family. It comprises more than 300 species scattered from Florida in the USA to Argentina. They are mostly epiphytes found at moderate altitudes, although some species occur in tropical lowlands and some at high altitudes. They have a long or short creeping rhizome. Some of the species have well-developed pseudobulbs that are commonly short and ovoid; others lack them. There are one or two leaves for each growth. The inflorescence arises from the rhizome near the base of a pseudobulb and bears a solitary flower, although there may be many flowers produced from one growth.

Maxillaria crassifolia

CULTIVATION

These plants like intermediate conditions with high humidity and bright light, but not full sunlight. The species without pseudobulbs should be kept evenly moist throughout the year, but those with pseudobulbs may be allowed a watering rest period when the growths are mature. Pots or baskets with a well-drained mixture that retains a little moisture are best. The few species with a climbing growth may do better on a slab. Care should be taken when repotting as some of these species do not like to be disturbed.

Maxillaria crassifolia (LINDL.) RCHB.F.

This is a widespread species occurring from Florida through the West Indies and Central America to Venezuela and Brazil. It is an epiphyte that grows in rain forests at low altitudes. Its ovoid, compressed pseudobulbs are about 2 in (5 cm) tall and have a single, straplike leaf up to 16 in (40 cm) long. The flowers, which arise from the base of the pseudobulbs, are about ⅘ in (2 cm) across. The flowers do not open widely, last for only a few days, and appear in late summer. **ZONES 10–12. I–H.**

Maxillaria cucullata

Maxillaria densa

Maxillaria cucullata LINDL.
syn: several names, including
M. *rhombea* LINDL., **M. *atrata*** RCHB.F.

This species ranges from
Mexico to Costa Rica. It
grows in wet forests at
altitudes of 5000–10,000 ft
(1500–3000 m). Several plants
form dense clumps of
pseudobulbs that are ovoid,
grooved, and compressed.
These are about 2½ in (6 cm)
tall and have a single straplike
leaf up to 16 in (40 cm) long.
One to three inflorescences
arise from bracts at the base
of the pseudobulbs. Each
inflorescence bears a single,
fleshy flower about 1¼ in
(3 cm) across. Flowering is
from autumn to early winter.
ZONES 10–11. I–H.

Maxillaria densa LINDL.
syn: *Ornithidium densum* (LINDL.) RCHB.F.

This species occurs from Mexico to Honduras
and features dense clusters of flowers. It grows as
a terrestrial in a range of habitats from pine or
rain forests in the lowlands to cloud forests at an
8300-ft (2500-m) altitude. The pseudobulbs are
compressed, ovoid, and up to 2¾ in (7 cm) long.
They are either clustered or, more commonly,
spread out on a rhizome that often hangs off a
tree trunk. The narrow leaf is up to 1 ft (30 cm)
long. Groups of up to 30 flowers arise from the
base of new growths. The flowers are fragrant
and about ⅘ in (2 cm) across, and they vary in
color from white to maroon or purple. Flowering
occurs in several bursts as the new growths
mature, and the flowers last for a few days.
ZONES 10–12. I–H.

Maxillaria elatior

Maxillaria elatior RCHB.F.

This species occurs from Mexico to Costa Rica at altitudes of
1300–5000 ft (400–1500 m). It is an epiphyte or, occasionally,
a terrestrial that grows in rain forests. The rhizome grows up
tree trunks or hangs off them. The pseudobulbs are at the end
of the rhizomes, and are compressed, ovoid, and up to 3⅔ in
(9 cm) long. There are one or two leaves which are up to 16 cm
(40 cm) long. The inflorescences arise from the bracts on the
rhizome and bear a single flower about 2 in (5 cm) across.
Flowering is from winter to spring. **ZONES 10–12. I–H.**

Maxillaria hematoglossa

Maxillaria hematoglossa
A. RICHARD & GAL.

This species, endemic
to Mexico, grows as
an epiphyte in
deciduous forests at
altitudes of about
3300 ft (1000 m).
The pseudobulbs are
ovoid, clustered, and
about 1 in (2.5 cm)
long. The slender leaf
is up to 1 ft (30 cm)
long. A solitary
flower is produced
from the base of a
pseudobulb on new
growth. The flowers
are about 1 in
(2.5 cm) wide.
Flowering is from late
summer to autumn.
ZONE 10. I.

Maxillaria lepidota

Maxillaria luteo-alba

Maxillaria lepidota LINDL.
syn: *M. pertusa* LINDL. EX RCHB.F., *M. saxicola* SCHLTR.

This species comes from Ecuador, Colombia,
and Venezuela. It grows at altitudes of
5000–6700 ft (1500–2000 m) in the Andes.
The pseudobulbs are clustered, ovoid or
cylindrical, and up to 2 in (5 cm) tall, with a
single, straplike leaf up to 14 in (35 cm) long.
The spidery flowers are about 4¾ in (12 cm)
across when spread out. These are borne on
a slender peduncle, up to 4¾ in (12 cm) long,
covered with inflated bracts. Flowering is
during spring and summer. **ZONES 10–11. C–I.**

Maxillaria luteo-alba LINDL.
syn: *M. luteo-grandiflora* HORT.

This very attractive species from Costa Rica,
Panama, Colombia, Ecuador, and Venezuela
grows at altitudes of 1700–5000 ft
(500–1500 m). The pseudobulbs are clustered,
ovoid, and about 2 in (5 cm) tall. There is a
single, straplike leaf up to 20 in (50 cm) long.
The inflorescence is more or less erect, up to
4¾ in (12 cm) long, and covered with bracts.
The fragrant and long-lasting flower is variable
in size, but no more than 4 in (10 cm) across.
Flowering is from spring to early summer.
ZONES 10–12. I.

Maxillaria marginata

Maxillaria meleagris

Maxillaria marginata LINDL.

syn: M. *punctulata* KLOTZSCH, M. *tricolor* LINDL.

This species is found at low to moderate altitudes in Brazil. The pseudobulbs are clustered, ovoid, and up to 2 in (5 cm) long with a single, narrow leaf up to 8 in (20 cm) long. There are one or a few inflorescences per growth, and these are up to 4 in (10 cm) long. Each one has a single flower about 1¾ in (4 cm) long. Flowering is from summer to autumn. **ZONES 10–12. I–H.**

Maxillaria meleagris LINDL.

syn: M. *lindeniana* A. RICH. & GALEOTTI, M. *punctostriata* RCHB.F.

This epiphytic species from Mexico, Guatemala, and Panama grows in rain forests at altitudes up to 6000 ft (1800 m). The pseudobulbs are clustered, ovoid, compressed, and up to 2 in (5 cm) long. There is a single, narrow leaf up to 16 in (40 cm) long. The inflorescence arises from the base of new growth and is about 2½ in (6 cm) long. It bears a single flower that is variable in size, but no more than 2 in (5 cm) across.
ZONES 10–11. I.

Maxillaria nigrescens LINDL.

syn: M. *rubrofusca* KLOTZSCH

The large, spidery flowers of this species make it a spectacular-looking plant when in bloom. It grows in rain forests at altitudes of 5000–8300 ft (1500–2500 m) in the Andes of Colombia and Venezuela. The pseudobulbs are narrowly ovoid, somewhat compressed, and up to 3⅔ in (9 cm) long. There is a single, straplike leaf up to about 14 in (35 cm) long. The inflorescence is much shorter than the leaf and bears a single flower up to 3¼ in (8 cm) across. Flowering is from summer to autumn. **ZONES 9–11. I.**

M

Maxillaria nigrescens

Maxillaria notylioglossa RCHB.F.

syn: *Maxillaria meirax* RCHB.F. & WARM.

This species occurs in Venezuela and Brazil at altitudes of
3300 ft (1000 m) or more. The pseudobulbs are up to 1 in
(2.5 cm) tall, and spaced about 1–2 in (2.5–5 cm) apart on a
creeping rhizome. The two narrow leaves are up to 6 in (15 cm)
long. The solitary flower is borne on a stem up to about 2 in
(5 cm) tall. The flower does not open widely and is about ⅘ in
(2 cm) wide. Flowering is during spring and this plant prefer
intermediate conditions with moisture all year. **ZONES 10–11. I.**

Maxillaria notylioglossa

Maxillaria ochroleuca

Maxillaria ochroleuca

LODD. EX LINDL.

This species occurs in Brazil
and Venezuela at moderate
to high altitudes. The ovoid,
compressed pseudobulbs are
up to 2¾ in (7 cm) long with
a single, straplike leaf up to
1 ft (30 cm) long. The
flowers, borne on a short
peduncle from the base of the
pseudobulbs, are about 1¼ in
(3 cm) across. They do not
open widely and appear
during spring and summer.
ZONE 10. C–I.

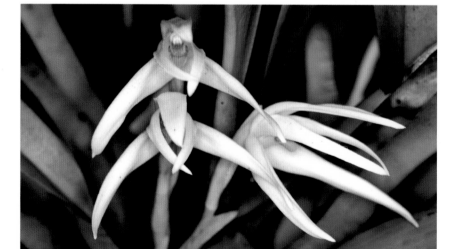

Maxillaria picta

HOOKER

syn: M. leucocheila

HOFFMANN-SEGG,

M. rupestris BARB. RODR.

This species occurs
in the southeastern
states of Brazil. It
grows as an epiphyte
or, occasionally, on
rocks at moderate
altitudes. The
pseudobulbs are
clustered or borne
at intervals along the
rhizome. They are
ovoid, compressed,
grooved, and up to
2¾ in (7 cm) long.
There are two or,
occasionally, one
narrow leaves up
to about 2 in (5 cm)
long. The flowers
are produced from
the base of the
pseudobulbs in large
numbers. Each flower
is about 2½ in (6 cm)
across, fragrant, and
long-lasting.
Flowering is during
winter. **ZONE 10. I–H.**

M

Maxillaria picta

Maxillaria porphryostele RCHB.F.

This species occurs in Brazil and grows at low
to moderate altitudes. The pseudobulbs are
ovoid to globose, slightly compressed, about
1¼ in (3 cm) tall, and become wrinkled with
age. There are two straplike leaves up to 1 ft
(30 cm) long on each pseudobulb. The flowers
are about 1¾ in (4 cm) across, long-lasting,
and borne singly on a peduncle up to 4¾ in
(12 cm) long. Flowering is from mid winter
to spring. **ZONES 9–10. C–I.**

Maxillaria porphryostele

Maxillaria sanguinea

Maxillaria sophronitis

Maxillaria sanguinea ROLFE

This species, related to *M. tenuifolia*, occurs in Costa Rica
and western Panama. It grows in lowland tropical and lower
mountain rain forests up to a 3000-ft (900-m) altitude. The
pseudobulbs are curved and $1/3$–1 in (1–2.5 cm) long. There
is one narrow, apical leaf about 8–14 in (20–35 cm) long and
$1/10$–$1/5$ in (2–4 mm) wide. The single flower is about 1 in
(2.5 cm) across and has a slight fruity fragrance. Flowering
is during late spring. **ZONES 10–11. I–H.**

Maxillaria sophronitis (RCHB.F.) GARAY

This miniature, creeping epiphyte is from Venezuela and
northeast Colombia, where it grows at altitudes of 2500–5300 ft
(750–1600 m). The pseudobulbs are ovoid, compressed, and
about $1/3$ in (1 cm) long. These are borne at intervals along the
creeping rhizome. The single leaf is about $4/5$ in (2 cm) long and
$1/3$ in (1 cm) wide. The flowers
are large for the size of the
plant, and are borne from the
base of mature pseudobulbs.
This species has a reputation
for being difficult to grow.
It requires intermediate
temperatures and good air
movement. **ZONES 9–10. C–I.**

Maxillaria tenuifolia
LINDL.

This species is related to
M. sanguinea. The difference
between the two is that
M. tenuifolia has spindle-
shaped pseudobulbs, broader
leaves, a coconut fragrance,
and a later flowering period.
This species is popular in
cultivation and grows in rain
forests at low altitudes, up to
about 4000 ft (1200 m), from
Mexico to Nicaragua. It climbs
or hangs from tree trunks, but
in cultivation it forms large
clumps. The pseudobulbs are
spaced about $1¾$ in (4 cm)
apart on the rhizome, and are
ovoid, wrinkled, compressed,
and up to about $2½$ in (6 cm)
long. The single, narrow leaf is
up to 20 in (50 cm) long. The
inflorescences arise from the
rhizome near the base of the
pseudobulbs and are about
$2½$ in (6 cm) long. The flowers
are about $1¾$ in (4 cm) across.
Flowering is during early
summer. **ZONES 10–12. I–H.**

Maxillaria tenuifolia

Maxillaria tenuis

Maxillaria ubatubana

Maxillaria variabilis

Maxillaria tenuis SCHWEINF.

This small species grows as an epiphyte in forests near Iquitos in northeast Peru. The pseudobulbs are clustered, more or less cylindrical, up to 1 in (2.5 cm) long, and partly covered with dried bracts. The single, straplike leaf is up to $5^2/_3$ in (14 cm) long and $^1/_3$ in (1 cm) wide. The inflorescence is about $1^1/_4$ in (3 cm) long and is covered with large bracts. It bears a single flower about $1^1/_4$ in (3 cm) long, which usually does not open fully. **ZONES 11–12. H.**

Maxillaria ubatubana HOEHNE

This species is restricted to Brazil where it occurs in the states of Espirito Santo, Rio de Janeiro, and São Paulo. It grows on trees and, occasionally, mossy rocks at moderate altitudes. The pseudobulbs have four angles and are about 2 in (5 cm) tall. The two straplike leaves are up to 16 in (40 cm) long and $^4/_5$ in (2 cm) wide. The single flower, about $1^3/_4$ in (4 cm) across, is borne on a peduncle about 4 in (10 cm) tall. Flowering is during autumn. In cultivation this species should be grown under semi-shade with heavy watering while actively growing and slightly less during winter. **ZONES 9–10. C–I.**

Maxillaria variabilis BATEM. EX LINDL.

syn: M. *angustifolia* HOOKER

This is a common species occuring from Mexico to Panama. It grows as an epiphyte, lithophyte, or terrestrial in rain forests from sea level to 6300 ft (1900 m). The pseudobulbs are ovoid, up to 2 in (5 cm) long, and spaced about $1^1/_4$ in (3 cm) apart on the rhizome. They have a single, narrow leaf up to 10 in (25 cm) long. The inflorescence is about 2 in (5 cm) long and bears a single flower about $^4/_5$ in (2 cm) across. The color of the flowers varies from white to pure yellow, yellow with red markings, or with a red lip, or dark red–brown or purple all over. Flowering occurs throughout the year. **ZONES 10–12. I–H.**

M

Mediocalcar decoratum

Mediocalcar bifolium

MEDIOCALCAR

Many of the 15 species in this genus are delightful miniatures, well suited to cultivation in cool climates. They occur in the rain forest mountains of New Guinea as well as some islands to the east and west of that island. Most grow as epiphytes at moderate to high altitudes, are small and mat-forming, and have one to four leaves on small pseudobulbs that may be crowded or well-spaced along the creeping rhizome. The small, brightly colored flowers are produced singly or in pairs from the apex of an old or developing pseudobulb. The connate sepals form a tube, and the petals and lip are small.

CULTIVATION

These species require moist, humid conditions year-round. The plants should be allowed to dry out for a day or two to help control fungi and algae. Light shade, never direct sunlight, is recommended. A shallow pan of a well-drained mixture that retains some moisture is best. Care is needed if plants are grown on slabs as they may dry out quickly.

Mediocalcar decoratum SCHUIT.

This species, restricted to the island of New Guinea, grows in forests at altitudes of 3000–8300 ft (900–2500 m). The pseudobulbs are cylindrical, about ⅓ in (1 cm) long, and spaced very close together on the rhizome. There are three or four leaves about ⅓ in (1 cm) long that spread out on one plane like the blades of a helicopter. The flowers are about ¼ in (6 mm) long and are borne on a short peduncle. Flowering is mostly during spring and a well-grown plant in flower can look spectacular as it may produce a mass of blooms. **ZONES 9–10. C–I.**

Mediocalcar bifolium
J. J. SM.
syn: several names, including
M. diphyllum SCHLTR., **M. monticola** SCHLTR.

This miniature, mat-forming species grows in rain forests, subalpine shrublands, on mossy rocks, and roadside cuttings at moderate to high altitudes in New Guinea. Its pseudobulbs are narrowly cylindrical, about ⅓ in (1 cm) long, and spaced about ⅓ in (1 cm) apart on the rhizome. There are one or two leaves about ⅘ in (2 cm) long. The flowers, borne on a peduncle about ⅓ in (1 cm) long, are also about ⅓ in (1 cm) long. Flowering occurs throughout the year. **ZONES 9–11. C–I.**

MEXICOA GARAY

There is only one species in this genus from southern Mexico. It grows on oak trees at elevations of 4700–7300 ft (1400–2200 m). It flowers during late spring.

CULTIVATION

This plant may be grown mounted or potted in a well-drained medium.

Mexicoa ghiesbreghtiana (RICH. & GAL.) GARAY

syn: *Oncidium ghiesbreghtiana* RICH. & GAL.

The pseudobulbs of this species are about 1¾ in (4 cm) long with two leaves emerging from the apex. These are up to 6 in (15 cm) long and up to ⅔ in (15 mm) wide. The inflorescence arises from the bases of the pseudobulbs. It is up to 8 in (20 cm) high and carries five to ten flowers, each about ⅘ in (2 cm) across. **ZONES 9–10. G–I.**

Mexicoa ghiesbreghtiana

MICROCOELIA LINDL.

There are some 30 species in this epiphytic genus from tropical Africa and Madagascar. The plants consist of a short stem and lack leaves—the photosynthetic and storage function of the leaves is taken over by a mass of green to gray–green roots. The mostly long inflorescences have small flowers.

CULTIVATION

The habit of these plants makes them best suited to a slab. Bright sunlight and humid conditions with regular watering are recommended.

Microcoelia exilis
LINDL.

This species has a wide distribution throughout tropical Africa and on Madagascar. It grows as a twig epiphyte in coastal and seasonally dry forests from sea level to a 6700-ft (2000-m) altitude. The plant has a mass of silver–gray roots up to 1 ft (30 cm) or more in length. These arise from a short stem. There are several inflorescences up to 10 in (25 cm) long with numerous small flowers. Flowering may occur at any time throughout the year but there tends to be an emphasis on November to April in the wild. **ZONES 10–12. I–H.**

Microcoelia exilis

Microcoelia ornithocephala

Microcoelia ornithocephala CRIBB.

This species from Malawi in tropical Africa occurs as a leafless, dwarf epiphyte at an altitude of about 2000 ft (600 m). It has several spreading roots that are prominent and flattened underneath. These are up to 1 ft (30 cm) long and ¼ in (6 mm) wide. Several inflorescences, about 1¾–2 in (4–5 cm) long, arise from a short stem and carry ten to 15 flowers, each about ⅓ in (1 cm) across. **ZONE 12. I–H.**

M

MICROPERA LINDL.

Most of the 15 monopodial species of this genus were originally placed in *Camarotis*. They range from India to Australia and the Solomon Islands, and grow mostly as epiphytes in wet forests at low to moderate altitudes. These plants have saccate lips and small but colorful flowers.

CULTIVATION

These plants require standard epiphytic cultivation conditions. The smaller species may be grown successfully in a pot, but the rambling species require a slab. Watering should be regular throughout the year.

Micropera philippensis (LINDL.) GARAY
syn: *Camarotis philippensis* LINDL.

This species is found in the Philippines on Luzon, Bohol, and Leyte islands. It grows as an epiphyte at an altitude of about 2700 ft (800 m). The erect stems are up to about 16 in (40 cm) tall with several leathery leaves about 6 in (15 cm) long. The upright inflorescence bears up to 20 flowers, each about ⅔ in (15 mm) across, with the lip held uppermost. Flowering occurs mostly during summer.
ZONES 10–11. I.

Micropera philippensis

Micropera rostrata (ROXB.) BALAKRISHNAN
syn: *M. purpurea* (LINDL.) PRADHAN, *Camarotis purpurea* LINDL.

This species occurs in northeast India and Thailand at low to moderate altitudes. The climbing stems are up to 3 ft (90 cm) long and have several straplike leaves up to 10 in (25 cm) long. The horizontal or pendulous inflorescences arise opposite the leaves and are up to 4 in (10 cm) long. They bear many fragrant, long-lasting flowers, each about 1 in (2.5 cm) across, with the lip held uppermost. Flowering is during spring.
ZONES 10–12. I–H.

Micropera rostrata

M

MILTONIA LINDL.

This genus of about ten species comes from low to moderate altitudes in Brazil. There is debate in botanical circles about *Oncidium* and *Miltonia*. The differences between the two genera are regarded by some authorities as insignificant and, if this view is accepted, *Miltonia* may be reclassified into *Oncidium*. In general, *Miltonia* has compressed pseudobulbs that are well spaced along the rhizome. There are two leaves on the apex of each pseudobulb and one or more large bracts with short leaves attached at the base. The inflorescences arise from the base of the pseudobulbs and have one to a few showy, moderately large flowers.

CULTIVATION

The best conditions for these plants are high humidity and bright light. Watering should be regular and heavy while the plants are in growth with a watering rest period after flowering. Those species with a rambling growth habit are best grown on a slab or in a large, shallow pan or basket. The others are suited to standard pots.

Miltonia candida

Miltonia candida LINDL.

syn: *Oncidium candidum* RCHB.F.

This species grows epiphytically at low to moderate altitudes in southeast Brazil. Its pseudobulbs are tapering, compressed, and up to $3\frac{2}{3}$ in (9 cm) tall. The leaves are straplike and up to 1 ft (30 cm) long. The erect or arching inflorescences bear up to eight long-lasting, fragrant flowers, each about $2\frac{3}{4}$ in (7 cm) across. Flowers appear during autumn. **ZONES 10–12. I–H.**

Miltonia flavescens

Miltonia clowesii

Miltonia clowesii LINDL.

syn: *Oncidium clowesii* RCHB.F., *Odontoglossum clowesii* (LINDL.) LINDL.

This species from southeast Brazil grows at low to moderate altitudes. Its pseudobulbs are narrow, ovate, compressed, and up to 4 in (10 cm) tall. The straplike leaves are up to 2 ft (60 cm) long. The inflorescence is up to 2 ft (60 cm) long and has five to ten flowers, each about 3¼ in (8 cm) long. This plant grows well in a pot but is better suited to a slab because of its rambling habit. Flowering occurs during autumn. **ZONES 11–12. I–H.**

Miltonia flavescens LINDL.

syn: *Cyrtochilum stellatum* LINDL., *Oncidium flavescens* (LINDL.) RCHB.F.

This species grows in hot lowlands from northern Brazil to Paraguay and Argentina. Its pseudobulbs are well spaced along the rhizome, ovate, strongly flattened, and up to 4¾ in (12 cm) in length. The two straplike leaves are about 1 ft (30 cm) long. The inflorescence is longer than the leaves and bears seven to ten fragrant flowers, each about 2¾ in (7 cm) across. Because this plant has a long rhizome it is best grown on a large slab. **ZONES 11–12. I–H.**

Miltonia regnellii RCHB.F.

syn: *Oncidium regnellii* (RCHB.F.) RCHB.F.

This epiphytic species comes from moderate altitudes in the eastern parts of Brazil. Its pseudobulbs are spaced about 2 in (5 cm) apart on the rhizome. They are compressed and tapering, and up to 4¾ in (12 cm) long. The straplike leaves are up to 1 ft (30 cm) long. The arching inflorescence is up to 20 in (50 cm) long with three to five flowers, about 2½ in (6 cm) across. This species does best if given a watering rest period after the flowering period in autumn. **ZONES 10–11. I.**

Miltonia regnellii

M

Miltonia russelliana (LINDL.) LINDL.

syn: *Oncidium russelliana* (LINDL.) LINDL.

This species occurs in the eastern states of
Brazil. It grows as an epiphyte at low to
moderate altitudes. The pseudobulbs are
spaced closely together on the rhizome and are
ovate, slightly compressed, and about 2–2¾ in
(5–7 cm) long. The leaves are straplike and up
to 10 in (25 cm) long. The inflorescence is
up to 2 ft (60 cm) long and has five to nine
flowers that do not open widely. These are
about 2 in (5 cm) across. Flowering is during
autumn and winter. **ZONES 10–11. I–H.**

Miltonia spectabilis LINDL.

syn: *Miltonia fryanus* KNOWLES & WESTCOTT,
Oncidium spectabile RCHB.F.

This species is found in eastern Brazil and,
perhaps, Venezuela. It grows at low to
moderate altitudes. The pseudobulbs are
spaced closely together on the rhizome. They
are compressed, ovate, and up to 4 in (10 cm)
long. The leaves are narrow, straplike, and up
to 1 ft (30 cm) long. The erect inflorescences
are up to 10 in (25 cm) long with one or two
flowers up to 4 in (10 cm) across. The flower
color varies from white or cream petals and
sepals with a purple lip, to entirely purple, as
in the variety "moreliana" shown here.
Flowering is during late spring or summer.
ZONES 10–11. I–H.

Miltonia spectabilis var. *morelliana*

Miltonia russelliana

MILTONIOPSIS GODEFROY-LEBEUF

"PANSY ORCHIDS"

This genus consists of about six epiphytic species from wet cloud forests at moderate to high altitudes in the Andes of Costa Rica. They have large, showy flowers with a large lip. The pseudobulbs are crowded closely together and have a single leaf.

CULTIVATION

These plants require cool to intermediate conditions with constant humidity and good air movement. They should not be given a watering rest period. The potting mixture should be well-drained but able to retain some moisture. Direct sunlight should be avoided, so grow these plants under filtered light.

HYBRIDS

Many hybrids have been made utilizing the bright colors and attractive flower shape that gave rise to these species' common name. They are well suited to temperate climates. Some of these hybrids are shown after the *Miltoniopsis* species section.

Miltoniopsis roezlii (RCHB.F.) GODEFROY-LEBEUF

syn: *Odontoglossum roezlii* RCHB.F., *Miltonia roezlii* (RCHB.F.) NICHOLSON

This species occurs in Colombia and Panama. It always grows in wet forests, not much above sea level to about 3300 ft (1000 m). The pseudobulbs are ovate, compressed, and about 2½ in (6 cm) long. The single, straplike leaf is up to 1 ft (30 cm) long. The flowers are flat, about 3¼–4 in (8–10 cm) across, and are borne on an inflorescence of two to five flowers. Flowering is during autumn.
ZONES 10–11. C–I.

Miltoniopsis roezlii

M

M

Miltoniopsis santanaei

Miltoniopsis vexillaria

Miltoniopsis santanaei GARAY & DUNSTERVILLE

This species occurs in the Andes of Colombia, Ecuador, and the northeastern corner of Venezuela. It grows in cloud forests and other moist environments at altitudes of 1300–3300 ft (400–1000 m). The flowers are about 2½ in (6 cm) across.
ZONES 10–11. I.

Miltoniopsis vexillaria
(RCHB.F.) GODEFROY-LEBEUF
syn: *Odontoglossum vexillarium*
RCHB.F., *Miltonia vexillaria* (RCHB.F.)
NICHOLSON

This species comes from Colombia and northern Ecuador. It grows on the margins of wet forests at altitudes of 4000–7300 ft (1200–2200 m). The pseudobulbs are ovoid to conical, strongly compressed, and up to 1¾ in (4 cm) long. A single, straplike leaf is up to 8 in (20 cm) long and there are three to six smaller leaves at the pseudobulb bases. The inflorescence bears about four flowers, each about 2½–4 in (6–10 cm) across. Flowering is from spring to summer.
ZONES 9–10. C–I.

Miltoniopsis Firewater "Red Butterfly"

Miltonia Jersey x Ace

Miltonia Hurricane Ridge "Silvia"

Miltonia Herralexandrae

MORMODES LINDL.

This genus of about 20 species occurs in Central and South America, mostly at lower altitudes. It is related to *Catasetum*. The plants have large pseudobulbs with several pleated, deciduous leaves. The inflorescences arise from nodes on the pseudobulbs. Some appear to have polymorphic flowers that are male and female, although whether these are truly unisexual is not clear. The column of the flowers is prominently twisted.

CULTIVATION

These plants should be watered regularly from the time new growth begins and while actively growing, with a watering rest period when the leaves fall. Pots or baskets with a standard well-drained epiphytic mixture are recommended. Bright light and good air movement are required.

Mormodes vinacea HOEHNE

This epiphyte occurs from Mexico to the northern part of South America. It grows in rain forests at low altitudes. Its pseudobulbs are clustered, broadly elliptical, and up to 10 in (25 cm) long with a few deciduous, rather narrow leaves. The inflorescences arise from the lower part of the pseudobulbs and bear up to 12 flowers, each about 2½ in (6 cm) across, that have a pungent fragrance. The color of the flowers varies and may include white, yellow to purple-brown or, sometimes, with stripes or spots. Flowering is from winter to spring.
ZONES 11–12. I–H.

M

Mormodes vinacea

MORMOLYCA FENZL.

This genus comprises about seven species ranging from Mexico to southeastern Brazil. Most of them grow at altitudes of 2500–6000 ft (750–1800 m) in the Andes of Venezuela and Brazil.

CULTIVATION

Most of these plants may be cultivated under intermediate conditions and potted in a well-drained mix or mounted on a suitable slab.

Mormolyca ringens (LINDL.) SCHLTR. (below)

This species is from Mexico, Belize, Guatemala, Honduras, El Salvador, and Costa Rica. It grows as an epiphyte in open oak and dense, humid forests from sea level to 4700 ft (1400 m). The slightly compressed pseudobulbs are about 2 in (5 cm) long with a solitary leaf to about 18 in (45 cm) long. Several erect inflorescences, up to 18 in (45 cm) tall, are produced simultaneously and each one bears a single flower about 2 in (5 cm) across. Flowering is mostly during summer.
ZONES 10–11. I–H.

Mormolyca ringens

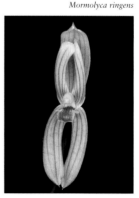

MYRMECOPHILA ROLFE

These species were originally part of *Schomburgkia*, and some
authorities still consider them part of that genus. *Myrmecophila*
are related closely to *Cattleya*, *Sophronitis*, and *Laelia*, and
have been hybridized with species from these genera to produce
complex forms. The genus comprises about eight species found
from Mexico and the West Indies to Venezuela. They are large,
robust epiphytes or lithophytes. The pseudobulbs are cylindrical
to conical, and gradually taper towards the end and become
hollow, creating a space in which ants often live. (It is thought
the plants provide the ants with a sheltered living area, and the
ants provide the plants with protection from other insects and,
possibly, provide a source of nitrogen.) The inflorescences are
terminal, long, and often branched, with a group of large,
showy flowers clustered near the end.

CULTIVATION

Some of these are large plants that will need a lot of room in
an orchid house. They should be grown in a basket or pot with
a coarse, free-draining mixture. Water heavily while in active
growth and allow a watering rest period after the plants have
finished growing. Care should be taken when repotting so that
the roots are not damaged.

Myrmecophila thomsoniana (RCHB.F.) ROLFE

syn: *Schomburgkia thomsoniana* RCHB.F., *Laelia thomsoniana* (RCHB.F.)
L. O. WILLIAMS

This species occurs on the Cayman Islands and in Cuba. It
grows on trees or eroded limestone rocks in lowland forests.
The hollow and curved pseudobulbs are up to 8 in (20 cm)
long, and the inflorescence is sometimes branched, and up
to 4 ft (1.2 m) long, but usually shorter. At the end of the
inflorescence are 12 to 20 flowers arranged in a dense head.
The flowers are about 2¾ in (7 cm) across and they appear
during spring.
ZONES 11–12. H.

Myrmecophila thomsoniana

Myrmecophila tibicinis (BATEMAN) ROLFE

syn: *Schomburgkia tibicinis* BATEMAN, *Schomburgkia grandiflora* HORT.,
Laelia tibicinis (BATEMAN) L. O. WILLIAMS

This common, robust species from Mexico, Belize, Guatemala, and
Honduras often grows on trees near the coast at low altitudes. The
pseudobulbs are crowded together, forming a large clump. They are up to
2 ft (60 cm) long, curved, slightly tapering, and hollow. In the wild, ants
live in these hollows. There are up to five oval, leathery leaves that grow
to 1 ft (30 cm) long.

The inflorescence, up
to about 8 ft 4 in
(2.5 m) long, is often
branched with several
flowers, each about
3¼ in (8 cm) across,
that crowd towards
the end. Flowering is
from spring to early
summer. **ZONE 12. H.**

Myrmecophila tibicinis

Myrmecophila wendlandii
(RCHB.F.) KENNEDY

syn: *Schomburgkia wendlandii* (RCHB.F.) H. G. JONES,
Laelia wendlandii (RCHB.F.) G. C. KENNEDY

This species occurs in Belize, Guatemala,
Honduras, and Nicaragua. It grows as an
epiphyte or lithophyte under full sun at
low altitudes. The pseudobulbs are curved,
cylindrical, grooved, and hollow, and up
to 8 in (20 cm) long. The two leathery leaves
are 8 in (20 cm) long and 2 in (5 cm) wide.
The inflorescence is up to 6 ft (2 m) tall and
bears up to 25 flowers arranged in a dense
group at the end of the inflorescence. The
fragrant flowers are about 4 in (10 cm) across
and appear during summer. **ZONES 11–12. H.**

Myrmecophila wendlandii

MYSTACIDIUM LINDL.

The species in this genus are all small monopodial epiphytes with a mass of roots, a short stem, and a few small, leathery leaves that may be deciduous in some species. These characteristics appear to be adaptations to the distinct dry season of their habitat in southeastern Africa. The inflorescences tend to be pendulous and bear a few white flowers with a long spur.

CULTIVATION

Most of these species are amenable to cultivation on a slab of bark or similar substrate. They should be given high humidity and strong light levels. Watering may be reduced during winter.

Mystacidium aliciae H. BOLUS

This miniature species is a twig epiphyte that grows in shady positions, often near rivers, in the Eastern Cape and KwaZulu Natal provinces of South Africa. Its extremely short stem has two to four leaves about 1¼ in (3 cm) long and a mass of gray–green roots. There are about three inflorescences and each one has four to seven flowers about ⅔ in (15 mm) across. Flowering is from late spring to the end of summer. **ZONES 10–11. I.**

Mystacidium aliciae

M

Mystacidium brayboniae

Mystacidium brayboniae
SUMMERH.

This miniature species is restricted to cloud forests at moderate altitudes in the mountains of northeastern South Africa. It is reported as growing on fig trees in shady positions. The stem is extremely short and the plant consists of a large mass of roots with about five leaves up to 2½ in (6 cm) long. During the dry season the plant may lose its leaves. The pendulous inflorescences have up to ten flowers, each about ⅘ in (2 cm) across, with a spur up to 1 in (2.5 cm) long. Flowers appear during late spring. **ZONE 10. I.**

NAGELIELLA L. O. WILLIAMS

This genus has about three species distributed from Mexico to Guatemala, El Salvador, and Honduras. The pseudobulb is slender and stemlike with a single, thick, fleshy, red-spotted leaf at the apex. The inflorescence is wiry and elongated, and carries several bell-shaped flowers that open successively.

CULTIVATION

These plants may be grown on slabs or in pots with intermediate conditions and ample water throughout the growing season.

Nageliella purpurea (LINDL.) L. O. WILLIAMS

This species grows on oak trees in mountainous forests, up to an altitude of 5000 ft (1500 m), from Mexico to Honduras. The thick stems are up to 1¾ in (4 cm) long and the leaves are up to 4¾ in (12 cm) long. The inflorescences arise from the apex of the stems and may be up to 16 in (40 cm) long. The ends of the inflorescences have clusters of several flowers, each about ¼ in (6 mm) wide. The flowers are produced from this same stem for several years, provided the tip is not damaged. Do not cut off the old inflorescence. Flowering is during summer. **ZONES 10–11. I.**

Nageliella purpurea

NEOBENTHAMIA ROLFE

This genus from East Africa has only one species. It is related to *Polystachya*.

CULTIVATION

The plant grows well in warm, humid conditions with bright light. It should be grown in a pot of terrestrial mix as would be used for *Phaius* or *Cymbidium* species. It commonly produces aerial growths with roots, and these may be used to propagate new plants.

Neobenthamia gracilis ROLFE

Restricted to Tanzania in east Africa, this species grows at low altitudes on rock faces in full sun. The plant is up to 6 ft (2 m) tall with slender, brittle, leafy, stems. The leaves are narrow, straplike, and up to about 8 in (20 cm) long. The erect, terminal inflorescences are about 4¾ in (12 cm) tall with numerous flowers, each about 1 in (2.5 cm) across, packed into a dense hemispherical head. Flowering may occur for most of the year. **ZONES 11–12. H.**

Neobenthamia gracilis

NEOFINETIA HU

This monotypic genus is widespread from China to Japan and Korea. It is a miniature epiphyte up to about 6 in (15 cm) tall. The leaves are arranged in two ranks, giving a fan-shaped appearance. The inflorescences are borne from the axils of the leaves and bear few flowers.

CULTIVATION

The species may be grown in small pots or baskets in intermediate conditions. Plenty of water should be provided during active growing periods, but this should reduced once new growth is complete.

Neofinetia falcata (THUMB.) HU
syn: *Angraecum falcatum* LINDL.

This plant is frequently branched from the base. The leaves are about 3 in (7.5 cm) long. The inflorescence is usually shorter than the leaves and has three to seven very fragrant flowers with a spur up to about 1¾ in (4 cm) long. **ZONES 9–10. I.**

Neofinetia falcata

N

NEOLEHMANNIA KRAENZL.

These species were once part of *Epidendrum*.
They range mainly from Mexico through
to Colombia and have similar vegetative
characteristics to those of the type of
Epidendrum species with reedlike stems.

CULTIVATION

These plants prefer similar cultivation
conditions to those of *Epidendrum*, and
Cattleya conditions also suit them well. The
smaller-growing species may be mounted.

Neolehmannia porpax (RCHB.F.) GARAY & DUNSTERVILLE

syn: *Epidendrum porpax* RCHB.F.

This species grows as an epiphyte in pine and
oak forests at altitudes up to 6700 ft (2000 m)
from Mexico to Panama, Venezuela, and Peru.
The plant lacks pseudobulbs but has a freely
branching habit with stems up to about 3¼ in
(8 cm) high. These are covered with alternating
leaves. The solitary flowers arise from the apex
of the stems. Flowering is during summer and
autumn. This species responds well to
cultivation on a slab or in a shallow pan with
a well-drained mixture. **ZONES 10–11. C–I.**

Neolehmannia porpax

N

Nervilia adolphii

NERVILIA COMM. EX GAUD.

There are about 70 species in this genus of terrestrial plants from tropical and subtropical areas. They occur in Africa, Madagascar, the Malay Archipelago, and Australia. Most of them grow in seasonal habitats and all of them have the habit of producing flowers at the start of the wet season, followed by the leaves a week or two later. The cycle from flowering to dispersal of seed is short, usually only two or three weeks. The single leaf is usually heart- or kidney-shaped and either lies on the ground or is slightly elevated.

CULTIVATION

The flowers and, in some cases, the leaves of these species are attractive—many of them are well worth a place in collections. A typical well-drained, terrestrial mixture of loam, sand, and leaf mold is best. The plants should be kept dry during the dry season (this is winter in most cases). Watering should be restarted in mid to late spring and continued until the leaves start to die back in autumn. These plants should be repotted every two years.

Nervilia adolphii SCHLTR.

This species grows on forest floors at moderate altitudes in central Africa, from northeast South Africa to Tanzania and Nigeria. The broadly ovate leaves are about 2 in (5 cm) across and are held on the ground. These are green above and, frequently, purple underneath. The inflorescence bears a single flower about $\frac{1}{3}$ in (1 cm) long and this is held about $3\frac{1}{4}$ in (8 cm) above the leaf. Flowering occurs from October to December in the wild. **ZONES 9–10. I.**

Nervilia holochila (F. MUELL.) SCHLTR.

This species is widespread in moist areas of the Australian tropics, on the islands of the Torres Strait, and in New Guinea. It grows in seasonally open forests from sea level to about 2700 ft (800 m). The broadly ovate leaf is pleated, held erect, and up to $6\frac{3}{4}$ in (17 cm) long. It emerges on a stalk about $1\frac{3}{4}$ in (4 cm) long. The inflorescence is up to 10 in (25 cm) tall and bears four to six flowers, each 1–2 in (2.5–5 cm) across. Flowering occurs during late spring or early summer, depending on the first heavy rains of the wet season. **ZONES 11–12. H.**

Nervilia holochila

N

Nervilia plicata

Nervilia reniformis

Nervilia plicata (ANDREWS) SCHLTR.
syn: many names, including N. *discolor* (BLUME) SCHLTR.,
Pogonia discolor (BLUME) BLUME

This widespread species ranges from India to China, New
Guinea, Australia, and all the areas in between. It grows on
the floor of seasonal, open forests from sea level to about
3300 ft (1000 m). The leaves lie flat on the ground and are
heart-shaped, circular, pleated, hairy, and up to 4¾ in (12 cm)
across. The inflorescence is about 7 in (18 cm) tall and it
becomes elongated after flowering to assist in scattering the
seed. There are two to four (most often only two) flowers, each
about 2 in (5 cm) across. Flowering occurs at the start of the
wet season, usually in early summer. **ZONES 11–12. H.**

Nervilia reniformis SCHLTR.

This small species occurs in Tanzania where it is common in
woodlands in the hills north of Lake Malawi. The leaf is kidney-
shaped to almost circular, hairy on the upper surface, and about
2 in (5 cm) across. The single flower points upwards and is
about ⅔ in (15 mm) long. Flowering is from November to
December in the wild. **ZONES 9–10. I.**

Nervilia uniflora (F. MUELL.) SCHLTR.

This small species occurs at low altitudes in northeast
Queensland, Australia. It has not been recorded in New Guinea
but it is possible it may occur there as well. It grows in moist,
open forests, usually in positions that are well shaded by tall
grass. The leaves are heart-shaped with undulate margins, green
above and purple underneath, and about 1¼–2¾ in (3–7 cm)
across. They are held above the ground, more or less horizontally. The inflorescence is up to 8 in (20 cm) tall with a single
flower about ⅘–1¼ in (2–3 cm) across. Flowering is from late
spring to early summer. **ZONE 12. H.**

Nervilia uniflora

NIGRITELLA RICH.

For many years this genus consisted only of two species. In the past few years, more and more have been described and added, making a total of 15. Because of the close relationship between this genus and *Gymnadenia*, some botanists consider *Nigritella* should be absorbed into that genus. The species in *Nigritella* are found above an altitude of about 3300 ft (1000 m) in the mountains in Europe, from the Pyrenees through the Alps and the Balkans to the Carpathians in Scandinavia, but most of them are more or less restricted to small, local areas in the Alps. Nine of the species have a peculiar behavior with respect to their propagation. They are apomicts, which means they form their seed without fertilization between male and female flowers. These plants are generally small with many basal leaves and densely flowered inflorescences. The flowers have a small, blunt spur.

CULTIVATION

Nigritella are not recommended for cultivation, in fact, none is known in cultivation. It would be almost impossible to replicate in an orchid house the habitat and climatic conditions of the high mountain regions in which they grow.

Nigritella corneliana (BEAUVERD) GÖLZ
& H. R. REINHARD

This orchid was first considered a subspecies but was elevated to species status in 1986. It is restricted to a small area in the western Alps—the southern Savoy Alps in southeast France and the Alps in France and Italy—where it grows in moist alpine meadows above 6000 ft (1800 m). The plants and flowers are relatively large for the genus and have an elongated, egg-shaped inflorescence. The flowers are white to pink tinged with red, with a lip less than $\frac{1}{3}$ in (1 cm) long. Flowers appear in mid summer.
ZONES 6–7. C.

Nigritella corneliana

N

Nigritella miniata

Nigritella miniata (CRANTZ) JANCH.
syn: *N. rubra* (WETTST.) RICHT.

This apomictic species has a larger distribution than most apomictic species. It occurs from the central Swiss Alps to the southern Carpathians in Scandinavia. It grows in calcareous soils, and also slate, at altitudes of 5300–7700 ft (1600–2300 m). The inflorescence has a cylindrical form with uniformly bright ruby–red flowers. The flowering season is early to mid summer. **ZONES 5–7. C.**

Nigritella rhellicani TEPPNER & E. KLEIN
syn: *N. nigra* L.

This species was first described as *N. nigra* by Linnaeus in 1753 from a plant found in Scandinavia. It was redescribed in 1990 when it became clear that it was not identical to the plants of other European mountain ranges, including the Alps. This one is widely spread from the French Alps to the Balkan Mountains and the Carpathians. It grows mostly in the calcareous soils of dry, sunny meadows at altitudes of 3300–9300 ft (1000–2800 m). The inflorescence is egg-shaped and the flower color is generally chocolate–brown, but pink (as in the variety *rosea*) and yellow (variety *flava*) forms do occur, even though they are rare, in some places. Flowers appear in mid summer. **ZONES 5–8. C.**

Nigritella rhellicani

NINDEMA BRITTON & MILLSP.

This genus comprises two species distributed from Mexico to Peru. They are epiphytes that grow in the wet forests from sea level to 4700 ft (1400 m). They have unifoliate pseudobulbs. The inflorescences arise from the apexes of these.

CULTIVATION

These plants are easy to cultivate in pots with a free-draining mix under intermediate to warm conditions.

Nindema boothii (LINDL.) SCHTLR.

This species occurs in Mexico, Panama, and Suriname. The pseudobulbs, about 1¼ in (3 cm) high, are clustered on a creeping rhizome. There are one or two apical leaves about 6 in (15 cm) long. The apical inflorescence is about 4 in (10 cm) long with a few flowers about 1¼ in (3 cm) wide. These flowers are pleasantly fragrant and arise from the new growth during summer. **ZONES 9–10. I.**

Nindema boothii

NOTYLIA LINDL.

This genus is found from Mexico through Colombia, Venezuela, and Trinidad and Tobago to Brazil and Bolivia. The species are epiphytes that grow in wet forests from sea level to about 2700 ft (800 m). The pseudobulbs have a single, flat apical leaf. The pendulous and densely flowered inflorescences are produced from the base of the pseudobulbs.

CULTIVATION

These plants grow best on slabs in intermediate to warm conditions with water and high humidity throughout the year.

Notylia barkeri LINDL.

This species ranges from Mexico to Panama. In Mexico it grows in sheltered situations at elevations between sea level and 3000 ft (900 m). Its pseudobulbs are clustered, up to 1 in (2.5 cm) long, and often concealed by overlapping green bracts. The solitary and leathery leaves are up to 7 in (18 cm) long. There are one or more densely flowered, arching or drooping inflorescences. These are produced from the base of the pseudobulbs and are about 1 ft (30 cm) long. The flowers are about ⅓ in (1 cm) long and appear during spring. This species is best cultivated on a slab. **ZONES 10–12. I–H.**

N

Notylia barkeri

OBERONIA LINDL.

This is a large genus of over 300 small species. These epiphytes occur at low to moderate altitudes in virtually all moist areas from Africa to the Pacific Islands. They have a long or short stem with fleshy, laterally flattened leaves that overlap at the base. The inflorescence is relatively long in relation to the size of the plant and has numerous tiny flowers.

CULTIVATION

Most of these species prefer shady conditions with good air movement. A small pot containing a mixture such as peat and perlite or fine bark, with a little added sphagnum moss, is recommended. A slab is equally suitable so long as the plants are kept moist.

O

Oberonia complanata
(CUNN.) M. CLEM. & D. L. JONES
syn: *O. muelleriana* SCHLTR.

This species is similar to the widespread *O. iridifolia* from the Himalayan region. *O. complanata* is a small plant found in northeast Queensland in Australia and, possibly, Papua New Guinea. It grows at low to moderate altitudes in rain forests, but usually in exposed situations. The plant consists of a short stem and several fleshy leaves to about 6 in (15 cm) long. The erect inflorescence is about 6 in (15 cm) long with numerous densely packed flowers about ⅛ in (3 mm) across. The flowers may appear at any time but there is an emphasis on spring.
ZONES 11–12. I–H.

Oberonia complanata

Oberonia drepanophylla
SCHLTR.

This attractive miniature occurs at moderate altitudes in the mountainous forests of Papua New Guinea. The species is pendulous, with stems up to about 8 in (20 cm) long. There are about seven to eight curved leaves, each about 6 in (15 cm) long. The inflorescence is about the same length as or longer than the leaves and it carries numerous small flowers. The flowers are arranged in whorls that each comprise about ten flowers. These are well spaced on the inflorescence. Flowering is throughout the year with an emphasis on summer.
ZONES 10–11. I–H.

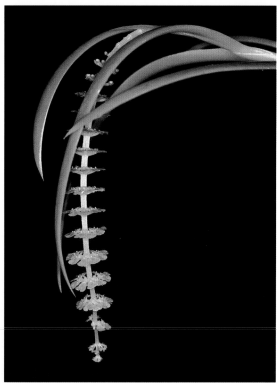

Oberonia drepanophylla

Oberonia titania LINDL.
syn: *O. palmicola* F. MUELL., *O. neocaledonica* SCHLTR.

This miniature species occurs on the east coast of Australia, from northern New South Wales to Cape York Peninsula. It is also found on Lord Howe Island, Norfolk Island, and New Caledonia. It grows in shady conditions on rain forest trees from sea level in the southern part of its range to about 3300 ft (1000 m) in the north. There is a short stem with several fleshy leaves, each up to 2½ in (6 cm) long. The arching inflorescence is up to 6 in (15 cm) long and bears numerous, very small flowers. Flowering is during autumn in the tropical north and spring in the south.
ZONES 10–11. I–H.

Oberonia titania

OCTOMERIA R. BR.

This genus, which is part of the pleurothallid alliance, is estimated to consist of about 150 species in Central and South America and the West Indies. Most of them occur in Brazil. They are diverse plants, but are usually small with flowers borne in bunches at the base of the fleshy or leathery leaves.

CULTIVATION

Most of these plants grow well in small pots with a free-draining medium or sphagnum moss, but some do equally well on a slab. Moisture and humidity are required throughout the year.

Octomeria crassifolia LINDL.

This species is found in the cool mountains of southeast Brazil, Paraguay, and Uraguay. The clustered stems are about 5½ in (13 cm) long. They are produced on a short creeping rhizome. The single, stiff, and erect leaf is about 4 in (10 cm) long. The three or four flowers borne from the base of the leaf are about ⅓ in (1 cm) across. Flowering is from autumn to spring. **ZONES 9–10. C–I.**

Octomeria crassifolia

Octomeria grandiflora

Octomera grandiflora LINDL.

This is one of the largest species in the genus. It is found in Guyana, Brazil, and Bolivia. The stems are clustered and each one is up to 7 in (18 cm) tall with a solitary, rigid leathery leaf up to 5½ in (13 cm) long. The inflorescence is produced at the leaf base and has numerous clustered flowers that open widely to nearly 1 in (2.5 cm). Flowering is from autumn to spring. This species may be grown mounted on a slab. **ZONES 10–12. I–H.**

ODONTOGLOSSUM H. B. K.

This genus occurs in the Andes of South America, mostly in cloud forests and constantly cool, wet habitats at altitudes above 5000 ft (1500 m). Many experts believe the differences between this genus and *Oncidium* are insignificant, but *Odontoglossum* remains in common use to date. Estimates of the number of species in this genus vary from about 60 to 175, depending on which groups are included. The pseudobulbs are usually laterally compressed and ovate, with one or two leaves at the apex. A few leaflike sheaths at the base enclose the inflorescence. The flowers are mostly large and showy.

CULTIVATION

Species from this genus are very popular among growers with cool orchid houses. They require constant watering and high humidity with good air movement and shade, particularly in hot conditions. A standard epiphytic mixture with some moisture-retaining capability is best. Care should be taken with watering when the new growths are emerging, so that water does not lodge in the leaf axils.

HYBRIDS

There has been extensive hybridization within this genus and with *Miltoniopsis*, *Miltonia*, *Oncidium*, *Cochlioda* and many other genera.

Odontoglossum luteopurpureum LINDL.

syn: *O. hystrix* BATEMAN, *O. radiatum* RCHB.F.

This species is an epiphyte from Colombia. It grows in cloud forests at altitudes of 7700–10,000 ft (2300–3000 m). The pseudobulbs are clustered, laterally compressed, and up to about 4 in (10 cm) tall. There are two straplike leaves, each about 1 ft (30 cm) long, at the apex, and two to three leaf-bearing sheaths at the base. The arching inflorescence is up to 1 ft (30 cm) long and carries up to 12 flowers, each 4 in (10 cm) across. Flowering is from spring to summer. **ZONES 9–10. C.**

Odontoglossum hallii LINDL.

This species occurs in the Andes of Ecuador. It is an epiphyte or terrestrial that grows in leaf litter in cloud forests at altitudes of 6700–10,000 ft (2000–3000 m). The pseudobulbs are close together, ovoid, laterally compressed, and about 3⅔ in (9 cm) long. There are two narrow, straplike leaves, each up to about 1 ft (30 cm) long, and two to four leaf sheaths near the pseudobulb bases. The inflorescence is up to 1 ft (30 cm) long and bears about ten flowers, each up to 4 in (10 cm) across. The flowers vary in size and color and appear from spring to summer. **ZONES 9–10. C.**

Odontoglossum luteopurpureum

Odontoglossum hallii

Odontoglossum nobile

Odontoglossum nobile RCHB.F.

syn: *O. pescatorei* LINDEN

This species occurs in Colombia, where it grows as an epiphyte in open cloud forests at about a 7700-ft (2300-m) altitude. It is a variable species with flower colors ranging from white to yellow and various combinations of purplish–red spots or stripes. About 12 flowers are borne in a raceme that may be occasionally branched. The flowers are faintly fragrant and about 2½in (6 cm) across. Flowering occurs during spring. **ZONES 9–10. C.**

Odontoglossum wallisii

Odontoglossum wallisii RCHB.F.

This species is recorded in Colombia, where it grows on cloud forest margins at altitudes of 6700–8300 ft (2000–2500 m). The pseudobulbs are clustered, compressed, furrowed, and up to about 1¾ in (4 cm) long. There are two leaves at the apex and two to three leaf-bearing sheaths at the base. The erect inflorescence has four to six star-shaped flowers about 2 in (5 cm) across. Flowering occurs during winter. **ZONES 9–10. C.**

Odontoglossum wyattianum

Odontoglossum wyattianum WILSON

This species from Peru and Ecuador grows on solitary trees in cloud forests at altitudes of 5300–7300 ft (1600–2200 m). The slender pseudobulbs are pear-shaped, furrowed, compressed, and up to 4 in (10 cm) long. There are one or two leaves at the apex, and these are up to about 1 ft (30 cm) long. There are also three or four leaf-bearing sheaths at the base. The erect to horizontal inflorescence has about eight flowers, each about 3¼ in (8 cm) across. **ZONES 10–11. C–I.**

OECEOCLADES LINDL.

syn: *Eulophidium* PFITZER

Until a few years ago, these 30 terrestrial species were placed in
Eulophidium. They are found in tropical Africa and on Madagascar
predominantly, but they also extend to Southeast Asia and Central and
South America. The pseudobulbs have two to three leaves at the apex.
The inflorescences are borne from the base of the pseudobulbs and are
either simple or branched with several small- to medium-sized flowers.

CULTIVATION

A terrestrial mixture of sand, loam, and leaf mold is usually successful.
The plants may be watered regularly but allow a brief watering rest
period after growth is complete. Some species require sun; others shade.

Oeceoclades maculata (LINDL.) LINDL.

syn: many names, including *Eulophia maculata* (LINDL.) RCHB.F., *Angraecum maculatum* LINDL., *Eulophidium maculatum* (LINDL.) PFITZER

The distribution
of this species is
inter-esting as it is in
tropical Africa, South
and Central America,
and Florida in the
USA. The plant grows
in shady situations,
mostly at low
altitudes. The
pseudobulbs are
ovoid to cylindrical,
and up to about
1¾ in (4 cm) tall.
There is a single leaf
about 10 in (25 cm)
long and 2 in (5 cm)
wide. The erect
inflorescence is either
simple or has a few
short branches. It is
up to 16 in (40 cm)
long and bears six
to 20 flowers, each
about ⅘ in (2 cm)
across. Flowering
time is variable, but
there is an emphasis
on autumn.
ZONES 10–12. I–H.

Oeceoclades maculata

OENIELLA SCHLTR.

This genus of about three species is from Madagascar and other
islands in the western Indian Ocean region. They are related to
Angraecum. The stems are well-developed with narrow, leathery
leaves in two ranks. The petals and sepals are narrow, but the
lip is broad. There is also a short spur.

CULTIVATION

In general, basket or pot culture is suitable for most species.
Most of them also benefit from a watering rest period during
the cool months. Both bright light and good air movement
are recommended.

Oeniella polystachys

(THOUARS) SCHLTR.

syn: *Angraecum polystachyum*
THOUARS, **Oeonia polystachyum**
(THOUARS) BENTH.

This species occurs on
Madagascar, the Seychelles,
and the Mascarene and
Comoro islands. It grows as
an epiphyte on tree trunks at
low altitudes. The erect, leafy
stems are up to 20 in (50 cm)
long. The leaves are fleshy
and about 1¾ in (4 cm) long.
The inflorescence is horizontal
to erect, and it bears up to
12 flowers, each about 2 in
(5 cm) across. Flowering is
from September to May in
the wild. **ZONE 12. H.**

Oeniella polystachys (left and above)

OERSTEDELLA RCHB.F.

Species now included in this genus were once considered part of
Epidendrum. They are easily distinguished from that genus by their
purple-warted stems. *Oerstedella* species are found from Mexico,
Costa Rica, and Panama to Bolivia.

CULTIVATION

These plants may be grown in pots with a water-retentive but well-
drained medium. Most require warm to intermediate conditions.

Oerstedella centradenia

Oerstedella centradenia (RCHB.F.) RCHB.F.

This species, native to Costa Rica and Panama,
grows at low elevations—up to about 4000 ft
(1200 m)—where there are wet and dry
seasons. The wiry stems are about 20 in
(50 cm) high and are clothed in narrow leaves
up to about 3⅔ in (9 cm) long. The terminal
inflorescence carries a few flowers, each about
1¼ in (3 cm) across. Flowering is during
summer. **ZONES 11–12. I–H.**

Oerstedella myriantha (LINDL.) HAGSATER

syn: *Epidendrum verrucosum* **var.** *myrianthum* (LINDL.)
AMES & CORRELL.

This species is found in Mexico, Guatemala,
and Honduras. It grows as a terrestrial on
grassy slopes and rocky banks, in thickets, and
in forests up to an altitude of 6700 ft (2000 m).
The habit and size of the plant is almost
identical to O. *verrucosa*, but the difference
lies in the flower color, which may range from
almost pure white to a deep purplish-red in this
species. The flowers also have a lilac scent and
appear during summer. **ZONES 11–12. I–H.**

Oerstedella myriantha

Oerstedella pseudoschumanniana
(FOWL.) HAGSATER

syn: *Epidendrum pseudoschumannianum* FOWL.

This species comes from Colombia and Costa Rica. It grows as both an epiphyte and terrestrial in open, light situations at altitudes of 4000–6700 ft (1200–2000 m). It is an erect plant that may be up to 80 in (2 m) tall. The upper part of the stem has leaves up to 4 in (10 cm) long. The drooping inflorescence is either terminal or lateral and may bear one to several flowers. The showy flowers are about 1¾ in (4 cm) across. Flowering is during spring. **ZONES 10–11. I.**

Oerstedella pseudoschumanniana

Oerstedella schweinfurthianum

Oerstedella schweinfurthianum (CORRELL.) HAGSATER
syn: *Epidendrum schweinfurthianum* CORRELL.

This species occurs in Guatemala, where it grows at altitudes of 7000–8000 ft (2100–2400 m). The leafy stems are up to 1 ft (30 cm) high, and the leaves are narrow and pointed, and up to about 2 in (5 cm) long. The terminal inflorescence has few to many flowers, each about 1¼ in (3 cm) across. Flowering is during spring. **ZONE 10. C–I.**

Oerstedella verrucosa (SW.)
syn: *Epidendrum verrucosum* SW.

This species is from Mexico, Guatemala, Honduras, Nicaragua, Colombia, and Jamaica. The clustered stems may grow up to 6 ft (1.8 m) tall. The stem is leafy above the leaf sheaths. The leaves are fleshy and up to 9 in (22 cm) long. The branched inflorescence, up to 18 in (45 cm) long, is erect and carries many flowers. The flowers are fragrant, long-lasting, and about ¾ in (18 mm) across. Flowering is during summer. **ZONES 11–12. I–H.**

Oerstedella verrucosa

ONCIDIUM SW.

This is one of the largest genera in the orchid family. It has more than 600 species, but the number depends on the taxonomic treatment of the group. There have been many name changes in the *Oncidium* alliance, and with such a large genus it will be some time before a stable nomenclature is achieved. The species are distributed throughout the American tropics, from Florida in the USA to Argentina. They occur from sea level to 13,300 ft (4000 m). The greatest diversity is in Brazil and the Andes. Most of the plants are epiphytes but a few are terrestrial.

CULTIVATION

With such a diverse genus it is difficult to generalize about cultivation. Most of them may be grown under the same

Oncidium ampliatum

conditions as *Cattleya*, *Epidendrum*, or *Encyclia*. Most do well in pots using a well-drained bark mix but some of the more robust species are better accommodated in wire or slatted baskets. The pendulous species should thrive on tree-fern slabs or cork mounts.

HYBRIDS

There are many hundreds of handsome hybrids made within the species of this genus and with other closely related genera. The genera most commonly used for hybridization are *Odontoglossum*, *Miltonia*, and *Brassia*. The following list indicates the make-up of the complex hybrids, and a selection of hybrids is at the end of the *Oncidium* species section.

Aspaia × Miltonia × Odontoglossum × Oncidium = Withnerara (With.)

Brassia × Miltonia = Miltassia (Mtssa.)

Brassia × Oncidium = Brassidium (Brsdm.)

Cochlioda × Miltonia × Odontoglossum × Oncidium = Burrageara (Burr.)

Cochlioda × Odontoglossum × Oncidium = Wilsonara (Wils.)

Miltonia × Odontoglossum × Oncidium = Colmanara (Colm.)

Odontoglossum × Cochlioda = Odontioda (Oda.)

Odontoglossum × Oncidium = Odontocidium (Odcdm.)

Note: The abbreviation in parentheses is the accepted form for the hybrid.

Oncidium ampliatum LINDL.

This species occurs from Guatemala to Panama, the West Indies, Venezuela, and Colombia. It is a robust plant with pseudobulbs that are large, ovoid to round, flattened, and about $3\frac{2}{3}$ in (9 cm) in diameter. There are two or three leathery leaves, each about $5\frac{1}{2}$ in (13 cm) long, at the apexes of the pseudobulbs. The erect inflorescence is branched and up to 40 in (1 m) high. It carries many flowers about 1 in (2.5 cm) wide. Flowering is during spring.
ZONES 11–12. I–H.

O

Oncidium barbatum

Oncidium barbatum LINDL.

This species is endemic to Bolivia and Brazil. The clustered pseudobulbs are about 2 in (5 cm) tall with a single leaf up to about 4 in (10 cm) long at the apex. The erect inflorescence is slender and about 16 in (40 cm) tall. It carries many flowers, each about 1¼ in (3 cm) wide. Flowering is during spring.
ZONES 10–12. I–H

Oncidium blanchettii
RCHB.F.

This species is a native of Brazil. Its clustered, erect pseudobulbs are ovoid to oblong in shape, and about 3⅔ in (9 cm) long. The three leaves are erect and rigid, and up to 20 in (50 cm) long. The robust, erect inflorescence is branched, up to 5 ft 4 in (1.6 m) long, and has many flowers, each 1 in (2.5 cm) in diameter. The flowers appear from late winter to spring.
ZONES 10–12. I–H.

Oncidium cariniferum

Oncidium blanchettii

Oncidium cariniferum BEER.
syn: *Odontoglossum cariniferum* RCHB.F.

This species occurs in Costa Rica, Panama, and Venezuela. The pseudobulbs are elliptic to oblong, compressed, and about 5½ in (13 cm) tall. The leathery leaves are about 18 in (45 cm) long and 3 in (7.5 cm) wide. The erect or arching inflorescence is about 4 ft 8 in (1.4 m) long, branched, and carries many flowers. The flowers are about 2 in (5 cm) wide and appear from autumn to spring. **ZONES 11–12. I–H.**

Oncidium cheirophorum

Oncidium concolor HOOK.

This species occurs in Brazil and Argentina. It has clustered, prominently ribbed pseudobulbs about 2 in (5 cm) high, with two or three leaves, about 6 in (15 cm) long, at each apex. The 8-in (20-cm) long inflorescence is pendulous due to the weight of the six to 12 flowers that are about 2 in (5 cm) wide. Flowering is during autumn. **ZONES 11–12. I–H.**

Oncidium cheirophorum
RCHB.F.

This species ranges from El Salvador to Colombia and Panama. Its clustered pseudobulbs are ovoid, compressed and around 1 in (2.5 cm) high. A solitary leaf arises from the apex and is about 4½ in (11 cm) long. The gracefully arching inflorescence is densely branched and about 1 ft (30 cm) long. It carries many flowers, each about ⅘ in (2 cm) wide. The flowers appear during autumn and winter. **ZONES 10–12. I–H.**

Oncidium concolor

Oncidium crispum

Oncidium crispum LODD.

This species is endemic to Brazil. Its dark-brown pseudobulbs are clustered, ribbed, and about 4 in (10 cm) tall. Two or three leaves up to about 6 in (15 cm) long arise from each apex. The inflorescence, up to (70 cm) long, is erect to pendulous, depending on the weight of flowers—there may be up to 80 of them. Each flower is about 3¼ in (8 cm) in diameter. Flowering is from spring to early summer. These plants require cool conditions as they come from high mountain regions. **ZONES 9–10. C–I.**

Oncidium cruciatum RCHB.F.

This species originates from cool mountainous areas in Brazil. The clustered pseudobulbs are almost terete and are up to 6 in (15 cm) tall. There are one or two leaves, each up to about 6 in (15 cm) long. The branched inflorescence is up to 1 ft (30 cm) long and carries up to 40 flowers. The flowers are about 1 in (2.5 cm) wide and appear during autumn and winter. **ZONES 9–10. C–I.**

Oncidium cruciatum

Oncidium dasystele RCHB.F.

This species is native to Brazil and has clustered and sharply angled pseudobulbs about 2 in (5 cm) high. Two thin-textured leaves arise from the apex and are about 6 in (15 cm) long. The slender inflorescence is about 20 in (50 cm) tall and is sparsely branched with a few flowers, each about 1¾ in (4 cm) across. Flowering is from summer to early winter. **ZONES 11–12. I–H.**

Oncidium dasystele

Oncidium divaricatum

Oncidium divaricatum LINDL.

This species is endemic to Brazil. The pseudobulbs are rounded, compressed, clustered, and have a diameter of about 1¾ in (4 cm). At the apex of each pseudobulb there is a single, rigid, leathery leaf up to about 1 ft (30 cm) long. The inflorescence may be up to 6 ft (1.8 m) long. It is branched and carries many flowers, each with a diameter of about ⅘ in (2 cm). Flowering is during autumn. **ZONES 11–12. I–H.**

Oncidium enderianum HORT.

Oncidium enderianum

This species is found in the cool mountainous areas of southeast Brazil. The oblong to elliptic pseudobulbs are about 2¾ in (7 cm) tall and each of these, generally, has two leaves up to 8 in (20 cm) long. The inflorescence spike is up to 40 in (1 m) long with several showy flowers about 2½ in (6 cm) wide. Flowering is during autumn and winter. This species may be grown mounted in an intermediate environment.
ZONE 10. I.

Oncidium flexuosum SIMS

Oncidium flexuosum

This species occurs in Brazil, Paraguay, and Argentina. The pseudobulbs are spaced up to 2 in (5 cm) apart on a creeping rhizome. They are compressed, with two distinctly acute edges and a diameter of about 3 in (7.5 cm). One or two leaves arise from the apex of the pseudobulbs. The inflorescence has short branches arising from near the top and each branch carries ten to 15 flowers with a diameter of about 1 in (2.5 cm). Flowering is during autumn and winter. This species is best cultivated on a slab because of its creeping habit.
ZONES 11–12. I–H.

Oncidium forbesii

Oncidium forbesii HOOK.

This species is endemic to Brazil. The oblong, compressed, and clustered pseudobulbs are about 3 in (7.5 cm) high, and each has one or two leaves at the apex. The erect or arching inflorescence is up to 40 in (1 m) long and branches towards its apex. The flowers are up to 2¾ in (7 cm) in diameter. Flowering is during spring. This plant may be grown on a mount in cool to intermediate conditions. **ZONES 9–12. C–I–H.**

Oncidium fuscatum RCHB.F.
syn: *Miltonia warscezwiczii* RCHB.F.

This species occurs on the lower slopes of the Andes from Panama to Peru. The clustered pseudobulbs are compressed and have sharp edges. They are up to 6 in (15 cm) tall and have one leaf, about 7 in (18 cm) long, at the apex. The inflorescence is up to 20 in (50 cm) long and carries several flowers about 2 in (5 cm) in diameter. The flowers open simultaneously during spring. **ZONES 9–12. I–H.**

Oncidium fuscatum

Oncidium fimbriatum LINDL

This species occurs in both the cool mountains and the hot lowlands of southeast Brazil and Paraguay. The pseudobulbs are up to 6 in (15 cm) long and about ⅓ in (1 cm) in diameter. They bear two leaves up to 8 in (20 cm) long. The arching or pendulous inflorescence is up to 3 ft (90 cm) long and has many flowers. The flowers are about 1 in (2.5 cm) wide and appear during autumn. This species is easy to grow on a mount in intermediate to hot conditions. **ZONES 11–12. I–H.**

Oncidium fimbriatum

Oncidium gardneri LINDL.

This species is endemic to Brazil. The plant has clustered pseudobulbs that are ovoid, flattened, grooved, and up to about 3 in (7.5 cm) tall. The erect inflorescence, up to 40 in (1 m) long, is usually branched. The flowers are about 2 in (5 cm) across, and they appear during winter. This species requires cool to intermediate conditions. **ZONES 10–11. C–I.**

Oncidium gardneri

Oncidium gracile

Oncidium harrisonianum

Oncidium gracile LINDL.

This species is found at altitudes of 1700–3300 ft (500–1000 m) in southeast Brazil. It grows as a terrestrial, lithophyte, or epiphyte in dry savanna woodlands. The tightly clustered pseudobulbs are up to 2 in (5 cm) tall and they sometimes produce new plantlets at their apex. There are also two leaves up to 4 in (10 cm) long at the apex. The inflorescence is up to 40 in (1 m) long and bears six to eight long-lasting, well-spaced flowers, each about $\frac{2}{3}$ in (15 mm) wide. Flowering occurs throughout the year. **ZONES 10–11. I.**

Oncidium harrisonianum LINDL.

This species was originally found in the Organ Mountains of Brazil. It is a small, epiphytic plant with pseudobulbs about 1 in (2.5 cm) long. The erect, single leaf is around 4 in (10 cm) long. The erect or arching inflorescence is up to 1 ft (30 cm) long and has branches with up to six flowers. The flowers are about $\frac{2}{3}$ in (15 mm) wide. Flowering is during summer and autumn. **ZONE 10. I.**

Oncidium hastilabium

Oncidium hastilabium (LINDL.) GARAY & DUNSTERV.

syn: *Odontoglossum hastilabium* LINDL.

This species occurs at moderate elevation in the Andes, from Venezuela to Peru. The clustered pseudobulbs are about 2½ in (6 cm) tall with a single leaf at each apex. The erect to arching inflorescence is branched and up to 40 in (1 m) long. The flowers are about 3¼ in (8 cm) wide. Flowering is during summer and autumn. **ZONES 10–12. I–H.**

Oncidium incurvum

Oncidium incurvum BORK.

This species from Mexico has ovoid, compressed, and ribbed pseudobulbs about 4 in (10 cm) tall. Two or three leathery leaves are produced and these are up to 18 in (45 cm) long. The erect to arching inflorescence is up to 5 ft 4 in (1.6 m) long with many branches. The fragrant flowers are about 1 in (2.5 cm) across and appear during autumn and winter. **ZONES 10–11. I.**

Oncidium laeve

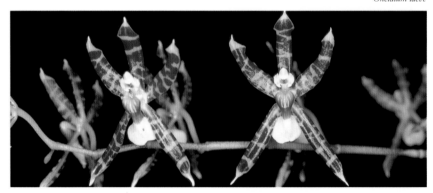

Oncidium laeve BEER.

syn: *Odontoglossum laeve* LINDL., *Miltonia karwinskii* PAXT.

This species from Mexico and Guatemala is found at altitudes of up to 5300 ft (1600 m). The pseudobulbs are ovoid to elliptic in shape,

and strongly compressed. They are about 5½ in (13 cm) long and carry two or three leaves, each up to 18 in (45 cm) long. The inflorescence, up to 4 ft 8 in (1.4 m) tall, is erect, robust, and branched with many flowers, each about 2½ in (6 cm) long. **ZONES 10–11. I.**

Oncidium leucochilum
BATEM.

This species occurs in Mexico, Guatemala, and Honduras. Its clustered pseudobulbs are compressed and about 5½ in (13 cm) high. The two leaves are about 1 ft (30 cm) long. The heavily branched inflorescence is about 1 ft (30 cm) long. Each branch has a few to many flowers, each about 1¾ in (4 cm) long. They are waxy and long-lasting, and appear mostly during winter and spring. **ZONES 11–12. I–H.**

Oncidium leucochilum

Oncidium longipes

Oncidium longipes LINDL.

This species is endemic to Brazil. It has elongated and ovoid pseudobulbs about 1 in (2.5 cm) high. The two leaves are about 6 in (15 cm) long. The erect inflorescence is about 6 in (15 cm) tall and carries three to five long-lasting flowers, each about 1¾ in (4 cm) wide. Flowering occurs during spring and early summer. **ZONES 11–12. I–H.**

Oncidium macranthum
LINDL.

syn: *Cyrtochilum macranthum* (LINDL.) KRAENZL.

This species is from high elevations in the Andes of northern Peru, Ecuador, and southern Colombia. Its clustered pseudobulbs are about 6 in (15 cm) high and each one carries two leaves at the apex. The wiry inflorescence, up to 80 in (2 m) long, is branched on the top half. Each branch carries three to five flowers about 4 in (10 cm) in diameter. Flowering is during winter. **ZONES 8–9. C.**

Oncidium macranthum

Oncidium macronix

Oncidium macropetalum LINDL.

This species occurs in
Paraguay, Bolivia, and Brazil.
It grows from near sea level
to about 3300 ft (1000 m).
The pseudobulbs are up to
2 in (5 cm) tall and carry one
or two arching inflorescences
up to 40 in (1 m) long. These bear a few to many well-spaced
flowers, each about 1¼ in (3 cm) long. Flowering is during
winter and spring. **ZONES 10–12. I–H.**

Oncidium maculatum LINDL.

This variable species is from Mexico, Guatemala, and Honduras.
The tightly clustered pseudobulbs are ovoid, compressed, and
become furrowed with age.
They are up to 5½ in (13 cm)
long and carry two leaves up
to 10 in (25 cm) long. The
inflorescence is about 18 in
(45 cm) long and bears many
flowers. These long-lasting
flowers are about 2 in (5 cm)
in diameter and appear from
winter to early summer.
ZONES 10–11. I.

Oncidium macronix RCHB.F.

In Brazil this species grows in both the cool mountains and hot
lowlands. It is also found in Argentina and Paraguay. The
pseudobulbs are about 2 in (5 cm) tall and spaced about ⅓ in
(1 cm) apart on the rhizome. They are narrow, compressed, and
strongly ribbed. The two leaves are up to 6 in (15 cm) long. The
branched inflorescence, about 16 in (40 cm) long, carries many
flowers about ⅔ in (15 mm) long. Flowering is during autumn.
This plant does well on a mount in intermediate conditions.
ZONES 9–10. C–I.

Oncidium macropetalum

Oncidium maculatum

Oncidium marshallianum
RCHB.F.

This species is a native of Brazil. Its clustered, ovoid, and compressed pseudobulbs are up to 6 in (15 cm) long. The two leaves may be up to 18 in (45 cm) long and the many-flowered inflorescence is up to 5 ft 4 in (1.6 m) long. Flowering occurs during winter. **ZONES 11–12. I–H.**

Oncidium marshallianum

Oncidium micropogon RCHB.F.

This species is native to Brazil. The clustered pseudobulbs are ovoid, compressed with sharp edges, and about 2 in (5 cm) long. The one or two leaves are up to 6 in (15 cm) long. The arching to pendulous inflorescence is about 18 in (45 cm) long with up to ten flowers. Each flower is about 1¾ in (4 cm) long. They appear during summer and autumn. **ZONES 11–12. I–H.**

Oncidium ornithorhyncum H. B. K.

This species grows from Mexico to Colombia. The pseudobulbs are clustered, compressed, and about 5½ in (13 cm) high. Two leaves emerge from each apex and they are about 1 ft (30 cm) long. The inflorescence is up to 2 ft (60 cm) long. It is branched with up to 15 flowers on each branch, and each flower is about ⅘ in (2 cm) in diameter. Flowering is during spring and summer. **ZONES 9–10. C–I.**

Oncidium micropogon

Oncidium ornithorhyncum

Oncidium phymatochilum LINDL.

This species occurs from Mexico through
Guatemala to Brazil. The ovoid to oblong and
clustered pseudobulbs are up to 4 in (10 cm)
tall. They may be brown and or purple in
color. The leathery leaves are usually solitary,
and up to 14 in (35 cm) long. The slender
inflorescence is 3–6 ft (90–180 cm) long and
carries many flowers, each about 2 in (5 cm)
long. Flowering is during spring and summer.
ZONES 11–12. I–H.

Oncidium phymatochilum

Oncidium retemeyerianum

Oncidium retemeyerianum RCHB.F.

This species is native
to Mexico and
Honduras. It has
small pseudobulbs.
The solitary leaf is
tough and leathery
and up to 10 in
(25 cm) long. It has
a strong keel shape
on the lower surface
and the leaf is often
a dull purplish–
green color. The
inflorescence is up
to 6 ft (1.8 m) long
and has many
flowers, which open
only a few at a time
over several months.
These are heavily
textured, waxy, about
$\frac{1}{3}$ in (1 cm) across,
and appear during
winter.
ZONES 11–12. I–H.

Oncidium sarcodes LINDL.

This species occurs in
Brazil. Its clustered
pseudobulbs are more or
less cylindrical, up to 6 in
(15 cm) high, and have two
or three apical leaves. The
leaves are up to 1 ft
(30 cm) long. The erect
to arching inflorescence
carries several flowers
about 1¼ in (3 cm) across.
Flowering is during spring,
and this species may be
grown on a mount.
ZONES 10–12. I–H.

Oncidium sarcodes

Oncidium sphacelatum

Oncidium sphacelatum
LINDL.

This species ranges from Mexico to Costa Rica, and it can quickly become a large specimen. The clustered pseudobulbs are compressed, about 7 in (18 cm) high, and have one or two narrow leaves, up to 2 ft (60 cm) long, at each apex. The branched inflorescence may be up to 80 in (2 m) long with many flowers, each one about 1 in (2.5 cm) wide. Flowering is from spring to early summer. This species may be grown outside in a rockery in warm climates. **ZONES 11–12. I–H.**

Oncidium sphegiferum LINDL.

This species is a native of Brazil. Its pseudobulbs are oval to almost rounded, very compressed, and about 1¾ in (4 cm) in diameter. The rigid, solitary leaf is erect up to about 8 in (20 cm) long. The inflorescence is up to 4 ft 4 in (1.3 m) long and has many branches. Each waxy flower is about 1 in (2.5 cm) wide. The flowers appear summer and autumn. **ZONES 11–12. I–H.**

Oncidium sphegiferum

Oncidium spilopterum LINDL.

This species is found in the hot lowlands and dry savannas of Brazil and Paraguay. Its clustered pseudobulbs, about 2½ in (6 cm) tall, are ovoid to conical in shape with one or two apical leaves up to 8 in (20 cm) long. The inflorescence is produced during autumn and winter and is up to 3 ft (90 cm) long. It has several flowers about 1¼ in (3 cm) long.
ZONES 9–10. I.

Oncidium spilopterum

Oncidium trulliferum LINDL.

This species occurs in the south and southeast of Brazil and inhabits both the cool mountains and hot lowlands. Its pseudobulbs are oblong, compressed, and are up to 8 in (20 cm) tall. The two or three leaves are about 8 in (20 cm) long. The gracefully arching spike is branched, up to 2 ft (60 cm) long, and carries many flowers, each one about ⅘ in (2 cm) wide. Flowering is during summer and autumn.
ZONES 10–12. I–H.

Oncidium varicosum LINDL. EX PAXT.

This species occurs in Brazil, Bolivia, and Paraguay. Its pseudobulbs are clustered, compressed with sharp edges, and about 5½ in (13 cm) high. One or two leaves arise from each apex. The inflorescence arises from the base of the pseudobulbs, is up to 32 in (80 cm) long, and has short branches along the top half. Each of these branches carries two to five flowers about 2 in (5 cm) wide. Flowering is during autumn and winter. This species may be grown on a slab or in a pot with a well-drained mix. **ZONES 10–12. I–H.**

Oncidium trulliferum

Oncidium varicosum

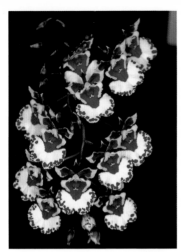

Oncidium Wilbur "Wilma"

Oncidium Liz "Full Moon"

Oncidium Keysa "Oka"

Colm. Wildcat "Carmela"

Oncidium Phyllis x Taffy

Wils. Ginger Meggs x *Oda.* Yellow Harry

Miltonia Goodale Moir "Golden Wonder"

Mtssa. Olmec "Kanno"

Burr. Nelly Isler

With. Ash Trees

Oda. Florence Stirling

Brsdm. Longlen

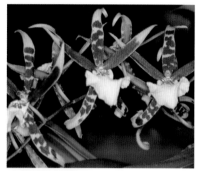

Oncidium Sharry Baby
"Sweet Fragrance"

Odcdm. Gloria Hill

Wils. Hamburen Stern
"Floriculture"

OPHRYS L.

This European and Middle Eastern genus is one of the most interesting of the region with respect to its distinctive flower appearance and pollination process (*see* below). A feature of the flower is the rather fleshy consistency and the hairy surface of the lip. In many cases the lip has a shiny white or blue area, which is called a "speculum." There are about 140 species in the genus, whereas a few decades ago only 21 were recognized. As each *Ophrys* species has its own specific insect pollinator, this has been an important consideration in defining the species in this genus. When not in flower, identification is nearly impossible as the plants all have similar leaf rosettes. The number of flowers per inflorescence varies between one and more than 20. These plants are generally from warm climates and are most abundant around the Mediterranean Sea. They prefer to grow in full sunlight, but can also tolerate partial shade. Only the species *Ophrys insectifera* likes shady, cool places, and its range extends as far as Scandinavia.

POLLINATION

Pollination is effected by different types of bees and wasps and each species of *Ophrys* has a flower that looks like a specific female insect and a scent that is nearly identical to that of the female insect. These traits attract the appropriate pollinating male, who initiates sexual movements that result in the pollen sticking to the male insect's head or abdomen. After a short time, the male insect realizes something is wrong, flies away with pollen stuck to it, and may repeat this mating ritual with other flowers, causing pollination. This process is known as "pseudocopulation." The reason the males are attracted to the flower is that the female insects do not emerge until one or two weeks after the males, so during this time the flowers have no competitors.

CULTIVATION

Species of this genus are not widespread in cultivation and can be seen mostly in botanical gardens. Consequently, there is limited knowledge about cultivation conditions, but this could change in the future when more hybrids come onto the market. In general, they may be potted in a mix of loam, coarse sand, leaf mold, and fine, slightly decomposed pine bark. The tubers should be repotted each autumn and watered well, after which the leaves will appear. The plants should be kept dry after flowering for a month or two.

Ophrys apifera HUDS.
"BEE ORCHID"

This is the only self-pollinating *Ophrys* species. Its distribution extends from Spain and north Africa to Great Britain and middle Europe, as far as the coastal regions of Turkey. The plant prefers dry to moist grasslands and wastelands between sea level and 6000 ft (1800 m). It varies in height between 6 in (15 cm) if the ground is dry and 2 ft (60 cm) if moist. Two to seven flowers are carried on the inflorescence, and each flower is about 1 in (2.5 cm) across. The flowering season is from late spring to summer. The variety *friburgensis* has pink petals which are especially attractive. **ZONES 7–9. C–I.**

Ophrys apifera

Ophrys holosericea

Ophrys holosericea (BURM.F.) GREUTER
syn: *Ophrys fuciflora* (F. W. SCHMIDT) MOENCH
"LATE SPIDER ORCHID"

The distribution of this species is from western middle Europe, with a few locations in Kent in England, France, and southern Germany, through Italy to the eastern Mediterranean coasts. It grows in the calcareous soils of grasslands, scrublands, and light coniferous forests between sea level and 4700 ft (1400 m). The plant is 6–20 in (15–50 cm) tall and carries two to ten flowers, each $\frac{4}{5}$–$1\frac{1}{4}$ in (2.5–3 cm) across. The lip has silky hairs and the color is a velvety dark brown. The relatively large, apical appendix on the lip is bent forward in a manner typical of this species. The flowering season is from late spring to summer. **ZONES 7–9. C–I.**

Ophrys incubacea

Ophrys insectifera

Ophrys incubacea BIANCA
syn: *Ophrys atrata* LINDL.
"BLACK SPIDER ORCHID"

This species is distributed in the northern and western parts of the Mediterranean area—from Portugal and southern Spain to Italy and the Balkan countries. It grows in grasslands and light coniferous forests between sea level and 2700 ft (800 m). The plants are 8–16 in (20–40 cm) tall. The inflorescence carries four to eight flowers, each about 1 in (2.5 cm) across. The lip is dark brown with a blue H-shaped marking that is sometimes framed in white. The flowering season is in spring. **ZONES 7–9. C–I.**

Ophrys insectifera L.
"FLY ORCHID"

This species was first described by Linnaeus in 1753 from a plant found on the Swedish island Öland. The distribution area is middle Europe and northern south Europe. It grows in dry grasslands, scrublands, and light coniferous forests from sea level to 6000 ft (1800 m). The slender plants are 8–24 in (20–60 cm) tall and carry three to 20 flowers, each about $\frac{4}{5}$ in (2 cm) long. In contrast to most *Ophrys* species, the leaves grow up the stem. The pollinators are the male Agrogorytes wasp. The plant flowers from late spring to summer, depending on the altitude. **ZONES 6–9. C–I.**

Ophrys lacaitae

Ophrys lacaitae LOJAC.
"LACAITA'S SPIDER ORCHID"

This species is restricted
to southern Italy, including
Sicily. It grows in slightly
acidic soils in dry grasslands
and light scrublands up
to 4000 ft (1200 m). This
plant is closely related to
O. *holosericea*, but it is
only 4–10 in (10–25 cm)
tall and carries three to nine
attractive, relatively large
flowers about 1¹/₄ in (3 cm)
across. The trapezoid form
of the lip and its yellow color
are features of these flowers.
Flowering is from spring to
early summer.
ZONES 7–9. C–I.

Ophrys reinholdii SPRUNER EX H. FLEISCHM.

The species is found in Greece and southwest
Turkey. It grows in the calcareous or sandstone
soils of dry grasslands and light coniferous forests
up to 4300 ft (1300 m). This species grows 8–16 in
(20–40 cm) tall. Its lax inflorescence carries two to
six flowers, each about 1 in (2.5 cm) across. The lip
is characteristically dark purple with two thick
white or pale-lilac lines. The flowering season is
during spring. **ZONES 6–9. C.**

Ophrys reinholdii

Ophrys scolopax

Ophrys scolopax CAV.
"WOODCOCK ORCHID"

This species comes from the western Mediterranean area—southern France, Corsica, and Spain. It grows in grasslands, scrublands, or light forests, especially on calcareous or, sometimes, acidic soils. The plants are about 3¹/₄–18 in (8–45 cm) tall with five or six leaves. There are three to 12 flowers, each about 1 in (2.5 cm) long. Flowering is during spring. **ZONES 8–9. I.**

Ophrys speculum

Ophrys speculum
LINK
syn: *Ophrys vernixia* BROT.
"MIRROR ORCHID"

This species comes from the coastal areas in the eastern and northern parts of the Mediterranean Sea, including the coast of northwest Africa. It grows in grasslands, scrublands, and under pine cover in light forests up to a low altitude of 2600 ft (800 m). This small plant is 4–12 in (10–30 cm) tall and carries two to ten flowers, each about ⁴/₅ in (2 cm) across. In the center of the lip is a shiny, blue oval speculum that resembles the iridescent wings of an insect. Flowering is during spring. **ZONES 7–9. I.**

Ophrys tenthredinifera WILLD.
"SAWFLY ORCHID"

This robust plant is found around the
Mediterranean region, excluding the area from
north Italy to Turkey. It grows in grassy and
stony wastelands, scrublands, and light forests,
often in slightly acidic soils, from sea level to
4000 ft (1200 m). It ranges in height from
4–18 in (10–45 cm). The loosely flowered
inflorescence bears three to eight flowers about
1 in (2.5 cm) across. The lip resembles a wasp
and the flowering season is spring.
ZONES 7–10. C–I.

Ophrys tenthredinifera

ORCHIS L.

The name of this genus is the origin of the
family name of all orchids, *Orchidaceae*. Carl
von Linnaeus named this species *Orchis* in
reference to the ovoid shape of the two tubers.
This shape separates the species from its close
relative *Dactylorhiza*, which has finger-shaped
tubers. *Orchis* comprises about 33 species
ranging from the temperate Mediterranean
areas of Europe through north Africa and the
Middle East to the temperate locales in Asia,
including north China and Japan. While two
tubers are present at the same time, one is an
old one from the previous year. The new one
produces the fresh shoots. The leaves may be
spotted and are mostly concentrated in a
rosette on the ground. Occasionally, they are
distributed along the stem. The inflorescence
has many densely packed flowers. Most of the
species have flowers with long spurs. Several
different kinds of insects, including social and
solitary bees and bumble bees, hoverflies, and
droneflies, are known as pollinators but,
surprisingly, little is known about the method
of pollination for these plants.

CULTIVATION

In general, some species seem to naturalize
easily, for example, *O. mascula*, *O. militaris*,
and *O. purpurea*. In some gardens they grow
readily in the open along with other species.
Few artificially raised plants are available at
present, but this situation may change in the
future. They grow best in a standard terrestrial
mix with conditions as for *Ophrys*.

Orchis coriophora

Orchis coriophora L.

"BUG ORCHID"

This species ranges from central and southern Europe to northwest
Africa and Turkey—in some areas of central Europe, such as Germany,
it is now rare and nearly extinct. It grows on slightly acidic soils in
grasslands between sea level and 7300 ft (2200 m). The plant is up
to 6–16 in (15–40 cm) tall and has densely flowered, cylindrical
inflorescences. These consist of 15 to 25 small, green to dark violet-
brown flowers, each about ⅔ in (15 mm) across. The sepals and petals
form a hood and the three-lobed lip is gently curved inwards and carries
dark-violet spots near the base. The flowering season is from late spring
to early summer. **ZONES 7–9. C.**

Orchis mascula (L.) L.
"EARLY PURPLE ORCHID"

This robust species is widely distributed in Europe. The plant grows in light deciduous and mixed forests and meadows from sea level in the north to 10,000 ft (3000 m) in the south. It reaches 8–20 in (20–50 cm) in height. The leaves are usually spotted. The inflorescence carries six to 20 flowers, each about ⅘ in (2 cm) across. The flower color varies between light rose and red-purple. The base of the lip is white with purple-red spots. The flower season is from late spring to early summer, depending on the region. **ZONES 5–8. C–I.**

Orchis mascula

Orchis militaris L.
"MILITARY ORCHID"

This is species on which the genus *Orchis* is based. It is widespread in central Europe, from England (where it is rare) to the Caucasus and Russia. It grows on calcareous soil in dry grasslands and light forests between sea level and 6000 ft (1800 m). It is a robust plant about 10–20 in (25–50 cm) tall. The rosette leaves are a glossy, light-green color. The inflorescence carries 20 to 30 flowers, each about ⅘ in (2 cm) across. The ground color of the lip varies from light to deep pink with small, dark-purple, hairlike tufts on it. Flowering is from mid spring to early summer, depending on the region. **ZONES 5–7. C–I.**

Orchis militaris

Orchis morio L.
"GREEN-WINGED ORCHID"

Due to intensive farming, occurrences of this species have been reduced dramatically in the wild during the past century. The distribution is most of Europe, except the southwestern and northern parts. This plant grows in calcareous to slightly acidic soil in meadows, dry grass-lands, and light forests. It is generally a small plant that reaches 4–12 in (10–30 cm) in height. The leaves grow in autumn and are present during winter. There are five to 25 flowers, each about ⅘ in (2 cm) across, that form a loose, short inflorescence. The flowering season is from mid spring to early summer, depending on the region. **ZONES 6–8. C.**

Orchis morio

Orchis pallens L.

"PALE-FLOWERED ORCHID"

The general distribution of this species is wide—central and northern south Europe—but the sites are rather small and uncommon. In central Europe it is rare and endangered. It grows in beech, pine, and fir forests, exclusively in calcareous soil, from sea level and mountainous areas up to 6700 ft (2000 m). It is one of the few European orchids with pure yellow flowers. The plant is 6–14 in (15–35 cm) tall. The flowers are ¾ in (18 mm) across, and they form a loose inflorescence. They have a strong, unpleasant scent. The flowering season is from mid spring to early summer, depending on the altitude. **ZONES 6–8. C–I.**

Orchis pallens

Orchis papilionacea

Orchis papilionacea L.

"BUTTERFLY ORCHID"

This species comes from the areas around the Mediterranean Sea, excluding northeast Africa. It grows in calcareous soils in dry grasslands, shrublands, and light forests between sea level and 6000 ft (1800 m). The plant varies from 6–16 in (15–40 cm) in height. The lax inflorescence carries five to 15 flowers, each about 1–1¼ in (2.5–3 cm) in diameter. The color varies considerably from pale to dark pink, with or without purple markings in the form of lines and spots. The plant flowers from late winter in the southern regions to late spring in north Italy. **ZONES 7–9. C–I.**

Orchis quadripunctata

ST. CYR EX TEN.

"FOUR-SPOTTED ORCHID"

The distribution range for this species is from the Balkans through southern Italy, including Sardinia and Sicily, to Greece and Cyprus. It grows in calcareous soils on stony grasslands or in light scrublands at altitudes from sea level to 5000 ft (1500 m). It is a slender orchid that is only 4–8 in (10–20 cm) tall. The inflorescence carries eight to 30 flowers, each ⅓ in (1 cm) across. The general color is from pink to deep purple–pink. Flowering occurs during spring. **ZONES 8–9. C–I.**

Orchis quadripunctata

Orchis simia

Orchis simia LAM.
"MONKEY ORCHID"

This species ranges from western and southern Europe through the coastal areas of Turkey to the Caucasus Mountains. It is rare in southeast England and southwest Germany. It grows in calcareous soils in dry grasslands, scrublands and light forests between sea level and 5000 ft (1500 m). The plant is 8–18 in (20–45 cm) tall. The inflorescence at first has an ovoid shape but then becomes cylindrical. Unlike most other orchids, the flowers at the top of the inflorescence open before those at the bottom. The flowering sequence is an effective way to distinguish it from the closely related O. militaris. The flowering season is in spring. **ZONES 7–9. C–I.**

Orchis spitzelii SAUT. EX W. KOCH

This is a rare and endangered species, although it is widely distributed from Spain through the Balkans to Turkey and the Caucasus Mountains, and through the Alps to the Swedish island of Gotland. It is a woodland plant that grows on calcareous soils in beech, oak, pine, and fir forests between sea level and 6000 ft (1800 m). The plants are 8–16 in (20–40 cm) tall. The inflorescence carries ten to 20 flowers, each about 1 in (2.5 cm) across. The flowering season is from late spring to early summer. **ZONES 6–9. C–I.**

Orchis spitzelii

Orchis ustulata

Orchis ustulata L.
"BURNT ORCHID"

The distribution area of this species is all of Europe, except the far west, south and north. It grows up to an altitude of 6700 ft (2000 m). This is one of the smallest species in the genus. Its stems are 4–10 in (10–25 cm) tall and the diameter of the flowers is $\frac{1}{3}$ in (1 cm). The loosely flowered inflorescence carries numerous, delicately scented flowers. The sepals and petals form a purplish–red to dark-brown hood which, in bud, looks like it has been burned. Flowering is from late spring to mid summer. **ZONES 4–9. C–I.**

ORNITHOCEPHALUS HOOK.

This genus of about 50 species is distributed throughout the American Tropics. The plants lack pseudobulbs and the stem is covered with overlapping leaf sheaths and fleshy leaves that are arranged in a fan shape. The inflorescences are borne on the leaf axils and the plants may flower several times during the year.

CULTIVATION

Typically, these orchids are twig epiphytes in their natural habitat and may be grown mounted on slabs. They may also be grown in small pots and should not be permitted to dry out. Intermediate to hot conditions with constant high humidity suits them well.

Ornithocephalus myrticola

Ornithocephalus iridifolius

Ornithocephalus myrticola LINDL.

This species from Brazil and Bolivia grows on trees belonging to the family myrtaceae. Its habitat ranges from cool mountains and dry savannas to hot lowlands. The plant is about 3 in (7.5 cm) high. The flowers are borne on a spike up to 3¼ in (8 cm) long, which may carry up to 15 flowers, each about ⅓ in (1 cm) across. **ZONES 10–12. I.**

Ornithocephalus iridifolius RCHB.F.

This species from Mexico and Guatemala grows on trees in oak forests at altitudes of 1800–3300 ft (550–1000 m). The leaves are up to about 3 in (7.5 cm) long. The slender inflorescence has a spreading zigzag shape and is up to 3 in (7.5 cm) long. There are many flowers up to about ¼ in (6 mm) across. This plant does best mounted and grown in a shady, moist intermediate environment. Flowering is during summer and autumn. **ZONES 10–11. I.**

ORNITHOPHORA BARB. RODR.

This genus of one species is from Brazil, where it is widespread in the southern states. It is easy to grow and accommodate on a slab, which allows for its rambling habit. It should be kept moist year-round with a brief watering rest period after the new growth has matured. Keep in cool to intermediate conditions.

Ornithophora radicans (RCHB.F.) GARY & PABST

The pseudobulbs are spaced ⅓–1¼ in (1–3 cm) apart on the creeping rhizome. They are thin and have two leaves, up to about 6 in (15 cm) long, at the apex. The flower spikes arise from the base of the pseudobulbs and carries up to ten flowers, each about ⅓ in (1 cm) long. Flowering is during late summer and autumn. **ZONES 10–11. C–I.**

Ornithophora radicans

OSMOGLOSSUM SCHLTR. (SCHLTR.)

This genus comprises about eight species occurring from Mexico to Panama.
They grow as epiphytes in pine–oak forests at altitudes of about 1600–6700 ft
(500–2000 m). They have unifoliate or bifoliate pseudobulbs of a single internode.
The flowers are dominantly white with the lateral sepals that unite.

CULTIVATION

These plants from moist or dry forests require intermediate to cool conditions.
They may be grown in pots with a free-draining mix or sphagnum moss.

Osmoglossum
candida

Osmoglossum pulchellum

Osmoglossum candida (LINDL.)

syn: *Palumbina candida* (LINDL.) RCHB.F.

This species occurs in Mexico and Guatemala.
Its pseudobulbs are narrowly ellipsoid, and are up
to about 2 in (5 cm) high. The solitary, fleshy leaf
is about 1 ft (30 cm) long. The erect inflorescence
is also up to about 1 ft (30 cm) tall and appears
with the new growth. Up to seven flowers are
produced and these are about 1 in (2.5 cm) across.
The fragrant, long-lasting flowers appear during
spring. **ZONES 9–11. C–I.**

Osmoglossum pulchellum (BATEM. EX LINDL.)
SCHLTR.

This species occurs in Mexico, Guatemala,
El Salvador, and Costa Rica. The clustered
pseudobulbs are narrowly ellipsoidal and up to
about 4 in (10 cm) long. The two or three leaves
are about 18 in (45 cm) long and the inflorescence
is about 14¾ in (37 cm) tall. They carry several
fragrant and long-lasting flowers, each about
1¾ in (4 cm) long. Flowering is during autumn
and winter. **ZONES 9–11. C–I.**

P

PABSTIA GARAY

This genus comprises about five species, all of which occur in tropical Brazil. They are showy plants with pseudobulbs that bear two leaves. The inflorescence arises from the base of the pseudobulbs and produces a few flowers.

CULTIVATION

These species may be grown in pots using a free-draining mix. They require abundant water year-round and warm to intermediate conditions.

Pabstia jugosa

Pabstia jugosa (LINDL.) GARAY
syn: *Colax jugosa* (LINDL.) LINDL.

This species, indigenous to southern Brazil, grows mostly as an epiphyte. Its clustered pseudobulbs are elongated, ovoid, and about 3 in (7.5 cm) high. The rather leathery leaves are up to 9 in (22 cm) long. The erect or arching inflorescence is up to 8 in (20 cm) long and bears two to four flowers, each about 3 in (7.5 cm) across. The flowers appear from late autumn to early winter.
ZONES 10–11. I–H.

Pabstia viridis LINDL. (GARAY)

This species is restricted to the mountains of southeast Brazil. The clustered pseudobulbs have four angles and are up to 4 in (10 cm) tall. At the apex are two leaves up to 8 in (20 cm) long. A solitary, fleshy flower is borne on a stem about 2 in (5 cm) tall, which arises from the base of the pseudobulbs. The flower is about 2 in (5 cm) across and appears during summer.
ZONES 10–11. I.

Pabstia viridis

PAPHIOPEDILUM PFITZER

"SLIPPER ORCHIDS," "LADY'S SLIPPERS"

This genus extends from India and southern China through Southeast Asia to the Philippines, New Guinea, and Guadalcanal in the Solomon Islands. It comprises about 60 species, although some authorities recognize a number of varieties as species. Many of the species were originally classified as members of *Cypripedium*. *Paphiopedilum* species grow mostly at moderate altitudes under dense shade on the rain forest floor or in leaf mold on rock faces and, occasionally, as epiphytes. They are usually compact and consist of fleshy roots, a short stem, and a few large, often mottled leaves with a terminal inflorescence of one or a few large flowers. The lip of the flower is shaped like a pouch. Many of these species are threatened in the wild due to over-collection.

CULTIVATION

These plants may be difficult to grow from seed but they can be propagated by division. Cultivation depends on the origin of the plants, but most of the species grow best with intermediate conditions and part shade. The potting mix should be well-drained but moisture-retentive, and the plants should be kept evenly moist throughout the year.

HYBRIDS

Thousands of hybrids have been registered in *Paphiopedilum*, more than in any other orchid genus. Unfortunately, many of the attempts have not resulted in improvements upon the original species, although there are some outstanding exceptions. Growers are attempting to create vigorous plants which have large, round flowers with interesting color combinations, and plants that will bloom several times a year. Another trend is to produce novelty plants, generally ignoring size and round flower shapes. Most of the hybrids come from about 25 species. King Arthur "Burgoyne," a typical hybrid, shows the strong influence of *P. insigne*—it has rich, coppery–red flowers with a white tip on the broad dorsal sepal. Grande Jersey is a hybrid bred from a small group of species with elongated, twisted petals and some of them have more than one flower per stem, a feature also apparent in this hybrid.

Paphiopedilum appletonianum

(GOWER) ROLFE

syn: several names, including
P. wolterianum (KRAENZL.) PFITZER,
P. hainanense FOWLIE, *P. hookerae*
subsp. *appletonianum* (GOWER)
M. W. WOOD

This species comes from China's Hainan Island, Vietnam, Laos, Cambodia, and Thailand. It grows on mossy rocks and in leaf mold on the floor of forests at low to moderate altitudes. The leaves are lightly mottled, about 2¾–10 in (7–25 cm) long and ⅘–1¾ in (2–4 cm) across. The inflorescence has one or, occasionally, two flowers, each 2½–4 in (6–10 cm) across. In cultivation, this plant benefits from slightly reduced watering during winter. Flowering time is variable, but there is an emphasis on late winter.
ZONES 10–12. I–H.

P

Paphiopedilum appletonianum var. *hainanense*

Paphiopedilum armeniacum
S. C. CHEN & F. Y. LIU

This unusual orchid has been heavily collected since its discovery in 1982 and is now under threat in the wild. It is restricted to southwest China, growing on rocks under light shade at moderate to high altitudes. The leaves are mottled, about 2½–6 in (6–15 cm) long and ⅘–1 in (2–2.5 cm) across. The bright-yellow flower is large for the size of the plant, about 2½–4½ in (6–11 cm) across. In its habitat the plant experiences a distinct dry season so a watering rest period may be beneficial when cultivating. Grow in a large pot to accommodate the long underground rhizome. **ZONES 9–10. C–I.**

Paphiopedilum armeniacum

Paphiopedilum bellatulum (RCHB.F.) STEIN

The spotted flowers of this species look spectacular against the limestone rocks and cliff faces of its habitat in Myanmar, northwest Thailand, and southwest China. It may be found growing under light shade at low to moderate altitudes. The leaves, up to 5⅔ in (14 cm) long and 2 in (5 cm) across, are strongly mottled on the upper surface and purple-spotted underneath. The short, upright or pendulous inflorescence bears one or, rarely, two flowers about 2–3¼ in (5–8 cm) across. Flowering occurs mostly during spring and early summer. In cultivation this species flowers well if provided with cool conditions, particularly during the night. **ZONES 9–10. C–1.**

Paphiopedilum bellatulum

Paphiopedilum bullenianum
(RCHB.F.) PFITZER

syn: *P. robinsonii* (RIDL.) RIDL., *P. linii* SCHOSER, *P. johorense* FOWLIE & YAP, *P. tortipetalum* FOWLIE

This species is widespread across the islands from the Malay Peninsula to Ceram in the Moluccas, including Sumatra, Borneo, and Sulawesi. It grows in leaf litter in moist, shaded positions from the edges of mangroves at sea level to a 6200-ft (1850-m) altitude. The leaves are strongly mottled on the upper surface, and about 2¾–5⅔ in (7–14 cm) long and 1–1¾ in (2.5–4 cm) wide. The single flower is up to 3¾ in (9.5 cm) across and appears during spring. In cultivation, this species should be kept moist throughout the year and grown under shade in order to achieve a good color for the leaves and flowers. **ZONES 10–12. H.**

Paphiopedilum bullenianum

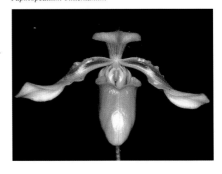

P

Paphiopedilum callosum

Paphiopedilum callosum (RCHB.F.) STEIN

syn: *P. sublaeve* (RCHB.F.) FOWLIE, *P. potentianum* O. GRUSS & J. ROTH

This species has been recorded from Thailand, Laos, and Cambodia. It grows at low to moderate altitudes in leaf litter on the forest floor, where the conditions are often misty with good air movement. It has been heavily collected from the wild and is now under threat. Its leaves are mottled on the upper surface, 4–8 in (10–20 cm) long and 1½–2 in (3–5 cm) wide. The single flower is 3¼–4½ in (8–11 cm) across. This plant is one of the more easy-to-grow species of the genus and will tolerate a range of cultivation conditions. **ZONES 10–12. I–H.**

Paphiopedilum charlesworthii (ROLFE) PFITZER

One of the most attractive in the genus, this species is found from Thailand through Myanmar to the Yunnan province of China. It grows on limestone peaks, usually under shade, in rock crevices, or in leaf litter at moderate to high altitudes. The leaves are up to 6 in (15 cm) long and 1¼ in (3 cm) wide, and often have a purple color at the base. The single, long-lasting flower is about 3¼ in (8 cm) across and has a large, colorful, and distinctive dorsal sepal. Flowering is during autumn. In cultivation, this plant requires a significant difference between day and night temperatures in order to flower well. **ZONES 10–11. I.**

Paphiopedilum charlesworthii

Paphiopedilum concolor

Paphiopedilum concolor
(BATEMAN) PFITZER

This delightful miniature is found in limestone hills in Indochina and southern China. It grows under dense shade on rocks or in leaf litter on the ground at low to moderate altitudes. The leaves, up to 5⅔ in (14 cm) long and 1¾ in (4 cm) wide, are attractively mottled on the upper surface and purple underneath. The inflorescence bears one to three flowers, about 2–2¾ in (5–7 cm) across. A watering rest period during winter is beneficial for good growth and flowering, which occurs during spring. **ZONES 10–12. I.**

Paphiopedilum delenatii
GUILLAUMIN

This species, restricted to Vietnam, grows in acidic soils in crevices on cliff faces and ledges in mountain habitats at altitudes of 2700–5000 ft (800–1500 m). The leaves, about 4 in (10 cm) long and 1¼ in (3 cm) wide, are mottled with light and dark green colors above, and purple-spotted below. The inflorescence is up to 8 in (20 cm) tall with one or two flowers about 3¼ in (8 cm) across. Flowering is during spring. In cultivation this plant should not be allowed to dry out completely. **ZONES 10–11. I.**

Paphiopedilum delenatii

P

Paphiopedilum dianthum TANG & WANG

syn: *P. parishii* (RCHB.F.) STEIN **var.** *dianthum* (TANG & WANG) KARASAWA & SAITO

This species occurs in the Yunnan, Guizhou, and Guangxi provinces of southwest China. It grows on limestone rocks and cliff faces in pockets of leaf litter at altitudes of around 1700–6700 ft (500–2000 m). The straplike leaves are dark green and 8–20 in (20–50 cm) long and $^4/_5$–2 in (2–5 cm) wide. The horizontal to erect inflorescence bears two to five flowers, about 6 in (15 cm) across when the petals are spread out. The flowers appear from autumn to winter. **ZONES 9–11. I.**

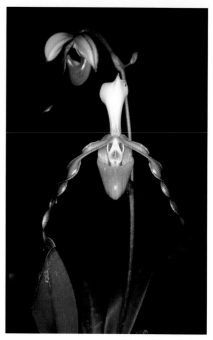

Paphiopedilum dianthum

Paphiopedilum druryi (left)

Paphiopedilum druryi (BEDD.) STEIN.

This species is of interest for several reasons. It occurs in the far south of India, in the state of Kerala, at an altitude of around 5000 ft (1500 m), and it is separated from other species in the genus by about 1200 miles (2000 km). It grows in low grass or other vegetation on rock faces in exposed conditions, and has suffered in the wild from over-collection and fires. The short stems are either spaced closely together or well-separated on the rhizome. The leaves are glossy green and up to 1 ft (30 cm) long and 1¼ in (3 cm) wide. The inflorescence is about 10 in (25 cm) tall and bears a single flower about 2½ in (6 cm) across. Flowering is during spring. In cultivation, this plant should be grown under stronger light than most other members of the genus. The long rhizomes will pose problems for pot culture, so baskets may be a better alternative. **ZONES 10–11. I.**

Paphiopedilum emersonii KOOP. & P. J. CRIBB

The distribution of this species is uncertain, but it appears to occur only in southern China. It grows on limestone rocks at an altitude of about 2000 ft (600 m). There are around six straplike, leathery, green leaves, each about 8 in (20 cm) long and 1¼ in (3 cm) wide. The inflorescence has a single or, rarely, two large flowers about 3¼–8 in (8–20 cm) across. Flowering is during spring. **ZONES 11. I–H.**

Paphiopedilum emersonii

Paphiopedilum fairrieanum

Paphiopedilum fowliei

Paphiopedilum fairrieanum (LINDL.) STEIN

This species was in cultivation in 1857, then
it virtually disappeared. In 1904, the sum of
£1000, an astonishing amount at that time,
was offered for its recovery. It is now common
in cultivation but is much reduced in numbers
in its habitat in Bhutan and the Indian states of
Sikkim and Arunachal Pradesh. It grows in tall
grass and in oak forests on limestone outcrops
at altitudes of 4700–7300 ft (1400–2200 m).
The straplike leaves, up to 10 in (25 cm) long
and ⅘–1¼ in (2–3 cm) wide, are darker green
above than underneath. The single flower
(occasionally there are two) is about 3¼ in
(8 cm) long. Flowering is during late winter
and spring. **ZONES 9–10. C–I.**

Paphiopedilum fowliei BIRK

syn: *P. hennisianum* (M. W. WOOD) FOWLIE
var. *fowliei* (BIRK) P. J. CRIBB

This species is restricted to Palawan Island
in the Philippines. It grows in leaf litter in
exposed situations, but not under direct
sunlight, on limestone rocks at altitudes of
2000–3300 ft (600–1000 m). The leaves are a
blue–gray color with faint tessellated patterns.
They are up to 5⅔ in (14 cm) long and 1¼ in
(3 cm) across. The single flower is about 3¼ in
(8 cm) long and is borne on a peduncle about
10 in (25 cm) tall. Flowering is during spring
and summer. **ZONES 10–12. I–H.**

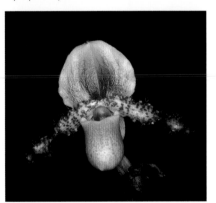

Paphiopedilum glaucophyllum

Paphiopedilum glaucophyllum J. J. SM.

syn: *P. victoria-regina* (SANDER) M. WOOD
subsp. *glaucophyllum* (J. J. SM.) M. W. WOOD

This species is found on the south coast of Java
in Indonesia. It grows in pockets of leaf litter
on steep limestone rock faces at low altitudes.
The leaves are dark green, up to 10 in (25 cm)
long and 2 in (5 cm) across. The erect to
horizontal inflorescence bears up to 20 flowers,
each about 3¼ in (8 cm) across. These open
successively throughout the year so that only
one or two are open at any one time. This
plant is recommended for beginner collections
as it does well in cultivation. **ZONES 11–12. H.**

P

Paphiopedilum godefroyae

Paphiopedilum gratrixianum

Paphiopedilum godefroyae (GOD.-LEB.) STEIN
syn: *P. leucochilum* (GOD.-LEB.) STEIN,
P. Xang-thong FOWLIE

This species occurs in the area of Thailand on the Malay Peninsula, and on adjacent islands. It grows in humus-filled crevices on limestone cliffs at low altitudes, sometimes just a few yards (meters) from the sea. The leaves are attractively mottled on the upper surface and purple underneath. They are up to 5⅔ in (14 cm) long and 1¼ in (3 cm) across. The short inflorescence bears one to two flowers on a short peduncle that is held close to the leaves. The flowers are up to 4¾ in (12 cm) across and appear during spring. This plant will not tolerate salt build-up in its soil, so fertilizers need to be well diluted. **ZONE 12. H.**

Paphiopedilum gratrixianum (MASTERS) ROLFE

This species occurs in Laos and Vietnam, where it grows in leaf-litter pockets on granite rock faces at moderate altitudes of about 3300 ft (1000 m). The leaves are straplike, evenly green, and up to 1 ft (30 cm) long and ⅘ in (2 cm) across. The single flower, up to 3¼ in (8 cm) across, is borne on an erect peduncle up to 10 in (25 cm) long. Flowering is during spring. This easy-to-grow species should be allowed a short watering rest period during mid winter. **ZONES 10–11. I–H.**

Paphiopedilum haynaldianum
(RCHB.F.) STEIN

This species occurs on the Philippine islands
of Luzon, Negros, and Mindanao. It grows on
serpentine cliffs or, occasionally, as an epiphyte
from sea level to a 5000-ft (1500-m) altitude.
The leaves are evenly green, straplike, and up
to 18 in (45 cm) long and 2 in (5 cm) across.
The arching inflorescence bears three to four
flowers, each 4–5^1/$_2$ in (10–13 cm) across.
Flowering is during late winter and spring.
This easy-to-grow species is tolerant of various
conditions. ZONES 10–12. I–H.

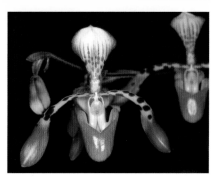

Paphiopedilum haynaldianum

Paphiopedilum hennisianum
(M. W. WOOD) FOWLIE

This species is from Mindanao, Negros, Panay,
and other Visayan islands in the Philippines.
It grows in leaf litter and moss on the floor
of rain forests at altitudes of 2000–3300 ft
(600–1000 m). The leaves are lightly mottled
on the upper surface, and up to 7 in (18 cm)
long and 1^3/$_4$ in (4 cm) across. The single
flower is about 2^1/$_2$ in (6 cm) across and is
borne on an erect peduncle up to 1 ft (30 cm)
long. Flowering occurs during spring. In
cultivation, this plant should be kept moist
throughout the year. ZONES 10–12. I–H.

Paphiopedilum hirsutissimum
(LINDL. EX HOOK.) STEIN

This species occurs in northeast India and
Myanmar. It grows in leaf-litter pockets in
the forks or at the base of trees on cliff faces
at altitudes of 660–6000 ft (200–1800 m).
The leaves are straplike, evenly green, and
about 18 in (45 cm) long and ^{4}/$_5$ in (2 cm)
across. The erect to horizontal inflorescence
is up to 10 in (25 cm) long, and has a single
flower up to 5^2/$_3$ in (14 cm) across. Flowering
is during spring. To achieve good flowering
in cultivation, this plant should be watered
copiously throughout spring and summer
and provided cooler temperatures and
reduced watering from autumn to spring.
ZONES 10–11. I.

Paphiopedilum hennisianum

Paphiopedilum hirsutissimum

Paphiopedilum insigne var. *sanderae*

Paphiopedilum insigne (WALL. EX LINDL.) PFITZER

This species from Nepal and northern India occurs on limestone cliffs at about 6700 ft (2000 m). It is a vigorous grower that reaches heights of about 12–18 in (30–45 cm) and often forms large clumps. The few straplike leaves are up to 15¼ in (38 cm) long and ⅘ in (2 cm) wide. The inflorescence is 1 ft (30 cm) long and has one or two glossy flowers about 4–6 in (10–15 cm) long. The flowers are in shades of brown with spots on the dorsal sepal. The variety *sanderae*, pictured here, has yellow flowers. The flowers appear during autumn and winter. This plant is the basis of many hybrids, some of which combine shades of green, russet, cream, and white with various patterns and markings. **ZONES 10–12. I.**

Paphiopedilum malipoense

Paphiopedilum malipoense

S. C. CHEN & Z. H. TSI

syn: *P. hiepii* AVER.,
P. jackii H. S. HUA

This species has been heavily collected and is now rare in its habitat of southern China and northern Vietnam. It grows in leaf litter on limestone in rain forests at altitudes of 2300–4300 ft (700–1300 m). The leaves are mottled above, with heavy purple spotting underneath. They are 4–8 in (10–20 cm) long and about 1¼ in (3 cm) wide. The peduncle is up to 1 ft (30 cm) long with a single flower 3¼–4¾ in (8–12 cm) across. Flowering occurs during spring. This plant is variable with two recognized varieties, *hiepii* and *jackii*. **ZONES 10–11. I–H.**

Paphiopedilum mastersianum

Paphiopedilum micranthum
T. TANG & F. T. WANG

When this species was first seen in London in 1984, it caused a sensation. It features large pink flowers on a small plant. It derives from the Yunnan, Guangxi, and Guizhou provinces in southern China, and grows in deep shade in the crevices of limestone rocks at altitudes of 1300–5000 ft (400–1500 m). The leaves are attractively mottled above with heavy purple spots underneath. They are up to 6 in (15 cm) long and 4/5 in (2 cm) across. There is a single flower up to 3 1/4 in (8 cm) across on an erect peduncle up to 8 in (20 cm) long. Flowering is during spring. This plant has been heavily collected and is now depleted in the wild. **ZONES 10–11. I–H.**

Paphiopedilum niveum (RCHB.F.) STEIN

This species is restricted to a small area near the border between Thailand and Malaysia, and on the Langkawi Islands to the west. It grows in pockets of leaf litter in the crevices of limestone cliffs at low altitudes. The leaves are heavily mottled on the upper surface and overlaid with purple spotting underneath. They are up to 7 2/3 in (19 cm) long and 1 1/4 in (3 cm) wide. The inflorescence has one or two flowers, each 2 1/2–3 1/4 in (6–8 cm) across, on a peduncle up to 10 in (25 cm) long. Flowering is during summer. This species is easy to grow, but is intolerant of any salt build-up in the potting mixture, so fertilizer must be well diluted. **ZONE 12. H.**

Paphiopedilum mastersianum
(RCHB.F.) STEIN

This species is recorded at altitudes of 3000–6700 ft (900–2000 m) on the islands of Ambon, Buru and, possibly, Ceram in Indonesia. Its leaves are mottled with dark and light green on the upper surface, and up to 16 in (40 cm) long and 1 3/4 in (4 cm) across. The erect inflorescence has a single flower about 3 2/3 in (9 cm) across on a peduncle up to 1 ft (30 cm) long. Flowering is from summer to autumn in cultivation. It needs consistent, warm temperatures and regular, year-round watering. **ZONES 10–11. I–H.**

Paphiopedilum micranthum

Paphiopedilum niveum

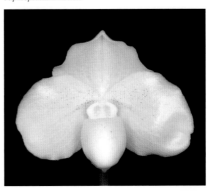

P

Paphiopedilum philippinense (RCHB.F.) STEIN
syn: *P. laevigatum* (BATEMAN) PFITZER

This species is widespread in the Philippines and in the extreme north of Sabah on Borneo. It grows in exposed conditions, but not in direct sunlight, on limestone rocks at low altitudes. The leaves are straplike, 8–20 in (20–50 cm) long and ⅘–2 in (2–5 cm) wide, and darker green on the upper surface than underneath. The erect to arching inflorescence comprises up to five flowers, each about 3½ in (8.5 cm) across. Flowering is during spring. This species does well in cultivation and is tolerant of any deterioration in the mixture. **ZONE 12. H.**

Paphiopedilum philippinense

Paphiopedilum parishii (RCHB.F.) STEIN

This species grows on trees or, occasionally, rocks at altitudes of 4000–7300 ft (1200–2200 m) in northeast Myanmar, Thailand, and the Yunnan province in southwest China. The leaves are darker green on the upper surface than underneath, straplike, and up to 18 in (45 cm) long and 2½ in (6 cm) wide. The arching to horizontal inflorescence has up to nine flowers, each about 4 in (10 cm) across. Flowering is during late winter and early spring. Reduced watering during winter is beneficial. **ZONES 9–10. C–I.**

Paphiopedilum parishii

Paphiopedilum primulinum var. *purpurascens*

Paphiopedilum purpuratum (LINDL.) STEIN
syn: *P. sinicum* (HANCE EX RCHB.F.) STEIN

This species occurs in Hong Kong, and the Guangdong province and Hainan Island in China. The plant is exposed to cool winds from mainland China during winter even though it is found at low altitudes—up to 2300 ft (700 m). It grows in leaf litter among the roots of bamboo and between rocks. The plant usually has a single leaf that is pale green underneath and attractively mottled on the upper surface. It is up to 6¾ in (17 cm) long and 1¾ in (4 cm) across. The single flower is up to 4 in (10 cm) across and is borne on an erect peduncle up to 8 in (20 cm) tall. Flowering is in late autumn. This species does well in areas with hot, humid summers and cool, humid winters. **ZONES 10–11. I.**

Paphiopedilum rothschildianum

Paphiopedilum primulinum
M. W. WOOD & P. TAYLOR

syn: **several names, including** *P. chamberlainianum*
var. *primulinum* (M. W. WOOD & P. TAYLOR) BRAEM

This species is found in a small area in the northern part of the island of Sumatra. It grows in humus on limestone hills from near sea level to about a 3300-ft (1000-m) altitude. The leaves are green on both sides, and 6½ in (16 cm) long and 1¼ in (3 cm) wide. The inflorescence is up to 14 in (35 cm) long with numerous flowers about 2¾ in (7 cm) across. The flowers open successively so the plant is in flower for an extended period of time. The variety shown here, *purpuascens*, is often found mingling with the type variety, which is evenly yellow all over. In cultivation, keep in a shaded position in an orchid house. **ZONES 10–12. I–H.**

Paphiopedilum purpuratum

Paphiopedilum rothschildianum
(RCHB.F.) STEIN

syn: *P. elliottianum* (O'BRIEN) STEIN

This rare species is known only from the lower slopes of Mount Kinabalu in Sabah on Borneo. It grows at altitudes of 2000–4000 ft (600–1200 m) on steep slopes and cliff faces. It is now considered endangered in the wild due to the combined effects of land clearing and over-collection. It forms clumps and has straplike, green leaves up to 2 ft (60 cm) long and 1¾ in (4 cm) across. The inflorescence has two to four, occasionally up to six flowers about 5⅔–12 in (14–30 cm) across with long, narrow petals. While it is quite easy to grow, this species should not be subdivided too early as this will prevent flowering. The flowers may appear at any time, but there is an emphasis on spring. **ZONES 10–11. I–H.**

P

Paphiopedilum spicerianum (RCHB.F.) PFITZER

This species occurs in northeast India, northern Myanmar and southwest China. It grows in shaded areas with pockets of leaf litter in the crevices of limestone cliffs at altitudes of 1000–4300 ft (300–1300 m). The leaves tend to be pendulous, evenly green, broadly straplike, and up to 1 ft (30 cm) long and 2 in (5 cm) across. The inflorescence has one or, rarely, two flowers up to 2¾ in (7 cm) across. These are borne on an erect peduncle up to 14 in (35 cm) tall. The flowers appear during autumn on the mature growths. In cultivation, this species should not be allowed to dry out. **ZONES 9–11. I.**

Paphiopedilum spicerianum

Paphiopedilum sukhakulii

Paphiopedilum sukhakulii

SCHOSER & SENGHAS

This species is known from a relatively small area in northern Thailand. It grows in sandy leaf litter near the streams of shady forests at a 3300-ft (1000-m) altitude. The leaves are attractively mottled on the upper surface, and 5½ in (13 cm) long and 1¾ in (4 cm) across. The single flower is up to 5⅔ in (14 cm) across, and is borne on a tall, erect peduncle. Flowering is during late winter and spring. In cultivation, this plant requires year-round humid conditions and frequent applications of diluted fertilizer. **ZONES 10–11. I.**

Paphiopedilum supardii

BRAEM & LOEB

This species is restricted to a small area in the southeast of Kalimantan province in Borneo. It grows in leaf mold in the crevices of limestone rocks at altitudes of 2000–3300 ft (600–1000 m). The leaves are evenly green, straplike, and 8–20 in (20–50 cm) long and 1¾ in (4 cm) wide. The erect inflorescence has three to seven flowers about 4 in (10 cm) across. **ZONES 10–11. I–H.**

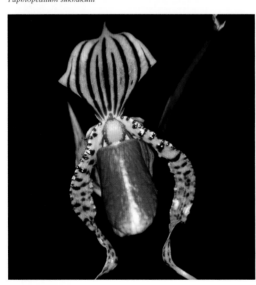

Paphiopedilum supardii

Paphiopedilum superbiens (RCHB.F.) STEIN
syn: *Cypripedium veitchianum* HORT. EX LEMAIRE

This species occurs in the northern and western parts of the Indonesian island of Sumatra. It grows in coniferous forest and on rock ledges at altitudes of 3000–4300 ft (900–1300 m). The leaves are gray-green and mottled with dark green on the upper surface, and green with some purple flushing at the base underneath. They are $9\frac{2}{3}$ in (24 cm) long and 2 in (5 cm) across. The single flower is up to $3\frac{1}{4}$ in (8 cm) across, and is borne on an erect peduncle about 8 in (20 cm) long. Flowering is during spring. A green and white variety, *sanderae*, is known. **ZONES 10–11. I–H.**

Paphiopedilum tonsum

Paphiopedilum tonsum (RCHB.F.) STEIN
syn: *P. braemii* H. MOHR

This species is restricted to the north and west of Sumatra. It has been reported as growing on and off limestone substrate, in pockets of leaf litter under shade at altitudes of 3300–6000 ft (1000–1800 m). The leaves are light gray–green

Paphiopedilum superbiens

and heavily mottled with dark green on the upper surface and some purple flushing underneath. They are up to 8 in (20 cm) long and $1\frac{3}{4}$ in (4 cm) across. The single flower is up to $4\frac{3}{4}$ in (12 cm) across and is borne on an erect peduncle up to 14 in (35 cm) long. Flowering is during spring. This species is easy to grow if watered regularly throughout the year and kept in humid conditions. **ZONE 10. I.**

Paphiopedilum urbanianum FOWLIE

This species is restricted to the Philippine island of Mindoro. It grows in humus pockets between rocks on forest floors at altitudes of 1300–2700 ft (400–800 m). The leaves are lightly mottled on the upper surface, and up to about 8 in (20 cm) long and $1\frac{3}{4}$ in (4 cm) across. The inflorescence has a single flower, very occasionally two, up to 4 in (10 cm) across, which is borne on an erect peduncle up to 10 in (25 cm) long. In cultivation, regular, year-round watering and constant humidity are required. Flowering is from winter to spring. **ZONES 11–12. I–H.**

Paphiopedilum urbanianum

Paphiopedilum venustum

P

Paphiopedilum venustum
(WALL EX SIMS) PFITZER
syn: *P. pardinium* (RCHB.F.) PFITZER

This species occurs in one of the wettest areas of the world—on the southern slopes of the Himalayas in northeast India, northern Bangladesh, Bhutan and, possibly, Nepal at altitudes of 200–4700 ft (60–1400 m). It grows in humus on the forest floors. The leaves, up to 10 in (25 cm) long and 2 in (5 cm) across, are heavily mottled with dark green and silver–green on the upper surface, with dense purple spots and striations underneath. The single flower is about $3^{2}/_{3}$ in (9 cm) across and is borne on an erect peduncle about 4–8 in (10–20) cm tall. Flowering occurs from winter to spring. In cultivation, keep moist year-round and the potting mixture should be free-draining.
ZONES 10–11. I–H.

Paphiopedilum victoria-regina (SANDER) M. W. WOOD
syn: *P. chamberlainianum* (SANDER) STEIN, *P. kalinae* BRAEM

This species is reported to grow on cliffs in a small area in western Sumatra at altitudes of 2700–5300 ft (800–1600 m). The leaves are green, and up to 1 ft (30 cm) long and $3^{2}/_{3}$ in (9 cm) wide. The inflorescence is long and bears up to 30 flowers, each $3^{1}/_{4}$–4 in (8–10 cm) across. The flowers open successively so only one or two are open at any particular time. This means the plant is in flower for a long period with the heaviest flowering during spring. It is easy to grow and will grow indoors for a period. It should be kept evenly moist year-round.
ZONES 10–11. I–H.

Paphiopedilum victoria-regina

Paphiopedilum villosum

Paphiopedilum villosum (LINDL.) STEIN
syn: *P. boxallii* (RCHB.F.) PFITZER

This species occurs in northeast India, Myanmar, and Thailand. It grows at altitudes of 3700–6700 ft (1100–2000 m), mostly as an epiphyte in tree forks or in clumps of ferns, but also on steep rock faces. The leaves are green, straplike, and up to 16 in (40 cm) long and 1¾ in (4 cm) wide. The single flower is 2¾–5½ in (7–13 cm) across, and is borne on a horizontal or pendulous peduncle up to 9⅔ in (24 cm) long. Flowering is from winter to spring or, sometimes, during autumn. It is easy to grow if watered heavily during growth with watering reduced during winter. It requires good air movement. **ZONES 9–10. I.**

Paphiopedilum wardii
SUMMERH.

This species occurs in northern Myanmar and, possibly, southern China. It grows at altitudes of about 4000–5000 ft (1200–1500 m) in deep leaf litter or on cliff faces. While some plants grow in exposed situations, the best plants are always under deep shade. The leaves are heavily mottled with dark green and silver–green on the upper surface and mottled with purple underneath. They are up to 6¾ in (17 cm) long and 2 in (5 cm) wide. The single flower is 3¼–4¾ in (8–12 cm) across. It is borne on an erect peduncle up to 18 in (45 cm) tall. Flowering is during early spring. In cultivation, good air circulation is required with heavy watering when the plant is actively growing. **ZONES 9–10. I.**

Paphiopedilum wardii

P

P

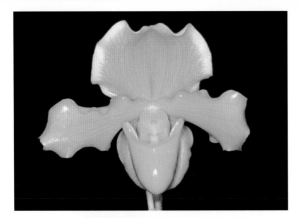

Paph. Marita

Paph. Langley's Pride

Paph. Magic Lantern

Paph. Raisin Jack x Red Maude

Paph. Iona

Paph. Transvaal

Paph. Nisqually

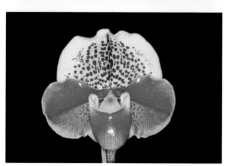

Paph. Warrawong "Kev"

PAPILIONANTHE SCHLTR.

This genus comprises about ten species, which were previously placed in the genera *Aerides* or *Vanda*. These scrambling epiphytes with terete leaves occur from India to Sulawesi, as far north as southern China. They grow mainly at low to moderate altitudes in exposed situations. Most of them have large flowers in shades of white or pink.

CULTIVATION

These plants do well in full sunlight with good air movement. In tropical climates they are grown on stakes and may be grown into a hedge. In an orchid house they require hot temperatures, bright light, and a slab or something similar on which to grow. The extremely popular form, "Vanda" Miss Agnes Joaquim, is a hybrid cross of *Papilionanthe hookeriana* and *P. teres*.

Papilionanthe teres
(ROXB.) SCHLTR.

syn: *Vanda teres* ROXB.

This species occurs in Nepal, Bhutan, northeast India, Myanmar, Thailand, Laos, Vietnam, and the Yunnan province of China. It is a large, scrambling epiphyte that grows at low altitudes. The stems are over 40 in (1 m) long and branched. The fleshy, terete leaves are up to 7 in (18 cm) long. The inflorescences are borne laterally and have two to five flowers, each about 2 in (5 cm) across. Flowering is during spring. **ZONE 12. H.**

Papilionanthe teres

P

Papilionanthe tricuspidata

Papilionanthe tricuspidata (J. J. SM.) GARAY
syn: *Vanda tricuspidata* J. J. SM.

This species occurs on the Lesser Sunda Islands of Indonesia. It is an epiphyte that grows at low altitudes. The stems are long and branched with terete leaves. The erect inflorescences bear a few flowers about 2¼ in (5.5 cm) across. These open successively over a long period, so large plants are almost always in flower.
ZONE 12. H.

Papilionanthe vandarum (RCHB.F.) GARAY
syn: *Aerides vandarum* RCHB.F., *A. cylindricum* HOOKER

This species occurs in Sikkim, the Khasi Hills, and Manipur in India, and in Myanmar. It grows on trees at altitudes of 4000–5000 ft (1200–1500 m). The branched stems are up to 2 ft (60 cm) long, and are pendulous with numerous narrow, terete leaves up to 10 in (25 cm) long. The inflorescences are short with up to three fragrant, long-lasting flowers, each about 2 in (5 cm) across. Flowering is during spring.
ZONES 9–10. I.

P

Papilionanthe vandarum

PARAPHALAENOPSIS A. D. HAWKES

This genus of four species was split from *Phalaenopsis* in 1980. The major distinction between the two genera is the leaves—they are terete in *Paraphalaenopsis*. Endemic to Borneo, none of the species in this genus will hybridize with *Phalaenopsis*. They grow in mountain rain forests at low altitudes.

CULTIVATION

A hanging pot or basket with a free-draining medium, or a slab suit the pendulous nature of these plants. Otherwise cultivation is as for *Phalaenopsis*.

Paraphalaenopsis serpentilingua (J. J. SM.) A. D. HAWKES

syn: *Phalaenopsis serpentilingua* J. J. SM., P. DENEVEI

The midlobe of the lip of this species' flower is split into two, and this bears a resemblance to a snake's tongue, which gives rise to the botanical name. It grows in swamp forests at low altitudes on the island of Borneo. The plant has a few pendulous, terete leaves about 1 ft (30 cm) long. The inflorescence is more or less upright with up to seven flowers, each about 1 in (2.5 cm) across. Flowering is during spring in cultivation and the flowers last for about two weeks. This plant needs bright, filtered light, year-round moisture, high temperatures, and good air movement to successfully cultivate. **ZONES 11–12. H.**

Paraphalaenopsis serpentilingua

Paraphalaenopsis labukensis SHIM., A. LAMB. & C. L. CHAN

syn: *Phalaenopsis labukensis* (SHIM., A. LAMB. & C. L. CHAN) SHIM.

This species grows as an epiphyte in hill forests at moderate altitudes near the Labuk River in eastern Sabah on Borneo. Its terete leaves reach 4 ft (1.2 m) in the wild, and have been known to reach 6 ft (1.8 m) in cultivation. The short inflorescence is more or less erect with a long pedicel and ovary—up to 4¾ in (12 cm). There are five to 15 flowers, each about 2½ in (6 cm) across with a cinnamon scent. In cultivation a hanging basket or slab are essential. Good air movement and year-round moisture are required. **ZONES 10–12. I–H.**

Paraphalaenopsis labukensis

PELATANTHERIA RIDL.

This genus of about five small species is from the regions between India and Sumatra. The species are monopodial epiphytes, which are related to *Cleisostoma*. The long climbing stems have short, fleshy leaves and roots along the whole length of the stems. The flowers are small and colorful.

CULTIVATION

The climbing habit of these plants means they need something to climb upon, so a slab rather than a pot is best. They also require bright light with regular watering.

Pelatantheria insectifera

P

Pelatantheria insectifera (RCHB.F.) RIDL.
syn: *Sarcanthus insectifer* RCHB.F.

This species occurs in the northwest Himalayas, the Deccan plateau and northeast India, Nepal, Myanmar and, possibly, southwest China. It grows as an epiphyte up to an altitude of about 3300 ft (1000 m). The erect stem is up to about 2 ft (60 cm) long. It has several stiff leaves, each about 6 in (15 cm) long and ⅔ in (15 mm) wide, that form two ranks. The short, lateral inflorescence has three to five flowers, each about ⅔ in (15 mm) across. Flowering is during summer.
ZONES 10–11. I–H.

PERISTYLUS BLUME

This genus has about 70 species that occur in regions
from India through Southeast Asia and the Malay
Archipelago to New Guinea, Australia, and the Pacific
Islands. These terrestrials grow from sea level up to
over 10,000 ft (3000 m), usually in grasslands or open
woodlands, with a few found in rain forests. They have
a tuber and a group of leaves near the base of the stem.
The flowers are mostly small and white or green in color.
These species are closely related to *Habenaria*.

CULTIVATION

A typical mix of loam, coarse sand, and leaf mold
is usually successful. The plants should be watered
regularly, as soon as growth commences during spring,
with reduced watering during autumn when the leaves
wither. They should be repotted each year in late winter.

Peristylus banfieldii (F. M. BAILEY) LAVARACK
syn: *Habenaria banfieldii* F. M. BAILEY

This species occurs in the northeast corner of Australia.
It grows in shaded areas along stream banks in open
forests at low altitudes. It is closely related to *Peristylus
goodyeroides*, a widespread species in Southeast Asia.
The plant is up to 40 in (1 m) tall, with four to seven
leaves about 1¼–10 in (3–25 cm) long and 2¾ in (7 cm)
wide. The leaves are grouped on the lower part of the
stem. The inflorescence is up to 10 in (25 cm) long with
numerous small flowers about ⅓ in (1 cm) long.
Flowering is during summer after the first rains of the
wet season. **ZONES 11–12. H.**

Peristylus banfieldii

Peristylus candidus J. J. SM.
syn: *Platanthera sumatrana* SCHLTR., *Habenaria sumatrana* (SCHLTR.) SCHLTR.

This species occurs in Vietnam and Cambodia, on the Malay
Peninsula, Indonesian islands, and New Guinea, and in
northeast Australia. It grows from sea level to about 3300 ft
(1000 m) in grasslands and open, grassy woodlands. The plant
is up to 20 in (50 cm) tall with about three elliptical leaves, each
about 2¾ in (7 cm) long, that lie on the surface of the ground.
The inflorescence is about 4¾ in (12 cm) long and bears up to
20 flowers, each about ⅓ in (1 cm) across. Flowering is mostly
during spring. **ZONES 11–12. H.**

Peristylus candidus

P

PESCATOREA RCHB.F.

This genus of about 15 species ranges from Costa Rica to Ecuador. They are epiphytic plants from wet forests at altitudes of 330–8700 ft (100–2600 m). There are no pseudobulbs but there are leaflike leaf sheaths arranged like a fan. The actual leaves are narrow and there is an inflorescence with one flower.

CULTIVATION

These species lack storage organs, such as pseudobulbs, so they should never be allowed to become dry. They may be potted in a well-drained mix and kept in cool to intermediate conditions.

Pescatorea cerina

Pescatorea cerina

(LINDL.) RCHB.F.

This tuft-forming plant from Costa Rica and Panama has erect to arching leaves up to 2 ft (60 cm) long. The inflorescence is short and arises from the leaf axil. The flower is large and showy, up to 3 in (7.5 cm) across, and has a waxy texture. It is also very fragrant. Flowering is from spring to autumn.
ZONES 9–10. C–I.

P

Pescatorea dayana

RCHB.F.

This species from Colombia grows at altitudes of 1000–5000 ft (300–1500 m). It is a large epiphyte with leaves up to 2 ft (60 cm) long and 2 in (5 cm) broad. The axillary inflorescence is up to about 4½ in (11 cm) tall. The flowers, about 3 in (7.5 cm) across, appear during winter.
ZONES 9–10. C–I.

Pescatorea dayana

PHAIUS LOUR.

This genus of about 50 species ranges from Africa through India and Southeast Asia, as far north as southern China, to New Guinea, Australia, and the islands of the Pacific. The species are almost all terrestrial, and are related to *Calanthe*. They are found in a variety of habitats and altitudes. They have squat or elongated pseudobulbs with large, pleated leaves. The inflorescence is usually erect with several large, colorful flowers.

CULTIVATION

Most of these species are easy to grow in an organically rich mix with additives, such as decomposed cow manure. They should be kept moist year-round and well fertilized while actively growing. They grow best in shady situations. For some species, the old flowering stalks may be used to propagate new plants by lying them on a bed of moss.

Phaius flavus

Phaius flavus (BLUME) LINDL.
syn: *P. maculatus* LINDL., *P. flexuosus* BLUME

This widespread species occurs from India and China through most of Southeast Asia and the islands of Indonesia and the Philippines to New Guinea and the islands in the southwest of the Pacific Ocean. It grows on humid, shady floors of forests at altitudes of about 1000–6700 ft (300–2000 m). The conical pseudobulbs are up to 4 in (10 cm) tall. There are several plicate leaves about 16 in (40 cm) long and 4 in (10 cm) across. The inflorescence arises from the base of the pseudobulbs and is 20–36 in (50–90 cm) tall with eight to 20 flowers, each up to 2¾ in (7 cm) across. Flowering is during spring.
ZONES 9–11. I.

P

Phaius pulchellus

Phaius pulchellus KRAENTZ

This species occurs on Madagascar and Réunion Island in the Indian Ocean. It grows as an epiphyte or a terrestrial in humid, evergreen forests at altitudes of 2300–5000 ft (700–1500 m). There are three varieties, including the type variety, which has purple flowers with some white on the lip, and variety *sandrangatensis*, which has a purple–red lip and yellow petals and sepals. Flowering is during winter. **ZONES 10–11. I.**

Phaius tankervilleae

Phaius tankervilleae
(BANKS EX L'HERITAGE) BLUME

syn: many names, including *P. grandifolius* LOUR., *P. blumei* LINDL.

This widespread species ranges from India and Sri Lanka through China, most of Southeast Asia, and the Malay Archipelago to Australia and the islands in the southwest of the Pacific Ocean. It grows most often in sheltered, moist or swampy conditions from sea level to about 6000 ft (1800 m). The conical pseudobulbs are up to 2½ in (6 cm) tall. There are several broad, pleated leaves, up to 40 in (1 m) long and 4¾ in (12 cm) across. The inflorescence may be up to 80 in (2 m) tall but is usually about 40 in (1 m). It bears up to 25 flowers, each up to 4¾ in (12 cm) across. Flowering occurs at various times across the range, but mostly during spring. Plants of this very popular species will grow and flower under direct sunlight, but the best results are achieved with shaded conditions. The mixture should not be allowed to dry out and some growers stand the plant pot in a saucer of water. **ZONES 10–12. I–H.**

P

PHALAENOPSIS BLUME

There are about 60 species in this genus, including some of the most popular orchids in cultivation. They range from Sri Lanka and southern India to New Guinea and northeast Australia, extending as far north as southern China. The Philippines and Borneo are rich with these species. Most of the species grow in hot, steamy lowlands, but a few are adapted to the cooler climates of higher altitudes. Generally, they grow in habitats that are moist and humid year-round, such as under dense- to partial-shade cover near streams in rain forests. They favor these types of habitats because they lack the storage organs that help them survive seasonal climates. A few cope with seasonally dry climates by dropping their leaves during the dry season. They have a few large leaves and a very short stem. The flowers are often large and colorful. Almost all are epiphytes or, occasionally, lithophytes, with the notable exception of three species formerly considered to be part of *Dorites* (see *Phalaenopsis pulcherrima*), which are always terrestrial or lithophytic species. The popularity of this genus has resulted in over-collection from the wild and a few species are threatened, including three considered to be endangered— *P. aphrodite*, *P. gigantea* and *P. javanica*.

CULTIVATION

The lack of storage organs means these species require year-round moisture and fertilizing. The species from lowland areas must be kept in warm conditions throughout the year so a heated greenhouse is required in temperate climates. While many of them grow in low-light situations, slightly higher light levels are usually used in cultivation as this produces better flowering. Where warm, moist, semi-shaded conditions are provided, they should also have good air movement to prevent diseases. The substrate should retain some moisture between waterings but should not become soggy.

Phalaenopsis amabilis

HYBRIDS

Phalaenopsis species have been used to make thousands of hybrids. Apart from the horticultural trade, the flowers of these plants are very popular in the florist trade due to their lasting qualities and large size. Various trends in breeding, along with the ever-present search for size, shape, and texture, concentrate on flower color, including varieties in white, pink, yellow, red, or white with colored lips, stripes, spots, and several others. The whites owe much to *P. amabilis* and *P. aphrodite*, while the pinks originate from *P. sanderiana* and *P. schilleriana*. Stripes come from *P.* x *intermedia* (a natural hybrid between *P. aphrodite* and *P. equestris*) and *P. lindenii*. Spots come from species such as *P. stuartiana* and *P. lueddemanniana*. Colorful miniatures have been made using *Doritis pulcherrima* (now considered to be *Phalaenopsis pulcherrima*) and *P. lobbii*, *P. maculata*, and *P. parishii*.

P

Phalaenopsis amboinensis

Phalaenopsis amabilis
(L.) BLUME

syn: *P. grandiflora* LINDL., *P. gloriosa* RCHB.F., *P. amabilis* F. M. BAILEY
"MOTH ORCHID"

The moth orchid is from the south of the Philippines, Sumatra, Java, Borneo, New Guinea, and northeast Australia. There are two subspecies and one or more varieties recognized, and the subspecies *rosenstromii* from New Guinea and Australia has slightly smaller flowers. *P. amabilis* is an epiphyte or lithophyte that grows year-round in warm, moist conditions in shaded or semi-shaded, humid locations at low to moderate altitudes. It has the largest flowers of the genus, up to 3¼ in (8 cm) across. Numerous, long-lasting flowers are borne on an arching, branched inflorescence up to 40 in (1 m) long. Flowering may occur at any time of the year but there is an emphasis on spring and summer. This plant must be kept warm and moist year-round and be provided with good drainage. A greenhouse is essential in all but subtropical and tropical climates. **ZONES 10–12. I–H.**

Phalaenopsis amboinensis J. J. SM.

This species occurs on the Moluccas and Sulawesi, where it grows in shady, humid forests with year-round rainfall at low altitudes. The thick-textured, long-lasting flowers are about 1¾ in (4 cm) across and have orange to brick-red markings in a more or less concentric pattern on a white or yellow background. There are two to four fleshy leaves up to 10 in (25 cm) long and 4 in (10 cm) across. **ZONES 11–12. H.**

Phalaenopsis bellina (RCHB.F.) CHRISTENSON
syn: *P. violacea* **var.** *bellina* RCHB.F.

Recognized as a separate species as recently as 1995, this plant is restricted to the Malay Peninsula and Borneo. It grows at low altitudes in shady, humid habitats, such as beside streams. It is pendulous with rounded leaves up to 10 in (25 cm) long and 4¾ in (12 cm) across. The flowers open progressively with one, two or three open at any one time. They are about 2 in (5 cm) across and are the most fragrant of the genus. They have a strong, fruity perfume. **ZONES 11–12. H.**

Phalaenopsis bellina

P

Phalaenopsis celebensis H. R. SWEET

This miniature species is known only from Sulawesi in Indonesia. Little is known of its habitat or altitude range. The plant has attractive dark-green leaves mottled with silver-gray, each about 6¾ in (17 cm) long and 2½ in (6 cm) across. There are numerous flowers about 1¼ in (3 cm) across, which are densely packed on an arching inflorescence. This species has only recently been introduced to cultivation. **ZONES 11–12. H.**

Phalaenopsis celebensis

Phalaenopsis cornu-cervi
(BREDA) BLUME & RCHB.F.

This widely distributed species occurs from northeast India to Java and Borneo. It grows as an epiphyte or, occasionally, a lithophyte at low to moderate elevations in humid forests in situations where there is bright light. The roots of this species are thicker than most of the others in the genus. The narrow leaves are up to 9 in (22 cm) long and 1¾ in (4 cm) wide. The flowers are about 1¾–2 in (4–5 cm) across and they open progressively, about one to three at a time, and last for about week. They are borne on a fleshy, serrated inflorescence. In cultivation, this species should be given warm, humid conditions with brighter light than for the other species in the genus. **ZONES 11–12. H.**

Phalaenopsis cornu-cervi

Phalaenopsis deliciosa RCHB.F.
syn: several names, including *Kingidium deliciosum* (RCHB.F.) H. R. SWEET, *Phalaenopsis bella* TEIJSM. & BINN., *P. hebe* RCHB.F., *Doritis philippinensis* AMES.

This medium-sized species has a widespread distribution over Asia, from Sri Lanka and India to the Philippines, Borneo, and Sulawesi. This has resulted in a long list of synonyms and it was considered, until recently, to be part of *Kingidium*. It grows as an epiphyte at low altitudes, often near streams. The inflorescences are from 2½–8 in (6–20 cm) long, with usually only one or two flowers open at any one time. The flowers are about ½ in (12 mm) across, and are usually suffused with a rose color, but some plants have pure-white flowers. **ZONES 11–12. H.**

Phalaenopsis deliciosa

P

Phalaenopsis equestris (SCHAUER) RCHB.F.
syn: *P. rosea* LINDL.

This small, upright species occurs naturally at low altitudes in the Philippines and Taiwan. It produces a simple or branched inflorescence with densely packed flowers, each about 1¼ in (3 cm) across. The flowers vary in color from rose to white suffused with rose. It flowers at any time in the wild, but mostly between February and May. The plant's small size makes it suited to a small pot with good drainage. It grows best in year-round humid conditions and warm temperatures, although a slightly drier period in winter may be acceptable. **ZONES 10–12. H.**

Phalaenopsis equestris

Phalaenopsis fasciata

Phalaenopsis fasciata
RCHB.F.

Sometimes incorrectly regarded as part of the *P. lueddemanniana* complex, this species from the Philippines has been used in hybridization to produce flowers with a dark-yellow coloring. It grows at low altitudes in hot, humid rain forests. The leaves are up to 8 in (20 cm) long and 2½ cm (6 cm) across. The flowers are about 1¾ in (4 cm) across and last for two or three weeks. Flowering may occur at almost any time with an emphasis on spring. **ZONES 11–12. H.**

Phalaenopsis fuscata RCHB.F.

The glossy, narrow, bicolored segments of this species are a feature. It has been recorded from Borneo, the Malay Peninsula, and the Philippines, although the latter region is doubtful. It grows in warm, humid areas beside streams in lowland hill forests below an altitude of 3300 ft (1000 m). The leaves are about 1 ft (30 cm) long and 4 in (10 cm) across. The flowers are about 1¼–1¾ in (3–4 cm) across and are borne on branched inflorescences up to 16 in (40 cm) long. If grown well, this species may reward with masses of flowers. **ZONES 10–12. I–H.**

Phalaenopsis fuscata

Phalaenopsis gigantea

Phalaenopsis gigantea
J. J. SM.

Noted for being the largest plant in the genus, this species has its drawbacks with modest flowers and a reputation for being slow to grow in cultivation. It is restricted to Borneo, where it grows in the understorey of lowland rain forests in humid, shady conditions. It is sometimes known as "elephant ears" for its extremely large leaves over 28 in (70 cm) long and 8–10 in (20–25 cm) wide. The pendulous inflorescence, up to 16 in (40 cm) long, is densely packed with flowers. The fleshy, sweetly scented flowers are about 2 in (5 cm) across. Despite its understorey habitat, experience indicates that relatively high light levels are necessary for flowering in cultivation. **ZONES 11–12. H.**

Phalaenopsis hieroglyphica

Phalaenopsis hieroglyphica
(RCHB.F.) H. R. SWEET

Named for its floral segment markings that look like hieroglyphs, this species is restricted to a few islands in the Philippines. It grows at altitudes of about 1700 ft (500 m) in humid, shady conditions. The leathery leaves are up to 1 ft (30 cm) long and 3⅔ in (9 cm) across. Numerous flowers, about 2 in (5 cm) wide, are borne on arching or pendulous inflorescences up to 1 ft (30 cm) long. This species will grow readily into a large specimen covered with flowers. **ZONES 10–12. I–H.**

Phalaenopsis kunstleri HOOK.F.

syn: *P. fuscata* **var.**
kunstleri Hort.

At first glance, this
species is extremely
similar to *P. fuscata*,
but the column of
P. kunstleri is squat not
slender. It is a medium-
sized epiphyte recorded
from Myanmar and the
Malay Peninsula, where
it grows at low to
moderate altitudes. There
are two to four leaves up
to $9\frac{2}{3}$ in (24 cm) long
and $3\frac{1}{4}$ in (8 cm) across.
The suberect to arching
inflorescences are
sometimes branched and
up to 16 in (40 cm) long.
The flowers are about
$1\frac{3}{4}$ in (4 cm) across.
ZONES 10–12. I–H.

Phalaenopsis kunstleri

Phalaenopsis lindenii LOHER

The famous "candy stripe" hybrids are due
in part to this charming miniature species.
It occurs in the mountains of northern
Luzon in the Philippines, where it grows
in cooler conditions than are usual for this
genus. The leaves are attractive, dark green,
mottled with silver, and up to 8 in (20 cm)
long and $1\frac{3}{4}$ in (4 cm) across. The densely
packed flowers are about $1\frac{1}{4}$ in (3 cm)
across. They are borne on an upright or
arching inflorescence. Most plants in the
wild have faint stripes on the flower parts,
but selected clones in cultivation have most
attractive stripes. In cultivation, this plant
requires significantly cooler conditions
than other species in the genus.
ZONES 9–11. C–I.

P

Phalaenopsis lindenii

Phalaenopsis lueddemanniana

Phalaenopsis lueddemanniana RCHB.F.

Several currently recognized species were
formerly considered part of *P. lueddemanniana*,
including *P. fasciata*, *P. hieroglyphica*,
P. pallens, *P. pulchra*, and *P. reichenbachiana*.
This variable species is widespread in the
Philippines where it grows as an epiphyte at
low altitudes. The leaves are 1 ft (30 cm) long
and 2¾ in (7 cm) across. The fragrant flowers,
up to 1¾ in (4 cm) across, are borne on a
branched, spreading inflorescence. Only a few
flowers are open at any one time, and they
may appear at any time of the year. The old
inflorescences often produce keikis, which may
be used for propagation. **ZONES 11–12. H.**

Phalaenopsis mannii

Phalaenopsis mannii RCHB.F.
syn: *P. boxallii* RCHB.F.

This species is found in forests with a distinct
dry season, ranging from Nepal and northeast
India to southern China and Vietnam. It grows
at low to moderate altitudes. The leaves are
spotted along the midrib and at the base, and
are up to 14¾ in (37 cm) long and 2¾ in
(7 cm) across. An inflorescence with many
branches bears numerous flowers, each about
1¼ in (3 cm) across. The flowers are variable
in color and the species is free-flowering.
ZONES 10–12. I–H.

Phalaenopsis pallens (LINDL.) RCHB.F.
syn: *Trichoglottis pallens* LINDL., *Phalaenopsis
foerstermannii* RCHB.F.

This small species is a member of the
P. lueddemanniana group and is endemic to
the Philippines. It grows in humid, shaded
habitats at low altitudes. The leaves are about
8 in (20 cm) long and 2½ in (6 cm) across
and the flowers are about 1¾ in (4 cm) wide.
A few flowers are carried on a more or less
upright inflorescence. Two varieties are
recognized, including the white-flowered *alba*.
ZONES 11–12. H.

Phalaenopsis pallens

P

Phalaenopsis parishii RCHB.F.
syn: *Aerides decumbens* GRIFF.

This miniature species occurs in habitats with
a distinct dry season in the foothills of the
Himalayas in India, and in Myanmar and
Thailand. It is deciduous, but cultivated plants
given moisture throughout winter do retain
their leaves. It is closely related to *P. lobbii*, but
is distinguished by its bright wine-colored lip.
The flowers are less than ⁴/₅ in (2 cm) across.
Five or six of these are borne on an upright
or arching inflorescence. **ZONES 10–12. I–H.**

Phalaenopsis parishii

Phalaenopsis philippinensis
GOLAMCO EX FOWLIE & TANG

This species is sometimes confused with the
natural hybrid *P.* x *leucorrhoda* (a cross between
P. aphrodite and *P. schilleriana*). It is restricted
to low to moderate altitudes in the Philippines.
The leaves, mottled with silver– gray, are up
to 14 in (35 cm) long and 5½ in (13 cm)
across. Numerous large, showy flowers,
each up to 2¾ in (7 cm) across, are borne
on sparsely branched, arching inflorescences
up to 4 ft (1.2 m) long, but usually less
than half this length.
ZONES 11–12. I–H.

Phalaenopsis philippinensis

Phalaenopsis pulcherrima (LINDL.) J. J. SM.
syn: *Doritis pulcherrima* LINDL., *Phalaenopsis esmerelda*
RCHB.F., *P. antennifera* RCHB.F.

For many years this terrestrial species was
placed in *Doritis*, but recent research resulted
in it being included in *Phalaenopsis*. It is a
widespread species from northeast India to
southern China, the Malay Peninsula, Sumatra,
and Borneo. It commonly grows under bright
sunlight in the crevices of rocks in coastal
locations up to a 4000-ft (1200-m) altitude.
The thick, leathery leaves are often tinged with
purple and are up to 6 in (15 cm) long and
1¼ in (3 cm) wide. Numerous flowers, about
⁴/₅ in (2 cm) across, are borne during summer
on an upright inflorescence that is up to 2 ft
(60 cm) tall. **ZONES 10–12. I–H.**

Phalaenopsis pulcherrima

Phalaenopsis pulchra (RCHB.F.) H. R. SWEET
syn: *P. lueddemanniana* **var.** *pulchra* RCHB.F.

This species, restricted to the Philippines, grows at low altitudes.
Its leaves are about 6 in (15 cm) long and 2½ in (6 cm) across.
The long-lasting flowers, about 1¼ in (3 cm) across, are borne
on inflorescences that may be either short and upright with a
few flowers or long, up to 40 in (1 m), with no flowers or,
occasionally, one or two flowers. In place of the flowers there
are keikis or small plantlets. **ZONES 11–12. H.**

Phalaenopsis schilleriana RCHB.F.

This spectacular pink-flowered species is restricted to the
Philippines. It occurs in rain forests at low to moderate altitudes.
The leaves are a feature, being dark green and richly mottled
with silver above and purple underneath. They are up to 16 in
(40 cm) long and 4 in (10 cm) across. The long, branched and
arching inflorescence bears fragrant flowers, each about 2–3¼ in
(5–8 cm) across. They are long-lasting and appear during spring.
This species does well in cultivation and may grow into
a large specimen plant with numerous flowers. A cool period
during winter is required for good flowering. **ZONES 10–12. I–H.**

Phalaenopsis stuartiana

Phalaenopsis venosa

Phalaenopsis pulchra   *Phalaenopsis schilleriana*

Phalaenopsis stuartiana RCHB.F.
syn: *P. schilleriana* **var.** *stuartiana* (RCHB.F.) BURB.

Similar to *P. schilleriana*, but with white flowers and a strongly
marked lip, this species occurs in lowland habitats in the
Philippines. The leaves, up to 16 in (40 cm) long and 4 in
(10 cm) across, are mottled with silver-gray above and purple
underneath. The long-lasting flowers, about 2¾ in (7 cm)
across, are borne on a long, arching, and branched inflorescence.
In cultivation this plant often grows into a large specimen that
may be covered with flowers. **ZONES 11–12. H.**

Phalaenopsis venosa
SHIM & FOWLIE
syn: *Polychilos venosa* SHIM EX FOWLIE

This medium-sized species
is known only from the
Indonesian island of Sulawesi.
It grows as an epiphyte at
moderate altitudes. There
are three to five glossy leaves,
each about 4–9 in (10–22 cm)
long and 2–2¾ in (5–7 cm)
across. The upright
inflorescences are sometimes
branched and up to 7 in
(18 cm) long. They carry
densely packed flowers,
each 1¾–2 in (4–5 cm)
across, that have a slightly
unpleasant scent. Flowers
may vary in color from brown
to yellow. **ZONES 10–11. I.**

Phal. Orchid World

Dpts. Miriko Seripes x Leopard Prince

Phal. Brother Kaiser

Dpts. Sogo Cherry

P

PHOLIDOTA LINDL. EX W. J. HOOK.

This genus of about 30 species has a widespread distribution
from Sri Lanka to New Guinea and Australia. It is related to
Coelogyne. The pseudobulbs may be large or small, clustered
or separated, with one or two leaves. The inflorescences arise
from the apex of young pseudobulbs. They are usually
pendulous with rather large bracts and numerous small
flowers in two ranks.

CULTIVATION

Species with clustered pseudobulbs grow best in a pot with
a well-drained mixture. Those with separated pseudobulbs
are better on a slab or in a basket to allow room for their
wandering style of growth. The plants need to be given a
brief watering rest period after the growth is complete and
should be grown under semi-shade.

P

Pholidota cantonensis

Pholidota cantonensis ROLFE

This species occurs in Hong Kong and in the south of mainland
China. It grows at moderate altitudes and is a small species with
well-separated ovoid pseudobulbs about ⅘ in (2 cm) long. There
are two leaves up to 3⅔ in (9 cm) long and ⅓ in (1 cm) wide.
The inflorescence arises from the base of a pseudobulb, and is
about 3¼ in (8 cm) long. It bears numerous flowers about ⅓ in
(1 cm) across. These appear during late winter and spring.
ZONES 10–11. I.

Pholidota chinensis LINDL.

This species is from Myanmar, Vietnam, and southern China, including Hong Kong. It grows as an epiphyte on rain forest trees or on rocks from low altitudes to about 8300 ft (2500 m). The pseudobulbs are spaced about ⅔ in (15 mm) apart on the rhizome. They are ovoid and ⅘–3¼ in (2–8 cm) long with three leaves up to 8 in (20 cm) long and 2 in (5 cm) across. The pendulous, zigzag-shaped inflorescence arises from the apex of the young pseudobulbs. It is up to 14 in (35 cm) long and has more than 20 flowers, each about ⅘ in (2 cm)across. Flowering is during spring.

ZONES 9–11. I–H.

Pholidota chinensis

Pholidota imbricata

Pholidota imbricata W. J. HOOK.
syn: several names, including *P. pallida* HOLT., *P. beccarii* SCHLTR.

This widespread species ranges from India to Australia and the Pacific Islands. It grows as an epiphyte or lithophyte from sea level to a 4000-ft (1200-m) altitude. The pseudobulbs are clustered, conical, angular, and up to 3¼ in (8 cm) long, but usually smaller. There is a single, leathery leaf up to 20 in (50 cm) long and 3¼ in (8 cm) wide. The inflorescence is initially erect then pendulous. It is zigzag-shaped and bears numerous flowers about ¼ in (6 mm) across that are in two rows and do not open widely. Flowering time is variable across the range—late spring in some areas, winter in others. **ZONES 11–12. H.**

P

PHRAGMIPEDIUM ROLFE

This genus of about 15 species is related to *Paphiopedilum* and *Cypripedium* but *Phragmipedium* species are generally larger. They range from southern Mexico to Bolivia and Brazil, and grow in moist areas, often in shady conditions at a range of altitudes. These plants are terrestrials, lithophytes or, rarely, epiphytes with several straplike leaves, often arranged in a fan. The erect inflorescence is usually unbranched with a few flowers that open successively. The inflated lip is slipper-shaped with united lateral sepals. The column has two fertile stamens and a staminode.

CULTIVATION

Most of these species require intermediate conditions with regular, year-round watering, semi-shade, and humidity. Use a well-drained but moisture-retentive potting mixture. It is best to allow the plants to form large clumps rather than divide them too often.

Phragmipedium caudatum

Phragmipedium besseae

Phragmipedium besseae DODSON & KUHN
syn: *Phragmipedium dalessandroi* DODSON & GRUSS

This very attractive species is found on the eastern slopes of the Andes from northern Peru to southern Colombia. It grows under semi-shade on or beside moist rock faces at an altitude of about 3300 ft (1000 m). The straplike leaves are up to 9 in (22 cm) long and 1¾ in (4 cm) wide. The erect inflorescence is often branched and up to 2 ft (60 cm) long. There are several flowers, each about 2½ in (6 cm) across, that open successively, with usually only one open at a time. Occasionally yellow flowers are reported. Flowering occurs over an extended period, but mostly during spring. Use only well-diluted fertilizer and keep this plant constantly wet. **ZONES 9–11. I.**

Phragmipedium caudatum (LINDL.) ROLFE
syn: *P. warscewiczianum* (RCHB.F.) GARAY

This species occurs from Panama and Colombia to Bolivia and Peru. It grows as an epiphyte or lithophyte, often in bright light, at altitudes of 5000–8300 ft (1500–2500 m). A number of plants form clumps. Each one has straplike leaves that are up to 2 ft (60 cm) long and 2 in (5 cm) wide. The erect inflorescence has up to six flowers, each up to 20 in (50 cm) long, most of this length comprising pendulous and twisted petals. Flowering is mainly during autumn. In cultivation, this species should be given a watering rest period during winter and a potting mix with extremely good drainage. **ZONES 9–10. C–I.**

P

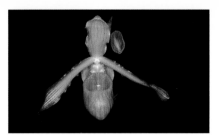

Phragmipedium lindleyanum

Phragmipedium lindleyanum (LINDL.) ROLFE
syn: *P. kaieteurum* (N. E. BROWN) GARAY

This species occurs from Venezuela to Brazil. It grows in pockets of leaf litter and soil on rock faces or among tree roots in exposed or semi-shaded areas at altitudes of about 2500–6700 ft (750–2000 m). The leaves are up to 20 in (50 cm) long and 2½ (6 cm) across. The inflorescence is branched and up to 40 in (1 m) tall with several flowers up to 3¼ in (8 cm) across. These open successively from autumn to winter. **ZONES 10–11. I.**

Phragmipedium schlimii

Phragmipedium schlimii
(LINDEN EX RCHB.F.) ROLFE
syn: *P. fischeri* BRAEM & MOHR

This species is found in Colombia at altitudes of 4300–6000 ft (1300–1800 m). It grows on the floor of forests, often near rivers. There are about eight straplike leaves, up to 14 in (35 cm) long and 1½ in (3.5 cm) wide. The erect inflorescence is about 1 ft (30 cm) tall and carries six to ten flowers, each about 2 in (5 cm) across. Flowers appear mostly during spring, but they may occur at other times. Some plants are self-pollinating with flowers that do not open properly. These should be avoided in cultivation. **ZONES 9–11. I.**

Phragmipedium pearcei

Phragmipedium pearcei
(RCHB.F.) RAUH & SENGHAS
syn: *P. ecuadorense* GARAY

This species occurs in Ecuador and Peru, where it grows on large boulders near small streams at low altitudes. The leaves are long and narrow, up to 2 ft (60 cm) long and ⅔ in (15 mm) wide. The inflorescence, up to 1 ft (30 cm) long, has up to six flowers about 2¾ in (7 cm) long that open successively. Flowering is during summer. **ZONES 11–12. I–H.**

Phragmipedium sargentianum (ROLFE) ROLFE

This species is from the Pernambuco state in northeast Brazil and it is closely related to *P. lindleyanum*, but it has smaller, more yellow flowers and drooping petals. It grows in leaf litter on forest floors or in shaded crevices among rocks at altitudes of 2000–3300 ft (600–1000 m). The leaves are 20 in (50 cm) long, or longer, and 1½ in (3.5 cm) wide. The inflorescence is up to 16 in (40 cm) long with up to four flowers, each 2¾–4 in (7–10 cm) across. Only one flower opens at any one time, and they appear from autumn to winter. In cultivation, this plant will grow in shade or bright, indirect light and requires year-round warm, humid temperatures. **ZONES 11–12. I–H.**

Phragmipedium sargentianum

Phrag. Hanna Popow

Phrag. Cardinale

Phrag. sedenii

Phrag. grande

PLATANTHERA L. C. RICHARD

This terrestrial genus of about 200 species inhabits temperate regions around the world. Many of the species occur in the northeast of North America, where they are among the most conspicuous wild flowers during July and August. Two subgroups contain most of the species. One, the *hyperborea/dilatata* complex, is usually white or green with a plain, narrow lip. It has a northerly, transcontinental range in the USA and Canada. The other subgroup comprises brightly colored fringed orchids, usually with incised lips. These extend inland from the coastal plain between Newfoundland and Texas. The habitat of *Platanthera* varies from woods to fields and peat bogs. All the species are erect, and are usually tall and leafy with dense, many-flowered, terminal inflorescences. The lip spur is typically long and curved downward. It contains nectar that attracts pollinating moths.

Platanthera aquilonis
SHEVIAK
"TALL NORTHERN GREEN ORCHID,"
"GREEN REIN-ORCHID"

This large American species was formerly included in *P. hyperborea* but was separated in 1999. It is one of a few orchids that live above the Arctic Circle in Alaska. It also ranges south to Illinois. It is part of a complex of closely related species that are actively undergoing evolution. This plant reaches 2 ft (60 cm) in height and has several slim, pointed leaves. The self-pollinating flowers are about $\frac{2}{3}$ in (15 mm) in diameter. The plant shown here was found growing at an abandoned gypsum quarry on Cape Breton Island in Nova Scotia. The flowers are withering as the ovaries swell.
ZONES 2–4. C.

P

Platanthera aquilonis

Platanthera ciliaris

Platanthera dilatata (PURSH) LINDL.

"TALL WHITE BOG ORCHID," "TALL WHITE NORTHERN ORCHID," "BOG CANDLES,"
"WHITE REIN-ORCHID"

This orchid blooms en masse in roadside ditches on Cape
Breton Island in Nova Scotia during July (summer). It is an
impressive species divided into several varieties, distinguishable
by their floral details. It occupies a transcontinental, northern
range similar to that of *P. aquilonis*. It exceeds a 40-in (1-m)
height, and there are two leaves up to 1 ft (30 cm) long.
The flowers number about 70, each one about 1 in (2.5 cm)
in diameter. The base of the lip is wide, and this gives rise
to its name. **ZONES 2–7. C.**

Platanthera grandiflora (BIGELOW) LINDL.

"LARGE PURPLE FRINGED ORCHID," "LARGE BUTTERFLY ORCHID"

This is perhaps the most spectacular North American orchid.
Often confused with *P. psycodes*, it is usually taller than that
species and has looser racemes with larger flowers, and it
generally blooms earlier. *P. grandiflora* is more likely to
be found in woodlands ranging from North Carolina to
Newfoundland. It reaches nearly 4 ft (1.2 m), and has two
to six leaves about 9 in (22 cm) tall and 2¾ in (7 cm) wide.
There are 30 to 60 flowers, each with a diameter over 1 in
(2.5 cm). The arrangement of the two pollen sacs and the
spur opening requires a different species of moth for
pollination than *P. psycodes*. **ZONES 4–7. C.**

Platanthera ciliaris (L.) LINDL.
"YELLOW FRINGED ORCHID"

This brilliant North American
species inhabits various habitats
from Texas to Maine, but it is
becoming uncommon. The height
of the plant is about 40 in (1 m).
There are several pointy leaves
up to 1 ft (30 cm) long and 2 in
(5 cm) wide. Up to 60 orange
flowers, each about 1 in (2.5 cm)
in diameter, have long spurs that
stretch downward behind deeply
fringed lips. The flowers appear
during August (summer).
ZONES 5–7. C.

Platanthera dilatata

Platanthera grandiflora

Platanthera huronensis

Platanthera macrophylla

Platanthera huronensis (NUTTALL) LINDL.
"TALL GREEN ORCHID," "GREEN REIN–ORCHID"

This species is widely distributed across northern North America, north to Alaska and the Aleutian Islands. It shares much of this range with *P. aquilonis*, a similar plant that belongs with it and *P. dilatata* in the *P. hyperborea* complex. *P. huronensis* is distinguishable from *P. aquilonis* by a lip dilated at the base and from *P. dilatata* by its green color. The plant pictured was growing in Denali National Park north of Mount McKinley in Alaska. The species is up to 40 in (1 m) tall and has a number of leaves and up to 30 flowers that are arranged tightly or loosely. Each flower has a diameter of about 1 in (2.5 cm). **ZONES 4–5. C.**

Platanthera integra
(NUTTALL) GRAY EX BECK.
"YELLOW FRINGELESS ORCHID"

This species ranges from New Jersey to Texas. The plant illustrated was photographed in a wet meadow near a shoreline in southern New Jersey. The upright plant is up to 2 ft (60 cm) tall, with one or two leaves up to 8 in (20 cm) long. The cylindrical flower head contains up to 60 yellow flowers, each with a diameter over $1\frac{3}{4}$ in (4 cm). The lip is only slightly fringed. **ZONES 5–7. C.**

Platanthera integra

Platanthera macrophylla (GOLDIE) P. M. BROWN
"LARGE ROUND-LEAFED ORCHID"

One of the largest and most striking North American orchids, this rare species is a resident of mixed woods ranging from Newfoundland to Pennsylvania. It closely resembles the better-known *P. orbiculata*, which has a wider range. The large specimen pictured was found in a mixed forest in southwest Nova Scotia during August. The two round, flat basal leaves are up to $9\frac{2}{3}$ in (24 cm) long and $7\frac{2}{3}$ in (19 cm) wide. The upright raceme, up to 2 ft (60 cm) tall, holds as many as 40 closely set flowers. The spur is longer than 1 in (2.5 cm). Flowering occurs during the summer months. **ZONES 4–6. C.**

P

Platanthera peramoena

Platanthera psycodes (L.) LINDL.
"SMALL PURPLE FRINGED ORCHID"

P

In bloom, this lovely species creates one of
the great wildflower vistas of eastern North
America. It is now confined to wooded
mountainous regions, but sometimes grows
in great colonies on wet fields in New England
and Nova Scotia. It is less common than its
larger-flowered relative, *P. grandiflora*, and has
a looser inflorescence. The plant is up to 40 in
(1 m) tall with two to five leaves, each about
8 in (20 cm) long. The dense flower head
holds up to 50 flowers, each with a diameter
of about 1 in (2.5 cm). The color ranges from
white to deep red-purple. **ZONES 5–6. C.**

Platanthera peramoena A. GRAY
"PURPLE FRINGELESS ORCHID"

This native of the eastern USA is largely
confined to the Ohio River valley and the
southern Appalachians. The plant shown
here was photographed in a grassy stream in
Delaware, at the eastern extreme of its range.
The species may be up to 40 in (1 m) tall and
has two to five leaves up to $5^1/_2$ in (13 cm)
long. The upright spike carries 30–50 purple
fringeless flowers, each about 2 in (5 cm) in
diameter. **ZONES 6–7. C.**

Platanthera psycodes

PLECTRELMINTHUS RAF.

This genus contains only one species which was previously placed in *Angraecum*. It is more closely related to *Aerangis*. The plant is found in west Africa and features large flowers with a long, corkscrew-shaped spur.

CULTIVATION

These species does well in pots with a very well-drained mixture or on a slab. They do not like being disturbed and may take some time to re-establish if repotted. They should be given hot, humid conditions and bright light.

Plectrelminthus caudatus
(LINDL.) SUMMERH.

syn: *Angraecum caudatum* LINDL., *Plectrelminthus bicolor* RAF.

This species ranges from Guinea to Cameroon in west Africa. It grows at low altitudes as an epiphyte in places where it receives mostly full sun. It has a woody stem less than 1 ft (30 cm) long with several leathery leaves up to 1 ft (30 cm) long and 1¼ in (3 cm) wide. The inflorescence is horizontal to pendulous, up to 20 in (50 cm) long, and carries up to 20 flowers, each about 2¾ in (7 cm) across. The corkscrew-shaped spur is about 10 in (25 cm) long. Flowering is during spring.
ZONES 11–12. H.

P

Plectrelminthus caudatus
(left and above)

PLEIONE D. DON

This genus consists of about 20 species. They are delightful miniatures that occur in the Himalayas from Nepal to China at moderate to high altitudes, with one species recorded as high as 14,000 ft (4200 m). They grow in deep moss and leaf litter, either on rocks or on tree trunks and branches. There is a pseudobulb, usually buried in the moss or leaf litter, with one or two long, pleated deciduous leaves. The inflorescence consists of a single flower, rarely two, which is large in comparison to the size of the plant. They are related to *Coelogyne*. *Pleione* hybrids are becoming popular and many are now available.

CULTIVATION

These plants require cold to intermediate conditions and are well suited to temperate climates. Use a shallow pan with a well-drained mixture with a significant component of chopped sphagnum to hold moisture, and perlite or polystyrene with some fine bark and charcoal. Water regularly, but decrease watering markedly when the leaves wither during late autumn. Keep the plants almost dry throughout most of winter. Repot each year when the new growth is about to appear and fertilize once the new growth starts during spring.

Pleione aurita

Pleione aurita P. J. CRIBB & H. PFENNIG

This species occurs in the Yunnan province of China, where it grows in *Rhododendron* forests on west-facing slopes at altitudes of about 9000 ft (2700 m). It is similar to *P. hookeriana*, but is larger in all its parts. There is a single leaf. Flowering is during spring. This species should be given a slightly more open mixture than others in the genus.
ZONE 9. C.

Pleione bulbocodioides
(FRANCH.) ROLFE

This species occurs in northern Myanmar and southwest China. It grows in deep leaf litter on steep banks under *Rhododendron* bushes in pine forests at high altitudes of 4000–12,000 ft (1200–3600 m). The pseudobulbs are clustered, pear-shaped, and about 1 in (2.5 cm) across. The single leaf is up to 20 in (50 cm) long and 2 in (5 cm) wide. The flower appears with the new leaf, and is about $3^{1}/_{4}$ in (8 cm) across. It is borne on a peduncle up to 7 in (18 cm) tall. For good flowering during spring, fertilize regularly. The pseudobulbs should be buried in the potting mix.
ZONES 9–10. C.

Pleione bulbocodioides

Pleione formosana

Pleione forrestii

Pleione formosana HAYATA

This species occurs in Taiwan and probably in mainland China. It grows on mossy rocks or as an epiphyte in deep moss on tree branches in moist forests at altitudes of 1700–8300 ft (500–2500 m). The pseudobulbs are flask-shaped, up to 2 in (5 cm) tall, and have a single leaf up to 1 ft (30 cm) long and 2 in (5 cm) wide. The pink or, occasionally, white flower is 2¾ in (7 cm) across, and is held about 2½ in (6 cm) above the pseudobulb. Flowers appear during spring. **ZONES 9–11. C–I.**

Pleione forrestii SCHLTR.

This species is restricted to northern Myanmar and the western Yunnan province in China. It forms mats on mossy tree trunks or mossy rocks in shady valleys or exposed sites at altitudes of 8000–10,700 ft (2400–3200 m). The pseudobulbs are conical and about 1 in (2.5 cm) tall, with a single leaf about 6 in (15 cm) long and 1¼ in (4 cm) wide. The single flower is up to 3¼ in (8 cm) across and sits about 2¾ in (7 cm) above the pseudobulb. The color of the flower ranges from orange to yellow, or even white. It appears during spring. This species has a reputation as being difficult to grow in cultivation. Sphagnum moss may be tried, or a mix of bark and moss. **ZONE 9. C.**

P

Pleione bookeriana

Pleione praecox (J. E. SM.) D. DON

This species occurs from Nepal and northeast India to the Yunnan province of China, northern Thailand, and Laos. It grows as an epiphyte on mossy branches or as a lithophyte in moss or pockets of humus on cliff faces at altitudes of 4000–11,300 ft (1200–3400 m). The pseudobulbs are barrel-shaped, about 1¾ in (4 cm) tall with two leaves up to 8 in (20 cm) long and 2½ in (6 cm) across. There is usually one or, occasionally two, flowers. It is white to purple-white, 2¾–4 in (7–10 cm) across, and borne about 4 in (10 cm) above the pseudobulb. Flowering is during autumn, when the leaves wither. The potting mixture should be very well drained.
ZONES 9–10. C.

Pleione bookeriana
(LINDL.) B. S. WILLIAMS

This is the most widespread species in the genus, extending from Nepal and the Yunnan province of China to Thailand and Laos. It grows on mossy branches or old tree stumps, or on the floor of conifer forests at altitudes of about 6000–14,000 ft (1800–4200 m), and is often covered with snow during winter. The pseudobulbs are ovoid, and about ⅘ in (2 cm) tall, and there is a single leaf up to 4 in (10 cm) long and 1 in (2.5 cm) wide. The flower is about 2½ in (6 cm) across and held about 3¼ in (8 cm) above the pseudobulb. Flowering is during spring. In cultivation this species should be kept cold for as long as possible during spring as it has a short growing season. Regular fertilizing is required when the plant is actively growing.
ZONES 8–9. C.

Pleione praecox

PLEUROTHALLIS R. BR.

This is one of the largest genera in the orchid family, probably more than 1000 species have been described. Recently, the genus has been studied using DNA technology and a new classification of its species is emerging. This will create many name changes, particularly at the generic level. In this account the genus has been maintained in the broad sense and any new names have been indicated as a synonym. The species are confined to tropical America. They are most abundant in the mountain regions but may range from near sea level in hot climates to cool cloud forests in excess of 10,000 ft (3000 m). Most of them are epiphytes but a few grow as lithophytes or terrestrials. They are very diverse in their habit, ranging from small, tufted plants to large, bushy ones. They lack pseudobulbs, and secondary stems arise from the rhizome and generally bear a single leaf which varies greatly in size and appearance. The inflorescence also varies considerably, but it is usually terminal and may have several flowers or just a single flower.

CULTIVATION

With such a large genus, it is difficult to generalize on the conditions required. Most of the plants, however, can be cultivated easily and grow best in small pots with a well-drained mix or mounted on tree-fern slabs. They are intolerant of stale conditions at the roots. When repotting, care should be taken so that the roots are not damaged. Most grow actively throughout the year, so they require constant moisture. Some shading is required for most species and the temperature will depend on the origin of the species.

Pleurothallis anceps LUER

This species occurs in seasonally wet forests at altitudes of 4800–6000 ft (1450–1800m) in northern Ecuador and southern Colombia. The leaf-bearing stems are up to 1 ft (30 cm) long and the rigid, leathery, ovate leaf is up to 4 in (10 cm) long and about 1 in (2.5 cm) broad. The inflorescence produces a succession of solitary flowers, each about ⅓ in (1 cm) wide. Flowering is during spring. **ZONE 10. I.**

Pleurothallis anceps

Pleurothallis alligatorifera RCHB.F.

syn: *Acianthera alligatorifera* (RCHB.F.) PRIDGEON & M. W. CHASE

This species is from southeast Brazil, where it grows as an epiphyte in the cool mountains. The stems are clustered and about 2 in (5 cm) long. The leathery, erect leaf is up to 4 in (10 cm) long and 1 in (2.5 cm) wide. The erect spike is up to 1 ft (30 cm) tall, has a slight zigzag shape, and up to 12 well-spaced flowers. The flowers are about ½ in (12 mm) long and appear during spring and summer. **ZONE 10–11. C–I.**

Pleurothallis alligatorifera

P

Pleurothallis atropurpurea LINDL.

syn: *Cryptophoranthus atropurpureum* (LINDL.)

This species comes from Cuba and Jamaica. The leaf-bearing stems are up to 5⅔ in (14 cm) tall. The solitary leaf is rigid and leathery, and up to 3⅔ in (9 cm) long and about 1¼ in (4 cm) wide. The inflorescence has either a solitary flower or a few flowers held in a tight cluster, each flower about 1 in (2.5 cm) long. Flowering is during autumn and winter. **ZONES 10–12. I–H.**

Pleurothallis atropurpurea

Pleurothallis endotrachys RCHB.F.

This medium-sized species is distributed from Mexico to Panama, Colombia, and Venezuela. It is an epiphyte that grows on trees in cloud forests at altitudes of 4300–8300 ft (1300–2500 m). The clustered stems are about 1 in (2.5 cm) tall. The fleshy leaf is up to 8 in (20 cm) long. The inflorescence is erect and carries a few to many flowers, each about ⅔ in (15 mm) long. The flowers open one at a time and appear during autumn. **ZONE 10. C–I.**

Pleurothallis endotrachys

Pleurothallis grobyi BATEM.

syn: *Specklina grobyi* (BATEMAN EX LINDL.) PRIDGEON & M. W. CHASE

This widespread and variable species ranges from the West Indies and Mexico to Central America and northern South America. It is common in dense forests up to a 5000-ft (1500-m) altitude. The plants are densely clustered, up to about 6 in (15 cm) tall, and the stems are barely discernible. The leaf may be up to 3 in (7.5 cm) long and usually has some purple mottling on the underside. The erect to arching inflorescence is up to 6 in (15 cm) long, threadlike, and carries several well-spaced flowers. Flowering is during spring. This species may be grown mounted on a tree-fern slab. **ZONES 10–12. C–I.**

Pleurothallis grobyi

P

Pleurothallis johnsonii

Pleurothallis johnsonii
AMES

syn: *Acianthera johnsonii* (AMES)
PRIDGEON & M. W. CHASE

This species is recorded from Mexico, Guatemala, and Honduras. It grows in the leaf litter of forest floors and moss on rocks up to an altitude of 9300 ft (2800 m). The stems are up to $5^{1}/_{2}$ in (13 cm) long and the leaf is about the same length. The inflorescences may arise from both the base of the leaf and the base of the stem. They are up to $1^{3}/_{4}$–3 in (4–7.5 cm) long. The flowers are about $^{1}/_{3}$ in (1 cm) long. Flowering is during winter or spring. This species may be grown mounted on a tree-fern slab. **ZONES 10–12. C–I.**

P

Pleurothallis marthae

Pleurothallis marthae LUER & ESCOBAR

This species from Colombia is one of the largest species in the genus—it may grow up to 10 in (25 cm) long and 4–8 in (10–20 cm) broad. The stems are up to 28 in (70 cm) tall and the leaf is large, spreading, thick, and broadly ovoid in shape. The inflorescence bears a few flowers at the tip. These flowers are showy, appear one at a time, are about 2 in (5 cm.) long, and occur during spring. **ZONE 10. C–I.**

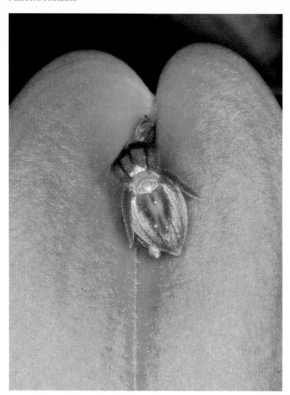

Pleurothallis matudiana

Pleurothallis mirabilis

P

Pleurothallis matudiana
C. SCHWEINF.

This species occurs in Mexico, Guatemala, and Belize, where it grows as an epiphyte on trees up to a 8000-ft (2400-m) altitude. It is an erect, clump-forming plant up to 14 in (35 cm) tall. The stems are up to 10 in (25 cm) tall and the leaf is up to 4 in (10 cm) long and 1¾ in (4 cm) wide. The flowers are about ⅔ in (15 mm) long. They are produced in clusters and appear during spring. **ZONE 10. I.**

Pleurothallis mirabilis
SCHLTR.

syn: *Anthereon mirabilis* (SCHLTR.) PRIDGEON & M. W. CHASE

This small, tufted plant with slender stems is from Brazil. It is about 2 in (5 cm) tall with leaves about 1¾ in (4 cm) long and about ⅓ in (1 cm) wide. The slender, erect inflorescence is up to about 2½ in (6 cm) tall and carries a few small flowers. Flowering is during spring. **ZONE 10. I.**

Pleurothallis praecipua
LUER.

This species from eastern Ecuador grows in cloud forests at altitudes of about 5300 ft (1600 m). There are clusters of stems, with the stems about 6 in (15 cm) long. The leathery leaves are up to 2 in (5 cm) long. The inflorescence has a cluster of flowers that open one at a time. They are about ⅓ in (1 cm) long and appear during spring. ZONE 10. I.

Pleurothallis praecipua

Pleurothallis quadrifida (LEX.) LINDL.
syn: *P. ghiesbreghtiana* A. RICH & GAL., *P. racemiflora* LINDL.

There is some controversy among botanists as to the correct name and synonym for this species. It is relatively common from Mexico and the West Indies to Central America and northern South America. It grows from sea level to a 5000-ft (1500-m) altitude. The stems are up to 7 in (18 cm) long and the leathery leaf is about 6 in (15 cm) long. The solitary inflorescence has a few to many flowers and is about the same length as the leaf. The nodding flowers are about ⅓ in (1 cm) in diameter and open widely. Flowering occurs during spring and summer. ZONES 10–11. C–I.

Pleurothallis quadrifida

Pleurothallis sarracenia

Pleurothallis sarracenia LEUR
syn: *Phloeophila pubescens* (BARB. RODR.) GARAY, *Physosiphon pubescens* BARB. RODR.

This species occurs in the cool mountains of southeast Brazil. The rhizome is creeping and, sometimes, branching with succulent, closely set leaves about ⅘ in (2 cm) long. The flowers are produced from the rhizome and are about ⅔ in (15 mm) long. Flowering is from late winter to spring. Because of its creeping habit, this species is best grown on a tree-fern slab. ZONE 10. C–I.

Pleurothallis schiedii
RCHB.F.

This species is found in Mexico, Guatemala, and El Salvador at altitudes of about 5000–8300 ft (1500–2500 m). It is a small species with a dense cushion of fleshy leaves, each about 2 in (5 cm) tall. Up to five flowers are produced on an inflorescence that may continue to elongate and produce flowers over several months. The flowers are about ¼ in (6 mm) across. This species grows well when mounted on a tree-fern slab and kept cool and moist. **ZONE 10. C–I.**

Pleurothallis schiedii

Pleurothallis sonderana
RCHB.F.

This species is restricted to southern Brazil, where it grows in the cool, moist mountain forests. The fleshy, erect leaves are on a short stem and reach a height of about 2 in (5 cm). They are narrow and channelled above. The inflorescence is up to 1¼ in (3 cm) long and carries three to five flowers, each about ¼ in (6 mm) long. Flowering is from summer to winter. This species may be grown in small pots or mounted on a tree-fern slab. **ZONE 10. C–I.**

Pleurothallis sonderana

Pleurothallis tribuloides

Pleurothallis tribuloides (SW.) LINDL.

This is a widely distributed species from Mexico through Central America to the islands of the West Indies. It grows at elevations up to 4700 ft (1400 m) in both dense, moist forests and drier oak forests. The plants are densely tufted and have leaves up to about 2¾ in (7 cm) long. The inflorescence is very short and carries up to four flowers, each about ¼ in (6 mm) long. Flowering may be at any time but the main season is during spring and summer. This species may be grown mounted or in a small pot. **ZONE 10–11. C–I.**

Pleurothallis tuerckheimii SCHLTR.

syn: *Stelis tuerckheimii* PRIDGEON & M. W. CHASE

This species is widely distributed from Mexico, Guatemala, Honduras, Nicaragua, and Costa Rica to Panama. It is a robust species with stems up to 10 in (25 cm) long. The rigid, leathery leaf is up to 10 in (25 cm) long and up to about 3 in (7.5 cm) wide. The inflorescence is up to 1 ft (30 cm) long and carries many flowers about 1 in (2.5 cm) long. Flowering is during summer. **ZONES 10–12. I–H.**

Pleurothallis viduata LUER

This species is from Ecuador, but little else is known of its distribution. It is a medium-sized, tufted plant with stems that may be up to 6 in (15 cm) long. The leaf is erect and leathery, and up to 4 in (10 cm) long. The inflorescence bears a succession of solitary flowers borne at the apex of the stem. The flowers are about ½ in (12 mm) long. Flowering is during spring. **ZONE 10. C–I.**

Pleurothallis tuerckheimii

Pleurathallis violacea A. RICH. & GAL.

syn: *Acianthera violacea* (A. RIC. & GALEOTTI) PRIDGEON & M. W. CHASE

This species occurs in Mexico, Belize, and Guatemala. It grows as an epiphyte on trees up to a 5000-ft (1500-m) altitude. This erect, tufted plant has stems to about 3 in (7.5 cm) long. The leaf is tinged with purple and is up to about 5½ in (13 cm) long. One to several inflorescences arise from the base of the leaf. They each bear a few flowers, about ¼ in (6 mm) long, during spring and summer. **ZONES 10–12. I–H.**

Pleurothallis viduata

Pleurathallis violacea

POGONIA JUSSIEU

This terrestrial genus comprises only two or three species. One is
from eastern North America and the other from Japan and China.
The separated distribution was caused by glaciers during the Ice Ages,
which caused *Pogonia* to disappear from the western side of North
America. The plants have fleshy roots and a single leaf. They have
proved difficult to grow in a pot, but some success has been achieved
in garden beds with a mix of sandy, acidic humus. Watering is required
throughout the year.

P

Pogonia ophioglossoides

Pogonia ophioglossoides (L.) JUSSIEU
"ROSE POGONIA"

This is a common species in North American peat bogs and wet
meadows from Newfoundland to Minnesota and Texas. It is one of
the four North American spring-blooming species with fragrant, pink
flowers and yellow "beards" that resemble the pollen of other species,
which deceive pollinating bumblebees. It grows to about 14 in (35 cm)
tall. The single leaf is about 4 in (10 cm) long and ⁴⁄₅ in (2 cm) wide.
The solitary flower is about 1¾ in (4 cm) in diameter and lasts for only
a few days. **ZONES 6–8. C.**

POLYSTACHYA HOOK.F.

This is a genus of about 120 epiphytes largely restricted to tropical Africa. A few species are widely distributed on Madagascar and in Asia and tropical America. They grow mostly in rain forests at low to high altitudes. The pseudobulbs vary markedly in shape—flattened or elongated, or upright or pendulous—and are held close to the branches of trees. The inflorescence is terminal, and typically bears several small flowers with a lip that is held uppermost. The paired lateral sepals form a mentum.

CULTIVATION

Most of these plants are relatively easy to cultivate in a pot or on a slab. If a pot is used, the medium should retain a little moisture without becoming soggy. Shade and high humidity are recommended, with temperatures comparable to those of the species' natural habitat.

Polystachya affinis LINDL.

This species is from west Africa—Zaire, Angola, and Uganda—and grows in rain forests at low to moderate altitudes. Its pseudobulbs are distinctive, being rounded and flattened like a disc. They are about ⅘–1 in (1–2.5 cm) across with two leaves at the apex. The leaves are up to about 8 in (20 cm) long and 1–2½ in (2.5–6 cm) wide. The arching or pendulous inflorescence has numerous flowers, each about ½ in (12 mm) across. They do not open fully and appear from July to August in the natural habitat. **ZONES 11–12. H.**

Polystachya affinis

P

Polystachya bella

Polystachya bella SUMMERH.

This attractive epiphyte is restricted to Kenya, where it grows in moist, shady conditions in rain forests at an altitude of about 6700 ft (2000 m). The plant is about 8 in (20 cm) tall. Each pseudobulb has two straplike leaves about 6 in (15 cm) long. The inflorescence arises from the new growth, and is erect, simple or branched, and up to 10 in (25 cm) long. The yellow or orange flowers are about 1 in (2.5 cm) across. Flowering occurs during December and January in the wild. **ZONES 9–11. C–I.**

Polystachya campyloglossa

Polystachya galeata (SW.) RCHB.F.

This species is restricted to the tropical west coast of Africa. It grows on the larger branches of rain forest trees under full sun or in light shade. The pseudobulbs are crowded, narrowly cylindrical, and up to 6 in (15 cm) long with a single, elliptic leaf. The inflorescence has a few relatively large flowers that appear from March to April in the wild. **ZONES 11–12. H.**

P

Polystachya campyloglossa ROLFE

This small species is found as an epiphyte or lithophyte in cloud forests at altitudes of 3300–9000 ft (1000–2700 m) in Kenya, Tanzania, Uganda, and Malawi. The pseudobulbs grow in clumps, are up to $4^3/_4$ in (12 cm) long, and have two or three narrow leaves, each about 4 in (10 cm) long. The inflorescence is terminal and erect, and bears two to eight flowers. The flowers vary in size, up to 1 in (2.5 cm) across, and appear from March to July in the wild. **ZONES 8–10. C–I.**

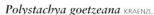

Polystachya galeata

Polystachya goetzeana

Polystachya goetzeana KRAENZL.

This slender, erect to pendulous epiphyte comes from the southern highlands of Tanzania and from Malawi. It grows in moist forests at altitudes of about 6000–8300 ft (1800–2500 m). The slender pseudobulbs are about $2/_3$ in (15 mm) long and have two to four grasslike leaves that may reach 9 in (22 cm) in length. The lax inflorescence has a few flowers, each about $2/_3$ in (15 mm) long. Flowering occurs during the dry season in the wild (September to November). **ZONES 9–10. C–I.**

Polystachya lawrenceana KRAENZL.

This species is recorded from Malawi at low to moderate altitudes. Its pseudobulbs are clustered and about 2 in (5 cm) tall with two to four leathery, straplike leaves, each about 4 in (10 cm) long. The erect or arching inflorescences are up to 6 in (15 cm) long with six to 12 flowers, each about ¾ in (18 mm) long. Flowering is from July to August in the wild.
ZONES 10–12. I–H.

Polystachya lawrenceana

Polystachya leonensis

Polystachya leonensis
RCHB.F.

This species from tropical west Africa—Guinea, Sierra Leone, Liberia, Côte d'Ivoire, and Cameroon—grows in rain forests above an altitude of 3300 ft (1000 m). The pseudobulbs are small and conical, with leaves about 3¼–8 in (8–20 cm) long, arranged in a fan. The inflorescence is branched and flowering is from February to March in the wild.
ZONES 9–11. I.

Polystachya piersii
P. J. CRIBB

This epiphytic species is restricted to the Northern Frontier district of Kenya. It grows at an altitude of about 8300 ft (2500 m). The slender and cylindrical pseudobulbs are about 1¾ in (4 cm) tall and have two narrow leaves, each about 7 in (18 cm) long and ⅘ in (2 cm) wide. The inflorescence is up to 6 in (15 cm) long and bears five to eight flowers, each about ⅘ in (2 cm) across. Flowering has been reported in August and January in the wild.
ZONE 9. C.

P

Polystachya piersii

Polystachya pubescens (LINDL.) RCHB.F.
syn: *Polystachya lindleyana* HARV.

This species occurs in eastern South Africa and Swaziland. It forms large clumps on rocks or trees in cool, moist, shady conditions at low altitudes. The conical pseudobulbs are about 1¼ in (3 cm) long with two to three straplike leaves, each about 3⅔ in (9 cm) long. The inflorescence bears seven to 12 flowers, each about ⅘ in (2 cm) across. Flowering is between October and December in the wild. **ZONES 10–11. I–H.**

Polystachya pubescens

Polystachya virginea SUMMERH.

This medium- to large-sized species is found in central Africa, in Zaire, Uganda, and Burundi. It grows at altitudes of about 6700–8000 ft (2000–2400 m). The pseudobulbs are narrowly cylindrical, up to 6 in (15 cm) long, and have a single straplike leaf about 4–10¾ in (10–27) cm long. The erect inflorescence bears up to ten flowers, each about 1 in (2.5 cm) long. **ZONES 9–10. C–I.**

Polystachya virginea

Polystachya zambesiaca ROLFE

This medium-sized species occurs in northeast South Africa, Zimbabwe, Mozambique, Malawi, and Zambia. It grows on trees or granite rocks at low to moderate altitudes. The pseudobulbs are crowded, flask-shaped, and up to about 1¼ in (3 cm) tall. There are two to three leaves up to 4 in (10 cm) long and ⅔ in (15 mm) wide. The inflorescence arises from young growth and bears about six flowers, each up to ⅘ in (2 cm) across. Flowering occurs from August to February in the habitat. **ZONES 10–11. I–H.**

Polystachya zambesiaca

P

POMATOCALPA BREDA

This genus, related to *Cleisostoma*, comprises about 40 species that range from Myanmar to the Pacific Islands. They grow as monopodial epiphytes or, occasionally, lithophytes at mostly low altitudes. The leaves are straplike and the simple or branched inflorescences are either erect or pendulous. Those species with erect inflorescences have the pouchlike lip held uppermost on the flower, and those with pendulous inflorescences have the lip lowermost.

CULTIVATION

Most of these species prefer bright light. The larger plants grow best in pots or baskets; the smaller one are best on slabs, particularly those with pendulous inflorescences. Constant high humidity and heavy watering during the warmer months are recommended.

Pomatocalpa arachnanthe

P

Pomatocalpa arachnanthe (RIDL.) J. J. SM.
syn: *Saccolabium arachnanthe* RIDL.

This species is restricted to the lowlands of the Malay Peninsula, where it grows in exposed situations. The climbing stem is long and has leaves up to $4^3/_4$ in (12 cm) long and $1^1/_4$ in (3 cm) wide along its length. The inflorescence, 8–16 in (20–40 cm) long, is branched. Each branch elongates for several weeks and always has a few flowers crowded near its apex. The flowers, about $^1/_3$ in (1 cm) long, face upwards and turn from white to greenish-yellow. **ZONE 12. H.**

Pomatocalpa macphersonii
(F. MUELL.) T. E. HUNT

syn: *Saccolabium macphersonii*
F. MUELL.

This species occurs in eastern tropical Queensland in Australia and in New Guinea. It grows as a rain forest epiphyte at low altitudes. The semi-pendulous stem is up to 6 in (15 cm) long with leaves along its length. The leaves are up to 10 in (25 cm) long and 1¼ in (3 cm) across. The pendulous inflorescence is up to 4 in (10 cm) long, and bears numerous densely packed flowers, each about ¹/₃ in (1 cm) across. Flowering is during spring. In cultivation, shaded conditions are best for this species. **ZONES 11–12. H.**

Pomatocalpa macphersonii

Pomatocalpa spicata

Pomatocalpa spicata BREDA
syn: several names, including *Cleisostoma wendlandorum* RCHB.F.
and *Saccolabium utiferum* (HOOK.F.) RIDL.

This species is widespread in Southeast Asia, from India to Java, as far north as the Philippines. It grows in hot, steamy lowlands. The stem is short with up to eight leathery leaves, each up to 10 in (25 cm) long and 1¼ in (3 cm) wide. There are usually a few pendulous inflorescences with numerous densely packed flowers, each about ¼ in (6 mm) across. These open progressively during spring, with about ten open at any one time. Because of the pendulous inflorescences, it is best to grow this species on a slab. **ZONES 12. H.**

PONTHIEVA

This genus of about 25 species occurs from the southern part of the USA through the West Indies and Central America to Chile. The plants are terrestrials with fleshy roots and leaves in a basal rosette. The erect inflorescences have either a few or many flowers, the lips of which are held uppermost.

CULTIVATION

The plants should be grown in a terrestrial mix of loam, sand, and leaf mold. Regular watering while actively growing is recommended, but watering should be reduced after flowering. However, the plants should not be allowed to dry out.

Ponthieva racemosa

Ponthieva racemosa (WALTER) MOHR
syn: several names, including *P. glandulosa* (SIMS) R. BR.,
P. oblongifolia RICHARD & GALEOTTI
"SHADOW WITCH"

This species occurs from southeast USA through the West Indies and Central America to northern South America. It grows in forests, on damp cliffs, and along stream banks, often in large colonies, from low altitudes to 6700 ft (2000 m). The plant is about 2 ft (60 cm) tall with three to eight leaves, up to 6 in (15 cm) long and 2 in (5 cm) wide, in a basal rosette. The inflorescence is up to 10 in (25 cm) long with numerous flowers about 2/3 in (15 mm) across. Flowering is from autumn to spring. **ZONES 8–10. I.**

P

PORROGLOSSUM SCHLTR.

This genus, a member of the *Pleurothallis* group, comprises about 30 species. They grow in the Andes of Colombia, Ecuador, and Peru, with one species in Bolivia and another in Venezuela. The genus is closely allied to *Masdevallia* and the leaves are similar. The flowers have a sensitive lip which, when touched, closes against the column and traps insects to cause pollination.

CULTIVATION

These species should be grown under similar conditions to those of the cool to intermediate species of *Masdevallia* or *Pleurothallis*.

Porroglossum mordax (RCHB.F.) SWEET

This is a medium-sized epiphyte from the western slopes of the Andes in Colombia. The plants are tufted with erect, blackish, leaf-bearing stems up to ⅘ in (2 cm) tall. The erect, leathery leaf is up to 3¼ in (8 cm) long. The inflorescence is erect, up to about 6 in (15 cm) in height, and bears a few flowers, each about 1 in (2.5 cm) long. These open in succession during spring. **ZONE 10. C–I.**

Porroglossum mordax

Porroglossum muscosum

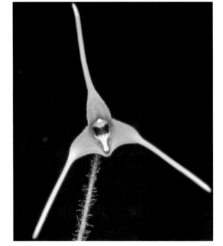

Porroglossum muscosum (RCHB.F.) SCHLTR.
syn: *P. echidna* (RCHB.F.) GARAY

This is a common, widespread, and variable species that ranges from the Andes of Ecuador and Colombia to Venezuela. It grows as a medium-sized epiphyte at altitudes below 8300 ft (2500 m). The plant is creeping to tufted with stems up to about 1¾ in (4 cm) tall. The erect, leathery leaf is about 6 in (15 cm) long. The surface of the leaf is notably bumpy and suffused with purple. The inflorescence is up to 10 in (25 cm) long. It is congested with flowers that open successively. The flowers are about 1 in (2.5 cm) across and appear during spring. **ZONES 10–11. C–I.**

Porroglossum teagueri LUER

This species is from Ecuador at elevations of about 7300 ft (2200 m). It is a medium-sized, tufted plant that grows as both a terrestrial or epiphyte. The erect stems are up to about ⅔ in (15 mm) long with an erect, leathery leaf that is slightly bumpy and up to 4 in (20 cm) long. The inflorescence bears a few, congested flowers, each up to about ⅓ in (1 cm) across, with tails about ⅘ in (2 cm) long. The flowers open successively during spring. **ZONE 10. C–I.**

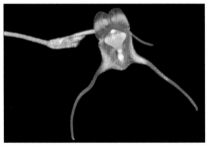

Porroglossum teagueri

P

PROMENAEA LINDL.

This is a genus of about 14 species endemic to central and southern Brazil. They grow as epiphytes in moist forests at moderate altitudes. They are compact plants with prominent pseudobulbs and they produce an attractive display of proportionately large flowers when well grown.

CULTIVATION

These plants are easy to grow in small pots with a well-drained mix and some added sphagnum moss. During the growing season they like plenty of water and high humidity with warm to intermediate conditions. They should never be allowed to dry out completely.

Promenaea stapelioides (LINDL.) LINDL.

This species grows in the cool mountains from Rio de Janeiro to Santa Catarina in Brazil. It grows on trees or rocks in shady, damp places at altitudes of about 3300 ft (1000 m). The pseudobulbs are slightly compressed and have four angles. There are two leaves at the apex of the pseudobulbs. The short inflorescence has one or two flowers, each about 2 in (5 cm) across. Flowering is during summer and autumn. This species grows well on a slab if kept moist, or in a hanging pot with a well-drained mixture with some added sphagnum moss. **ZONES 10–11. I–H.**

Promenaea xanthina (LINDL.) LINDL.
syn. *Promenaea citrina* D. DON

This attractive miniature is from the mountains of southern Brazil. It grows on trees or rocks at an altitude of about 5700 ft (1700 m). The pseudobulbs are clustered, four-angled, and about 1¼ in (3 cm) long. There are two leaves, each about 2–2¾ in (5–7 cm) long. The inflorescence is 2–4 in (5–10 cm) tall with one or two very fragrant flowers about 1¾ in (4 cm) in diameter. The heavily textured and long-lasting flowers appear during spring or summer. **ZONES 10–11. I–H.**

Promenaea rollisonii

Promenaea rollisonii (LINDL.) LINDL.

The pseudobulbs of this species are clustered, round, and about 1 in (2.5 cm) high. The leaves are a gray-green color and about 2 in (5 cm) long. The slightly arching inflorescence is about 2 in (5 cm) long and carries one to three flowers, each about 1¾ in (4 cm) wide. Flowering is during summer. **ZONES 10–11. I–H.**

Promenaea stapelioides

Promenaea xanthina

P

PROSTHECHEA KNOWLES & WESTC.

This genus of about 100 species occurs from Mexico to Brazil. They were
originally placed in *Epidendrum* and then in *Encyclia*, but were reclassified
because of the pseudobulbs and lips. The pseudobulbs are spindle-shaped
and, often, somewhat flattened, while those of *Encyclia* are usually ovoid.
The flowers usually have the lip held uppermost, while in most *Encyclia*
species it is lowermost. *Prosthechea* species have one to five leaves with
a rather thin texture. The inflorescence is rarely branched and there are
usually several flowers of a medium size.

CULTIVATION

These plants like bright, indirect light, high humidity, and good air
movement. Grow them in a pot with a standard epiphytic mix of bark or
similar, with some added moss. Water regularly while the plants are in active
growth, and reduce watering during winter. Diluted fertilizer should be
applied regularly during the growing season.

Prosthechea baculus

Prosthechea baculus (RCHB.F.) W. E. HIGGINS
syn: **several names, including** *Encyclia baculus*
(RCHB.F.) DRESSLER & POLLARD, *Epidendrum baculus* RCHB.F.,
E. pentotis RCHB.F.

This species occurs from Mexico to Colombia
and Brazil. It grows in wet forests at altitudes
of 1300–5700 ft (400–1700 m). The
pseudobulbs are well spaced apart on the
rhizome. They are narrow, spindle-shaped,
and flattened, and up to 14 in (35 cm) long
with two to three straplike leaves up to about
1 ft (30 cm) long. The inflorescence is short
with two flowers, each about 2¾ in (7 cm)
across, placed back to back. Flowering is
during spring. **ZONES 9–11. I–H.**

Prosthechea brassavolae

Prosthechea brassavolae (RCHB.F.) W. E. HIGGINS
syn: *Encyclia brassavolae* (RCHB.F.) DRESSLER, *Epidendrum*
brassavolae RCHB.F.

This species occurs from Mexico to Panama.
It grows on trees or, occasionally, rocks in wet
pine–oak and evergreen forests at altitudes
of 4000–8300 ft (1200–2500 m). The
pseudobulbs are clustered or well spaced apart,
ovoid or pear-shaped, and somewhat flattened.
They are up to 7 in (18 cm) long with two to
three leaves up to 11 in (28 cm) long. The
simple inflorescence bears up to 15 faintly
fragrant flowers, each about 3¼ in (8 cm)
across. Flowering is during winter.
ZONES 9–10. C–I.

Prosthechea cochleata (L.) W. E. HIGGINS
syn: *Encyclia cochleata* (L.) LEMÉE, *Epidendrum cochleatum* L.

This species occurs from Florida in the USA and the West Indies through Mexico to Colombia and Venezuela. It grows in a range of forests from sea level to 6700 ft (2000 m). The pseudobulbs are loosely clustered, pear-shaped, flattened, and up to 10 in (25 cm) long. There are two to three straplike leaves about 8–12 in (20–30 cm) long. The inflorescence is about 20 in (50 cm) long with numerous flowers, each about 3⅔ in (9 cm) across. The flowers open successively throughout the year. **ZONES 9–11. I.**

Prosthechea fausta
(RCHB.F. EX COGN.) W. E. HIGGINS
syn: *Encyclia fausta* (RCHB.F. EX COGN.) PABST, *Epidendrum faustum* RCHB.F. EX COGN.

This species occurs in the southern states of Brazil at low to moderate altitudes on forested hills where it is often subjected to mist and light rain. The pseudobulbs are spaced closely together on the rhizome. They are spindle-shaped and about 4½ in (11 cm) long with two narrow, straplike leaves up to 4¾ in (12 cm) long. The inflorescence is short, erect, and has four to ten fragrant flowers, each about 2 in (5 cm) across. Flowering is from summer to autumn. **ZONES 9–10. C–I.**

Prosthechea chacaoensis (RCHB.F.)
W. E. HIGGINS
syn: *Encyclia chacaoensis* (RCHB.F.) DRESSLER & G. E. POLLARD, *Epidendrum chacaoense* RCHB.F., *E. ionophlebium* RCHB.F.

This species occurs from Mexico to Colombia and Venezuela. It grows on trees or rocks in oak forests at altitudes of 2500–3700 ft (750–1100 m). The pseudobulbs are clustered, ovoid, somewhat flattened, gray-green in color, and up to 4 in (10 cm) long. The two to three gray-green leaves are up to 8 in (20 cm) long and 2 in (5 cm) wide. The inflorescence is up to 4 in (10 cm) long with two to seven fragrant flowers, each 1¾–4 in (4–10 cm) long. Flowering is during spring. **ZONES 10–11. I–H.**

Prosthechea chacaoensis

Prosthechea cochleata

Prosthechea fausta

P

Prosthechea fragrans (SW.) W. E. HIGGINS
syn: *Encyclia fragrans* (SW.) LEMÉE, *Epidendrum fragrans* SW.

This species occurs from Mexico through
Central America to most of South America. It
grows at altitudes of 660–3000 ft (200–900 m).
The pseudobulbs are spaced fairly close
together, are narrowly ovoid, and slightly
flattened. They are up to 4½ in (11 cm) long.
There is one straplike leaf up to 1 ft (30 cm)
long. The inflorescence is up to 6¾ in (17 cm)
long with two to six highly fragrant flowers,
each about 2 in (5 cm) across. Flowering is
during spring and they are long-lasting.
ZONES 10–12. I–H.

Prosthechea garciana (GARAY & DUNST.)
W. E. HIGGINS
syn: *Epidendrum garcianum* GARAY & DUNST.

This species from Venezuela has a creeping
rhizome with pseudobulbs spaced up to about
⅘ in (2 cm) apart. They are ellipsoidal and
about 1 in (2.5 cm) high. The single apical leaf
is up to 4 in (10 cm) long. The inflorescence
generally has a single flower up to 2 in (5 cm)
tall and 1¾ in (4 cm) wide. Flowering is during
spring and early summer.
ZONES 11–12. I–H.

Prosthechea fragrans

Prosthechea garciana

Prosthechea glumacea (LINDL.) W. E. HIGGINS
syn: *Epidendrum glumaceum* LINDL.

This species occurs in Brazil at low to moderate
altitudes. The pseudobulbs are clustered, ovoid,
and up to 2½ in (6 cm) long, with two straplike leaves about 4 in (10 cm) long. The
fragrant flowers are about 2 in (5 cm) across.
These appear from summer to autumn.
ZONES 10–11. I–H.

Prosthechea glumacea

Prosthechea prismatocarpa (RCHB.F.) W. E. HIGGINS
syn: *Epidendrum prismatocarpum* RCHB.F.

This species grows at low to moderate altitudes in Costa Rica and Panama. The pseudobulbs may be clustered or are separated on the rhizome. They are narrow, ovoid, up to 6 in (15 cm) long, and become wrinkled with age. There are two to three straplike, leathery leaves up to 14 in (35 cm) long and 2 in (5 cm) wide. The inflorescence is up to 14 in (35 cm) tall with a few to many fragrant, waxy, long-lasting flowers, each about 2 in (5 cm) across. Flowering is from summer to autumn.
ZONES 10–11. I–H.

Prosthechea prismatocarpa

Prosthechea radiata

Prosthechea radiata (LINDL.) W. E. HIGGINS
syn: *Encyclia radiata* (LINDL.) DRESSLER, *Epidendrum radiatum* LINDL.

This species occurs from Mexico to Costa Rica and, possibly, Venezuela. It grows in rain forests, oak forests, and pine–oak forests from sea level to 6700 ft (2000 m). The pseudobulbs are spaced about 1 in (2.5 cm) apart on the rhizome. They are ellipsoid, somewhat flattened, and up to $4\frac{1}{2}$ in (11 cm) long with two to four leaves up to 14 in (35 cm) long. The inflorescence is up to 8 in (20 cm) long with two to eight flowers, each $1\frac{1}{4}$ in (3 cm) across. The flowers last for several weeks and appear intermittently throughout the year.
ZONES 10–12. I–H.

P

Prosthechea rhynchophora
(A. RICH. & GALEOTTI) W. E. HIGGINS
syn: *Encyclia rhynchophora* (A. RICH. & GALEOTTI) DRESSLER, *Epidendrum rhynchophora* A. RICH. & GALEOTTI

This species ranges from Mexico to Nicaragua. It grows pine or pine–oak forests, or wet forests, at altitudes of about 3000–5000 ft (900–1500 m). The pseudobulbs are loosely clustered, ovoid, and up to $2\frac{1}{2}$ in (6 cm) long. The leaves are straplike and up to 10 in (25 cm) long. The inflorescence arises from new shoots, and is up to 1 ft (30 cm) long with three to seven flowers, each about $1\frac{3}{4}$ in (4 cm) across. Flowering is during spring and summer. **ZONES 10–11. I.**

Prosthechea rhynchophora

Prosthechea trulla

(RCHB.F.) W. E. HIGGINS

syn: *Epidendrum trulla* RCHB.F.

This species occurs in western Mexico in oak or pine–oak forests, occasionally on rocks, at altitudes of 1000–5000 ft (300–1500 m). The spindle-shaped pseudobulbs are loosely clustered and up to 5⅔ in (14 cm) long. There are two straplike leaves up to 10 in (25 cm) long. The inflorescence is up to 4¾ in (12 cm) long with four to ten fragrant flowers, each about 1¾ in (4 cm) long. Flowering is during spring and summer. **ZONES 10–11. I–H.**

Prosthechea trulla

Prosthechea vitellina (LINDL.) W. E. HIGGINS

This species occurs in Mexico and Guatemala. It grows in pine and oak forests, cloud forests, and in scrublands or on lava fields at altitudes of 5000–8700 ft (1500–2600 m). The pseudobulbs are conical, slightly flattened, and up to 2 in (5 cm) long with one to three leaves up to 9 in (22 cm) long and 1¼ in (3 cm) wide. The inflorescence is up to 1 ft (30 cm) long, and is simple or sparsely branched with four to 12 orange-red flowers, each about 1¾ in (4 cm) across. This species flowers sporadically throughout the year. **ZONES 9–10. C–I.**

Prosthechea vitellina

PSYCHILIS RAFIN.

This is a genus of about 15 species from the Caribbean. It is closely related to *Encyclia* and *Epidendrum*. The plants are easily distinguished from these genera by their spindle-shaped pseudobulbs, which consist of several internodes and are marked by a scar from the leaf bracts. (*Encyclia* has only one major internode on pear-shaped or spherical pseudobulbs.) The old inflorescence stem often produces new, condensed racemes for up to three years. The leaves have serrated margins that are rough to the touch. These plants grow in exposed conditions on rocks or as epiphytes.

CULTIVATION

Grow these species on slabs or in hanging baskets and position them where they will get plenty of sun and light. They may be grown outside on trees or in a rockery in warm climates. They like high humidity, and watering should be reduced during the cooler months.

Psychilis atropurpurea

Psychilis atropurpurea

(WILLD.) SAULEDA
syn: *Epidendrum atropurpureum* WILLD., *Encyclia atropurpurea* (WILLD.) SCHLTR.

This species is from Hispaniola in the West Indies. It has pseudobulbs up to 5½ in (13 cm) long and 2½ in (6 cm) in diameter. The two to five leaves are rigid and leathery, and up to 18 in (45 cm) long. The erect inflorescence is up to 2 ft (60 cm) long and carries up to 18 flowers, each about 3 in (7.5 cm) long. Flowering is mostly during summer but may occur at any time. **ZONE 12. I–H.**

Psychilis dodii SAULEDA

This species grows in forests between 1000 and 4000 ft (300 and 1200 m) in the Dominican Republic. The plants are similar in habit to *P. atropurpurea* and may be up to 5 ft (1.5m) tall. Flowers are about 2.5 in (6 cm) in diameter. Flowering is mainly in summer. **ZONE 12. I–H.**

Psychilis dodii

PSYCHOPSIELLA LUCKEL & BRAEM

This genus contains only one species. It was given a genus separate from *Psychopsis* because of its unique vegetative habit, flower characteristics, and several other less visible aspects.

CULTIVATION

The species grows best on a mount and should be given warm to intermediate conditions with high humidity and daily watering during summer. Conditions around the roots should not be allowed to become stale or overly wet.

Psychopsiella limminhgei

Psychopsiella limminhgei (E. MORR. EX LINDL.)

This small, creeping epiphyte occurs in Brazil and Venezuela. The rhizome is branched and the pseudobulbs are spaced about ⁴/₅ in (2 cm) apart. They are prostrate, ellipsoidal, compressed, and about ⁴/₅ in (2 cm) long and ⅔ in (15 mm) wide. The solitary leaf is produced at the apex of each pseudobulb, and is elliptic, about 1¾ in (4 cm) long, and held close to the substrate. The color of the leaf is light brown and green with conspicuous red–brown markings. The inflorescence arises from the base of a new pseudobulb and is up to 4 in (10 cm) long. It carries two to five flowers about 1¾ in (4 cm) wide. Flowering occurs throughout most of the year, but peaks from late spring to autumn. **ZONES 11–12. I–H.**

PSYCHOPSIS RAFIN.
"BUTTERFLY ORCHIDS"

This genus of about four species ranges from Costa Rica to Peru. The plants grow in wet and moist forests from sea level to about 2700 ft (800m). The pseudobulbs have a single internode and a single leaf that is red–brown in color with conspicuous spots and blotches of green. The flowers are produced one at a time from the apex of the inflorescence.

CULTIVATION
The species in this genus are ideally suited to slab culture, but may be grown in a pot with a free-draining mix. This mix must not be allowed to become acidic as it breakdowns as these plants are intolerant of stale conditions at the roots.

Psychopsis papilio

Psychopsis papilio (LINDL.) H. G. JONES
syn: *Oncidium papilio* LINDL.

This species occurs from the West Indies, to Guyana, Brazil, and Colombia. Its pseudobulbs are clustered, orbicular, bilaterally compressed, and brown in color. They are up to 2 in (5 cm) high and have an oblong, leathery, and conspicuously mottled leaf up to 8 in (20 cm) long. The erect inflorescence is up to 40 in (1 m) long. It bears a spectacular flower up to 4 in (10 cm) long. Flowering occurs throughout the year. **ZONES 11–12. I–H.**

Psychopsis versteegiana
(PULLE) LEUCKEL & BRAEME
syn: *Oncidium versteegianum* PULLE

This species is distributed from Suriname to Ecuador, Peru, and Bolivia. It grows in wet mountain forests at altitudes of 2000–4000 ft (600–1200 m). The pseudobulbs are broadly ovate to almost orbicular, compressed, and up to 2 in (5 cm) high. The exposed surfaces of these are dark red–purple. The single, mottled, red–purple leaf is up to 1 ft (30 cm) long and arises from the apex of the pseudobulb. The inflorescence is up to about 40 in (1 m) long and carries three to five flowers. These are produced one at a time, and are about 4 in (10 cm) long. Flowering occurs mostly during summer. **ZONES 10–11. I–H.**

Psychopsis versteegiana

PSYGMORCHIS DODSON & DRESSLER

This is a genus of about four species that range from Mexico to Brazil. They grow as twig epiphytes, particularly in trees overhanging water, from sea level to about 4700 ft (1400 m). The plants are small and fan-shaped with flattened leaves that overlap at the base. The inflorescence arises laterally and the flowers open one at a time.

CULTIVATION

These plants are short lived, and they should be mounted on twigs or small slabs.

Psygmorchis pusilla
(L.) DODSON & DRESSLER

syn: *Oncidium pusillum* L.

This widespread species ranges from Mexico and the West Indies to Guyana, Bolivia, and Brazil. The plant lacks pseudobulbs and the leaves are up to about 2 in (5 cm) long. Several flowers are produced in succession from the same inflorescence. These are large in proportion to the size of the plant, up to 1 in (2.5 cm) long. Flowers appear throughout the year.
ZONES 11–12. I–H.

Psygmorchis pusilla

PTEROSTYLIS R. BR.

"GREENHOODS"

This genus comprises more than 150 species, the majority of which are found in southern and eastern Australia, with a few extending to New Guinea, New Zealand, and New Caledonia. Most of them grow in cool, moist forests. All of the species are terrestrial and either solitary or grow in colonies—the latter reproducing by means of tubers. Most of the species bear a rosette of leaves during the growing season. These die back during the months of dormancy, which is usually summer.

CULTIVATION

Most of these species are easy to grow and flower well in cultivation. Those that form colonies multiply readily and may be grown in a terrestrial mix. When in active growth the plants should be watered regularly. When the plants reach the dormant phase, the pots should be allowed to dry out. Repot every two years to eliminate over-crowding of the plants. The solitary species may be treated in a similar manner, but the potting mix must be perfectly drained and not allowed to become excessively wet. Tuber removal may increase the number of plants.

Pterostylis biseta

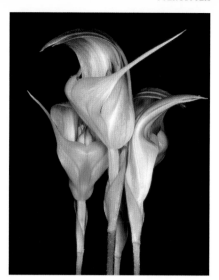

Pterostylis baptistii

Pterostylis baptistii FITZG.

This easy-to-grow species is distributed in eastern Australia, from Queensland through New South Wales to Victoria. It often forms large, dense, and extensive colonies, and has the largest flower of any species in the genus. The leaves, about 3¼ in (8 cm) long, form a basal rosette. The flower stem, about 16 in (40 cm) tall, bears a single flower about 2½ in (6 cm) long. This species may flower in autumn or in spring, depending on the population to which it belongs. **ZONES 8–10. C–I.**

Pterostylis biseta BLACKMORE & CLEMESHA

This species belongs to the so-called "rufa" group, which includes drought-tolerant species that range into arid regions of Australia. All the species in this group have sepals that bend over to form a lower lip below the labellum. This species is endemic to New South Wales, Victoria, and South Australia, and it grows in open forests or arid scrublands. Its rosette-shaped leaves are about 1¾ in (4 cm) long and the flower stem is up to 14 in (35 cm) tall. The stem bears one to seven flowers, each about 1¾ in (4 cm) long. Flowering occurs during late spring. **ZONES 8–9. C.**

P

Pterostylis curta R. BR.
"BLUNT GREENHOOD"

This is a widespread species that extends from the eastern coast of
Australia to Tasmania and South Australia. It forms a colony and has
a rosette of leaves, each of which is about 4 in (10 cm) long. The flower
stem is about 1 ft (30 cm) tall and bears a single flower about 1¾ in
(4 cm) long. Flowering is from late winter to spring. **ZONES 8–10. C–I.**

Pterostylis curta

P

Pterostylis nutans (above and right)

Pterostylis nutans R. BR.
"NODDING GREENHOOD"

This species is one of the most widespread of
the genus. It ranges from north Queensland to
Tasmania, South Australia in Australia, and
in New Zealand. It forms a colony and has a
basal rosette of leaves; each leaf is about 3⅔ in
(9 cm) long. The flowering stem is up to about
1 ft (30 cm) tall and bears a solitary, nodding
flower about 1 in (2.5 cm) long. Flowering is
from late autumn through to spring. This is an
easy-to-grow species. **ZONES 8–10. C–I.**

Pterostylis plumosa

P

Pterostylis plumosa CADY

This species occurs in the Australian states of New South Wales, Victoria, Tasmania, and South Australia, and also in New Zealand. It grows in open woodlands and heathlands. It is a solitary species with rosette leaves. Each leaf is about 1¾ in (4 cm) long. The flower stem is about 1 ft (30 cm) tall and bears a single flower about 1¾ in (4 cm) long. The flowers appear from late winter to early summer. It may be difficult to maintain in cultivation.
ZONES 8–9. C.

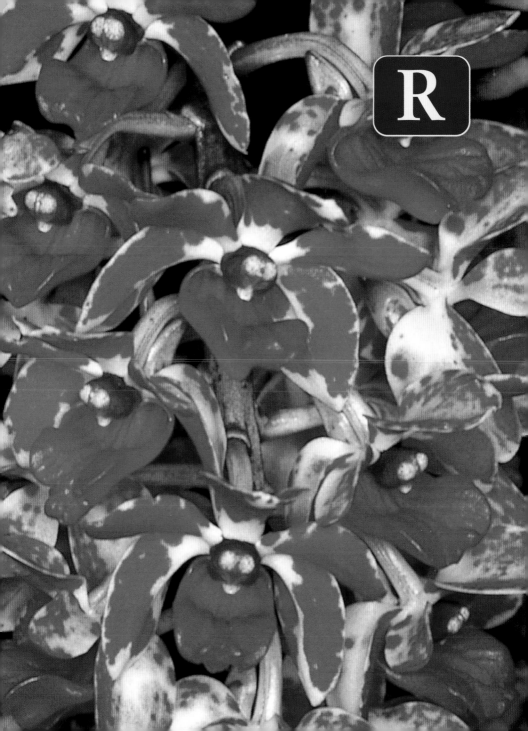

RANGAERIS SUMMERH.

This genus of about six monopodial species is widespread across tropical Africa. It occurs in dry habitats and rain forests at a range of altitudes. The species were originally placed in *Aerangis*, but were separated because of the folded, narrow leaves and some aspects of the flower, which have a lip with a long spur.

CULTIVATION

These plants grow best on slabs so their long spurs are on display. Place them under semi to heavy shade, and a watering rest period after flowering is beneficial.

R

Rangaeris amaniensis
(KRAENZL.) SUMMERH.

The dry regions of central Africa are the habitat for this species. It occurs in Ethiopia, Kenya, Uganda, Tanzania, and Zambia at altitudes between 3300 and 7700 ft (1000 and 2300 m). It grows in dry, evergreen forests and on isolated trees in grasslands or on rocks in semi-shaded conditions. This species forms large clumps of branched stems up to about 18 in (45 cm) long with leathery leaves in two ranks. The inflorescences are pendulous and bear five to 12 flowers, each about $1^3/_4$ in (4 cm) long; the spur about is 6 in (15 cm) long. The flowers appear in a couple of bursts during the year. **ZONES 9–11. C–I.**

Rangaeris amaniensis

RENANTHERA LOUR.

There are about 15 species in this monopodial genus which is related to both *Vanda* and *Arachnis*. They range from India to the Philippines and New Guinea. Most grow in hot, steamy lowland areas. The plants tend to have long, scrambling stems with leaves and roots along their lengths. The inflorescences are branched with numerous red, orange, or yellow, long-lasting flowers.

CULTIVATION

These species require hot or, occasionally, intermediate conditions with bright light and good air movement. They are often grown in tropical gardens on a stake. In orchid houses they grow best if placed in a hanging basket or tied to a long slab so that they can climb. If grown in a pot or basket, the drainage must be excellent.

Renanthera imschootiana

Renanthera imschootiana ROLFE

This species comes from northeast India, the Yunnan province of China, Myanmar, and Vietnam. It grows on tree trunks and along the sides of gorges at altitudes of 1700–5000 ft (500–1500 m). The stems are branched, scrambling, and over 40 in (1 m) long. The leaves are narrow, leathery, and up to $4^{1}/_{2}$ in (11 cm) long. The inflorescence is simple or branched with many flowers about $1^{3}/_{4}$ in (4 cm) across. Flowering is from spring to summer. **ZONES 10–11. I–H.**

R

Renanthera monachica AMES

This attractive species occurs on the islands
of Luzon and Mindanao in the Philippines.
It grows on trees below a 1700-ft (500-m)
altitude. The climbing stems are usually less
than 40 in (1 m) long. The leaves are thick
and stiff, and have a purple tinge. They are
up to 6 in (15 cm) long and $\frac{1}{3}$ in (1 cm) wide.
The arching and branched inflorescence has up
to 50 long-lasting flowers, each about $1\frac{3}{4}$ in
(4 cm) across. It grows best in a hanging basket
as the roots can be difficult to contain in a pot.
Flowering is during late winter and spring.
ZONES 11–12. I–H.

Renanthera pulchella ROLFE

This rare species is restricted to Myanmar,
where it grows at moderate altitudes. The stem
is usually unbranched and up to 1 ft (30 cm)
long. The leathery leaves are about $3\frac{2}{3}$ in
(9 cm) long, and they form two ranks. The
horizontal inflorescence is branched and up to
1 ft (30 cm) long with many flowers. Flowering
is during autumn. **ZONE 10. I.**

Renanthera storei

Renanthera monachica

Renanthera pulchella

Renanthera storei RCHB.F.

syn: *Vanda storei* (RCHB.F.) RCHB.F.

This large, robust species is restricted to the
Philippines where it occurs on several islands,
including Luzon, Palawan, and Mindanao.
It grows in exposed positions from sea level
to 3300 ft (1000 m). It has been extensively
hybridized with species from other genera.
The stems may reach up to 13 ft 4 in (4 m)
long with roots produced along their lengths.
The leaves are leathery, narrow, and up to
$4\frac{3}{4}$ in (12 cm) long. The inflorescences are
produced opposite the leaves and are branched
with about 100 long-lasting flowers, each
about $2\frac{1}{2}$ in (6 cm) across. The flowers
appear during summer. This plant needs
plenty of room and may grow too large for
a small orchid house. It does best tied to a
post in a tropical garden. **ZONES 11–12. H.**

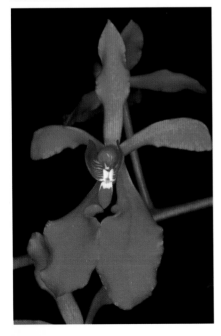

R

RESTREPIA HUMBOLT, BONPLAND & KUNTH.

This genus is a member of the pleurothallid alliance and is most distinctive in that group. It is found in Central America and the Andean region of South America. There are more than 30 species known, and many of these are poorly defined. The species are the ideal "miniature" plants. They lack pseudobulbs and the stems bear oblong to ovate leaves. The inflorescence commonly appears on the reverse surface of the leaf and bears a single flower.

CULTIVATION

Most of these species are easy to grow. They require constant, year-round moisture, and cool to intermediate conditions. The potting mix should be free-draining and sphagnum moss is often used. Because of the small size of the plants, they require small pots.

Restrepia antennifera

Restrepia antennifera
HUMBOLT, BONPLAND & KUNTH.

This species is distributed from Ecuador and Colombia to Venezuela. It is a medium- to large-sized, clump-forming, epiphytic species that grows at altitudes of 5000–11,700 ft (1500–3500 m). The stems are up to 8 in (20 cm) tall, and the erect and leathery leaf is often suffused with purple. The leaf is up to 4 in (10 cm) long and 2 in (5 cm) wide. Solitary flowers are produced in succession from the reverse side and at the base of the leaf. The joined lateral sepals are up to 2 in (5 cm) long. Flowering occurs during spring. **ZONES 10–11. C–I.**

Restrepia elegans H. KARST.

This is a common species in the mountains of Venezuela, found at altitudes of about 5000–9300 ft (1500–2800 m). It is a small, clumping epiphyte with stems up to about 3¼ in (8 cm) tall. The erect, leathery leaf is often suffused with purple underneath and is up to 2½ in (6 cm) long. Solitary flowers are produced in succession from the reverse side and at the base of the leaf. The joined lateral sepals are up to 1 in (2.5 cm) long. Flowering is during spring. **ZONES 10–11. C–I.**

Restrepia elegans

R

Restrepia guttulata LINDL.

This species has been recorded from western Venezuela, Colombia, Ecuador, and Peru at altitudes of 5700–10,000 ft (1700–3000 m). It forms clumps with stems up to 8 in (20 cm) tall. The erect, leathery leaf is up to 4 in (10 cm) long and is often suffused with purple underneath. Solitary flowers are produced in succession from the reverse side and at the base of the leaf. The joined lateral sepals are up to 2 in (5 cm) long. Flowering is during spring. **ZONES 10–11. C–I.**

Restrepia lansbergii RCHB.F. & WAGENER

This species has been recorded from Peru, Ecuador, and Venezuela at altitudes of 1700–5000 ft (500–1500 m). It is a small, densely tufted epiphyte with stems up to about 3¼ in (8 cm) high. The leaf is erect, leathery, and up to 2 in (5 cm) long. It is often suffused with purple on the underside. Solitary flowers are produced in succession from the back side and the base of the leaf. The joined lateral sepals are up to ⅘ in (2 cm) long. Flowering is during spring. **ZONES 10–11. C–I.**

Restrepia guttulata

Restrepia lansbergii

Restrepia muscifera

(LINDL.) RCHB.F.

syn: *R. xanthophthalma* RCHB.F.

This species varies in size and has a wide distribution in Mexico, Guatemala, Honduras, El Salvador, Nicaragua, Costa Rica, Panama, Colombia, and Ecuador. It grows at altitudes of about 1000–8300 ft (300–2500 m). The plants form clumps with stems about 7 in (18 cm) high. The erect, leathery leaf is often suffused with purple underneath. It is up to 3¼ in (8 cm) long. Solitary flowers are produced successively from the reverse side and at the base of the leaf. The joined lateral sepals are up to ⅔ in (15 mm) long. The flowers appear mainly during spring. **ZONES 10–11. C–I.**

Restrepia muscifera

Restrepia sanguinea ROLFE

This species is restricted to Colombia, where it grows at elevations between 5000 and 8300 ft (1500 and 2500 m). The plant is a medium-sized, clump-forming epiphyte with stems to 5½ in (13 cm) tall. The erect, leathery leaf is suffused with purple and is up to 4 in (10 cm) long. Solitary flowers are produced in succession from the reverse side and at the base of the leaf. The joined lateral sepals are up to 1¼ in (3 cm) long. Flowering is during spring. **ZONES 10–11. C–I.**

Restrepia sanguinea

Restrepia trichoglossa

Restrepia trichoglossa F. LEHM EX SANDER

This small- to medium-sized species is widely distributed in Mexico, Guatemala, Costa Rica, Panama, Colombia, Ecuador, and Peru at altitudes of about 1000–8000 ft (300–2400 m). The plants form clumps and the stems are up to about 4 in (10 cm) high. The erect, leathery leaf is often suffused with purple underneath and is up to 2½ in (6 cm) long. Solitary flowers are produced in succession from the back of and near the base of the leaf. The joined lateral sepals are about 1¼ in (3 cm.) long. Flowering is during spring. **ZONES 10–11. C–I.**

R

RESTREPIELLA GARAY & DUNSTERV.

This monotypic genus is found in riverine forests at low altitudes of about 230–660 ft (70–200 m) in Mexico, Belize, Guatemala, El Salvador, and Costa Rica. It is closely allied to *Restrepia* and *Pleurothallis* but differs from the former through its mobile lip that lacks hairlike attachments, and from the latter genus through the four pollinia as opposed to two.

CULTIVATION

This species may be cultivated using similar mixes and conditions as those used for *Pleurothallis* species.

R

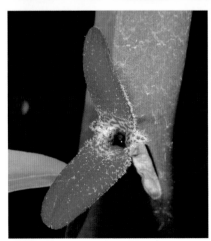

Restrepiella ophiocephala
(LINDL.) GARAY & DUNSTERV.

This medium- to large-sized plant forms dense clumps. It has stout stems about 10 in (25 cm) high. The erect leaf is leathery and about 8 in (20 cm) long and 1¾ in (4 cm) wide. The inflorescence produces a succession of single flowers that emerge from near the apex of the stem. These flowers, up to ⅘ in (2 cm) long, are produced in the axils of the conspicuous papery bracts and appear during winter and spring. **ZONES 11–12. I–H.**

Restrepiella ophiocephala (above and left)

RHYNCHOLAELIA
SCHLTR.

This genus of two epiphytes is from Central America. Both species were formerly placed in *Brassavola* and they are closely related to that genus and to *Cattleya*. The pseudobulb has a single, large, showy flower.

CULTIVATION

These plants grow best when treated like *Cattleya* species, and they should be provided with bright light and a watering rest period after growth is complete.

Rhyncholaelia digbyana
(LINDL.) SCHLTR.

syn: *Brassavola digbyana* LINDL.

This species occurs in Central America from Mexico to Honduras. It grows as an epiphyte in rather dry scrub in lowlands and up to an altitude of 5000 ft (1500 m). The pseudobulbs are club-shaped and up to 8 in (20 cm) long. The single, erect leaf is about 8 in (20 cm) long and 1¾ in (4 cm) wide. There is a single, large, waxy flower up to 6 in (15 cm) across, which is extremely fragrant, particularly at night. The flowers last for about a week and appear from spring to summer. **ZONES 10–12. I–H.**

Rhyncholaelia digbyana

Rhyncholaelia glauca

Rhyncholaelia glauca (LINDL.) SCHLTR.
syn: *Brassavola glauca* LINDL.

This epiphytic or, occasionally, terrestrial species occurs in Central America from Mexico to Honduras. It grows in moist forest at altitudes of 2000–5000 ft (600–1500 m). The pseudobulbs are spindle-shaped, slightly compressed, and about 3⅔ in (9 cm) long. The erect leaf has a slight blue-gray color, and is up to 5½ in (13 cm) long and 1½ in (3.5 cm) wide. The showy, fragrant, long-lasting, waxy flower is about 4 in (10 cm) across. Flowering is during spring. **ZONES 10–11. I–H.**

R

RHYNCHOSTELE RCHB.F.

This genus of about 16 species is found in Central
America and the northern part of South America.
They have had a confused classification history,
formerly belonging to both the genera *Odontoglossum*
and *Lembroglossum*. These epiphytes grow mostly
at moderate to high altitudes in moist cloud forests.
They have ovoid, compressed pseudobulbs and large,
colorful flowers.

CULTIVATION

These species should be given cool, humid, and semi-
shaded conditions, and kept moist throughout the year.
Pot in a free-draining but moisture-retentive mixture.

Rhynchostele bictoniensis

(BATEMAN) SOTO ARENAS & SALAZAR

syn: *Lembroglossum bictoniense* (BATEMAN) HALBINGER,
Odontoglossum bictoniense (BATEMAN) LINDL.

This large species grows from Mexico to Panama.
It grows on the trees, rocks, or in leaf litter on the
ground of wet forests at altitudes of 5300–10,000 ft
(1600–3000 m). The pseudobulbs are ovoid, compressed,
and up to 7 in (18 cm) long. There are one to three
straplike leaves up to 18 in (45 cm) long and 2 in
(5 cm) wide. The erect inflorescence is either simple
or, occasionally, branched and has numerous flowers,
each about 2 in (5 cm) across. Flowering is from
winter to spring. **ZONES 9–10. C–I.**

Rhynchostele bictoniensis

Rhynchostele cervantesii

(LA LLAVE & LEX) SOTO ARENAS & SALAZAR

syn: *Lembroglossum cervantesii* (LA LLAVE)
HALBINGER, *Odontoglossum cervantesii*
LA LLAVE & LEX

This species grows on pine trees
in cloud forests at altitudes of
5000–10,000 ft (1500–3000 m)
in central Mexico and Panama. The
pseudobulbs are ovoid, compressed,
and up to $2^{1}/_{2}$ in (6 cm) long. There
are one to three straplike leaves, each
10 in (25 cm) long and $^{4}/_{5}$ in (2 cm)
across. The pendulous inflorescence
bears three to six fragrant flowers,
each about $1^{1}/_{2}$–2 in (3.5–5 cm)
across. Flowering is from autumn
to spring. **ZONES 9–10. C–I.**

Rhynchostele cervantesii

R

Rhynchostele cordata (LINDL.) SOTO ARENAS & SALAZAR

syn: *Lembroglossum cordatum* (LINDL.) HALBINGER, *Odontoglossum cordatum* LINDL.

Rhynchostele cordata

This species occurs from Mexico through Central America to Venezuela. It grows on tree trunks or, occasionally, as a terrestrial up to a 10,000-ft (3000-m) altitude. The ovoid, compressed pseudobulbs, about 2 in (5 cm) long, are well-spaced along the rhizome. The single leaf is up to 8 in (20 cm) long and 2 in (5 cm) wide. The arching, branched inflorescence is 1–2 ft (30–60 cm) long, and bears many flowers, each about 3 in (7.5 cm) across. The plant shown is the sulphureum form. Flowering is from summer to autumn. **ZONES 9–10. C–I.**

Rhynchostele maculata (LA LLAVE & LEX) SOTO ARENAS & SALAZAR

syn: *Lembroglossum maculatum* (LA LAVE & LEX) HALBINGER, *Odontoglossum maculatum* LA LAVE & LEX

Rhynchostele maculata

This species occurs in Mexico and Guatemala, where it grows in pine and oak forests at altitudes of 3300–10,000 ft (1000–3000 m). The ovoid, compressed pseudobulbs are up to 3²⁄₃ in (9 cm) long. There are one or two straplike leaves up to 1 ft (30 cm) long and 2 in (5 cm) wide. The pendulous, occasionally branched inflorescence is up to 16 in (40 cm) long and bears a few to many flowers, each 2¹⁄₂ in (6 cm) across. Flowering is during summer. **ZONES 9–10. C–I.**

Rhynchostele rossii (LINDL.) SOTO ARENAS & SALAZAR

syn: *Lembroglossum rossii* (LINDL.) HALBINGER, *Odontoglossum rossii* LINDL.

This small species occurs in Central America from Mexico to Nicaragua. It grows in forests at altitudes of around 3300–10,000 ft (1000–3000 m). The pseudobulbs form loose clumps and are ovoid, compressed, and up to 2¹⁄₂ in (6 cm) long. There is a single leaf about 2–8 in (5–20 cm) long and ⁴⁄₅–1³⁄₄ in (2–4 cm) wide. The erect or arching inflorescence has up to four flowers, each about 2³⁄₄ in (7 cm) across. Flowering is mostly during spring. **ZONES 9–10. C–I.**

Rhynchostele rossii

R

Rhynchostele stellata (LINDL.) SOTO ARENAS & SALAZAR

syn: *Lembroglossum stellatum* (LINDL.) HALBINGER, *Odontoglossum stellatum* LINDL.

This small species occurs in Mexico and Guatemala up to a 10,000-ft (3000-m) altitude. The pseudobulbs are clustered, narrow, almost cylindrical, and up to 2 in (5 cm) long. They form dense clumps. There is a single leaf up to 6 in (15 cm) long. The inflorescence is short with one or two flowers, each about 2 in (5 cm) across. Flowering is during spring. **ZONES 9–10. C–I.**

Rhynchostele stellata

Rhynchostele uro-skinneri (LINDL.) SOTO ARENAS & SALAZAR

syn: *Lembroglossum uro-skinneri* (LINDL.) HALBINGER, *Odontoglossum uro-skinneri* LINDL.

This robust species occurs in Guatemala and Honduras and grows on rocks at high altitudes. The pseudobulbs are ovoid, compressed, and up to 4 in (10 cm) long. There are one or two leaves, each about 8–12 in (20–30 cm) long and 2 in (5 cm) wide. The inflorescence is either simple or branched, and up to 28 in (70 cm) long. The flowers are about $2^1/_2$ in (6 cm) across. Flowering is from summer to autumn. **ZONES 9–10. C–I.**

Rhynchostele uro-skinneri

R

RHYNCHOSTYLIS BLUME

This genus of about four monopodial species, related to *Vanda*, ranges from India to the Malay Peninsula, Indonesia, and the Philippines. The plants grow in brightly lit situations at low to moderate altitudes. They have short, thick stems and straplike, fleshy leaves in two ranks. The inflorescences are either erect or arching and bear many densely packed, medium-sized, and colorful flowers.

CULTIVATION

These plants require hot, humid conditions with bright light, but not direct sunlight. Baskets would best accommodate the thick roots of the plants. Any open, free-draining epiphyte mix is suitable.

Rhynchostylis coelestris RCHB.F.

syn: *Vanda pseudocoerulescens* GUILL.

This species occurs in Thailand, Cambodia, and Vietnam at low to moderate altitudes. The stout stem is about 8 in (20 cm) long with several straplike, fleshy leaves up to 8 in (20 cm) long and ⅘ in (2 cm) wide. The erect inflorescence bears numerous densely packed, waxy, fragrant flowers, each about ⅘ in (2 cm) across. Flowering is from summer to autumn. **ZONES 11–12. I–H.**

Rhynchostylis coelestris

Rhynchostylis gigantea (LINDL.) RIDL.

syn: *Saccolabium giganteum* LINDL., *Vanda densiflora* LINDL.

This species occurs in the Yunnan province of China, Myanmar, Thailand, Laos, and Vietnam at low to moderate altitudes. The stout stem is about 8 in (20 cm) long with several leathery leaves on the upper part. Each leaf is about 1 ft (30 cm) long and 2¾ in (7 cm) across. The plant has two to four pendulous, cylindrical inflorescences up to 14 in (35 cm) long, each bearing many flowers about 1¼ in (3 cm) across. The forms with rose–purple and pure-white flowers are popular. Flowering is from autumn to winter. **ZONES 11–12. I–H.**

R

Rhynchostylis gigantea

Rhynchostylis retusa

Rhynchostylis violacea RCHB.F.

syn: *Vanda violacea* RCHB.F., *Rhynchostylis retusa*
subspecies *violacea* (LINDL.) E. A. CHRISTENSON

This species occurs in the Philippines at low
altitudes, where it grows as an epiphyte.
Some authorities regard it as a subspecies of
the widespread *Rhynchostylis retusa*. The stout
stems are up to 7 in (18 cm) long with several
thick, leathery leaves up to 20 in (50 cm) long.
The pendulous inflorescence has many loosely
packed, fragrant flowers, each about ⁴⁄₅ in
(2 cm) across. Flowering is during winter.
ZONES 11–12. I–H.

Rhynchostylis retusa (L.) BLUME
syn: *R. praemorsa* (WILLD.) BLUME, *Saccolabium blumei* LINDL.

This species ranges from Sri Lanka and India
to Southeast Asia. It grows in areas with a
seasonal climate, anywhere from sea level to
about a 5000-ft (1500-m) altitude. The stems
are about 2 ft (60 cm) long, the bottom half
of which is covered with old leaf bases while
the upper part has several fleshy, straplike
leaves. Each leaf is 10–20 in (25–50 cm) long.
The pendulous inflorescence is 10–18 in
(25–45 cm) long and bears many waxy,
fragrant flowers, each about ⁴⁄₅ in (2 cm)
across. Flowering is from summer to autumn.
ZONES 10–12. I–H.

Rhynchostylis violacea

ROBIQUETIA GAUD.

This epiphytic genus is related to *Saccolabium*. It comprises about 40 monopodial species that range from Sri Lanka to the islands in the southwest of the Pacific Ocean. They grow mostly at low altitudes in rain forests in shade. The pendulous inflorescences bear many small, but often brightly colored flowers with a well-developed spur.

CULTIVATION

These species grow best on a slab as the plants and inflorescences are pendulous. They prefer shady, humid conditions with year-round watering.

Robiquetia wassellii DOCKRILL

This species occurs on eastern Cape York Peninsula in northeast Australia. It is an epiphyte that grows in shady positions in seasonal rain forests at about a 600-ft (200-m) altitude. The pendulous stems are up to 32 in (80 cm) long with several leaves on the apical part. The leaves are straplike, about 4¾ in (12 cm) long and ⅘ in (2 cm) wide. The pendulous inflorescence is up to 6 in (15 cm) long with numerous flowers, each about ½ in (12 mm) long. Flowering is mostly during spring.
ZONES 11–12. H.

Robiquetia wassellii

Robiquetia spatulata

(BLUME) J. J. SM.
syn: many names, including
Cleisostoma spatulatum BLUME,
C. spicatum LINDL.

This widespread species occurs across Asia, from India to the Hainan province of China and the islands of Sumatra, Java, and Borneo. It grows as an epiphyte in rain forests from sea level to about a 2700-ft (800-m) altitude. The stems are semi-pendulous, up to 32 in (80 cm) long, with leaves along the upper part. The leaves are up to 6½ in (16 cm) long and 1¾ in (4 cm) wide. The pendulous inflorescence is up to about 4 in (10 cm) long with numerous small flowers about ⅓ in (1 cm) long. Flowering is during summer.
ZONES 11–12. H.

R

Robiquetia spatulata

RODRIGUEZIA RUIZ & PAVON

The home for the 40 epiphytic species in this genus is tropical America. They are related to *Oncidium* and grow in wet cloud forests from sea level to about a 5000-ft (1500-m) altitude. The pseudobulbs are small, often flattened, and surrounded by leaflike bracts. There are one or two straplike leaves at the apex of the pseudobulbs. The inflorescences are produced from the axils of the bracts at the base of the pseudobulbs. The inflorescences bear a few to many brightly colored, small- to medium-sized flowers.

CULTIVATION

All these species require humid conditions with moderate shade. They may be grown, with the exception of *Rodriguezia decora*, in small pots with a free-draining mix and abundant water throughout most of the year. They may also be grown mounted. Conditions should be intermediate to hot.

Rodriguezia bracteata

(VELL.) HOEHNE

syn: *R. fragrans* RCHB.F., *R. venusta* COGN.

This species occurs from the warm lowlands to the cool mountain areas of southeast Brazil. The oblong, compressed pseudobulbs are about 1¼–2 in (3–5 cm) tall. There are three or four leaflike bracts surrounding each pseudobulb and a single, straplike leaf up to 10 in (25 cm) long at the apex. The inflorescence is up to 8 in (20 cm) long and arises from the base of the pseudobulbs. The inflorescence is arching and has several crystalline-white flowers, each about 1¼ in (3 cm) across. This plant grows best on a slab as its wiry roots tend to hang freely. Flowering is during autumn and early winter.

ZONES 10–12. I–H.

Rodriguezia bracteata

R

Rodriguezia decora

Rodriguezia maculata (LINDL.) RCHB.F.
syn: *Burlingtonia maculata* LINDL.

This species from Brazil grows at low to moderate altitudes. The pseudobulbs are ovoid, compressed, and about 1 in (2.5 cm) tall. The single, straplike leaf is about 5¹/₂ in (13 cm) long and ¹/₂ in (12 mm) wide. The pendulous inflorescence is about 6 in (15 cm) long and bears five to ten flowers, each about 1¹/₄ in (3 cm) long. Flowering is during spring. **ZONES 10–11. I–H.**

Rodriguezia decora (LEMAIRE) RCHB.F.
syn: *Burlingtonia decora* LEMAIRE

The mountains in the southeast of Brazil are the home of this species. It grows at moderate altitudes in forests and savannas. It is a small epiphyte with ovoid, compressed pseudobulbs that are well separated along the rhizome. The single leaf is straplike and about 6 in (15 cm) long and 1 in (2.5 cm) wide. The inflorescence is 12–16 in (30–40 cm) long with five to 15 slightly fragrant flowers, each about 1¹/₂ in (3.5 cm) long. Because of its rambling habit, this species requires a long mount. Flowering is during autumn and winter. **ZONES 10–11. I–H.**

Rodriguezia lanceolata RUIZ & PAVON
syn: *R. secunda* H. B. K.

There remains some debate over whether this species is synonymous with or separate from *R. secunda*. *R. lanceolata* is known from the West Indies and Panama to Venezuela, Guyana, Brazil, and Bolivia. It grows as an epiphyte in humid forests at low to moderate altitudes. The pseudobulbs are ovoid, compressed, and about 1¹/₄ in (3 cm) tall. There are one or two straplike leaves up to 10 in (25 cm) long and 1¹/₄ in (3 cm) wide. Up to six inflorescences arise from each pseudobulb. They are arching, up to 14 in (35 cm) long, and have many flowers, each about ²/₃ in (15 mm) across. These flowers vary in color from pale pink to bright red. This species does not require a watering rest period. Flowering occurs throughout the year. **ZONES 11–12. I–H.**

Rodriguezia lanceolata

R

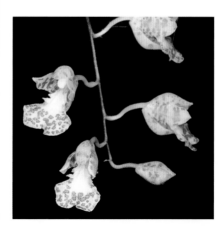

Rodriguezia maculata

RODRIGUEZIELLA O. KTZE.

The five species in this genus, related to *Gomesa* and *Rodriguezia*, are all endemic to Brazil. They are small- to medium-sized epiphytes. The pseudobulbs are ovoid and clustered, with one or two leaves at the apex. The inflorescence is upright to arching with many small flowers.

CULTIVATION

The plants are small and they grow best when tied to a slab of cork or similar material. They should be grown under moderate shade with high humidity. Regular watering is required while the plants are growing, but watering can be reduced when growth has finished for the season.

Rodrigueziella gomezoides (BARB. RODR.) O. KTZE.
syn: *Gomesa theodorea* COGN., *Theodorea gomezoides* BARB. RODR.

This small epiphyte occurs in eastern Brazil at low to moderate altitudes. The pseudobulbs are elongated, compressed, and about 2 in (5 cm) long. There are usually two leaves, each 2¾–6 in (7–15 cm) long and about ⅓ in (1 cm) wide. The erect or arching inflorescence is shorter than the leaves and has many flowers arranged so that they are all on one side of the rachis. The fragrant flowers are about 1¾ in (4 cm) long and appear from summer to autumn.
ZONES 10–12. I–H.

Rodrigueziella gomezoides

ROSSIOGLOSSUM GARAY & KENNEDY

This genus comprises about six species, all from Central America between Mexico and Panama. They are epiphytes from moist cloud forests at moderate to high altitudes. All the species were formerly included in *Odontoglossum*. They have rounded, laterally compressed pseudobulbs with two or three rather thick leaves. The erect inflorescence has a few large, colorful flowers, usually dark red–brown with yellow bars on the segments, or vice versa.

CULTIVATION

These plants require intermediate conditions, bright light, and a free-draining potting mix. They should be given a short watering rest period after the new growths have matured.

Rossioglossum grande (LINDL.) GARAY & KENNEDY
syn: *Odontoglossum grande* LINDL.

This species occurs from Mexico to Honduras, where it grows as an epiphyte in moist forests up to a 9000-ft (2700-m) altitude. The clustered pseudobulbs are ovoid and up to 4 in (10 cm) long. There are one to three leaves up to 16 in (40 cm) long and 2 in (5 cm) wide. The inflorescence is up to 1 ft (30 cm) long with four to eight waxy, long-lasting flowers, each up to 6 in (15 cm) across. The flowers appear from autumn to spring.
ZONES 9–10. C–I.

Rossioglossum grande

R

Rossioglossum insleayi (BARKER EX LINDL.) GARAY & KENNEDY

syn: *Oncidium insleayi* BARKER EX LINDL., *Odontoglossum insleayi*
(BARKER EX LINDL.) LINDL.

This species occurs in Mexico at moderate to high altitudes.
The pseudobulbs are ovoid, compressed, and up to 4 in (10 cm)
tall. There are two or three leaves about 4¾ in (12 cm) long.
The inflorescence is up to 1 ft (30 cm) long with five to ten
faintly fragrant flowers, each about 3⅔ in (9 cm) across.
Flowering is mostly during autumn. **ZONES 9–10. C–I.**

Rossioglossum insleayi

Rossioglossum schlieperianum (RCHB.F.)
GARAY & KENNEDY

syn: *Odontoglossum schlieperianum*
RCHB.F.

This species occurs in Costa
Rica and Panama. It grows
in rain forests at moderate
to high altitudes. The plant
form is similar to that of
Rossioglossum grande. The
erect inflorescence is about
8 in (20 cm) long with
six to eight flowers, each
about 3⅔ in (9 cm) across.
Flowering is during autumn.
ZONES 9–10. C–I.

Rossioglossum schlieperianum

R

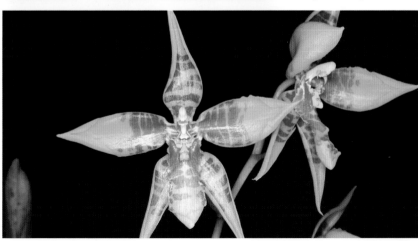

S

SARCOCHILUS R. BR.

Some species from Southeast Asia were once placed in this genus, but they have now been moved to other genera, such as *Thrixspermum*, *Pteroceras* and *Chiloshista*. There are about 15 species in *Sarcochilus*, and these are found in Australia and New Caledonia. They are small epiphytes or lithophytes that grow under shade or, in one or two cases, on hot, exposed rock faces from sea level to about 4000 ft (1200 m). They have a short stem, a few leaves, and colorful flowers on short inflorescences. These plants have been hybridized with *Phalaenopsis* and related genera.

CULTIVATION

The smaller plants of this genus are usually grown on small slabs of hardwood or cork, while the larger plants are grown in pots and baskets. High humidity and cool to intermediate temperatures are required by most of the species.

HYBRIDS

Sarcochilus hybrids are attractive, compact plants particularly suited to cooler climates. Intergeneric hybrids of note have been made with *Vanda* (*Sarcovanda* = Srv.) and *Plectorrhiza* (*Plectochilus* = Plchs.). Some of these hybrids are shown at the end of the *Sarcochilus* species section.

Sarcochilus falcatus

Sarcochilus falcatus R. BR.

syn: *S. montanus* FITZG.
"ORANGE BLOSSOM ORCHID"

This species occurs along the eastern coast of Australia, from Victoria to north Queensland. It is an epiphyte that often grows on the outer twigs of canopies or on mossy branches in misty forests at altitudes of 600–4000 ft (200–1200 m). It is a miniature plant with a short stem and a few curved leaves up to 6 in (15 cm) long. The inflorescences are semi-pendulous with three to 12 flowers, each ⅘–1½ in (2–3.5 cm) across. The fragrance resembles orange blossoms and the flowers appear during spring. In cultivation a mossy slab is best. The plant should be given good air movement, no direct sunlight, and moist, humid, cool to intermediate conditions. **ZONES 9–10. C–I.**

Sarcochilus ceciliae

Sarcochilus ceciliae F. MUELL.

syn: *S. eriochilus* FITZG.
"FAIRY BELLS"

This species occurs in the mountains along the eastern coast of Australia. It grows on rocks in exposed situations from a little above sea level up to about a 4000-ft (1200-m) altitude. The plant forms clumps and the stem is short and branching. Each growth has several narrow leaves up to 3¼ in (8 cm) long, and the leaves are a brownish–green color with some dark spots. The erect or arching inflorescences bear up to 15 bell-shaped flowers, each about ¼ in (6 mm) across. Flowering is during late spring or early summer and lasts for about two weeks. This species requires bright light, even full sun, good air movement and perfect drainage. It grows best in a shallow pan. **ZONES 9–11. C–I–H.**

Sarcochilus fitzgeraldii

Sarcochilus hartmannii

Sarcochilus fitzgeraldii F. MUELL
"RAVINE ORCHID"

This attractive, small species from the central eastern coast of Australia occurs in a relatively small area on either side of the Queensland–New South Wales border. It grows in sheltered situations, often beside streams where there is good air movement, high humidity, and shade, from near sea level up to about a 2300-ft (700-m) altitude. The stems are mostly pendulous, may grow up to 40 in (1 m) long, but are usually up to 20 in (50 cm) long, and form loose clumps. The curved leaves are about 2½–8 in (6–20 cm) long. The arching to pendulous inflorescence bears about ten fragrant flowers, each 1–1½ in (2.5–3.5 cm) across. Flowering is during spring. It is best to grow this species in terra cotta pots or saucers, keep them in an area that is cool and shaded with good air movement, and provide even moisture throughout the year. **ZONES 9–10. C–I.**

Sarcochilus hirticalcar
(DOCKR.) CLEMENTS & B. WALLACE
syn: *Parasarcochilus hirticalcar*
DOCKR., *Pteroceras hirticalcar*
(DOCKR.) GARAY
"HARLEQUIN ORCHID"

This miniature species is restricted to a small area in Australia—eastern Cape York Peninsula. It is a small, semi-pendulous epiphyte that grows on small trees along creeks at a low altitude, where there are

Sarcochilus hirticalcar

dry winters and wet summers. The stems are up to 1¼ in (3 cm) long with a few curved thin leaves up to 4 in (10 cm) long. The inflorescence is up to 1¼ in (3 cm) long, with up to eight flowers, but usually only two or three are open at any one time. The flowers are about ½ in (12 mm) across and appear from late spring to early summer. This plant grows best on slabs in a semi-shaded position with regular water. **ZONES 10–12. I–H.**

Sarcochilus hartmannii F. MUELL.

This species is restricted to a small area near the Queensland–New South Wales border in eastern Australia. It grows in the humus of rock crevices and cliffs, both in exposed situations and sheltered places, at altitudes of 660–3000 ft (200–1000 m). The erect, branched stems form small or large clumps, and are up to 6 in (15 cm) long, occasionally much longer. The curved leaves are about 6 in (15 cm) long and ⅔ in (15 mm) wide. The inflorescence is erect to arching with five to 25 flowers, each up to 1¼ in (3 cm) across. The flowers vary in shape and color, and appear during spring. This species requires bright light and good air movement. **ZONES 9–10. C–I.**

S

Sarcochilus weinthalii

Sarcochilus weinthalii F. M. BAILEY

syn: *S. longmannii* F. M. BAILEY, *Parasarcochilus weinthalii* (F. M. BAILEY) DOCKR.

This miniature species is from northern New South Wales and southern Queensland in Australia. It is a small, pendulous epiphyte that grows in open rain forests, often on the edges of clearings, on the slopes of the ranges at altitudes of up to 2300 ft (700 m). There is a short stem and a few thin, curved leaves about 3¼ in (8 cm) long. The inflorescence is up to 3¼ in (8 cm) long with up to 17 flowers, each about ⅔ in (15 mm) across. Flowering is during late winter and spring. This species is regarded as difficult to grow in cultivation. It should be mounted on a slab in an area with good air movement, and kept constantly moist. **ZONES 9–10. C–I.**

Plchs. Richard Jost

Sarcochilus Burgundy on ice No 2

Sarcochilus First Light "Pepper"

Sarcochilus Melody Pink Spots

S

Satyrium kitimboense

Satyrium monadenum SCHLTR.

This species occurs in Tanzania, Zambia, and Malawi. It grows in open grasslands at altitudes of 6700–8000 ft (2000–2400 m). The plant is robust and up to about 2 ft (60 cm) tall. The inflorescence, up to 5²/₃ in (14 cm) long, is dense with many small flowers. Flowering is from December to January in the habitat. **ZONES 8–9. C.**

SATYRIUM SW.

There are about 100 terrestrial species in this genus, which is related to *Disa*. The majority occur in Africa, with a few on Madagascar and two species in Asia. The lip is uppermost on the flower and is shaped like a helmet. There are usually two long, pendulous spurs at the base of the lip. In some species the leaves are on separate shoots from the flowers.

CULTIVATION

The African species have proved difficult to grow, suffering from either rot or insect infestation after a couple of years. They should be potted in a standard terrestrial mixture and kept cool and dry after the growth period.

Satyrium kitimboense KRAENZL.

This species is widespread in eastern tropical Africa, occurring in Zaire, Tanzania, Angola, Zambia, Mozambique, Zimbabwe, and Malawi. It grows in wet, grassy *Brachystegia* woodlands at an altitude of around 5000 ft (1500 m). It is a robust species up to 26 in (65 cm) tall. There are two basal leaves; the largest ones are 1¹/₄–3 in (3–7 cm) long and 1³/₄–4¹/₂ in (4–11 cm) wide. The inflorescence is up to 5²/₃ in (14 cm) long and bears up to ten loosely arranged flowers. Flowering is from January to February. **ZONES 9–10. C–I.**

S

Satyrium monadenum

Satyrium trinerve LINDL.

syn: *S. atherstonei* RCHB.F.

This species is recorded from
the eastern part of South
Africa, parts of tropical Africa
and Madagascar, although
some authorities regard the
Madagascar plants as a
separate species from those
on the mainland. They grow
in swampy grasslands from
about sea level to a 6700-ft
(2000-m) altitude. The plants
are slender, 8–32 in (20–80 cm)
tall, and bear two to five
leaves, each 2½–10 in
(6–25 cm) long. There are
numerous small flowers that
are tightly bunched together
on an inflorescence, which is
up to 7 in (18 cm) long. The
floral bracts are prominent,
being at least twice the length
of the flowers. Flowering time
varies, but is during late
spring and summer in South
Africa. **ZONES 9–10. C–I.**

Satyrium trinerve

Satyrium woodii SCHLTR.

syn: *S. acutirostrum* SUMMERH., *S. sceptrum* SCHLTR.

This species is widespread in tropical Africa,
extending south to South Africa and north to
Sudan. It grows in damp places in grasslands,
and is a high-altitude species—occurring as high
as 6700–10,000 ft (2000–3000 m) in the northern
part of the range and as low as 1000 ft (300 m)
in the southern part. The plant is up to 40 in (1 m)
tall and is covered with leaflike sheaths. There are
two to five leaves on a separate shoot, the upper
two are the largest at 4–18 in (10–45 cm) long
and ⅘–2¾ in (2–7 cm) wide. The inflorescence
has many flowers, each about ⅔ in (15 mm) long.
These vary in color from yellow to orange and
appear mostly during spring and summer, but the
timing depends on the climate. **ZONES 8–10. C.**

S

Satyrium woodii

SCAPHOSEPALUM PFITZ.

This is a genus of more than 50 species. They are found mostly in the cloud forests of central and southern America, ranging from Guatemala to Peru. They are closely allied to *Pleurothallis* and *Masdevallia*. Vegetatively, the plants may be short and prostrate or form clumps. The leathery leaves are borne on short stems. The inflorescence emerges low on the stem and bears a succession of flowers with lips held uppermost.

CULTIVATION

These are cool to intermediate species that should be cultivated in a manner similar to that of *Pleurothallis* or *Masdevallia* species from similar climatic regions.

Scaphosepalum lima

Scaphosepalum odontochilum

Scaphosepalum lima (LEHM. & KRANZL.) SCHLTR.

This species is from Colombia, where it grows in cloud forests at altitudes of 6000–8300 ft (1800–2500 m) as both an epiphyte and as a terrestrial, commonly in disturbed soil. The plants form clumps with erect stems up to about 1¾ in (4 cm) high. The erect, leathery leaf is about 6 in (15 cm) long. The loose and flexuous inflorescence is up to about 2 ft (60 cm) long. It bears many flowers that appear in succession. These are about ⅓ in (1 cm) wide. Flowering is during autumn. **ZONE 10. C–I.**

Scaphosepalum odontochilum KRAENZL.

This species is from Colombia and Ecuador and grows at an altitude of about 6700 ft (2000 m). It is a medium-sized, clumping epiphyte with stems up to about 1¾ in (4 cm) high. The erect, thick, leathery leaf is about 6 in (15 cm) long and 1¾ in (4 cm) wide. The inflorescence, up to 8 in (20 cm) long, produces several flowers, each one appearing successively. The flowers are about ⅓ in (1 cm) long, and they appear during autumn. **ZONE 10. C–I.**

S

SCAPHYGLOTTIS POEPPIG & ENDL.

This genus ranges from Mexico and the West Indies through Central America to Brazil and Bolivia. It comprises more than 50 species that are variable in plant form. Many of them have an unusual growth habit—the pseudobulbs are borne on top of each other and each successive growth arises from the apex of the former growth. All of them have fairly small but attractive flowers.

CULTIVATION

These plants may be grown in a well-drained pot and many also do well mounted on a slab. When in active growth they need abundant watering, and this may be reduced after flowering. The temperature requirements vary, depending on the origin of the species, but most of the plants do well in intermediate conditions.

Scaphyglottis amethystina

Scaphyglottis livida

Scaphyglottis amethystina (RCHB.F.) SCHLTR.

This small, epiphytic species ranges from Guatemala to Costa Rica. The plant is up to 14 in (35 cm) long and the pseudobulbs are up to about 5½ in (13 cm) long. The short stem may be branching, and many roots grow from the nodes. The leaves are horizontal and up to about 5½ in (13 cm) long and ½ in (12 mm) wide. The inflorescence grows from the apex of the pseudobulb and bears a few to many densely clustered flowers. Each flower is about ¼ in (6 mm) across, and they appear during spring and summer. **ZONES 11–12. I–H.**

Scaphyglottis livida (LINDL.) SCHLTR.

This orchid, common in Mexico, Guatemala, and Honduras, grows at altitudes up to 6700 ft (2000 m), often on fence posts and in coffee plantations. The erect plants are densely branched and up to 14 in (35 cm) tall. The pseudobulbs are up to 5½ in (13 cm) long and the horizontal leaves are up to 8 in (20 cm) long and ¼ in (6 mm) wide. The inflorescence emerges from the apex of the pseudobulb and the flowers are about ¼ in (6 mm) wide. Flowering is during spring and summer. This species does well mounted on a slab. **ZONES 11–12. I–H.**

SCHOENORCHIS REINW.

This genus of about 25 epiphytic, monopodial species is widely
distributed from Sri Lanka and India to the islands in the southwest
of the Pacific Ocean. These plants were once placed in *Saccolabium*.
Most of them are miniatures, some have terete leaves, and most have
small flowers in a long or short inflorescence.

CULTIVATION

Plants from this genus are usually grown on a slab rather than in a pot.
The species with terete leaves should be watered regularly throughout
the year, while the broad-leaved species should be kept considerably
drier. They need bright, filtered light and intermediate to hot conditions.

Schoenorchis fragrans

(PAR. & RCHB.F.) SEIDENF.
& SMITINAND

syn: *Saccolabium fragrans*
PAR. & RCHB.F., *Gastrochilus*
fragrans (PAR. & RCHB.F.)
KTZE., *Schoenorchis*
manipurensis PRADHAN

This tiny species
occurs in northeast
India, Myanmar, and
Thailand. It grows at
an altitude of about
3300 ft (1000 m).
The stem is about
$\frac{1}{3}$ in (1 cm) long, and
it branches as it ages.
The leaves are fleshy
and up to $\frac{3}{4}$ in
(18 mm) long. The
inflorescence is up
to $\frac{4}{5}$ in (2 cm) long
and bears about ten
fragrant flowers, each
about $\frac{1}{8}$ in (3 mm)
across. Flowering is
during summer, and
these plants often
produce several
inflorescences, which
provide a mass of
flowers. **ZONE 10. I.**

Schoenorchis fragrans

Schoenorchis seidenfadenii PRADHAN

This tiny species from Thailand
grows at altitudes of about
2700–4000 (800–1200 m).
The entire plant is only about
$1\frac{3}{4}$ in (4 cm) across. The stem
is short with several fleshy
leaves about $\frac{2}{3}$ in (15 mm)
long. The inflorescence is
about $\frac{4}{5}$ in (2 cm) long and
has about six to eight tiny,
fragrant flowers, each about
$\frac{1}{4}$ in (6 mm) long. This plant
often produces several
inflorescences, which provide
a mass of flowers. **ZONE 10. I.**

S

Schoenorchis seidenfadenii

SCHOMBURGKIA LINDL.

This genus of about 16 species is distributed from Mexico and the West Indies to Bolivia and Brazil. They are related to *Laelia* and *Cattleya*. These large epiphytes or lithophytes grow below an altitude of 3300 ft (1000 m). They have elongated pseudobulbs made up of several nodes, with two or three large, flat leaves at the apex. The inflorescence is long with several large, showy flowers grouped at the end. In most of the species the petals and sepals have undulated margins.

CULTIVATION

These plants should be grown in a pot with a free-draining mixture. Bright light and good air movement are required. They should be watered regularly during the growing season and given a short watering rest period only. Repotting should be avoided, except when absolutely necessary.

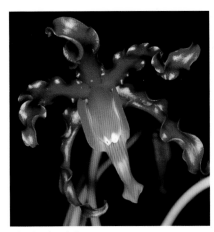

Schomburgkia schultzei

Schomburgkia superbiens (LINDL.) ROLFE
syn: *Laelia superbiens* LINDL.

This species occurs in Mexico, Honduras, and Guatemala. It grows on trees in open or damp forests or on rocks in low altitudes, up to about 6700 ft (2000 m). The curved pseudobulbs are somewhat compressed, up to 18 in (45 cm) tall, and have one or two rigid, leathery leaves. The leaves are 1 ft (30 cm) long and 2½ in (6 cm) wide. The inflorescence is about 4 ft (1.2 m) long, but some are recorded as long as 13¹/₃ ft (4 m). There are several fragrant, long-lasting flowers, each about 5½ in (13 cm) across. These are arranged in a dense group at the end of the inflorescence and appear during winter. **ZONES 10–12. I–H.**

Schomburgkia schultzei SCHLTR.
syn: *S. rosea* var. *schultzei* (SCHLTR.) JONES

This species is restricted to Colombia, where it grows on rocks at about a 5300-ft (1600-m) altitude. The pseudobulbs are short for the genus, being about 6–6¾ in (15–17 cm) tall. There are two leaves, and a few large, glossy flowers. The flowers are borne in a cluster at the end of a long inflorescence and are 2½–4 in (6–10 cm) across. The floral bracts are about as long as the flowers. **ZONES 9–10. I.**

Schomburgkia superbiens

SEDIREA GARAY & SWEET

This genus contains only one species, and it is closely allied to *Aerides*.
It is found in Japan, on the Ryukyu Islands, and in Korea. It is an
epiphyte with monopodial growth and leathery leaves that are arranged
alternately on opposite sides of the growths. The inflorescence arises
from a leaf axil and has several loosely arranged flowers.

CULTIVATION

This plant should be grown in a pot with a free-draining mix, as you
would for *Aerides* species, or mounted on a slab. Intermediate conditions
suit the species best.

Sedirea japonica

(LINDEN & RCHB.F.) GARAY
& SWEET

syn: *Aerides japonica*
LINDEN & RCHB.F.

This species occurs
at low altitudes in
Japan, Korea, and the
Ryukyu Islands. The
stems are very short
and carries five to
seven leaves up to
6 in (15 cm) long
and about 1¼ in
(3 cm) wide. The
arching or pendulous
inflorescence is up to
6 in (15 cm) long and
it carries many fleshy
flowers, each about
1¾ in (4 cm) across.
Flowering is during
summer.
ZONES 8–9. C–I.

S

Sedirea japonica

SEIDENFADENIA GARAY

The one species of this genus was originally placed in *Aerides*, to which it is related. It is distinguished from that genus through its almost terete leaves and by some details of the flower. It occurs in Myanmar and Thailand.

CULTIVATION

This plant grows best on a slab as it is pendulous in habit. It should be provided with bright light, good air movement, and heavy watering and fertilizing during active growth. Reduce watering after seasonal growth is complete.

Seidenfadenia mitrata (RCHB.F.) GARAY
syn: *Aerides mitrata* RCHB.F.

This species grows on trees in exposed situations at altitudes of 1000–5000 ft (300–1500 m), in areas where there is heavy seasonal rainfall. Its stem is very short and there are a few semi-terete, whiplike, pendulous leaves, each up to 18 in (45 cm) long. The leaves have a deep groove on the upper surface. The upright inflorescence has many densely packed, fragrant flowers, each ⅘ in (2 cm) long. Flowering is in spring. **ZONES 10–11. I–H.**

Seidenfadenia mitrata

Serapias cordigera

Serapias cordigera L.
"HEART-FLOWERED SERAPIAS"

SERAPIAS L.

The genus consists of about eight or, according to some botanists who have elevated subspecies to the species status, nearly 20 species. Most of them occur around the Mediterranean region. The sepals and side lobes of the lip form a short tube, which provides a pollinating insect shelter from the elements. The temperature inside this tube is slightly higher than the temperature surrounding it. When the insect leaves the flower tube it carries the pollinia on its head.

CULTIVATION

Serapias species are not common in private collections, although a few, including S. *neglecta*, are occasionally cultivated. These plants should be potted in a mix of loam, coarse sand, leaf mold, and fine composted pine bark. Protect from frost, water well during growth, and allow a watering rest period for a month or two after flowering. The tubers should be dug up after the plants have died back and repotted each autumn.

This species occurs in western coastal areas of the Mediterranean Sea, as far east as Greece and Crete. It grows in dry or wet grasslands, scrubs, or light pine, oak, or chestnut forests between sea level and 2000 ft (600 m). The plant is 8–14 in (20–35 cm) tall, and it has five to eight lanceolate leaves at the base. It is one of the showiest plants of the genus with its four to ten large, colorful flowers on a spike. The flowers are about 1½ in (3.5 cm) long, and they appear in April and May (spring). **ZONES 8–9. C–I.**

S

Serapias lingua L.
"TONGUE ORCHID"

This species occurs on western coastal areas of the Mediterranean Sea, as far east as Greece and Crete. It grows mostly in wet grasslands (for example, beside creeks), scrubs, and light pine and oak forests from sea level to 6700 ft (2000 m). It sometimes forms large colonies, and it is a slender plant up to 1 ft (30 cm) tall. There are two to six flowers, each about 1 in (2.5 cm) long, on a rather open inflorescence. The color of the midlobe varies from yellow through light pink to purple with veining in a dark-red color. A distinguishing feature is the single dark-brown hump on the lip base, which can be seen easily inside the flower tube. The flowering season starts in late March in north Africa and ends in early June in the south of France (spring to early summer). **ZONES 8–10. C–I.**

Serapias lingua

Serapias nurrica

Serapias nurrica CORRIAS
"NURRAN SERAPIAS"

This rare species has a very limited distribution in Corsica, Sardinia, and northeast Sicily. It grows on dry grasslands, but not on limestone, near the coast at altitudes between 660 and 3300 ft (200 and 1000 m). The plant is 8–14 in (20–35 cm) tall. The inflorescence carries four to eight flowers, each about 1¼ in (3 cm) long. A distinguishing feature of the flower is its bicolored lip. Flowering is from April to June (spring to summer). It appears that there are less than 1000 plants left in the wild, and for preservation reasons these should never be taken from the habitat. **ZONES 8–9. C–I.**

S

Serapias neglecta DE NOT.
"SCARCE SERAPIAS"

This species occurs in southeast France, northwest Italy, Corsica, and Sardinia. It grows in wet grasslands, olive groves, scrubs, or light pine forests near the coast up to a 2000-ft (600-m) altitude. The compact plant is 4–12 in (10–30 cm) tall. The inflorescence has three to eight large flowers. The midlobe of the lip varies from pale cream or yellow to orange–brown. Flowering is from late March to early May (spring). **ZONES 8–9. C–I.**

Serapias neglecta

Serapias vomeracea (BURM.) BRIQ.
"LONG-LIPPED SERAPIAS"

This species ranges from Portugal to Greece, as far north as northern Italy and southern Switzerland. It grows in dry or wet grasslands, scrubs, and light pine forests from sea level to a 3300-ft (1000-m) altitude. The plant is 8–20 in (20–50 cm) tall and there are four to ten well-spaced flowers, each about 1¼ in (3 cm) long. The lip color varies from light red to reddish-brown. Flowering is from April to early June (spring to early summer). **ZONES 6–9. C.**

Serapias vomeracea

SMITINANDIA HOLTTUM

This genus consists of three monopodial species ranging from the Himalayas to the island of Sulawesi in Indonesia. The species were previously placed in *Ascocentrum* and *Saccolabium*. They have slender stems with a few straplike leaves. The flowers are small and fleshy and are borne on a long, slender inflorescence.

CULTIVATION

These plants grow well in cultivation and quickly develop into large, branched specimens. They may be grown in a small pot or on a slab. They should be kept evenly moist in humid conditions with bright light.

Smitinandia micrantha
(LINDL.) HOLTTUM

syn: several names, including
Saccolabium micranthum LINDL.,
Ascocentrum micranthum (LINDL.)
HOLTTUM

This species ranges from northern India to Vietnam, Cambodia, and the Malay Peninsula. It grows on trees at altitudes of 2000–3300 ft (600–1000 m). The slender stems are about 4 in (10 cm) long, and are more or less erect. The leaves are fleshy, straplike, and about 4 in (10 cm) long. The erect or pendulous inflorescence is about 2¾ in (7 cm) long with many fleshy flowers, each up to about ¼ in (6 mm) across. The inflorescence in flower lasts for about a month. **ZONES 10–11. I.**

Smitinandia micrantha

SOBENNIKOFFIA SCHLTR.

This small genus of three monopodial species is restricted to Madagascar. They grow mostly in seasonally dry habitats under partial shade. The genus is related to *Angraecum* but is distinguished by its three-lobed lip. Cultivate these plants as for *Angraecum* species.

Sobennikoffia robusta (SCHLTR.) SCHLTR.

This species grows in seasonally dry forests and scrubs on trees and rocks or, occasionally, as a terrestrial, at about a 4700-ft (1400-m) altitude. The stem reaches about 16 in (40 cm) in length. The leaves are 10–15 in (25–38 cm) long and 1¼ in (3 cm) wide. The inflorescence is up to 20 in (50 cm) long and has 12 to 17 flowers, each 2–2½ in (5–6 cm) across. The spur is about 2 in (5 cm) long. The flowers last for several weeks and turn an apricot color as they age. ZONES 10–11. I.

Sobennikoffia robusta

SOBRALIA RUIZ & PAV.

This is a genus of perhaps 75 species distributed from Mexico to South America. They grow from sea level to high altitudes, mostly as terrestrials, but some are epiphytes. The plants have long, canelike stems with thin, heavily veined leaves along their length. The flowers are borne terminally or from the upper nodes. They are fragrant, large, and showy, but last for only a day or two.

CULTIVATION

These plants are grown easily in a large pot or a garden bed under partial shade. A standard terrestrial mix of leaf mold and sand is best. The plants often seem to flower well when pot-bound. They should be watered and fertilized heavily while actively growing, with watering reduced when growth is complete.

Sobralia macrantha LINDL.

This large, robust species ranges from Mexico to Costa Rica. It grows as a terrestrial or, occasionally, an epiphyte in pockets of leaf litter on rocks or in sandy soil near streams from about sea level to a 6700-ft (2000-m) altitude. The clustered, leafy stems are up to 80 in (2 m) tall. The leaves are rigid, and

Sobralia macrantha

6–12 in (15–30 cm) long and 2–3 in (5–7.5 cm) wide. The short inflorescence bears several flowers that open over a few months, one at a time. The showy, fragrant flowers last for about two days, vary in color, and are 6–10 in (15–25 cm) across. Flowering occurs throughout the year. ZONES 9–12. I–H.

S

Sobralia xantholeuca HORT EX B. S. WILLIAMS

This large, robust species from Mexico and
Guatemala grows on trees and rocks at
altitudes of up to 5000 ft (1500 m). The plants
are up to 6 ft (1.8 m) tall. The slender stems
have leaves along their length and are covered
with leaf sheaths that are green speckled with
red–brown. The leaves are up to 1 ft (30 cm)
long and 2³/₄ in (7 cm) wide. The solitary
flower is terminal, short-lived, showy, fragrant,
and 6–9¹/₃ in (15–23 cm) across. Flowering is
during summer. **ZONES 10–12. I–H.**

Sobralia xantholeuca

SOPHRONITELLA
SCHLTR.

There is only one species in
this genus and it comes from
eastern Brazil. It is closely
related to *Sophronitis* and
Laelia, but distinguishable
by the details of the flower
structure and color. It has
pseudobulbs with shallow
furrows and a narrow,
grasslike leaf. The flower is
violet and borne on a short
peduncle.

CULTIVATION

This species grows best
on a slab of cork or similar
material under shade. It should
be kept moist for most of the
year, but allowed to dry out
between waterings with a
watering rest period during
winter.

Sophronitella violacea

Sophronitella violacea (LINDL.) SCHLTR.
syn: *Sophronitis violacea* LINDL., *Cattleya violacea* (LINDL.) BEER

This species occurs in the Minas Gerais, Rio de Janeiro, and
São Paulo states of Brazil. It grows in mountainous and dry
savanna habitats at moderate altitudes. The pseudobulbs are
ovoid and up to about 1¹/₄ in (3 cm) long. There is a single,
narrow, grasslike leaf that is up to 3¹/₄ in (8 cm) long. The
inflorescence is short with a single flower or, occasionally,
two flowers, about ⁴/₅ in (2 cm) across. Flowering is during
winter and early spring. **ZONES 10–11. I.**

SOPHRONITIS LINDL.

This genus consists of about 70 species from Brazil, Bolivia, and Paraguay. They are closely related to the genera *Cattleya* and *Laelia*—most of the species shown here were, until recently, placed in *Laelia* and were known as "rupicolous" (rock-dwelling) *Laelia* species. A few collections and nurseries have changed the labels of the plants to reflect the recent reclassification but most are still referred to as *Laelia* in horticultural circles. These plants are mostly small with large, colorful flowers. The pseudobulbs are small in most cases, and some are extremely small. There is a single, leathery or succulent leaf and an inflorescence with usually one or a few flowers.

CULTIVATION

Among this group are some of the most attractive miniature species in cultivation. Most of them are from moderate to high altitudes and grow in harsh, exposed situations on rocks. To grow them successfully, the conditions need to reflect those of their habitats. They do well under bright light with humid conditions and good air movement. All of the species require excellent pot drainage and must not remain wet for a long period after watering. Many are well suited to slab culture. They require a watering rest period during winter with water completely withheld—only a light misting every day or so is required. The exceptions to this are the "original" species, for example, *S. cernua* and *S. coccinea*. These should be kept moist year-round and have regular watering while in growth.

Sophronitis blumenscheinii

(PABST) VAN DEN BERG & M. W. CHASE
syn: *Laelia blumenscheinii* PABST

This species occurs in the state of Espírito Santo in Brazil. It grows on exposed rock faces at about a 4000-ft (1200-m) altitude. The pseudobulbs are up to 6 in (15 cm) long and ⅘ in (2 cm) wide at the base. The single leaf has a keel on the lower surface and is up to 6¾ in (17 cm) long and 1¼ in (3 cm) wide. The inflorescence is up to 6¾ in (17 cm) long with about ten flowers, each 1¾ in (4 cm) across. This species grows best in a pot with a free-draining mix under bright light and with a short watering rest period during winter. Flowering is from autumn to early winter. **ZONE 10. I.**

S

Sophronitis blumenscheinii

Sophronitis brevipedunculata

(COGN.) FOWLIE

This species occurs in Brazil on the plateau of Minas Gerais at altitudes of 5000–6700 ft (1500–2000 m). It grows on *Vellozia* bushes or in pockets of humus on rocky outcrops. The pseudobulbs wrinkle with age and are arranged in two rows on the rhizome. They are globose to cylindrical and up to 1/3 in (1 cm) long. There is a single, stiff, leathery leaf up to 1¾ in (4 cm) long and 4/5 in (2 cm) wide. The inflorescence is short with one to three flowers, each 1¾–3 in (4–7.5 cm) across. Flowering is from autumn to winter. This plant grows best on a slab of cork or similar material. **ZONES 9–10. C–I.**

Sophronitis brevipedunculata

Sophronitis briegeri (BLUMENSCH. EX PABST) VAN DEN BERG & M. W. CHASE

syn: *Laelia briegeri* BLUMENSCH.

This species is restricted to the state of Minas Gerais in Brazil. It grows in moss and lichens on sandstone at altitudes of about 3300–4700 ft (1000–1400 m). The pseudobulbs are squat or short and cylindrical, and up to 4 in (10 cm) tall. The leaf is succulent and about 4 in (10 cm) long. The inflorescence is about 8 in (20 cm) long with three to five flowers, each about 2 in (5 cm) across and grouped near the end of the inflorescence. This species should not be watered during winter, but given regular misting. Flowering is during spring or early summer. **ZONES 9–10. I.**

Sophronitis briegeri

Sophronitis caulescens

Sophronitis caulescens

(LINDL.) VAN DEN BERG & M. W. CHASE

syn: *Laelia caulescens* LINDL.

This species occurs in the state of Minas Gerais in Brazil. It grows on rocks at an altitude of about 3300 ft (1000 m). The pseudobulbs are enlarged at the base and around 1¼–3¼ in (3–8 cm) tall. There is a leathery leaf up to 4¾ in (12 cm) long. The inflorescence is taller than the leaf and has five or six well-spaced flowers, about 1¾ in (4 cm) across. Flowering is during spring. **ZONE 10. I.**

S

Sophronitis cernua LINDL.

syn: *S. modesta* LINDL.,
S. hoffmannseggii RCHB.F., *S. nutans*
HOFFMANSEGG.

This species occurs in Brazil
and Paraguay. It grows on
trees and rocks in coastal
lowlands and inland savannas.
The pseudobulbs are slightly
flattened, about ⅘ in (2 cm)
long, and lie close to the tree
or rock. The single leaf is
rigid, ovate, up to 1¼ in
(3 cm) long, and usually
gray–green colored above
with some purple underneath.
The inflorescence is terminal
and short with two to six
flowers, each about 1 in
(2.5 cm) across. Flowering is
in autumn. **ZONES 11–12. I–H.**

Sophronitis cernua

Sophronitis crispa

Sophronitis coccinea

RCHB.F.

syn: several names, including
S. grandiflora LINDL.

This species occurs in the
mountains in the southeast of
Brazil. It grows on mossy tree
branches or sheltered sites on
cliff ledges at altitudes of
2000–5000 ft (600–1500 m).
The pseudobulbs are clustered,
ovoid to cylindrical, and up to
1¾ in (4 cm) long. There is a
single, rigid, leathery leaf up
to 1¾ in (4 cm) tall. The
inflorescence is up to 2¾ in
(7 cm) long with a single
flower about 2¾ in (7 cm)
across. There are many
varieties and forms of this
species, and the flower color
ranges from scarlet to yellow
or orange. Flowering is from
autumn to winter.
ZONES 9–11. I.

Sophronitis crispa (LINDL.) VAN DEN BERG & M. W. CHASE

syn: *Laelia crispa* (LINDL.) RCHB.F., *Cattleya crispa* LINDL.

This species occurs in the Brazilian states of Espírito Santo,
Rio de Janeiro, and Minas Gerais. It grows in the upper
branches of tall trees or, sometimes, on rocky outcrops at
altitudes of 2700–5000 ft (800–1500 m). The pseudobulbs are
club-shaped and 8–12 in (20–30 cm) long with an oblong, fleshy
leaf about 6–12 in (15–30 cm) long. The inflorescence is up to
1 ft (30 cm) long with up to ten flowers, each 4–6 in (10–15 cm)
across. This species grows well mounted or in a pot under bright
light with humid conditions. Flowering is during late spring and
summer. **ZONES 10–11. I.**

S

Sophronitis coccinea

Sophronitis dayana
(RCHB.F.) VAN DEN BERG & M. W. CHASE

syn: *Laelia dayana* RCHB.F., *L. pumila* **var.** *dayana* BURBRIDGE EX DEAN.

This species occurs in the Organ Mountains of Rio de Janeiro and north to Minas Gerais. It grows among lichens on trees along river banks at altitudes of 1700–4300 ft (500–1300 m). The pseudobulbs are cylindrical, covered in white sheaths, and about 1¼–2¾ in (3–7 cm) long. The leaf is fleshy, broad, and up to 4 in (10 cm) long. The single flower is about 2 in (5 cm) across and is borne on a peduncle about 1¼ in (3 cm) tall. This species is proven to grow well on a tree-fern slab, but a pot with a free-draining mix is also successful. Flowering is from summer to autumn and, occasionally, during spring. **ZONES 10–11. I.**

Sophronitis esalqueana

Sophronitis esalqueana
(BLUMENSCH. EX PABST) VAN DEN BERG & M. W. CHASE

syn: *Laelia esalqueana* BLUMENSCH.

This species is restricted to a small area on the Rio São Francisco in the state of Minas Gerais in Brazil. It grows in crevices of rocks at altitudes of 3700–4000 ft (1100–1200 m). The pseudobulbs are cylindrical and up to 2 in (5 cm) long and ⅓ in (1 cm) wide. The succulent leaf is boat-shaped and up to 3¼ in (8 cm) long. The inflorescence is up to 4 in (10 cm) long with two to four flowers, each about 1¼ in (3 cm) across. Flowering is from late spring to early summer. The plant requires bright light with no watering during winter, just regular misting. **ZONES 9–10. C–I.**

Sophronitis grandis (LINDL.)
VAN DEN BERG & M. W. CHASE

syn: *Laelia grandis* LINDL.

This species comes from the states of Bahia and Espírito Santo in Brazil. It grows on the upper branches of tall trees at low altitudes. The pseudobulbs are slightly compressed, club- to spindle-shaped, and about 8 in (20 cm) tall. The leaf is stiff and leathery, and 8–14 in (20–35 cm) long. The inflorescence is up to 10 in (25 cm) long with two to six flowers, each about 4–5⅔ in (10–14 cm) across. Flowering is during spring or early summer and the flowers last for about two weeks. This species should be kept moist throughout the year and grown in a hot, humid environment. **ZONES 11–12. H.**

Sophronitis dayana

Sophronitis grandis

Sophronitis harpophylla

(RCHB.F.) VAN DEN BERG & M. W. CHASE
syn: *Laelia harpophylla* RCHB.F.,
L. geraensis BARB. RODR.

This species occurs in the states of Minas Gerais and Espírito Santo in Brazil. It grows as an epiphyte in shady, humid habitats at altitudes of 1700–3300 ft (500–1000 m). The pseudobulbs are narrow, cylindrical, and about 4–20 in (10–50 cm) tall. The leaf is lance-shaped with a long, tapering apex. It is

Sophronitis harpophylla

about 1 ft (30 cm) long. The inflorescence is up to 6 in (15 cm) long with five to 15 flowers, each about 2¾ in (7 cm) across. Flowering is during winter or spring. This plant grows well in a pot with a free-draining mix or on a slab. It should be kept a little moister than most of the other species in the genus, but it still requires reduced watering during winter. **ZONES 10–11. I–H.**

Sophronitis jongheana (PABST) VAN DEN BERG & M. W. CHASE
syn: *Laelia jongheana* RCHB.F.

This species from the state of Minas Gerais in Brazil is now nearing extinction in the wild due to over-collection. It grows in small patches of forests at altitudes of 4300–5300 ft (1300–1600 m). The pseudobulbs are slightly compressed and about 2 in (5 cm) long. They become wrinkled with age. The leaf is thick and stiff, and about 3¼–4¾ in (8–12 cm) long. The inflorescence is about 1¾ in (4 cm) long with two flowers, each about 4–6½ in (10–16 cm) across. Flowering is from winter to spring. This plant does well under very bright light on a slab. It requires a watering rest period during winter. **ZONES 9–10. I.**

Sophronitis kettieana

Sophronitis jongheana

S

Sophronitis kettieana (PABST) VAN DEN BERG & M. W. CHASE
syn: *Laelia kettieana* PABST

This miniature species is restricted to the Minas Gerais state in Brazil, where it grows on rocks at moderate altitudes in areas with hot, moist summers and cold, dry winters. The pseudobulbs are clustered, almost globose, and ⅘–1¾ in (2–4 cm) tall. The single, succulent, boat-shaped leaf is up to 2 in (5 cm) long. There are one to three flowers on an inflorescence about 2 in (5 cm) long. The flowers are about 1¼ in (3 cm) across and appear during spring or summer. This plant should be grown in a small pot with a free-draining, coarse mix. A watering rest period during winter is required. **ZONES 9–10. C–I.**

Sophronitis liliputana

Sophronitis mantiqueirae FOWLIE

syn: *S. coccinea* **subsp.** *mantiqueirae* (FOWLIE) FOWLIE

This species is restricted to the Minas Gerais plateau and a few other locations in Brazil at altitudes of about 4000–6000 ft (1200–1800 m). It grows on mossy branches in gullies or exposed sites. It is similar to *S. coccinea*, but the pseudobulbs are smaller. The flowers are about 1¼ in (3 cm) across, and they appear during summer. This plant may be grown on slabs or in pots and should be given a short watering rest period during winter. **ZONES 9–10. C–I.**

Sophronitis mantiqueirae

Sophronitis milleri (BLUMENSCH. EX PABST) VAN DEN BERG & M. W. CHASE

syn: *Laelia milleri* BLUMENSCH.

This showy species is endangered and may even be extinct in the wild due to mining and over-collection. It is known only from the Minas Gerais state in Brazil. It grows around the bases of *Vellozia* shrubs at altitudes of 2700–4300 ft (800–1300 m). The pseudobulbs are clustered, narrow with a swollen base that tapers, and about 1¼–3¼ in (3–8 cm) tall. The single leaf is fleshy, tinged with purple underneath, and about 4 in (10 cm) long. The inflorescence is up to 14 in (35 cm) long with four to ten flowers, each about 2 in (5 cm) across. Despite its rarity in nature this species is quite common in cultivation. It is easy to grow in a free-draining mix and needs a watering rest period during winter. Flowering is from late spring to early autumn. **ZONES 9–10. C–I.**

Sophronitis milleri

Sophronitis liliputana

(PABST) VAN DEN BERG & M. W. CHASE

syn: *Laelia liliputana* PABST.

As the name suggests this is a tiny miniature species. It is restricted to a small area in the Minas Gerais state in Brazil, where it grows on granite rocks at about a 5300-ft (1600-m) altitude. The plant grows under direct sunlight and experiences a long dry season with only dew providing moisture. The pseudobulbs are tinged with purple, globose, and ⅔ in (15 mm) tall. The single leaf is also purple-tinged, succulent, boat-shaped, and ⅓–1¼ in (1–3 cm) long. The inflorescences are about 1¼ in (3 cm) long with one or two white to pale-pink flowers, each about ⅘–1¼ in (2–3 cm) across. Flowering is during late spring and summer. This plant grows best in a small pot with a coarse mix. It should be kept dry during winter with occasional misting. **ZONES 9–10. C–I.**

S

Sophronitis mirandai
VAN DEN BERG & M. W. CHASE
syn: *Laelia crispata* (THUNB.) GARAY,
L. rupestris LINDL.

Most orchid growers know
this species as *Sophronitis
crispata*, a name incorrectly
applied. It occurs in the state
of Minas Gerais of Brazil,
where it grows on exposed
ledges partly sheltered by
shrubs at altitudes of
1300–2700 ft (400–800 m).
The cylindrical pseudobulbs
vary from $1\frac{3}{4}$–8 in (4 to
20 cm) long and are about
$\frac{1}{3}$ in (1 cm) wide. There is
a single, fleshy leaf up to
8 in (20 cm) long. The
inflorescence is longer than
the leaf with three to five
flowers, about 2 in (5 cm)
across, crowded at the end.
Flowering is during winter
and spring. This species grows
best in a pot with a free-
draining mix and a winter
watering rest period.
ZONES 10–11. I.

Sophronitis praestans

Sophronitis praestans
(LINDEN & RCHB.F.) VAN DEN BERG
& M. W. CHASE
syn: *Laelia praestans* LINDL. & RCHB.F.

This species occurs in the
Espírito Santo and Minas
Gerais states of Brazil, where
it grows in forests at altitudes

Sophronitis mirandai

Sophronitis perrinii

of about 2000–3300 ft
(600–1000 m). The spindle-
shaped pseudobulbs are about
$1\frac{1}{4}$–$2\frac{1}{2}$ in (3–6 cm) long with
a single, leathery leaf up to
$4\frac{1}{2}$ in (11 cm) long and
$\frac{1}{3}$ in (1 cm) wide. The single
flower, about $4\frac{3}{4}$ in (12 cm)
across, is borne on a peduncle
shorter than the leaf.
Flowering is during summer
or autumn or, occasionally, at
other times of the year. This
species does best on a slab
under bright light and with
a short watering rest period
during winter. **ZONES 10–11. I.**

Sophronitis perrinii (LINDL.)
VAN DEN BERG & M. W. CHASE
syn: *Laelia perrinii* LINDL.,
Cattleya intermedia GRAHAM
var. *angustifolia* HOOKER

This species is restricted to
Brazil, where it is recorded
from the states of Minas
Gerais, Espírito Santo, Rio
de Janeiro, and São Paulo
at altitudes of about 2300–
3300 ft (700–1000 m). The
pseudobulbs are clustered,
club-shaped, and up to $6\frac{1}{2}$ in
(16 cm) long. The leaf is stiff,
straplike, and up to 10 in
(25 cm) long. The
inflorescence arises from a
compressed sheath and is up
to 10 in (25 cm) long with
two to three flowers about
$4\frac{3}{4}$–6 in (12–15 cm) across.
Flowering is from autumn to
winter. This species may be
grown on a slab or in a pot
with coarse material, and
needs a watering rest period
during winter.
ZONES 10–11. I–H.

S

Sophronitis pumila (HOOKER) VAN DEN BERG & M. W. CHASE
syn: *Laelia pumila* (HOOKER) RCHB.F., *Cattleya praestans* HOOKER

This miniature from Brazil grows in the states of Minas Gerais and Espírito Santo. It is found in open forests low on trees near water courses at altitudes of 2000–4300 ft (600–1300 m). The ovoid pseudobulbs are spaced about ⅓ in (1 cm) apart on the rhizome, and are about 1¼ in (3 cm) tall. There is a single, straplike, leathery leaf about 4¾ in (12 cm) long. The inflorescence is about 3⅔ in (9 cm) long with one or, occasionally, two fragrant, long-lasting flowers, each about 4 in (10 cm) across. Flowering is during autumn, and the plant should be grown on a slab under bright light. **ZONES 10–11. I.**

Sophronitis pumila

Sophronitis purpurata (LINDL. & PAXTON) VAN DEN BERG & M. W. CHASE
syn: *Cattleya brysiana* LEMAIRE, *C. casperiana* RCHB.F.

This variable species occurs in southern Brazil in the states of Rio de Janeiro, São Paulo, Santa Catarina, and Rio Grande do Sul. It grows on tall trees in swampy areas near the coast and on some islands, mostly at low altitudes. The pseudobulbs are club-shaped and about 10 in (25 cm) long with a single, fleshy leaf up to 18 in (45 cm) long. The inflorescence is 8–12 in (20–30 cm) long with two to eight flowers, each about 6 in (15 cm) across, but some forms are recorded as being up to 10 in (25 cm) across—there are over 20 color forms recorded. Flowering is during late spring or summer. This plant is easy to grow in a pot with a free-draining medium or on a slab. **ZONES 10–12. I–H.**

Sophronitis purpurata

Sophronitis pygmaea

Sophronitis pygmaea (PABST) C. L. WITHNER
syn: *Sophronitis coccinea* **subsp.** *pygmaea* PABST

This species occurs in the coastal mountains of the state of Espírito Santo in Brazil. It grows on trees and rocks, sometimes in exposed situations, at about a 5000-ft (1500-m) altitude. The pseudobulbs are clustered, globose, and only ¼–⅘ in (6–20 mm) long. There is a single, stiff leaf up to 1½ in (3.5 cm) long with some purple spotting underneath. The single flower is about ⅘ in (2 cm) across and sits almost on the top of the pseudobulb. Flowering is during autumn and winter. **ZONES 9–10. C–I.**

S

Sophronitis reginae

Sophronitis tenebrosa

Sophronitis reginae (PABST) VAN DEN BERG & M. W. CHASE

syn: *Laelia reginae* PABST

This species is restricted to Brazil in the Minas Gerais state, where it grows on rock ledges at altitudes of about 4000–6700 ft (1200–2000 m). The pseudobulbs are clustered, conical, and about 1¼ in (3 cm) tall. There is a single succulent, boat-shaped leaf about 1¾ in (4 cm) long. This is often tinged with purple underneath. The inflorescence is up to 2 in (5 cm) long with two to six flowers, each about ⅔–1 in (15–25 mm) across. This plant should not be watered during winter; it should be given an occasional misting only. **ZONES 9–10. C–I.**

S

Sophronitis tenebrosa (ROLFE) VAN DEN BERG & M. W. CHASE

syn: *Laelia tenebrosa* ROLFE, *L. grandis* **var.** *tenebrosa* GOWER

This showy species from the states of Bahia and Espírito Santo in Brazil grows at low to moderate altitudes. The pseudobulbs are club-shaped and up to 7 in (18 cm) long, with a single, leathery leaf up to 3¼ in (8 cm) long. The inflorescence is up to 1 ft (30 cm) long with about four fragrant flowers, each about 5⅔ in (14 cm) across. Flowering is during spring. **ZONES 10–11. I–H.**

Sophronitis wittigiana

Sophronitis xanthina (LINDL.) VAN DEN BERG & M. W. CHASE

syn: *Laelia xanthina* LINDL. EX HOOKER, *L. wetmorei* RUSCHI.

This Brazilian species is from the south of the state of Bahia and the center of the state of Espírito Santo. It grows in shady forests at about a 2700-ft (800-m) altitude. It is a robust epiphyte with club-shaped pseudobulbs about 8 in (20 cm) long. There is a single, stiff, leathery leaf up to 10 in (25 cm) long. The inflorescence is up to 9⅔ in (24 cm) long with two to eight greenish–yellow to canary–yellow flowers up to 3⅔ in (9 cm) across. Flowering is during summer. Both pots and slabs are suitable for this plant, which grows best under bright, filtered light in hot, humid conditions. **ZONES 10–11. I–H.**

Sophronitis wittigiana
RODRIG.

syn: *S. purpurea* RCHB.F., *S. rosea* HORT. EX GASTLING, *S. violacea* O'BRIEN

This species comes from the state of Espírito Santo in Brazil, where it grows on mossy, rough-barked trees in swampy conditions at altitudes of 2300–6700 ft (700–2000 m). The pseudobulbs are arranged in two rows. They are more or less globular and about 1 in (2.5 cm) tall. The single, ovate leaf is stiff and leathery and about 1–2 in (2.5–5 cm) long. The single flower is 1¾–2½ in (4–6 cm) across. Flowering is during winter. This species is suited to cultivation on a slab of cork or similar material. **ZONES 9–11. C–I.**

Sophronitis xanthina

S

SPATHOGLOTTIS BLUME

There are about 40 species in this widespread genus that occurs from India through Southeast Asia and the Malay Archipelago to New Guinea, Australia, the islands in the southwest Pacific Ocean. They are all terrestrial species, and grow mostly at low to moderate altitudes in grasslands and open forests in moist places. The plants have small, compact pseudobulbs on or just below the surface of the soil. There are a few large, broad, pleated leaves. The inflorescence arises from the base of a pseudobulb and is tall and erect with a few to many colorful flowers of a medium size.

CULTIVATION

These plants may be grown in a pot with garden loam and some added peat or other organic material, so long as the mix drains freely. They should be kept moist throughout the year, particularly when in active growth. In tropical areas some species, such as S. plicata, are grown as a garden plant.

Spathoglottis affinis

Spathoglottis affinis DE VRIESE
syn: *S. lobbii* RCHB.F.

This species occurs from Myanmar to Vietnam, the Malay Peninsula, and the island of Java. It grows in open, rocky areas at altitudes of 2000–3300 ft (600–1000 m). The small, flattened pseudobulbs are just below the surface of the ground. There are about four leaves per pseudobulb, each about 1 ft (30 cm) long and 1¼ in (3 cm) wide. The deciduous leaves are usually not present at flowering. The inflorescence is up to 28 in (70 cm) tall with about 15 flowers, six of which are open at one time. The flowers are 1¼ in (3 cm) across and appear during summer.
ZONES 10–11. I–H.

Spathoglottis kimballiana HOOK.F.

This species is restricted to Borneo, where it grows at sea level to 5000 ft (1500 m). It grows in lower hill forests and among stones beside rivers. The leaves are pleated, narrow, and about 2 ft (60 cm) long. The inflorescence is 2 ft (60 cm) or more tall with several flowers, each about 3 in (7.5 cm) across. Flowering is during spring.
ZONES 11–12. I–H.

Spathoglottis kimballiana

S

Spathoglottis petri RCHB.F.

This species occurs on the Pacific islands of Vanuatu and New Caledonia. It grows from sea level to about 2300 ft (700 m) on grassy slopes that are subject to regular fires. The pseudobulbs are conical and about 2 in (5 cm) tall. The leaves are pleated and about 18 in (45 cm) long and 2 in (5 cm) wide. The inflorescence is about 32 in (80 cm) long and bears six to 20 flowers, each about 1¾ in (4 cm) across. Flowering is during spring in cultivation, but may occur at any time in the wild. **ZONES 11–12. H.**

Spathoglottis plicata BLUME
syn: several names, including S. vieillardii RCHB.F. **and** Bletia angustata GAUD.

This widespread species extends from Sri Lanka to Australia and the islands in the southwest of the Pacific Ocean, as far north as Vietnam and the Philippines. It often grows on roadsides or other disturbed sites but can be found in grasslands and swamp margins, mostly at low altitudes but also as high as 4700 ft (1400 m). The pseudobulbs are ovoid and up to 2¾ in (7 cm) tall. There are four to five pleated leaves per pseudobulb, and these are up to 3 ft (90 cm) tall and 3⅔ in (9 cm) wide. The erect inflorescence is up to 40 in (1 m) tall with many flowers, each about 1¾ in (4 cm) across. White-flowered forms of this species are relatively common. Only three or four flowers are open at any one time, and these may appear at any time throughout the year. This species is commonly cultivated as a garden plant throughout Southeast Asia, Papua New Guinea, and tropical Australia. **ZONES 11–12. H.**

Spathoglottis petri

Spathoglottis plicata

Spathoglottis portusfinchii KRAENZL.
syn: S. hollrungii KRAENZL.

This medium- to large-sized species is found north of the central mountain range in Papua New Guinea. It occurs in grasslands, on rocky hillsides, and in gullies from sea level to at least a 4000-ft (1200-m) altitude, often in areas subject to regular fires, to which the plants are well adapted.

The pseudobulbs grow on the soil surface, are globose and about ⅘–1¼ in (2–4 cm) in diameter. There are four to five pleated leaves, each 16–32 in (40–80 cm) long and ⅘–3¼ in (2–8 cm) wide. The inflorescence arises from the base of the pseudobulb and is up to 40 in (1 m) tall with many flowers, but only about six open at any one time. The flowers are up to 2 in (5 cm) across. Flowering is throughout the year. **ZONES 11–12. H.**

Spathoglottis portusfinchii

S

Spathoglottis pubescens LINDL.

syn: several names, including *S. parviflora* LINDL.,
S. fortunei LINDL., *S. khasyana* GRIFF.

This species ranges from northeast India
through several provinces in south China to
Myanmar, Thailand, Laos, Cambodia, and
Vietnam. It grows in open woodlands and
on grassy slopes at altitudes of 2300–6700 ft
(700–2000 m). The pseudobulbs are flattened
and about 1 in (2.5 cm) in diameter. There are
up to three pleated leaves, each about 16 in
(40 cm) long and ⅔ in (15 mm) wide. The
inflorescence is up to 20 in (50 cm) tall with
two to eight flowers about 1 in (2.5 cm) across.
The ovary and back of the sepals are hairy. The
flowering time varies from summer to winter,
depending on the locality. **ZONES 10–11. I–H.**

Spathoglottis pubescens

Sphyrarhyncus schliebenii

SPHYRARHYNCUS

MANSFELD

This genus contains only
one species. It is related to
Aerangis but is distinguishable
by the very short inflorescence
and club-shaped spur. It is
restricted to a few mountain
sites in Tanzania and Kenya.

CULTIVATION

These plants grow well on
small pieces of cork, bark,
or hardwood under moderate
shade with humidity. They
grow best in areas where there
is a sharp drop in temperature
at night. Water regularly
throughout the year.

Sphyrarhyncus schliebenii MANSFELD

This charming miniature species occurs in Tanzania and Kenya. It
grows at about a 5000-ft (1500-m) altitude. The plants have a short
stem with three to five fleshy, gray–green, curved leaves up to 1¾ in
(4 cm) long and ¼ in (6 mm) wide. There is a mass of gray–green,
flattened roots and usually a few inflorescences about 1¼ in (3 cm)
long with three to ten flowers. The flowers vary in size, ⅓–1 in
(1–2.5 cm) across, with the larger ones at the apex. The spur is
usually less than ⅓ in (1 cm) long. Flowering is during October
in the habitat. **ZONES 9–10. I.**

SPIRANTHES L. C. RICHARD

This genus of terrestrial orchids nearly has a worldwide distribution—it is found on all the continents except Antarctica. Most of the species occur in tropical and subtropical areas, but a few are found in temperate North America, temperate Asia, and Europe. They have thick, fleshy, tuberlike roots, a basal rosette of leaves, and a tall inflorescence with a few to many small flowers arranged in a spiral fashion around the upper part of the inflorescence. The sepals unite to form a partial tube and the flowers do not open widely.

CULTIVATION

Some of these species have proved to be difficult to grow, but most of them may be grown in a pot of loam and leaf mold. They should be watered well while actively growing, with reduced watering after growth has finished.

Spiranthes cernua

Spiranthes cernua (L.) L. C. RICHARD
"NODDING LADIES' TRESSES"

This is a common autumn-blooming species in the eastern half of North America, where it inhabits wet fields and quickly colonizes disturbed ground, such as roadsides and embankments. There are many variations of the species over this wide range. The plant grows up to about 20 in (50 cm) tall and has several pointed leaves, each 8 in (20 cm) long and 2 in (5 cm) wide. The inflorescence has up to 60 closely spaced, nodding white flowers. **ZONES 6–8. C–I.**

Spiranthes elata (SW.) L. C. RICHARD
syn: many names, including S. peruviana C. PRESL, **Cyclopogon elatus** (SW.) SCHLTR.

This widespread species occurs from Florida in the USA through Central America and the West Indies to South America. It grows in a range of habitats, from dense, moist forests to open woodlands, at low altitudes in Florida and up to 10,000 ft (3000 m) in Peru. The plants vary in height from 10–32 in (25–80 cm). There are about six dark-green leaves in a basal rosette on a well-developed stalk up to 6 in (15 cm) long. The inflorescence bears many flowers, each about 1/4 in (6 mm) long. Flowering is during spring. **ZONES 8–10. C–I.**

Spiranthes elata

S

Spiranthes lacera

Spiranthes sinensis

Spiranthes lacera (RAFIN.) RAFIN.

syn: *S. gracilis* (BIGELOW) BECK

This species occurs in the northeast of the USA and into Canada, while the variety *gracilis* extends south to the eastern part of Texas. The plant grows up to 2 ft (60 cm) tall with a basal rosette of leaves. The inflorescence has many tightly packed flowers about ¼ in (6 mm) long. Flowering is from summer to autumn. **ZONES 4–8. C.**

Spiranthes romanzoffiana

Spiranthes romanzoffiana

CHAMISSO

"HOODED LADIES' TRESSES"

This species has a northern distribution across North America, and also occurs in Ireland and the Hebrides. It is at home in various habitats, including bogs and roadsides, with scattered plants often appearing on disturbed ground. The plant is up to 20 in (50 cm) tall with several slim, pointed leaves, each about 10 in (25 cm) long and ⅔ in (15 mm) wide. The three-ranked inflorescence carries up to 60 small, creamy flowers, which are distinguished by their reflexed lip which looks like a receding chin and the prominent hood made up of the five sepals and petals. Flowering is during autumn. **ZONES 4–7. C.**

Spiranthes sinensis (PERS.) AMES

syn: *S. australis* (R. BR.) LINDL., *S. pucida* LINDL.

This widespread species extends from India to Australia and New Zealand, as far north as China, Japan, and Siberia. It grows in grasslands, open forests, and swamp margins, and is a common lawn weed in some areas. It grows at sea level to moderate altitudes in temperate climates or moderate to high altitudes in the tropics. The plant is up to 20 in (50 cm) tall with a few leaves in a basal rosette. There are numerous flowers arranged in a spiral along the upper part of the inflorescence. Each flower is up to ¼ in (6 mm) long and only about one third of them are open at any one time. The color varies from purple with a white lip to all white. Flowering varies over the range, but is mostly from summer to autumn. **ZONES 9–11. C–I–H.**

S

STANHOPEA FROST EX HOOKER

This genus contains about 60 species that range from Mexico to Brazil. They are epiphytes or lithophytes from moist forests at low to moderate altitudes. The pseudobulbs are small with a large, pleated, leathery leaf. The inflorescence is pendulous with a few large flowers. These are usually strongly fragrant, waxy, and often do not last for more than two or three days. Most of the plants are similar and can only be accurately identified when they are in flower.

CULTIVATION

The inflorescences grow straight down, therefore the plants should not be grown in a pot. Wire baskets with a fiber lining are used most commonly, but a slab is a alternative. The plants should be grown under bright light with humid conditions, and watered throughout the year.

Stanhopea embreei DODSON

This species is endemic to western Ecuador, where it grows in cloud forests between 2000 and 3300 ft (600 and 1000 m). Three to seven large, attractive flowers are produced. Flowering is during late spring and early summer.
ZONES 10–11. C–I.

Stanhopea embreei

S

Stanhopea inodora RCHB.F.

This species occurs in Mexico, Belize, and Nicaragua. It grows on trees in wet mountain forests at low to moderate altitudes. The pseudobulbs have ribs and are about 2 in (5 cm) long. The leaf is 1 ft (30 cm) long and 4 in (10 cm) wide. The pendulous inflorescence has several showy flowers up to 4¾ in (12 cm) across. Flowering is during spring and summer. **ZONES 10–12. I–H.**

Stanhopea insignis FROST EX HOOKER

This species occurs in Peru, Ecuador, and Brazil. It grows in the mountains from a low altitude to about 5000 ft (1500 m). The pseudobulbs are ovoid to round, ribbed, and 1¼–2¾ in (3–7 cm) tall. The leaf is 12–18 in (30–45 cm) long and about 4 in (10 cm) across, with a short stalk. The pendulous inflorescence is 10 in (25 cm) long with two to three heavily fragrant flowers, each about 3⅔–4¾ in (9–12 cm) long. Flowering is during autumn. **ZONES 10–12. I–H.**

Stanhopea inodora

Stanhopea insignis

Stanhopea jenischiana

KRAMER EX RCHB.F.

This species has a wide distribution in southern Colombia, Ecuador, and Peru, where it grows in moist forests with a pronounced dry season on the western slopes of the Andes at altitudes of about 2700–5000 ft (800–1500 m). Five to seven medium-sized flowers are produced in summer and the inflorescences may emerge laterally instead of directly downward. Flowering is during autumn.
ZONES 10–11. I–H.

Stanhopea lietzii

(REGEL) SCHLTR.

This species is widespread in eastern Brazil at moderate altitudes. It comes in a variety of color forms and requires a distinct watering rest period during the cooler months.
ZONES 10–11. I–H.

Stanhopea jenischiana

Stanhopea lietzii

S

Stanhopea nigroviolacea (MOOR.) BEER

This large-flowered species has been classified
as a variety of *S. tigrina* by some authorities.
It is native to the eastern slopes of the
Mexican plateau at altitudes of 4000–6700 ft
(1200–2000 m). Each inflorescence produces
two or three heavily fragrant flowers up to
7 in (18 cm) across. Flowering is during late
spring and summer. **ZONE 10. I.**

Stanhopea wardii LODD. EX LINDL.

This species from Nicaragua, Costa Rica,
Panama, Colombia, and Venezuela grows in
cloud forests at altitudes of about 2700–9000 ft
(800–2700 m). It is a large epiphyte but
occasionally grows as a lithophyte. The
pseudobulbs are ovoid, slightly compressed,
and up to 2½ in (6 cm) tall. The leaves are up
to 1 ft (30 cm) long and about 5½ in (13 cm)
wide. The inflorescence produces eight to ten
flowers that are strongly scented. Flowering is
from summer to autumn. **ZONES 10–11. I.**

Stanhopea wardii

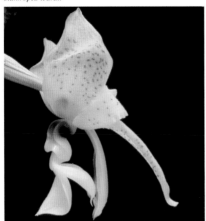

Stanhopea nigroviolacea

Stanhopea oculata

Stanhopea oculata (LODD.) LINDL.
syn: many names, including *S. bucephalus* LINDL.
and *S. guttata* LINDL.

This widespread species occurs from Mexico
to Colombia and the Amazon Basin in
northern Brazil. It grows in moist rain forests
on trees, rocks or even on the ground from
about a 2300–5000-ft (700–1500-m) altitude.
The pseudobulbs are ovoid, ribbed, and about
2½ in (6 cm) long. The leaves have a long
stalk and are up to 28 in (70 cm) long and
8 in (20 cm) wide, although usually smaller.
The pendulous inflorescence is up to 20 in
(50 cm) long with five to seven vanilla-scented
flowers, each 4–5½ in (10–13 cm) long.
Flowering is from summer to autumn. This
species prefers to be moderately dry during
winter. **ZONES 10–12. I–H.**

Stanhopea tigrina BATEM. EX LINDL.

This species is restricted to Mexico. It is a large
epiphyte with clustered pseudobulbs that are
ovoid, grooved, and up to 2½ in (6 cm) tall.
The leaves are up to 14 in (35 cm) long and
up to 4 in (10 cm) broad. The flowers are large
and fragrant. Flowering is from summer to
autumn. **ZONES 10–11. I.**

Stanhopea tigrina

S

STAUROCHILUS RIDL. EX PFITZER

Many of the 12 to 14 species in this genus
were formerly placed in *Trichoglottis*. The
inflorescence of *Staurochilus* species are longer,
erect, branched, and carry more flowers
than those of *Trichoglottis*. The center of
distribution is the Philippines, with about
nine species, and the rest are spread throughout
Southeast Asia. All are climbing monopodial
epiphytes, mostly from low to moderate
altitudes. Some make fine horticultural species.

CULTIVATION

Bright, filtered light with good air movement
and even moisture throughout the year are the
basic requirements for this genus. As plants
become larger, it is useful to provide something
for them to climb on. A coarse mixture and
regular fertilizing are suggested.

Staurochilus luchuensis

Staurochilus loheriana

Staurochilus luchuensis (ROLFE) FUKUY.

This species is present in many collections but
is incorrectly labelled as *Trichoglottis ionosma*.
It occurs on Luzon and Mindanao islands
in the Philippines, the Ryukyu Islands, and
Taiwan. The stem is erect and up to 1 ft
(30 cm) or more tall. The leaves are leathery
and about 6 in (15 cm) long and 1¼ in (3 cm)
wide. The inflorescence is erect, branched,
longer than the leaves, and bears many flowers,
each about 1¼ (3 cm) across. Flowering is
during spring. **ZONE 11. I–H.**

Staurochilus loheriana (KRAENZL.)
E. A. CHRISTENSON
syn: *Trichoglottis loheriana* (KRAENZL.) L. O. WILLIAMS

This species occurs on Luzon Island in the
Philippines. It grows as an epiphyte at elevations
up to 3000 ft (900 m). The stem is erect, stiff,
and up to 1 ft (30 cm) long. The leathery leaves
are 1 ft (30 cm) long, and arranged in two
ranks. The erect inflorescence is longer than the
leaves and bears up to 12 flowers, each about
1¼ (3 cm) across. Flowering is during spring.
ZONES 11–12. H.

S

STELIS SW.

This is a large pleurothallid genus with several hundred species known to date. They range from Cuba and Mexico to Brazil and Peru. Their greatest diversity is probably in the Andes, where they are found in moist habitats at moderate to high altitudes. They are mostly epiphytes but occasionally occur as lithophytes. In habit, they closely resemble *Pleurothallis* species.

CULTIVATION

Depending on their place of origin, these plants should receive similar conditions to those for *Pleurothallis*. Small pots with a well-drained medium are ideal. Being without pseudobulbs and unable to store water, these species should be kept evenly moist throughout the year. High humidity and good air movement are recommended.

Stelis gracilis AMES

This species is widespread from Mexico, Guatemala, Honduras, and Nicaragua to Costa Rica. It is a small, tufted plant with stems up to about 1¾ in (4 cm) tall. The rigid leaf is up to about 5½ in (13 cm) long. The very slender inflorescence is up to 6 in (15 cm) long and has numerous scattered flowers that are each less than ¼ in (6 mm) in diameter. Flowering is during summer. **ZONES 11–12. I–H.**

Stelis ciliaris

Stelis ciliaris LINDL.

This species extends from Mexico to Panama, Brazil, and Peru. It forms clumps and the stems are up to 1¼ in (3 cm) tall. The erect, leathery leaf is up to 6 in (15 cm) long and 1¼ in (3 cm) wide. The erect inflorescence may be up to 6 in (15 cm) tall and has many loosely arranged flowers, each about ½ in (12 mm) across. Flowering is mostly during spring. **ZONES 11–12. I–H.**

Stelis gracilis

Stelis micrantha (SW.) SW.

This species occurs in Jamaica. The long, clustered stems are up to about 6 in (15 cm) and the leathery leaf is about the same length. The solitary or paired inflorescences are up to 6 in (15 cm) long, and these have densely packed flowers, each about ⅓ in (1 cm) in diameter. Flowering may occur at any time during the year. **ZONES 11–12. I–H.**

Stelis micrantha

Stelis ophioglossoides (JACQ.) SW

This species is widely distributed in the West Indies. The plants are small and tufted with erect stems up to 3 in (7.5 cm) long. The leaf is elongated to oblong in shape, and up to about 4 in (10 cm) long. The solitary inflorescence is dense with many flowers, each up to 6 in (15 cm) long. The flowers are about ¼ in (6 mm) in diameter. Flowering may occur at any time during the year. This plant can be grown on a mount. **ZONE 11–12. I–H.**

Stelis ophioglossoides

Stelis tubatus LODD.

syn: *Physosiphon tubatus* (LODD.) RCHB.F., *Pleurothallis tubata* (LODD.) STEUD.

This species is common in both rain forests and dry forests up to 11,700 ft (3500 m) in Mexico and Guatemala. It is a small clumping epiphyte with erect stems up to about 5½ in (13 cm) long. The single leaf is erect and leathery and is about the same length as the stems. The arching inflorescence is up to 10 in (25 cm) long and carries many flowers that open simultaneously. It emerges from near the top of the stem. Flowers are about ⅘ in (2 cm) long. Flowering is during summer. **ZONES 9–11. C–I.**

Stelis tubatus

STENIA LINDL.

Stenia has about eight species distributed from Trinidad and Tobago through the Andes in South America to Bolivia. They are epiphytes growing in wet forests up to a 5000-ft (1500-m) altitude. They are related to *Zygopetalum*. The plants do not have pseudobulbs and the leaves are arranged in a fan shape. The inflorescences are lateral and short with a single large flower.

CULTIVATION

These plants should be grown in pots with a well-drained mix. They should never be allowed to dry out and should be kept in constantly humid conditions under moderate shade.

Stenia pallida

Stenia pallida LINDL.

This species is distributed from the West Indies to Brazil and Bolivia. The leaves are arranged in a fan shape. They are about 5½ in (13 cm) long and 1¼ in (3 cm) across. The inflorescence arises from the base of the short stem. There is a single flower about 1¾ in (4 cm) across. The lip is deeply pouch-shaped. **ZONES 10. I.**

S

STENORRHYNCHOS L. C. RICH. EX SPRENG.

This genus of perhaps 60 or more species is closely related to *Spiranthes*. They can be distinguished by the flowers, which are not arranged in a spiral in *Stenorrhynchos*. The distribution is from Florida in the USA through the West Indies and Central America to South America. They are mostly terrestrial, but some species grow in moss on trees. There is a basal rosette of leaves and a tall inflorescence with many tubular flowers. Some have spectacular, colorful flowers.

CULTIVATION

Most of the species may be grown in a pot of loam and leaf mold. They should be watered while in active growth, with watering reduced after the leaves die back. They should be kept in shaded, humid conditions.

Stenorrhynchos speciosus

Stenorrhynchos speciosus (JACQ.) L. C. RICH. EX SPRENG.
syn: *Spiranthes speciosus* (JACQ.) L. C. RICH.

This species occurs from Mexico and the West Indies to northern South America. It grows in forests and grasslands up to a 10,000-ft (3000-m) altitude as an epiphyte or terrestrial. The plants are 4–20 in (10–50 cm) tall with a rosette of basal leaves. The leaves are 1¾–8 in (4–20 cm) long and ⅘–2½ in (2–6 cm) wide, and they sometimes have silver spots. The inflorescence has a few to many red to purple-red flowers, each about ¾ in (18 mm) long. Flowering is from autumn to winter.
ZONES 9–11. I.

Stenorrhynchos australis LINDL.
syns: many names, including
Stenorrhynch lanceolatus (AUBLET)
L. C. RICH., *Spiranthes lanceolata*
(AUBLET) LEON, *Sacoila lanceolata*
var. *australis* (LINDL.) SZLACH.

There is considerable confusion over which name to use for this species, with many authorities using *Spiranthes lanceolata*. It is a widespread species occurring from Florida in the USA through Central America to much of South America. It grows in grasslands and dry forests up to a 5000-ft (1500-m) altitude. The plants are up to 2 ft (60 cm) tall when in flower. The leaves are basal and appear after flowering. They are lancelike and about 2–14 in (5–35 cm) long and ⅘–3¼ in (2–8 cm) wide. The inflorescence has numerous red flowers about 1¼ in (3 cm) long. Flowering is from spring to autumn. This species will grow in full sun. **ZONES 8–11. I–H.**

Stenorrhynchos australis

STENOCORYNE LINDL.

There are about 12 species in this genus from Brazil. It is closely related to *Bifrenaria*. They are medium-sized epiphytes with egg-shaped pseudobulbs and a single, leathery leaf. The erect inflorescences arise from the base of the pseudobulbs and have a few showy flowers.

CULTIVATION

The plants do best in a pot with a standard epiphytic mix. They should be grown under semi-shade with good air movement. Watering and fertilizing should be heavy while the plants are in growth. This should be stopped for two or three weeks before watering again at reduced levels until the new growths appear.

Stenocoryne vitellina

Stenocoryne vitellina (LINDL.) KRAENZL.
syn: *Bifrenaria vitellina* LINDL.

This species is from Brazil. It has clustered pseudobulbs that are egg-shaped and strongly angular, and are up to 2 in (5 cm) tall. The solitary, leathery leaf is about 6 in (15 cm) long. The loosely flowered inflorescence is erect to arching and about 8 in (20 cm) tall. Five to eight flowers are produced and these are about ¾ in (18 mm) long. Flowering is during summer. **ZONES 11–12. I–H.**

S

STENOGLOTTIS LINDL.

This genus of three or four species occurs
in eastern, central, and southern Africa. They
grow in shady situations on moss-covered
rocks, in sheltered crevices in cliffs, or on
rotting logs in forests. They are all terrestrials
related to *Habenaria*. They grow from
underground tuberlike roots and have a short
stem with several leaves in a basal rosette.
The inflorescences are tall with numerous
small flowers that are attractively colored.
The plants are in flower over several months
as the flowers open successively.

CULTIVATION

These species do well in cultivation if potted
in a shallow pot or pan with a mix of sand
and leaf mold or peat moss. They should
be watered and fertilized regularly when in
growth, but given a watering rest period of
at least one month during winter. They are
best if grown under semi-shade in cool to
intermediate conditions.

Stenoglottis longifolia HOOKER

This species is
restricted to a few
sites in the KwaZulu
Natal province of
South Africa. It
grows on mossy
rocks at altitudes
of 1000–2300 ft
(300–700 m). It is
closely related to
S. *fimbriata*, but is
larger in all its parts.
The plant is up to
40 in (1 m) tall with
a basal rosette of
many uniformly light,
green leaves about 10 in

Stenoglottis longifolia

(25 cm) long. There are up to 80 flowers, each
about 1/3 in (1 cm) long. The flower color and
the degree of spotting varies. Flowering is
during autumn. **ZONES 10–11. I.**

Stenoglottis fimbriata LINDL.

syn: *Stenoglottis zambesiaca* ROLFE

This species occurs from the Eastern Cape and
KwaZulu Natal provinces in South Africa
to Tanzania. It grows on the forest floor or
on mossy rocks and tree trunks from sea level
to a 6000-ft (1800-m) altitude. The plant is
up to 16 in (40 cm) tall with up to 16 maroon-
spotted leaves about 6 in (15 cm) long and in
a basal rosette. The inflorescence has up to
50 flowers, each about 1/8 in (3 mm) long. The
flower color and the degree of spotting varies.
Flowering is during autumn. **ZONES 9–11. C–I.**

Stenoglottis fimbriata

S

Stenoglottis woodii SCHLTR.

This species is restricted to a few localities in the KwaZulu Natal and Transkei provinces of South Africa. It grows on mossy rocks at low to moderate altitudes. The dull-green-colored leaves are in a basal rosette and are up to 6 in (15 cm) long. This species can be separated from the others by its white or pale-pink flowers. There are up to 40 flowers about ¼ in (6 mm) long. Flowering is from late summer to early autumn. **ZONES 10–11. I.**

Stenoglottis woodii

SYMPHYOGLOSSUM
SCHLTR.

This genus comprises about six species in Venezuela, Colombia, Ecuador, and Peru. Most of them grow as epiphytes in wet forests in the Andes at altitudes of 3300–8300 ft (1000–2500 m). They have clustered pseudobulbs with one or two leaves at the apex.

CULTIVATION

These species do best when cultivated under cool to intermediate conditions similar to those for *Odontoglossum*. A pot with a well-drained medium is suitable.

Symphyoglossum sanguineum (RCHB.F.) SCHLTR.
syn: *Cochlioda sanguinea* (RCHB.F.) BENTH.

This species is from Ecuador and northwest Peru. The pseudobulbs are oval to oblong, compressed, and up to 2 in (5 cm) long. The two leaves are narrow and about 8 in (20 cm) long. The arching or drooping inflorescence is up to 40 in (1 m) long and carries many flowers, each about 1 in (2.5 cm) in diameter. Flowering is from autumn to spring. **ZONE 10. C–I.**

S

Symphyoglossum sanguineum

TELIPOGON HUMBOLDT, BONPLAND & KUNTH

This is a genus of more than 100 species ranging from Costa Rica to Bolivia. They grow as epiphytes or terrestrials at altitudes of 5000–11,300 ft (1500 to 3400 m). The plants are often dwarfed by the large, showy flowers. The pseudobulbs are either very small or absent and the few-flowered inflorescence arises from the axils of the leaves.

CULTIVATION

This genus is generally regarded as difficult to grow. The plants require cool to intermediate conditions with constant high humidity and good air movement. They resent disturbance and should be grown in small pots.

Telipogon vampyrus BRASS & HORICH.

This species grows in the cloud forests of Costa Rica at an altitude of about 5000 ft (1500 m). The plants are about 2 in (5 cm) tall with two or three inflorescences, each around 8 in (20 cm) long. Each inflorescence carries four or five flowers, each about 2 in (5 cm) wide. Flowering is during spring. ZONE 10. I.

Telipogon vampyrus

THECOSTELE RCHB.F.

There is only one species in this genus from Southeast Asia and the western islands of the Malay Archipelago. It is related to *Acriopsis*, but differs through some details of the flower.

CULTIVATION

Slab culture or pots prove to be equally successful when growing this species. If potted, the plant should be given a coarse, free-draining medium, and in some situations it will tolerate bright light, even full sun. Water regularly throughout the year.

Thecostele alata (ROXB.) PAR. & RCHB.F.
syn: *Thecostele zollingeri* RCHB.F., *T. maculosa* RIDL.

This species is widespread from northeast India to Java and the Philippines, including most areas in between. It grows on trees, mostly in the lowlands, but also in the mountains up to a 6000-ft (1800-m) altitude. The pseudobulbs are clustered, egg-shaped to cylindrical, and about 2½ in (6 cm) long. The single leaf is about 6–12 in (15–30 cm) long and 2 in (5 cm) wide. The pendulous inflorescence is up to 20 in (50 cm) long and has many flowers, each one about ½ in (12 mm) across. Only a few flowers open at any one time and they appear mostly during autumn. ZONES 10–12. I–H.

Thecostele alata

T

THELYMITRA J. R. FORST. & G. FORST.
"SUN ORCHIDS"

There are about 70 species in this genus, predominantly from southern Australia. There are a few species in New Zealand and one in New Caledonia, Papua New Guinea, and the Philippines. They are known as sun orchids as the flowers tend to open fully only with sunshine; they remain closed on cloudy days. These terrestrials grow in sandy soils in forests and heathlands in areas with a hot, dry summer. There is a pair of underground tubers and a single leaf. The erect inflorescence has a few to many flowers. These are unusual in that the lip is almost identical to the other petals.

CULTIVATION

Most of the species can be grown in a terrestrial mix of leaf mold, wood shavings, peat moss, and coarse sand. They require a reduced watering period, followed with a period of no watering at all. When the first sign of growth is seen in autumn, recommence watering.

Thelymitra sargentii

Thelymitra pauciflora

Thelymitra pauciflora R. BR.
"SLENDER SUN ORCHID"

This species is widespread in eastern Australia from north Queensland to Tasmania and South Australia. It grows in a range of habitats, including open woodlands and heathlands at low to moderate altitudes. The leaf is straplike, up to 8 in (20 cm) long, and ⅘ in (2 cm) wide. The inflorescence is up to 20 in (50 cm) tall with one to 15 flowers, each about 4¾–8 in (12–20 mm) across. Usually only one or two flowers are open at any one time and, in cool, cloudy weather, the flowers may not open at all. Flowering is from spring to summer. This species does well in cultivation. **ZONES 8–10. C–I.**

Thelymitra sargentii R. S. ROGERS
"FRECKLED SUN ORCHID"

This species is restricted to the southwest corner of Western Australia. It grows in low-rainfall, inland areas in open forests and yellow sandplains, often in the shade of shrubs. The leaf is thick and fleshy, and up to 5½ in (13 cm) long and 1¼ in (3 cm) wide. The inflorescence is up to 20 in (50 cm) tall with five to 17 flowers, each about 1½ in (3.5 cm) across. The flowers are long-lasting and they open on hot sunny days during spring. **ZONES 9–10. I.**

T

THRIXSPERMUM LOUR.

This genus has somewhere between 100 and 150 monopodial species. They occur in north and south China, Southeast Asia, the Malay Archipelago, the islands in the southwest of the Pacific Ocean, and Australia. They are small epiphytes growing mostly at low altitudes. Some species have long climbing stems and some have very short stems. The inflorescences are usually long with several to many flowers that open one or two at a time and last for only a day. The inflorescence has persistent fleshy bracts which may be arranged in two rows or all around the stem.

CULTIVATION

A slab of cork or similar material is usually the best sort of mount for these plants. They usually do well under moderate shade with humid conditions and year-round watering.

Thrixspermum centipedum

Thrixspermum centipedum LOUR.
syn: many names, including *T. arachnites* (BLUME) RCHB.F.,
T. serraeformis (LINDL.) RCHB.F.

This species is widespread from India through southern China through the Malay Peninsula to the Indonesian islands, as far east as Sulawesi. A very similar species occurs in Papua New Guinea and Australia and may prove to be the same species. The plants grow on trees at a 660–4700-ft (200–1400-m) altitude and are erect with a short stem up to 8 in (20 cm) long, but are usually shorter. The leaves are thick and fleshy and about 4 in (10 cm) long and ⅘ in (2 cm) wide. The erect to horizontal inflorescence is up to 6 in (15 cm) long. The apex of it is strongly flattened and has two rows of persistent floral bracts. The flowers are about 2 in (5 cm) across and last for only one day. One or two of these are open at any one time, and they appear at any time of the year, but there is an emphasis on summer. **ZONES 10–11. I–H.**

T

THUNIA RCHB.F.

There are about six species in this genus, occurring from India through southern China to Southeast Asia. They grow as terrestrials or, rarely, as epiphytes at moderate to high altitudes. The stems are canelike, long, and slender with deciduous leaves in two ranks. The inflorescence is short and drooping with several showy flowers.

CULTIVATION

These plants grow best in a terrestrial-type mix, such as a mix used for *Cymbidium* species. They should be grown in a shady position and watered heavily until the leaves wither and fall. Then they should be kept dry until the new shoots are about 8 in (20 cm) tall and the new roots appear.

Thunia alba

Thunia alba (LINDL.) RCHB.F.
syn: *T. marshalliana* RCHB.F., *Phaius albus* LINDL.

Thunia alba and *T. marshalliana* are often regarded as separate species. Generally, they are very similar but *T. alba* is smaller in all its parts. This robust species occurs along the Himalayas from Nepal to southern China, and south to the Malay Peninsula. It grows in the ground, on rocks, and in forks of trees at altitudes of 3300–7700 ft (1000–2300 m). The stems are up to 4 ft (1.2 m) tall with deciduous, thin-textured leaves, each about 6–8 in (15–20 cm) long, arranged in two ranks. The inflorescences are short, terminal, and pendulous with up to ten fragrant, long-lasting flowers, each about 5½ in (13 cm) across. Flowering is during summer. **ZONES 9–10. I.**

T

TICOGLOSSUM LUCAS RODRIGUEZ EX HALBINGER

There are two species in this genus. Both were formerly included in *Oncidium* and *Odontoglossum*. *Ticoglossum* species have a shorter column than either of those genera. The distribution is at high altitudes in the central mountain range of Costa Rica and western Panama.

CULTIVATION

These plants grow best in pots in cool, moist shaded or semi-shaded positions. Good air movement is required.

Ticoglossum krameri (RCHB.F.) LUCAS RODRIGUEZ EX HALBINGER
syn: *Odontoglossum krameri* RCHB.F.

This species occurs in Costa Rica. It grows on trees in cloud forests at moderate to high altitudes. The pseudobulbs are round, compressed, green or bluish–green in color, and about 2 in (5 cm) tall. The leaf is about 10 in

Ticoglossum krameri

(25 cm) long and 1¾ in (4 cm) across. The inflorescence is erect or pendulous with three flowers that are about 1½–2 in (3.5–5 cm) across. Flowering occurs sporadically throughout the year. **ZONES 9–10. I.**

TIPULARIA NUTTALL

There are three species in this genus—one in the Himalayas, one in Japan, and one in eastern USA. They are all terrestrials with a broad leaf that arises from a series of underground, jointed tubers. The inflorescence is tall and slender with numerous small flowers.

CULTIVATION

These plants are relatively easy to grow in a slightly acidic terrestrial mix. They must be given a watering rest period, in which water is withheld after the flowers have finished, for several weeks during winter.

Tipularia discolor (PURSH.) NUTTALL
"CRANE FLY ORCHID"

This species occurs in the USA from the northeastern states to Nebraska in the west, eastern Texas, and Florida in south. It is an uncommon orchid growing in coniferous and deciduous forests and along stream banks. The plant is up to 2 ft (60 cm) tall and arises from a series of tubers, each about ⅘ in (2 cm) long. The solitary leaf is dark green above and purple below, and about 3¼–4 in (8–10 cm)

Tipularia discolor

long and 2½ in (6 cm) wide. The inflorescence appears in mid summer after the leaf has withered. There are 20–40 flowers, each about ½ in (12 mm) across. **ZONES 5–9. C–I.**

TOLUMNIA RAFINESQUE

Plants of this genus are native to the Caribbean islands and were called "equitant" *Oncidiums*, a term that referred to their unique growth habit of overlapping leaves. Generally, they are small epiphytic plants that lack pseudobulbs or have a very small one. The leaves are three-sided and V–shaped in cross section.

CULTIVATION

These species are best cultivated on slabs that allow their roots to dry rapidly after watering. Watering should be reduced during the cooler months. Most require bright light in hot to intermediate conditions.

Tolumnia guianensis

Tolumnia guianensis (AUBL.) GARAY
syn: *Oncidium guianense* (AUBL.) G. J. BRAEM

This species is from the island of Hispaniola in the West Indies. The fan of bronze–green leaves reach about 3 in (7.5 cm) tall. The inflorescence is up to 6 in (15 cm) long and bears ten to 15 flowers, each about 1 in (2.5 cm) wide. Flowering is from spring to autumn.
ZONES 11–12. I–H.

Tolumnia henekenii (SCHOMB. EX LINDL.) M. A. NIR
syn: *Oncidium henekenii* SCHOMB. EX LINDL.
"BEE ORCHID"

This species is from very dry areas in northwest Hispaniola in the West Indies. It forms a fan of stiff, sharply curved, red–green leaves. The inflorescence gradually increases in length as each flower dies and another is formed. It can produce up to 15 flowers over several months, with each flower about 1 in (2.5 cm) long. This species is best cultivated on a narrow hardwood slab in bright conditions. It does not like excessive moisture at the roots.
ZONES 11–12. I–H.

Tolumnia henekenii

T

Tolumnia pulchella

Tolumnia pulchella RAFIN.
syn: *Oncidium pulchellum* HOOK.

This species is indigenous to higher elevations in Jamaica and Hispaniola in the West Indies. The leaf clusters are well separated along the elongated rhizomes. The pseudobulbs are very small and the three to five leaves overlap at the base. The erect inflorescence is about 20 in (50 cm) long and is often branched. The flowers are about 1 in (2.5 cm) in diameter, and they appear during spring and summer. **ZONES 10–11. I.**

Tolumnia sasseri (MOIR) G. J. BRAEM
syn: *Oncidium sasseri* MOIR

This species is restricted to the Bahamas, where it grows on the islands of Andros and Great Abaco. In appearance the plant looks similar to other species in the genus. The inflorescence is up to 10 in (25 cm) long and carries three to 20 flowers. Flowering is during summer. **ZONES 11–12. I-H.**

Tolumnia sasseri

Tolumnia triquetra

(SW.) M. A. NIR

syn: *Oncidium triquetra* (SW.) R. BR.

This species is from Jamaica, where it grows in moist environments. It has a short inflorescence with many branches. It continues to branch and flower throughout much of the year. The plant has closely spaced leaf clusters and the three to five narrow leaves are thick, fleshy, and up to about 6 in (15 cm) long. The erect inflorescence is up to about 4 in (10 cm) long and produces up to 15 flowers, each about 1 in (2.5 cm) wide. Flowering is mostly during summer. **ZONE 11. I–H.**

Tolumnia triquetra

Tolumnia urophylla

Tolumnia urophylla

(LODD. EX LINDL.) G. J. BRAEM

syn: *Oncidium urophyllum* LODD. EX LINDL.

This species is from the northern islands of the Lesser Antilles, where it grows in dry, windy conditions, and in Brazil. It is a vigorous plant with long, climbing rhizomes and a flower stem that reaches up to 3 ft (90 cm). The species is known to produce plantlets from the unflowered nodes of the flower stem. The flowers are up to 1 in (2.5 cm) in diameter. Flowering is during summer and autumn. **ZONES 11–12. I–H.**

T

TRAUNSTEINERA RCHB.

This genus is named after Joseph Traunsteiner, a chemist from Kitzbühel in Austria. It consists of only two species that grow in moist, mountain meadows in middle Europe, the northern parts of south Europe, and in the Caucasus. The two ovoid tubers without divided ends and the arrangement of the leaves—arising in the middle of the stem—separate this genus from the closely related *Orchis*, which has a basal rosette. The flowers are relatively small, about ⅓ in (1 cm) across. The apexes of the petals and sepals are narrow with a thickened tip.

CULTIVATION

These species are not known to be in cultivation. It would be difficult to cultivate them, as plants from high mountain regions have special requirements.

Traunsteinera globose (L.) RCHB.

This rather slender plant is restricted to the European mountain regions and the Caucasus. It grows in soils with limestone or slate or granite in moist meadows, usually above a 5000-ft (1500-m) altitude. The plant is 8–28 in (20–70 cm) tall. The dense, ovoid to globose inflorescence is about 1¾ in (4 cm) in diameter. The flowering season is from May to August (spring to summer), depending on the altitude of origin. **ZONES 5–7. C.**

Traunsteinera globose

T

TRICHOCENTRUM POEPPIG & ENDL.

Many species included in this genus were once regarded as part of *Oncidium*, including the species referred to as "mule-ear" and "rat-tail" *Oncidiums*. (Mule-ear species have large, flat leaves; rat-tail species have narrow, terete leaves.) *Trichocentrum* species are mostly epiphytes with short rhizomes and small pseudobulbs. Typically, the leaves are thick and fleshy.

CULTIVATION

Many of these species prefer to be mounted on a slab, in particular the rat-tail types. Those of the mule-ear type may be grown in pots. Whatever means are used, these orchids do not like staleness at the roots, therefore good drainage is important. Most of the species do best in hot to intermediate conditions with copious watering during the growing period and a watering rest period during the cooler months. Bright light is important to encourage good flowering.

Trichocentrum bicallosum (LINDL.) M. W. CHASE & N. H. WILLIAMS
syn: *Oncidium bicallosum* LINDL.

This species occurs in Mexico, El Salvador, and Guatemala up to an altitude of about 5000 ft (1500 m). The plant is stout, up to 2 ft (60 cm) tall, and has very small pseudobulbs, less than $\frac{2}{3}$ in (15 mm) long. The solitary leaf is fleshy to leathery and up to 14 in (35 cm) long and $3\frac{2}{3}$ in (9 cm) wide. The erect inflorescence is up to 3 ft (90 cm) tall and is rarely branching. It carries many flowers, each about 2 in (5 cm) long. Flowering is during autumn. Cultivation is as for the mule-ear group.
ZONES 11–12. I–H.

T

Trichocentrum bicallosum

Trichocentrum carthagenense

(JACQ.) M. W. CHASE & N. H. WILLIAMS

syn: *Oncidium carthagenense* (JACQ.) SW.

This species occurs from southern Florida in
the USA through the West Indies and Mexico
to Venezuela and Brazil. It grows from sea level
to 3300 ft (1000 m). The pseudobulbs are
incredibly small and a single leaf is borne from
a robust rhizome. The leaf is rigid and fleshy
and can be spotted with brown or maroon.
It is up to 2 ft (60 cm) long and 3 in (7.5 cm)
wide. The erect or arching inflorescence has
many flowers, is branched and up to 5 ft
(1.5 m) tall. Flowers are about ¾ in (18 mm)
in diameter. Flowering is during summer.
Cultivation is as for the mule-ear types.
ZONES 11–12. I–H.

Trichocentrum carthagenense

Trichocentrum cavendishianum

Trichocentrum cebolleta

Trichocentrum cavendishianum

(BATEM.) M. W. CHASE & N. H. WILLIAMS

syn: *Oncidium cavendishianum* BATEM.

This species occurs in Mexico and Guatemala,
where it grows as an epiphyte at altitudes up
to 9300 ft (2800 m). The pseudobulbs are
incredibly small and the one or two leaves are
up to 2 ft (60 cm) long and 8 in (20 cm) wide.
They are erect, rigid, leathery, and prominently
keeled. The erect inflorescence is up to about
3 ft (90 cm) tall and carries many fragrant
flowers, each about 1¾ in (4 cm) wide.
Flowering is during winter and spring.
Cultivation is as for the mule-ear type.
ZONES 10–12. I–H.

Trichocentrum cebolleta

(JACQ.) M. W. CHASE & N. H. WILLIAMS

syn: *Oncidium cebolleta* (JACQ.) SW.

This is a common species in the American
tropics, where it grows from near sea level
to about 5700 ft (1700 m) in areas that have
a fairly long, hot, dry period. It is an epiphyte
with indistinct pseudobulbs and a single, terete
leaf up to 16 in (40 cm) long. The erect or
arching inflorescence is up to 5 ft (1.5 m) long
and may have short branches. It carries many
flowers, each up to about 1¼ in (3 cm)
in diameter. Flowering is during summer.
Cultivation is as for the rat-tail species.
ZONES 11–12. I–H.

T

Trichocentrum jonesianum

Trichocentrum microchilum

Trichocentrum microchilum

(BATEM.) M. W. CHASE & N. H. WILLIAMS
syn: *Oncidium microchilum* BATEM.

This species occurs in Mexico and Guatemala, where it grows on rocks as well as epiphytically, up to an altitude of 7700 ft (2300 m). The pseudobulbs are tiny and the solitary leaf is rigid, thick, and up to 1 ft (30 cm) long and 3 in (7.5 cm) wide. Both the pseudobulbs and leaves are a dull brownish– green color. The inflorescence is up to 4 ft (1.2 m) tall, densely branched, and bears many flowers, each about 1 in (2.5 cm) wide. Flowering is during summer. Cultivation is as for the mule-ear types. **ZONES 10–12. I–H.**

Trichocentrum jonesianum (RCHB.F.)

M. W. CHASE & N. H. WILLIAMS
syn: *Oncidium jonesianum* RCHB.F.

This species is found in southern Brazil, Paraguay, and Uruguay. The pseudobulbs are incredibly small and the fleshy, terete leaves are pendulous and up to 2 ft (60 cm) long. The erect inflorescence is up to 2 ft (60 cm) tall. Ten to 15 flowers are produced and these are about 3 in (7.5 cm) in diameter. Flowering is during autumn. This species should be cultivated on a slab as for the rat-tail species. **ZONES 11–12. I–H.**

Trichocentrum lanceanum (LINDL.)

M. W. CHASE & N. H. WILLIAMS
syn: *Oncidium lanceanum* LINDL.

This species occurs from Trinidad and Tobago to Guyana, Venezuela, and Colombia. The thick rhizome produces tiny pseudobulbs and the thick, leathery leaves are up to 20 in (50 cm) long and 5½ in (13 cm) wide. These are a dull-green color with dense purple spotting. The erect inflorescence is up to 18 in (45 cm) tall and has a few to many flowers, each up to 2½ in (6 cm) long. The flowers are fragrant, long-lasting, and appear during summer. Cultivation is as for the mule-ear types. **ZONES 11–12. I–H.**

T

Trichocentrum lanceanum

Trichocentrum pumilum
(LINDL.) M. W. CHASE & N. H. WILLIAMS

syn: *Oncidium pumilum* LINDL.

This miniature species from Brazil, Paraguay, Uruguay, and Argentina grows from the hot lowlands to the cool mountains. It is the smallest of the "mule ear" type of species, and it has clustered, tiny pseudobulbs. Each bears a single, fleshy leaf up to about 4 in (10 cm) long and ⅕ in (2 cm) wide. The erect inflorescence is up to about 6 in (15 cm) tall, branches, and carries many small flowers, each about ¼ in (6 mm) wide. Flowering is during spring and summer. This species grows well on a mount, but may be grown in a small pot. **ZONES 10–12. I–H.**

Trichocentrum pumilum

Trichocentrum splendidum (A. RICH. EX DUCHARTE) M. W. CHASE & N. H. WILLIAMS

syn: *Oncidium splendidum* A. RICH. EX DUCHARTE

This species from Honduras and Guatemala is rare in the wild. The clustered pseudobulbs are almost round, compressed, dull brown–green in color, and up to 2 in (5 cm) tall. The solitary leaf has a similar color and is up to 1 ft (30 cm) long and 3 in (7.5 cm) wide. It is rigid, thick, and leathery. The erect inflorescence is up to 4 ft (1.2 m) tall and bears a few to many long-lasting flowers, each about 3 in (7.5 cm) long. Flowering is from late winter to spring. Cultivation is as for the mule-ear types. **ZONES 11–12. I–H.**

Trichocentrum stramineum (LINDL.) M. W. CHASE & N. H. WILLIAMS

syn: *Oncidium stramineum* LINDL.

This species, endemic to Mexico, has a limited distribution. It grows at an altitude of about 3300 ft (1000 m) and is one of the smaller mule-ear types. It has fleshy, leathery leaves up to 1 ft (30 cm) long. The branching inflorescence is up to 20 in (50 cm) long and carries many flowers, each about ⅔ in (15 mm) wide. Flowering is from winter to spring. Cultivation is as for the mule-ear species. **ZONE 10. I.**

Trichocentrum splendidum

Trichocentrum stramineum

TRICHOGLOTTIS BLUME

Trichoglottis is a genus of about 60 species ranging from mainland Asia through the Philippines and Indonesian islands to New Guinea and Australia, which has one species. Two of the species, *T. atropurpurea* and *T. philippinensis*, are particularly well known in cultivation. These monopodial species are elongated with leaves along their length. The flowers are borne singly or in a group of two to ten on the opposite side of the stem to the leaves. Most of the plants are small, but a few species have attractive large flowers.

CULTIVATION

Many of these species have a tangled mass of aerial roots that arise from the nodes and are difficult to confine in a pot. They are often grown in a basket or pot without any medium or with a coarse mixture. Any roots that are in a medium which starts to break down will soon die. So if grown in a pot, regular fertilizing is necessary. A long slab can be provided for the plants to climb on. They also require bright light, constant high humidity, daily watering, and most of them require hot temperatures.

Trichoglottis amesiana L. O. WILLIAMS

This species is restricted to the mountains in central Luzon in the Philippines. It grows in shady conditions at an altitude of about 4000 ft (1200 m). The pendulous stems reach 2 ft (60 cm) long and the leathery leaves are about 5⅔ in (14 cm) long and ⅔ in (15 mm) wide. The short inflorescences are opposite the leaves and bear up to ten flowers, each about ⅔ in (15 mm) across. **ZONES 10–11. I.**

Trichoglottis amesiana

Trichoglottis atropurpurea RCHB.F.

syn: *T. brachiata* AMES

In most collections this attractive species is incorrectly labelled *T. brachiata*. It is also sometimes regarded as a variety of *T. philippinensis*. This upright species is restricted to the Philippines, where it grows in the lowlands on several islands. It is as high as 1 ft (60 cm) and has ovate leaves 3¼ in (8 cm) long and 1¾ in (4 cm) wide. The single flowers are borne opposite the leaves and are up to 2½ in (6 cm) across. Flowering is during spring and summer. **ZONES 11–12. H.**

Trichoglottis atropurpurea

T

Trichoglottis cirrhifera TEIJSM. & BINN.

syn: *Trichoglottis tetraceras* RIDL., *Saccolabium cornigerum* RIDL., *Cleisostoma tenuicaule* KING & PRANTL.

This species occurs in Indochina and on the island of Java. It grows at low to moderate altitudes. The pendulous stems are up to 10 ft (3 m) long and have narrow leaves up to 4¾ in (12 cm) long and ⅔ in (15 mm) wide. The very short inflorescences bear one to three flowers, each about ⅓–⅔ in (10–15 mm) across. **ZONES 11–12. I–H.**

Trichoglottis cirrhifera

Trichoglottis geminata J. J. SM.

syn: *T. wenzelii* AMES

This species is recorded from the islands of Borneo, Sulawesi, Ambon, and Seram, and in the Philippines. It grows on rocks and trees at low altitudes, often near the sea. The stems are upright to semi-pendulous and up to about 20 in (50 cm) long. The leathery leaves are 4¾ in (12 cm) long and ⅘ in (2 cm) wide. The flowers are about ⅔ in (15 mm) across and are borne singly or in pairs opposite the leaves. **ZONES 11–12. H.**

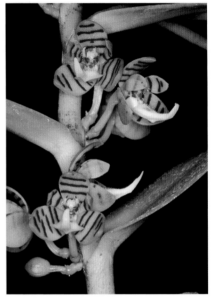

Trichoglottis geminata

Trichoglottis philippinensis LINDL.

This species is closely related to *T. atropurpurea*, but has lighter colored flowers. It occurs in the lowlands of the Philippines and Borneo. The stems are up to about 2 ft (60 cm) long. The leaves are about 2¾ in (7 cm) long and 1½ in (3.5 cm) wide along their length. The flowers are about 1¾ in (4 cm) across and are borne singly opposite the leaves. Flowering is during spring and summer. **ZONES 11–12. H.**

Trichoglottis philippinensis

Trichoglottis seidenfadenii AVERYANOV
syn: *T. tomentosa* SEIDENF.

This species is labelled
T. sagarikii in most
collections, but this name was
never formally accepted. It is
a lowland species recorded
in Thailand and Vietnam
and on the islands in the Gulf
of Thailand, among other
locations. It grows into large,
tangled clumps with stems
up to 40 in (1 m) long. The
leaves are about 3¼ in (8 cm)
long and 1¼ in (3 cm) wide.
These are arranged along
the length of the stems. The
flowers are about ⅘–1¼ in
(2–3 cm) across and last
for about four weeks. They
are produced singly or,
occasionally, in pairs opposite
the leaves. **ZONES 11–12. H.**

Trichoglottis seidenfadenii

Trichoglottis smithii CARR
syn: *T. quadricornuta* J. J. SM.,
T. appendiculifera HOLTTUM

This species is found on
Borneo and, possibly,
Sumatra. It grows as an
epiphyte or lithophyte in
lightly shaded situations in
mountain forests at low to
moderate altitudes. The stems
are upright to semi-pendulous
and reach 6 ft (1.8 m) in
height, but more often about
12–16 in (30–40 cm). The
leaves are about 2 in (5 cm)
long and ⅔ in (15 mm)
across. The single, faintly
fragrant flowers are about
1 in (2.5 cm) across.
Flowering occurs several
times throughout the year.
ZONES 11–12. I–H.

T

Trichoglottis smithii

TRICHOPILIA LINDL.

This is a genus of about 30 species that occur from Mexico to Bolivia and Brazil. They are mostly epiphytes but may also occur as lithophytes and, occasionally, terrestrials, and they grow in wet forests at altitudes of 1700–6700 ft (500–2000 m). The plants in this genus have flattened pseudobulbs with a single leaf. The inflorescence is produced from the axils of the bracts surrounding the pseudobulbs.

CULTIVATION

Most species in this genus are easy to grow. They are most suited to pot culture but may be grown in hanging baskets. A well-drained medium should be used. When actively growing, these plants should be given copious amounts of water and given a watering rest period during the cooler months. Moderate shade and intermediate to hot conditions suit most of the species.

Trichopilia marginata

Trichopilia suavis

Trichopilia marginata
HENFR. EX. MOORE

This species ranges from Guatemala through Costa Rica and Panama to Colombia. The clustered pseudobulbs are strongly compressed and up to 5⅔ in (14 cm) long. The leathery leaf is up to 1 ft (30 cm) long. The inflorescence is short and arching and carries two to five flowers. These are highly fragrant and about 4 in (10 cm) wide. Flowering is during spring.
ZONES 11–12. I–H.

Trichopilia tortilis LINDL.

This species occurs in Mexico, Guatemala, El Salvador, and Honduras. The pseudobulbs are up to 4 in (10 cm) tall and are more or less covered with brown spotted bracts. The single leaf is up to 10 in (25 cm) long. The inflorescence carries one or two fragrant flowers, each up to 6 in (15 cm) across. Flowering is during winter.
ZONES 11–12. I–H.

Trichopilia tortilis

Trichopilia suavis
LINDL. & PAXT.

This species occurs in Costa Rica, Panama and Colombia. The pseudobulbs are clustered and about 3 in (7.5 cm) long, with a solitary leaf up to about 14 in (35 cm) long. The short inflorescence is pendulous or arching and carries between two and five flowers. These are highly fragrant and about 4 in (10 cm) wide. Flowering is mostly during spring.
ZONES 11–12. I–H.

TRIDACTYLE SCHLTR.

There are about 40 species in this genus of monopodial orchids that are related to *Angraecum* and were originally included in that genus. *Tridactyle* species have a three-lobed lip, often with two or more of the lobes having fringes. They are mostly small epiphytes or lithophytes from moist habitats in shaded conditions. Cultivation is as for *Angraecum* species.

Tridactyle gentilii

Tridactyle tricuspis (BOLUS) SCHLTR.

This small epiphyte occurs along the east African coast, from Kenya to KwaZulu Natal province in South Africa. It is found in moist, cool, mountain forests above an altitude of 5000 ft (1500 m). It grows as a single plant or in untidy clumps with stems up to 4 in (10 cm) long. The leaves are arranged in a fan and are up to 6 in (15 cm) long. There are two to four inflorescences per stem, each with seven to 30 small flowers in two ranks. The flowers, each about 1/3 in (1 cm) across, are light green to yellow–brown in color and appear from February to April in the wild. **ZONES 9–10. C–I.**

Tridactyle tricuspis

Tridactyle gentilii (DEWILD) SCHLTR.

This species is widespread from the west African coastal regions through central Africa to KwaZulu Natal province in South Africa. It grows in rain forests and riverine forests at low to moderate altitudes. It forms robust clumps of long stems. The inflorescences are spreading and bears numerous flowers, each about 4/5 in (2 cm) across. The spur is 1¾–3¼ in (4–8 cm) long. Flowering is from February to April in the wild. **ZONES 10–11 I–H**

Tridactyle tanneri P. J. CRIBB

This small species is known from Kenya and Tanzania at altitudes of about 4000–5000 ft (1200–1500 m). It grows on tree trunks in shady, humid, rain forest conditions. The stems are about 1¾ in (4 cm) long with a few mottled leaves about 2½–4 in (6–10 cm) long. The short inflorescences are arching with two to eight small flowers, each about ⅔ in (15 mm) across. The spur is up to 4/5 in (2 cm) long. **ZONES 10–11. I.**

Tridactyle tanneri

T

TRIGONIDIUM LINDL.

The 20 species in this genus are epiphytes that grow in tropical Central and South America. They are related to *Maxillaria*. They have medium-sized pseudobulbs with one or two straplike leaves. The single flowers are borne on a long, upright peduncle. The sepals overlap at the base to form a tube.

CULTIVATION

These species grow best in pots or baskets with a well-drained mixture that retains a little moisture. They prefer intermediate to hot conditions with high humidity, bright but not full sunlight, and a slightly reduced watering when the growths are mature. Care should be taken when repotting as some of the species do not tolerate being disturbed.

Trigonidium ergertonianum

Trigonidium ergertonianum
BATEMAN EX LINDL.
syn: *T. seemanii* RCHB.F.

This species occurs from Mexico to Colombia at low to moderate altitudes. It is a common epiphyte in Central America and is often seen on isolated trees that are left after land clearing. The pseudobulbs are clustered, ovoid, ridged, and up to 3²⁄₃ in (9 cm) long. There are one or two straplike, erect leaves up to 18 in (45 cm) long and 1 in (2.5 cm) wide. The inflorescences arise from the base of the pseudobulbs. They are slender, erect, almost as tall as the leaves, and bear a single, long-lasting, cuplike flower about 1¼ in (3 cm) long. Flowering is mostly during spring.
ZONES 10–12. I–H.

Trigonidium latifolium LINDL.

This epiphytic species grows in Brazil in the hot, humid lowlands and the cool mountains in the south. The pseudobulbs are ellipsoidal and compressed with grooves on both sides. They are about 2½ in (6 cm) tall. There are two leaves up to 8 in (20 cm) long and 1¼ in (3 cm) wide. The single-flowered inflorescence arises from the base of the pseudobulb and is about 3¼ in (8 cm) long. The flower is triangular when seen from above and is about 1 in (2.5 cm) across. **ZONES 10–12. I–H.**

Trigonidium latifolium

TRUDELIA GARAY

This genus of six species was formerly placed in *Vanda* and the species are often seen in collections under that name. They are mostly small- to medium-sized monopodial plants, ranging from northeast India and Nepal to Thailand and Java. All of them have fleshy leaves and inflorescences with a few waxy flowers. Cultivation is the same as for *Vanda* species.

Trudelia cristata

Trudelia cristata (LINDL.) GARAY
syn: *Vanda cristata* LINDL.

This species occurs in the Himalayas in northeast India, Bhutan, Nepal, and the Yunnan and Xizang Gaoyuan provinces of China. It grows on trees or rocks at moderate to high altitudes in areas with a cool, dry winter. The stems are upright and up to 8 in (20 cm) tall with short inflorescences of about four fragrant flowers, each 1¾–2 in (4–5 cm) across. In cultivation this species should be kept moist throughout the year and given medium light. **ZONES 9–11. C–I.**

Trudelia pumila (J. D. HOOK.) SENGHAS
syn: *Vanda pumila* J. D. HOOK.

This species from the Himalayan region occurs from northeast India and Nepal to southern China and Indochina. It grows epiphytically at moderate to high altitudes in forests with a distinct dry season during the winter, usually in areas with bright light. The plant is about 10 in (25 cm) long and upright, and it bears short, lateral inflorescences of two to four fragrant flowers up to 2 in (5 cm) across. Flowering may occur at any time with an emphasis on spring. This species will not tolerate hot, tropical conditions. **ZONES 9–10. C–I.**

T

Trudelia pumila

VANDA JONES EX R. BR.

This is one of the most popular genera in horticulture. It is found in the area bound by Sri Lanka and India in the west, Bougainville and Guadalcanal islands in the east, southern China and the Philippines in the north, and Australia in the south. There are about 40 species evenly spread across India, Thailand, the Philippines, and Indonesia, however the distribution tails off in the east. They grow mostly in mountain forests from sea level to high altitudes (over 6700 ft / 2000 m) in areas with year-round rainfall; a few grow in areas with seasonally dry climates. Most of them prefer moderate to strong light and sometimes they are found in exposed conditions. They may be epiphytes or lithophytes, and many form large, scrambling clumps.

Vanda species range from miniatures to large plants up to 5 ft (1.5 m) tall. Most of them have leathery, straplike leaves in two ranks. The flowers vary in size, up to 4 in (10 cm) in diameter, and many last for more than a week. Many of the flowers are fragrant. Some species, such as the spectacular blue-flowered *V. coerulea* found from northern India to southern China and Thailand, have suffered from over-collection; they are now considered threatened in the wild.

CULTIVATION

While the flowers are attractive, many *Vanda* species have an untidy growth habit with thick roots that are difficult to contain in a pot. Most of the species should be grown under bright light, although full sunlight should be avoided for the majority of them. Year-round moisture and good air circulation are recommended. In some areas *Vanda* species are grown hanging in baskets with no medium surrounding the roots. In such cases regular fertilizing is required. If grown in a pot, a very coarse medium is necessary. In the tropics they may be grown in the garden successfully, but they require glasshouse conditions in temperate climates.

HYBRIDS

Thousands of hybrids have been made over the past 50 or so years with *Vanda* species. These are extremely popular as pot plants and as cut flowers. The large, colorful flowers last well and are used in countless bouquets and floral arrangements around the world. Almost all the hybrids with straplike leaves originated from five species—*Euanthe sanderiana*, *Vanda coerulea*, *V. tricolor*, *V. luzonica*, and *V. dearei*.

As with other genera, hybridists are always striving to produce large, well-shaped, long-lasting, colorful flowers on a compact plant. The influence of *V. coerulea* can be seen in the large, blue flowers with attractive tessellations. The primary hybrid, *V. rothschildiana*, has been around for many years but retains its popularity as new, improved strains of the parents (*V. coerulea* and *Euanthe sanderiana*) are used. Many crosses involving *E. sanderiana* produce large, well-rounded, heavily textured flowers with dark lateral sepals and spotted, light-colored petals and dorsal sepal. Much potential still remains to use some of the qualities of the other 35 *Vanda* species. These species are also crossed successfully with several other genera. The most notable are the hybrids produced with *Ascocentrum* (*Ascocendra* or *Ascda.*). These have smaller but colorful flowers on compact plants well suited for the hobbyist's orchid house.

Ascda. Crown Fox "Golden Dawn"
for further hybrid photographs
see the end of *Vanda* species section.

Vanda bensonii

Vanda bensonii BATEMAN

This small plant has been recorded in Myanmar and Thailand. The habitat is reported to be deciduous forests at low to moderate altitude in areas with a pronounced dry season. It has upright, leafy stems up to about 1 ft (30 cm) long. Up to 20 fragrant flowers, each about 2 in (5 cm) across, are borne on inflorescences about 14 in (35 cm) long. Flowering may occur at any time, but most often during spring. **ZONES 10–12. I–H.**

Vanda coerulescens

Vanda coerulea GRIFF. EX LINDL.

This is one of the few genuinely blue orchids. It is a spectacular species found in the Himalayas from northeast India, the Yunnan province in China, Myanmar, and Thailand. It grows at moderate altitudes in deciduous forests in areas with a distinct seasonal climate. It is a robust species with stems up to 5 ft (1.5 m) in length. The inflorescences, up to 30 in (75 cm) tall, are upright with ten to 14 long-lasting flowers, each 3¼–4 in (8–10 cm) across. The flower color ranges from almost white to violet with tessellations more or less obvious on the floral parts. Flowering in the wild is during autumn and winter but it may occur at any time, particularly in cultivation. This species is from cool climates and does not do well in lowland tropical areas. **ZONES 9–11. C–I.**

Vanda coerulescens GRIFF.

This miniature is similar to *V. coerulea* in that it also has blue flowers. It comes from northeast India, southern China, Myanmar, and Thailand, growing at moderate altitudes in deciduous forests under strong light. The plants are 1–2 ft (30–60 cm) tall. Many flowers, about 1–1¾ in (2.5–4 cm) across, are borne on an upright or arching inflorescence up to 14 in (35 cm) long. The long-lasting flowers open during spring. Intermediate conditions are required for successful cultivation. **ZONES 9–11. I.**

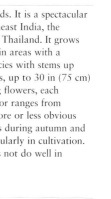

V

Vanda coerulea

Vanda denisoniana BENSON & RCHB.F.

While many *Vanda* species have flowers that are fragrant during the middle of the day, the flowers of this medium-sized plant are fragrant during the evening. It occurs in southern China, Myanmar, and Thailand, growing at low to moderate altitudes. The flowers are long-lasting, about 2–2¾ in (5–7 cm) long, and are borne on a more or less horizontal inflorescence with up to eight flowers. **ZONES 10–12. I–H.**

Vanda hindsii LINDL.

syn: *V. whiteana* D. A. HERB. & S. T. BLAKE

This robust species occurs in New Guinea, on Bougainville Island, and in northeast Australia. It commonly grows along streams in lowland habitats. In Australia it grows in climates that are dry during winter and spring. The stems are up to 40 in (1m) long. The short, lateral inflorescences bear up to eight fragrant flowers, each 1¼–1¾ in (3–4 cm) across. They last for about three weeks and appear at any time of the year with an emphasis on spring. Yellow forms occur occasionally. This species should be given a slight watering rest period during winter. **ZONES 11–12. H.**

Vanda denisoniana

Vanda hindsii

Vanda javierae TIU EX FESSEL & LUCKEL

The white flowers of this recently discovered species are unique within the genus. It is restricted to one area in the Philippines, where it grows at moderate altitudes, often near streams. The plant is about 14 in (35 cm) tall with leaves about 8 in (20 cm) long. The inflorescences are upright with five or six flowers, each about 2½ in (6 cm) across. **ZONES 10–11. I.**

Vanda lamellata LINDL.

syn: *V. cumingii* LINDL. EX PAXTON

This species occurs in hot, seasonally dry, lowland climates in Taiwan, Borneo, and the Philippines. It often grows under full sun near the sea. It is a medium-sized plant with stems up to about 16 in (40 cm) long. The flowers are about 1¼ in (3 cm) across, last for about three weeks, and are borne on lateral, suberect inflorescences 8–12 in (20–30 cm) long. Flowering is throughout the year. This variable species has several, recognized varieties, and these are based on flower color. **ZONES 11–12. H.**

Vanda javierae

Vanda lamellata

V

Vanda liliacina TEIJSM & BINNEND.

syn: *V. laotica* GUILL.

This species occurs in the Yunnan province of China, Myanmar, Thailand, Laos, Cambodia, and Vietnam. It grows from sea level to a 3300-ft (1000-m) altitude. The stems are about 4¾ in (12 cm) long with a few straplike leaves, each about 4 in (10 cm) long. The erect inflorescence has about eight flowers, each about 1 in (2.5 cm) across. Flowering is during winter or spring. **ZONES 10–12. I–H.**

Vanda liouvillei FINET

This species is restricted to Myanmar, Thailand, and Laos. In many collections it is incorrectly labelled *V. brunnea*, which has slightly smaller flowers. The inflorescence is up to 20 in (50 cm) long with about 12 flowers, each about 1¾ in (4 cm) across. **ZONES 10–11. I.**

Vanda liliacina

Vanda liouvillei

Vanda luzonica

Vanda luzonica LOHER EX ROLFE

This is one of the most attractive and robust species in the genus, with stems reaching 5 ft (1.5 m) in length with many side branches. It is from Luzon in the Philippines and grows as an epiphyte at low or moderate altitudes. The upright inflorescence bears up to 12 flowers, each about 1¾–2½ in (4–6 cm) across. They last for about two weeks and occurs at any time of the year. **ZONES 10–12. I–H.**

Vanda merrillii AMES & QUISUMB.

This epiphytic species is confined to the Philippines, where it grows at low to moderate altitudes on Luzon and Negros islands. It is a robust species growing up to 5 ft (1.5 m) in length. The upright inflorescences bears up to ten flowers, which vary in color. Some forms are almost pure red. The glossy flowers have a strong, spicy fragrance and are up to 1¾–2 in (4–5 cm) across. Flowering is during spring. **ZONES 10–12. I–H.**

Vanda merrillii

V

Vanda roeblingiana ROLFE

This species is restricted to mountain forests at moderate to high altitudes on Luzon in the Philippines. It is reported as growing in shady conditions. The plant is up to about 20 in (50 cm) tall. It has an upright inflorescence which bears eight to 15 flowers, each about 2 in (5 cm) across. The large, fringed midlobe of the lip is split in two and is unusual for the genus. Flowering is mostly during summer. This is a cool-growing species that is suited to temperate climates.
ZONES 9–11. C–I.

Vanda roeblingiana

Vanda tessellata (ROXB.)
HOOK. EX G. DON
syn: *V. roxburghii* R. BR.

This is a medium-sized species from Sri Lanka, northeast India, Nepal, and Myanmar. It grows at low to moderate altitudes. The plant is about 2 ft (60 cm) tall with several leaves 6–10 in (15–25 cm) long and $\frac{1}{3}$ in (1 cm) across. The inflorescences bear up to ten long-lasting, fragrant flowers, each about 2 in (5 cm) across. Flowering occurs during summer. **ZONES 10–12. I–H.**

Vanda testacea

Vanda testacea (LINDL.) RCHB.F.
syn: *V. parviflora* LINDL.

This widespread species from Sri Lanka, India, southern China, Myanmar, and Thailand grows at moderate altitudes. It has flowers that are somewhat similar to *V. coerulescens*, but differ in the petals and sepals, which are brownish–yellow in *V. testacea*. The plant is about 12–20 in (30–50 cm) tall. The flowers are about 1 in (2.5 cm) across and are borne on an upright or arching inflorescence. Flowering is during spring. **ZONES 10–12. I.**

Vanda tessellata

V

Vanda (Pissamiax Varavuth) x Sakura

Vasco. Pine rivers "Esau"

Ascda. Fuch's "Spotted Cat"

Ascda. Sun Fun Beauty

Ascda. Gwen

V

VANDOPSIS PFITZER

There are about eight species in this genus distributed from Southeast Asia, as far north as southern China, to the Malay Archipelago. They are monopodial orchids related to *Vanda* and are large epiphytes that often grow in exposed situations, mostly in the lowlands. The inflorescences bear many flowers, which are large, fleshy, showy and long-lasting.

CULTIVATION

Most of these species are robust and large and need room in an orchid house when mature. They may be grown in a pot with an extremely coarse medium, but grow best when planted in a tropical garden bed—the bed should have a coarse material rather than garden soil. Water year-round and grow under bright light, even full sun for some species.

Vandopsis gigantea

Vandopsis gigantea (LINDL.) PFITZER
syn: *Vanda gigantea* LINDL., *Vandopsis chinensis* (ROLFE) SCHLTR.

This large epiphyte occurs in southern China, Myanmar, Thailand, Cambodia, Laos, Vietnam, and the Malay Peninsula. It grows on trees on the margins of forests from sea level to a 5700-ft (1700-m) altitude. The stout, branched stem is up to 20 in (50 cm) long. The fleshy leaves are arranged in two ranks and are up to 14 in (35 cm) long and 3 in (7.5 cm) wide. The pendulous inflorescence is about 1 ft (30 cm) long with many densely packed flowers, each about 3 in (7.5 cm) across. The flowers have a heavy texture and last for several weeks. Flowering is from spring to summer. **ZONES 10–12. I–H.**

Vandopsis lissochiloides (GAUD.) PFITZER
syn: *Vanda batemannii* LINDL., *Vanda lissochiloides* (GAUD.) LINDL.

This robust species grows in lowlands in Thailand, Laos, the Philippines, and several islands as far east as New Guinea. The robust stem may be up to 80 in (2 m) or more long. The leaves are stiff and leathery, and up to 1 ft (30 cm) long and 2 in (5 cm) wide. The inflorescence is up to 8ft 4 in (2.5 m) tall with 12 to 30 flowers that open successively over several months. These fragrant, heavily textured flowers are about 2¾ in (7 cm) across and last for several months. Flowering is mostly during summer, but in the tropics a large plant is seldom out of flower. This species grows well under full sun in a tropical garden, but may become too large for a small orchid house. **ZONES 11–12. H.**

Vandopsis lissochiloides

V

VANILLA MILLER

Over 50 species are contained within this genus. They occur
throughout the tropics in Africa, Asia, and the Americas.
V. planifolia is grown on farms for the vanilla essence that is
made from the seed pods. The plants grow as vines that often
reach more than 100 ft (30 m) long. The roots are produced at
the nodes and grow up trees, over rocks, or on cliff faces. The
leaves are succulent and well spaced along the stem. The short
inflorescences bear a few large flowers that last for only a day
or two. These species usually do not flower until they have
reached a large size.

CULTIVATION

Commercial plants are grown over large frames under full sun.
In a private collection a basket is probably best, although the
plants do better if provided with something to grow over.
A mixture of sand and peat moss or other organic material
works well so long as it drains freely. Intermediate to hot
temperatures, year-round watering, fertilizing, and bright
light are recommended.

Vanilla planifolia

Vanilla planifolia ANDREWS
syn: *V. fragrans* (SALISB.) AMES

This well-known plant is widely cultivated commercially for its
vanilla seed pods. It occurs naturally in the West Indies, Florida
in the USA, and Central America and, as a result of commercial
production, has become naturalized in areas outside its original
habitat. The stems are 60 ft (18 m) or more long. The succulent
leaves are well separated along the stem and are about 6 in
(15 cm) long and 1¾ in (4 cm) wide. The seed pods are up to
6 in (15 cm) long. The inflorescences are borne laterally along
the stem and bear several fleshy, fragrant flowers, each about
2½ in (6 cm) long. The flowers open one at a time, but not
widely, and last for only about a day. Flowering does not occur
until the plant is well established, then the flowers will appear
throughout the year. **ZONES 11–12. I–H.**

Vanilla polylepis SUMMERH.

This species occurs in tropical
Africa—Angola, Zaire, Kenya,
Malawi, Zambia, and
Zimbabwe. It grows as an
epiphyte or terrestrial under
deep shade along stream
banks and over cliff faces at
an altitude of about 5000 ft
(1500 m). The stems reach
several yards (meters) in
length and are up to 1 in
(2.5 cm) in diameter. The
leaves are succulent, ovate,
and 4–8 in (10–20 cm) long
and 1¼–3¼ in (3–8 cm) wide.
The inflorescences are borne
laterally along the stem and
bear several flowers, each
about 4¾ in (12 cm) across.
The flowers open one at
a time and last for about
three days. Flowering is from
September to January in the
habitat. **ZONES 10. I.**

V

Vanilla polylepis

XYLOBIUM LINDL.

This genus of 25 species ranges from Mexico to southeast Brazil, with the greatest diversity in the Andes. These species have clustered pseudobulbs that are spherical to cylindrical with one to four leaves. The inflorescence is short and arises from the base of the pseudobulbs.

CULTIVATION

Most of these vigorously growing species require hot to intermediate conditions. They may be potted in a free-draining mix and they require bright light, but not direct sunlight. Water well during the growing period but reduce the amount during the cool months when growth has ceased.

Xylobium squalens

Xylobium squalens (LINDL.) LINDL.
syn: *X. variegatum* (RUIZ & PAVON) GARAY & DUNSTERV.

This species ranges from Costa Rica to Brazil and grows at altitudes of 660–3300 ft (200–1000 m). The pseudobulbs are up to 2½ in (6 cm) tall and 1¼ in (3 cm) in diameter. The leaves are about 18 in (45 cm) long. The erect inflorescence arises from the base of the pseudobulbs and is up to 6 in (15 cm) tall. It carries 12 to 15 flowers, each up to 1¾ in (4 cm) wide, that appear during summer. **ZONES 11–12. I–H.**

Zelenkoa onusta

ZELENKOA M. CHASE & N. WILLIAMS

This genus was separated from *Oncidium* and consists of only one species. It is distributed from Panama, Colombia, and Ecuador to Peru where it grows in coastal areas, often as a lithophyte or as an epiphyte in dry forests, from sea level to about 4000 ft (1200 m).

CULTIVATION

This species does well on a suitable mount or potted in a free-draining mix. Reduce watering in winter.

Zelenkoa onusta (LINDL.) M. CHASE & N. WILLIAMS

This species has clustered, ovoid, compressed pseudobulbs up to 1¾ in (4 cm) high. The leaf is solitary, leathery, and up to 5½ in (13 cm) long. Both the leaves and pseudobulbs may be spotted with red–brown or red–purple colors. The inflorescence is up to 20 in (50 cm) long and bears many flowers about 1 in (2.5 cm) wide. Flowering is from spring to early autumn. **ZONES 11–12. I–H.**

X

ZYGOPETALUM
HOOK.

This genus of about 16 species occurs in Brazil, Peru, and other South American countries. The plants grow as epiphytes or terrestrials at moderate altitudes in wet forests. The pseudobulbs are round or egg-shaped with two or three straplike leaves at the apex. There are usually two or more leaflike bracts that arise from the base of the pseudobulbs. The inflorescence arises from the base of the pseudobulbs and bears several fragrant, long-lasting flowers. The flowers are moderately large and showy.

CULTIVATION
The thick and fleshy roots of these species need to be contained in a large pot with a well-drained mix similar to that used for *Cymbidium* species. Water throughout the year, but reduce slightly after the plants have finished growth. However, do not allow the plant to dry out for more than a day or two.

HYBRIDS
Apart from hybrids made with other species in the genus, *Zygopetalum* has been hybridized with several other genera, such as *Lycaste, Oncidium, Colax, Epidendrum* and *Chondrorhyncha*. The complex hybrid genus *Hamelwellsara* (*Aganisia* x *Batemannia* x *Otostylis* x *Zygopetalum* x *Zygosepalum* = Hmwsa.) has produced some attractive and interesting hybrids. The other genus that has been of importance is *Neogardeneria*. Hybrids made with this genus and *Zygopetalum* are known as *Zygoneria* (Zga.) They have upright spikes with many strongly scented and attractive flowers. These hybrids are particularly suited to cooler climates but are very adaptable. Some of these hybrids are show at the end of the *Zygopetalum* species section.

Zygopetalum crinitum

Zygopetalum crinitum
LODDIGES

This species occurs in the mountains in southern Brazil. It grows as a terrestrial, often with the pseudobulbs partly buried in leaf litter at moderate altitudes. The ovoid pseudobulbs are clustered, and about 1¾–4 in (4–10 cm) long. There are three to five lanceolate leaves, each about 12–16 in (30–40 cm) long and 1¼ in (3 cm) wide. The inflorescence is up to 20 in (50 cm) long with three to ten long-lasting, highly fragrant flowers, each about 3¼ in (8 cm) across. Flowering is from late autumn to early spring. **ZONES 9–10. C–I.**

Z

Zygopetalum maculatum (H. B. & K.) GARAY

This species grows as a terrestrial in cool, shady situations at moderate altitudes in Brazil. The pseudobulbs are more or less globose and about 1¼–2¾ in (3–7 cm) tall. The pseudobulb has two or three straplike leaves up to 20 in (50 cm) long and 2 in (5 cm) wide. The erect to arching inflorescence is 2–3 ft (60–90 cm) tall with four to ten highly fragrant, long-lasting flowers, each about 2¾ in (7 cm) across. Flowering is from late autumn to winter. This plant does well in a pot of *Cymbidium* type mix and placed in a shady position. **ZONES 9–10. I.**

Zygopetalum maxillare LODDIGES

This species is recorded from southeast Brazil and Peru. It is reported as growing as an epiphyte on tree ferns at moderate to high altitudes. The ovoid, slightly compressed pseudobulbs are about 2¾ in (7 cm) tall and are well spaced along the rhizome. The leaves are straplike, about 8–12 in (20–30 cm) long, and 1 in (2.5 cm) wide. The inflorescence is erect with five to eight waxy, fragrant, long-lasting flowers, each about 2⅔ in (6.5 cm) across. Flowering is from winter to spring. This plant grows best on a slab and care should be taken if remounting to disturb the roots as little as possible. **ZONES 9–10. C–I.**

Zygopetalum maculatum

Zygopetalum maxillare

Zygopetalum triste BARB. RODRIG.

This species grows on rocks in wet forests at altitudes of about 6000 ft (1800 m) in the state of Minas Gerais in southeast Brazil. The flowers crowd together near the end of the inflorescence and are about 2¾ in (7 cm) across. **ZONES 9–10. C–I.**

Zygopetalum triste

Zygoneria Adelaide Meadows

Zygoneria Adelaide Meadows

Zygoneria Rebecca

Hmwsa. June "Indigo Sue"

Z

ZYGOSEPALUM RCHB.F.

This genus comprises about four or five species from Venezuela, Guyana, and northern Brazil. They are related to *Zygopetalum*. They have an elongated rhizome and pseudobulbs with one to three leaves. These are showy, epiphytic orchids and they may be grown in slatted baskets or shallow pans. Provide them with hot and humid conditions throughout the year.

Zygosepalum labiosum

Zygosepalum labiosum (L. C. RICH.) COGN.

syn: *Menadenium labiosum* (L. C. RICH.) COGN., *Epidendrum labiosum* L. C. RICH.

This species is from Venezuela, Guyana, and Brazil. It has an elongated rhizome that often branches to form large masses. The ovoid and laterally compressed pseudobulbs are well spaced along the rhizome and about 1¾ in (4 cm) tall. They bear one or two leaves up to about 10 in (25 cm) long and 1¾ in (4 cm) wide. The erect inflorescence is generally shorter than the leaves and has one to three flowers. These large, attractive flowers are heavily textured and about 4 in (10 cm) long. The long-lasting flowers appear during spring and early summer. **ZONE 12. H.**

Zygosepalum lindeniae (ROLFE) GARAY & DUNST.

This species is from Venezuela through to Peru and Brazil. It occurs at low elevations on the eastern slopes of the Andes. The pseudobulbs are spaced about 3 in (7.5 cm) apart on a creeping rhizome. They are about 2 in (5 cm) tall and carry one or two linear leaves up to about 1 ft (30 cm) long. The inflorescence is up to 4 in (10 cm) long and arises from near the base of the new growth. One or two flowers are produced, each about 3¼ in (8 cm) across. Flowering is during spring and summer. Because of its creeping habit, this plant grows best on a slab. **ZONES 11–12. I–H.**

Z

Zygosepalum lindeniae

ZYGOSTATES LINDL.

This genus comprises about seven species from central and southern Brazil, where they grow as epiphytes in moist forests. The plants are fan-shaped and may lack pseudobulbs. If there are no pseudobulbs, the leaves are flattened and overlap at the base. The inflorescence arises from an axil.

CULTIVATION

These plants require intermediate conditions and year-round moisture at the roots. They may be grown either mounted or in small pots.

Zygostates grandiflora (LINDL.) COGN.

This species is from Brazil. The arrangement of the leaves gives the plant a fanlike appearance. The leaves are up to 4 in (10 cm) long. The arching to pendulous inflorescence is up to 4 in (10 cm) long and carries many small flowers, each about ¼ in (6 mm) wide. Flowering is from spring to summer. **ZONES 10–11. I.**

Zygostates grandiflora

Zygostates lunata
LINDL.

This species occurs in the southern part of Brazil, where it grows on mossy trees at moderate altitudes. It is similar vegetatively to Z. grandiflora but differs principally by having slightly larger flowers, up to about ⅓ in (1 cm) wide, in a different color. Flowering is during spring and summer. **ZONES 10–11. I.**

Zygostates lunata

Z

Glossary

ADAPTATION An alteration in the structure or function of an organism which enables it to survive and multiply in a changed environment.

ADNATE A fusion of parts, for example, a labellum with the column.

AERATION Allowing the free penetration of air.

ALLIANCE A group of species or genera that share certain features in common. For example, genera such as *Stelis*, *Restrepia* and *Scaphosepalum* are regarded as being part of the "pleurothallid alliance" because they have a similar growing habit to that of *Pleurothallis*.

ANTHER The male part of the flower that contains the pollen.

APEX (n); APICAL (adj) The end or top of something, as in the tip of a stem.

APOMICTS Plants that reproduce by seed but the ovule (embryonic seed) is not fertilized by pollen. This results in seedlings genetically identical to the mother plant.

AXIL (n); AXILLARY (adj) The angle between the two parts, for example, the petiole and stem.

BARRING Marks on flower parts, particularly the lip or the column of some orchids.

BIFOLIATE Having two leaves.

BRACT A modified, usually small leaf. Often reduced to a small scale on the stem.

CALCAREOUS Contains calcium.

CALLI (pl); CALLUS (singular) An unusually thickened part. In orchids it is generally applied to appendages on the labellum.

CAPITATE (adj); CAPITULUM (n) A closely packed head of flowers that do not have flower stalks.

CLOUD FOREST A forest on a mountain top or its slopes that is regularly covered in cloud. This is a wet habitats with trees covered in mosses and other epiphytic plants.

COLUMN The body in the central part of the flower; consists of fused male and female parts.

COMPLEX A group of closely related species. Used where there is some doubt about whether the species involved should have status as separate species or not.

CONNATE (adj); CONNATION (n) Two or more things joined or fused together.

CORM The swollen base of a stem containing stored plant food.

DAUGHTER TUBER A new tuber formed from the original tuber, which may be used for propagation.

DECIDUOUS The habit of some plants of dropping their leaves when the climate is unfavorable, such as during winter or a prolonged dry season.

DORSAL SEPAL The sepal uppermost on the flower when the lip is lowermost, as in the normal orchid flower.

ELLIPTIC Shaped like an ellipse.

ENDEMIC Confined to a given area or country.

EPIPHYTE (n); EPIPHYTIC (adj) A plant that grows on another plant, but is not a parasite.

EVERGREEN Plants that do not drop their leaves seasonally.

FAMILY A major subdivision of the plant kingdom, for example, the orchid family (Orchidaceae), the daisy family (Asteraceae) etc.

FIMBRIATE Having a hairy or fringed margin.

FLEXUOUS Full of curves, winding.

FLORAL TUBE The sepals and, sometimes, the petals may be joined at their bases to form a tube, as in the genus *Masdevallia*.

FREE-FLOWERING Produces flowers frequently and prolifically.

FUSIFORM Spindle-shaped, as in a leaf with a wide mid section and tapering ends.

GENERA (pl); GENUS (singular) A subdivision within the plant kingdom. A genus is the first major level below the family and it consists of one or more species.

GLOBOSE Shaped like a globe or sphere.

GLOBULAR A small, spherical shape.

HABIT The growth form that is characteristic of a plant, for example, an upright habit or a pendulous habit.

HYBRID A plant originating from the cross pollination of two or more different species. Hybrids may occur naturally or may be artificially made.

INFLORESCENCE The flowering stem and the flowers.

INTERNODE The part of the stem between nodes, for example, between the attachment points of leaves.

KEIKI A small plant that forms on the pseudobulb of some species, such as *Dendrobium*. These can be removed and used for propagation.

LABELLUM The lip or modified third petal in an orchid flower, which often consists of three lobes, two side (lateral) lobes, and a mid lobe. In most orchid species the lip is on the lower side of the flower.

LANCEOLATE Shaped like a lance—narrow and tapered at both ends.

LATERAL SEPAL The two paired sepals on either side of the flower, where the lip is lowermost.

LEAF SHEATH A bract that encloses the base of the leaf.

LIP *See* "labellum."

LITHOPHYTE (n); LITHOPHYTIC (adj) A plant that grows on rocks or cliffs.

MENTUM A chinlike projection at the base of some orchid flowers.

MONOPODIAL The type of orchid in which new leaves continue to grow from the stem apex.

MONOTYPIC Something that consists of a single unit, as in a genus with only one species.

MOUNT A piece of material, such as cork, onto which an orchid plant is tied for cultivation.

MUCILAGINOUS Covered with mucilage, a thick, sticky fluid.

NECTARY The organ that secretes nectar.

NODE The point on a stem, often with a small swelling, where the leaf is attached.

OVARY The lowest part of the flower containing the embryonic seeds (ovules).

OVATE; OVOID Shaped like the outline of an egg; the largest part below the middle.

PEAT A substance comprising partly decomposed plants from old swamps that is used in potting mixtures.

PEDICEL The stalk of a single flower.

PEDUNCLE The basal stalk of an inflorescence.

PENDULOUS Hangs or swings freely, as in an inflorescence.

PERENNIAL Lasts for several years, at least.

PERIANTH The sepals and petals.

PERLITE A material made from heating a mineral until it expands to form small granules. It is used for potting to "open" up the mixture and allow aeration and drainage. It holds a little water, but has no nutritional value for a plant.

PETAL A segment of a flower. In orchids, there are usually two petals with the labellum (lip) being a modified third petal.

PETIOLE The stalk of a leaf.

pH The measure of acidity. A potting mix with a pH of 1 is highly acidic; one of 14 is highly alkaline, and a value of 7 is neutral. Most orchid mixes are neutral or slightly acidic (about pH 6). As a mix breaks down it can become more acidic.

PLANTLETS Small plants formed on an old pseudobulb or flowering stem. They are used for propagation.

PLICATE Pleated; referring to leaves with several longitudinal veins, with each one usually folded.

POLLEN Tiny grains of genetic material which, when united with ovules (embryonic seeds) in the ovary, form seeds.

POLLINATION The process of transferring pollen from one plant to the stigma of another plant.

POLLINIA In orchids, pollen grains that are united into small bundles.

POLYMORPHIC Having more than one distinct form.

PSEUDOBULB A thickened stem used to store food and water.

RACEME An inflorescence or flowering stem with several flowers, each borne on a pedicel or flower stalk.

RACHIS The central axis of an inflorescence from which the flowers arise.

RANK A number of leaves in a row.

RHIZOME A stem that creeps on or below the surface, forming roots along its length as it grows. The rhizome is often thickened and it contains food reserves for the plant.

ROSTELLUM A part of the stigma that has been modified to assist in attaching the pollinia to the pollinator.

SACCATE Shaped like a sack or cup.

SAPROPHYTE (n); SAPROPHYTIC (adj) A plant that gets its nourishment from decaying organic matter with the aid of a symbiotic fungus. Usually these plants lack leaves and chlorophyll.

SCAPE A leafless inflorescence arising directly from the base of a pseudobulb or corm.

SELF POLLINATING (OR "SELFING") A plant pollinated by its own pollen. Self pollination produces offspring genetically identical to the parent plant.

SEPAL The outer whorl of flower parts that, together with the petals, makes up the perianth.

SLAB *See* mount.

SPHAGNUM A type of moss collected from wet environments and sold for use in the nursery industry. It is a useful component of orchid growing/potting mixtures.

SPECIES (singular and pl) The basic unit of plant classification. It is below the genus level and comprises a group of similar organisms that can interbreed to produce fertile offspring similar to the parents.

SPECIMEN A single plant. The term is sometimes used in horticultural circles to denote a particularly large plant—a "specimen" plant.

SPIKE A term often used instead of inflorescence, particularly when it is unbranched.

SPUR A hollow, slender projection at the base of the labellum (lip).

STAMEN The basic male organ of a flower. In orchids, there is mostly only one fertile stamen, and it is fused to the styles to form the column.

STAMINODE A sterile stamen that does not have an anther or pollen.

STIGMA In orchids, the part of the column that receives the pollen if fertilization is to be effected.

STYLE The female part of the flower that bears the stigma. In orchids, styles are fused with the stamen(s) to form the column.

SUBSPECIES (abbrev. subsp. or ssp.) The level of classification below a species. Subspecies have some important differences to the other plants in the species, but these are not sufficient enough to raise them to the status of species.

SUBSTRATE Material on which an orchid grows, for example, a tree, rock, or leaf litter.

SYMBIOSIS (n); SYMBIOTICALLY (adv) A relationship between two organisms where both derive benefit.

SYMPODIAL The type of orchid where each stem grows to a certain defined size and new stems are produced each year.

SYNONYM (abbrev. syn.) A scientific name which, although no longer accepted, still lingers in use.

TERETE Having a long, narrow cylinder shape that is usually solid, not hollow, and circular in cross section.

TERMINAL At the end of the stem.

TERRESTRIAL A plant that grows in the ground.

TRIBE A level in the classification system between the family and the genus. It consists of a group of related genera.

TUBER An underground storage organ that provides food for the plant during the period when there are no leaves.

UMBEL An inflorescence in which the pedicels arise from almost the same point.

UNIFOLIATE Having a single leaf.

VARIETY (abbrev. var.) A level in the classification of plants below the species. It is often used loosely by gardeners to describe any different form, such as plants with a different flower color.

WHORL A circular arrangement of similar parts, for example, several leaves arising from the one point on a stem. The petals and sepals are whorls within the flower.

Index for Synonyms
and Common Names

Acknowledgments

Photographs taken by **Wayne Harris** excluding the following:

Jim Comber: 281t

Gary Yong Gee: 17, 42t, 43tr, 52l, 53l, 54b, 55l, 56b, 59t, 65, 72, 74bl, 75b, 81t, 88, 103b, 119b, 130t, 134b, 142, 144t, 161, 175t, 236tl, 248b, 249, 253tl, 274t, 275t, 284t, 286, tr, 286cl, 289t, 303t, 304b, 305t, 312b, 313t, 314t, 315, 316t, 321t, 321bl, 324b, 364, 365t, 371b, 380br, 387b, 391br, 394b, 409b, 410t, 432, 433b, 443b, 444t, 444b, 446b, 459br, 485b, 487b, 495, 496bl, 499tr, 500b, 501t, 510t, 520l, 522tl, 536c, 546bl, 546br, 550, br, 554/5, 556t, 559, 560t, 563t, 575t, 577b, 578cl, 588b

Bill Lavarack: 10, 11, 12, 14, 15t, 15c, 15b, 22, 28, 67t, 97b, 101tr, 105b, 110b, 113b, 118l, 139b, 154c, 162t, 163r, 186/7, 192t, 192b, 193tr, 193b, 194c, 194b, 195t, 196t, 196b, 197t, 197c, 197b, 198t, 199t, 199b, 200b, 202t, 202b, 203tr, 203b, 204t, 205t, 205b, 206bl, 207b, 210c, 210b, 212b, 213t, 213b, 215t, 215c, 215b, 216b, 218c, 222, 227c, 232, 233l, 240b, 241c, 241b, 242b, 270b, 271b, 272b, 273tl, 277tl, 281b, 296br, 298t, 299b, 300bl, 300br, 317t, 350tl, 367b, 368tl, 368b, 375t, 434t, 434b, 436t, 436b, 441t, 496t, 547t, 569b, 571t, 578cr, 583t

Royal Botanic Gardens, Kew: 45t, 46b, 47t, 82t, 82b, 135t, 135b, 178t, 185c, 185b, 234t, 234b, 235t, 235c, 235bl, 235br, 236tl, 236tr, 236b, 237, 276b, 277tr, 277b, 278r, 280, 298cl, 299t, 300bc, 352b, 367t, 368tr, 471t, 472t, 472c, 472b, 473tr, 474cl, 494, 517t, 517b, 518t, 518b, 573t, 573bl, 573br, 583b

Wolfgang Rysy: 57, 136t, 136b, 137t, 137b, 179, 180t, 180b, 181t, 181c, 181b, 182t, 182b, 183t, 183b, 188t, 189tl, 189tr, 189b, 190t, 190c, 190b, 267t, 267b, 268t, 268bl, 268br, 269tl, 269tr, 302bl, 302br, 369, 370t, 370b, 400, 401t, 401bl, 401br, 402t, 402b, 403t, 403b, 404, 405, 406t, 406c, 406b, 407t, 407c, 407b, 408t, 408c, 408b, 460t, 460b, 461b, 462t, 462b, 524b, 525t, 525b, 526cl, 564

Geoff Stocker: p40b, 68b, 229, 330t, 330b

Howard Wood: 67b, 69, 80t, 85t, 85br, 87b, 119l, 160bl, 160br, 188b, 228t, 255bl, 256t, 257b, 285, 307t, 307b, 318b, 319t, 320, 455, 456t, 456c, 456b, 457t, 457cr, 457b, 458t, 458b, 470, 477, 542t, 543tl, 543cr, 548b, 549tr, 560b

Random House Photo Library: 328/9, 372/3, 412/3

Global Book Publishing: 2,8

Code:
number = page number
t = top
c = centre
b = bottom
l = left
r = right

Illustrations on pages 16, 20 and 21 were rendered by Ian Faulkner.